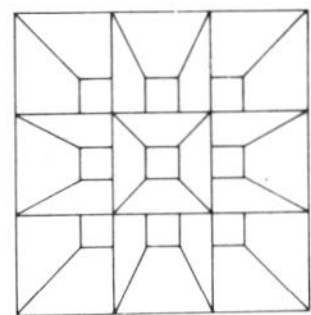

BENJAMIN/CUMMINGS SERIES IN DATABASE SYSTEMS AND APPLICATIONS

S. B. Navathe, Series Editor

L. Kerschberg
EXPERT DATABASE SYSTEMS
Proceedings From the First International Workshop **(1986)**

S. B. Navathe and R. Elmasri
FUNDAMENTALS OF DATABASE SYSTEMS (1987)

OTHER TITLES OF INTEREST

E. V. B. Software Engineering, Inc.
OBJECT ORIENTED DESIGN HANDBOOK (1987)

D. Maier and D. Warren
LOGIC PROGRAMMING WITH PROLOG (1987)

F. McFadden and J. Hoffer
DATA BASE MANAGEMENT (1985)

C. Negoita
EXPERT SYSTEMS AND FUZZY SYSTEMS (1985)

PREFACE

The fields of Expert Systems (ES) and Database Management Systems (DB) have well-defined concepts and architectures. There are also many commercially available products. However, the concept of an "Expert Database System" connotes diverse definitions and decidedly different architectures.

One can envision several scenarios: 1) an expert system loosely-coupled with a database system, 2) a database management system enhanced with reasoning capabilities to perform knowledge-directed problem solving, 3) a logic programming system, or a knowledge representation system, enhanced with database access and manipulation primitives, or 4) an intelligent natural language interface to a database system. All of these architectures are meaningful and interesting; there are certainly others.

A unique aspect of Expert Database Systems is that they represent the *confluence* of ideas from Artificial Intelligence, Database Management, Logic Programming, Information Retrieval, and Fuzzy Systems Theory. It is precisely this *synergism* that makes the field so fascinating and will lead to new architectures for intelligent systems.

In order to foster research and development in the field of Expert Database Systems, the Institute of Information Management, Technology and Policy of the College of Business Administration at the University of South Carolina sponsored the First International Workshop on Expert Database Systems. The Workshop was held at Kiawah Island, South Carolina, during October 24–27, 1984, and brought together 110 researchers and practitioners from 13 countries to present their research work and to discuss the issues related to Expert Database Systems. Many of the architectures mentioned above were presented and discussed during the Workshop.

In response to the Workshop's Call for Papers, 96 papers were submitted. The Program Committee accepted 37 full-length papers and 30 position papers representing a total of 115 authors.

This volume contains the Keynote Address entitled "Expert Database Systems: A Database Perspective," delivered by Dr. John Miles Smith of the Computer Corporation of America, three Working Group reports, and the 37 full-length papers.

Scope of the Papers

In the keynote paper, John Smith defines an Expert Database System as a "system for developing applications requiring knowledge-directed processing of shared information." He envisions an architecture in which multiple expert systems access a common, shared database.

EXPERT DATABASE SYSTEMS

Proceedings From the First International Workshop

LARRY KERSCHBERG, EDITOR

University of South Carolina

THE BENJAMIN/CUMMINGS PUBLISHING COMPANY, INC.

*Menlo Park, California • Reading, Massachusetts •
Don Mills, Ontario • Wokingham, U.K. • Amsterdam •
Sydney • Singapore • Tokyo • Mexico City • Bogota •
Santiago • San Juan*

Sponsoring Editor: **ALAN APT**
Production Supervisor: **MARY PICKLUM**
Cover Designer: **EDITH ALLGOOD**

Library of Congress Cataloging-in-Publication Data

Main entry under title:

Expert database systems.

Papers presented at the First International Workshop on Expert Database Systems during Oct. 24–27, 1984 at Kiawah Island, S.C. and sponsored by the Institute of Information Management, Technology, and Policy of the College of Business Administration at the University of South Carolina.

Includes index.

1. Expert systems (Computer science)—Congresses. 2. Data base management—Congresses. I. Kerschberg, Larry. II. International Workshop on Expert Database Systems (1st : 1984 : Kiawah Island, S.C.) III. University of South Carolina. Institute of Information Management, Technology, and Policy.

QA76.76.E95E95 1986 006.3'3 85–28600
ISBN 0–8053–3270–7
BCDEFGHIJ–AL–8 9876

THE BENJAMIN/CUMMINGS PUBLISHING COMPANY, INC.

2727 Sand Hill Road
Menlo Park, California 94025

Dr. Smith discusses the tradeoffs involved in trying to interface an expert system inferencing mechanism with a database's associative retrieval and triggering mechanisms. To improve performance, he suggests that the database system be enhanced to perform high-speed integrity constraint management so as to alert the expert systems to "database states" that require their attention. He also suggests that database data models should be enhanced to represent both temporal and spatial concepts and relationships.

Part II contains the reports from the Working Groups that were held in the evenings, after the Workshop. Some Working Group meetings ran well past midnight. These reports present the major research issues that must be addressed in the next few years to make Expert Database Systems a reality.

Part III, on theory of Knowledge Bases, contains papers that provide formal approaches to the acquisition, specification, representation, and manipulation of knowledge.

Part IV focuses on the relationship between Logic Programming and Databases. Several proposals are given to integrate logic programming and databases by endowing the language PROLOG with database access primitives, rule management facilities, and concurrency control mechanisms. In addition, PROLOG is shown to be a "natural" query language for graph-oriented semantic data models, and can also be used as a "front-end" knowledge system for a commercial database management system.

Part V, Expert Database System Architectures, Tools and Techniques, contains various frameworks for the specification and design of Expert Database Systems. Techniques include the use of constraints for knowlege/data specification and semantic integrity enforcement, as well as modal logic for the specification of schemas, queries, and integrity constraints. Also discussed is the role of active and extensible data dictionaries in handling database meta-data. Several working prototype systems are presented in this Part.

Part VI, on reason in Expert Database Systems, discusses how database techniques can manage Artificial Intelligence reasoning environments, the role of heuristic search in database systems, the distinction between abductive and deductive reasoning in Expert Systems, and temporal reasoning on changing databases in the context of natural language question-answering systems.

Part VII, Intelligent Database Access and Interaction, focuses on ways to make databases more accessible to users, including transportable natural language interfaces, forgiving query languages that infer the user's intended query and even generalize its scope, knowledge-based helpers to aid in the specification of database applications, and knowledge-based semantic query optimization techniques.

Overall, this book is an excellent reference for researchers and practitioners who want to understand the central issues and architectures of the next generation of intelligent systems. It would make an ideal textbook for a graduate level course in this area.

Acknowledgments

I would like to acknowledge the support of all those individuals and organizations that made the Expert Database Systems Workshop possible. First, I want to thank the Organizing Committee, all of whom provided invaluable assistance and encouragement.

Without the foresight and support of Dr. Donald A. Marchand, Director of the Institute of Information Management, Technology and Policy at the University of South Carolina, the Workshop would have remained only an interesting concept. His support and organizational backing were crucial to the Workshop's success.

Ms. Cathie Hughes served as Workshop Coordinator and her tireless efforts and enthusiasm made the organizational aspects of the Workshop seem simple. She was assisted by several Institute staffers, especially Ann Brannon, Margie Martens, and Jackie Davis.

My Program Committee was extremely helpful in providing cogent advice, publicizing the Workshop, and reviewing the 96 submitted papers. Every paper was reviewed by three referees. In a few cases Program Committee members referred papers to outside reviewers. Special thanks go to Marco Casanova, Terry Huntsberger, S. Jayaramamurthy, Frank Manola, and Don Potter for reviewing papers. Don Potter also served as "recorder" during the Workshop Plenary Sessions.

The Working Group organizers deserve special praise for the professional manner in which they ran their groups. Shamkant Navathe served as Working Group coordinator and the following individuals organized and chaired the groups: Michael L. Brodie, James Bezdek, Charles Kellogg, John Mylopoulos, D. Stott Parker, Jr., Enrique Ruspini, Richard Tong, Gio Wiederhold, and Carlo Zaniolo.

Two professional societies cooperated with the Workshop. The ACM through its Special Interest Groups on Management of Data (SIGMOD) and Artificial Intelligence (SIGART), and the IEEE Computer Society through its Technical Committee on Data Base Engineering. We extend our thanks to Beatrice Yormark (SIGMOD Chair), Jaime Carbonell and Ronald J. Brachman (SIGART Chair and Vice-Chair, respectively), and Bruce Berra, Gio Wiederhold, and Mas Tsuchiya (IEEE) for their assistance.

Closer to home, I want to express my sincere appreciation to the College of Business Administration, especially the Division of Research which awarded me a Research Fellowship that allowed me to develop the Expert Database Systems concept, and to the Department of Management Science and its Program Director, Professor Robert E. Markland, for providing the stimulating research environment and support that spawned the Workshop concept.

As Adjunct Associate Professor of Computer Science, I have shared many interesting conversations with department members, and I especially want to thank Professor James Bezdek, the Department Chairman, for his support of the Workshop. The Computer Science Department allowed me to use the VAX11/780 computer for much of the text processing associated with the Workshop and this book. Mr. Ken Sallenger, the System Manager, was very helpful in solving problems associated with the TROFF text formatting program.

The NCR Corporation of Columbia graciously allowed me to typeset portions of this book using the TROFF formatter operating on an NCR TOWER computer. Special thanks go to Mr. Tom Mays, Mr. Bob Wyatt, and Ms. Jo Stanton for their assistance.

Alan Apt, my editor at Benjamin/Cummings, deserves special recognition for his continued interest and support in getting this book to press. His enthusiasm and patience have made our working relationship very pleasant and productive.

Finally, I want to express my sincerest love and appreciation to my wife, Nicole, and to my son, Benjamin, for their support during those many months of planning for the Workshop.

Larry Kerschberg

College of Business Administration
University of South Carolina
Columbia, South Carolina

CONTENTS

This book is dedicated to my parents
Fanny Zajac Kerschberg
and
Samuel Kerschberg

First International Workshop on Expert Database Systems

Organizing Committee

General Chairman

Donald A. Marchand
University of South Carolina

Program Chairman

Larry Kerschberg
University of South Carolina

Program Committee

Bruce Berra
Syracuse University

James Bezdek
University of South Carolina

Michael L. Brodie
Computer Corporation of America

Janis Bubenko
University of Stockholm

Peter Buneman
University of Pennsylvania

Antonio L. Furtado
PUC — Rio de Janeiro

Jonathan King
Teknowledge

John L. McCarthy
Lawrence Berkeley Laboratory

John Mylopoulos
University of Toronto

Erich Neuhold
Hewlett — Packard Laboratory

Sham Navathe
University of Florida

D. Stott Parker, Jr.
University of California — UCLA

Michael Stonebraker
University of California — Berkeley

Yannis Vassiliou
New York University

Adrian Walker
IBM Research Laboratory, San Jose

Bonnie L. Webber
University of Pennsylvania

Gio Wiederhold
Stanford University

Carlo Zaniolo
MCC Corporation

Workshop Coordinator

Cathie Hughes
Institute of Information Management,
Technology and Policy
University of South Carolina

PART I:
Keynote Address

Expert Database Systems: A Database Perspective

John Miles Smith

Computer Corporation of America

ABSTRACT

This paper characterizes a new class of computer systems to be called "Expert Database Systems." An expert database system (EDS) involves a combination of expert system (EDS) and database management system (DBMS) technology. EDS's will be used for developing applications requiring knowledge-directed processing of shared information. An increasing number of applications, including CAD/CAM, office automation and military command and control, have a requirement for this capability. Today, the integration of ES and DBMS systems is an emerging research area. By the 1990's, EDS's are expected to become one of the most important application development tools. This paper focuses on identifying system architectures and design principles to meet 1990's application requirements.

1. INTRODUCTION

This paper characterizes a new class of computer systems to be called here "Expert Database Systems." Generally speaking, an expert database system (EDS) involves a combination of database management system (DBMS) and expert system (ES) technology. The ES is used to perform intelligent processing of information being stored in, or retrieved from, the DBMS. An increasing number of applications, including CAD/CAM, office automation and military command and control, require this combination of technology. Today, the integration of ES and DBMS systems is an emerging research area. By the 1990's, EDS's are expected to become one of the most important application development products. This paper focuses on identifying system architectures and design principles to meet 1990's application requirements.

The paper begins by reviewing the fundamental objectives of DBMS and ES systems. An EDS is then defined as "a system for developing applications requiring knowledge-directed processing of shared information." Search is the common underlying function of ES's and DBMS's. The inappropriate combination of two powerful search engines can lead to a multiplicative explosion in computation time. It is argued that performance is a key challenge in the development of EDS's.

A strawman architecture of an EDS is proposed. In addition to DBMS and ES components, a key architectural feature is the presence of components to handle specialized datatypes such as images and speech. These latter components are placed under the auspices of the DBMS. The key architectural question is identified as the distribution of system functionality between the DBMS and ES components. In principle, due to the considerable overlap of technologies, major functions could be provided in either component. It is proposed that the distribution criteria should be based on maximizing overall system performance.

The two principal performance bottlenecks are identified as inferential search in ES's and access to secondary storage devices in DBMS's. To explore the first performance bottleneck, an in-depth comparison is made between inferential search in ES's and query evaluation search in DBMS's. It is concluded that query evaluation can provide some but not all the capabilities of inferencing in ES's. However, the DBMS can provide these capabilities much more efficiently than an ES. In essence the DBMS is sacrificing flexibility in exchange for increased performance. The proposed solution is to move as much as possible of the search requirements from the ES down to the DBMS. In this way, the expensive inferential search mechanism in the ES is only being used where it is essential. By moving more capabilities to the DBMS, the DBMS gets a higher-level specification of search requirements. The DBMS then has more scope for optimization and exploitation of parallel processing. This is seen as the solution to the second performance bottleneck.

These design principles are applied to two applications of EDS's which are particularly challenging from a performance viewpoint. The first application involves CAD/CAM for the production of maps. Multiple ES's are required on the data input path to the DBMS. While performance in keeping up with the workload is critical, real-time delays are acceptable. The second application is to tactical command and control. This requires multiple ES's on the data output path from the DBMS. In this application, real-time response is required.

From an analysis of these applications, specific capabilities are identified for moving down into the DBMS component of the EDS. These capabilities include: space and time semantics, logic rule processing and production (situation-action) rule processing. Furthermore, the DBMS needs to be distributed across multiple processors for parallel access by multiple ES's. It is not suggested that these capabilities only be provided within the DBMS. Instead, these capabilities need to be within both the ES and the DBMS components. Loosely speaking, the ES's will use these capabilities for problem solving, while the DBMS will use them for smarter, and more efficient, information storage and retrieval.

2. EDS ARCHITECTURE

This section reviews the principal characteristics of DBMS's and ES's, introduces an architecture for EDS's, and describes the technical challenges in the EDS design.

2.1. Database Systems

A DBMS is a software tool for developing applications requiring access to shared information. A DBMS is needed when multiple users (application programs) require access to the same collection of information for purposes of update and/or retrieval. Under these circumstances, a separate software facility is required between the users and the database to protect the shared information. This facility provides consistency control, recovery control, concurrency control and security control.

A DBMS provides these functions via a high-level transaction specification language. Users generate transactions in this language and the DBMS assumes the responsibility for managing physical data access, interleaving of overlapped operations, recovery from system failures, and managing access rights. To insulate users from the details of the physical data representations, the DBMS provides a special knowledge representation language called a "data model."

While protecting shared information is the raison d'etre of DBMS's, they can also provide other advantages in controlling data redundancy and distribution, and in making application programs easier to develop and maintain.

The functionality of a DBMS is required whether the volume of shared information is large or small, and whether the data is primarily resident in main memory or secondary storage. However, most DBMS designs today are tailored towards large data volumes (10**10 bytes) resident on secondary storage. This situation is likely to change in the future as main memories get larger and the demand for increased performance continues to build.

In applications with dedicated (non-shared) information, a DBMS may still be a useful tool although a lot of its functionality will be unnecessary. The use of a DBMS becomes a trade-off between the advantages of rapid application development and the disadvantages of decreased performance engendered by overly general software.

The bottom line is this. If the application requires access to shared information, the functionality of a DBMS is required. If the application uses dedicated information, and performance is critical, then a DBMS is probably undesirable.

2.2. Expert Systems

Expert knowledge is a collection of principles and procedures used by human experts in solving a certain domain of problems. An ES is an application system built around a direct representation of such expert knowledge. In general, an ES represents expert knowledge in small discrete chunks as logic rules, production rules, or frames. The attempt is made to preserve a one-to-one correspondence between a separable piece of expert knowledge and a rule or frame in the knowledge representation.

The rationale for ES's is that, in complex and ill-structured applications, such a knowledge representation makes applications easier to develop, debug and evolve. In addition, it is argued that interactive messages (explanations) can be made more meaningful for the user.

There is of course a price to be paid for achieving these benefits. The knowledge representation can only be kept discrete and simple if performance-oriented computational details are omitted. These missing details have to be made up by powerful, and inefficient, control strategies which must search for the order in which to apply knowledge rules. The performance of such general-purpose search mechanisms is currently the major factor limiting the utilization of the technology.

The prevailing trend in ES's is to use multiple representations for capturing expert knowledge. Pure logic rules have very simple semantics and are effective for representing knowledge that does not involve side-effects. Production rules are necessary to handle side-effects. Frames are well suited to clustering rules based on their applicability at different stages of the problem solving process.

2.3. Expert Database Systems

It is most logical to define an EDS as a tool for developing applications requiring both a DBMS and one or more ES's. There are clearly many applications which require such a tool. In fact, the majority of the applications where a DBMS is currently being used today would benefit from such a tool. Accordingly, an EDS is defined here as "a system for developing applications requiring knowledge-directed processing of shared information."

A strawman architecture for an EDS is shown in Figure 2.1. There are three kinds of system components between the users and the information: ES's for knowledge-directed processing, a DBMS for shared information management, and specialized processors for handling special format data. The number and type of specialized processors will depend on the application. The pathways between the components reflect a hierarchy of control rather than data or command paths. Any of the components may allow direct access for data or commands to lower level components. The user will access the EDS via the ES interfaces.

The specialized processors are used for specific data operations such as image enhancement or finite element analysis. These specialized data processors operate on data stored in particular formats and perform a fixed menu of functions. The structure of this data is of no interest to the user other than its manifestation via the fixed functions. The data structure is therefore not captured in any knowledge representation language (or data model). The ability to handle specialized data is a requirement in a growing number of ES and DBMS applications. It is essential that a general-purpose EDS have this ability.

There are important advantages to placing the specialized processors under the control of the DBMS, as shown in Figure 2.1. The functions performed by these processors can be integrated into the DBMS query language. All data passed to, or generated by, the specialized processors can be catalogued away by the DBMS. The DBMS capabilities for information protection, and representation hiding, are then extended to all kinds of information.

In general, the DBMS will be distributed across multiple processors and storage devices. The multiple processors may be loosely-coupled across a computer network, or tightly-coupled using shared memory. This allows each ES to interact with its own node of the DBMS. A DBMS node may store information in main memory for rapid access by the ES. Clustering and replication of data can maximize the parallel processing opportunities within the DBMS.

It is difficult to imagine any substantially different alternative to this basic architecture. The DBMS needs to be a separate module so as to protect shared information. The specialized processors need to be separate modules so as to limit access to their built-in function menus. Each ES needs to be a separate module to encapsulate a particular problem-solving activity within the application. While this modularity needs to be adopted internally, there is no necessity to reveal the internal architecture to the application system developer.

There are two really basic issues about this architecture. First, how should functionality be dispersed across the ES's and the DBMS. Should the DBMS data model, query language, and other system functionality, be stripped to a bare minimum and all other services be provided by the ES's? Or should the ES's be stripped instead? Second, how should the total EDS functionality appear to the application system developer. Should the applications development interface reveal the boundaries between the ES and DBMS? Should the applications developer need to consciously move information between DBMS and private work areas within an ES? The subsequent discussion focuses on the first of the two issues.

The major challenge to developing a general-purpose EDS will be performance. An EDS is essentially the composition of two powerful search engines. One engine will be searching knowledge rules to solve an application problem and, in so doing, generating queries over shared information. The other engine will be searching the shared information to answer the queries. The result could be a multiplicative explosion in processing time.

Performance should be the criterion for the dispersion of functionality between ES's and DBMS. A function should be allocated to the system where it can be executed most efficiently. The two primary performance concerns are the secondary storage search patterns of the DBMS and the search cycle of an ES.

Consider the first concern about secondary storage search. A fundamental observation here is that the more the DBMS "understands" about the overall goal of an access request, the more scope the DBMS has for optimizing that request. The worst situation for DBMS optimization is when the DBMS receives a large number of isolated information requests. Without knowing the overall goal of these requests, the DBMS has no choice but to respond to them individually. All opportunities for global optimization, which is where the highest payoffs can be attained, are lost. Thus moving functionality down to the DBMS can result in more efficient access to secondary storage.

The remaining concern is to reduce the load on the search cycle of the ES. The question of whether the DBMS can taken over some of this load, so that overall efficiency is increased, is discussed in the next section.

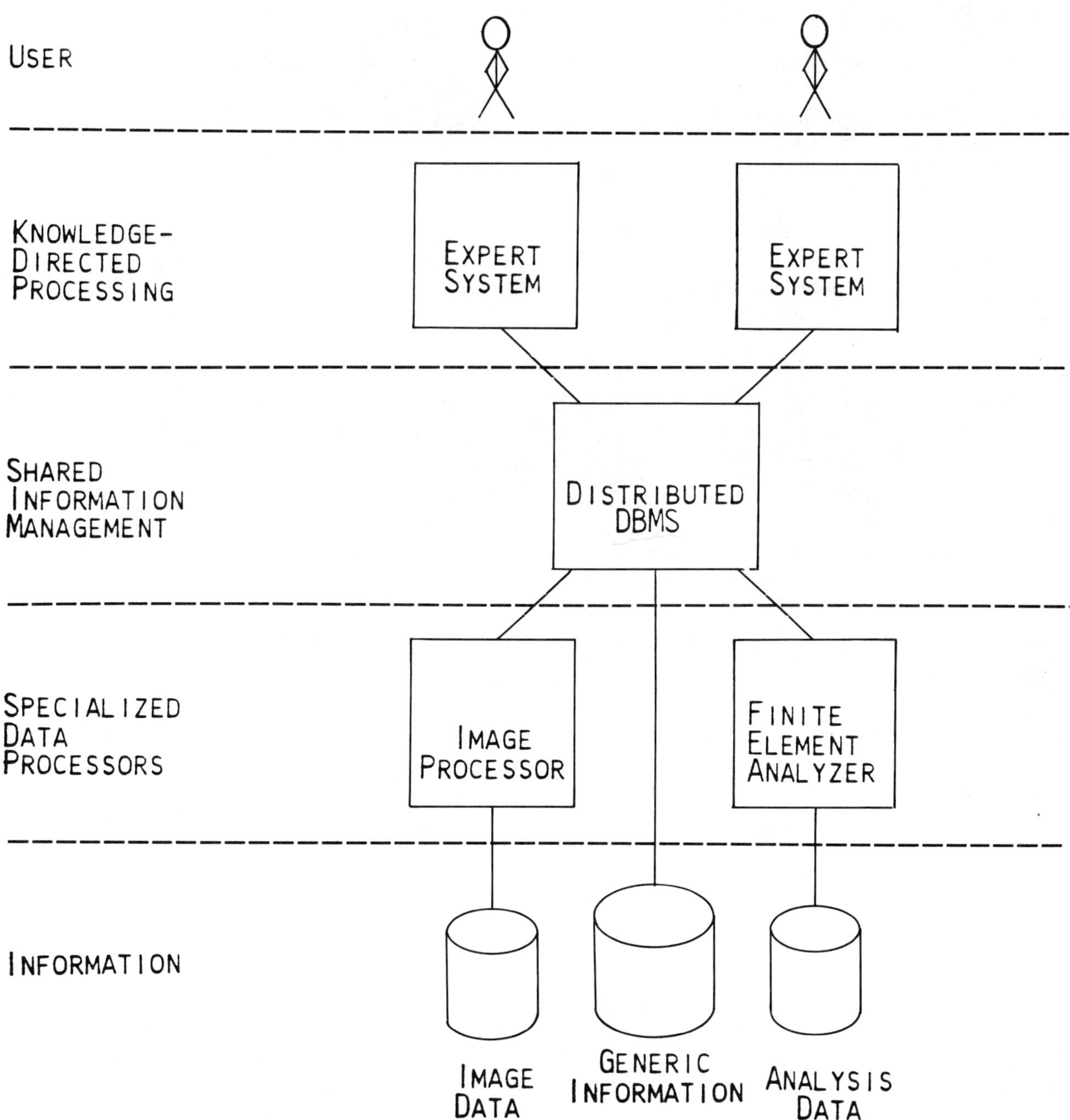

Figure 2.1 EDS Architecture

3. SEARCH: INFERENCING VERSUS QUERY EVALUATION

Search is the fundamental process underlying both ES's and DBMS's. In ES's search supports inferencing, while in DBMS's it supports query evaluation. However, the two types of system employ search in quite distinct ways. This section provides a comparison between ES search and DBMS search. The objective is to draw conclusions about how the two different uses of search should be combined in an EDS.

Given the wide variety of ES's, it is practically impossible to identify a generic inferencing method. So deductive inferencing in first-order predicate logic will be selected as a representative ES inferencing method. Deductive inferencing will be contrasted with query evaluation in relational DBMS's. The search process required for deductive inferencing will be characterized first.

3.1. Deductive Inferencing

In deductive inferencing, knowledge is represented in the language of logic as a set of formulae (axioms) A. A query is another formula Q(v) with free variables v. The result of a query is the set of free variable instantiations s, such that Q(s) is provable from A.

Consider the example in Figure 3.1 which is concerned with the positions of ships. There are two axioms. The first axiom asserts that the Kennedy is positioned at either point_U or point_V. The second asserts that the Kennedy is not at point_V. The query asks for the position of the Kennedy. Since position(Kennedy, point_U) is provable from the axioms A, but position(Kennedy, point_V) is not, the result is point_U.

Axioms:

1. position(Kennedy, point_U) or position(Kennedy, point_V)

2. not (position(Kennedy, point_V))

Query:

?position(Kennedy, p)

Inference:

find p's such that position(Kennedy, p) is provable
from the axioms

Results:

p = point_U

Figure 3.1 Deductive Inferencing

Let's use the standard symbols "$\vdash$" and "$\models$" to mean "is provable" and "is a logical consequence," respectively. The search involved in inferencing can be characterized as the search required to demonstrate $A \vdash Q(s)$. By using well-known metatheorems of logic, $A \vdash Q(s)$ is equivalent to $\models A \supset Q(s)$. Inferential search can then be characterized as the search required to demonstrate $A \supset Q(s)$ is true under every possible interpretation of the predicate symbols. An interpretation of an n-ary predicate symbol is an n-ary relation over a given set.

Notice that inferential search involves a "second-level" demonstration. It is not sufficient to demonstrate on the first level that A⊃Q(s) holds for a specific interpretation. Instead, it is necessary to demonstrate that A⊃Q(s) holds for all possible interpretations. It is this second level demonstration that makes inferential search computationally expensive, and potentially non-terminating.

3.2. Query Evaluation

In query evaluation, knowledge is represented by a set of definitions D and by an interpretation I. I gives an interpretation to set of primitive predicate symbols. D defines derived predicate symbols in terms of the primitive symbols. A query is a formula Q(v) with free variables v. Let Q(v)/D be the result of substituting definitions for the derived symbols in Q(v). The result of a query is the set of free variable instantiations s, such that Q(s)/D evaluates to true under interpretation I.

The example in Figure 3.2 represents the same knowledge as in Figure 3.1. The derived predicate symbol "position" is defined by a (rather lengthy) formula over the primitive predicate symbol "report," which, in turn, has the given relation as its interpretation. Reports are of two types: positive reports and negative reports. Positive reports state that a ship might be at the given position. Moreover, among positive reports with the same id# and ship, the ship is in exactly one of the given positions. Negative reports state that the ship is not in the given position. The id#'s for negative reports occur only once.

As far as a user is concerned, the knowledge content of this representation is indistinguishable from the one in Figure 3.1. Moreover, the syntax and semantics of predicate logic is used for both representations. Nevertheless, the representations appear very different.

The search involved in query evaluation can be characterized as that required to find the truth-value of Q(s)/D under the interpretation I. Only one level of demonstration is required: the evaluation of one query under one interpretation. The search is guaranteed to terminate since the interpretation is finite.

3.3. A Comparison

Let's compare the search process in query evaluation with the previous one in deductive inferencing.

The search in query evaluation is much simpler than the search in deductive inferencing. Only one interpretation needs to be searched as opposed to an arbitrarily large number of them. On the other hand, the formula Q(s)/D involved in query evaluation is usually more complex than the formula A⊃Q(s) involved in deductive inference. In most cases, formula complexity is a minor factor in comparison to the number of interpretations. In general, query evaluation can be expected to be orders of magnitude faster than deductive inference.

The knowledge representation for deductive inference is more powerful than the knowledge representation for query evaluation. Specifically, there are sets of axioms which cannot be captured by the combination of an interpretation and a set of definitions. To see this, notice that the interpretation I is a specific encoding of the axioms A. The definitions D determine a particular strategy for searching the encoded axioms to determine whether or not Q(s) is provable. While any axioms can be encoded as an interpretation, predicate logic is not powerful enough to express the required definitions D.

The deductive inferencing approach is more flexible than the query evaluation approach. Specifically, with deductive inferencing, any new knowledge can be added to the representation without impacting knowledge already represented. With query evaluation, the addition of new knowledge in the form of new tuples in the relations of I may invalidate the definitions D. In the example of Figure 3.2, adding a negative report, with the same id# as one already stored, will invalidate the definitions. In DBMS parlance,

Definition:

position(x, y) is

range r1 : report, type(r1) = pos

r2 : report, r1 ≠ r2, id#(r1) = id#(r2)

r3 : report, type(r3) = neg

$(\exists r1)(\forall r2)(\exists r3)(ship(r1) = x\ \&$

$position(r1) = y\ \&$

$position(r2) = position(r3)\ \&$

$ship(r2) = ship(r3))$

Interpretation:

report

id#	type	ship	position
b-2	pos	Kennedy	point_U
b-2	pos	Kennedy	point_V
f-4	neg	Kennedy	point_V

Query:

?position(Kennedy, p)

Evaluation:

Find p such that position(Kennedy, p) evaluates to true under the interpretation.

Result:

p = point_U

Figure 3.2 Query Evaluation

constraints on I to maintain the validity of D are called "integrity constraints."

The flexibility of deductive inferencing is an unneeded luxury in many applications. In most applications, there is some knowledge which will never change. It is best to build this knowledge into the search process, as an integrity constraint, so that one can benefit from the knowledge in the form of improved performance. In deductive inferencing, integrity constraints are not distinguished from other knowledge and the search process cannot take advantage of them. In many applications, integrity constraints are used for detecting and/or correcting errors in input data. In this situation, constraint knowledge must be distinguished from other knowledge.

The query evaluation approach has a comparable query explanation capability to the deductive inferencing approach. In deductive inferencing, explanation involves backtracking the proof tree. In query evaluation, it involves backtracking the query evaluation tree. The query evaluation approach may have to deal with a lower level of detail than is required for the deductive inferencing approach. This can easily be handled by exploiting intermediate definitions. It is reasonable to assume that the defined terms are understood by the user, and so explanations need only be given in terms of the current state of the interpretation I.

Consider the addition of the following intermediate definitions to the example of Figure 3.2. Two reports are "from the same source" if they both have the same id#. A negative report "cancels" a positive report if they both have the same ship and position. Position can then be defined in terms of these intermediate definitions as given by a positive report when all other reports from the same source are canceled. The response to the explanation request "Why is the Kennedy shown at point-U?" might be "There is a positive report for point-U, and all other reports from this source are canceled." Intermediate definitions fit naturally into the query evaluation approach.

This concludes the comparison of deductive inference in ES's with query evaluation in DBMS's. Let's give a proof-theoretic explanation for the results. It is generally known that a more efficient deductive search is possible if the axioms are restricted to conjunctions of simple predicate clauses (i.e. no negations, disjunctions, or existential quantifiers). Disregarding some minor complications, the tuples in an interpretation I can be regarded as axioms in this form.

The effect of moving from a knowledge representation for deductive inference to one for query evaluation, is to transform the axioms to a simpler form. However, queries are correspondingly transformed to a more complex form. The overall effect is to transfer complexity from the axioms to the queries. Such a transfer would be pointless, if it were not for the fact that it allows a more efficient deductive search mechanism to be employed.

3.4. Conclusions

We will assume that the properties of deductive inferencing are typical of other types of ES inferencing. On this basis the following conclusions about the relative capabilities of ES's and DBMS's can be reached.

When first-order logic is employed for predicate definitions in DBMS's, DBMS's cannot represent as large a class of knowledge as ES's. However, this situation could be improved significantly if a more powerful definition language were adopted, for example a recursive form of predicate definition.

In cases where ES's and DBMS's represent the same knowledge, both systems can support similar querying and explanation functions. However, DBMS's can answer queries much more efficiently than ES's.

ES's have a more flexible form of knowledge representation, but it is not clear that this flexibility is needed in most applications.

ES's employ a very powerful, yet computationally expensive, search mechanism. The search mechanism is the same for all knowledge. DBMS's employ a far less powerful, yet computationally economical, search mechanism. To offset the lack of power, DBMS's allow the search mechanism to be extended, via definitions, to handle additional kinds of knowledge.

The key design criterion for dispersing functionality between ES's and DBMS in an EDS can now be stated. The ES should only be used for those cases of inferencing where the power of its search mechanism is really needed. In other cases, simpler search mechanisms should be used. In particular, the DBMS should be delegated maximum responsibility for searching shared information. The goal is to minimize the amount of knowledge involved in the search cycle of the ES. This goal is entirely compatible with the second goal of giving the DBMS maximum scope for optimization, so as to reduce secondary storage access costs.

In the next section, this design criterion is applied to two examples of an EDS.

4. EXAMPLE EDS APPLICATIONS

As defined above, an EDS is intended for applications involving knowledge-based processing of shared information. Two such applications will be examined in this section. The objective is to develop a better understanding about interactions between ES and DBMS components in an EDS.

The two applications described here are based on real applications that we have been involved with at CCA. Some of the details of the real applications have been omitted so as to focus more clearly on the larger issues. The first application involves multiple expert systems on the data input path to the DBMS. While system performance is a critical factor, substantial real time delays are acceptable. The second application involves multiple expert systems on the output path from the DBMS. In this case, real time response is required.

The first application is an automated map production system. The DBMS must maintain a model of the world's surface which reflects changes over time. The surface model is being continuously updated on the basis of raw image data received from satellites. The raw images must be analyzed to extract information about significant features. This structured information is then used to update the surface model. On the output side, the surface model is used to automatically generate (hardcopy or softcopy) maps according to given map specifications. The size of the database is estimated to be on the order of 10**19 bytes.

The arrival rate of raw image data is so great that human analysts cannot keep up with it using manual methods. Each human analyst must be aided by an expert system for feature analysis. Given a raw image, an ES must interpret the image and identify features. Typically, when the ES is forming hypotheses about certain features, related information must be retrieved from the existing surface model in the DBMS. When features have been extracted, the ES must update the surface model accordingly. Up to one thousand human analysts may each be simultaneously using an ES.

Let's consider the interactions between ES and DBMS components in this application.

A key fact is that, when processing a particular raw image, all relevant database information comes from a localized geographical area. The ES needs to have as rapid access as possible to this local information. This suggests that the surface model database should be distributed and that the ES should have access to its own node. Local information can be replicated at this node prior to the start of an image analysis session.

During a session, the ES will need to retrieve information (from its DBMS node) to help with hypothesis formation and also to corroborate hypotheses already formed. For efficiency, it is essential that these retrievals return as little information as possible into the search cycle of the ES. This means that the retrieval queries must be formulated as tightly as possible. This can only be done if the DBMS query language captures the principal semantics of the application. In this case, it is the semantics of space and time that dominate the application. It is essential that the DBMS query language support these semantics.

There is no real-time requirement for newly extracted features to appear in maps. This means that surface model updates can be retained during the session in the ES's own node of the distributed database. When the session ends, all updates can be integrated with the main database in one step. In this way, time-consuming distributed concurrency control operations are avoided during a session. However, this is not a standard form of concurrency control provided by distributed DBMS.

In summary, the secret to optimizing the EDS performance for this application is to develop a new kind of distributed DBMS which supports:

— a query language and data model with space and time semantics,

— batched reintegration of updated replicated information.

The second example of an EDS application is a system for Naval Tactical Situation Assessment for use on board ship. The DBMS in this system must store both static and dynamic information. The static information includes maps, charts, ship characteristics and weapon characteristics. Dynamic information includes real-time "contact" reports describing the positions and actions of other ships and aircraft in the vicinity. The change over time of the dynamic information is important as well as the current state.

On the data input side, the DBMS must be able to rapidly receive, store, and commit contact reports. The reports are received at high and bursty rates. Each report must be made available through the database to users very quickly after it is received.

On the data output side, there must be application programs to meet a variety of standard command and control reporting functions. In addition, multiple expert systems are required for threat analysis. The ES's will specialize in different kinds of threats, for example air, surface, subsurface, and mine threats. The ES's must identify contacts, try to determine their intentions, analyze the threats they pose, alert users, and suggest alternative courses of action.

Let's examine the interactions between the DBMS and ES components in this application.

The key problem in this application is alerting users to impending threats in real-time. As soon as the database commits data relevant to a threat, the appropriate ES's must act on it. It does not make sense for the ES's to keep on repeatedly polling the DBMS to see if relevant new data has arrived. This just wastes effort in both the ES's and the DBMS. Instead, the DBMS should alert the appropriate ES's when they need to respond to a situation.

This means that certain production (situation-action) rules should be moved down from the ES's to the DBMS. When the DBMS discovers that a certain situation holds, its action is to interrupt an ES, and supply it with sufficient information that it can take charge of the situation. The more analysis the DBMS performs on the situation, the less likely it is to interrupt the ES unnecessarily.

In general, the DBMS may have to check several hundred situation predicates in real-time whenever new contact reports are received. It could be argued that DBMS's cannot hope to do this efficiently. While this is true of existing DBMS designs, there is vast scope for innovative hardware/software solutions to this problem.

Typically, after an ES has taken charge of a potential threat situation, it will start analyzing the situation in higher-level terms than the information actually stored in the database. These higher-level terms would usually be defined using logic rules. Now consider what should happen when the ES needs to retrieve some additional information from the database.

For efficiency reasons, these additional queries should return as little information as possible back into the search cycle of the ES. This means that the queries should be expressed to the DBMS in the higher-level terms used by the ES. Otherwise the DBMS will return much more information than is necessary, and the ES will have to extract the required information using a search directed by the logic rules. In general then, all logic rules that may relate to follow-up queries should be moved down to the DBMS where they can be processed as part of the query.

Currently, DBMS's are unable to process recursive logic rules. This is unfortunate as these rules are computationally the most expensive, and thus the rules which can benefit most from being moved down. A major thrust is required to develop techniques for processing and optimizing recursive queries in DBMS's.

In summary, the key steps to optimizing EDS performance in this application are to develop a new class of DBMS that can:

— efficiently process a large number of situation-action rules over the database on the arrival of new information,

— optimize and process recursive logic rules over the database in response to query requests.

5. RESEARCH ISSUES

The analysis of the applications in the previous section identified three capabilities which should be moved into the DBMS component of an EDS, specifically: space and time semantics, situation-action rules, and recursive logic rules. A deeper analysis of these, and other, applications will doubtlessly reveal additional capabilities. The full impact of moving capabilities to the DBMS will be understood only when processing and optimization techniques have been developed. However, the removal of activities from the expensive search cycle of the ES into the cheaper search mechanism of the DBMS should give a major performance improvement.

Let's consider some of the research issues in moving the above three capabilities to a DBMS. There have been several proposals for handling time in DBMS's. The basic idea is to retain and timestamp old information versions. Several semantic problems remain to be resolved, and performance issues are largely unexplored. Most work on spatial databases has been application specific and involved ad-hoc extensions to a DBMS. Full integration of spatial capabilities into the data model, physical structures, and query language of a DBMS is only partially understood.

Logic rules can already be processed in a DBMS. These correspond to the definitions in a DBMS knowledge representation. However, these definitions are not recursive. Recursive definitions would provide a dramatic increase in the knowledge representation power of DBMS's, and allow more processing to be offloaded from the ES. Some research has been done on adding recursion to relational query languages. However, this has focussed on the power of the resulting language, and little has been done on optimization strategies for recursive queries. It is known that various forms of recursion can be processed efficiently using algorithms such as Warshall's, or Schnorr's. It remains to be seen whether these forms of recursion can be detected by the DBMS, and efficient algorithms utilized.

Situation-action rules are related to DBMS integrity constraints. Integrity constraints are checked at the time of information entry. However, when integrity constraints are triggered, they normally lead to the raising of an error condition. When situation-action rules are triggered, they would lead to alerting of the ES or the user. Research has been done on the efficient checking of integrity conditions. However, this work has normally focussed on the processing of single rules. In the context of an EDS, there may be several hundred rules to check. A lot more research is required in this area.

ACKNOWLEDGEMENTS

The ideas in this paper have resulted from interactions with the Internal Research Group at CCA. This group, led by Umesh Dayal, includes Michael Brodie, Hai-Yann Hwang, Frank Manola, Arnon Rosenthal, Sunil Sarin and Susan Seltzer.

PART II:
Working Group Reports

Knowledge Base Management Systems:

Discussions from the Working Group

Michael L. Brodie

Computer Corporation of America
Working Group Chairman and Organizer

Speakers:

Robert Balzer

Information Sciences Institute

Gio Wiederhold

Stanford University

Ron Brachman

Fairchild Lab for AI Research

John Mylopoulos

University of Toronto

The concept of a Knowledge Base Management System (KBMS) provided a framework within which to place most topics relevant to the workshop. Hence, there were more than 65 attendees (i.e., 60 percent of the workshop registration). The following is the chairman's summary of the Working Group discussions along with comments received before the Working Group began.

Introduction

Michael Brodie: A major reason for the interest in interactions between AI and Databases is the realization that, on one hand, significant improvements in productivity and functionality of information systems require AI techniques such as those provided by knowledge-directed and reasoning systems. On the other hand, practical application of the same AI technology requires progress in systems and efficiency issues such as those addressed by database management research. A meeting point for the two technologies is the concept of a **knowledge base management system** (KBMS) which could be defined as:

> **A system providing highly efficient management of large, shared knowledge bases for knowledge-directed systems.**

KBMSs are being proposed in order to provide friendly environments for the construction, retrieval, and manipulation of large, shared knowledge bases with functionalities such as deductive reasoning, concurrent access, distribution of a knowledge base over several geographic locations, error recovery, and security.

The necessity of integrating AI and Database technologies has been widely recognized, particularly in projects that build tools for developing knowledge-directed applications. Table 1 is an incomplete list of 40 such projects or tools. Although all projects claim some form of database, most of them use simple file system concepts. However, fifteen of the systems make significant use of database, and AI technology and could be considered to have prototype KBMSs.

At this early stage of KBMS development, we might ask four important questions:

1. What is a KBMS's potential functionality, knowledge representation capabilities, and architecture?
2. What are the potential requirements and application classes for a KBMS? That is, what services will a KBMS provide to what human user or software system?
3. What important research questions must be answered in order to make KBMSs a reality?
4. What approaches are being taken to the research questions and to KBMSs in general? In particular, which of the following four approaches are being taken to the "integration" of AI and Database technology to realize KBMSs?
    1. Loosely couple an existing AI system with a DBMS.
    2. Extend a DBMS by enhancing the data model with knowledge representation and other AI capabilities.
    3. Enhance an AI system with database functionality.
    4. Tightly integrate database and AI system functionality including data model and knowledge representation concepts.

The current situation for KBMSs is reminiscent of the early days of Database Management when there was an open discussion of desirable features and capabilities for database management systems (DBMSs).

KBMS Functionality

Michael Brodie: The functionality of a KBMS will be inherited from Database, AI, and possibly other technologies.

From DBMSs, KBMSs might inherit traditional database management functions for large, shared databases including: (semantic) data models, languages (i.e., definition, query/browsing, manipulation, transaction), semantic integrity definition and maintenance, multiple views, storage/search structures, search and update optimization, concurrency, security, error recovery, and possibly distribution of data and processes.

To support knowledge-directed applications, KBMSs might inherit facilities from AI for: rich knowledge representation schemes and languages; deductive reasoning/search with backtracking; control structures for deductive, plausible, and inductive reasoning; knowledge refinement and validation; automatic classification of knowledge; explanation; and dynamic human intervention. For example, a KBMS that provides deductive search over a knowledge base also must provide appropriate explanations related to the deductions.

KBMSs also might inherit features from other areas, such as programming languages and software engineering, and concepts such as powerful, user-friendly, development environments.

John Mylopoulos: KBMSs also might provide implementation facilities. Having built and validated a knowledge base using a KBMS, one also should be provided with implementation tools with which to generate efficient code.

Alex Borgida: The increased knowledge capacity and problem solving capabilities expected of KBMSs will lead to a requirement for powerful exception handling. KBMSs should combine the flexibility of AI knowledge bases (e.g., LISP structures) and the efficiency of a DBMS. That is, KBMSs should combine the benefits of strong typing and compilation with those of run-time type checking and run-time specification of alternative actions.

Experience with databases strongly suggests having an integrated language for describing and accessing knowledge bases and the associated programs.

William Mark: Due to the large size and complexity of knowledge bases, KBMSs should take substantial responsibility for organizing new knowledge. When human modellers modify a knowledge base, the KBMS should automatically classify the change and check for possible errors. Automatic classification is for a knowledge base what an error-checking compiler is for a complex program. It will encourage more precise and more comprehensive modelling.

Ulrich Reimer: The roles suggested for KBMSs will result in both people and software being heavily dependent on KBMSs for knowledge and data. Hence, knowledge base validity will be critical. It also will be extremely difficult to ensure if knowledge bases are to support multiple knowledge representations and are to be large, complex, shared, and frequently updated.

KBMS Knowledge Representation Capabilities

Michael Brodie: There is general agreement that KBMSs support multiple knowledge representation schemes and languages, as well as powerful means for structuring knowledge. Typically, the power of first order logic is considered a measure of the minimum representation power required. The knowledge representation requirements lead to some of the most challenging research issues.

John Mylopoulos: The most important KBMS feature is the knowledge representation language (KRL). This is similar to the importance of the data model in a DBMS. Since knowledge is both complex and voluminous, the KRL must provide organization principles. These principles must be grounded in epistemology rather than in efficiency as is the case with data model organizational principles. The KRL must have the power of first order logic and must provide means to represent control knowledge.

KBMS Architecture

Michael Brodie: The typical view of a KBMS is that it support multiple, cooperating knowledge-directed applications and tools, and provide multiple interfaces (e.g., natural language; interactive graphical; query/browsing; database transaction; knowledge base update; integrated definition, access, and manipulation). KBMS architectures were viewed as consisting of two levels (i.e., a kernel supporting extended DBMS functions and a second level supporting more AI and knowledge engineering functions) or three levels (i.e., a special processor level, an integrated KBMS level, and an application level). Performance concerns will determine both the functionality and interfaces of components in a KBMS architecture.

Roles of a KBMS

John Mylopoulos: A KBMS could provide a computational environment for a new software development paradigm in which the most important task is the construction of the knowledge base rather than the construction of programs or the database. Once we are convinced that the knowledge base is adequate, we use the KBMS to address the computational issues.

Rolf Stachowitz: The basic function of a KBMS should be to provide context-free information and context-sensitive advice. It should cooperate with the user to accomplish tasks such as software development, knowledge acquisition (e.g., natural language analysis of text), and knowledge base access. A KBMS should be able to work autonomously without advice about the input, output, and algorithms to be used. As a software development tool, a KBMS could have expert systems to assist with software development issues such as which knowledge representation should be used for a given problem. All these functions would require large knowledge bases and significant knowledge-directed processing.

Bob Balzer: KBMSs should support a higher level of discussion and do more for us. In particular, a KBMS should assume responsibility for maintaining consistency that has been specified declaratively. A KBMS also should provide tools to support evolution and the iterative development of large systems. For example, we need tools to assist in modifying the schema, which requires changes to the data and to the code.

Gio Wiederhold: Current DBMSs provide reports that humans use to produce the appropriate information for human decision makers. A KBMS should apply knowledge to databases to produce the appropriate information directly.

Sham Navathe: Unlike current DBMSs, a KBMS should provide intelligent assistance. For example, a KBMS should be able find possible alternative budgets for a manager who is attempting to cut her budget by 20 percent.

Marco Valtorta: A KBMS should provide tools similar to those being developed for new expert system writing systems (e.g., for developing, refining, evaluating, validating, and debugging knowledge bases). For example, there might be tools to validate certainty factors both in terms of meaning (e.g., to assist knowledge engineering) and in terms of precision (i.e., validating the numeric values and ensuring the desired effect on the system). Other tools might check for ambiguity and consistency. Such tools will be problematic for systems such as MYCIN and PROLOG which encourage the use of ad hoc programming tricks that go beyond the paradigm of the language.

Jonathan King: The following roles have been proposed for KBMSs: decision support system, cognitive model, software development environment, special purpose problem solver, tool kit for application building, and system for better presentation of data. A possible way out of this muddle is to identify the services or functions that we expect of a KBMS. These might include: assimilation of new information of many kinds and associated confidence levels, question answering, explanation, remembering, and roadmaps to other systems. For a particular class of applications or tasks, we can choose a subset of services. A valuable job would be to ennumerate the kinds of tasks (e.g., customers, types of systems) and services, and the task-service mapping to produce types of KBMSs.

Knowledge Representation

Ron Brachman: It may be useful to point out to those not familiar with AI jargon that the following pairs are not equivalent:

Artificial Intelligence	and	expert systems (ES)
ES	and	rule-based systems
commercial ES	and	ES
ES development tools	and	ES
logic programming	and	Prolog
knowledge representation	and	programming languages

Knowledge representation will be a fundamental research issue for KBMSs. We must be able to establish the competence of a knowledge representation system. Important knowledge representation issues include expressive power, representing sentences of certain declarative forms, epistemological adequacy, inference (that must be well-defined by formal semantics), and the computation need for inference.

Two issues that are not relevant to the question "What is a knowledge bases?" are inheritance and procedural attachments. Inheritance is an implementation technique for certain kinds of inference. It is not essential and in some cases, such as in large, complex networks, may not be optimal. Procedural attachments tend to provide escapes from the knowledge representation system. Although these may be useful for programming they do not permit analysis to determine what functions are being computed and whether the computation will halt.

Rolf Stachowitz: Just as inheritance is an implementation issue so is inference, since databases can be completely extensional.

Gene Lowenthal: Ron, could you clarify your comment that KRLs are not programming languages? In that context, is PROLOG a reasonable knowledge representation language for databases?

Ron Brachman: Programming and representation languages are typically designed with different concerns in mind. For example, programming languages generally are not designed for the issues just mentioned whereas representation languages are not designed for, say, iteration and recursion. PROLOG and LISP are used in AI as programming languages. Since they do not strictly address knowledge representation issues, they are not KRLs per se. Up to the point where the language paradigm fits the problem being programmed, you are using the language as a representation language. To go outside the paradigm is to treat the language as a programming language. PROLOG is a representation language for the Horn clause subset of first order logic (modulo the nonlogical features). Is that paradigm appropriate for databases? To branch outside PROLOG or to use a nonlogical feature is to treat PROLOG as a programming language.

Knowledge Base Architecture

Ron Brachman: To understand the term "knowledge base" and its role in a KBMS we must look at the "knowledge level" and consider how it operates. A knowledge base may have an architecture consisting of multiple reasoning components. In KRYPTON, a knowledge representation system at Fairchild, knowledge is divided into two parts. One part deals with terminology in a domain (i.e., the definition of complex logical terms and predicates). The other part deals with facts or contingencies of the domain and the related assertional reasoning. Each kind of knowledge has different demands on the representation framework. Within each of the two parts, we may want progressively more complex reasoners. For example, PROLOG may be used for a certain class of problems whereas a more complex reasoning component (e.g. Stickel's first order theorem prover) is used for a richer class of deduction. This leads to a two-dimensional integration of reasoning components: terminological with assertional, and more complex with less complex. Hence, the knowledge representation deductive component could consist of multiple, hopefully integrated, reasoning components.

Knowledge versus Data

Gio Wiederhold: The distinction between databases and knowledge bases (hence DBMSs and KBMSs), is based on the distinction between data and knowledge. The following table contrasts the attributes that I associate with knowledge and data.

KNOWLEDGE	DATA
small volumes	large volumes
intentional (schema level)	extensional (database level)
imprecise	verifiable, often erroneous
statements applicable to large groups of facts	factual, atomic statements
supplied by "experts"	maintained by clerks

These differences lead me to the following operational definition of data versus knowledge:

If you would let a clerk update it, then it is "data." If you let experts update it, then it is "knowledge."

For example, the statement that "a person is 45 years old" can be verified and entered by a clerk, hence it is data. Definitive statements such as "a person is middle-aged" and "middle aged people are careful" are evaluations to be made by experts and are therefore knowledge. In situations such a research environment, a person may play the roles of both a clerk and an expert. In most data processing environments, the roles are distinct.

This intuitive distinction is useful in designing KBMS architectures and tools but not in representation or storage management. For example, it may be reasonable to have distinct update interfaces for data and knowledge since the effects of updating shared knowledge can be much more widespread than those of updating facts. However, the same representation and query language could be used for both data and knowledge. Tools for verifying databases can be based on metrics for correctness. However, tools for examining belief and precision of knowledge would require judgement; hence, they would be completely different in nature. An interesting quote from Turing in this context is: "If a machine is expected to be infallible, it cannot also be intelligent".

John Mylopoulos: Several attributes of what you call knowledge (e.g., verifiability, justification, correctness, inconsistency, informality, generality) also are applicable to what you call data.

Rolf Stachowitz: There is nothing small about knowledge. 50,000 rules frequently are are being discussed for the near future. Within ten years, I expect KBMSs to handle 10**6 rules. The Japanese are discussing rule bases of 10**9 rules.

Francisco Corella: Gio's distinction seems to be between propositional (data) and quantified (knowledge) logic. Databases are restricted to model theory (i.e., ground clauses without functors, which is an interpretation of logical symbols) so that database deduction (i.e., search) terminates and is efficient.

Rudolf Bayer: Gio's distinction is evident and useful. There is a clear distinction between factual knowledge and the knowledge used to deduce other facts. This produces a useful operational distinction. For example, data acquisition (e.g., database maintenance) is a quite different process from knowledge base design.

Knowledge Bases versus Databases

John Mylopoulos: To distinguish DBMSs and KBMSs we must distinguish databases and knowledge bases. A **database** consists of mathematical structures together with a computational theory that states how the structures can be implemented efficiently. A **knowledge base** contains symbolic structures with a notion of interpretation of a specific subject matter. The different emphasis on computation versus interpretation has always distinguished database and AI research. The distinction emphasizes the extremes. In practice, much AI and Database research lies between the extremes.

Rolf Stachowitz: Databases can be considered models that have associated interpretations.

David Beech: Although your characterization may distinguish AI and Database research, it does not distinguish databases and knowledge bases. Most existing DBMSs, such as IMS, do not have mathematical structures with an associated computational theory.

AI versus Database Approaches

Bob Balzer: Although the AI and Database communities have common interests (e.g., integrity constraints and multiple views), they typically have different approaches to realizing systems. One difference concerns physical representation. AI systems tend to be memory-based whereas database systems are disk-based. However, the two communities are beginning to use each other's techniques. A second difference concerns evaluation. AI systems emphasize interpretation (i.e., delayed binding) to retain flexibility and permit prototyping. Database systems attempt to take advantage of compilation (i.e., early commitment). From this background, the choice of approaches for a particular system is based on data and transaction volumes as well as on expected system stability (e.g., prototyping versus optimization).

Ron Brachman: Gio's distinction between knowledge and data suggests to me a fundamental difference between assumptions underlying AI and Database research. The assumption that DBMSs have different types of users may lead to architectural and language decisions about DBMSs. AI systems do not support different types of users. Since AI research is motivated by human reasoning, AI systems are intended for all (i.e., complete) individuals and are intended to be self-contained (e.g., contain all types of knowledge: common sense knowledge, expert knowledge, simple facts, complicated rules, heuristics, definitions).

Mike Stonebraker: AI and Database research has a fundamental difference in timeframes. The AI timeframe is at least a decade away. Rather than discussing how to improve and integrate existing AI and database technology now, AI researchers concentrate on longer term issues such as developing the next generation of AI systems. The databases timeframe is tomorrow.

Bob Balzer: The solution to integrating AI and Database technology is not to simply stick them together now. We must determine how the two technologies might fit together. This is clearly supported by the many discussions that point out mismatches between the two technologies. Hence, KBMS technology cannot be produced tomorrow.

Implementation versus Knowledge Level Approaches

Mike Stonebraker: I do not see many of the distinctions being made here. First, an expert system is simply an application program for which there are many tool kits. OPS-5 was used to write DEC's expert system that configures DEC equipment. PL/1 was used to write IBM's program that configures IBM equipment. We seem to be talking about which tool kits apply to which application programs. Second, we seem to be putting binary order (i.e., expert system or not) on a large collection of applications that range from simple rule based systems (e.g., in automatic teller machines) to very complex expert systems.

John Mylopoulos: In AI systems there are two levels, the knowledge level and the implementation level. Concerns at the knowledge level include knowledge representation (including organization), knowledge acquisition, and adequacy and relevance of the knowledge for the desired task. Having completed work at the knowledge level, any language can be used at the implementation level. When talking about tool kits, Mike Stonebraker has ignored the level and issues of primary importance in AI (e.g., what is the relevant knowledge, how should it be organized, how should the system reason to solve the identified task). An expert system is not an application program. It is a system with a knowledge base that uses a KRL and a reasoning component (all developed at the knowledge level) and can be implemented in any language. The implementation language does not make an application an expert system.

Eugene Lowenthal: Before there were DBMSs, application programs had to provide database management. How they were written and whether they were DBMSs is irrelevant. Similarly, how current knowledge management programs are implemented and whether they are expert systems is irrelevant. The goal for KBMSs is to produce a high level tool for knowledge management.

Revolutionary versus Evolutionary Approaches

John Mylopoulos: We can move from existing AI systems and DBMSs to KBMSs by evolution or by revolution. Of the four approaches identified in the introduction, the first three are evolutionary and the fourth, tight integration, is revolutionary. I prefer a revolutionary approach that would address issues at the knowledge level. We need to jump from the more computational level of DBMSs to the higher knowledge level, just as we needed to jump from assembler language to higher level languages many years ago.

Ron Brachman: The database community may be less interested in the revolutionary approach than in looking for evolutionary ways to improve DBMSs and for problems to avoid. For example, database researchers may wish to avoid computational problems by restricting the expressive power of their data models. They also may be looking to AI for techniques to make DBMSs easier to use (hence, seem more intelligent). However, these techniques may not come from the knowledge representation area or from the expert systems area.

Gio Wiederhold: The revolutionary approach is currently impossible since there are still significant problems with large databases.

Nigel Derrett: I prefer an evolutionary approach in which knowledge-directed processes can be used to improve and augment DBMS functionality and performance. For example, KBMSs should improve data presentation.

Michael Brodie: We do not yet know enough about KBMSs to start a revolution. Whereas we understand data independence, the major DBMS goal, we know little about knowledge independence (i.e., isolation of knowledge from changes in use and in logical and physical structure) which presumably will be a major KBMS goal. (Knowledge independence is related to the AI requirement for knowledge to be used in multiple ways.) We also know little about the proposed ingredients of KBMSs. We know very little about programming paradigms such as OPS and logic programming in comparison with the appropriate application classes and application development. We must understand the requirements, concepts, goals, functionality, and techniques needed for knowledge management before we start to be revolting.

Conclusions

Michael Brodie: At this early stage, the KBMS concept suggests a class of potential and actual (See table 1) systems that integrate selected features from both AI systems and DBMSs. The particular features of a given KBMS will be chosen from a menu of AI features and a menu of DBMS features to meet specific requirements (i.e., to offer specific services to software components and human users). Currently, KBMSs are in a concept formulation stage in which requirements are being formulated, and prototype KBMSs are being built in response to specific needs.

The key research issues concern how to integrate the selected AI and DBMS functions. The most challenging issues fall, not surprisingly, into two levels: the knowledge level and the computational level. The knowledge level requires an integration of AI knowledge representation concepts in order to meet requirements for expressive power, reasoning, and truth management, with concepts from database data models if it is to meet requirements for data/knowledge management. This research should take advantage of the common interest in what the database area calls semantic integrity constraints. Clearly, AI can bring a lot to research at the knowledge level.

The central research issues at the conceptual level concern performance. Existing processing techniques must be applied and new techniques must be developed to efficiently support KBMS functionality. The existence of techniques will determine the KBMS architecture (i.e., the functionality and interfaces of KBMS components and of the KBMS itself with respect to the knowledge-directed systems to be supported). For example, currently optimal database search techniques are being extended to include recursion. This strongly suggests that the DBMS component of a KBMS handle all model theoretic deduction. It is an open issue whether proof theoretic deduction be handled by the knowledge-directed systems to be supported, by the KBMS, or through some cooperation between the two. Clearly, database research can bring a lot to research at the computational level.

Approaches to integrating AI and Database technology must accommodate distinctions between them. Many distinctions have been observed: semantic versus computational theories of information, intentional versus extensional statements, complex versus simple statements, general versus specific statements, complex versus simple update semantics, propositional versus quantified logic, and proof theory versus model theory. The distinctions are useful if they suggest how to integrate AI and Database technologies or how to design KBMSs. Applying labels such as "knowledge" and "data" to the two sides of these distinctions is a terminological exercise that does not aid integration or KBMS design.

A KBMS is intended to be a high-level tool that provides knowledge management for knowledge-directed applications, just as a DBMS provides data management for data-intensive applications. KBMSs will be developed by both evolutionary processes that enhance existing AI systems with DBMS functionality, or vice versa, and revolutionary processes aimed at tight integrations of AI and DBMS technologies. Due to the large number of open issues ranging from KBMS requirements to deep knowledge and computational problems, the revolution will not be starting this evening. However, the evolution towards particular KBMSs has already started (see Table 1). To view these processes as programming problems is to avoid the knowledge level issues, and most of the computational issues, neither of which can be adequately addressed with your favorite programming language.

Development Tools for Knowledge-Directed Applications

NAME	SOURCE	Database	Features
PROBE	Computer Corporation of America, Cambridge, MA (CCA)	YES	semantic DBMS with space & time semantics supports logic rules and recursion
CAT/SDMS	CCA and Carnegie Mellon University	YES	KBMS with database support for graphical database interface and multiple ES applications (in OPS)
STROBE	Sclumberger-Doll, Ridgefield, CT	PLANNED	object-oriented SMALLTALK-like KRL with expert systems features, DBMS, and InterLisp-D environment
KBMS	Stanford University	YES	project on intelligent processing in large databases: design, human interfaces, performance models
KRYPTON	Fairchild, Palo Alto, CA	NO	based on KL-ONE; structures knowledge base into a dictionary of terms and a collection of assertions about the application domain
ARGON	Fairchild, Palo Alto, CA	NO	knowledge representation system
PRISM	University of South Carolina	YES	object-oriented KB system supporting rules for DBMS semantic integrity management
PRISM	University of Maryland	YES	logic programming language compiled on a VAX and executed on ZMOB, a parrallel processor
PRISM	IBM, Yorktown Heights, NY	NO	prototype inference system for building expert systems
EMYCIN	Stanford University	NO	domain independant MYCIN for deductive problems involving diagnosis; production-rules, inheritence, certainty values, backward-chaining

AGE	Stanford University	NO	tool for developing different ES frameworks; supports many AI mechanisms, representations, and control schemes
UNITS	Stanford University	NO	expert system building tool: hierarchies, frames, rules
KAS	SRI	NO	domain independant PROSPECTOR; probabilistic inference rules, partitioned semantic nets
HP-KL	Hewlett-Parkard, Palo Alto, CA	YES	KRL with supporting DBMS
TAXIS	University of Toronto	YES	object-oriented design environment and tools for building information systems; compiles design specifications into PASCAL code

Commercial Application Development Environments

NAME	SOURCE	Database	Features
LOOPS	Xerox, Palo Alto, CA	NO	extended programming environment; integrates procedure-, object-, access-, and rule-oriented paradigms
Automated Reasoning Tool (ART)	Inference Corp., Los Angeles, CA.	NO	interactive development system with superset of knowledge engineering tools: KRL, rule base, viewpoint mechanism, rule compiler, graphics interface
Expert-Ease	Export Software Int'l, Edinburg, Scotland	NO	low-cost knowledge engineering tool
KEE	Intellicorp, Menlo Park, CA	NO	interactive development environment with superset of knowledge engineering tools: rules, frames, descriptive and procedural KRLs, graphics interface, rule compiler & debugger
Knowledge Workbench	Silogic, Los Angeles, CA	YES	development environment; natural language (English) processing system; built on Logic Workbench(see next section)
M.1	Teknowledge, Palo Alto, CA	NO	micro computer based tools for small expert systems applications: KRL, knowledge base debugger, certainty factors
S.1	Teknowledge, Palo Alto, CA	NO	tools for large-scale diagnostic and structured selection applications: KRL, procedural language, inference system
Personal Consultant	Texas Instruments, Houston, TX	NO	Lisp-based, low-cost expert system development package

Picon	LISP Machines Inc., Cambridge, MA	NO	expert system configuration designer for real-time process control systems
EXPLAIN	Knowledge Engineering, Boston, MA	SOME	rule based language with novel mathematical representation and equation solving deduction engine
SRL+	Carnegie Group, Pittsburgh, PA	PLANNED	integrated knowledge engineering environment with logic, rule base, and a frame-based, object-oriented programming language
TIMM	General Research Corp.	NO	frame-based system using a partial-match and analogical inference
FDS	USC/ISI, Marina Del Ray, CA	YES	E-R data model based KBMS for formal software specification
Rosie	Rand Corp., Santa Barbara, CA	SOME	general purpose rule-based programming system; English like syntax, relational database; state-, goal-, and change-driven inference

AI Languages

NAME	SOURCE	Database	Features
KL-TWO	Bolt, Beranek & Newman, Cambridge, MA (also ISI)	NO	KRL with automatic classification
OPS5	Digital Equipment Corporation, Maynard, MA	NO	Vax-based language for developing rule-based expert systems
OPS83	Production Systems Technologies, Pittsburgh, PA	NO	Pascal-like extension of OPS5
YAPS	University of Maryland	SOME	Franz-Lisp based tools: Flavors, Interlisp-like environment, YAPS (OPS-like language allowing LISP expressions, Flavors objects, multiple "databases")
Commonlisp	DEC, LMI, Symbolics	NO	proposed standard Lisp
Interlisp	Xerox, ISI	NO	mature programming environment
Franzlisp	Berkeley	NO	Unix-based Lisp
Prolog	approximately 20 vendors/developers for PCs, micros, minis, and mainframes	SOME	logic programming languages; some with database support
Logic Workbench	Silogic Los Angeles, CA	YES	integrated Prolog-Database system; transparent Prolog access to various DBMSs; interface to C
POP-2	Systems Designers, Ltd.	NO	language integrating PROLOG with a procedural language
PEARL	University of California Berkeley	SOME	frames, strong typing, hashed access to files, pattern matching retrieval

AI Machines

NAME	SOURCE	Database	Features
3600/3640/3670	Symbolics, Cambridge, MA	NO	Zeta-Lisp, KEE, Fortran-77, C, LM-Prolog, Pascal, MACSYMA, Interlisp compatibility package
Chapparal	Texas Instruments, Houston, TX	NO	Common Lisp, Zeta-Lisp, LM-Prolog
Lambda series	Lisp Machines, INC., Los Angeles, CA	NO	Common Lisp, Zeta Lisp-LM-Prolog, C, Fortran 77, Pascal
Dandelion/Dolphin/Dorado	Xerox, Palo Alto, CA	NO	Interlisp-D, LOOPS, Smalltalk, programmers assistant, inspector, structure editor
4404 AI Workstation	Tektronix, Inc., Beaverton, OR	NO	Franzlisp, Prolog, Smalltalk-80, C

Database Machines

NAME	SOURCE	AI	Features
IDM 500/2	Britton-Lee Inc., Los Gatos, CA	NO	relational database backend machine; used in prototype KBMS
CAFS (content addressible file store)	ICL, Great Britain	NO	relational database machine for mutilple, real-time transactions against
DBC/1012	Teradata Corp., Inglewood, CA	NO	multiprocessor relational database machine with parrellel microprocessors and intelligent distribution of data and queries
IDBP	Intel Corp., Austin, TX.	NO	relational, network, and hierarchical back end database machine

Logic Programming and Databases

D. Stott Parker, Jr.
UCLA and Silogic, Inc.

Michael Carey
University of Wisconsin

Forouzan Golshani
Arizona State University

Matthias Jarke
New York University

Edward Sciore
Boston University

Adrian Walker
IBM Research, Yorktown Heights

ABSTRACT

Logic Programming outlines the future of Databases. It permits storage of complex information structures as well as records, blends deduction and procedural constructs into information management, and 'amalgamates' intensional (schema) information with extensional (instance) information. It is elegant and formally based. It also rests at the center of an exciting confluence of many fields, including Programming Languages, Artificial Intelligence, and Databases.

The interface between Logic Programming and Databases is only beginning to be explored. Both fields have much to offer the other. We discuss problems that must be addressed in the incorporation of Database applications within Logic Programming systems. Specifically, we discuss

(1) Extending Logic Programming for Database applications

(2) Adding Database Storage & Query Capability to Logic Programming

1. Introduction

The interface between Logic Programming and Databases is an important aspect of a much larger phenomenon: *the confluence of the information sciences.* As the emphasis on information processing has grown, previously independent symbolic processing disciplines have begun borrowing concepts heavily from one another.

A great deal of excitement is resulting from this confluence. Unfortunately, a great deal of confusion is resulting as well, since the fields all refer to similar concepts with different terminology, and use concepts that are ad hoc or lack a solid foundation. Logic

Programming offers a direction out of the confusion. It is unique in that it offers a consolidation of what has already been done, as well as a sound formal basis on which to build: predicate calculus with Horn clauses.

It is surprising that the merging of Logic Programming and Databases has taken this long to occur. The two fields followed parallel lines of development throughout the 1970's, but have largely ignored one another in spite of a great deal of work at the interface. The references [Gallaire79,81a,81b, Kowalski81] provide excellent surveys of this interface. Perhaps only the selection of Prolog [Clocksin81] by the Japanese FGCS project has precipitated reevaluation of inaccurate perceptions of Logic Programming, such as difficulty of use or of learning (Prolog is taught in some British elementary schools [Ennals82]), inferiority to LISP, inefficiency, etc. It has been observed [Hayes77, Moore82] that most complaints against logic are grounded in misconception.

Much has been written recently about *Knowledge Bases* (also called Inferential Databases, Deductive Databases, and Expert System kernels). These are the information management systems of the future, and will incorporate the results of several decades of work in the Database, Knowledge Representation, Expert System, and Automated Theorem Proving fields. They are now being developed directly using Logic Programming systems.

Both Databases and Logic Programming have much to obtain from confluence. Logic Programming extends Relational Databases with deduction, storage of non-record-oriented information, and the ability to combine schema, metadata, and constraints with database facts [Bowen82]. Logic Programming also provides an elegant and uniform way of implementing views, query languages, and null values.

However, Logic Programming systems such as Prolog do not yet have all the qualities one would want of a Database system. Prolog does not directly support some types of queries, integrity constraints, schema definition, and so forth. Moreover most Prolog implementations are *in-memory* systems: *all* information is loaded into memory (possibly virtual memory) before execution. Secondary storage media are not used to store and query the current state of the information, unless the underlying operating system uses paging.

Clearly there are many issues to be resolved. We have chosen to focus on two key issues:

(1) *Extending Logic Programming for Database Applications*

How can Logic Programming systems be augmented to support query interfaces that are more responsive to user needs? What ways can Logic Programming be used to support modeling, in particular knowledge representation, data definition, and incomplete information? Which Database notions (transactions, concurrency, sophisticated indexing, and so forth) should be incorporated into Logic Programming?

(2) *Adding Database Storage & Query Capability to Logic Programming*

What techniques are useful in implementation of combined Logic Programming/Database systems? Problems range from the most basic architectural issues to optimization of queries.

For Logic Programming examples in this paper we (arbitrarily) use the Edinburgh Prolog notation of [Clocksin81].

2. Extending Logic Programming for Database Applications

By 'extending' Logic Programming here we mean adding new primitives that permit greater support for database users. There are a multitude of extensions of Logic Programming, such as generalized equality predicates instead of simple unification, functional systems, lambda expressions, first-order predicate calculus beyond Horn clauses, typed logics, etc. [Brodie85] discusses issues here. Each of these extensions may help some database applications.

In this paper we shall examine ways to extend Logic Programming to support powerful query handling, data modeling, and aspects of database management (like transactions and integrity constraints) that should make Logic Programming systems more desirable in Knowledge Base applications.

2.1. Extending Logic Programming for Support of Queries

There are two key problems with using Logic Programming as a query interface. The first problem is whether a language like Prolog can be developed for the naive user. First, it is often asked whether something like Prolog can be developed that the naive user (a nonprogrammer) can relate to more directly. It is possible to develop standard database query interfaces straightforwardly using Logic Programming (see, for example, [Neves83]); and Logic Programming supports rapid development of 'natural language' interfaces (for example, [Dahl82]). Still, it is hard to write programs declaratively, and large Prolog programs often depend on procedural features. Zaniolo [Zaniolo85] takes the position that Prolog makes a better navigational query interface, and should be procedural.

Second, it is interesting to speculate on how query interfaces may be made more responsive to user needs. Conventional database systems are mainly concerned with storage and retrieval of data, and the efficiency of these activities. Generally, all of the data must be explicitly stored and the only mechanisms for deriving new facts from the existing information are queries and views. In addition to giving precise and complete answers to questions, knowledge bases should be able to cope with modal queries such as:

- What would be the consequence if X happens? (hypothetical queries)
- Why would X happen?
- What are the objects that are directly or indirectly related to a certain object? (transitive closure)
- Which objects can be candidates for solutions (in addition to the definite answers obtained from the database)?

An interesting problem is how Logic Programming systems can provide the machinery to cope with such queries efficiently.

2.1.1. Making Prolog Queries behave 'Declaratively'

There appear to be two main reasons why Prolog must be extended for use by nonprogrammers. First, many nontechnical people have some difficulty expressing their thoughts in Prolog's logic-like syntax. Second, although a Prolog program has a declarative reading, corresponding to the formal Logic Programming proof-theoretic meaning or the commonsense reading behind it, the procedural reading (i.e., what the Prolog interpreter actually does) is not always the same. For example, the rule

```
fly(X, Z) :- fly(X, Y) , fly(Y, Z)
```

expresses declaratively that a way to fly from X to Z is to fly from X to Y and from Y to Z. Unfortunately this rule cannot be run successfully as a Prolog program to find all answers. In more subtle cases the two readings diverge, and considerable programming skills are needed to bring them into line.

The Syllog system [Walker81b,83b] provides an alternative approach. Syllog is currently implemented in Prolog, and runs experimentally on IBM mainframe computers. It is more declarative than Prolog and provides error checking. The above rule is written in the following form

```
one can fly from eg_place1 to eg_place2
one can fly from eg_place2 to eg_place3
---------------------------------------
one can fly from eg_place1 to eg_place3
```

The premises appear above the line, the conclusion below it, as in a classical syllogism. The syllogism works exactly as one would expect: the procedural meaning is the same as the declarative one. Syllog handles some other recursions that are not possible in Prolog. Some related theory of recursion-handling is developed in [Brough84].

The system forms a syllogistic, expert system-like user interface to a relational data base. The prompt consists of the sentences the system knows about. Facts and syllogisms can be retrieved by picking a sentence from the prompt. The retrieved items can be changed directly on the screen. Explanations of both 'yes' and 'no' answers are generated automatically when needed, and are displayed using the English sentences from the syllogisms [Walker83a]. In fact, the syllogisms can equally well be in French, German, or other natural languages; no dictionary construction is needed.

The above underscores the problems that can arise with recursive or iterative constructs, such as transitive closure, in Logic Programming systems. This is not possible with relational algebra or most other existing database query languages, and is now a major area of research [Henschen84, Ullman84]. The Syllog system uses a mixed backchain and forwardchain approach to give declarative meaning at the user level to a spectrum of recursive queries over a relational data base.

2.1.2. Modality in Query Systems

One way to deal with the modal queries mentioned above is to consider a combination of semantic evaluation and proof-theoretic techniques as tools for the design of knowledge bases, whereby ordinary queries are computed straightforwardly and deduction is used for more sophisticated ones. It is not difficult to achieve this.

Database systems can be seen as dynamically changing objects, but frequently we are interested in every instance of an dynamic object. The reason is an obvious one; updates change the state of the database while the instances are used for answering queries. The distinction between query level and update level enables us to distinguish clearly between, for example, static and dynamic integrity constraints.

For the dynamic aspects we can develop a modal logic system. Modal logic originally began as a vehicle to deal with *necessity* and *possibility.* A collection of possible worlds is considered with an accessibility relation to determine which world is accessible from which. A proposition is called 'necessary' if it can be satisfied in all worlds, and it is called 'possible' if it is satisfied in some.

Modal logic has been used for different purposes in the field of computer science and is particularly suited for the study of dynamic systems as databases. The domain of interpretation (or the universe) of a modal system for databases is the set of database instances and the accessibility relation is determined by the update functions. Depending on what aspects of databases we wish to study, we can use (or define) one or more modal operators. These operators allow us to reason about the past or the future states of the system. For example, we can specify transition constraints or support hypothetical queries.

The database instances can be defined in a number of ways. For example we can consider an instance as:

- an algebra of relations (as in the relational approach)
- a set of Horn clause expressions (as in Prolog)
- a collection of first order assertions (i.e. a many-sorted logic)
- functions and combinators (as in functional query languages)
- a collection of sets and functions (i.e. a many-sorted algebra).

Obviously each approach will suggest a certain method for computation and may enforce some limitations. The universal algebra approach is the least well-known and, surprising enough, has a great deal of power. Here we will expand on it further.

A database instance can be seen as a collection of sets together with a collection of functions mapping these sets to each other. This view should not be totally unfamiliar for the reader as it has similarities to the entity-relationship model. As in abstract data type specification methodology, we can use the signature of the algebra as the basis for the type checker and the syntax checker of the database language.* Computation power is provided by including a sufficiently rich collection of operations (such as arithmetic, set theoretic, etc.) which would be fixed across all applications. Ordinary database queries are then simply expressions which are built up out of the symbols in the signature together with the operation symbols and which comply with the precise formation rules given by the query language. Integrity constraints are expressed as boolean valued expressions that must hold in all instances (or algebras).

The power of deduction can be provided by allowing inference rules which are activated by programs (queries) or users. The inference rules are also boolean expressions, like integrity constraints. The distinction between constraints and inference rules may be a fine one. Although both groups are used for making correct inferences, it is only the integrity constraints that must be considered in updates. Sometimes, however, it is more difficult to make a distinction between the two. For example, if we wish to include the statement 'certain diseases once caught cannot be cured', it is not clear whether this should be a constraint or a rule. Although the deduction rules can be invoked by the language processor, it is possible to define operators which explicitly trigger the inference mechanism. See [Golshani85] for details.

2.2. Modeling and Knowledge Representation in Logic

The Database Modeling field faces a quantum jump as it expands into the Knowledge Representation area. One is no longer required to model just static or even dynamic record structure, but all sorts of knowledge. Fortunately, Logic Programming provides the modeler/knowledge representer with an embarrassment of riches as far as modeling/KR capability is concerned.

An excellent example of the issues involved is in incomplete information. The unbound 'logical variable' of Logic Programming appears to provide many of the properties one wants in modeling the '*Value Unknown*' null values of the Database field. While the notion of 'generalization' in Database Modeling is frequently restricted to **is_a** hierarchies, in Logic Programming a variety of concepts relate to generalization. Generalization diminishes the distinction between 'intension' and 'extension' that is strongly enforced in

*In many-sorted algebra, each set and each function has a name (a symbol) associated it. These names together with the appropriate typing rules for the mappings are contained in the *signature* of the algebra. Readers familiar with database terminology will find it similar in ways to the schema or data dictionary of a database.

Databases: there is a spectrum between intension and extension, and between unknown and known. For example there is a spectrum between generic, or 'most general', newspapers, and a particular copy of a newspaper.

```
newspaper(  Name,      City,            Day,          Edition,     Owner)
newspaper(  'Times',   City,            Day,          Edition,     Owner)
newspaper(  'Times',   'Los Angeles',   Day,          Edition,     Owner)
newspaper(  'Times',   'Los Angeles',   '12/25/84',   Edition,     Owner)
newspaper(  'Times',   'Los Angeles',   '12/25/84',   'Evening',   Owner)
newspaper(  'Times',   'Los Angeles',   '12/25/84',   'Evening',   'Mr. S. Clause')
```

Logic Programming supports this spectrum naturally, and permits intensional information to coexist with extensional information, just as partial information can coexist with total. Furthermore, Logic Programming permits rules to be defined, generalizing collections of tuples or records (static information) with computed information.

The modal framework discussed above accommodates the use of incomplete information, as well as dealing with possible inconsistencies in the database. First order logic and universal algebra (with an appropriate set of primitive operators) have similar expressive power. This equivalence is best demonstrated in cylindrical algebra literature, e.g. in [Henkin71].

The treatment of incomplete information in existing Databases is primitive by comparison. The existence of *'Not Applicable'* null values in relational databases arises only because the relational model is too rigid to permit tree-structured information. For example, to represent information about clothes in a relation, we must supply attributes for each possible clothing attribute (shirt sleeve length, hat size, dress style, etc.) and mark these inapplicable where they do not describe the clothing in question. In Logic Programming systems, however, we can use structures to describe these attributes appropriately:

```
clothes( Item, Manufacturer, Qty )
clothes( shirt(SleeveLength,NeckSize,Color,Style), Manufacturer, Qty )
clothes( hat(HatSize,Color,style(bowler,band(BColor))), Manufacturer, Qty )
clothes( Item, manufacturer(Name,normaladdress(Street,City,Zip),Phone),Qty )
```

Past emphasis on First Normal Form databases is now being actively reconsidered.

It is clear, then, that Logic Programming offers a great deal of power in modeling. Unfortunately, it is not clear *how* this power should be used in modeling. Only experience will determine what is useful here. Goebel's DLOG system is an impressive example of a Logic Programming-based Knowledge Representation system, however [Goebel83]. It provides interesting solutions to fundamental problems involved in representing knowledge with first-order Horn clause logic, such as representation of Negation, Definitions ('iff' is hard to represent in general), and Disjunction [Kowalski79].

2.3. Database Primitives

The past decade has seen impressive advances in database research. Many interesting problems arise from considering their introduction into Logic Programming. Parsaye sketches how schemas, functional dependencies, integrity constraints, and explanations can be implemented easily in Prolog [Parsaye83]. However, the following concepts do not really exist in currently available Logic Programming systems, and their introduction is nontrivial: Transactions, Indexing, and Triggers. It is straightforward to develop experimental implementations of each of these, but the nontriviality arises if we seek a true implementation that is efficient and blends nicely with the Logic Programming paradigm.

We would like an implementation of transactions, for example, that permits our Logic Programming system to recover from crashes.

Also it seems extremely difficult to implement an efficient integrity checker. Integrity checking can equate to theorem proving. (For a logic programming approach that can reduce the need to back out bad transactions, see [Walker81a]). The Syllog system [Walker81b,83b] contains some simple checks for possible user errors, such as rule subsumption and underspecified updates into views. It is also possible to write integrity constraints as syllogisms. However, these will only be checked if the user so indicates. It might be desirable to have the system check updates automatically.

Logic Programming systems tend to have very poor control over updates to the database. The operators **assert** and **retract** are used to update clauses, and thus the notion of a consistent update is problematic. There have been many approaches to this problem, including proof-theoretic ones [Fagin82, Reiter84], and modal logic [Warren84]. This second approach accounts for updates to facts, but general updates to clauses have not yet been considered. [Jarke85] proposed a multi-level hierarchy of theories where each lower-level theory has to be a model of its immediate superior. For example, integrity constraints may control the database state but themselves be controlled by a knowledge base that defines when to apply them. In this way, updates to the integrity constraints are treated on a higher level than updates to the database.

In general, there is a need for more work on metalevel concepts, such as types, triggers, and scheme definition.

3. Adding Database Storage & Query Capability to Logic Programming

In this section we consider how to extend a logic programming system with database features. The goal is to have a system that is as efficient as a conventional DBMS, but has more powerful query and meta- languages. We will address open problems in four areas: system architecture, query optimization, constraint management, and data sharing.

3.1. System Architecture

There are three main approaches to designing a system that has both database and logic programming capabilities. One can

(1) add more powerful inference facilities to a conventional database system [Stonebraker84],

(2) couple an existing database system with a logic programming system [Chang85, Jarke85],

(3) or add database facilities to a logic programming system [Chomicki83, Lloyd83, Naish83, Sciore85].

The approaches share many open questions, but there also are important differences.

The first architecture does not completely cover the inferences of Prolog, since it does not take into consideration function symbols (hence data structures such as lists). Research in this area seems to be focused on providing general abstract data type facilities to the query language instead. Query languages of this type are far afield from Horn clause logic; more results are needed in order to verify the power of such systems as database backends.

A disadvantage of the third architecture is that it seems to require writing a large portion of a database system. The potential effectiveness of an integrated system is large; designing such a system could produce new insights about the relationship between databases, programming languages, and operating systems.

The second architecture is faced with the problem of coupling two existing systems. There are increased optimization problems because of a possible mismatch between logic programs and the DBMS [Zaniolo85], and the cost of communication is quite high. Initial experiences indicate that this architecture performs well on typical queries, but is less efficient in a concurrent or dynamic environment.

A simple example of such an architecture is the PROSQL interface between Prolog and the SQL/DS database system, running in experimental form on the VM/CMS operating system [Chang85]. SQL/DS resides on its own virtual machine, handling queries and data manipulation requests from one or more Prolog tasks on other virtual machines.

A query in PROSQL is a special Prolog predicate of the form

sql('*<well-formed SQL command>*')

When the predicate is encountered during Prolog execution, the SQL command is executed on the server machine, and the results are deposited in the Prolog workspace. If the SQL command contains an INTO phrase, then Prolog variables can be bound to the results of the query.

Recently Silogic Inc.'s *'Logic Workbench'*® has become available. This commercial system encompasses the second *and* third architectures above. The Logic Workbench comprises a Prolog system together with a Prolog knowledge base system (a database manager for Prolog clauses), and a general interface connecting Prolog to existing DBMS. Access is extended to outside DBMS by writing a 'DBMS server', a module which converts Logic Workbench requests into DBMS commands.

An effort has been made to integrate the Logic Workbench architecture both with Prolog and DBMS features. In some cases the result has been features that are new, and otherwise unavailable in today's DBMS or Prolog systems. The Logic Workbench offers schema management, various kinds of pattern retrieval (or, in Logic Programming terms, extended unification), nested transactions, and flexible dynamic indexing. It is one of the first systems bridging the gap between existing AI and DBMS technology.

3.2. Implementation Considerations

Let us consider a performance-oriented, integrated Logic Programming/Database system, built using conventional database system implementation techniques interfaced with the Logic Programming system. Here we sketch some of the ways in which database technology might contribute to the construction of a multi-user Prolog system with a large knowledge base stored on disk.

3.2.1. Access Methods

A number of good disk-based indexing techniques are known and used in implementations of conventional database systems, including tree-based structures for range queries (e.g., B+ trees and ISAM files) and hashing techniques for exact-match queries (e.g., linear and extendible hashing). These indices and their associated access methods can also be used to improve query processing efficiency in a Prolog database system. Existing Prolog/Database systems [Chomicki83, Lloyd83, Naish83] all support advanced methods such as these.

In order to interface with the disk, a logic programming system may implement its own access methods, or it may be coupled with an existing DBMS. An advantage of the first approach is that the access methods can be a simple extension of the logic programming language. In this way the system becomes closely integrated, providing less redundancy and overhead. [Sciore85] describes a few, well-defined built-in primitive predicates that need to be added; more research in this direction needs to be done, especially in regard to 'blocking' (grouping information together on the disk). In coupled architectures, the questions of how to buffer values of views, and how to manage very large rule bases have to be addressed.

3.2.2. Data Sharing

In a system with multiple users, some sort of concurrency control mechanism is needed. Ideally, these mechanisms can be adapted from the usual database techniques.

Prolog systems do not currently accommodate multiple users or provide support for resilient data storage. Prolog database systems will have to provide shared, resilient knowledge bases if they are to be the next generation of database systems (as some researchers claim). Fortunately, a great deal of effort has gone into the design of concurrency control and recovery techniques for multi-user database systems. This work can be adapted for use in Logic Programming environments [Carey85], although certain recovery issues (such as what to do with knowledge base updates from failed subqueries) must be resolved in a satisfactory manner.

3.2.3. Query Optimization

Database query optimization techniques relieve users of relational database systems from having to worry about efficiency issues when formulating their queries. Cost models are employed to select the best plan for processing queries based on estimates of the CPU and I/O costs for each of the possible plans. Many of these same techniques can be used in a Prolog database system to choose the best indices, evaluation orders, join methods, etc., for processing Prolog queries against a large, disk-based knowledge base.

There are several key areas where enhanced query processing capabilities are needed.

Logical Transformations.

Prolog uses variable binding to reduce its search space, and its evaluation mechanism corresponds to a nested loop strategy for joins. Thus goal reordering heuristics [Warren 1981] need to be more closely investigated. The nested loop strategy has little overhead, since it does not need to sort or create intermediate relations. However, it is not as efficient on large relations as, for example, a database sort-merge strategy. It therefore seems necessary to reexamine the strategies used in Prolog and in conventional DBMSs. The proposed mechanisms for lazy evaluation by collecting database calls (using setof predicates [Kunifuji82] or metalevel evaluation [Vassiliou84]) have to be refined. Progress toward a solution of the problem of recursion optimization [Henschen84, Ullman84] appears promising. Finally, view processing, which is at the heart of logic programming, inevitably introduces redundancies at the base relation level. Semantic query simplification based on integrity constraints of the database [Jarke84a,84b, Chakravarthy85] must be further investigated, especially in multiple-query contexts such as recursion.

A great deal of effort has gone into finding efficient join methods for relational database systems. A Logic Programming/Database system should benefit from these techniques. As an example, consider the following rule:

a(X, Y) :- r(X, Z), s(Z, Y).

Suppose that there are a large number of r and s entries in a fact base, and that the two queries 'a(foo,Y)' and 'a(X,bar)' both occur frequently. Both are join queries in relational database terms, but a typical Prolog system would execute the first query much more efficiently than the second one due to Prolog's order of evaluation conventions. If both queries are indeed frequent, then neither order for the clauses in the rule can provide good overall performance. If Prolog's order of evaluation conventions are relaxed, database join methods (e.g., sort-merge, hashing, nested loops) can be applied for processing both queries. The query optimizer can then select the best method from among the available options based on estimates of the costs of the alternatives.

View Maintenance.

Thus far, the bulk of deductive databases have applied their rules at query time only. In contrast, [Nicolas78] proposed a generative database in which all rules are applied at update time to store all derivable facts explicitly. A compromise between these extreme positions is needed, where the system pre-stores selected predicates. The question of how to maintain such "concrete views" has been addressed in [Shmueli85] but the question of when they should be used is open. It should also be possible to pre-evaluate and store predicates during query execution; such a facility enables the system to deal with common sub-expressions, and bottom up query processing. The analogy with typical cacheing strategies needs to be explored.

3.3. Problems of Integration

Aside from the deeper technical issues listed above, and ignoring the various political aspects of integration that complicate the task, a number of implementation problems confront the implementor of an integrated Logic Programming/Database system. The following problems are typical of those that must be dealt with:

(1) Most Logic Programming systems have a finite *atom space*, containing all symbols currently defined in a logic program. This atom space can *overflow* when the logic program retrieves a large amount of information from a knowledge base. How can we avoid such overflows? (Interestingly, early relational systems like RAM and XRM [Lorie74] worked with an atom space-approach.)

(2) Logic Programming systems may index relations on certain fields just as in Databases. But these fields may be *structures* instead of atoms. Worse, the fields may be currently unbound. How can indexing be accomplished on these fields?

Generally speaking, both the *degree of integration* of Logic Programming with Databases and the *performance* of a connected system are difficult goals to achieve simultaneously, since the two kinds of systems have historically different architectures and applications.

In the short run, there is a need for coupling because of the many existing commercial databases. In the long run, we expect the integrated methods to become more and more important. However, there remains much technical work to be done in coupling Logic Programming systems and Relational Databases.

4. Conclusions

The confluence of the various information sciences — Databases, Artificial Intelligence, Programming Languages; all fields dealing with symbolic computation — raises many questions. We have surveyed the questions in connecting Logic Programming with Databases, discussing (1) the extension of Logic Programming for Database applications, and (2) the addition of Database storage and query capabilities to Logic Programming. The outlook is extremely positive, in spite of the many challenging problems that arise in each of these endeavors.

Keeping in mind the power of Logic Programming and the drive towards automation of information access, it is tempting also to conjecture that Logic Programming will grow to *subsume* Relational Databases. The resulting Knowledge Bases will set the standard for the next generation of Information Management systems. Some argue to the contrary that by modest additions to Relational Databases, this subsumption will not be necessary. For example, adding recursion to existing query languages and permitting heavy use of 'views' will give Relational Databases some of the power of Logic Programming. Unfortunately, it does not give all of the power, since Logic Programming combines recursion with the use of recursive *structures* (data structures built up with 'function symbols', such as lists). Adding storage of structures to Relational Databases is *not* a modest addition.

It appears difficult to obtain the full power of either Logic Programming or Databases without taking all that each field has to offer.

In any event, it is clear that Databases and Logic Programming have much to learn from each other, and that the upcoming years hold great promise from the exchange of ideas among these fields.

References

[Bowen82] Bowen, K., & R.A. Kowalski, "Amalgamating language and metalanguage in logic programming," *Logic Programming,* K.L. Clark and S.-A. Tarnlund, eds., NY: Academic Press, 1982.

[Brodie85] Brodie, M.L.,& M. Jarke, "On Integrating Logic Programming and Databases," in this book.

[Brough84] Brough, D., and A. Walker, "Some practical properties of logic programming interpreters," Proc. FGCS Conference, November 1984, Tokyo, Japan.

[Carey85] Carey, M., DeWitt, D., and Graefe, G., "Mechanisms for Concurrency Control and Recovery in Prolog - A Proposal," in this book.

[Chakravarthy85] Chakravarthy, U., D. Fishman, and J. Minker, "Semantic Query Optimization in Expert Systems and Database Systems," in this book.

[Chang85] Chang, C.L., and A Walker, "PROSQL: A Prolog programming interface with SQL/DS," Report RJ 4314, IBM Research Laboratory, San Jose, California, 1984. Also in this book.

[Chomicki83] Chomicki, J., "A database support system for Prolog," *Proc. Logic Programming Workshop,* Algarve, Portugal, 1983.

[Clark82] Clark, K., & S-A. Tarnlund, *Logic Programming,* Academic Press, 1982.

[Clocksin81] Clocksin, W.F., & C.S. Mellish, *Programming in Prolog,* Springer-Verlag, 1981.

[Dahl82] Dahl, V., "On Database Systems Development through Logic," *ACM Trans. Database Systems 7,* pp. 102-123, 1982.

[Ennals82] Ennals, R.P., *Beginning Micro-Prolog,* John Wiley.

[Fagin82] Fagin, R., "Horn Clauses and Database Dependencies," *Journal of the ACM 29:4,* October 1982.

[Gallaire78] Gallare, H. and J. Minker, eds., *Logic and Data Bases,* New York: Plenum Press, 1978.

[Gallaire81a] Gallaire, H., "Impacts of Logic on Databases," *Proc. 7th International Conference on Very Large Data Bases,* Cannes, France, 1981.

[Gallaire81b] Gallaire, H., J. Minker, and J-M. Nicolas, *Logic and Data Bases,* New York: Plenum Press, 1981.

[Goebel83] Goebel, R., "DLOG: An experimental Prolog-based database management system," Technical Report, Computer Science Dept., Univ. of Waterloo.

[Golshani85] Golshani, F., "*Specification and Design of Expert Database Systems,*" in this book.

[Hayes77] Hayes, P.J., "In Defense of Logic," *Proc. 5th Intl. Joint Conf. on Artificial Intelligence,* Cambridge, MA, August 1977.

[Henkin71] Henkin, L., J.D. Monk, and A. Tarski, *Cylindrical Algebras,* Part 1, North Holland, 1971.

[Henschen84] Henschen, L.J., and Naqvi, S.A., "On Compiling Queries in Recursive First-Order Databases," *Journal of the ACM 31:1,* 1984.

[Jarke84a] Jarke, M., & Y. Vassiliou, "Coupling Expert Systems with Database Management Systems," in: Artificial Intelligence Applications for

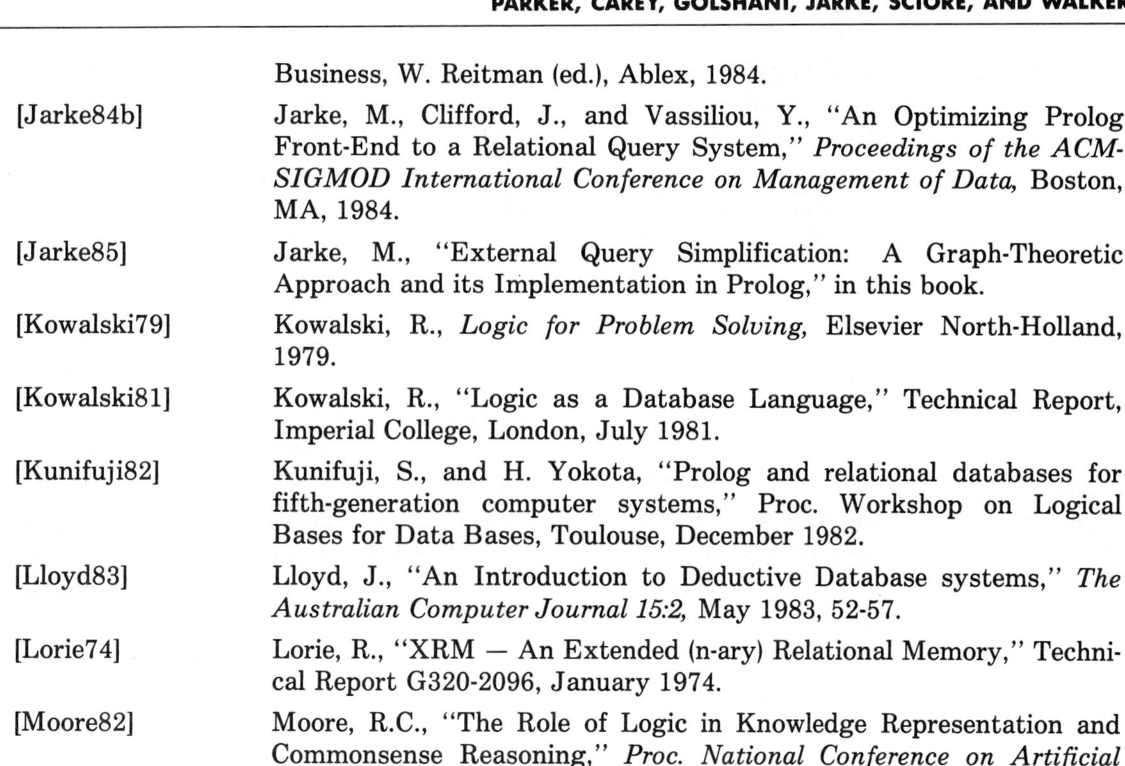

Business, W. Reitman (ed.), Ablex, 1984.

[Jarke84b] Jarke, M., Clifford, J., and Vassiliou, Y., "An Optimizing Prolog Front-End to a Relational Query System," *Proceedings of the ACM-SIGMOD International Conference on Management of Data*, Boston, MA, 1984.

[Jarke85] Jarke, M., "External Query Simplification: A Graph-Theoretic Approach and its Implementation in Prolog," in this book.

[Kowalski79] Kowalski, R., *Logic for Problem Solving*, Elsevier North-Holland, 1979.

[Kowalski81] Kowalski, R., "Logic as a Database Language," Technical Report, Imperial College, London, July 1981.

[Kunifuji82] Kunifuji, S., and H. Yokota, "Prolog and relational databases for fifth-generation computer systems," Proc. Workshop on Logical Bases for Data Bases, Toulouse, December 1982.

[Lloyd83] Lloyd, J., "An Introduction to Deductive Database systems," *The Australian Computer Journal 15:2*, May 1983, 52-57.

[Lorie74] Lorie, R., "XRM — An Extended (n-ary) Relational Memory," Technical Report G320-2096, January 1974.

[Moore82] Moore, R.C., "The Role of Logic in Knowledge Representation and Commonsense Reasoning," *Proc. National Conference on Artificial Intelligence*, CMU, August 1982.

[Naish83] Naish, L., and J.A. Thom, "The MU-Prolog Deductive Database," Technical Report 83/10, Dept. of Computer Science, The University of Melbourne, Australia.

[Neves83] Neves, J.C., R.C. Backhouse, S.O. Anderson, and M.H. Williams, "A Prolog Implementation of Query by Example," *7th International Computing Symposium*, Germany, 1983.

[Nicolas78] Nicolas, J.-M., & K. Yazdanian, "Integrity checking in deductive databases," in [Gallaire78].

[Parsaye83] Parsaye, K., "Database Management, Knowledge Base Management, and Expert System Development in Prolog," Proceedings International Workshop on Logic Programming, Algarve, Portugal, August 1983. Also appeared in ACM SIGMOD Database Week, June 1983.

[Reiter84] Reiter, R., Towards a Logical Reconstruction of Relational Database Theory, in *Conceptual Modeling*, M. Brodie, J. Mylopoulos, and J. Schmidt, eds., Springer-Verlag, 1984.

[Sciore85] Sciore, E., and Warren, D., "Towards an Integrated Database-Prolog System," in this book.

[Shmueli85] Shmueli, O., H. Tsfirah, S. Tsur, "Rule Support in Prolog," in this book.

[Stickel84] Stickel, M., "A Prolog Technology Theorem Prover," *Proc. International Conference on Logic Programming*, Atlantic City, NJ, February 1984.

[Stonebraker84] Stonebraker, M., "Extending a Relational Interface for Expert Systems Applications," preprint, Dept. of Computer Science, Univ. of California, Berkeley, 1984.

[Ullman84] Ullman, J.D., "Implementation of Logical Query Languages for Databases," Technical Report STAN-CS-84-1000, Dept.of Computer Science, Stanford University, May 1984.

[Vassiliou84] Vassiliou, Y., J. Clifford, M. Jarke, "Access to Specific Declarative Knowledge by Expert Systems: the Impact of Logic Programming," *Decision Support Systems 1:1,* 1984.

[Walker81a] Walker, A., and S. Salveter, "Automatic modification of transactions to preserve data base integrity without undoing updates," Report 81/026, Department of Computer Science, State University of New York at Stony Brook, 1981.

[Walker81b] Walker, A., "Syllog: a knowledge-based data management system," Report No. 34, Department of Computer Science, New York University, 1981.

[Walker82a] Walker, A., "Automatic generation of explanations of results from knowledge bases," Report RJ 3481, IBM Research Laboratory, San Jose, California, 1982.

[Walker83a] Walker, A., "Prolog/Ex1, an inference engine which explains both yes and no answers," Report RJ 3771, IBM Research Laboratory, San Jose, California, 1983. Also *Proc. 8th Int. Joint Conf. Artificial Intelligence,* Karlsruhe, West Germany, August 1983.

[Walker83b] Walker, A., "Syllog: an approach to Prolog for non-programmers," Report RJ 3950, IBM Research Laboratory, San Jose, California, 1983. Chapter in *Logic Programming and its Applications,* M. van Caneghem and D. H. D. Warren (Eds.), Ablex, 1984.

[Walker84] Walker, A., "Data bases, expert systems, and Prolog," In *Artificial Intelligence Applications for Business,* W. Reitman, (Ed.), Ablex, 1984.

[Warren81] Warren, D.H.D., "Efficient Processing of Interactive Relational Database Queries Expressed in Logic," *Proc. 7th International Conference on Very Large Data Bases,* Cannes, France, 1981.

[Warren84] Warren, D.S., "Database Updates in Pure Prolog," Proc. FGCS Conference, November 1984, Tokyo, Japan.

[Zaniolo85] Zaniolo, C., "Prolog: A Database Query Language for All Seasons," in this volume.

Object Oriented Database Systems and Knowledge Systems

Carlo Zaniolo
MCC

Hassan Ait-Kaci
MCC

David Beech
Hewlett-Packard

Stephanie Cammarata
UCLA and the Rand Corporation

Larry Kerschberg
University of South Carolina

David Maier
Oregon Graduate Center

ABSTRACT

Object Orientation represents a most successful unifying paradigm in various areas of computing, including Programming Languages, Databases, Knowledge Representation, Computer Aided Design and Office Information Systems. This paper provides an overview of the key technical concepts that form the common basis of the Object Oriented approach, enphasizing the selective and specialized use of these concepts made by the different computing disciplines. Various problem areas are then reviewed, and some current research projects addressing topical problems are discussed. One is the use of Object Oriented architectures for integrating data with metadata and for constraint management in database systems. Another is the design of an integrated system that unifies databases, logic languages and object-oriented programming.

Object Oriented Database Systems and Knowledge Systems

Carlo Zaniolo
MCC

Hassan Ait-Kaci
MCC

David Beech
Hewlett-Packard

Stephanie Cammarata
UCLA and the Rand Corporation

Larry Kerschberg
University of South Carolina

David Maier
Oregon Graduate Center

1. Introduction

The concepts of objects and object-oriented architectures represent a most promising unifying paradigm in the design of Knowledge-Based Systems, Databases, and Programming Languages. Versatility and flexibility constitute proven virtues of this approach, that has been successfully applied to a wide spectrum of applications and programming environments, including:

(1) Programming Languages [Dahl et al. 68, Liskov & Zilles 74, Wulf et al. 76, Goldberg & Robson 83, Cannon 82].

(2) CAD Systems and Engineering Design Databases [Cammarata & Melkanoff 84, Gerzso & Buchmann 84].

(3) Office Information Systems [Adiba & Nguyen 84].

(4) Knowledge Representation Systems [Bobrow & Stefik 83].

(5) Database Management Systems [Copeland & Maier 84].

The term "Object-Oriented," $O-O$ for short, has often been used to denote different concepts in different discipline and applications; thus, in the next section (Section 2) we attempt to provide a better characterization of the concept, by delineating its most salient features and contrasting their relative usage in different application domains. In Section 3 we discussed briefly some of the research issues confronting the designers of $O-O$ systems. Sections 4 and 5 of the paper focus on two promising areas of opportunities for object-oriented architectures.

One area of great opportunity (and technical challenges) involves the unification of different programming paradigms and systems. For instance, the Flavors package features a simple $O-O$ extension of Lisp [Cannon 82], and C++ is an O-O extension of C [Stroustrup 84]. More ambitious schemes propose the integration of object-based programming languages with database systems [Ahlsen et al. 84], [Copeland & Maier 84], [Gerzso & Buchmann 84]. Finally, systems, such as those discussed in [Beech et al. 84] and in Section 4 of this paper, pursue the goal of ultimate integration by seeking a "Grand Unification" of database systems, logic languages and object-oriented programming.

A second important application of object-oriented architectures is the integration of data and metadata discussed in Sections 5 and 6. The traditional approach of first designing a schema and then populating the database is ineffective with CAD applications, where the two processes need to be merged [Maier & Price 84]. A dynamic object-based dictionary organization represents the solution of choice [Cammarata & Melkanoff 84].

In order to operate with intelligence and expertise, a system must make good use of the available knowledge — in the knowledge lies the power. Now the main source of knowledge for a DBMS is represented by its metadata (contained in the data dictionary), which, therefore, must be accessible and manageable as if it were regular data. The problem of constraint and specification management illustrates the advantages of object-oriented architectures in dealing with the integration of data and metadata [Shepherd & Kerschberg 84a/b].

2. What Does Object-Oriented Mean?

A number of related notions are currently associated with the $O-O$ approach. They can be listed as follows:

(1) Data abstraction and encapsulation,

(2) Object identity independent of (mutable) values of properties,

(3) Property inheritance,

(4) Messages,

(5) Overloading,

(6) Late binding,

(7) Interactive interfaces with windows, menus and mice.

The discussion that follows should help clarifying the relationships between these notions and place them in an historical perspective.

2.1. Programming Languages

The proselyting work done by Smalltalk and its supporters [Goldberg & Robson 83] is largely responsible for the visibility of the $O-O$ paradigm in the field of Programming Languages, and for demonstrating its merits for interactive user interfaces. The seeds of many concepts incorporated in Smalltalk can, however, be traced back to previous systems. In particular, Simula 67 should be credited with the notions of data abstraction and encapsulation that lie at the core of the $O-O$ approach [Birtwistle et al. 73]. The basic idea is that every object comes endowed with a set of operators, which are used to operate upon and change the state of the object. An object consists of an interface part, which is public, and of an implementation part, which is kept private.

Objects communicate and perform all computations via *messages*. In Smalltalk, a message consists of three parts respectively used to identify (i) an object (the receiver),

(ii) a method, and (iii) a possibly empty list of arguments. An object consists essentially of a private memory with a public interface. The private memory is structured as a list of named or numbered *instance variables*. Objects are organized into classes that contain the methods that the objects use to respond to messages. Classes are organized in a (strict) hierarchy, so that they can inherit the structures and methods of their superclasses.

Smalltalk's object-method paradigm was designed, and is ideally suited, for programming graphic and menu-based interfaces. While a verb-object form is used for stating imperatives in the English language, systems such as Smalltalk and the popular Macintosh adopt an object-operation style of commands. For instance, the user may first specify an object by pointing at its icon with a mouse, and then select the operation from a small object-specific menu that has appeared on the screen. It is unfortunate that, because of its success with the "windows and mice" style of interfaces, the Object-Oriented approach is often improperly identified with them.

Another salient feature of object orientation is *operator overloading*. Operator overloading describes the useful notion of using the same operator symbol to denote distinct operations on different data types (e.g., it may possible to use the minus sign to denote both integer difference and set difference). The meaning of an operator is therefore overloaded and can be resolved only on the basis of its operand type(s). In interpreting a message, an $O-O$ Language first binds the message head to an object class, then binds the rest of the message to a method for that class. Overloading follows from the fact that distinct methods can be given the same name in two different classes.

As will be discussed in the Section 3, there is a fairness problem when operators have two or more operands. Then one operand must be selected as the message receiver that controls the overloading, while the others (message arguments) are relegated to appendices to the method.

The advantages of overloading become apparent if we take, for instance, an application where the printout of different objects, each with their own format, is requested via a print message. Then, new objects, each with their own print method, can simply be appended on with no further program modification required. In the case of Smalltalk, the *late binding* of methods means that no recompilation is needed, either, favoring flexibility at the expense of speed.

While Smalltalk has found only limited use in the commercial world, perhaps due to this lack of speed (see also discussion in the next section), it has also inspired Lisp- based extensions such as Flavors [Cannon 82] or Loops [Bobrow & Stefik 83], which have gained widespread acceptance. Similar extensions proposed for languages such as Prolog [Zaniolo 84a], or functional languages [Lindstrom 85], reemphasize the flexibility and portability of the approach.

Other systems, such as Actors [Hewitt 77] or Concurrent Prolog [Shapiro 83] are based on the concept of processes communicating through messages. These systems view computation as being carried out by interacting processes each keeping some private state information.

2.2. Databases

The database field has arrived at the notion of objects along an independent, although perhaps equally tortuous, trail. Here the object-based approach can be contrasted to the valued-based paradigm espoused by the original relational approach to databases. While in relational systems, tuples can only be distinguished on the basis of their values, in object-based systems a hidden permanent unique identifier is assigned to each entity record (in a database context the terms "entity" and "object" are normally used as synonymous). An entity occurrence can therefore be implemented to refer to another using the latter's unique identifier. This policy provides a simple means to support relationships between entities and referential integrity constraints, as needed to implement semantic data models such as the Entity-Relationship [Chen 76] model, and Database Aggregation and Generalization [Smith & Smith 77].

The $O-O$ framework also provides better support for managing time and changes in databases. *Referential transparency* represents a first benefit, since any change in an entity value is automatically seen by all entities which refer to it — unlike relational systems, where a change in the key value of an entity is not propagated automatically to other tuples sharing that value.

A second advantage involves *version management*. Old versions of objects can be archived, and later retrieved, using their unique identifier end a time stamp [Copeland & Maier 84], or version number. This feature is invaluable in many applications, including Software or CAD databases where, frequently, there is a need to reestablish the original environment in which software modules or design plans were once operational.

2.3. Knowledge Representation and AI

In the field of AI, frames are the most widely used primitives for Knowledge Representation [Minsky 75]. Although frames were conceived independently of the object-oriented paradigm they are in fact consistent with it, and provide an excellent demonstration of its power and flexibility; indeed frames are capable of representing both specific and general knowledge, and of accommodating both descriptive and prescriptive computations. In a frame system, the properties of both specific objects and generic objects (classes) are described by their slots, which may contain references to other frames (defining their relationships), actual values or procedural attachments to compute them. Of particular importance are ontological relationships between frames, which are, e.g., essential in defining semantic constraints and assigning default values to slots. Thus, generic objects are classified using the $is-a$ relationship, and the membership of an instance-object in a class-object is described using the $as-a$ relationship.

2.4. CAD Systems

The capability of unifying the treatment of data and metadata exemplified by frame systems represents an important strength of $O-O$ systems. As discussed in Section 5, systems for the management of engineering information need this capability, since information at the schema level frequently must be manipulated as regular data [Cammarata & Melkanoff 84]. Moreover, typical VLSI/CAD applications require objects having a complex internal structures, and support for object versions and multiple design transactions [Batory & Buchmann 84].

The second important obstacle encountered in developing DBMS-based CAD applications is an *impedance mismatch* between the programming language used to develop the application and the data manipulation language used to access the database.

(Naturally, this problem is not unique to CAD applications.) A first aspect of this mismatch is the conflict between the prescriptive (imperative) paradigm, typically used by existing programming languages, and the descriptive (declarative) paradigm favored by databases. A second aspect is that the DBMS and the programming language often do not support the same data types and structures; e.g., programming languages may manipulate single records with complex internal structures, while relational systems support sets of unstructured tuples.

The work of [Copeland & Maier 84] and [Gerzso & Buchmann 84] attack the impedance mismatch problem by proposing an integration of databases and programming languages using objects. An even more complete and ambitious "grand unification" scheme is described in Section 4.

2.5. Office Information Systems

A final area, where there is widespread interest in the object-oriented approach, is that of Office Information Systems [Ahlsen et al. 84]. Reasons for this interest are similar to those found in other areas, e.g., the ease-of-use of menus and icons, but there is also a special emphasis on multimedia document management [Beech et al. 84], often in a distributed environment [Adiba & Nguyen 84].

3. Problem Areas

It should be of little surprise that the $O-O$ approach that holds such great promise, also presents significant research challenges and an assortment of technical problems.

3.1. Performance

A main problem area of practical concern is the need for an efficient implementation. The comparatively poor performance of Smalltalk is partially due to the fact that the language is interpreted rather than compiled. Thus, a deeply nested inheritance hierarchy may have to be traversed at run time to fetch the original definition of a method [Borning & Ingalls 81], with an obvious impact on performance. Clearly, performance could be improved by using compilation, since much of this search can be done at compile time. Yet, if a truly dynamic binding and full overloading is desired, there are situations in which the binding of methods to objects must be resolved at run time [Ait-Kaci 85]. In this respect the $O-O$ paradigm may be be more demanding than the functional programming paradigm which is amenable to static typing using polymorphic compilation techniques [Milner 78]. In spite of these limitations, it appears that compilation is crucial in building an efficient $O-O$ systems, and a closer identification of Smalltalk's classes with types should help in this respect [Beech et al. 84]. Performance issues pertaining to $O-O$ mass storage management are discussed in Section 4.

There is no lack of interesting theoretical issues in the $O-O$ approach. Among these, we have the following three problems.

3.2. Overloading

Overloading should be over *all* arguments rather than only the *first* one. There is a certain "unfairness" in the object-oriented computation of existing systems which biases function code retrieval based only on the type of the *first* argument. Full object-oriented computation should consider *all* argument types as characterizing the function to be applied. For example,

Multiply (x: *real* , y: *real*)

and

Multiply (x: *real* , y: *vector*)

should be clearly understood as, respectively, real number multiplication, and scalar-vector multiplication. Such a disambiguation can be done only if the type *tuple* is used as the overloaded type, instead of just the first argument's type.

3.3. Higher Order

Higher-order type hierarchies pose a non-trivial problem to solve. Indeed, to our knowledge, such systems as Smalltalk's classes or Lisp's Flavors are strictly *first-order* type systems. The natural "type-as-set" semantics implicit in a type hierarchy has a strange order-theoretic behavior if extended to functional types. Consider the types $CAR \subseteq VEHICLE$ and $INTEGER \subseteq REAL$. Any function of type $VEHICLE \rightarrow INTEGER$ is also a function of type $CAR \rightarrow REAL$, in the sense that it is defined for all objects of type *CAR* and maps its arguments into objects of type *REAL*, as illustrated by the following diagram.

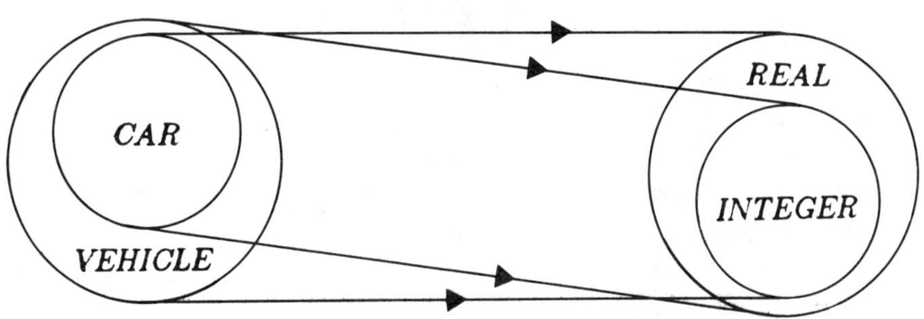

This phenomenon was first pointed out by D. MacQueen, G. Plotkin, and R. Sethi [MacQueen et al. 84], as *anti-monotonic* behavior of the first argument type in functional types.

It is not obvious, hence, how one may define a flexible type system allowing functional types as arguments to function. The problem is made even more complex if *polymorphic* types (i.e., parameterized types) are allowed; which brings us to the third point.

3.4. Parameterized Types

Parameterized types must be supported by object-oriented systems. Anyone having attempted to implement a generic package on a Lisp machine finds it frustrating to express a type such as LIST(x) or SET(x) where x is a type variable. This clearly is a shortcoming. By the point made above, a tricky problem would thus be integrate a *type inference* mechanism a la ML [Milner 78]. Indeed, the ML typing" algorithm uses first-order unification to infer most general types of to functions at compile-time. This process is an immense help for grams, and allows the removal of type-checking at run-time, with th no run-time error may occur because of ill-typing. The benefi efficiency.

Now, to extend this to *partially−ordered* types is at best non-trivial. Monotonic extensions of the unification algorithm are easy to obtain [Ait-Kaci 84], but it is not clear what a non-monotonic extension could be. For example, in the type "t $\rightarrow$ t", where t is a type variable, the right occurrence of t denotes an *upper bound* constraint while the left occurrence of t denotes a *lower bound* constraint. Much is needed to explore the meaning of such types in an object-oriented system.

In summary, it seems that little has been done to define formal semantics of object-oriented models of computation. Much insight in designing better and more adequate systems is bound to follow from more research.

4. Grand Unification

The line between programming language and database language is becoming indistinct. Logic languages, such as Prolog, provide declarative programming, similar to domain and tuple calculus for relational databases, but with recursion and structured data values. Object-oriented languages, such as Smalltalk, provide a rich milieu in which to model the world, reminiscent of semantic data models, embodying object identity, class hierarchies and operational semantics, all powerful modeling tools, along with good support for graphical interfaces. Neither language currently provides much in the way of data schemas or associative access. Both have only rudimentary support for secondary storage management, and next to nothing for other database amenities, such as concurrency, authorization and recovery.

A "Grand Unification" of database systems, logic languages and object-oriented programming, is being investigated in projects such as those at Hewlett-Packard [Beech and Feldman 83, Beech et al. 84] and at Oregon Graduate Center. The goal of the project at Oregon Graduate Center is to create an object-oriented database system with a single language for data manipulation and application programming. In the next sections we discuss pieces of this work: graphical interaction with database objects, organizing secondary storage in an object-oriented system, and unified languages for data manipulation and application programming.

4.1. Graphical Interaction with Data Objects

In most relational systems, the formats for displaying data are fairly rigid, generally giving users control only over ordering of rows and columns. These data display capabilities are often enough, as the data being displayed all have a simple tabular structure. In object-oriented database systems, however, there is more variation in the structure of the data. Objects can have complex structures as subparts, and objects can be multiply connected. Thus, we need more control over how objects are displayed, in order to control the complexity and portray the connectivity.

To explore this problem, a system was built to construct interactive displays of data objects in Smalltalk [Nordquist 85]. The system is called SIG, for Smalltalk Interaction Generator. SIG produces displays from high-level descriptions, called *display types*, which are associated with classes. (A *class* in Smalltalk is a collection of objects sharing structure and behavior.) A class can have multiple display types, to give a choice as to how the object is displayed. For example, a binary tree can have one display type to portray it in indented, outline form, and another display type to portray it with nodes [illegible] arrows. Each display type has one or more *recipes*. Recipes are selected based on [illegible] of the particular object being displayed. For a binary tree, a different recipe is used for a leaf, a tree with no left subtree, a tree with no right subtree, and a tree with both subtrees. A display type for Employee objects has different recipes for salaried and hourly employees. Each recipe describes what the display for the object should look like, and how the user interacts with the display. Interaction takes the form of sending update messages to the object, the messages being selected from a menu or by pointing to parts of the display. The display itself can be a standard one for text or graphics, or a compound one, composed of displays for subparts of the object. Since the subparts are themselves objects, they can have display types. The display description says where to display the subobjects, and what display type to use for each.

The hope is that many database applications on object-oriented databases will be nothing more than some interactive displays and browsers. A *browser* is a special display for scanning the objects in a class and selecting the ones of interest for more detailed display.

4.2. Secondary Storage in Object-Oriented Databases

Storing complex objects on disk presents some challenging problems. Consider Employee objects with fields Number, Name, Dept and Salary, where Name itself is a compound object with fields First and Last, and Dept is a compound object. There are two basic ways to store Employee objects. One is to decompose them into their fields, and represent each field as a binary relation. Thus we would have one relation storing Employees and their Numbers, another storing Employees and their Names, and so forth. Actually, since Name is a complex object, a surrogate is stored for each Name in the Employee-Name relation, and that surrogate is related to the First field and Last field in two binary relations. The other way to store objects is to group all the fields of one object together on disk.

Comparing the two representations, the binary relation representation is better for associative access [Copeland & Khoshafian 85]. If we want to find all Employees making more than $16,000, we can scan the Employee-Salary relation to pick out such Employee objects (their surrogates, actually). Since all these tuples are presumably stored in disk blocks together, few blocks need be read for the scan. If that relation is sorted by Salary, then an index could cut further the number of blocks read. Binary relations are not very good if we want to look at all fields for a particular Employee, as those fields are dispersed through many disk blocks.

For the object-based storage scheme, we need read only one block to get all the fields for a single Employee (if objects do not span blocks). However, to find employees with salaries over $16,000, many disk blocks must be read, because Salary fields are separated by all the other fields in Employee. Even with an index, there are still many blocks to read, because Employees are not clustered by Salary. (If they are, they cannot be clustered on any other field.) The situation for associative access has further complications. Many Employees work in each Department. If we duplicate a Department object with each Employee with that Department in the Dept field, we have a host of problems with redundancy and update. Duplicating Departments within Employees is not even feasible if Departments reference their Employees in some field. Thus, each Department object is represented once, and Employees in that Department point to that one representation. Now an associative access, say to find Employees in a Department with a certain Manager, is even more cumbersome, because in scanning Employees, we have to access other disk blocks to pick up the value of the Dept field.

One storage representation is not clearly better than the other. However, most queries have an associative access phase, where a few objects are selected out of a larger set, followed by a computation phase, where more complex selection conditions are applied and the few objects are otherwise manipulated. In the hybrid organization under investigation at the Oregon Graduate Center, binary relations are used on disk to speed associative access, with an object-based representation used in main memory, to aid manipulations on single objects.

4.3. Unified Languages for Database Programming

The problem of *impedance mismatch* between data manipulation language and application programming language has been pointed out previously [Copeland and Maier 84] [Maier and Price 84]. The mismatch is that the two languages may support vastly different programming paradigms and data structures. Thus, structure in one language can be reflected back at the interface to the other. For example, in a Cobol interface to SQL, the structure of relations is reflected back, and only records pass through.

Most application programming languages are procedural. However, data manipulation languages benefit from being declarative, as that property provides more opportunities for using indices and planning secondary storage access. In the OPAL language, being developed at Servio Logic Corporation [Copeland and Maier 84], the syntax of Smalltalk was extended with a declarative notation for set expressions. The form of a set expression is

{ <bindings> | <result expression> | <selection condition> }

The semantics are: form a Cartesian product with the <bindings>, apply the <selection condition> to those tuples, and evaluate the <result expression> for all tuples that satisfy the selection. The results of applying the <result expression> to the tuples are collected in a set, which is returned as the value of the query. The <result expression> is any OPAL expression. The <selection condition> is any Boolean OPAL expression. It may contain arbitrary pieces of embedded OPAL code. However, only certain constructs are recognized for associative processing. An example set expression is:

```
{ Dept:d  Employee:e | #[d name . e name] |
  (e in: d staff) and:
  ((e name last = d manager name last) or:
   (e salary >= d budget))}
```

which returns pairs of department name and employee name such that the employee has the same last name as his department's manager, or the employee's salary is more than his department's budget. To process such queries, we must add typing information to OPAL, so that we know, for example, that the manager field of a department holds an employee, and that an employee's last name is a string.

Another language for programming in object-oriented databases, called DMDM, is being developed at Oregon Graduate Center. DMDM queries resemble Prolog clauses, and the language has also been influenced by the lattice-theoretic model for computation proposed by Ait-Kaci [Ait-Kaci 84a]. In DMDM, evaluating a query is separate from viewing the value. The query

```
BothWork:*(workIn→:D,
            spouses→Pair:*(spouse1→:S1,
            spouse2→:S2)) <=
        Employee:S1(assignedTo→:D,
                spouse→Employee:S2(assignedTo→:D))..
```

consists of a *pattern* to the right of the double arrow, and an *action* to the left. The pattern is matched against the database to instantiate object variables, such as D, S1 and S2. The action is performed for each instantiation. In this case, the action calls for creating a new objects of type BothWork, containing a department and a pair of spouses. After this query is evaluated, the user may browse the set of BothWork objects to see the answer.

5. Data Dictionaries and Constraint Management

In a DBMS, the data dictionary/directory is used to control access to the database, ensure data integrity, and supervise the distribution of data. In the past, the data dictionary has been viewed as a collection of static record structures designed and built after an in-depth study of the enterprise to be modeled. For this reason, the dictionary was fixed throughout the life of the data base applications. Thus in the past, dictionaries have been mostly viewed as static tools for the control of data and information resources.

Now, however, particularly in CAD/CAM and knowledge-based applications, dictionaries are asked to play a much more dynamic and active role in the design and management of databases. A new scenario is emerging where the cycles of database design, dictionary definition, and even data acquisition, are intertwined and need to be integrated [Maier & Price 84]. Thus the trend is to use the dictionary as the *knowledge base* for *database design* and for *planning.* In this new scenario, the dictionary becomes the main vehicle for requirement analysis and system design and documentation. This new trend has two major implications on the organization of the dictionary. One is the need for more dynamic structures capable of evolving over time and with changing requirements, the second is a closer integration between data and metadata.

Traditional database management systems (DBMS) make a clear distinction between data (the database) and meta-data (the data dictionary/directory). This separation of function, that has proved effective in making DBMSs the "workhorses" of modern corporations that manage data as a resource, needs now to be removed since it now represents an impedement to use of the available knowledge.

The key idea is:

In the meta-data lies the knowledge.

For intelligent applications to make full use of the power that knowledge entails, we need a new approach that supports the *integration* of database and data dictionary functions. This will allow us to build the next generation, the Expert Database System or Knowledge Base Management System. Future systems will not distinguish between data and meta-data, rather, there will be a continuum of concepts, from tokens representing database instances, to objects representing goal and learning criteria.

An approach is therefore proposed to integrate the data and meta-data making them co-resident in the same "knowledge base." In this approach, database tokens, types, operations, and transactions are all considered typed "objects." The rest of this section outlines the use of objects to support data-dictionary dynamics, while Section 6 discusses constraint management in such an environment.

5.1. Problems with Current Dictionary Organizations

The purpose of a data dictionary is to enforce the structure of new data instances and keep track of existing ones. Some of the objects referenced in a data dictionary include records, fields, groups, data types, sets and relations. Once these items are defined, they cannot be easily modified. For instance, new fields or relations cannot be dynamically added to the data base schema because current dictionaries are not robust and do not have facilities to adequately handle changing meta-data. Domains such as design, engineering, and manufacturing are starting to recognize the advantages of data base management systems, but are also finding that existing DBMS do not have all the facilities they need to model and maintain their applications. One deficiency is the lack of an "active" or "dynamic" schema, i.e., a data dictionary which can be referenced, accessed, and modified during DBMS processing. The need for a dynamic schema is motivated by the following characteristics of a domain: the structure (schema) of the data is defined as the data is generated; the structure of the data is not uniform across data objects; there exist many different instances of data with many different formats. The desired functionality includes schema viewing, schema modification, and consistency checking among schema items. For these reasons, existing data dictionary facilities are not sufficient.

5.2. Object-Oriented Organizations

An object-oriented dictionary facility uses an $O-O$ organization to represent and describe a data dictionary schema. Instead of using static record structures to represent the format of domain data, think instead of using objects to represent classes and instances of schema structures. Properties of the objects are used to describe both the characteristics of classes of data structures, and characteristics of specific instances of the class. Properties are also used to indicate behaviors or methods that represent the operational aspects of a schema structure by prescribing how an object should respond to requests. In this way, knowledge about representations, i.e., how to add, modify, or delete schema definitions, is maintained.

5.3. Advantages

Building and managing a data base schema requires an enormous bookkeeping effort to maintain consistency between records, fields, relations, data types, and values. For this reason, dictionary facilities have been static in nature. By building a schema description as an object-oriented hierarchy, we are now able to provide a "data structure management facility" to serve as an assistant for automatically describing data representations and transparently maintaining them. Schema descriptions are represented as object properties, and procedures for adding, modifying, or deleting dictionary objects are represented as behaviors or methods associated with the schema object. These procedures prescribe how to maintain consistency of the schema and data objects when schema modifications are made.

6. Constraint Management

In object-oriented models the various objects (or concepts) are organized in a "semantic net" using primitives such as: 1) the notion of a class of objects of a certain type, 2) *isa*-links that relate subtypes to supertypes, 3) *asa*-links stating that a token is a member of a type, and 4) certain primitive maps and functions that provide access to meta-data that can be used for reasoning about the knowledge base.

This general semantic organization is complemented with the "behavioral specification" of the objects, that is, how they relate to one another, and how they behave when accessed and manipulated by database operations and transactions. We propose that this *behavioral specification* be given in terms of constraints. These include not only the concepts of integrity, security, cardinality constraints, but also .ul dynamic constraints that affect the knowledge base state due to update operations and transactions. The notion of a database "trigger" is also considered a constraint. Thus, a constraint can be used to specify "condition/action" rules as well as "antecedent/consequent" rules. By including the notion of dynamic constraints we embody the architecture with reasoning capabilities, as will be discussed shortly.

6.1. Constraint Specification Language

In order to specify the behavior semantics of objects, we will need a *constraint language*. The language will be a specification language for all types of constraints: integrity, security, transactional, and goal.

Both Alan Borning [Borning 79] and Guy Steele [Steele 80] have suggested the need for such a language. We feel that the language should be declarative so that the constraints can be examined and reasoned about. Examples of reasoning about constraints will be given shortly. Explicitly specified constraints can be shared by various tools, and can be translated and distributed to tools such as application program generators, and query optimizers.

6.2. Reasoning about Constraints

The fact that constraints can be explicitly specified means that they can be interpreted and reasoned about. Some examples are given below:

A. *Query Optimization.* Constraints are used to determine the best strategy to evaluate queries against a database. Rather than evaluate all possible processing strategies, one would prefer to examine those that are most feasible. Constraint information in the database meta-data can limit the search space. For example, statistics can be maintained about usage patterns, the distribution of attribute values, the most likely join-attributes for multi-relational queries, etc., so that reasonable strategies can be proposed. Also, query processing *heuristics* can be used to limit the search space.

In the design of genetic experiments, [Stefik 81a,81b] uses constraints to do hierarchical planning, wherein each level uses appropriate meta-data for planning the use and manipulation of objects at the next lower level. These ideas could be used in planning query processing strategies.

B. *Semantic Concurrency Control.* In systems where constraints are available in a knowledge base, they may be used to predict the interaction and impact of database transactions. Thus, by computing the set of objects involved in one or more (concurrent) transactions, one can find the set of common objects that must be "locked" for concurrency control. Although a run-time check may be costly, we propose that with proper transaction "packaging" the set of associated objects could be pre-computed and stored as meta- data. The use of semantic information can help to determine the appropriate locking granularity.

C. *Knowledge Translation.* The object-oriented approach does not favor any particular "knowledge paradigm" such as logic, logic programming, frames, semantic nets, or production systems. However, the object-oriented approach may be used to provide *external views* of the knowledge base so that specialized interpreters can be used for reasoning about the knowledge.

D. *Intelligent User Agents.* In constraint-based object-oriented systems it is possible to have the system reason about its capabilities as they pertain to user goals, perceptions, and expectations. Thus, one might expect these systems to inform the user of how certain capabilities work. In addition such systems should provide adaptive user interfaces that learn the user's usage patterns and preferences.

6.3. The PRISM System

PRISM [Shepherd and Kerschberg 84a] is a constraint- based object-oriented system that embodies many of the concepts discussed above. The entire specification of the system is stored in a knowledge base of "constraints." Constraints are specified in a Constraint Language (CL) and are stored as text in a UNIX* file. Examples of constraint specifications are provided in this volume [Shepherd & Kerschberg 84b].

When PRISM is initiated, the constraints are read in and an "internal representation" of the *knowledge kernel* is constructed. This internal representation is in the form of an associative net the uses the primitive concepts discussed earlier. The current implementation has about 100 constraints specified.

The user can interact with PRISM and its knowledge kernel to specify a database schema, to populate a database according to a database schema, to define a *data model* in terms of the rules (constraints) that govern the behavior of the data model concepts, and to extend the meta-level primitives. This capability is very powerful and some levels of the system could be protected from manipulation. For example, the Knowledge Base Administrator (KBA) might have access to the meta-level primitives, the Database Administrator (DBA) to the database schemas, and clerks to application schemas and transactions.

7. Conclusion

Object Orientation has emerged as a very pervasive and useful paradigm in several areas of computer science. In the first part of this paper, we have reviewed the key technical concepts on which the $O-O$ approach is based and have discussed some its most useful applications.

While the results of this review confirm the merits and versatility of the $O-O$ approach, they also suggest that different disciplines enphasize and build upon markedly different aspects of the $O-O$ paradigm. Thus, many research issues remain to be solved before an $O-O$ Expert Database System can be built to support data, knowledge and application programming within one integrated framework.

---

* UNIX is a trademark of AT&T Bell Laboratories.

In the second part of the paper, we have discussed current research that addresses some of these open problems, including the management of secondary storage in a $O-O$ database, the unification of languages for database programming, and dictionary design for the integration of data and metadata and for constraint management.

References

[Adiba 84]
Adiba M. and G.T. Nguyen, "Handling Constraints and Meta- Data on Generalized Data Management Systems," *Proc. First Int. Workshop on Expert Database Systems,* 1984.

[Ahlsen et al. 84]
M Ahlsen, M., A. Bjornerstedt, S. Britts, C. Hulten and L. Suderlund," An Architecture for Object Management in OIS," *ACM TOOIS,* Vol. 2, no. 3, July 1984.

[Ait-Kaci 84a]
Ait-Kaci, H. *A Lattice Theoretic Approach to Computation Based on a Calculus of Partially Ordered Type Structures,* doctoral dissertation, Univ. of Pennsylvania, 1984.

[Ait-Kaci 84b]
Ait-Kaci, H., "Type Subsumption as a Model of Computation," *in this volume.*

[Ait-Kaci 85]
Ait-Kaci, H., private communication, 1985.

[Batory & Buchmann 84]
Batory, D.S. and Buchmann, A. P., "Molecular Objects, Abstract Data Types and Data Models: A Framework," *Proc. 10th Int. Conference on Very Large Data Bases,* pp. 172-184, 1984.

[Beech & Feldman 83]
Beech, D., and J.S. Feldman, "The Integrated Data Model: A Database Perspective," *Proc. 9th Int. Conference on Very Large Data Bases,* Florence, 1983.

[Beech et al. 84]
Beech, D., N. Derrett, A. Shepherd and T. Wilson, "Overview of the IRIS Information Model," *Proc. First Int. Workshop on Expert Database Systems,* 1984.

[Birtwistle et al.]
Birtwistle, G. M., O.-J. Dahl, B. Myrhaug and K. Nygaard, *Simula Begins,* Auerbach, Philadelphia, 1973.

[Bobrow & Stefik 83]
Bobrow, D.G. and M. Stefik, "The LOOPS Manual," Xerox Corporation, 1983.

[Borning 79]
Borning, A., "ThingLab: A Constraint-Oriented Simulation Laboratory", SSL-79-3, Xerox Palo Alto Research Center, July 1979.

[Borning & Ingalls 81]
Borning, A.H. and D.H.H. Ingalls, "A Type Declaration and Inference System for Smalltalk," University of Washington Computer Science TR 81-08-02a, November 1981.

[Cammarata & Melkanoff 84]
Cammarata S., and M.A. Melkanoff, "An Interactive Data Dictionary Facility for CAD/CAM Databases," *Proc. First Int. Workshop on Expert Database Systems,* 1984.

[Cannon 82]
Cannon, H.I., "Flavors: a Non-hierarchical Approach to Object-oriented" Programming", unpublished manuscript, 1982.

[Chen 76]
Chen P.P.S., "The Entity Relationship Model-Journal of Unified View of Data," *ACM Trans. Database Systems, Vol. 1,* No. 1, pp. 9-36, 1976.

[Copeland & Maier 84]
Copeland, G. and Maier, D., "Making *SMALLTALK* a Database System," *Proc. ACM SIGMOD Conference, pp. 316-325, 1984.*

[Copeland & Khoshafian 85]
Copeland, G.P. and S.N. Khoshafian, "A Decomposition Storage Model," *Proc. ACM SIGMOD Conference, pp. 268-279, 1985.*

[Dahl et al. 68]
Dahl, O., Myrhaug, B., and Nygaard, K., "Simula67 Common Base Language," Norvegian Computing Centre S-2, 1968.

[Gerzso & Buchmann 84]
Gerzso J.M. and A.P. Buchmann, "TM-An Object-Oriented Language for CAD and Required Database Capabilities," Submitted for publication.

[Goldberg & Robson 83]
Goldberg, A .D., Robson, "*SMALLTALK-80: The Language and its Implementation,*" Addison Wesley, 1983.

[Hewitt 77]
Hewitt, C. E., "Viewing control Structures as Pattern of Passing Messages," *Artif. Intell.,* vol. 8, no. 3, June 1977.

[Liskov & Zilles 74]
Liskov, B., and Zilles, S., "Programming with Abstract Data Types," *ACM SIGPLAN Notices, 9:4,* April, 1974.

[Maier & Price 84]
Maier D. and D. Price, "Data Model Requirements for Engineering Applications," *Proc. First Int. Workshop on Expert Database Systems,* 1984.

[McQueen et al. 84]
MacQueen, D., G. Plotkin, and R. Sethi, "An Ideal Model for Recursive Polymorphic Types", in *Proceedings of the 11th POPL Symposium , pp. 165-75, 1984.*

[Minsky 75]
Minsky, M., "A Framework for Representing Knowledge," in P. H. Winston (ed.), *The Psychology of Computer Vision,* McGraw Hill, 1975

[Milner 78]
Milner, R., "A Theory of Type Polymorphism in Programming," *JCSS*, vol. 17, no. 3, 378-375, 1979.

[Nordquist 85]
P. Nordquist, "Interactive Display Generation in *SMALLTALK*," Master's thesis, Oregon Graduate Center, 1985.

[Lindstrom 85]
Lindstrom, G., private communication, 1985.

[Shapiro 83]
Shapiro E. Y. and A. Tokeuchi, "Object-Oriented Programming in Concurrent Prolog," *Journal of the New Generation Computing,* Vol. 1, No. 1, pp. 25-48, 1983.

[Shepherd & Kerschberg 84a]
Shepherd, A., and L. Kerschberg, "PRISM: A Knowledge-Based System for Semantic Integrity Specification and Enforcement in Database Systems," *Proc. ACM SIGMOD Conference,* pp. 307-315, 1984.

[Shepherd & Kerschberg 84b]
Shepherd, A., and L. Kerschberg, "Constraint Management in Expert Database Systems," *Proc. First Int. Workshop on Expert Database Systems,* 1984.

[Smith & Smith 77]
Smith, J. M. and D. C. P. Smith, "Database Architectures: Aggregation and Generalizations," *ACM Trans. Database Systems,* Vol. 6, No. 1, 160-173, 1977.

[Steele 80]
Steele, G.L., *The Definition and Implementation of a Computer Programming Language Based on Constraints,* Ph.D. Dissertation, MIT VLSI Memo. 80-32, 1980.

[Stefik 81a]
Stefik, M., "Planning with Constraints (MOLGEN: Part 1)," *Artificial Intelligence 16,* pp. 111-140, 1981.

[Stefik 81b]
Stefik, M., "Planning and Meta-Planning (MOLGEN: Part 2)," *Artificial Intelligence 16,* pp. 141-170, 1981.

[Stroustrup 84]
Stroustrup, B., "Data Abstraction in C," Computing Science Technical Report No. 109, AT&T Bell Laboratories, 1984.

[Wulf et al. 76]
Wulf, W., London,R., and Shaw, M., "An introduction to the construction and Verification of Alphard Programs," *IEEE Transactions on Software Engineering,* SE-2:4, 1976.

[Zaniolo 84a]
Zaniolo, C., "Object-Oriented Programming in Prolog," *Proc. Logic Programming Symposium,* pp. 265-270, 1984.

PART III:

Theory of Knowledge Bases

What Makes a Knowledge Base Knowledgeable? A View of Databases from the Knowledge Level

Ronald J. Brachman
Hector J. Levesque

Fairchild Laboratory for Artificial Intelligence Research
4001 Miranda Avenue
Palo Alto, California 94304

Abstract

At least one view of the potential relation between knowledge bases in Artificial Intelligence (AI) and the databases of Database Management Systems (DBMS) is that each can contribute techniques and mechanisms to the other: inheritance networks or natural language interfaces from AI, and inverted files or B-trees from DBMS. In other words, the sharing is at what has been called the "Symbol Level". We propose that the interaction between knowledge representation and databases is better considered at a more fundamental "Knowledge Level". Under this view, databases are interpreted as large knowledge bases of a certain limited form. This limitation in representation form can be motivated by a fundamental tradeoff that all knowledge representation and reasoning systems are faced with. The nature of this tradeoff, the role of a representation and reasoning system as a component of a knowledge-based system, and a view of databases as knowledge bases are all discussed here.

1 Introduction

At least one current view of the differences between knowledge bases and databases has it that the former (but presumably not the latter) "describe and operate on classes of objects rather than on individual objects," and that the latter (but presumably not the former) represent and manage "facts" [14]. Roughly speaking, knowledge bases contain the equivalent of universally quantified statements (*e.g.*, "People of middle age are careful"), while databases have the equivalent of ground atomic assertions (*e.g.*, "Mr. Lee's age is 43 years"). While this is perhaps a reasonable point from which to start considering how AI work on knowledge bases relates to that on databases, it is our contention that such differences between knowledge bases and databases are rather shallow.[1] Instead, we would like to emphasize a deep and significant *commonality* between knowledge bases and databases, one that stems from more fundamental concerns about knowledge and inference. This paper is an attempt to explicate those fundamental concerns and their relation to AI and databases.

The position we take here is that databases *are* (or at least can be profitably viewed as) knowledge bases of a certain sort.[2] Both try to provide reliable and timely *fact management* services. And by considering

[1] It is not even clear that these are real differences: many knowledge bases handle both individuals and classes, and moreover, statistical databases deal almost exclusively with classes of objects. It is also hard to see why general statements about the world (*e.g.*, middle-aged people are careful) are any less factual than ground atomic assertions.

[2] We do not claim, however, that this view is necessarily compatible with the views of Database Management practitioners. At best, ours is a reconstruction of database theory that we believe explains most clearly how it relates to other representational practices.

a database as a very large but limited knowledge base we can see clearly the implications of adding more complex representational machinery (*e.g.*, universally quantified statements), and can understand the relation of traditional databases to other mainstream AI representation frameworks (logic programs, semantic nets, frames, etc.). In fact, we might propose that the principal contribution that AI research in knowledge representation can make to databases is the very point of view that facilitates this understanding, a point of view that encourages a semantically rationalized account of the logical import of a database.

This point of view has been called the *Knowledge Level* [10,9], and involves looking at what an agent (or a fact management system of some sort) knows[3] about the world, not in terms of the symbolic representation and inference techniques used, but in terms of *the world itself*—what it would have to be like if what the agent held as true were in fact true. Specifically, the Knowledge Level does not distinguish among the different ways of capturing the same information, or even between the information that is explicitly available to the agent and that which is implied. The only thing that counts from this perspective is what the entire body of information taken together says about the world.

The view from the Knowledge Level is in sharp contrast to the more common view that emphasizes the contribution that AI *techniques* (*i.e.*, data structures, data structure-manipulating routines, etc.) can make to database systems (see for example, [5], as well as [14]). This is certainly not to deny that AI techniques can be of pragmatic interest to database designers, just as proposed in [5]. As well, knowledge representation systems will soon need to be able to deal with large amounts of information, typically managed much more efficiently in database systems. However, a marriage at what has been called the *Symbol Level*, without an understanding of the *knowledge* a database is to carry, is likely to lead to trouble.[4] This paper is in part a tutorial on a view of knowledge representation that can help avoid that kind of trouble. In other words, one major goal of this paper is to explain what we think is meant by "knowledge representation system", so that we can understand exactly what it means to say that a database system is one.

In order to see a database as a knowledge base, and to understand the implications of that view, we first look at the functional role a knowledge base is to play in a knowledge-based system. The kind of functional analysis we propose strongly distinguishes our view of representation systems from the more common view that takes them as elaborate data-structuring packages (for example, packages for manipulating wffs or links and nodes). To the extent that a database management system is to be used for fact storage and management in a larger system, it is subject to the same analysis as any knowledge base management system; in particular, its position with respect to an expressiveness/computational tractability tradeoff becomes relevant. We say a few words about that tradeoff, analyze the case of databases, and add a few thoughts in conclusion about the deep relationship between knowledge bases and databases.[5]

2 The Role of Knowledge Representation

While it is generally agreed that knowledge representation (KR) plays an important role in knowledge-based systems, the exact nature of that role is often hard to define. In some cases, a KR subsystem does no more than manage a collection of data structures, providing, for example, suitable search, indexing and inheritance facilities; in others, the KR subsystem is not really distinguished from the rest of the system at all and does just about everything—make decisions, prove theorems, solve problems, and so on. Here we discuss in very general terms the role of a KR subsystem within a knowledge-based system.

[3] While we use cognitive terms like "knowledge" here, it will become clear below that our emphasis is on a propositional interpretation of a body of information, and not on any kind of psychological modelling.

[4] This has already proven to be the case in the AI subfield that studies semantic networks, for example. There, overmuch attention to the level of mechanism at the expense of knowing what function the system was computing has lead to serious difficulties [1,6].

[5] Significant portions of the rest of this manuscript have been borrowed from [8].

2.1 The Knowledge Representation Hypothesis

A good place to begin a discussion of KR as a whole is with what Brian Smith has called in [13] the *Knowledge Representation Hypothesis:*

> *Any mechanically embodied intelligent process will be comprised of structural ingredients that a) we as external observers naturally take to represent a propositional account of the knowledge that the overall process exhibits, and b) independent of such external semantical attribution, play a formal but causal and essential role in engendering the behaviour that manifests that knowledge.*

This hypothesis seems to underly much of the research in KR. In fact, we might think of *knowledge-based systems* as those that satisfy the hypothesis by design. Also, in some sense, it is only with respect to this hypothesis that KR research can be distinguished from any number of other areas involving symbolic structures such as programming languages and data structures.

Granting this hypothesis, there are two major properties that the structures in a knowledge-based system have to satisfy. First of all, it must be possible to interpret them as *propositions* representing the overall knowledge of the system. Otherwise, the representation would not necessarily be of *knowledge* at all, but of something quite different, like numbers or circuits. Implicit in this constraint is that the structures have to be expressions in a language that has a *truth theory.* We should be able to point to one of them and say what the world would have to be like for it to be true. The structures themselves need not *look* like sentences—there are no syntactic requirements on them at all, other than perhaps finiteness—but we have to be able to understand them that way.

A second requirement of the hypothesis is perhaps more obvious. The symbolic structures within a knowledge-based system must play a *causal role* in the behaviour of that system, as opposed to, say, the role played by comments in a programming language. Moreover, the influence they have on the behaviour of the system should agree with our understanding of them as propositions representing knowledge. Not that the system has to be aware in any mysterious way of the interpretation of its structures and their connection to the world; but for us to call it knowledge-based, *we* have to be able to understand its behaviour as if it believed these propositions, just as we understand the behaviour of a numerical program as if it appreciated the connection between bit patterns and abstract numerical quantities.

2.2 Knowledge Bases

To make the above discussion a bit less abstract, we can consider a very simple task and consider what a system facing this task would have to be like for us to call it knowledge-based. The amount of knowledge the system will be dealing with will, of course, be very small.

Suppose we want a system in PROLOG that is able to print the colors of various items. One way to implement that system would be as follows:

```
printColor(snow) :-  !, write("It's white.").
printColor(grass) :- !, write("It's green.").
printColor(sky) :-   !, write("It's yellow.").
printColor(X) :- write("Beats me.").
```

A slightly different organization that leads to the same overall behaviour is

```
printColor(X) :-  color(X,Y), !, write("It's "),
                        write(Y), write(".").
printColor(X) :-  write("Beats me.").
```

```
color(snow,white).
color(grass,green).
color(sky,yellow).
```

The second program is characterized by explicit structures representing the (minimal) knowledge[6] the system has about colors and is the kind of system that we are calling knowledge-based. In the first program, the association between the object (we understand as) referring to grass and the one referring to its color is implicit in the structure of the program. In the second, we have an explicit *knowledge base* (or KB) that we can understand as propositions relating the items to their colors. Moreover, this interpretation is justified in that these structures determine what the system does when asked to print the color of a particular item.

One thing to emphasize about the example is that it is not the use of a certain programming language or data-structuring facility that makes a system knowledge-based. The fact that PROLOG happens to be understandable as a subset of first-order logic is largely irrelevant. Further, we note that if the knowledge base is simple enough (as it is in this example), it is indistinguishable from what has typically been thought of as a *data*base. Thus, in terms of *what knowledge is represented* (as opposed to what kinds of data structures, relations, etc., are used to encode it), the distinction here between database and knowledge base is nonexistent.

2.3 The KR Subsystem

In terms of its overall goals, a knowledge-based system is not directly interested in what specific structures might exist in its KB. Rather, it is concerned about what the application domain is like, for example, what the color of grass is. How that knowledge is represented and made available to the overall system is a secondary concern and one that we take to be the responsibility of the KR subsystem. The role of a KR subsystem, then, is to manage a KB for a knowledge-based system and present to it a picture of the world based on what it has represented in the KB.[7]

If, for simplicity, we restrict our attention to the yes-no questions about the world that a system might be interested in, what is involved here is being able to determine what the KB says regarding the truth of certain sentences. It is not whether the sentence itself is present in the KB that counts, but whether its truth is *implicit* in the KB. Stated differently, what a KR system has to be able to determine, given a sentence α, is the answer to the following question:

Assuming the world is such that what is believed is true, is α also true?

We will let the notation KB $\models \alpha$ mean that α is implied (in this sense) by what is in the KB.

One thing to notice about this view of a KR system is that the service it provides to a knowledge-based system depends only on the truth theory of the language of representation. Depending on the particular truth theory, determining if KB $\models \alpha$ might require not just simple retrieval capabilities, but also *inference* of some sort. This is not to say that the *only* service to be performed by a KR subsystem is question-answering. If we imagine the overall system existing over a period of time, then we will also want it to be able to

[6]Notice that typical of how the term "knowledge" is used in AI, there is no requirement of *truth*. A system may be mistaken about the color of the sky but still be knowledge-based.

[7]One of the most important things to emphasize here is that we need to carefully distinguish between *knowledge-based systems* and their *knowledge representation components*. It seems that in many people's minds these two are indistinguishable. A knowledge-based system is any system that uses an explicit knowledge base in some capacity. The knowledge representation component is the part of the overall system that manages the knowledge base. Equating this knowledge base management with the full knowledge-based system is a mistake. Unfortunately, while [14] tries admirably to move AI into databases, it exhibits a number of examples of confusion of the knowledge base management subtask with the system as a whole (see esp. p. 64).

augment the KB as it acquires new information about the world.[8] In other words, the responsibility of the KR system is to select appropriate *symbolic structures* to represent knowledge, and to select appropriate *reasoning mechanisms* both to answer questions and to assimilate new information, in accordance with the truth theory of the underlying representation language.

So our view of KR makes it depend only on the semantics of the representation language, unlike other possible accounts that might have it defined in terms of a set of formal symbol manipulation routines (*e.g.*, a proof theory). This is in keeping with what we have called elsewhere a *functional* view of knowledge representation (see [4] and [9]), where the service performed by a KR system is defined separately from the techniques a system might use to realize that service.

3 Computational Tractability

The Knowledge Level import of a knowledge base can be conveniently analyzed using a formal logic. We can use, say, first-order logic (FOL) to write down the contents of a knowledge base. The end result of this process would be a first-order knowledge base—a collection of sentences in FOL representing what was known about the domain.[9] A major advantage of FOL is that given a yes-no question also expressed in this language, we can give a very precise definition of KB $\models \alpha$ (and thus, under what conditions the question should be answered *yes*, *no*, or *unknown*):

KB $\models \alpha$ iff every interpretation satisfying the sentences in the KB also satisfies α.[10]

There is, moreover, another property of FOL which helps solidify the role of KR. If we assume that the KB is a finite set of sentences and let *KB* stand for their conjunction, it can be shown that

$$\text{KB} \models \alpha \quad \text{iff} \quad \vdash (KB \supset \alpha).$$

In other words, the question as to whether or not the truth of α is implicit in the KB reduces to whether or not a certain sentence is a *theorem* of FOL. Thus, the question-answering operation becomes one of *theorem-proving* in FOL.

The good news in looking at the KR service as theorem-proving is that it gives us a very clear and specific notion of what the KR system should do; the bad news is that it is also clear that *this service cannot be provided.* The sad fact of the matter is that deciding whether or not a sentence of first-order logic is a theorem (*i.e.*, the decision problem) is unsolvable. Moreover, even if we restrict the language practically to the point of triviality by eliminating the quantifiers, the decision problem, though now solvable, does not appear to be solvable in anywhere near reasonable time.[11] It is important to realize that this is not a property of particular algorithms that people have looked at but of the *problem* itself: there *cannot* be an algorithm that does the theorem-proving correctly in a reasonable amount of time. This bodes poorly, to say the least, for a service that is supposed to be only a part of a larger knowledge-based system.

There are at least two fairly obvious ways to minimize the intractability problem. The first is to push the computational barrier as far back as possible. The area of automatic theorem-proving has concentrated

[8] It is this management of a KB over time that makes a KR subsystem much more than just the implementation of a static deductive calculus.

[9] This fact that FOL is convenient for expressing the knowledge of a knowledge base has been a serious source of confusion in AI, since there are those who indeed advocate first-order logic as the *implementation* language for knowledge bases at the Symbol Level. The advantages and disadvantages of that point of view are not at issue here; our concern is with making transparent the distinctions allowed by the knowledge representation language underlying a knowledge base, and concomitantly, the computational cost of doing inference.

[10] The assumption here is that the semantics of FOL specify in the usual way what an interpretation is and under what conditions it will satisfy a sentence.

[11] Technically, the problem is now co-NP-complete, meaning that it is strongly believed to be computationally intractable.

on techniques for avoiding redundancies and speeding up certain operations in theorem-provers. Significant progress has been achieved here, allowing open questions in mathematics to be answered. Along similar lines, VLSI architectural support stands to improve the performance of theorem-provers at least as much as it would any search program.

The second way to make theorem-provers more usable is to relax our notion of correctness. A very simple way of doing this is to make a theorem-proving program always return an answer after a certain amount of time.[12] If it has been unable to prove either that a sentence or its negation is implicit in the KB, it could assume that it was independent of the KB and answer *unknown* (or maybe reassess the importance of the question and try again). This form of error (*i.e.*, one introduced by an incomplete theorem-prover), is not nearly as serious as returning a *yes* for a *no*, and is obviously preferable to an answer that never arrives. This is of course especially true if the program uses its resources wisely, in conjunction with the first suggestion above.

However, from the point of view of providing a dependable fact management (KR) service, both of these are only pseudo-solutions. Clearly, the first one alone does not help us guarantee anything about an inferential service. The second one, on the other hand, might allow us to guarantee an answer within certain time bounds, but would make it very hard for us to specify what that answer would be. If we think of the KR sevice as reasoning according to a certain logic, then the logic being followed is immensely complicated (compared to that of FOL) when resource limitations are present. Indeed, the whole notion of the KR system calculating what is implicit in the KB (which was our original goal) would have to be replaced by some other notion that went beyond the truth theory of the representation language to include the inferential power of a particular theorem-proving program. In a nutshell, we can guarantee getting an answer, but not necessarily the one we wanted.

One final observation about this intractability is that it is *not* a problem that is due to the formalization of knowledge in FOL. If we assume that the goal of our KR sevice is to calculate what is implicit in the KB, then as long as the truth theory of our representation language is upward-compatible with that of FOL, we will run into the same problem. In particular, using English (or any other natural or artificial language) as our representation language does not avoid the problem as long as we can express in it at least what FOL allows us to express.

4 Databases as Knowledge Bases

There is one other pseudo-solution to the tractability problem that we might consider. In a sense, it is the *incompleteness* or uncertainty of knowledge allowed by first-order logic that makes theorem-proving so hard. The kind of incompleteness we are thinking of here is that which results from the ability (among others) to state that one of two conditions is true without saying which (using a disjunction operator), or to state that something satisfies a certain condition without saying what that thing is (using an existential quantifier). One of the ways to deal with the tractability issue, then, is to simply limit the incompleteness expressible in the language of the knowledge base. This is still a pseudo-solution, of course; indeed, provably, there cannot be a *real* solution to the problem. But, as argued in [8], this one has the distinct advantage of allowing us to calculate exactly the picture of the world implied by the KB, precisely what a KR service was supposed to do. Our main claim is that at the Knowledge Level, databases are simply knowledge bases that are limited in precisely this way and for more or less these reasons.

Consider, for example, a very simple database that talks about university courses. It might contain a relation (or record type or whatever) like

[12]The resource limitation here should obviously be a function of how important overall it might be to answer the question.

COURSE

Id	Name	Dept	Enrollment	Instructor
csc248	ProgrammingLanguages	ComputerScience	42	S.J.Hurtubise
mat100	HistoryOfMathematics	Mathematics	137	R.Cumberbatch
csc373	ArtificialIntelligence	ComputerScience	853	T.Slothrop
		...		

If we had to charaterize in FOL the information that this relation contains, we could use a collection of function-free atomic sentences like[13]

Course(csc248)   Dept(csc248,ComputerScience)   Enrollment(csc248,42)   . . .
Course(mat100)   Dept(mat100,Mathematics)   . . .
. . .

In other words, the tabular database format characterizes exactly the positive instances of the various predicates. But more to the point, since our list of FOL sentences never ends up with ones like

Dept(mat100,mathematics) ∨ Dept(mat100,history),

the range of uncertainty that we are dealing with is quite limited.

There is, however, additional information contained in the database not captured in the simple FOL translation. To see this, consider, for instance, how we might try to determine the answer to the question,

How many courses are offered by the Computer Science Department?

The knowledge expressed by the above collection of FOL sentences is insufficient to answer this question: nothing about our set of atomic sentences implies that Computer Science has at least two courses (since csc373 and csc248 could be names of the same individual), and nothing implies that it has at most two courses (since there could be courses other than those mentioned in the list of sentences). On the other hand, from a database point of view, we could apparently successfully answer our question using our miniature database by phrasing it as

Count c in COURSE where c.Dept = ComputerScience;

this yields the definitive answer, "2". The crucial difference here, between failing to answer the question at all and answering it definitively, is that we have actually asked *two different questions*. The formal query addressed to the database must be understood as

How many tuples in the COURSE relation have ComputerScience in their Dept field?

This is a question *not* about the world being modelled at all, but about the *data* itself. In other words, the database retrieval version of the question is a Symbol Level operation that asks about the structures in the database itself, and not about what these structures represent.[14]

To be able to reinterpret the database query as the intuitive question originally posed about courses and departments (rather than as one about tuples and fields), we must account for additional information at the Knowledge Level that takes us beyond the stored data itself. In particular, we need FOL sentences of the form

[13]This is not the only way to characterize this information. For example, we could treat the field names as function symbols or use *Id* as an additional relation or function symbol. Also, for the sake of simplicity, we are ignoring here integrity constraints (saying, for example, that each course has a unique enrollment), which may contain quantificational and other logical operations, but typically are only used to verify the consistency of the database, not to infer new facts. None of these decisions affect the conclusions we will draw below.

[14]The hallmark, it would appear, of conventional Database Management is that its practitioners take their role to be providing users access to the data, rather than using the data to answer questions about the world. The difference between the two points of view is especially evident when the data is very incomplete [7].

$$c_i \neq c_j, \qquad \text{for distinct constants } c_i \text{ and } c_j,$$

stating that each constant represents a unique individual. In addition, for each predicate, we need a sentence similar in form to

$$\forall x[\text{Course}(x) \supset x = \text{csc248} \lor \cdots \lor x = \text{mat100}],$$

saying that the only instances of the predicate are the ones named explicitly.[15] If we now consider a KB consisting of all of the sentences in FOL we have listed so far, a KR system could, in fact, conclude that there were exactly two Computer Science courses, just like its Database Management counterpart. We have included in the imagined KB all of the information, both explicit and implicit, contained in the database.

One important property of a KB in this final form is that it is much easier to use than a general first-order KB. In particular, since the first part of the KB (the atomic sentences) does not use negation, disjunction, or existential quantification, we know the exact instances of every predicate of interest in the language. There is no incompleteness in our knowledge at all. Because of this, *inference reduces to calculation.* To find out how many courses there are, all we have to do is count how many appropriate tuples appear in the *COURSE* relation. We do not, for instance, have to reason by cases or by contradiction, as we would have to in the more general case. For example, if we also knew that either *csc148* or *csc149* or both were Computer Science courses but that no Computer Science course other than *csc373* had an odd identification number, we could still determine that there were three courses, but not by simply counting. But a KB in database form does not allow us to express this kind of uncertainty and, because of this expressive limitation, the KR service is much more tractable. Specifically, we can represent what is known about the world at the Symbol Level using just these sets of tuples, exactly like a standard database system. From this perspective, a database is a knowledge base whose limited form permits a very special form of inference.

This limitation on the logical form of a KB has other interesting features. Essentially, what it amounts to is making sure that there is very close structural correspondence between the (explicit) KB and the domain of interest: for each entity in the domain, there is a unique representational object that stands for it; for each relationship that it participates in, there is a tuple in the KB that corresponds to it. In a very real sense, the KB is an *analogue* of the domain of interest, not so different from other analogues such as maps or physical models. The main advantange of having such an analogue is that it can be used directly to answer questions about the domain. That is, the calculations on the model itself can play the role of more general reasoning techniques much the way arithmetic can replace reasoning with Peano's axioms. The disadvantage of an analogue, however, should also be clear: within a certain descriptive language, it does not allow anything to be left unsaid about the domain.[16] In this sense, an analogue representation can be viewed as a special case of a propositional one where the information it contains is relatively complete.

5 Conclusion

In this paper, we have primarily attempted to set out our view of the knowledge representation service—a view that we think is appropriate for relating knowledge bases and databases. We advocate thinking of knowledge representation systems not as collections of links and nodes, or routines for indexing and inheritance, but as providers of timely, dependable fact management services.

The implications of this view are numerous. For one thing, we see that it is best to consider database systems as comparable to knowledge representation systems and *not* full knowledge-based systems. In fact,

[15] This is one form of what has been called the *closed world assumption* [12].

[16] The same is true for the standard analogues. One of the things a map does not allow you to say, for example, is that a river passes through one of two widely separated towns, without specifying which. Similarly, a plastic model of a ship cannot tell us that the ship it represents does not have two smokestacks, without also telling us how many it does have. This is not to say that there is no *uncertainty* associated with an analogue, but that this uncertainty is due to the coarseness of the analogue (*e.g.*, how carefully the map is drawn) rather than to its content.

under the Knowledge Level view, databases *are* knowledge bases (we can easily understand the data as sentences and how the data can contribute in the right way to the behaviour of programs). The kind of distinction that Wiederhold draws in [14] between universally quantified knowledge and ground atomic assertions is a relevant one, although it is not a matter of one being "knowledge" and the other "data"—both kinds of facts are legitimate knowledge.[17]

If databases are just knowledge bases at the Knowledge Level, the only real issue is what is to be gained by this Knowledge Level understanding. There are a number of things. First of all, it leads to better semantic or conceptual models, free of inadvertent implementation biases. The *only* relevant issue at the Knowledge Level is what knowledge is represented. Even the data itself is regarded as just a means to a representational end. Semantic accounts are thus much less likely to be phrased in terms of entities like "conceptual records" and "conceptual fields" that seem to show their origins in the underlying implementation structures. It should be stressed, however, that nothing is gained by replacing database Symbol Level terminology by Symbol Level terminology from any other representational language, even FOL. For instance, accounts that rely on the theorem-proving part of FOL (with talk of clauses, Skolemization, resolution, or modulation) beg the issue. What counts is the *semantic* interpretation of sentences in the language insofar as they tell us what the world could be like.

Secondly, the Knowledge Level provides a good vantage point from which to examine potential generalizations to database languages. Attempting to analyze, say, null values in databases and the corresponding retrieval algorithms only at the Symbol Level is somewhat odd. It is at the Knowledge Level that the meaning of null values (that is, the information about the world they do or do not carry) is determined and the correctness of representations and algorithms can be judged. Moreover, the effect of a proposed extension can often be assessed with respect to the tradeoff discussed here without even discussing algorithms and representations at the Symbol Level. We know, for example, that we cannot simply add universally quantified statements to databases without being careful about their computational impact. (We might, in fact, have to consider hybrid approaches to fact management, such as those advocated in [4] and [11].) Nor can we simply incorporate AI techniques at the Symbol Level without paying careful attention to their Knowledge Level import. In sum, a major advantage of the Knowledge Level perspective is that it allows us to examine computational properties of representational formalisms that will continue to hold no matter what Symbol Level decisions are made.

Finally, the Knowledge Level provides a basis from which to compare databases to other representation schemes in terms of the range of knowledge that can be represented. All too often, such comparisons have been plagued by discussions of representation techniques like connection graphs, inheritance taxonomies, and production rules, without a good understanding of what (if anything) these symbol structures were saying. It is only by analyzing the represented knowledge that we will discover the areas of overlap among these schemes, the positions they occupy with respect to the expressiveness/tractability tradeoff, and finally the areas where sharing is both desirable and feasible.

In the end, we might even consider that the single most important contribution that AI can make to databases is the notion of the Knowledge Level itself, and the semantically rationalized view of the import of databases that it provides.

Acknowledgement

We are especially grateful to Peter Patel-Schneider for his help with early versions of this paper.

[17]There are other distinctions in kinds of knowledge that are also useful to draw. For example, in Krypton [4] we advocate distinguishing between *terminological* and *assertional* competence. This bears some relation to the intension/extension relation that is perhaps a bit confused in [14]. We could also distinguish procedural advice (*e.g.*, knowledge about the combinatorics of the domain as a whole) from declarative world knowledge, knowledge of simple facts from knowledge of laws, etc.

Bibliography

[1] Brachman, R. J. "What IS-A Is and Isn't: An Analysis of Taxonomic Links in Semantic Networks." *IEEE Computer*, Vol. 16, No. 10, October, 1983, pp. 30–36.

[2] Brachman, R. J., and Levesque, H. J. "Competence in Knowledge Representation." *Proc. AAAI-82*, Pittsburgh, PA, 1982, pp. 189–192.

[3] Brachman, R. J., and Levesque, H. J. "The Tractability of Subsumption in Frame-Based Description Languages." *Proc. AAAI-84*, Austin, TX, 1984, pp. 34–37.

[4] Brachman, R. J., Fikes, R. E., and Levesque, H. J. "KRYPTON: A Functional Approach to Knowledge Representation." *IEEE Computer*, Vol. 16, No. 10, October, 1983, pp. 67–73.

[5] Deering, M., and Falletti, J. "Database Support for Storage of AI Reasoning Knowledge." This volume.

[6] Etherington, D., and Reiter, R. "On Inheritance Hierarchies with Exceptions." *Proc. AAAI-83*, Washington, D. C., 1983, pp. 104–108.

[7] Levesque, H. J. "The Logic of Incomplete Knowledge Bases." In M. L. Brodie, J. Mylopoulos, and J. W. Schmidt (*eds.*), *On Conceptual Modelling: Perspectives from Artificial Intelligence, Databases, and Programming Languages*. New York: Springer-Verlag, 1984, pp. 165–186.

[8] Levesque, H. J. "A Fundamental Tradeoff in Knowledge Representation and Reasoning." *Proc. CSCSI-84*, London, Ontario, 1984, pp. 141–152.

[9] Levesque, H. J. "Foundations of a Functional Approach to Knowledge Representation." *Artificial Intelligence*, Vol. 23, No. 2, July, 1984, pp. 155–212.

[10] Newell, A. "The Knowledge Level." *The AI Magazine*, Vol. 2, No. 2, 1981, pp. 1–20.

[11] Patel-Schneider, P. F., Brachman, R. J., and Levesque, H. J. "ARGON: Knowledge Representation Meets Information Retrieval." *Proc. First Conference on Artificial Intelligence Applications*, Denver, 1984.

[12] Reiter, R. "On Closed World Data Bases." In H. Gallaire and J. Minker (*eds.*), *Logic and Data Bases*. New York: Plenum Press, 1978, pp. 55–76.

[13] Smith, B. C. *Reflection and Semantics in a Procedural Language*, Ph.D. Thesis and Tech. Report MIT/LCS/TR-272, MIT, Cambridge, MA, 1982.

[14] Wiederhold, G. "Knowledge and Database Management." *IEEE Software*, January, 1984, pp. 63–73.

INTERACTIVE CLASSIFICATION

as a Knowledge Aquisition Tool

Tim Finin
Computer and Information Science
University of Pennsylvania
Philadelphia PA

David Silverman
IntelliCorp
Meno Park, CA

1. ABSTRACT

The practical application of knowledge-based systems, such as in expert systems, often requires the maintenance of large amounts of declarative knowledge. As a knowledge base (KB) grows in size and complexity, it becomes more difficult to maintain and extend. Even someone who is familiar with the knowledge domain, how it is represented in the KB and the actual contents of the current KB may have severe difficulties in updating it. Even if the difficulties can be tolerated, there is a very real danger that inconsistencies and errors may be introduced into the KB through the modification. This paper describes an approach to this problem based on a tool called an **interactive classifier**. An interactive classifier uses the contents of the existing KB and knowledge about its representation to help the maintainer describe new KB objects. The interactive classifier will identify the appropriate taxononomic location for the newly described object and add it to the KB. The new object is allowed to be a generalization of existing KB objects, enabling the system to learn more about existing obects.

2. INTRODUCTION

The practical application of knowlege-based systems, such as in expert systems, requires the maintenance of large amounts of declarative knowledge. As a knowledge base (KB) grows in size and complexity, it becomes more difficult to maintain and extend. Even someone who is familiar with the domain, how it is being represented and the current KB contents may introduce inconsistencies and errors whenever an addition or modification is made.

One approach to this maintenance problem is to provide a special **KB editor**. Schoen and Smith, for example, describe a display oriented editor for the representation language STROBE [25]. Freeman, et. al., have implemented an editor/browser for the KNET language [13, 14]. Lipkis and Stallard are developing an editor for the KL-ONE representation language [21]. There are several problems inherent in the editor paradim, for example:

- The system must take care that constraints in the KB, such as those defined via subsumption, are maintained.
- The system must distinguish at least two different kinds of reference to a KB object: reference *by name* and reference *by meaning*. A reference *by name* to an object should not be effected if the underlying definition of the object is changed by the editor. If one refers to an object *by meaning*, however, and later edits the object refered to, then the reference should still refer to the original description.

- The system must keep track of the origin of the subsumption relationship to distinguish between those explicitly sanctioned by the KB designer and those inferred by the system (e.g. by a classifier).

- Editors tend to be complex formal systems requiring familiarity with the editor and with the structure and content of the KB being modified.

This paper describes another approach to the KB maintenance problem based on a tool called an interactive classifier. This kind of tool is not as general or powerful as a full KB editor but avoids many of the problems described above. The interactive classifier can only be used to make monotonic changes to the KB. New objects can be added to the taxonomy and additonal attributes can be added to objects already in the KB. It does not allow object to be deleted or their existing attributes changed or overridden.

Although this may sound like a severe restriction, we believe that there are many situations where this is just the kind of KB update that is to be allowed. Consider, for example, the *computer configuration* problem which has been the domain of several recent expert system projects [18, 13, 20]. Such a system needs to have an extensive KB describing a large number computer components and their attributes, including their decomposition and interconnection constraints. An important feature of this domain is that new components are constantly being introduced as the underlying technology advances. Older components still need to be represented in the KB since there are many instalations in the field which may still need them. We may, however, want to predicate additional attributes of these older components to distinguish them from newer ones. For example, at some point in time we may add a new *laser printer* to the line of hardcopy devices. At a later time, we may want to add a new model, a *high speed laser printer*. This might involve adding two new objects: one to represent a generic laser printer with a attribute *printing speed* and another to represent the new high-speed laser printer. The original *laser printer* object would be seen as a specialization of the newly created generic laser printer.

Knowledge-based systems often represent declarative knowledge using a set of nodes, corresponding to discrete "concepts" or descriptions, which are partially ordered by a subsumption, or inheritance relation. One concept subsumes another if everything that is true about the first is also true about the second. Whenever a new node is added to the knowledge base, either during its initial construction or later maintenance, it must be placed in the appropriate position within the ordering - i.e. all subsumption relationships between the new node and existing nodes must be established. This is called *classification* because a subsuming node can be considered as a representation of a more abstract category than its subsumees. The notions of subsumption and automatic classification are very useful and have been offered as centeral features of several recent knowledge representation languages (see [5], [23], [7], and [2] for example).

Current classifiers require a complete description of the node to be added before they begin. (See [30] for a description of classification, and [17] or [24] for examples of a classifier for the representation language KL-ONE [4].) When the classifier is used directly by a user to add a new node, the user must know the descriptive terms in use in the existing KB and something of its structure in order to create a description which will be accurately classified. If the classifier places the new node in the wrong place, or if the description of the node contains errors or omissions, the user must repeatedly modify the node and redo classification until he is satisfied. The process of adding a node is much more efficient if done interactively, so that immediate feedback based on the contents of the KB is available to the user as each piece of information about the new node is entered.

The rest of this paper describes an interactive classification algorithm, which has been implemented in Prolog. Together with a simple knowledge representation language, this implementation forms a system called KuBIC, for Knowledge Base Interactive Classifier. The system takes a user's initial description of a new node and a (possibly empty) KB and either classifies the node immediately, if enough information has been specified, or determines relevant questions for the user that will help classify it. Thus a user who is familiar with the knowledge base may completely avoid the question/answer interaction with KuBIC, and use it only as a classifier, while someone who has never seen the knowledge base before may use the interaction to be presented with just those portions of the KB which are relevant to the classification of the new concept. The algorithm could be applied, for example, to knowledge representation systems or environments for building expert systems which contain classifiable knowledge bases, such as KEE [15], HPRL [16], SRL [12] or LOOPS [3].

3. THE REPRESENTATION LANGUAGE

In order to explore the underlying ideas of interactive classification, a simple knowledge representation language was chosen. The KB is constrained to be a tree structure, so each node has at most one parent. Nodes have single-valued attributes which represent components or characteristics that apply to the object or concept described. Values of attributes can be numbers, intervals, symbols, sets of symbols. The meaning of a set or range with multiple values is *disjunctive*; children of a node with an attribute with multiple values can have any subset or subrange (including single values) of the parent's value. Each node inherits all the attributes of its parent node, but its values can be restrictions of the parent attribute's values. Finally, no procedural attachment is allowed.

The Subsumption Relation

The tree structure of the knowledge base is formed by the partial ordering of its nodes with respect to the subsumption relation. The intended meaning of "*X subsumes Y*" is that whatever is represented by description Y, is also represented by the more general description *X*. All of *X*'s characteristics are inherited by *Y*, perhaps with some restriction. Since the subsumption relation is transitive, *Y* also inherits the characteristics of *X*'s subsumers (i.e. all its ancestors in the tree). In KuBIC, subsumption information is used to achieve *economy of description* and to *localize distinguishing information*.

Economy of description is a direct consequence of the inheritance of attributes and attribute values. Each description is considered to be a *virtual* description whose attributes are either local to the real description, or inherited from an ancestor. Only the most restricted value of an attribute appears in the attribute of the virtual description, even if the value occurs in an attribute of more than one ancestor description.

Classification is aided by the structure of the knowledge base. In such a taxonomic data base, distinguishing information is localized. Once a new description has been determined to be subsumed by node X, only X's subsumees are possible candidates for a more specific subsumer of the new description. The information stored at X's immediate subsumees allows the classifier to select questions which will determine which node is this more specific subsumer.

4. INTERACTIVE CLASSIFICATION

The interactive classification process is divided into three phases: acquiring the initial description of the new concept, finding the appropriate parent concept in the existing taxonomy (the most specific subsumer) and finding the apropriate immediate descendants in the existing taxonomy (the most general subsumees).

4.1. Acquiring the Initial Description

To make the interaction more efficient and minimize the number of questions the user has to answer, the user is allowed to specify an initial description of the new node. Attributes of the new node can be given, and a subsumer can be stated directly if known. Note that the user can say only that a node subsumes the new node, not that it is the **most specific** subsumer. If enough information is given, it is possible to classify the new node immediately without any further interaction. If not, KuBIC must determine what attributes to ask about so that classification can be completed.

If the initial description includes an attribute which in not currently in the KB, then the user is asked to supply certain information about the new attribute. In the simplified representation language used in KuBIC, this information is just the general constraint on possible values that the attribute can take on and a *question form* that the system can use to ask for a value for this attribute.

4.2. Establishing the Most Specific Subsumer

Because the characteristics of a node are shared by all its descendants, it is most efficient to search the tree for the new node's most specific subsumer (MSS) in a top-down manner, starting with the root. Two strategies are used to speed the search for the most specific subsumer: classification by *attribute profile* and classification by *exclusion*. The first stategy is used to take the partial description of the new KB object the user initialy presents and to identify a likely ancestor as low in the taxonomy as possible. The second strategy, classification by exclusion, is used to *push* the new KB concept lower in the taxonomy, eliciting new information from the user as needed. This second strategy is more basic to the interactive classifier and will be described in detail first.

Classifying Using Exclusion

Classifying by exclusion makes use of the fact that every node (except the root) has exactly one immediate subsumer, or parent. At all times during classification, there is one node which has been verified to be a subsumer of the new node, and is the most specific such node (the current most specific subsumer, or MSS). Only subsumees of this node need be considered as more-specific subsumers. Moreover, at most one of the immediate subsumees of this node may be a more-specific subsumer.

Exclusion therefore proceeds by looking for inconsistencies between the current description of the new node and the immediate subsumees of the current MSS. If no subsumees are consistent, the current MSS remains the actual MSS, and classification continues with the search for the new node's subsumees. If only one node is consistent, it must be verified to be a subsumer of the new node. This is done by asking the user, if necessary. If two or more nodes are consistent, attributes must be found to ask the user about which will help exclude as many of them as possible, until less than two nodes remain consistent.

The word "consistent" is a bit inadequate - what is actually meant by *"node S is consistent with the new node N"* is *"node S subsumes the* **current** *description of the new node."* (Note that this consistency relation is not symmetric.) Because the new node's description changes during its interactive classification as the user adds new information, it is possible for S to become inconsistent with it. Thus the meaning of the term *consistant* that we are using is similar to that used in discussions of non-monotonic logic [19].

Verifying Subsumption of a Consistent Node

Because the new description is entered interactively, one attribute at a time, it is incomplete during classification. Suppose that there is only one candidate node in the set of consistent children of the current MSS. This is not enough to ensure that the candidate is a more specific subsumer of the new node since the candidate may have additional attributes that the new node does not. We are assuming, of course, that the user is giving us a *partial description* of the new KB object. If the canadiate has additional attributes, we must verify that is indeed subsumes the new node. For each such attribute, the user is presented with its value in the candidate node and is asked to confirm, deny, or restrict the value as appropriate for the new node (see figure 4-2). This is done to ensure that the values of the new node's attributes are restrictions of the values of the candidate's values. Note that the new node may have attributes which the candidate does not; this does not affect subsumption. If the user does **not** verify that the single candidate node is a subsumer of the new node, then the current MSS of the new node is established as the final MSS.

An example showing a KB fragment which requires such verification is shown in figure 4-1, and the verification interaction is shown in figure 4-2. For each node in figure 4-1, only the attributes which are either defined locally or locally restricted are displayed at that node. The new description, *tandemBicycle*, has been determined to be subsumed by *unmotorizedWheeledVehicle*. Since one attribute of *tandem Bicycle* is that it has two wheels, only *bicycle* is a consistent candidate for a more specific subsumer of *tandemBicycle*. Before asserting that *tandemBicycle* is subsumed by *bicycle*, the user is asked to verify that *tandemBicycle* also has a *cargo* attribute whose value is *people* and has a *driveMechanism* whose value is a subset of {*directDrive, chain*}. If the user does not agree, *tandemBicycle*'s MSS remains *unmotorizedWheeledVehicle*.

Determining the Next Question

If there are two or more candidate nodes in the set of consistent children of the current MSS, more information about the new node is required to exclude some of them. This is done by selecting an attribute to ask about, getting the answer from the user, and repeating until the set of consistent children has been reduced to zero or one node, or there are no more attributes which will help reduce the set. Two strategies are used to select an attribute to ask about from the set of attributes which apply to the set of

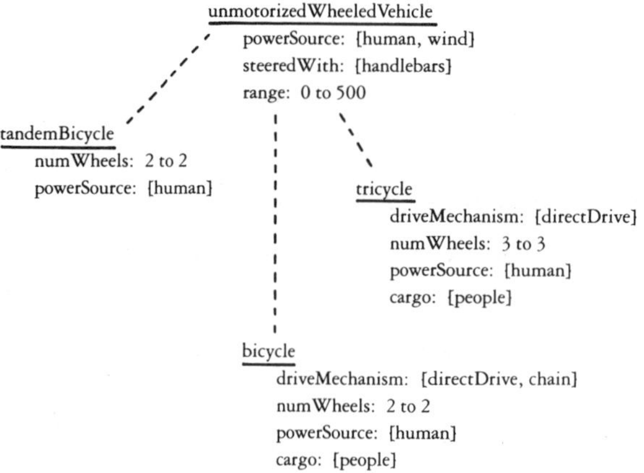

Dashed lines mean "subsumes," with subsumer above subsumee

Figure 4-1: KB Fragment Just Before Verification

There is evidence that the new description is a *bicycle*. I will now question you on each unverified aspects of *bicycle*. Please confirm, deny, or restrict the value, for each attribute.

What is the cargo?
cargo = [people]
Enter yes, no, or a restriction of the answer: ***yes.***

What is the drive mechanism?
driveMechanism = [directDrive,chain]
Enter yes, no, or a restriction of the answer: ***[chain].***

I've verified that *bicycle* subsumes *tandemBicycle*

Is this acceptable?: ***yes.***

Subsumer changed from *unmotorizedWheeledVehicle* to *bicycle*.

Figure 4-2: Interaction During Verification

(user's response in ***bold italics***)

---

consistent children: *explicit attribute ranking* and *maximal restriction*.

In our simple representation language, one can attach to a concept a list of some of the concept's attributes which are ranked with respect to their importance in classifying by exclusion. If such a ranking has been defined, then the attributes are selected in the given order. This strategy supercedes the next one, because the ranking contains external information which is not otherwise available to the system. The ranking could be based on numerical weights, but here it is a non-numerical ordering.

If there are no more attributes in the ranked list, the attribute selected to ask about is the one which *maximally restricts* the set of consistent children, in the worst case. In other words, no matter what answer is given as the value of this attribute, the minimum number of consistent children which are excluded by the answer is greater than or equal to the same minimum for any other relevant attribute. If more than one attribute is best, one is selected without regard to other considerations.

The above strategies could be augmented by using information about the particular user. Since not all questions need to be asked to perform one classification, questions which the user is more likely to be able to answer should be asked first. The user's ability to answer can be decomposed into his or her ability to understand the question, determine an appropriate response, and communicate the response to the system. The user model could be created initially by asking the user several questions intended to establish a stereotype of the user, and refined later as the user answers (or doesn't answer) questions. (See [22] and [10] for examples of this use of stereotypes.)

Classifying Using Attribute Profiles

The second classification strategy is a heuristic for searching the tree more quickly. Given the operations of determining consistency and asking the user to verify subsumption described above, if a guess could be made about possible subsumers of the new node, it would be a simple matter to verify the subsumption. A good guess is necessary, however, because the user must get involved in the verification.

The particular heuristic used in KuBIC examines the set of attributes specified by the user in the initial description to try to restrict the possible subsumers of the new node. The heuristic could also be used whenever volunteered information is allowed. It works by picking an attribute of the initial description, finding the common ancestor of all nodes in the KB which have the attribute, and using this common ancestor as a guess. The guess must be a subsumee (immediate or not) of the current MSS of the new node.

If the user verifies the guess, then it becomes the current MSS and the process continues. The user has been spared from having to answer questions about attributes of concepts which lie between the original MSS and the guess. The deeper the guess in the tree, the more questions avoided. If the user does not verify the guess, perhaps because the attribute has more than one meaning in the current KB, all is not wasted. Questions asked during verification can contribute information to the new node, or, if the attribute in question is not an attribute of the new node, KuBIC knows not to ask the question again. The system can keep guessing, whether a previous guess succeeded or not, until it runs out of attributes, or until the user becomes weary of incorrect guesses.

4.3. Establishing the Most General Subsumees

The task of classification is half completed once the most specific subsumer of the new node has been established. Finding the most general subsumees (MGS's) is the other half. Fortunately, this half is much less work because of the constraint that the KB form a tree structure.

The only possible candidates for most general subsumees are children of the MSS of the new node - i.e. siblings of the new node. (This assumes that the KB is well-constructed, so that the immediate subsumer of each node is its MSS, and the immediate subsumees are its MGS's.) Thus to find all the MGS's, it is only necessary to check whether the new node is "consistent" with each sibling in turn, and to ask the user to verify that there is no missing information about either node which misled the classifier. Note that by establishing a node as the MGS of the new node, the interactive classifier can implicitly change the descriptions of the MGS and all its subsumees - nodes which were already in the KB - because they inherit new attributes from the new node.

If the subsumption relationship is alloweed to define a latice rather than a tree, then determining the MGS's is more difficult. A newly entered node may not subsume its siblings, but could subsume some of its sibling's descendants. For example, consider a taxonomy for living things which includes a concept *livingThing* with two immediate children: *animal* and *plant*. We could use the interactive classifier to enter a new node *genderedLivingThing* to represent the concept of a *livingthing* with an attribute gender whose values come from the set {male,female}. This concept would initially be an immediate descendant of the concept *livingThing*. Neither *animal* nor *plant*, however, is a descendant of this new concept, since there are genderless animals and genderless plants. Many of their descendants, however, are subsummed by the new concept *genderedLivingThing*.

5. FURTHER WORK

There are two areas on which our current work is focused. First, we are extending the idea of an interactive classifier to a more complete representation language. Second, we are incorporating a more sophisticated *user model* to guide the interaction.

5.1. More Expressive Representation Languages

The limitations of the current work stem from the simplified nature of the knowledge representation language we have used. Using this simplified language was a conscious research stategy choice. It allowed us to focus on the notion of an interactive classifier in a simple surrounding. The two major shortcomings in KuBIC's representation language are that nodes are organized in a tree rather than a lattice, and that values of attributes must be explicit sets or intervals. Neither of these limitations should be an obstacle to extending the interactive classifier to a more general representation language. This section sketches our planned approach to such an extension (we anticipate developing an interactive classifier for the representation language HPRL [16]).

Suppose nodes were organized in a lattice structure, so that they would be allowed to have multiple subsumers. In the course of finding the new node's most specific subsumers, this would require the interactive classifier to search all paths from the current most specific subsumer down the subsumption links until a node is found that is inconsistent with the new node, or until there are no more consistent paths below a node on the path. The user would have to give enough information about the new node so that *each* child of the current MSS could be determined to be inconsistent or a subsumer of the new node, instead of stopping when the user verified one subsumer.

If attribute values are allowed to be pointers to nodes (e.g. as in KL-ONE's *value/restrictions*) then the description of a new node would depend in part on the nodes it refers to in its attributes. The algorithm described in this paper will work when the nodes referred to are already classified in the KB; only the subsumption relation would have to be changed. If they are new nodes, however, they must be interactively classified before the new node which refers to them.

5.2. More Sophisticated User Models

The second area we are working on is the incorporation of a more sophisticated model of the user. Such a model could be used to select attributes to ask about next and also to provide the user with appropriate help and guidance is answering questions. This is related to work in the context of interfaces to expert systems (see [28, 29] for example).

There has been some previous research on how expert systems get information from their users. For example, Fox [11] considered integrating reasoning with knowledge aquisition from a resource management perspective. Aikins [1] addressed the seemingly random question-asking behavior of systems which pursued lines of reasoning opportunistically, jumping around to whatever line looked most promising and asking for whatever information they needed at that point. This randomness annoyed and confused users. Aikins suggested an organization for reasoning that would result in related questions being asked together. Brooks [6] considered the amount of information systems may end up requesting from their users and found that a large number (30 or more) of requests is generally considered unacceptable. He suggested ways of cutting down on the amount of information requested, by enriching systems' models of their domains. These same sorts of considerations can be employed in the context of interactive classification.

Expert systems vary as to when they ask the user for information and when they rely on their own deductions. However, in this decision, they do not take into account the user's ability to understand and respond reliably. In Prospector [8] for example, goals are simply marked as being either "askable" or "unaskable" (never both). If the goal is "askable", the user is asked for the information. If "unaskable", the system attempts to deduce it. There are no other criteria. (On the other hand, Prospector does allow the user to change his/her answer to any question and will recompute its conclusions accordingly.) In Mycin [26], the user is only asked for information if either the system's attempt to deduce a subgoal fails - i.e., if no rules were applicable or if the applicable rules were too weak or offset each other - or the user's answer would be conclusive (e.g., lab results). In Knobs [9], a system for assisting users in mission planning, the user is asked for preferences, not facts. If the user prefers not to answer at any point, s/he can turn over control to the system and let it compute an appropriate value.

Any attempt to customize a system's way of interacting to the user at hand must allow for the fact that at times, the system is going to guess wrong - the user is not going to be able to answer its question or will answer it incorrectly or will find it annoying. Thus what we are proposing has two aspects - (1) <u>recovering</u> from a wrong decision (i.e., from having asked a "bad" question, and (2) <u>modifying</u> subsequent decisions about what sort of questions to ask. It is based on our belief that one can <u>structure</u> and <u>annotate</u> a system's inferential space in such a way that it can modify its behavior in response to the user at hand. For example, one approach might be to evaluate strategies according to how much work is required of the user to provide the information requested of him/her. This can be factored into how much work is required to: (1) understand the question; (2) acquire the information and (3) communicate the information to the system.

Of course there might be several alternative procedures the user could employ in acquiring the information the system wants, each of different difficulty for him/her, each requiring somewhat different resources. While the system's evaluation of a strategy might be based on the assumption that the user can and will use the easiest of these procedures, more refined evaluations might take into account the resources available to the particular user as well. (This information about alternative procedures - their level of difficulty and resource requirements would also be useful for certain cases where a user cannot answer the system's question, as will be discussed in the next section.)

A strategy evaluation based solely on how much work is required of the user would not be sufficient however. Another factor in the system's choice of reasoning strategy must be its a priori beliefs about the reliability of the user's information. The system should prefer a line of reasoning which depends on facts it believes the user can supply reliably over one which it believes the user can supply with less reliability.

6. SUMMARY

This paper presented the design and implementation of an interactive, incremental classifier which is used to add nodes to a hierachical frame oriented knowledge base. A knowledge representation language was defined, complex enough to resemble in certain aspects representations of current knowledge-based systems yet simple enough to allow focusing on interactive classification (for more detail and the Prolog implementation of KuBIC, see [27]). The problem of classification was described as determining most-specific and most-general subsumption relationships between the new node and nodes already in the knowledge base. Two components to the classification strategy were presented: classification using exclusion, which uses a special "consistency" relation and asks questions to exclude whole portions of the KB at a time, and classification using attributes, which uses a heuristic based on what attributes the user says the new node has to take short-cuts in the search. Both of these serve to establish the most specific subsumer; the most general subsumees are then relatively simple to find. Current work is focused on extending the concept of an interactive classifier to a more powerful representation language and incorporating a more sophisticated user model.

7. BIBLIOGRAPHY

1. Aikins, J. Prototypes and Production Rules: A knowledge representation for computer consultations. HPP-80-17, Heuristic Programming Project, Stanford University, August, 1980.

2. Hassan Ait-Kaci. Type Subsumption as a Model of Computation. In Larry Kerschberg, Ed., *Expert Database Systems*, Benjamin/Cummings Publishing Co., Menlo Park CA, 1985.

3. Bobrow, D.G. and Stefik, M. The Loops Manual. Technical report KB-VLSI-81-13, Xerox PARC, 1981.

4. Brachman, Ronald. A Structural Paradigm for Representing Knowledge. Technical Report 3605, Bolt Beranek and Newman Inc., May, 1978.

5. Brachman, R. R. Fikes and H. Levesque. KRYPTON: A Functional Approach to Knowledge Representation. 16, Fairchild Lab for AI Research, 1983.

6. Brooks, R., Heiser, J. Controlling Question Asking in a Medical Expert System. Proc. IJCAI-79, Tokyo Japan, 1979, pp. 102-104.

7. Francisco Corella. Semantic Retrieval and Levels of Abstraction. In Larry Kerschberg, Ed., *Expert Database Systems*, Benjamin/Cummings Publishing Co., Menlo Park CA, 1985.

8. Duda, R., Gaschnig, J., & Hart, P. Model Design in the PROSPECTOR Consultant System for Mineral Exploration. In *Expert Systems in the Micro-electronic Age*, D. Michie, Ed., Edinburgh University Press, Edinburgh, 1979.

9. Engleman, C., Scarl, E. & Berg, C. Interactive Frame Instantiation. Proc. First National Conference on Artificial Intelligence (AAAI), Stanford CA, 1980.

10. Finin, T. and D. Drager. GUMS1 - A General User Modeling System. technical report MS-CIS-85-30, Computer and Information Science, U. of Pennsylvania, 1985.

11. Fox, M. S. Reasoning with Incomplete Knowledge in a Resource Limited Environment: Integrating Reasoning with Knowledge Aquisition. Proc. 7th Int'l. Joint Conf. on Art. Intelligence, IJCAI, University of British Columbia, Vancouver, Canada, August, 1981.

12. Fox, M and J. Wright and D. Adam. Experiences with SRL: An Analysis of a Frame-based Knowledge Representation. In Larry Kerschberg, Ed., *Expert Database Systems*, Benjamin/Cummings Publishing Co., Menlo Park CA, 1985.

13. Freeman, M., L. Hirschman and D. McKay. A Logic Based Configurator. technical memo LBS 9, SDC, A Burroughs Company, May, 1983.

14. Freeman, M., L. Hirschman and D. McKay. KNET - A logic Based Associative Network Framework for Expert Systems. technical memo LBS 12, SDC, A Burroughs Company, September, 1983.

15. Kehler, T.P. and Clemenson, G.D. "An Application Development System for Expert Systems". *Systems & Software* (January 1984).

16. Lanam, D, R. Letsinger, S. Rosenberg, P. Huyun and M. Lemon. Guide to the Heuristic Programming and Representation Language Part 1 : Frames. AT-MEMO-83-3, Application and Technology Laboratory, Computer Research Center, Hewlett-Packard , January, 1984.

17. Lipkis, Thomas. A KL-ONE Classifier. Consul Note 5, USC/Information Sciences Institute, October, 1981.

18. McDermott, J. R1: A Rule-Based Configurer of Computer Systems. Carnegie-Mellon University, 1980.

19. McDermott, D and J. Doyle. "Non-Monotonic Logic I". *Artificial Intelligence 13*, 1-2 (1980), 41 - 72.

20. McDermott, J. XSEL: A Computer Saleperson's Assistant. In *Machine Intelligence 10*, Ellis Horwood Ltd, Chichester UK, 1982, pp. 325-337.

21. personal communication.

22. Rich, Elaine. "User Modeling via Stereotypes". *Cognitive Science 3* (1979), 329-354.

23. James Schmolze and David Israel. KL-ONE: Semantics and Classification. 5421, Bolt Beranek and Newman Inc., Cambridge MA, 1983.

24. Schmolze, J.G., and Lipkis, T.A. Classification in the KL-ONE Knowledge Representation System. Proc. IJCAI-83, Karlsruhe, W. Germany, 1983.

25. Schoen, E. and R. Smith. IMPULSE: A Display Oriented Editor for STROBE. Proceedings of the National Conference on Artificial Intelligence, AAAI, Washington, D.C., August, 1983, pp. 356-358.

26. Shortliffe, E.. *Computer-based Medical Consultations: MYCIN.* Elsevier, New York, 1976.

27. Silverman, David L. An Interactive, Incremental Classifier. Technical Report MS-CIS-84-10, University of Pennsylvania, Apr., 1984.

28. Webber, B. and T. Finin. In Response: Next Steps in Natural Language Interaction. In *Artificial Intelligence Applications for Business*, W. Reitman, Ed., Ablex Publ. Co., Norwood NJ, 1984.

29. Webber, B. and Tim Finin. Expert Questions - Adapting to Users' Needs. technical report MS-CIS-84-19, Computer and Information Science, University of Pennsylvania, 1984.

30. Woods, W. Theoretical Studies in Natural Language Understanding: Annual Report. Technical Report 4332, Bolt Beranek and Newman Inc., 1979.

Semantic Retrieval and Levels of Abstraction

Francisco Corella
Schlumberger Palo Alto Research
Artificial Intelligence Laboratory

Abstract

Some important bodies of information should be properly modelled, not as collections of individual objects, but as collections of predicates, or "concepts", whose extensions are not explicitly represented in the knowledge base because they are immaterial. Previous work in knowledge representation has focussed on the representation and automatic classification of concepts, and on the retrieval of their extensions. Here we focus on the retrieval of those concepts themselves.

We propose a knowledge-level view of taxonomies as tools for sorting sets of concepts. We introduce the notions of composition of taxonomies, level of abstraction, retrievable concept, and semantic space. This leads to a formal definition of what it means to retrieve and sort concepts in response to a query, at a given level of abstraction. Finally we give sufficient conditions on the structure of the semantic space, the predicate of a query and the level of abstraction specified for the response, under which the answer to the query is exhaustive.

1 Introduction

The ideas presented in this paper are early results of research that was triggered by the unexpected finding of a whole class of applications that lie in between the fields of database management and knowledge representation, and seem to have been left out of both fields. It is difficult to characterize this set of applications precisely, at this point, except maybe as "catalog-type" systems. We discovered a representative of this class when we attempted to build, using the retrieval system Argon [9,10] (which is based on the knowledge representation system Kandor), an on-line catalog of TTL devices, with data from the Fairchild TTL Data Book [7]. The enterprise immediately raised a number of problems "at the knowledge level" which, we believe, have not been addressed before.

We must insist that the problems that we are referring to are not at the "Symbol Level" but at the "Knowledge Level". We are not proposing fast or *optimized* retrieval algorithms. We are not discussing computational tractability either. More fundamentally, we are trying to determine what the basic notions of retrieval mean for applications of the above-mentioned category.

One would expect a catalog of integrated circuits to be an easy application for database management systems. The information in a catalog is repetitive, well structured, "tabular". More importantly, it is complete in the sense of [2], which properly characterizes databases as knowledge bases with complete information about their domain. Indeed, the TTL Data Book never tells us that a given chip is either a gate or a flip-flop, without specifying which is the actual type. In spite of this, we will show that a proper treatment of this domain lies out of the scope of the ongoing work in object-oriented data modelling [4,5,6,8,12], because it requires the representation of concepts.

Frame systems such as KL-ONE [3,11] and Kandor do have the capability of defining and representing concepts. However, they do not provide some of the tools that would be necessary to build an information retrieval system targetted to these concepts themselves. And this, as we shall see, is necessary in catalog-type domains.

1.1 Organization of the paper

We have made an effort to give precise definitions to the concepts that we introduce and to prove all non-trivial results. For the sake of readability, we have grouped definitions, theorems and proofs in the appendix, in the form of a small self-contained theory. In the body of the paper we concentrate on motivating that theory. For that purpose, we rely on the TTL Data Book example, which has proved to be so fruitful. Step by step, we try to show how a proper treatment of this information retrieval problem conflicts with current approaches and leads naturally to the ideas that we propose.

2 Semantic Retrieval

2.1 TTL Numbering System

Since we are going to use the TTL Data Book as a running example, it is necessary to describe briefly the industry-wide convention for designating TTL devices. Each device is assigned a serial number, consisting of two or three digits. For example, the 00 designates a "quad 2-input nand gate", i.e. a device providing 4 logic blocks, each of which is a 2-input nand gate, while the 73 is a "dual JK flip-flop", consisting of two blocks each of which is a JK flip-flop. Each device can be available in various versions, having different grades (military or commercial) and belonging to different subfamilies of TTL (standard, High-Power, Low-Power, Schottky or Low-Power-Schottky). Each such version is designated by a code consisting of the digits 54 (for military grade) or 74 (for commercial grade), followed by zero, one or two letters indicating the family (zero letters for standard TTL; H, L, S, or LS for non-standard TTL) followed by the serial number of the device. Thus a 5400 is a military-grade standard-TTL quad 2-input nand gate while a 74LS73 is a commercial-grade Low-Power-Schottky-TTL dual JK flip-flop.

It is posssible to specify the family but not the grade, by replacing the grade code (54 or 74) by an apostrophe. Thus a 'LS73 is a Low-Power-Schottky flip-flop of either grade, while a '73 is a standard-TTL flip-flop of either grade. It is unfortunate that the "standard TTL" subfamily is designated by the absence of a subfamily code. That makes it difficult to distinguish the specification of the standard subfamily from the absence of a subfamily specification. In this paper we shall adopt the convention that a number preceded by the #-sign designates a device where only the serial number has been specified. Thus a 'LS73 is a Low-Power-Schottky #73, and a '73 is a standard-TTL #73.

Finally, each version can be offered in various packages and each manufacturer feels free to designate the package type and embellish the standard code by adding characters in front of it or at the end, to form the full Ordering Code. Fairchild adds one letter designating the package type (D for Ceramic, F for Flatpak, M for Metal, P for Plastic) and a second letter, M or C, that redundantly designates the grade. Thus a 74LS73PC is a Low-Power Schottky flip-flop of commercial grade in a plastic package.

2.2 Concepts vs. Individuals

Let us now assume the existence of an on-line catalog of TTL devices, and let us consider a simple query that one might want to issue:

```
(Q1)     ''List the flip-flops''.
```

What should the answer be? It could be a list of serial numbers designating flip-flops:

(1) #70, #71, #72, #73, #74, #76, #78, #101, #102...

But it could also be a list of codes indicating both the serial number and the TTL subfamily, maybe ordered by serial number:

(2) '70, 'H71, '72, 'H72, '73, 'H73, 'LS73...

(#70 is offered in Standard-TTL version only, #71 in High-Power version only, #72 in both standard and "H" version, etc.) Or a list of codes specifying grade and family:

(3) 5470, 7470, 54H71, 74H71, 5472, 7472, 54H72, 74H72, 5473, 7473, 54H73, 74H73, 54LS73, 74LS73...

Or even a much longer list of fully specified Ordering Codes:

(4) 5470DM, 5470FM, 7470PC, 7470DC, 7470FC, 54H71DM...

Answer (1) may seem preferable because it is the shortest. However, (2) has the advantage that it indicates what devices are available in what subfamilies. Also, if we ask: "What are the Toggle Frequencies of the flip-flops?", then we will have to give (2), because the frequency depends on the family.

We will expand on these issues later in the paper. All we need to notice at this point is that the information retrieval system must be able to give various "kinds of answers" in various circumstances. Hence, it must be able to display, and therefore have knowledge of "entities" such as "#73", "'LS73", "74LS73PC", etc.

What is the nature of such entities? How can we model them adequately? The answer becomes clear if we consider the relationships in which they stand to each other. We can certainly say, for example that:

(5) "Every 'LS73 is a #73"

(6) "A #73 is either a '73 or a 'H73 or a 'LS73"

This shows that these "entities" are concepts, i.e. sets, or one-place, set-defining predicates. In set notation, (5) and (6) become:

(5') $'LS73 \subset \#73$

(6') $\#73 = '73 \cup 'H73 \cup 'LS73$

and in logic notation:

(5") $\forall x \ 'LS73(x) \rightarrow \#73(x)$

(6") $\forall x \ \#73(x) \leftrightarrow '73(x) \vee 'H73(x) \vee 'LS73(x)$

Now, if these "entities" are sets, what are their elements? We could decide that the most specific designators, namely the Ordering Codes, correspond to individuals, and that these individuals are members of sets designated by less specific codes. Thus 74LS73PC would be an ELEMENT of 74LS73, while the latter would be a SUBSET of 'LS73. However, this is arbitrary and counterintuitive. Also, it will not work if we need to consider concepts which are even more specialized, e.g. in a database used by a Manufacturing Division, variants of a given device obtained by variations on the manufacturing procedure. Maybe the individuals should be the material chips that come out of a fabrication line.

Obviously, such considerations are irrelevant to the problem of computerizing a TTL catalog. But this means that the nature of the elements of the sets under consideration is irrelevant. We need an information retrieval system capable of dealing with concepts whose extensions are immaterial.

In the remainder of the paper we shall assume the existence of a domain D (also called DEVICE(x) when considered as a predicate), which is the set of the devices covered by the catalog (whatever those devices are). Predicates have extensions over D, which are subsets of D. We shall identify each predicate with its extension, referring to it alternatively as a concept, a predicate or a set, and freely switching between set and logic terminology. In particular, we shall say that 2 predicates are equal when they have the same extension, i.e. when they are logically equivalent over the domain.

2.3 Retrieval of Concepts

Because the data in the information retrieval system that we wish to construct consists of concepts, we must rule out using an object-oriented database system and turn instead to frame systems, such as KL-ONE and Kandor, which focus precisely on the representation and classification of concepts, and information retrieval systems based on them, such as Argon. The capability provided by these systems for defining and classifying concepts is very valuable. We have actually been able to represent, using Kandor, all the concepts needed for a demonstration system covering a fraction of the TTL Data Book (gates and flip-flops)

However, these frame-based systems lack the notion of "Semantic Retrieval", by which we mean retrieval of concepts. Argon has a retrieval capability, but it applies to elements of the extensions of concepts. As we have seen, in the problem domain the extensions of the concepts are immaterial. We need therefore a system capable of both representing concepts, and retrieving them in response to queries.

Now, the notion of retrieval of concepts is problematic. It is clear what it means to retrieve a set of individuals as the answer to a query. The query has a condition C, which is a predicate, and the answer is simply the extension of the predicate:

$$\{x \in D \mid C(x)\}$$

It is reasonable to say that a concept p satisfies a query C if:

$$\forall x\, P(x) \rightarrow C(x)$$

(in which case we shall equivalently say that C subsumes P, or P implies C, or C contains P (referring to their extensions), or P is included in C (again referring to the extensions)). But, of course, listing all subsets of the condition of the query is out of question. Which ones, then, should be part of the answer?

Let us consider again query Q1, whose condition is simply the predicate flip-flop(x), and a few predicates subsumed by the condition:

$$P1 = \#73$$

$$P2 = 'H76$$

$$P3 = 'LS73 \vee 'H76$$

$$P4 = master - slave$$

Although all these concepts satisfy the condition of the query (the #76 is also a flip-flop, and does have an "H" version), it would be surprising to see P3 or P4 in the answer to the query, while it would not be suprising to see P1 or P2. Intuitively, the disjunction P3 of two version codes with different serial numbers is not a very "interesting" concept. As for concept P4, it is certainly interesting, and a necessary part of a TTL catalog, but it does not seem to belong in the answer.

We are going to postulate that the knowledge engineer who is building a catalog-type application of this kind using a general purpose tool should be able to choose a set Z of concepts which can be retrieved and listed in answers to queries, and which we shall call the *retrievable concepts* of the domain. We shall later require Z to have some properties, but for now we only assume it to be finite. For lack of a better term, we will call the structure consisting of a domain D together with a set Z of retrievable concepts over D a *semantic space*. In our example domain, Z would be the set of all the concepts that can be named according to the TTL numbering system described in 2.1. Thus P1 and P2 would be retrievable concepts, while P3 and P4 would not.

Consider now two retrievable concepts that satisfy the above query and such that one of them subsumes the other:

$$P1 = \#73$$

$$P5 = 'LS73$$

It is clear that both of them should not appear simultaneously in the answer. If P1 is part of the answer, then it would be redundant and confusing to include P5. Saying that C subsumes P1 carries more information than saying than C subsumes P5. Thus, if there is no reason for excluding P1 from the answer, we should include P1 and exclude P5. If we apply the same argument globally to the set of all retrievable concepts subsumed by C, we can see that we should include only those which are not subsumed by any other concepts in that same set, i.e. those which are maximal for subsumption. Therefore we propose the following rule:

Rule 1 *"In the absence of any other constraints, the answer to a query with condition C should comprise the maximal retrievable concepts subsumed by C."*

The above rule would produce, in response to query Q1, the set:

```
(A1)    #70, #71, #72, #73, #74, #76, #78, #101...
```

But consider a modification of that query:

```
(Q2)    ''List the edge-triggered flip-flops''
```

A JK (or D) flip-flop is "edge-triggered" when it reads its inputs on the active edge of the clock pulse, while it is said to be a "master-slave" flip-flop if it will accept a toggle command at any time during the half cycle preceding the active edge of the clock and then toggle on the active edge. The #70, #74, #101, and others, are edge-triggered. The #71, #72 and others are master-slave. As for the #73, #76 and #78, their "LS" versions are edge-triggered, while the other versions in which they are offered are master-slave. In the set S of retrievable concepts subsumed by the condition "edge-triggered flip-flop", 'LS73 is maximal because #73 is not in S, while 'LS74, say, is not maximal because #74 is in S. Thus 'LS73 and #74 are part of the answer, A2, while #73 and 'LS74 are not:

```
(A2)    #70, 'LS73, #74, 'LS76, 'LS78, #101...
```

This answer is correct, but has a serious competitor, namely the list obtained by expanding each serial number in A2 into subfamily/serial-number codes:

```
(A2')   '70, 'LS73, '74, 'H74, 'S74, 'LS74, 'LS76, 'LS78, 'H101...
```

In addition to showing what versions can be chosen for each serial number, A2' is also more uniform than A2, in the sense that all the items in the response have the same "granularity", they are at the same "level of abstraction". Clearly, it would be desirable to allow the user to specify the "granularity", or "level of abstraction" of the elements of the response, together with the condition. In the TTL domain, there are 4 sets of concepts that stand out as candidates to be considered levels of abstraction, corresponding to the 4 types of codes described in section 2.1. We shall refer to them as levels of abstraction I, II, III and IV. Concepts described by a serial number will be at level I, concepts such as 'LS73 where the family is specifed in addition to the serial number will be at level II, codes that specify both family and grade will be at level III and codes that specify family, grade and package at level IV.

A query would then have two components, a condition and a level of abstraction. The condition "edge-triggered flip-flop" at level of abstraction II would produce the answer A2'. The same condition at level of abstraction III would give:

```
(A2'')  5470, 7470, 54LS73, 74LS73, 5474, 7474, 54H74, 74H74...
```

But what if the user specifies level I? The answer should contain #70, #74, etc, but it cannot contain #73, since '73 and 'H73 are not edge-triggered. Should any reference to serial-number 73 be omitted? That would be misleading. It would be better to show 'LS73, as an "exception". Thus it appears that A2 is the appropriate answer at level I. In general, we want the specification of a level of abstraction to impose an upper bound on the granularity of the items in the response. This leads us to redefine our 4 levels so that each of them contains those "below it". Thus #74 would be at level I only, 'H74 would be part of level II, but also of level I, 54H74 would be part of I, II and III, and a fully specifed Ordering Code would be part of all 4 levels of abstraction. Inside the level of abstraction specified for a given query, the same argument that led to rule 1 applies, and shows that the answer should include only those retrievable concepts which are maximal for subsumption. Thus the level of abstraction acts as an upper bound on the granularity of the elements of the answer, while the maximality condition "pushes them up" as high as possible. This mechanism allows for "exceptions" such as 'LS73 to be properly handled. It can be codified in the following rule:

Rule 2 *"The answer to a query with condition C, at a level of abstraction L, should comprise the maximal retrievable concepts among those subsumed by C which are at level of abstraction L."*

In the discussion leading to this rule, we have avoided giving a precise definition of the notion of "level of abstraction". We have identified and numbered 4 levels in our example domain, and indicated what retrievable concepts lie at each of those levels. But the specification that we have given of those levels is based on the TTL numbering convention, and thus narrowly domain-dependent. The main goal of this paper is to give a domain independent definition of the notion of "level of abstraction", which will confer general validity to rule 2 over the range of catalog-type domains. However, this must wait until we have explored, in section 3, the notions of taxonomy, composition of taxonomies, and classification. The analysis in section 3 will show that it is often necessary for the answer of a query to satisfy some "classifiability constraints". At the same time, it will prepare the ground for the proposal, in section 4, of a domain-independent notion of "level of abstraction", which embodies these classifiability constraints and also accounts for the 4 levels that we have identified in the example domain.

3 Taxonomies

3.1 Composition and Classification

Database Management Systems provide facilities for sorting the result of a query, which are an essential part of the retrieval function. The printed TTL Data Book, on the other hand, provides selection guides, which list all the devices, sorted in various ways.

Let us consider a small sample of a selection guide:

```
Device                    (T1)
    Gate
        Nand
            2-input
                #00
                #01
                #03
            3-input
                #10
                #12
        Nor
            2-input
                #02
            3-input
                #27
```

```
    Flip-flop
        JK-type
            #70
            #71
            #72
            #73
            #76
            #78
        D-type
            #73
```

We have simplified and rearranged the sample in order to make its logical structure apparent. It is clearly a tree, whose nodes are labeled by concepts (Device, Gate, Nand, 2-input, #00, #01, etc.). We will say that a tree of concepts is a *taxonomy*[1]. Notice that some concepts (2-input and 3-input, in this case) label more than one node. A related remark is that a node does not necessarily subsume its descendants (2-input appears below Nand, however not all 2-input devices are nand gates, there can also be 2-input nor gates, as the taxonomy suggests). However, the retrievable concepts that appear as leaves of the taxonomy are subsumed by the concepts labelling all the nodes in the path leading from the root to the leaf.

We will say that a taxonomy is strict if any two siblings are labeled by incompatible concepts, i.e. by disjoint sets (definition 4 in the appendix is slightly more general). We will not assume that a taxonomy is strict unless we say so explicitly.

It is easy to imagine other ways of composing selection guides using the same concepts. For example, we could distinguish the gates according to the number of inputs before distinguishing them according to the logic function:

```
Device                    (T2)
    Gate
        2-input
            Nand
                #00
                #01
                #03
            Nor
                #02
        3-input
            Nand
                #10
                #12
            Nor
                #27
    Flip-flop
        JK-type
            #70
            #71
            #72
            #73
            #76
```

[1]Our taxonomies are not to be confused with what is usually called "THE taxonomy" in a frame system. We justify this terminology below, in section 3.2.

```
        #78
    D-type
        #73
```

All these observations can be "explained" by considering these selection guides as obtained from smaller building blocks by several operations. Thus, in order to obtain T1 we can start with T3:

```
Device                    (T3)
    Gate
    Flip-flop
```

and *compose* it with T4:

```
Gate                      (T4)
    Nand
    Nor
```

by *grafting* T4 at the "Gate" node of T3, which gives T5:

```
Device                    (T5)
    Gate
        Nand
        Nor
    Flip-flop
```

Then we graft, twice, T6:

```
Device                    (T6)
    2-input
    3-input
```

on the Nand and Nor nodes of T5, obtaining T7:

```
Device                    (T7)
    Gate
        Nand
            2-input
            3-input
        Nor
            2-input
            3-input
    Flip-flop
```

Notice that the root of the grafted taxonomy can be labeled by a concept other than the label of the node on which it is grafted, and does not appear in the resulting taxonomy. The only requirement is that it must must subsume the conjunction of the nodes in the path from the root to the leaf where the graft occurs[2].

The next step is to graft T8:

```
Flip-flop                 (T8)
    JK-type
    D-type
```

on node Flip-flop, obtaining T9:

[2]Definition 8 in the appendix provides a precise and more general specification of the *composition* operation

```
Device                    (T9)
    Gate
        Nand
            2-input
            3-input
        Nor
            2-input
            3-input
    Flip-flop
        JK-type
        D-type
```

Finally from T9 we obtain T1 by *classifying the concepts*:

```
(7)     #00, #01, #02, #03, #10, #12, #27, #70, #71, #72,
        #73, #74, #76, #78
```

on taxonomy T9. A concept is classifiable at a tip of a taxonomy if it is subsumed by all the nodes in the path from the root to the tip. The result of the classification is the taxonomy obtained by installing the concept as an immediate descendant of the tip[3].

The alternative selection guide T2 is obtained from the same building blocks, by a similar procedure, but composing with T6 before T4.

3.2 Sorting and Stability Result

We have motivated the notions of composition and classification by observation of the selection guides provided in printed catalogs. It is clear that an on-line information retrieval system should allow the usage of taxonomies as tools for organizing information in more flexible ways. It should be possible to provide any number of selection guides instead of only one or two. Better, the user should be allowed to build his own taxonomies by composition of elementary ones, and use them to sort the result sets of queries. Indeed, from the operation of classification of a concept by a taxonomy we can derive the following operations:

- To *sort a list of classifiable concepts according to a taxonomy*, classify each concept in the sequence, then remove all nodes that do not have any newly added concept among their descendents.

- To *order a list of classifiable concepts according to a taxonomy*, classify each concept in the list, then traverse the tree and collect the nodes into a new list, in the order in which they are encountered.

These notions correspond directly to the more traditional notions of sorting or ordering a result set of "individuals" with respect to one or more attributes, found in database management.

For example, the two grades, "commercial" and "military", can be viewed as sets of devices, or as values of a "grade" attribute. In the second case the concept of a "commercial-grade" ["military-grade"] device can be defined as a device having the value "commercial" ["military"] for the grade attribute. Then the taxonomy:

```
Device                    (T10)
    Commercial-grade
    Military-grade
```

is *the taxonomy induced by the grade attribute*[4]. Similarly, if we choose to view the TTL subfamilies as values of a "subfamily attribute", the "subfamily taxonomy":

[3]Again, the appendix gives a precise definition (no. 5) which is more general

[4]A formal definition of the notion of induced taxonomy is given in the appendix (definition 9)

```
Device                    (T11)
    Standard-TTL
    High-Power
    Low-Power
    Schottky
    Low-Power-Schottky
```

is the one induced by this attribute. But then sorting a list of ("individual") devices x1, x2 ... xp by, e.g., family and grade is clearly the same as sorting the singletons x1, x2 ... xp, in the sense defined above, with respect to the taxonomy:

```
Device                    (T12)
    Standard-TTL
        Commercial-grade
        Military-grade
    High-Power
        Commercial-grade
        Military-grade
    Low-Power
        Commercial-grade
        Military-grade
    Schottky
        Commercial-grade
        Military-grade
    Low-Power-Schottky
        Commercial-grade
        Military-grade
```

This taxonomy is the result of grafting the grade taxonomy T10 at each terminal node of the subfamily taxonomy T11. This is what we call the product[5] of T10 by T11.

In this sense the notion of sorting introduced above for concepts is a generalization of the traditional notion of sorting.

The following Stability Result is proven in the appendix (theorem 1): if a concept is classifiable by two taxonomies, it is also classifiable by any (legal) composition of these two taxonomies. This result is important from a practical point of view. It implies that, if each concept in the result set of a query is classifiable by a group of elementary taxonomies, then the result set can be sorted and displayed according to any selection guide that can be obtained by composition of these taxonomies[6].

3.3 Taxonomies vs. Subsumption Graph

The notions of taxonomy and classification that we have defined coincide with the ordinary meaning of these words. The term *taxonomy* evokes a carefully thought out hierarchy (i.e. tree) of concepts with respect to which other concepts are classified. When more than one such classification system is considered for a given set of concepts, they are referred to as alternative taxonomies, rather than as "a single taxonomy which is not a tree". This is to be contrasted with what is usually called "the taxonomy" in a frame system. Such a taxonomy is a collection of all the frames, or concepts, that happen to have been defined in the system,

[5] A formal definition of the product of two taxonomies is given in the appendix (definition 8)

[6] There are other operations besides composition which may be useful in building taxonomies and which are stable with respect to classification. They are described in definition 8 and also covered by theorem 1.

linked by all the subsumption relationships that have been determined among them. It should be more properly called "the subsumption graph" of the system.

The subsumption graph is clearly *at the symbol level*, as has been properly emphasized in [1]. On the other hand, even though we are accustomed to thinking of trees as data structures, the taxonomies here cannot be suspected of being implementation tools: they are present in the printed catalog! They are *at the knowledge level*. But thus we have a knowledge level notion that cannot be accounted for in terms of the so-called "first order" logic, a taxonomy being a graph labeled by concepts. We have previously introduced another "second order" notion: the distinction between retrievable and non-retrievable concepts requires the explicit representation of "the concept of a retrievable-concept", a predicate applying to predicates! Levels of abstraction are also "second order entities".

There is, of course, nothing mysterious or even remarkable about this. The set of retrievable concepts is a set of sets, a taxonomy is a graph with nodes labeled by sets. These notions can thus be trivially described in set theory.

3.4 Classifiability Constraints

We have seen how the result set of a query in a catalog-type environment can be "sorted" by classifying its elements with respect to a taxonomy. But of course, not all result sets are classifiable by all taxonomies. For example, result sets that contain concepts defined by serial numbers, such as A1 and A2, are not classifiable by the subfamily taxonomy T11, nor by any product of taxonomies that includes T11 as one of the factors. For a less obvious example, consider the elementary taxonomy that distinguishes between master-slave and edge-triggered flip-flops:

```
Flip-flop                (T13)
    Master-slave
    Edge-triggered
```

and the simple flip-flop selection guide obtained by grafting T13 at the end of the "JK-type" node of T8:

```
Flip-flop                (T14)
    JK-type
        Master-slave
        Edge-triggered
    D-type
```

One would like to be able to sort the result set of query Q1 ("List the flip-flops") by T14, but, as we have seen, the answer A1 contains concepts, e.g. #73, which are not classifiable.

The impossibility of sorting a given result set with respect to a given taxonomy is what we call a "classifiability conflict". A classifiability conflict may also arise if we attempt to display "the values of an attribute A for the result set" of a query. For example, in response to the query:

```
(Q3)    ''List the propagation delays of the gates''
```

we would like to show, for each gate, the value of the attributes tPLH and tPHL. The parameter tPLH (respectively tPHL) is defined for a gate as the propagation delay of a change in the inputs that causes the output to go from Low to High (respectively High to Low). The answer of a query whose condition is the predicate "Gate", according to rule 1 (or rule 2 vat level of abstraction I) is a list of the serial numbers corresponding to gates:

```
(A3)    #00, #01, #02, #03, #12, #27...
```

But the propagation delays depend on the family. For example, a standard-TTL #00 has a tPLH of 8.0, while a faster High-Power-TTL #00 has a tPHL of 16.8. Thus no value[7] of tPLH can be given for the concept #00.

In general, if A is an attribute over D and C is a concept, C "has a value for A" if A is constant over C, and C "has no value" for A if none of the elements in the extension of C has a value for A. In both cases we can say that C is consistent with A. But if some elements of the extension of C have a value for A while others don't, or if two elements have different values for A, then C is inconsistent with A. This notion is not new, C is consistent with A exactly when it is classifiable by the taxonomy induced by A. This is again a classifiability conflict.

Classifiability problems occur when the "grain size" of the concepts in the answer is too large, and it should be possible to solve them by limiting the "granularity" of the result set. But this is precisely the effect produced by the specification of a level of abstraction in rule 2. For example, in all the above cases, the conflict is resolved at level of abstraction II. On the other hand, in order to be able to sort with respect to the grade taxonomy T10, or with respect to any product of taxonomies having T10 as a factor, and in order to be able to show values of attributes that depend on the grade (e.g. the fan-out) it is necessary to require level III.

Clearly it is important, given a level of abstraction, to determine what taxonomies can be used to sort the answers at that level, and what attributes are consistent with the answers at that level. We will say that such attributes and taxonomies are *compatible* with the level of abstraction. But before we discuss that question, we need to define what a level of abstraction is, in domain-independent terms. We have now the tools needed to give and justify the definition.

4 Levels of Abstraction

4.1 A Domain-Independent Definition

In section 2, we introduced levels of abstraction I, II, III and IV for the TTL domain, and defined them according to the 4 types of codes derived from the TTL numbering convention. In section 3 we have introduced a grade taxonomy (T10) and a family taxonomy (T11). Let us also consider the "package" taxonomy:

```
Device                  (T15)
    Ceramic
    Plastic
    Metal-can
    Flatpak
```

The definition of the 4 levels can be based on these taxonomies. Level I is simply the set of all retrievable concepts, level II contains the retrievable concepts classifiable by the family taxonomy T11, level III contains those classifiable by both the family taxonomy T11 and the grade taxonomy T10, and level IV those which, in addition, are classifiable by the package taxonomy T15. This leads us to propose the following definition:

The level of abstraction generated by a set of taxonomies S is the set of all concepts which are classifiable by all the taxonomies in S. [8]

[7] These values are actually manufacturer-specified upper bounds. As such, they are by definition constant over the extension of the concept for which they are given (e.g. '00, 'H00). Actual propagation delays, of course, will be different for each physical device, and will depend on the environment and circumstances under which the device is operating.

[8] In the appendix, prior to this definition, we define a level abstraction independently of any taxonomies. Then we prove that the set of concepts classifiable by a group of taxonomies is actually a level of abstraction in that sense. But we only need to consider, in practice, levels of abstraction which are generated by taxonomies.

Level I is then the level of abstraction generated by the empty set, level II is generated by T11, level III by T11,T10 and level IV by T11,T10,T15.

Notice that, according to this definition, a concept does not have to be retrievable in order to be at the level of abstraction generated by a set of taxonomies S. Thus the level of abstraction depends only on S, not on a particular choice of retrievable concepts. On the other hand, a taxonomy T is compatible with a level of abstraction L if it classifies all the retrievable concepts contained in L. The result set of any query at level L can then be sorted by T. An attribute A is compatible with L if the taxonomy induced by A is compatible with L, since each retrievable concept at level L will then have a consistent value (or none at all) for the attribute.

The stability result given in section 3.2 is useful in determining what taxonomies are compatible with a given level of abstraction. Any taxonomy obtained by composition (and other operations on taxonomies described in definition 8) from elementary taxonomies which are compatible with a level of abstraction L will also be compatible with L. It is thus sufficient to know what elementary taxonomies are compatible with L. Moreover, if L is generated by S, then all taxonomies in S are compatible with L.

As an example, consider the following selection guide for gates and flip-flops:

```
Device                  (T16)
    Gate
        Nand
            2-input
            3-input
        Nor
            2-input
            3-input
    Flip-flop
        JK-type
            Master-Slave
            Edge-triggered
        D-type
```

and those obtained from it by taking the product by the family, grade and package taxonomies:

```
T17 = T16 X T11         (family)
T18 = T17 X T10         (family, grade)
T19 = T18 X T15         (family, grade, package)
```

T16 can be built from T3, T4, T6, T8, and T13. Observation of the TTL Data Book shows that T3, T4, T6 and T8 are compatible with level I. T13, which distinguishes between master-slave and edge-triggered flip-flops, is compatible with level II. From the definitions of the levels, T11 is at level II, T10 at level III and T15 at level IV. From the Stability Result we can then conclude that the selection guides T17, T18 and T19 are at levels II, III and IV respectively.

4.2 Exhaustive Answers

We have proposed two specifications (rules 1 and 2) of what the answer of a query should be in an environment of concepts whose extensions are immaterial. We have arrived at these rules in several steps. Given a query with condition C we have postulated that the answer should contain concepts subsumed by C. At this stage of the argument, the specification is grossly underconstrained: there are "too many" such concepts. We have then proposed to select a set of ***retrievable concepts*** from which all answers would have to be extracted, and shown that it is often necessary to impose a level of abstraction on the result set. Have we not then overconstrained the specification of the answer? Unfortunately, yes. For an arbitrary choice of retrievable concepts, level of abstraction, and condition, the answer given by rule 2 may not be adequate.

The problem is that the answer of the query may be incomplete, in the sense that the extension of the answer, i.e. the union of the subsets of D listed in the answer, will certainly be contained in, but may not be equal to the extension of the condition of the query.

However it is possible to determine conditions under which the answer is exhaustive, i.e. equiextensional to the condition of the query. This is the purpose of sections A.4 and A.5 of the appendix. The argument, that we summarize here, procedes in two steps.

In section A.4, we explore this question as far as we can without imposing any conditions on the semantic space, and can actually establish that the answer will be exhaustive if and only if the condition of the query is *decomposable* and the level of abstraction is *consistent*. The notions of *decomposable concept* and *consistent level of abstraction* (definitions 15 and 18), are relative to the set of retrievable concepts and can be characterized using the notion of *irreducible retrievable concept* (definition 20). The irreducible retrievable concepts form a subset of Z, Z'. A concept is decomposable iff it is a disjunction of elements of Z', a level of abstraction is consistent if it contains Z'.

In section A.5 we study the case where the semantic space is *decomposable*, i.e. satisfies the conditions given in definition 21. These conditions are "natural" requirements on a set of retrievable concepts and we show that they are met by the set Z that we have been considering in our example. These requirements being satisfied, the picture becomes very clear. The irreducible retrievable concepts are simply the minimal retrievable concepts, which partition D, while all other retrievable concepts are disjunctions of minimal ones. A concept is decomposable iff it does not *cut through* any minimal retrievable concept, i.e. if it is disjoint with those that it does not contain. A boolean combination of decomposable concepts is decomposable. A level of abstraction generated by one or more taxonomies whose nodes are labeled by decomposable concepts is consistent.

In our example domain, which is decomposable, all concepts which we have encountered so far in the examples, and all other *reasonable* (in a sense which is discussed in the appendix) concepts are decomposable. Therefore, in practice, conditions will be decomposable, levels of abstraction generated by taxonomies will be consistent, and queries will be exhaustive.

5 Conclusion

Taking a TTL catalog as an example, we have shown the existence of a class of potential applications which are special, among other things, in that the entities to be retrieved in response to queries are concepts whose extensions are immaterial. In an environment of that type, the traditional information retrieval notions found in both database management and knowledge representation systems are inadequate and have to be revised. It is non-trivial to decide what it means to answer a query and sort a result set in such an environment.

We have presented a view of taxonomies as composite objects useful for organizing and sorting information. We have proposed that, for a catalog-type application, there should be a class of "retrievable concepts" from which the elements of all result sets should be chosen, and have shown how classifiability constraints may have to be taken into account in order to determine the response. We have introduced the notion of levels of abstraction, which can embody these constraints, and have specified what the answer of a query should be at a given level of abstraction. Finally we have determined conditions under which such answers are exhaustive.

Besides shedding light on general knowledge representation issues, we believe that this work sets up a framework in which it is possible to take, in an informed way, the human interface and data engineering decisions that would lead to a practical information retrieval system for this special but important class of applications.

A Appendix

We present here precise definitions for all the concepts introduced in the paper, and precise statements of the results, with proofs for those which are non-trivial.

CONTEXT. We consider a domain D (the set of "devices" in our example), whose extension is immaterial (we do not even need to assume that it is finite), and *concepts* relative to D. A concept is a one-place predicate defined over D, or equivalently a subset of D (the extension of the predicate). We shall consider that two concepts having the same extension over D are equal. We shall use both set terminology (union, intersection, complementation, set inclusion...) and logic terminology (disjunction, conjunction, negation, subsumption) when referring to concepts. We shall say *X contains Y* to mean that Y is a member or a subset of X. The context should suffice to disambiguate.

A *query* consists sometimes simply of a *condition*, which is a concept, and sometimes of both a condition and a *level of abstraction* (the notion of level of abstraction is formally defined below). The *result set* or *answer* of a query is a list, or sequence, of concepts. The ordering of the list is left unspecified by rules 1 and 2 below, but in a practical system, of course, some ordering would have to be chosen. Operations that *order* and *sort* the result set are formally specifed below, but these operations themselves take as operand an ordered result set: the relative placement of identically classifiable concepts is determined by the previous ordering (stable sort).

A.1 Semantic Spaces

Definition 1 *A SEMANTIC SPACE is a structure (D,Z) where D is a set ("the domain") and Z is a subset of P(D) (i.e. a set of subsets of D) which is finite, non-empty and which does not contain the empty set. The elements of Z are the RETRIEVABLE CONCEPTS of the space.*

Rule 1 *"In the absence of any constraint other than the condition of the query, the answer to a query with condition C should comprise the maximal retrievable concepts subsumed by C".*

A.2 Taxonomies

Definition 2 *A* taxonomy *is a (finite) tree whose nodes are labeled by concepts. The successors of each node are ordered, i.e. each node has a list of successors. The list of successors is empty for a leaf node. The depth, or "number of levels" of a taxonomy is the maximum length of a path minus one (a taxonomy consisting only of the root and the successors of the root is a one-level taxonomy).*

Definition 3 (Paths) *A* rooted path *is either the empty path, or a path that starts at the root. A* terminal path *is a path ending at a tip node. A* full path *is a rooted terminal path. The* successors of a path *are the successors of the last node in the path, if the path is not empty. The empty path has one successor, the root of the tree. A terminal path has of course an empty list of successors. The* concept associated with a path *is the conjunction of:*

- the concepts that label the nodes in the path, if any

- and the negation of the concepts that label the successors of the path, if any.

We will say that a path P subsumes a concept C when the concept associated with P subsumes C.

NOTATION. We shall use a Unix-like notation to designate paths in a taxonomy. For non-terminal paths, we shall indicate the successors of the last node in the path in addition to the nodes along the path. In taxonomy T7, for example:

```
Device                    (T7)
    Gate
        Nand
```

```
            2-input
            3-input
        Nor
            2-input
            3-input
    Flip-flop
```

the rooted path leading to 2-input nand gates is:

```
\Device\Gate\Nand\2-input
```

while the path containing the nodes Device and Gate will be described by:

```
\Device\Gate.Nand/Nor/
```

Definition 4 *The* decomposition of a rooted non-terminal path *of a taxonomy is the list of the intersections of each one of the successors of the path with the intersection of the nodes along the path. (The* decomposition of a non-leaf node *is that of the rooted path leading to the node.) A decomposition is* exhaustive *if the union of its elements is equal to the intersection of the nodes along the path, i.e. if the concept associated with the path has an empty extension. A taxonomy is* exhaustive *if the decompositions of all its non-terminal paths are exhaustive. A decomposition is* disjoint *if its elements are disjoint. A taxonomy is* strict *if the decompositions of all its non-terminal paths are disjoint.*

Definition 5 *A concept C is* classifiable by a taxonomy T *if it is subsumed by at least one rooted path P (there can be at most one such path if the taxonomy is strict). In that case the result of* classifying C at the end of P *is a taxonomy derived from T as follows:*

- If P is not empty, a node labeled by C is created and added at the end of the list of successors of the last node of P.

- If P is empty, T is first modified by "adding a new root on top of T", i.e. by creating a new node, labeled by the domain D, which becomes the new root of T, and installing the old root as the only successor of the new node. Then C is classified at the end of the path of length 1 containing the new root.

REMARK. Consider classifying a Nand gate (#00), a Nor gate (#02) and an Exclusive-or gate (#86) with respect to taxonomy T5:

```
Device                  (T5)
    Gate
        Nand
        Nor
    Flip-flop
```

The Nand and Nor gates will be classified at the end of the terminal paths:

```
\Device\Gate\Nand
\Device\Gate\Nor
```

while the Exclusive-or gate will be classified at the end of the non-terminal path:

```
\Device\Gate.Nand/Nor/
```

The result is thus:

```
Device                    (T5')
    Gate
        Nand
            #00
        Nor
            #02
        #86
    Flip-flop
```

Now consider classifying a flip-flop such as #70 according to (T4):

```
Gate                      (T4)
    Nand
    Nor
```

The concept #70 is classifiable at the end of the empty path of T4 because it is disjoint from the concept Gate. The result is:

```
Device                    (T4')
    Gate
        Nand
        Nor
    #70
```

Thus classification at the end of a non-terminal path is a mechanism similar to the "otherwise" label found in switching statements of computer languages. Anticipating on what follows, it is necessary to allow for this mechanism because we want a level of abstraction to limit the granularity of the answer to a query without limiting its extension, thus acting orthogonally to the condition of the query in determining the answer.

Definition 6 Sorting a list of classifiable concepts *according to a taxonomy is an operation that takes as operands a taxonomy and a list of concepts, and produces a new taxonomy as its result. The concepts to be sorted have to be classifiable according to the taxonomy. Each one of them, in order, is classified at the end of each rooted path that subsumes it. Then all subtrees of the original taxonomies that do not contain any of the newly classified concepts are pruned to obtain the result.*

Definition 7 Ordering a list of classifiable concepts *according to a* strict *taxonomy is an operation that takes as operands a strict taxonomy and a list of concepts, which must be classifiable by the taxonomy, and produces a rearranged list as its result. The new list is obtained by classifying each concept at the end of the only rooted path that subsumes it, then traversing the taxonomy (in pre- or post-order) and collecting the newly classified nodes in the order in which they are encountered.*

Definition 8 (Operations on Taxonomies) Composition *is an operation which takes as operands a taxonomy T, a rooted path P of T, and a second taxonomy T'. The root R of T' must subsume (the concept associated with) P. The result is a taxonomy obtained by* grafting T *at the end of P' as follows:*

- If P is not empty, the root of T' is removed and its successors are added at the end of the list of successors of the last node of P.

- If P is empty, T is first modified by "adding a new root on top of T", i.e. by creating a new node, labeled by the domain D, which becomes the new root of T, and installing the old root as the only successor of the new node. Then T' is grafted at the end of the path of length 1 containing the new root.

The body of the paper has many examples of composition at the end of a terminal path. For an example of composition at the end of a non-terminal path, we can "complete" the taxonomy T5 by grafting the following taxonomy:

```
Gate                    (T17)
    And
    Or
    Xor
```

at the end of the path of T5:

```
\Device\Gate.Nand/Nor
```

The result is:

```
Device                  (T18)
    Gate
        Nand
        Nor
        And
        Or
        Xor
    Flip-flop
```

The product *of a taxonomy T by a taxonomy T' is the result of grafting T' at the end of every rooted terminal path of T. The root of T' must subsume the rooted terminal paths of T.*

Example: The product of

```
Gate                    (T4)
    Nand
    Nor
```

and

```
Device                  (T6)
    2-input
    3-input
```

is:

```
Gate                    (T19)
    Nand
        2-input
        3-input
    Nor
        2-input
        3-input
```

Splitting a node *is an operation that takes as operands a taxonomy T and one of its nodes, N, and whose result is the taxonomy obtained as follows:*

- If N has a parent M, then in the list of successors of M, N is replaced by its decomposition. To each node in the decomposition is then attached the subtree rooted on the corresponding descendant of N in T.

- If N is the root, then a new root labeled D is first added "on top of T" then N, whose parent is now the new root, is split as described above.

Simplifying a terminal decomposition *is an operation which takes as operands a taxonomy T and a node N of T which is the root of a terminal subtree of depth 1, and results in the taxonomy obtained by removing, among the successors of N, those that do not terminate maximal paths.*

By successive applications of the last two operations it is possible to reduce each taxonomy to a canonical form, a taxonomy of depth 1 whose root is labeled by D and where none of the successors of the root subsumes another.

Theorem 1 *The operations described in definition 8 preserve the classifiability of concepts. A concept C which is classifiable by each one of a set of taxonomies S is also classifiable by any taxonomy that can be built from those in S by the operations described in definition 8. (As a partial converse, if C is classifiable by the product of T and T', and T is exhaustive, then C is classifiable separately by T and by T'.)*

PROOF. We shall prove that, if C is a concept classifiable by two taxonomies T and T', and if T" is a composition of T and T' (obtained by grafting T' at the end of a path P of T), then C is also classifiable by T". The rest of the theorem and the converse are clear.

We can assume, without loss of generality, that P is not empty (otherwise T is modified by adding a new root labeled D before grafting T', and the modified taxonomy obviously classifies C if T does) and that C does not have an empty extension (otherwise C is trivially classifiable by any taxonomy).

For any path of T other than P, there exists in T" a path having exactly the same nodes and the same successors. Thus if C is classifiable at the end of a path of T other than P, it is also classifiable by T". Otherwise, C must be classifiable by T precisely at the end of P, i.e. C must be subsumed by P.

The root of T', R, subsumes P, hence subsumes C. Since C is not empty, it cannot be disjoint from the root of T'. This means that C is not classifiable at the end of the empty path of T'. Let P' be a non-empty path of T' that subsumes C. We must now distinguish two cases.

If P' consists of only one node, R, then let P" be the rooted path of T" whose nodes are those of P. The successors of P" are those of P in T plus thus of R in T'. The nodes of P subsume C. The negations of the successors of P in T subsume C. The successors of R in T' being the successors of P' in T', their negations also subsume C. Hence P" subsumes C.

If P' consists of more than one node, let P" be the rooted path of T" whose nodes are those of P followed by the nodes of P' other than R. The successors of this path are those of P' in T'. The nodes of P subsume C. The nodes of P' (and in particular those other than R) subsume C. The negations of the successors of P' in T' also subsume C. Hence P" subsumes C.

Definition 9 *Let A be an attribute defined on D and taking a finite number of values on some other domain D', over which is defined some total ordering (D' does not have to be finite, e.g. it could be the set of real numbers). In all generality A is a binary relation, i.e. a subset of D X D'. The* taxonomy induced by A *is a one-level tree whose root is labeled by D, the successors of the root being labeled by the subsets of D:*

$$E(y) = \{x \mid A(x,y)\}$$

for each y in D' such that E(y) is not the empty set. The list of successors is ordered according to the ordering of D'.

Proposition 1 *If each element of D has at most one value for attribute A, then the taxonomy induced by A is strict. If each element has at least one value, then the taxonomy is exhaustive (i.e. the decomposition of the root is exhaustive).*

Proposition 2 *A concept C is classifiable by the taxonomy induced by attribute A if and only if all the elements of the extension of D have a value for A in common or none of them has a value for A.*

A.3 Levels of Abstraction

A.3.1 Taxonomies and Levels of Abstraction

Definition 10 *A level of abstraction L can be defined as a subset of P(D), i.e. as a set of subsets of D, satisfying the following properties:*

(a) if X is in L and Y is a subset of X, then Y is in L.
(b) L is a cover of D, i.e. the union of the elements of L is D.
A concept is said to be at a level of abstraction L *simply when it is an element of L.*

Theorem 2 *The set of concepts classifiable by a taxonomy is a level of abstraction. (Conversely, a level of abstraction having a finite number of maximal elements trivially coincides with the set of concepts classifiable by the one-level taxonomy whose root is D and where the succesors of the root are these maximal concepts.)*

PROOF. Let T be a taxonomy and L the set of concepts that it classifies. Part (a) of definition 10 is clear. In order to prove that L covers D, we observe that L contains the complement of the root, hence we just have to show that L covers the root, which can be proved by induction on the depth of T.

Proposition 3 *The intersection of a set of levels of abstraction is a level of abstraction.*

Definition 11 *Hence the set of concepts classified by each taxonomy in a finite set of taxonomies S is a level of abstraction,* the level of abstraction generated by S, loa(S).

Definition 12 *A taxonomy T is above a level of abstraction L if it classifies all the elements of L.*

Proposition 4 *Let S be a set of taxonomies. Each taxonomy in S is above loa(S). A taxonomy T is above loa(S) if and only if loa(S) is equal to loa(S'), where S' is the union of S anc T.*

Proposition 5 *All taxonomies that can be derived from a set of taxonomies S by the operations described in definition 8 are above loa(S).*

A.3.2 Result Set And Levels Of Abstraction

Rule 2 *"The answer to a query with condition C, at a level of abstraction L, should comprise the maximal retrievable concepts among those subsumed by C at a level of abstraction L."*

Definition 13 *Two levels of abstraction are* equivalent *if they contain the same retrievable concepts. A level of abstraction is* passive *if it contains all the retrievable concepts.*

Proposition 6 *The answers to a query at equivalent levels of abstraction are identical. The answer to a query at a passive level of abstraction is the same as the answer when no level of abstraction is specified (i.e. as the answer defined by rule 1).*

Definition 14 *A taxonomy T is* compatible with a level of abstraction L *if it classifies all the retrievable concepts which are at level of abstraction L.*

Proposition 7 *The result set of a query at level of abstraction L can be sorted by any taxonomy compatible with L.*

Definition 15 *A taxonomy is passive if it classifies all the retrievable concepts. (A passive taxonomy is therefore compatible with all levels of abstraction.)*

Proposition 8 *A taxonomy T is compatible with the level of abstraction generated by a set of taxonomies S if and only if loa(S) is equivalent to loa(S'), where S' is the union of S and T.*

Proposition 9 *If all taxonomies in a set of taxonomies S are compatible with a level of abstraction L, then all taxonomies that can be derived from them by the operations described in defintion 8 are also compatible with L.*

A.4 Exhaustive Answers

A.4.1 Decomposable Concepts and Consistent Levels of Abstraction

Definition 16 The components of a concept C *are the retrievable concepts subsumed by C.* A concept is decomposable *if it is equal to the union of its components.* A concept C is decomposable at level of abstraction L *(in other words* L decomposes C*) if it is equal to the union of its components at level L. (The union of zero sets being the empty set, this definition implies that the empty set is decomposable.)*

Definition 17 The extension of the answer of a query *is the union of the concepts in the result set. The answer of a query (respectively the answer at level L) is* exhaustive *if its extension is equal to the extension of the condition of the query, i.e. if the condition of the query is decomposable (respectively decomposable at level L).*

Definition 18 A level of abstraction L decomposes a level of abstraction L' *if it decomposes all the retrievable concepts in L'.*

Proposition 10 *If a level of abstraction L decomposes a level of abstraction L', then, for any query, the extension of the answer at L contains the extension of the answer at L'. (And conversely, if answers at L always contain answers at L', then L must decompose L'). If two levels of abstraction decompose each other, they produce equiextensional answers.*

Definition 19 *A level of abstraction is* consistent *if it decomposes all the retrievable concepts.*

Proposition 11 *The answer to a query at a consistent level of abstraction has the same extension as the answer when no level of abstraction is specified (i.e. as the answer defined by rule 1).*

Definition 20 *A taxonomy is consistent if the set of concepts that it classifies is a consistent level of abstraction.*

Proposition 12 *A set of consistent taxonomies generates a consistent level of abstraction.*

A.4.2 Irreducible Retrievable Concepts

Definition 21 *A retrievable concept C is* irreducible *if it is NOT a union of retrievable concepts all of which are contained in but not equal to C.*

Lemma 1 *Any retrievable concept is a disjunction of irreducible retrievable concepts (IRCs).*

Theorem 3 *A level of abstraction L decomposes a level of abstraction L' iff it contains all the IRCs in L'. Two levels of abstraction decompose each other iff they contain the same IRCs. A level of abstraction is consistent iff it contains all the IRCs. A taxonomy is consistent iff it classifies all the IRCs.*

A.5 Decomposable Semantic Spaces

Definition 22 A semantic space is decomposable *if:*

- *the intersection of any two retrievable concepts is the union of zero or more retrievable concepts*
- *the complement of any retrievable concept, is the union of zero or more retrievable concepts*

Proposition 13 *A semantic space is decomposable iff the set of its decomposable concepts is stable by intersection, union and complementation, i.e. constitutes a finite sigma-algebra. In logic terminology, this implies that, in a decomposable semantic space, a boolean combination of decomposable concepts is a decomposable concept.*

Theorem 4 *In a decomposable semantic space:*

- *The minimal retrievable concepts (MRCs) partition D*
- *Each retrievable concept is the union of the MRCs that it subsumes.*

Conversely, given a set D, a finite set S of concepts that partitions D, and a finite set S' of unions of elements of S, containing all the elements of S, (D,S') is a decomposable semantic space.

PROOF. Let us first prove that the MRCs of a decomposable semantic space partition D. If the intersection of two MRCs is not empty, it is a union of retrievable concepts, hence it contains at least one retrievable concept, which must be equal to both MRCs. Therefore two distinct MRCs are disjoint. On the other hand, the complement of the union of all the MRCs is decomposable (by proposition 13). If not empty, it would contain a retrievable concept, which itself would contain an MRC (the set of retrievable concepts being finite). Therefore the MRCs must cover D.

Now let us prove that a retrievable concept is a union of minimal retrievable concepts. If a retrievable concept C intersects an MRC M it must contain it, since the intersection will contain a retrievable concept R, which must be equal to M. Hence every MRC is either contained in C or disjoint with C. Let U be the union of the MRCs contained in C, and V the complement of the union of the MRCs disjoint with C. V contains C which contains U. But, since the MRCs partition D, U is equal to V. Hence C is equal to U, which is a disjunction of MRCs.

The converse is trivial.

Corollary 1 *In a decomposable semantic space, a concept is decomposable iff it is a union of zero or more MRCs, i.e. iff it contains each MRC that it intersects.*

Corollary 2 *In a decomposable semantic space, the IRCs are the MRCs. A level of abstraction is consistent iff it contains all the MRCs. A taxonomy is consistent iff it classifies all the MRCs.*

Definition 23 *A taxonomy is* regular *if its nodes are decomposable.*

Theorem 5 *In a decomposable semantic space, each regular taxonomy is consistent. As a partial converse, each taxonomy which is (1) consistent, (2) strict, (3) such that each non-leaf node subsumes its successors, is regular.*

PROOF. Let T be a regular taxonomy and M an MRC. Let us show that T classifies M. Each node of T either contains M, or is disjoint with M. In particular, if the root R does not contain M, then M is classifiable at the end of the empty path of T. Let us show, by induction on the depth of T, that, when R contains M, T classifies M at the end of a non-empty path. The result is obvious when the taxonomy is of depth 0, i.e. when R is the only node of T. If the depth is n, greater than zero, then R has one or more successors. If M is disjoint from all of them, it is classifiable at the end of the path consisting of the only node R. Otherwise M is contained in a node N which is a successor of R. The subtree T' rooted at N is of depth n' less than n, hence, by the induction hypothesis, classifies M at the end of a non-empty path P'. Clearly, T classifies M at the end of the path which is the concatenation of R and T'.

Now let T be a strict taxonomy where each non-leaf node subsumes its successors and which classifies all the minimal retrievable concepts. In order to prove, by contradiction, that all the nodes of T are decomposable, let us assume that there is a node N which is not. N must then intersect some MRC M without containing it. M is classifiable at the end of a certain path P. It is clear that, in T, each node is disjoint with each path that does not contain it. N intersects M, and hence P, therefore is in P, therefore subsumes M, a contradiction.

OBSERVATION. Our example semantic space is trivially decomposable. The concepts corresponding to fully specified Ordering Codes are clearly disjoint. Whether they cover the domain is a non-issue: we just define the domain of the catalog as the set of what can be ordered, hence as the union of the sets defined by the Ordering Codes. Thus the Ordering Codes partition the domain. The other concepts that we have chosen as retrievable can be defined as unions of Ordering Codes. A concept such as 'LS00, e.g. can be considered to be the union of the Ordering Codes for the 5 combinations of grades and packages in which the 'LS00 is offered: 74LS00PC, 74LS00DC, 54LS00DM, 74LS00FC and 54LS00FM. Therefore, by the converse of theorem 4, the space is decomposable.

By corollary 1, a concept C is NOT decomposable iff there exists an Ordering Code M which is neither subsumed by, nor incompatible with C, i.e. if it is possible to have devices with ordering code M that satisfy the predicate C, while other devices with the same ordering code do not satisfy it. It is easy to think of such concepts. For instance, the propagation delays that we have discussed are manufacturer-specfied upperbounds. Thus, by definition, they are constant over the retrievable concepts for which their values are specified, and the taxonomies that they induce are consistent. Actual propagation delays determined experimentally will be slightly different for each physical device. Thus devices with the same Ordering Codes will have different experimental propagation delays. But of course, nobody would want to include such an attribute in the computerized catalog, it is not "what the catalog is about". In general, when a concept is not decomposable with respect to a given semantic space, one has a very strong intuition that "it is out of place" in the catalog. Thus, it is clear that all the concepts that have been used in examples in the paper are decomposable, all the taxonomies are consistent, and all the levels of abstraction that they generate are also consistent. The conclusion is that, without taking any special precautions, one will consider only decomposable conditions and consistent levels of abstraction, therefore answers will be exhaustive.

Acknowledgement

The research presented in this paper was carried out at the Artificial Intelligence Laboratory - Schlumberger Palo Alto Research, formerly Fairchild Laboratory for Artificial Intelligence Research. I would like to thank many people for their comments on early drafts and presentations of this paper, in particular Ron Brachman, Norman Haas, Julia Hirschberg, Arthur Keller, Hector Levesque, Martha Pollack, and Bonnie Weber.

References

[1] R.J. Brachman, R.E. Fikes and H.J. Levesque "KRYPTON: A Functional Approach to Knowledge Representation" IEEE Computer, Vol. 16, No. 10, October 1983, pp. 67-73

[2] R.J. Brachman and H.J. Levesque "What Makes a Knowledge Base Knowledgeable?" This volume.

[3] R.J. Brachman and J.G. Schmolze "An Overview of the KL-ONE Knowledge Representation System" To appear in Cognitive Science, Vol. 9, No. 2, Apr-June, 1985

[4] O.P. Bunemal and R.E. Frankel "FQL - A Functional Query Language" Proc 1979 ACM SIGMOD Intl. Conf. on Management of Data

[5] P.P.S. Chen "The Entity-Relationship Model - Toward a Unified View of Data" TODS, Vol. 1, No. 1, March 1976

[6] E.F. Codd "Extending the Database Relational Model of Data to Capture More Meaning" TODS, Vol.4, No.4, December 1979

[7] TTL Data Book Fairchild Camera and Instrument Corporation

[8] W. Kent. Data and Reality. North-Holland (1978)

[9] P.F. Patel-Schneider "Small can be beautiful in Knowledge Representation" Proc. IEEE Workshop in Principles of Knowledge-Based Systems Denver, Co, Dec. 1984

[10] P.F. Patel-Schneider, R.J. Brachman, H.J. Levesque "ARGON: Knowledge Representation meets Information Retrieval" Proc. First Conference on AI Applications, Denver, Co, Dec. 1984

[11] Schmolze, J.G. and Lipkis, T.A. "Classification in the KL-ONE Knowledge Representation System" Proceedings of the Eighth I.J.C.A.I. (1983)

[12] D. Shipman "The Functional Data Model and the Data Language DAPLEX" TODS, Vol. 6, No. 1, March 1981

Type Subsumption as a Model of Computation

Hassan Ait-Kaci

Microelectronics and Computer Technology Corporation[1]
9430 Research Boulevard
Austin, Texas 78759-6509
(512) 834-3354

Abstract

A design for a programming language based on a calculus of type subsumption is presented. A close analysis of the notion of *term* in universal algebra and logic shows how the concept of *subsumption* may be extended to bear more semantic power. A mathematical semantics is proposed for a particular language where type structures are first-class objects, which can be practically implemented. In this language, computation amounts to type checking. Possible connections of this model of computation with logic are discussed. Finally, further extensions of the language are described which can be given well-defined semantics without loss of the basic language philosophy.

1. Introduction

This paper attempts to analyze the notion of representation and classification of objects. It is advocated that structured types and program schemes can be conceived as the same kind of objects. The following sections elaborate a new model of computation based on data type specification.

1.1. Thesis

Subtyping is concerned with capturing the notion of *subsumption*[2] among objects. Thus, I would like to define a notational system for representing *approximations* of objects of which one conceives in one's mind. Moreover, I want this system to contain some mechanism which could automatically classify thus represented objects in a fashion which is congruent with their interpretation as approximations.

An example of such a system is provided by first-order *terms* or *trees* in universal algebra and logic. In PROLOG [6], the underlying logic model means first-order terms as *functions*. However,

[1]Research described in this paper was done while the author was at the University of Pennsylvania, Philadelphia.

[2]I am borrowing this term from G.Plotkin [20]. Although his definition is different from what will be presented here, it inspired its approach.

operationally, term structures are *uninterpreted* constructors. Hence, one often finds it very practical to use them as *record structures*, completely forgetting their functional semantics. For example, I would like to express the fact that a person has a name, a birth date, and a sex. Representing a thus specified generic person as a term could be `person(x,y,z)`. Then, by a convention remembered at interpretation, the symbol `person` at the root of a term denotes a person object, and the variables `x, y, z` as *place markers* for a person's name, date of birth, and sex, respectively. The classification mechanism in this model is *term instantiation*. The meaning of variables is that they stand for incomplete information and may be substituted for by terms. Thus,

```
person(Hassan,y,z)
```

denotes any person named Hassan, and

```
person(Hassan,date(14,June,y),z)
```

designates any person named Hassan and born the 14th of June. The term appearing as the date of birth in the latter `person` illustrates the substitution process. If I choose to define a type to be a first-order term as shown, and the type classification ordering to be term instantiation, then I have at hand a type system as wished. Indeed, the types thus defined form a *lattice* whose *meet* operation (*i.e.*, greatest lower bound) is first-order unification [22], and whose *join* operation (*i.e.*, least upper bound) is first-order *anti-unification*, or *generalization* [21]. PROLOG programmers are well familiar with this model which is unlike any other available in conventional programming languages and turns out to be very handy in practice.

1.2. Antithesis

There is however a certain amount of inflexibility inherent to the definition of types as terms. Firstly, a term is a finitely branching tree. In particular, it has a *fixed number of arguments*. If I want to extend the definition of a person to have also a marital status, I must entirely redefine the type `person` to take one more argument, and hence revise all previously used instances of a person. Secondly, a term has a *fixed order of arguments*. This is very convenient to interpret consistently *position* within a term as having a fixed meaning. For example, in a `person` term, the first argument is once and for all meant to denote the person's name. Indeed, this is also taken advantage of by the unification process; *i.e.*, in order to match, two terms are expected to have their corresponding subterms in the same order. This is the same principle used in most programming languages to pass procedure parameters. As a result, one must constantly keep in mind the original intended interpretation of the order of arguments. Thirdly, type subsumption as one-way pattern-matching is forcing a *common syntactical pattern* for all terms in a chain in the lattice. For example, if I define a type `student(x,y,z)`, then I cannot express that I also intend a student to be a person, since a type is identified by its constant root symbol and `student` is distinct from `person`. Finally, there is no provision in the definition of a term for specifying any *restriction on the pattern* of subterms. For example, restricting the name of a person to terms whose root symbols belong to, or better yet do *not* belong to a given set, is not syntactically possible.

The foregoing shortcomings of the first-order term model of types make it look rather limited. However, it has appeal because of its solid formal grounds, its simplicity, and its use as the basic model of types of such clear and clean programming languages as PROLOG.[3] It would be of great advantage if this model of types could be enhanced so that it may keep its elegance and sound formal basis, lend itself to a powerful interpretation scheme, and yet overcome the limitations explicated above.

1.3. Synthesis

I propose to modify the notion of a type by extrapolating on the classical definition of a term. Since first-order term structures are not operationally used as functions but rather as record structures, it is senseless to have them syntactically restricted as functions constructors must be. Let us first relax the fixed-arity constraint; *i.e.*, a term may have an unbounded number of arguments. Next, let us relax the fixed-position constraint by *explicitly* indexing or labeling the arguments. The reader familiar with ADA [14] will note that this language allows a procedure call's actual parameters to be specified either by position, or possibly out of order by explicit labeling. However, in ADA *all* actual parameters *must* be present at run-time, possibly by default. In our case, since a type can now have a *potentially infinite* number of attributes, all that is ever needed is to specify only those which are relevant at any given time. For example, `person(name:Hassan)` denotes the type of persons named Hassan, and `person(sex:Male)` stands for the type of male persons. Furthermore, let us assume some partial ordering on the root symbols. This can easily be extended to an ordering on terms in a way very similar to a homomorphic extension. For example, if the symbols `person` and `student` are such that

`student` $<$ `person`

then I can consistently say that

`student(name:Hassan,sex:male)`

is a subtype of

`person(name:Hassan,sex:male)`.

The idea behind this kind of extension of a term is based on the concept of *multi-sorted* terms with the very peculiar difference that the sorts are implicitly denoted by terms themselves. This is quite a new formal window through which to look at data and program structures that makes them syntactically undistinguishable, and it forces re-thinking of many related familiar notions. The concepts of *variable* and *symbol* which are central in programming as well as formal languages are to be construed in a completely different yet more general way. A variable in a first-order term term has *two* distinct purposes: it is a *wild card* and a *tag*. As a wild card, it specifies that any term may be substituted for it; and as a tag, it

[3] I am not referring to any particular implementation, but rather to the *pure* language as defined in [23].

constrains all positions in the term where it appears to be substituted for by the *same* term. I contend that these two roles ought to be explicitly separated. In fact, it is explained in [1] that if symbols are partially ordered, the familiar notion of variable has but the restrictive designation of a term which is a *maximal element*. Symbols, and extended terms for that matter, may be specified as *upper bound constraints* within other terms. I shall try and show how a natural extension of a partial ordering on the symbols may be consistently defined on extended terms. Such classical operations as *variable substitution, term unification, etc.*, also take on a radically new interpretation, of which the familiar well-known notions are but special cases.

A specific *desideratum* can be informally sketched as follows. a structured data type must have:

- a *head symbol* which determines a class of objects being restricted;
- *attributes (or fields, or slots, etc.,)* which describe some sort of features possessed by this type, which are typed by structured types themselves;
- *coreference constraints* between attributes, and attributes of attributes, *etc.*, denoting the fact that the *same* substructure is to be shared by different compositions of attributes.

Then, a type structure t_1 is a *subtype* of a type structure t_2 if and only if:

- the class denoted by the head of t_1 is contained in the class denoted by the head of t_2; *and,*
- *all* the attributes of t_2 are present in t_1 and have types which are subtypes of their counterparts in t_2; *and,*
- *all* the coreference constraints binding in t_2 are also binding in t_1.

For example, understanding the symbols student, person, philadelphia, cityname to denote sets of objects, and if student $<$ person and philadelphia $<$ cityname denote set inclusion, then the type:

```
student(id => name(last => X:string);
        lives_at => Y:address(city => philadelphia);
        father => person(id => name(last => X);
                         lives_at => Y));
```

should be a subtype of:

```
person(id => name;
       lives_at => address(city => cityname);
       father => person);
```

The letters X, Y in this example denote coreference constraints as will be explained.

Formalizing the above informal wish is attempted in the next section. There is presented a formal calculus of type subsumption upon which I shall rest the design of a programming language called KBL[4] where types are *first-class objects*. Then, a discussion on how this relates to logic and theorem-proving follows. Finally, extensions of the basic design are proposed.

[4]Knowledge Base Language.

2. A Calculus of Type Subsumption

In this section, I propose to develop a step-by-step presentation of *extended terms* and how they can be made to capture enough semantics to be actually used computationally. The semantics described here is essentially operational. However, a complete algebraic fixed-point semantics is presented in [1]. I shall mix intuitive and formal descriptions; the former generally introducing the latter.

2.1. A Syntax of Structured Types

In section 1.3, I sketched a description of what I call extended terms. These objects will constitute the syntactic basis of the language which I am to outline. In what follows, examples will be used to introduce *implicitly* the syntax of the language of terms.

Let Σ be a partially ordered *signature* of *type symbols* with a *top* element $\top$, and a *bottom* element $\bot$. Let $\mathcal{L}$ be a set of *label symbols*, and let $\mathcal{T}$ be a set of *tag symbols*, both non-empty and countably infinite. I shall represent type symbols and labels by strings of characters starting with a *lower-case* letter, and tags by strings of characters starting with an *upper-case* letter.

A simple "type-as-set" semantics for these objects is elaborated in [1]. It will suffice to mention that type symbols in Σ denote sets of objects, and label symbols in $\mathcal{L}$ denote the *intension* of functions. This semantics takes the partial ordering on type symbols into set inclusion, and label concatenation as function composition. Thus, the syntax of terms introduced next can be interpreted as describing commutative composition diagrams of attributes.

In a manner akin to tree addressing as defined in [7, 8, 9], I define a *term domain on* $\mathcal{L}$ to be the *skeleton* built from label symbols of a such a commutative diagram. This is nothing but the graph of arrows that one draws to picture functional maps. Formally,

Definition 1: A *term (or tree) domain* Δ on $\mathcal{L}$ is a set of finite strings of labels of $\mathcal{L}$ such that:

- Δ is *prefix-closed; i.e.*, if u, v $\in \mathcal{L}^*$ and u.v $\in \Delta$ then u $\in \Delta$;
- Δ is *finitely branching; i.e.*, if u $\in \Delta$, then the set {u.a $\in \Delta$ | a $\in \mathcal{L}$} is finite.

It follows from this definition that the empty string e must belong to all term domains. Elements of a term domain are called *(term) addresses*. Addresses in a domain which are not the prefix of any other address in the domain are called *leaves*. The empty string is called the *root* address. For example, if $\mathcal{L}$ = {id, born, day, month, year, first, last, father}, a term-domain on $\mathcal{L}$ may be Δ_1 = {e, born, born.day, born.month, born.year, id, id.last, father, father.id, father.id.first}. A term domain need not be finite; for instance, the regular expression Δ_2 = a(ba)*+(ab)*, where a, b $\in \mathcal{L}$, denotes a regular set (on {a,b}, say) which is closed under prefixes, and finitely branching; thus, it is a term domain and it is infinite.

Given a term domain Δ, an address `w` in Δ, we define the *sub-domain of Δ at address* `w` to be the term domain $\Delta\backslash$`w` = {`w'` | `w.w'` $\in \Delta$}. In the last example, the sub-domain at address `born` of Δ_1 is the set {*e*, `day`, `month`, `year`}, and the sub-domain of Δ_2 at address `a.b` is Δ_2 itself.

Definition 2: A term domain Δ is a *regular* term domain if the set of all sub-domains of Δ defined as **Subdom**(Δ) = {$\Delta\backslash$`w` | `w` $\in \Delta$} is finite.

In the previous examples, the term domain Δ_1 is a finite (regular) term domain, and Δ_2 is a regular infinite term domain since **Subdom**(Δ_2) = {Δ_2, `b`.Δ_2}. In what follows, I will consider only regular term-domains.

The "flesh" that goes on the skeleton defined by a term domain consists of signature symbols labelling the nodes which are arrow extremities. Keeping the "arrow graph" picture in mind, this stands for information about the origin and destination sets of the arrow representation of functions. As for notation, I proceed to introduce a specific syntax of terms as record-like structures. Thus, a term has a *head* which is a type symbol, and a *body* which is a (possibly empty) list of pairs associating labels with terms in a unique fashion -- an *association list*. An example of such an object is shown in figure 2-1.

```
person(id => name;
       born => date(day => integer;
                    month => monthname;
                    year => integer);
       father => person);
```

Figure 2-1: An example of a term structure

The domain of a term is the set of addresses which explicitly appear in the expression of the term. For example, the domain of the above term is the set of addresses {*e*, `id`, `born`, `born.day`, `born.month`, `born.year`, `father`}.

The example in figure 2-1 shows a possible description of what one may intend to use as a structure for a person. The terms associated with the labels are to *restrict* the types of possible values that may be used under each label. However, there is no explicit constraint, in this particular structure, *among* the sub-structures appearing under distinct labels. For instance, a person bearing a last-name which is not the same as his father's would be a legal instance of this structure. In order to capture this sort of constraints, one can *tag* the addresses in a term structure, and *enforce* identically tagged addresses to be identically instantiated. For example, if in the above example one is to express that a person's father's last-name must be the same as that person's last-name, a better representation may be the term in figure 2-2.

```
person(id => name(last => X:string);
       born => date(day => integer;
                    month => monthname;
                    year => integer);
       father => person(id => name(last => X:string)));
```

Figure 2-2: An example of tagging in a term structure

Definition 3: A *term* is a triple (Δ,ψ,τ) where Δ is a term domain on $\mathcal{L}$, ψ is a *symbol* function from $\mathcal{L}^*$ to Σ such that $\psi(\mathcal{L}^*-\Delta) = \{\top\}$, and τ is a *tag* function from Δ to $\mathcal{T}$. A term is finite (*resp.* regular) if its domain is finite (*resp.* regular).

Such a definition illustrated for the term in figure 2-2 is captured in the table in figure 2-3. Note the *"syntactic sugar"* implicitly used in figure 2-2. Namely, I shall omit writing explicitly tags for addresses which are not sharing theirs. In the sequel, by "term" it will be meant "regular term".

Addresses (Δ)	*Symbols* (ψ)	*Tags* (τ)
e	person	X_0
id	name	X_1
id.last	string	X
born	date	X_2
born.day	integer	X_3
born.month	monthname	X_4
born.year	integer	X_5
father	person	X_6
father.id	name	X_7
father.id.last	string	X

Figure 2-3: (Δ,ψ,τ)-definition of the term in figure 2-2

Given a term $t = (\Delta,\psi,\tau)$, an address w in Δ, the *subterm of t at address* w is the term $t\backslash w = (\Delta\backslash w, \psi\backslash w, \tau\backslash w)$ where $\psi\backslash w\colon\ \mathcal{L}^* \to \Sigma$ and $\tau\backslash w\colon\ \Delta\backslash w \to \mathcal{T}$ are defined by:

- $\psi\backslash w(w') = \psi(w.w')\ \forall w' \in \mathcal{L}^*$;
- $\tau\backslash w(w') = \tau(w.w')\ \forall w' \in \Delta\backslash w$.

From these definitions, it is clear that $t\backslash e$ is the same as t. In example of figure 2-2, the subterm at address `father.id` is `name(last => X:string)`.

Given a term $t = (\Delta,\psi,\tau)$, a symbol f, (*resp.*, a tag X, a term t') is said to *occur* in t if there is an address w in Δ such that $\psi(w) = f$ (*resp.*, $\tau(w) = X$, $t\backslash w = t'$). The following proposition is immediate and follows by definition.[5]

Proposition 4: Given a term $t = (\Delta,\psi,\tau)$, the following statements are equivalent:

- t is a regular term;
- The number of subterms occurring in t is finite;
- The number of symbols occurring in t is finite;
- The number of tags occurring in t is finite.

It follows that a coreference relation on a regular term domain has finite index.

Definition 5: In a term, any two addresses bearing the same tag are said to corefer. Thus, the *coreference* relation κ of a term $t = (\Delta,\psi,\tau)$ is a relation defined on Δ as the

[5] Also established in [7]

kernel of the tag function τ; *i.e.*, κ = Ker(τ) = $\tau \bullet \tau^{-1}$.

We immediately note that κ is an equivalence relation since it is the kernel of a function. A κ-class is called a *coreference class*. For example, in the term in figure 2-2, the addresses `father.id.last` and `id.last` corefer.

A term `t` is *referentially consistent* if the same subterm occurs at all addresses in a coreference class. That is, if C is a coreference class in Δ/κ then `t\w` is *identical* for *all* addresses `w` in C. Thus, if a term is referentially consistent, then by definition for any w_1, w_2 in Δ, if $\tau(w_1) = \tau(w_2)$ then for all `w` such that $w_1.w \in \Delta$, necessarily $w_2.w \in \Delta$ also, and $\tau(w_1.w) = \tau(w_2.w)$. Therefore, if a term is referentially consistent, κ is in fact more than a simple equivalence relation: it is a *right-invariant* equivalence, or a *right-congruence*, on Δ. That is, for any two addresses w_1, w_2, if $w_1 \kappa w_2$ then $w_1.w \kappa w_2.w$ for any `w` such that $w_1.w \in \Delta$ and $w_2.w \in \Delta$.

Definition 6: A *well-formed term* (wft) is a term which is referentially consistent.

I shall use this property to justify another syntactic "sweetness": whenever a tag occurs in a term without a subterm, what is meant is that the subterm elsewhere referred to in the term by an address bearing this tag is implicitly present. If there is no such subterm, the implicit subterm is $\top$. For example, in the term foo(l_1 => X; l_2 => X:bar; l_3 => Y; l_4 => Y), the subterm at address l_1 is `bar`, and the subterm at address l_4 is $\top$. In what follows, $\top$ will never be written explicitly in a term.

Note that it is quite possible to consider *infinite* terms such as shown in figure 2-4. For example, at the addresses `father` and `father.son.father`, is a phenomenon which I call *cyclic tagging*.

```
person(id => name(last => X:string);
       born => date(day => integer;
                    month => monthname;
                    year => integer);
       father => Y:person(id => name(last => X:string);
                          son => person(father => Y)));
```

Figure 2-4: An example of simple cyclic tagging in a term structure

Syntactically, cycles may also be present in more pathological ways such as pictured in figure 2-5, where one must follow a path of cross-references.

```
foo(l1 => X1:foo1(k1 => X2);
    l2 => X2:foo2(k2 => X3);
    ...
    li => Xi:fooi(ki => Xi+1);
    ...
    ln => Xn:foon(kn => X1));
```

Figure 2-5: An example of complex cyclic tagging in a term structure

A term is ***referentially acyclic*** if there is no cyclic tagging occurring in the term. A *cyclic term* is one which is not referentially acyclic. Thus, the terms in figures 2-4 and 2-5 are ***not*** referentially acyclic. A wft is then best pictured as a ***labelled directed graph*** as illustrated in figure 2-6 which is the ***graph representation*** of the wft below. Thus, labels act as arcs between nodes bearing type symbols. Tags are ***physical pointers*** to nodes, indicating which nodes are shared.

$$
\begin{array}{l}
\mathtt{X_0:f_1(l_1 \Rightarrow X_1:f_2(l_2 \Rightarrow X_2;} \\
\qquad\qquad\qquad\quad \mathtt{l_3 \Rightarrow f_3);} \\
\qquad \mathtt{l_4 \Rightarrow X_2;} \\
\qquad \mathtt{l_5 \Rightarrow f_4(l_6 \Rightarrow X_1;} \\
\qquad\qquad\quad \mathtt{l_7 \Rightarrow X_3:f_5;} \\
\qquad\qquad\quad \mathtt{l_8 \Rightarrow X_3);} \\
\qquad\qquad\quad \mathtt{l_9 \Rightarrow X_0))}
\end{array}
$$

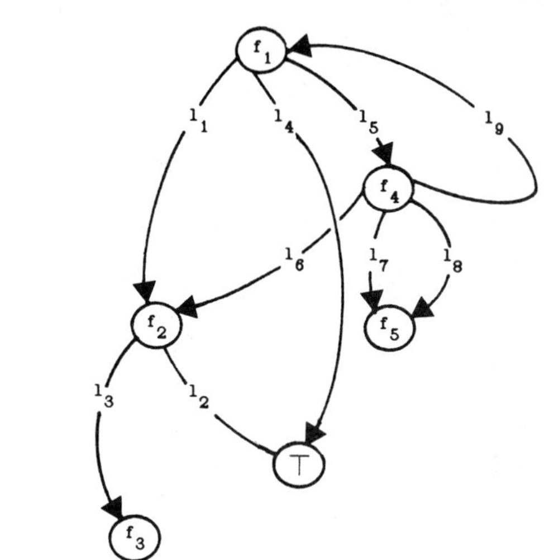

Figure 2-6: Graph representation of a wft

In figure 2-6, the similarity with finite states diagrams is not coincidental. And thus, it follows that a term is referentially acyclic if and only if its term domain is finite. Also, any term (cyclic or not) expressed in the above syntax is a regular term.

The set of well-formed terms is denoted $\mathcal{WFT}$. The set of well-formed acyclic terms is denoted $\mathcal{WFAT}$ and is a subset of $\mathcal{WFT}$.

I shall not give any semantic value to the tags aside from the coreference classes they define. The following relation α on $\mathcal{WFT}$ is to handle *tag renaming*. This means that α is relating wft's which are identical up to a renaming of the tags which preserves the coreference classes.

Definition 7: Two terms $t_1 = (\Delta_1, \psi_1, \tau_1)$ and $t_2 = (\Delta_2, \psi_2, \tau_2)$ are ***alphabetical variants*** of one another (noted $t_1 \ \alpha \ t_2$) if and only if:

1. $\Delta_1 = \Delta_2$;
2. $\mathrm{Ker}(\tau_1) = \mathrm{Ker}(\tau_2)$;

3. $\psi_1 = \psi_2$.

Interpreting these structures as commutative diagrams betweens sets, it comes that the symbols $\top$ and $\bot$ denote, respectively, the whole universe -- *"anything"* -- and the empty set -- *"inconsistent"*. Hence, a term in which the symbol $\bot$ occurs is to be interpreted as being inconsistent. To this end, we can define a relation $\Downarrow$ on $\mathcal{WFT}$ -- *smashing* --, where $t_1 \Downarrow t_2$ if and only if $\bot$ occurs in both t_1 *and* t_2, to be such that all equivalence classes except $[\bot]$ are *singletons*. Clearly, if $\bot$ occurs in a term, it also occurs in all terms in its α-class. In the way they have been defined, the relations α and $\Downarrow$ are such that their *union* $\approx\, = \alpha \cup \Downarrow$ is an equivalence relation. Thus,

Definition 8: A *ψ-type* is an element of the quotient set $\Psi = \mathcal{WFT}/\approx$. An *acyclic* ψ-type is an element of the quotient set $\Psi_0 = \mathcal{WFAT}/\approx$.

2.2. The Subsumption Ordering

The partial ordering on symbols can be extended to terms in a fashion which is reminiscent of the algebraic notion of *homomorphic extension*. I define the *subsumption* relation on the set Ψ as follows.

Definition 9: A term $t_1 = (\Delta_1, \psi_1, \tau_1)$ *is subsumed* by a term $t_2 = (\Delta_2, \psi_2, \tau_2)$ (noted $t_1 \preceq t_2$), if and only if *either*, $t_1 \approx \bot$; *or*,

1. $\Delta_2 \subseteq \Delta_1$;
2. $\mathrm{Ker}(\tau_2) \subseteq \mathrm{Ker}(\tau_1)$;
3. $\psi_1(w) \leq \psi_2(w),\ \forall w \in \mathcal{L}^*$.

It is easy to verify that a subsumption relation on Ψ defined by $[t_1] \preceq [t_2]$ if and only if $t_1 \preceq t_2$ is well-defined (*i.e.*, it does not depend on particular class representatives) and it is an *ordering* relation.[6]

This notion of subsumption is related to the (in)famous *IS-A* ordering in semantic networks [4, 5], and the *tuple ordering* in the so-called semantic relation data model [3]. It expresses the fact that, given a ψ-type t, any ψ-type t' defined on at least the same domain, with at least the same coreference classes, and with symbols at each address which are less than the symbols in t at the corresponding addresses, is a subtype of t. Indeed, such a t' is *more specified* than t.

The "homomorphic" extension of the ordering on Σ to the subsumption ordering on Ψ can be exploited further. Indeed, if *least upper bounds* (LUB) and *greatest lower bounds* (GLB) are defined for any subsets of Σ, then this property carries over to Ψ.

Theorem 10: If the signature Σ is a lattice, then so is Ψ.

---

[6] In the sequel, I shall use the (*abusive*) convention of denoting a ψ-type by one of its class representatives, understanding that what is meant is modulo *tag renaming* and *smashing*.

Rather than giving formal definitions for the meet and join operations on Ψ, let us illustrate the extended lattice operations with an example. Figure 2-7 shows a signature which is a finite (non-modular) lattice.

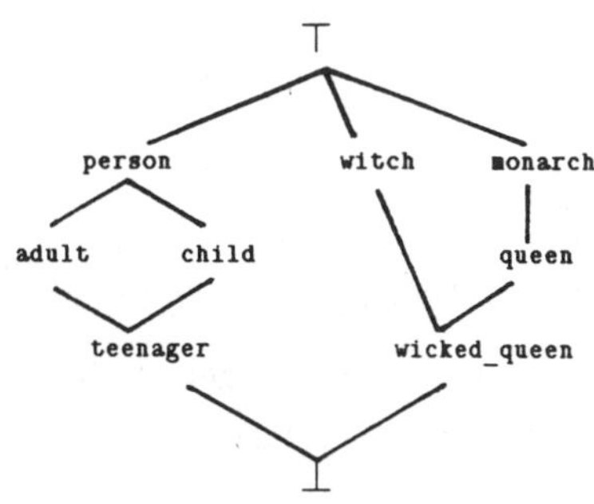

Figure 2-7: A signature which is a lattice

Given this signature, the two types in figure 2-8 admit as meet and join the types in figure 2-9.

```
child(knows => X:person(knows => queen;
                        hates => Y:monarch);
      hates => child(knows => Y;
                     likes => wicked_queen);
      likes => X);

adult(knows => adult(knows => witch);
      hates => person(knows => X:monarch;
                      likes => X));
```

Figure 2-8: Two wft's

```
person(knows => person;
       hates => person(knows => monarch;
                       likes => monarch));

teenager(knows => X:adult(knows => wicked_queen;
                          hates => Y:wicked_queen);
         hates => child(knows => Y;
                        likes => Y);
         likes => X);
```

Figure 2-9: LUB and GLB of the two types in figure 2-8

The reader is referred to [1] for the detailed definitions of the meet and join operation on Ψ. It suffices here to say that they are essentially extensions of the *unification* [11, 22] and *generalization* [21] operations on regular first-order terms. Indeed, these operations are special cases of my definitions when *(i)* Σ is a *flat* lattice, *(ii)* a coreference class may contain more than one element *iff* all of its elements are leaves and the symbols occurring at these leaves are restricted to be $\top$.

An important remark is that the set Ψ_0 of acyclic ψ-types also has a lattice structure.

Theorem 11: If Σ is a lattice, then so is Ψ_0. However Ψ_0 is *not* a sublattice of Ψ.

The join operation is the same, but the meet operation is modified so that if the GLB in Ψ of two acyclic terms contains a cycle, then their GLB in Ψ_0 is $\perp$. However, Ψ_0 is not a sublattice of Ψ, since the meet in Ψ of two acyclic wft's is not necessarily acyclic. Consider, for example[7]

t_1 = f(l_1 => X : f; l_2 => f(l_3 => X))

t_2 = f(l_1 => X : f; l_2 => X)

$t_1 \wedge t_2$ = f(l_1 => X : f(l_3 => X) ; l_2 => X)

2.3. A Distributive Lattice of Types

Accepting the "type-as-set" interpretation of the calculus of ψ-types, it is yet necessary to wonder whether lattice-theoretic properties of meet and join reflect those of intersection and union. Unfortunately, this is not the case with Ψ. The lattice of ψ-types is not so convenient as to be ***distributive***, even if the signature Σ is itself distributive. As a counter-example, consider the flat (distributive) lattice Σ = {$\top$, a, f, $\perp$}. Indeed,

f $\wedge$ (f(l => a) $\vee$ a) = f

(f $\wedge$ f(l => a)) $\vee$ (f $\wedge$ a) = f(l => a)

and this proves that $\mathcal{WFT}$ is not distributive.[8]

This is not the only ailment of $\mathcal{WFT}$ as a type system. Recall that in order to obtain the benefit of a lattice structure as stated in theorem 10, there is a rather strong demand that the type signature Σ be itself a lattice. For a signature that would be any poset, this nice result is unfortunately lost. In practice, programs deal with finite sets of primitive types. Even then, it would be quite unreasonable to require that all meets and joins of those primitive types be explicitly defined. What should be typically specified in a program is the minimal amount of type information which is to be relevant to the program. Clearly, such a signature of type symbols should be not necessarily more than a finite incompletely specified poset of symbols.

It is hence necessary to go further than the construction of $\mathcal{WFT}$ in order to obtain a satisfactory type system which would not make unreasonable demand for primitive type information. Fortunately, it is possible not to impose so drastic demands on Σ and yet construct a more powerful lattice than $\mathcal{WFT}$; *i.e.*, a distributive lattice. The idea is very simple, and is based on observing that the join operation in Ψ is too "greedy". Indeed, if one wants to specify that an object is of type foo or bar when no explicit type symbol in Σ is known as their GLB, then $\top$ is returned. Clearly, it is not correct to infer that the given object is of type *"anything"* just because Σ does not happen to contain explicitly a symbol for the GLB

[7] A similar phenomenon happens in unification of first-order terms where it is reason for the so-called *"occur-check"* testing whether a variable occurs in a term when trying to unify that variable with the term.

[8] A similar result was pointed out by G.Plotkin in [20].

foo and bar. All that can be correctly said is that the given object is of *disjunctive* type foo$\vee$bar.

I next give a brief summary of a construction of such a more adequate type lattice. It may be construed as a powerdomain construction to handle indeterminacy [19]; in our case, *variant records*. It is not possible to detail this construction here. The interested reader is referred to [1].

A poset is *Noetherian* if it does not contain infinitely ascending chains. Given a set S, the set $\mathcal{Q}^{(S)}$ of finite non-empty subsets of *maximal elements* of S is called the *restricted power of* S. If S is a Noetherian poset, the set $\mathcal{Q}^{[S]}$ of *all* such subsets of maximal elements is called the *complete* restricted power of S. Given a Noetherian poset S, and S'$\subseteq$S, $\Re$(S') is the set of maximal elements of S'.

I shall call £ the set $\mathcal{Q}^{[\Psi]}$, and $£_0$ the set $\mathcal{Q}^{[\Psi_0]}$. Clearly, $£_0$ is a subset of £. I shall denote a singleton {t} in £ simply by t.

Definition 12: Subsumption in £ is defined by, $T_1 \sqsubseteq T_2$ if and only if *every* ψ-type in T_1 is subsumed by *some* ψ-type in T_2.

Let's define a notational variant of elements of £ which will have the advantage of being more *compact* syntactically. Consider the object shown in figure 2-10. The syntax used is similar to the one which has expressed ψ-types up to now. However, *sets* of terms rather that terms may occur at some addresses.

```
person(sex => {male, female};
       father => Y:person(sex => male);
       mother => Z:person(sex => female);
       parent => {Y, Z});
```

Figure 2-10: Example of an ϵ-term

This notation may be viewed as a compact way of representing a sets of ψ-types. For example, the object in figure 2-10 represents a set of *four* ψ-types which can be obtained by expansion, keeping *one* element at each address. Such terms are called ϵ-terms. I shall denote the set of ϵ-terms by E.

Definition 13: A *basic ϵ-term* is a quadruple (f, A, λ, θ) where:

- $f \in \Sigma - \{\bot\}$;
- A is a finite subset of $\mathcal{L}$;
- $\lambda: A \rightarrow E$;
- $\theta: A \rightarrow \mathcal{T}$.

Definition 14: An *ϵ-term* is a non-empty set of *basic ϵ-terms*.

To be exact, E is rather the set of *well-formed* ϵ-terms. That is, ϵ-terms whose expansion into sets of terms contains only well-formed terms.

An ϵ-term can be transformed into a set of ψ-types -- its *ψ-expansion*. The ψ-expansion of an ϵ-term is the set of all possible ψ-types which can be inductively obtained by keeping only one ψ-type at each address. The reader familiar with first-order logic could construe this process as being similar to transforming a logical formula into its disjunctive normal form.

1. *pick some* $\epsilon = (\mathtt{f}, \Lambda, \lambda, \theta)$ *in* E;

2. *let* $\Lambda = \{\mathtt{l}_i\}_{i=1}^{n}$ *and* $\mathtt{t}_i = (\Delta_i, \psi_i, \tau_i)$ *be some element of the ψ-expansion of* $\lambda(\mathtt{l}_i)$, *for* $i = 1, \ldots, n$.

3. $\Delta = \{e\} \cup (\cup_{i=1}^{n} \mathtt{l}_i . \Delta_i)$;

4. $\psi(e) = \mathtt{f}$; $\psi(\mathtt{l}_i . \mathtt{w}) = \psi_i(\mathtt{w})$; $\psi(\mathtt{l} . \mathtt{w}) = \top$ *if* $\mathtt{l} \notin \Lambda$;

5. $\tau(\mathtt{l}_i) = \theta(\mathtt{l}_i)$; $\tau(\mathtt{l}_i . \mathtt{w}) = \tau_i(\mathtt{w})$, *if* $\mathtt{w} \in \Delta_i$.

This process defines the ψ-expansion of an ϵ-term E by reduction into an element of £. A more detailed algorithm is presented in section [1].

We are now ready to construct a distributive lattice of ϵ-types. First, we relax the demand that the signature Σ be lattice. Assuming it is a Noetherian poset we can embed it in a meet-semilattice $2^{[\Sigma]}$ preserving existing GLB's. Then, we can define the meet operation on Ψ so that whenever the meet of two symbols in not a singleton, the result is expanded using ψ-expansion.

Theorem 15: If the signature Σ is a Noetherian poset then so is the lattice Ψ_0; but the lattice Ψ is *not* Noetherian.

The following counter-example exhibits an infinitely ascending chain of wfts in Ψ. For any a in L and any f in Σ, define the sequence $\mathtt{t}_n = (\Delta_n, \psi_n, \tau_n)$, $n \geq 1$ as follows:

$$\Delta_n = a^*;$$
$$\psi_n(\Delta_n) = f;$$
$$\Delta_n / \kappa_n = \Delta_n / \mathrm{Ker}(\tau_n) = \{\{e\}, \{a\}, \ldots, \{a^{n-1}\}, a^n . a^*\}.$$

This clearly defines an infinite strictly ascending sequence of regular wft's since, for all $n \geq 0$:

$$\Delta_{n+1} \subseteq \Delta_n;$$
$$\psi_n(\Delta_n) \leq \psi_{n+1}(\Delta_{n+1});$$
$$\kappa_{n+1} \subset \kappa_n.$$

In our syntax, this corresponds to the sequence:

```
t0 = X : f(a => X),
t1 = f(a => X : f(a => X)),
t2 = f(a => f(a => X : f(a => X))), ... ,
tn = f(a => f(a => ... f(a => X : f(a => X))...)), ...
          <---- n+1 a's ---->
```

We define two binary operations $\sqcap$ and $\sqcup$ on the set $\mathcal{L}_0$. For any two sets T_1 and T_2 in $\mathcal{L}_0$:

$$T_1 \sqcap T_2 = \Re(\{t \mid t = t_1 \wedge t_2,\ t_1 \in T_1,\ t_2 \in T_2\});$$

$$T_1 \sqcup T_2 = \Re(T_1 \cup T_2).$$

where $\wedge$ is the meet operation defined on Ψ_0. Then, for *any* poset Σ containing $\top$ and $\bot$,

Theorem 16: The poset $\mathcal{L}_0$ is a *distributive* lattice whose meet is $\sqcap$, whose join is $\sqcup$, and whose top and bottom are $\{\top\}$ and $\{\bot\}$.

It is not possible to define lattice operations for $\mathcal{L}$ because Ψ is not Noetherian. Hence, the set of maximal elements of a set cannot be defined for *all* sets. However, if only finite sets of regular wft's are considered, then:

Theorem 17: The poset $\mathcal{Q}^{(\Psi)}$ of *finite* sets of incomparable regular wft's is a distributive lattice.

However, it is not complete. It is also true that $\mathcal{Q}^{(\Psi_0)} \subseteq \mathcal{Q}^{(\Psi)}$ and $\mathcal{Q}^{(\Psi_0)}$ is a distributive lattice, but it is not a sublattice of $\mathcal{L}$. In general, the GLB of elements of $\mathcal{Q}^{(\Psi_0)}$ is a lower bound of the GLB of these elements taken in $\mathcal{Q}^{(\Psi)}$.

3. Programs as Recursive Type Equations

Consider the equations in figure 3-1. Each equation is a pair made of a symbol and an ϵ-term, and may intuitively be understood as a *definition*. I shall call a set of such definitions a *knowledge base*.[9]

Definition 18: A *knowledge base* is a function from $\Sigma-\{\bot\}$ to $\mathcal{L}_0$ which is the identity almost everywhere except for a finite number of symbols.

Definition 19: A knowledge base KB is said to be in *standard form* if, for any symbols f and g in Σ,

1. whenever $KB(f) = \{t_1, \ldots, t_n\}$ and $n>1$ then $t_i \in \Sigma$ for all $i=1,\ldots,n$; *and,*

2. whenever $KB(f) \in \Sigma$ then $KB(f) = f$; *and,*

3. if f and g are such that $KB(f)$ and $KB(g)$ are not singletons, then $KB(f)$ cannot be a subset $KB(g)$.

---

[9] Or *program*, or *type environment*... Nevertheless, *knowledge base* is a deliberate choice since what is defined is in essence an *abstract semantic network*.

```
list = {nil, cons};

append = {append_0, append_1};

append_0 =
      (front => nil;
       back => X:list;
       whole => X);

append_1 =
      (front => cons(head => X; tail => Y);
       back => Z:list;
       whole => cons(head => X; tail => U);
       patch => append(front => Y; back => Z; whole => U));
```

Figure 3-1: A specification for appending two lists

That is, (1) whenever the definition of `f` in KB is more than a singleton, its elements are only symbols; (2) there cannot be symbol aliases; and, (3) no symbol definition is contained is some other symbol definition. The knowledge base in figure 3-1 is in standard form. Any knowledge base KB can be put in standard form as follows:

1. If a ψ-type element t_1 of KB(f) is not a symbol (*i.e.*, it has non-$\top$ subterms) then replace it by a new symbol **s** not already in Σ and augment the knowledge base with KB(s) = t_1.
2. Whenever KB(f) = **g**, replace all occurrences of **g** by **f** in KB, and delete **g** from Σ.
3. Whenever KB(f) $\subseteq$ KB(g), remove KB(f) from KB(g) and replace it with a new symbol **s** not already in Σ and augment the knowledge base with **s** = KB(f).

Hence, without loss of generality, I shall only consider knowledge bases in standard form.

So far, the partial order on Σ has been assumed predefined. However, given a knowledge base, it is quite easy to quickly infer what I shall call its *implicit symbol ordering*. For example, examining the knowledge base in figure 3-1, it is evident that the signature Σ must contain the set of symbols {list, cons, nil, append, append_0, append_1}, and that the partial ordering on Σ is such that nil < list, cons < list, append_0 < append, append_1 < append. In general, this ordering can be extracted from the specification of a knowledge base as explained in the following definition.

Definition 20: Given a knowledge base KB, its *implicit symbol ordering* is the least *strict* ordering relation < on Σ, if one exists, such that:

- *if* $KB(f) = (g, A, \lambda, \theta)$ *then* f<g;
- *if* $KB(f) = \{f_1, \ldots, f_n\}$, $n > 1$, *then* $f_i < f$, *for all* $i=1, \ldots, n$.

Definition 21: A knowledge base is *well-defined* if and only if it admits an implicit symbol ordering.

The knowledge base in figure 3-1 is well-defined. It specifies four types:[10]

[10] In the following description, "*head*" is the head of a structure as defined on page 6 and must not be confused with the label **head** of a **cons** type...

`list`	which is to be matched by something whose head is `nil` or `cons`;
`append`	which is to be matched by something whose head is `append_0` or `append_1`;
`append_0`	whose head is $\top$, and describes a type whose `front` must be a `nil`;
`append_1`	whose head is $\top$, and describes a type whose `front` must be a `cons`.

I want to describe an *interpretation* of any given type in the context of this knowledge base so that *expanding* the input according to the specifications will produce a consistently typed object.

Given a well-defined knowledge base KB, I define the functional $\mathcal{EVAL}_{KB}$ which maps $\pounds_0$ into itself. The functional $\mathcal{EVAL}_{KB}$ defines an *operational semantics* of KBL interpreting an ϵ-term in the knowledge base by *evaluating* ϵ-types as follows:

$$\mathcal{EVAL}_{KB}[\![\{t_i\}_{i=1}^{n}]\!] = \sqcup_{i=1}^{n} \mathcal{EVAL}_{KB}[\![t_i]\!];$$

$$\mathcal{EVAL}_{KB}[\![(f, \Lambda, \lambda, \theta)]\!] = \textit{if } KB(f) \neq f$$
$$\textit{then } \mathcal{EVAL}_{KB}[\![KB(f) \sqcap (\top, \Lambda, \lambda, \theta)]\!]$$
$$\textit{else } (f, \Lambda, \mathcal{EVAL}_{KB} \circ \lambda, \theta).$$

The functional $\mathcal{EVAL}_{KB}$ defines the interpreter for KBL. It evaluates ϵ-types as follows:

- A set of ψ-types is evaluated by evaluating all its elements and keeping only maximal elements;
- A ψ-type is evaluated by *"expanding"* its root symbol if its knowledge base value is not itself; *i.e.*, substituting the root symbol by its knowledge base value by taking the meet of this value and the ψ-type whose root symbol has been erased (replaced by $\top$). If the root symbol is mapped to itself by the knowledge base, the process is applied recursively to the subterms.

Recalling the "type-as-set" semantics of ϵ-types and ψ-types, this process essentially computes unions and intersections of sets. The symbol substitution process is to be interpreted as *importing* the information encapsulated in the symbol into the context of another type.

Let's *trace* what the interpreter does, one step at a time, on an example. Let's suppose that the knowledge base in figure 3-1 is defined. Consider the following input:

```
append(front => cons(head => 1;
                     tail => cons(head => 2;
                                  tail => nil));
       back => cons(head => 3;
                    tail => nil));
```

Next, the interpreter expands `append` into `{append_0, append_1}`:

```
{append_0(front => cons(head => 1;
                        tail => cons(head => 2;
                                     tail => nil));
          back => cons(head => 3;
                       tail => nil)),

 append_1(front => cons(head => 1;
                        tail => cons(head => 2;
                                     tail => nil));
          back => cons(head => 3;
                       tail => nil))};
```

Each of these two basic ϵ-terms is further expanded according to the definitions of their heads. However, the first one (append_0) yields $\perp$ since the meet of the subterms at front is $\perp$. Hence, by $\Re$-reduction, we are left with only:

```
(front => cons(head => 1;
               tail => cons(head => 2;
                            tail => nil));
 back => cons(head => 3;
              tail => nil);
 whole => cons(head => 1;
               tail => U);
 patch => append(front => cons(head => 2;
                               tail => nil);
                 back => cons(head => 3;
                              tail => nil);
                 whole => U));
```

The process continues, expanding the subterms:[11]

```
(front => cons(head => 1;
               tail => cons(head => 2;
                            tail => nil));
 back => cons(head => 3;
              tail => nil);
 whole => cons(head => 1;
               tail => cons(head => 2;
                            tail => U));
 patch => (front => cons(head => 2;
                         tail => nil);
           back => cons(head => 3;
                        tail => nil);
           patch => append(front => nil;
                           back => cons(head => 3;
                                        tail => nil);
                           whole => U);
           whole => cons(head => 2;
                         tail => U)));
```

Finally, the following term is obtained which cannot be further expanded. The interpretation of append has thus correctly produced a type whose whole is the concatenation of its front to its end. The result could be isolated by projection on the field whole if desired. The attribute patch is the history of the computation.

[11]For what remains, I shall leave out the details of cleaning-up $\perp$ by reduction.

```
(front => cons(head => 1;
               tail => cons(head => 2;
                            tail => nil));
 back => cons(head => 3;
              tail => nil);
 whole => cons(head => 1;
               tail => cons(head => 2;
                            tail => cons(head => 3;
                                         tail => nil)));
 patch => (front => cons(head => 2;
                         tail => nil);
           back => cons(head => 3;
                        tail => nil);
           patch => (front => nil;
                     back => cons(head => 3;
                                  tail => nil);
                     whole => cons(head => 3;
                                   tail => nil));
           whole => cons(head => 2;
                         tail => cons(head => 3;
                                      tail => nil))));
```

More elaborate programs which can be similarly interpreted can be found in [1, 2].

4. A Perspective

At this stage, it is beneficial to put things into perspective. The following is a discussion on the nature of KBL, and how it relates to logic programming and automated reasoning.

4.1. Declarative and Procedural Semantics

Among all acclaimed aspects of the use of Horn logic as a programming language, the most underscored has been its *dual* semantics: a *declarative* semantics and a *procedural* semantics. Kowalski [13] proposes *"reading"* a Horn clause A_0 <- $A_1, \ldots, A_n$ in two ways:

declaration: The fact A_0 holds if all facts $(A_i)_{i=1}^{n}$ hold.

procedure: In order to prove goal A_0, prove all goals $(A_i)_{i=1}^{n}$.

Thus, logic programming proponents have advocated that a program should be nothing but the *specification* of some *axiomatic system*. That is, one ought to solve a problem just by stating it. Thus, description of a grammar (*declaration*) becomes a parsing program (*procedure*) [18], description of actions and states (*declaration*) becomes a planning program (*procedure*) [24], description of relations (*declaration*) becomes a database management program (*procedure*) [12], and so on.

This is a very nice aspect which I claim is the essence of KBL. Indeed, as can be further seen in detail in the examples shown in [2, 1], KBL has a *dual* semantics as well, in a fashion which I claim is less constraining than the Horn logic model.[12] I propose *"reading"* an ϵ-term definition s = t in two ways:

declaration: Anything which is describable as an s must be also describable as a t.

[12] See section 4.2.

procedure: In order to check s, check the head of t and the components of the body of t.

It should be pointed out that I have not yet claimed any connection with logic or theorem-proving aside from the mention of the familiar notion of term. I next expose some ideas about such a connection.

4.2. Disjunctive Reasoning

In his master's thesis [16], R.Moore discusses a particular form of reasoning; namely, *disjunctive* reasoning, or reasoning *by cases*. He gives the following example, also pictured in figure 4-1.

> There are three colored cubes stacked one on top of another. The cube on top is green, the cube at the bottom is blue, and the cube in the middle is hidden from view and hence has an unspecified color. Does one have enough information to decide whether there is a green cube immediately on top of a non-green cube?

```
+---+
| G |
+---+  Q = "Is there a green cube on top of a non-green cube?"
| ? |
+---+  A = YES!
| B |
+---+
```

Figure 4-1: An example of disjunctive reasoning

Surprisingly, the answer is *yes!* One arrives at this conclusion following a reasoning by cases. Indeed, either the middle cube is green or non-green. If it is green, then the middle cube and the bottom cube constitute such a green cube over a non-green (blue) cube. If the middle is not green, then the top and the middle cubes constitute such a pair of cubes. Hence, the conclusion follows.

Moore shows that so-called *AND/OR tree* deduction systems *a la* PROLOG or *PLANNER* [10] cannot deal effectively with disjunctive reasoning without a special rule which he calls *restricted goal resolution* which essentially proves *tautologies* of the form P *or* ¬P.[13] The awkwardness of such systems stems from the fact that deduction chains along separate *OR* branches are independent of each other. By contrast, the semantics of my KBL makes it very easy to express disjunction, and therefore reasoning by cases is achieved with no supplementary aid. Figure 4-2 shows a program solving the cubes problem and the value it computes. It is worth observing that the latter captures *exactly* the form of the proof that I described above.

The foregoing discussion on disjunctive reasoning points out a weakness of PROLOG. It is in fact linked to a feature of PROLOG which, paradoxically, has been advertised as an asset; namely, the so-

[13] See also [17], pp.234-341.

```
color = {green, blue, other};

non_green = {blue, other};

threecubes = stack(top => green; middle => color; bottom => blue);

on = {on1, on2};

on1 = threecubes(top => X; middle => Y; above => X; below => Y);

on2 = threecubes(middle => X; bottom => Y; above => X; below => Y);

question = on(above => green; below => non_green);
```

input:

```
question;
```

output:

```
{stack(top => green;
       middle => {blue, other};
       bottom => blue;
       above => green;
       below => {blue, other}),

 stack(top => green;
       middle => green;
       bottom => blue;
       above => green;
       below => blue)};
```

Figure 4-2: Program, query, and answer for the cubes problem

called *closed world assumption*.

5. A Prospective Overview

Section 2 presented a basis for a programming language. This section is a presentation of issues whose adoption would not lose on the crux of the philosophy underlying the proposed design.

5.1. Complemented Types

I want to outline how the semantics of KBL can be augmented to deal with *generic* negative information. More precisely, I shall allow both *positive and negative* types to appear under labels of ϵ-terms in the form of pairs $t_1\backslash t_2$. Intuitively, this specifies anything which is subsumed by t_1 but not by t_2. For example, expressing the type of something which is an animal but not a cat can be written: `animal\cat`.

Consider the set $\mathcal{L}\times\mathcal{L}$. I need to express that $t_1\backslash t_2$ has no meaning if $t_1 \sqsubseteq t_2$. Thus, I define the following *smash* function from $\mathcal{L}\times\mathcal{L}$ to $\mathcal{L}\times\mathcal{L}$:

$$smash(t_1\backslash t_2) = \textit{if } t_1 \sqsubseteq t_2 \textit{ then } \bot \textit{ else } t_1\backslash(t_1 \sqcap t_2). \qquad (1)$$

Next, I define the following binary operation $\wedge$ on $smash(\mathcal{L}\times\mathcal{L})$:

$$t_1\backslash t_2 \wedge t_3\backslash t_4 = smash((t_1 \sqcap t_3)\backslash \Re(\{t_2, t_4\}). \qquad (2)$$

It is straighforward to check that

Proposition 22: The operation defined in 2 is associative, commutative and idempotent.

Hence,

Proposition 23: The operation $\wedge$ defined in 2 defines a meet-semi-lattice structure on $\mathcal{L} \times \mathcal{L}$ for the ordering defined by:

$$t_1 \backslash t_2 \preceq t_3 \backslash t_4 \textit{ iff } t_1 \backslash t_2 \wedge t_3 \backslash t_4 = t_1 \backslash t_2. \tag{3}$$

We can then can proceed to the same lattice construction used for KBL and justify the definition of the $\sqcap$ and $\sqcup$ operations on the set of sets of pairs of ϵ-terms in exactly the same fashion. The lattice thus constructed is then distributive, and complete if limited to finite wft's on a Noetherian signature.

The point made here is that one can use the same operational semantics detailed for KBL to interpret the language of complemented types outlined above.

5.2. Polymorphic Types

I want to show that KBL could easily be extended to provide for the possibility of defining *parameterized* or *polymorphic* types [15].

Let me give an example. If I want to specify a type representing a list of integers, the following will work:

```
integer_list = {nil, cons(head => integer;
                          tail => integer_list)};
```

However, If I want to define, in a generic way, a *homogeneous* list type for any base type and not only for `integer`, the language fails me.

Again, looking at what is needed provides a straightforward solution. Indeed, the original terms in $\mathcal{WFT}$ are built on a signature which is a poset of symbols. This is *all* which has been needed to construct the lattice of ϵ-types. Therefore *any* poset shall do as well. A poset which does *better* is the set of first-order algebraic terms on a given partially ordered signature of symbols Σ and a set of *type variables* $\mathcal{V}$, ordered by first-order term instantiation, also called *matching* or *one-way unification*. With this poset rather than Σ, KBL gains polymorphism.

If type variables are denoted by small greek letters, the definition of a polymorphic list type can therefore be:

```
list[α] = {nil, cons(head => α, tail => list[α])};
```

It is not difficult to extend the syntax to accommodate this feature.

6. Conclusion

I have tried to present a potentially promising design for a programming language based on a calculus of type subsumption. I have shown that a close analysis of the notion of *term* in universal algebra and logic provides a clear insight about how the concept of *subsumption* may be extended to bear more semantical power. I have proposed a mathematical semantics for a particular language where type structures are first-class objects, and which can be practically implemented. I have tried to point out connections of this model of computation with logic. Finally, I have described further extensions in the language design which can be given well-defined semantics without loss of the basic language philosophy.

References

[1] Ait-Kaci, H.
A Lattice Theoretic Approach to Computation Based on a Calculus of Partially Ordered Type Structures.
PhD thesis, Computer and Information Science, University of Pennsylvania, 1984.

[2] Ait-Kaci, H.
A New Model of Computation Based on a Calculus of Type Subsumption.
Technical Report MS-CIS-83-40, Department of Computer and Information Science, University of Pennsylvania, Philadelphia, PA, December, 1983.

[3] Borkin, S.A.
Series in Computer Science. Volume 4: *Data Models: A Semantic Approach for Database Systems.*
The M.I.T. Press, Cambridge, MA, 1980.

[4] Brachman, R.J.
A New Paradigm for Representing Knowledge.
BBN Report 3605, Bolt Beranek and Newman, Cambridge, MA, 1978.

[5] Brachman, R.J.
What IS-A Is and Isn't: An Analysis of Taxonomic Links in Semantic Networks.
Computer 16(10):30-35, October 1983.

[6] Clocksin, C.F., Mellish, W.M.
Programming in PROLOG.
Springer-Verlag, Berlin, W.Germany, 1980.

[7] Courcelle, B.
Fundamental Properties of Infinite Trees.
Theoretical Computer Science 25:95-169, 1983.

[8] Gorn, S.
Explicit Definitions and Linguistic Dominoes.
In J.F. Hart and S. Takasu (editors), *Systems and Computer Science*, pages 77-105. University of Toronto Press, Toronto, Ontario, 1965.

[9] Gorn, S.
Data Representation and Lexical Calculi.
Information Processing & Management 20(1-2):151-174, 1984.
Also available as technical report MS-CIS-82-39, Department of Computer and Information Science, University of Pennsylvania, Philadelphia, PA.

[10] Hewitt, C.
Description and Theoretical Analysis (Using Schemata) of PLANNER: A Language for Proving Theorems and Manipulating Models in a Robot.
PhD thesis, Massachussetts Institute of Technology, June, 1971.

[11] Huet, G.
Resolution d'Equations dans des Langages d'Ordre 1, 2, ..., ω.
PhD thesis, Universite de Paris VII, France, September, 1976.

[12] Kowalski, R.A.
Logic for Data Description.
In Gallaire, H., and Minker, J. (editors), *Logic and Data Bases*, pages 77-103. Plenum Press, 1978.

[13] Kowalski, R.A.
Logic for Problem Solving.
North-Holland, New York, 1979.

[14] Ledgard, H.
ADA: An Introduction; ADA Reference Manual.
Springer-Verlag, Berlin, W.Germany, 1980.

[15] Milner, R.
A Theory of Type Polymorphism in Programming.
Journal of Computer and System Sciences 17(3):348-375, 1978.

[16] Moore, R.C.
Reasoning from Incomplete Knowledge in a Procedural Deduction System.
Master's thesis, Massachussetts Institute of Technology, October, 1975.

[17] Nilsson, N.J.
Principles of Artificial Intelligence.
Tioga Publishing Co., Palo Alto, CA, 1980.

[18] Pereira, F.C.N., and Warren, D.H.D.
Definite Clause Grammars for Language Analysis -- a Survey of the Formalism and a Comparison with Augmented Transition Networks.
Artificial Intelligence 13(3):231-278, 1980.

[19] Plotkin, G.D.
A Powerdomain Construction.
SIAM Journal on Computing 5, 1976.

[20] Plotkin, G.D.
Lattice Theoretic Properties of Subsumption.
Memorandum MIP-R-77, Department of Machine Intelligence and Perception, University of Edinburgh, June, 1977.

[21] Reynolds, J.C.
Transformational Systems and the Algebraic Structure of Atomic Formulas.
In D. Michie (editor), *Machine Intelligence 5*, chapter 7. Edinburgh University Press, 1970.

[22] Robinson, J.A.
A Machine-Oriented Logic Based on the Resolution Principle.
Journal of the ACM 12(1):23-41, 1965.

[23] Van Emden, M.H., and Kowalski, R.A.
The Semantics of Predicate Logic as a Programming Language.
Journal of the ACM 23(4):733-742, 1976.

[24] Warren, D.H.D.
WARPLAN: A System for Generating Plans.
Memorandum 76, Department of Computational Logic, School of Artificial Intelligence, University of Edinburgh, June, 1974.

CONSTRUCTING AND UTILIZING LARGE FACT DATABASES USING ARTIFICIAL INTELLIGENCE TECHNIQUES

Gian Piero ZARRI

Centre National de la Recherche Scientifique, Paris, France
and
TECSIEL SpA
Via Barnaba Oriani, 32
00197 Roma
Italy

ABSTRACT

In this paper, I shall describe two fundamental aspects of the RESEDA project : a) the study, which is still in a preliminary phase, concerning the possibility of constructing automatically or semi-automatically the "fact database" part of RESEDA's "knowledge base" ; b) the working prototype which makes use of inference techniques of different levels of complexity to carry out "intelligent" information retrieval within the fact database.

I. INTRODUCTION

The aim of the RESEDA system is to retrieve information from large fact databases making use of inference techniques borrowed from Knowledge Engineering (Feigenbaum 1977). The information contained in the fact database is complex biographical data ; the term "biographical data" must be understood in its broadest possible sense, i.e. referring to any elementary event, located by space-time coordinates, that it is possible to isolate within the life-cycle ("biography") of a given "personage". The personage can be a human being, in which case "biographical data" refers to any event, in the public or private life, physical or intellectual, etc., that it is possible to gather about this human personage ; but one can also speak of "biographical data" concerning the vicissitudes in the journey of a nuclear submarine (the "personage") or the various avatars in the life of a commercial product. From this point of view, the French terme "**vedette**" which is normally used to mean "personage" within RESEDA is less strictly linked to the context of a human character than the latter. The system has been developed using a fact database concerning human personages from the history of France ; the examples appearing later in the paper will refer to this particular application. But the system has already been used in other fields, the military, for example ; other applications are being studied, concerning the "intelligent" analysis of cancer patients' records or the legal field.

As regards the system's architecture, the fundamental decision taken when designing RESEDA was to establish that the "fact database" should be considered as an integral part of the system's general "knowledge base", on an equal footing with the "rule base" which enables inference operations to be performed. More precisely, one could say that RESEDA's "knowledge base" is made up of the knowledge, in its entirety, represented in **declarative form** inside the system. This base is divided into two subsets which, from a strictly functional point of view, have quite different roles :

- the "fact database" contains the data, in the usual sense of the word, on which the system will operate, that is the true "biographical data" and the system's general information about the specific field it is meant to manipulate (extensional data) ;

- the "rule base" contains the reasoning schemata which allow the system to search for data in the fact database by instantiating particularly complex inference strategies (intensional data).

This differentiation disappears completely when one considers the knowledge representation language ("metalanguage", in our terminology) used to describe the information contained in the two parts of the knowledge base. This language is the same in both cases ; the only difference being that **extensional data do not have any quantified variables** ; they represent assertions of individual facts. The intensional data involve quantified variables because of the need to write inference rules applicable to large classes of events.

This uniformity of representation has considerable advantages from the point of view of both logical perspicuity and computational efficiency ; for example, it makes it possible to avoid continually translating from one system of representation to another when formulating, in the terms of the fact database, the search strategies suggested by rule base. Note that this "integrated approach" to the problem of introducing Artificial Intelligence techniques into the domain of databases contrasts with the "classical" approach which consists in using a "traditional" (relational) database as a "fact database". Well known works which, despite their differences in approach, can be placed in the classical mold, are those of Kellog (1982), Stonebraker (1984), Tsur and Zaniolo (1984). All the "tools" popular today which allow the construction of "second generation" knowledge systems are, on the other hand, closer to an integrated approach ; amongst these tools - inspired by KRL (Bobrow and Winograd 1977) and "object oriented programming" (Goldberg and Robson 1983) - I would mention LOOPS (Bobrow and Stefik 1981), STROBE (Smith 1983; Lafue and Smith 1984), KEE (INTELLICORP 1984) and LOOKS (Mizoguchi **et al.** 1984).

The integrated approach doesn't have only advantages : its bottleneck occurs at the level of the construction of the fact database. Since this base requires a complex knowledge representation language (frames, semantic nets, etc.) its construction can be a long and delicate process ; a solely "interactive manual" approach to the problem is inconceivable for building large systems. Thus the first part of this paper describes a new direction of enquiry, recently opened within the framework of the RESEDA project, which aims at the automatic or semi-automatic construction of the fact database, starting from texts in natural language containing the information to be entered into the base : this research is still in the stage of the construction of a prototype. The second part of this paper describes some characteristics of the "Knowledge Processing Unit" (KPU) of a system which, on the other hand, is perfectly operational and which, at the moment, uses knowledge bases constructed interactively at the terminal. This is written in VSAPL and is implemented at the "Centre Inter-Régional de Calcul Electronique" (CIRCE) at Orsay, France.

II. THE AUTOMATIC CONSTRUCTION OF THE FACT DATABASE

In the rest of this section, I shall concentrate mainly on the construction of the more strictly "biographical data" part of the fact database.

II.1 The RESEDA metalanguage.

The biographical information which constitutes the system's database is organized in the form of units called "planes", which can be equated to "frames". There are several different types of planes, see Zarri (1984a); the "predicative planes", the most important, correspond to a "snapshot" illustrating a particular moment, an event, in the "life story" of one or more personages. A predicative plane is made up of one of five possible "predicates" (BE-AFFECTED-BY, BEHAVE, BE-PRESENT, MOVE, PRODUCE) ; one or more "modulators" may be attached to each predicate. The modulator's function is to specify and delimit the semantic role of the predicate. Each predicate is accompanied by "case slots" which introduce its arguments ; dating and space location is also given within a predicative plane, as is the bibliographic authority for the statement. The knowledge representation language ("metalanguage") we have chosen in the RESEDA project is basically, therefore, a kind of "case grammar", according to the particular meaning attached to the term in an AI context (Bruce 1975; Charniak 1981; etc.). Predicative planes can be linked together in a number of ways ; one way is to use explicit links ("labelled pointers") of "coordination", "alternativeness", "causality", "goal", etc. Besides the "predicative planes", which report a detailed event, and the "parenthetical planes", which collect the explicit links between events , a third type of plane, the "relational planes", is used to simply note the existence of a particular relationships between people.

The coding of information must be done on two distinct levels : an "external" coding, up until now performed manually by the analyst, gives rise to a first type of representation, formalized according to the categories of the RESEDA metalanguage; a second, automatic stage results in the "internal" numerical code.

For instance, the external "manual" coding of the data "Robert de Bonnay is appointed **bailli** of Mâcon by the King's council on 27th September 1413", results in the predicative plane shown in figure 1, see also section III.1. The **bailli** was an officer who dispensed justice, administered finances, etc., for a particular area, the **bailliage**, in the name of a king or lord.

```
114)    begin+soc+BE-AFFECTED-BY   SUBJ     Robert-de-Bonnay
                                   OBJ      bailli:Mâcon
                                   SOURCE   king's-council
                                   date1 :  27-september-1413
                                   date2 :
                                   bibl. :  Demurger1,234
```

figure 1

The code in capital letters indicates a predicate and its associated case slots. The predicative plane is characterized by a pair of "time references" (date1-date2) which give the duration of the episode in question. In the above plane, the second date slot (date2) is empty because the modulator ("begin") specifies a change of state associated with a punctual event. "Robert de Bonnay" is an historical personage known to the system ; "bailli", "king's-council" are terms of RESEDA's lexicon. The classifications associated with the terms of the lexicon provide the major part of the system's socio-historical knowledge of the period. "Mâcon" is the "location of the object" . If the historical sources analyzed gave us the exact causes of these events, we would introduce into the database the corresponding predicative planes and associate them with the above plane by an explicit link (parenthetical plane) of type "CAUSAL(ity)".

Among the intellectual contributions to the development of the metalanguage, it is reasonable to quote here Silvio Ceccato's correlational theory (Ceccato 1961) and, of course, the work of Schank (Schank 1973; 1975; Schank and Abelson 1977; etc.).

II.2 The method of automatic coding.

To describe our methodology, I shall use the simple example given in II.1 - for more complete examples, see Zarri (1983a). The initial text in natural language is first (pre)processed to obtain its constituent structure. For this purpose, we have used in a first approach the French surface grammar implemented in DEREDEC, a software package developed at the University of Quebec in Montreal by Pierre Plante (1980a; 1980b). This system, comparable to an ATN parser, permits a breakdown of the surface text into its syntactic constituents, and establishes, between these constituents, syntagmatic relationships of the type "topic-comment", "determination" and "coordination". This preliminary analysis provides a context for subsequent processing, without necessarily removing all the ambiguities.

The specific tools that we intend to develop for this aspect of the RESEDA project are of two types : a main control procedure , and a system of heuristic rules. For works which - whilst being much more ambitious than ours - present some similarities to the approach we have chosen, see DeJong (1979), Wilensky and Arens (1980), Dyer (1983).

II.21 **Main Control Strategy.** The first stage of the general procedure consists of marking the "triggers", defined as lexical units which call for one or more of the "predicative patterns" allowed for in RESEDA's metalanguage ; these patterns correspond to the "skeletons" of the different types of predicative planes. Thus we do not take into consideration every one of the lexical items met in the surface text, retaining only those directly pertaining to the "translation" to be done.

However, we do not limit ourselves to a simple keyword approach, since a number of operations utilizing data provided by the morpho-syntactic analysis executed by DEREDEC are necessary before the predicative patterns which will be actually used afterwards can be selected.

One of the results of the DEREDEC analysis is a kind of lemmatization enabling the reduction of surface forms in the text to a canonical form ; for example, infinitive in the case of verbs. The canonical forms found in the text under examination are compared with a list of potential triggers stored permanently in the system. In the case of the sentence given above : "He (Robert de Bonnay) is appointed **bailli** of Mâcon by the King's council on 27th September 1413", the following sub-list of triggers can be constructed : verbal form : "appoint" ; a term pertaining directly to the metalanguage : "bailli", which is a specification of the "generic" term "post" ("head" of a "sub-tree" in RESEDA's lexicon). The results of the pre-analysis executed by DEREDEC enable the elimination of potential patterns associated with the trigger "appoint" which would correspond to surface constructions of type "active", as in the example : "The Duke of Orleans appointed Robert de Bonnay **bailli** of Mâcon ...". The patterns which will actually be utilized afterwards are therefore those shown in figure 2. Note that in the case of a trigger "appoint (active form)" the personage who appears as surface object would have been found as the "SUBJECT" of "BE-AFFECTED-BY", whilst the surface subject would have been associated with the slot "SOURCE" of "BE-AFFECTED-BY".

```
appoint (passive form) = begin+(soc+)BE-AFFECTED-BY
                 SUBJ   <personage> - surface subject of the trigger
                 OBJ    <post> - surface complement
                 (SOURCE <personage>|<social body> - surface
                                     complement of the agent of the
                                     trigger)
                 date1 : obligatory
                 date2 : prohibited
                 bibl. : obligatory

bailli  =  (soc+)BE-AFFECTED-BY  SUBJ  <personage>
                                 OBJ   <post> - trigger
                                 (SOURCE <personage>|<social body>)
                                 date1 : obligatory
                                 date2 : prohibited
                                 bibl. : obligatory
```

figure 2

In reality, the predicative structures selected are not limited to those shown in figure 2. They are in fact repeated with predicative patterns of the type "BE-AFFECTED-BY" which have, as "SUBJECT", "social-body", and as "OBJECT", "personage" accompanied by the specification ("SPECIF") of a "post". These constructions each correspond to the description : "A personage receives a post in a certain organization (the organization in question, SUBJECT, is "augmented", BE-AFFECTED-BY, by the personage, OBJECT, in relation, SPECIF, to a given post)". A corresponding surface expression would be, for example, the following : "Robert de Bonnay (personage) is appointed secretary (post) of the papal court (social body)".

Therefore, for example, the pattern in figure 3 is also associated with the trigger "appoint (passive form)". But it will be eliminated at the end of the construction procedure, since, as it is not possible to obtain a surface realization of the concept "social-body" in the position "SUBJECT", it cannot provide a complete predicative structure.

```
appoint (passive form) = begin+(soc+)BE-AFFECTED-BY
                         SUBJ     <social-body>
                         OBJ      <personage>  - surface subject
                                   of the trigger, SPECIF <post>-
                                   surface complement
                         (SOURCE    <personage>|<social-body>)
                         date1 : obligatory
                         date2 : prohibited
                         bibl. : obligatory
```

figure 3

The last stage of the general procedure consists of examining the triggers belonging to the same morpho-syntactic environments, as defined by the results of the DEREDEC analysis. If there are several triggers pertaining to the same environment, and if the predicative patterns triggered are the same - which means that the predicates and case slots must be the same and that the modulators, dates and space location information must be compatible - then it can be said that the triggers refer to the same situation. As a result, the predicative patterns are merged as to obtain the most complete description possible; the predictions about filling the slots linked with the cases of the resulting patterns together govern to search for fillers in the surface expression.

Thus, the two triggers in figure 2, recognized as relevant to the same environment, are combined in the formula in figure 4, which gives the general framework of the plane given in figure 1.

```
begin+(soc+)BE-AFFECTED-BY  SUBJ <personage> - surface  subject of
                                           "is appointed"
                            OBJ    <post> - "bailli"
                            (SOURCE <personnage>|<social-body> -
                                           surface complement of the
                                           agent of "is appointed")
                            date1 : obligatory
                            date2 : prohibited
                            bibl. : obligatory
```

figure 4

The example we are considering illustrates a particularly simple case, in which it is not necessary to establish links between the planes to be created. If we had to process the sentence "Philibert de St Léger is nominated seneschal of Lyon on 30th July 1412, in lieu of the late A. de Viry", three planes should be generated : one for the nomination of Philibert de St Léger, one for the death of A. de Viry, and another (parenthetical plane) establishing a weak causality link ("CONFER", in our metalanguage) between the first two planes. Surface items such as conjunctions, prepositions and sentential adverbs can be used to infer links between planes : links of causality, goal, coordination, etc. More precisely, in the last example, "in lieu of" is a potential trigger according to the following rule : if the main noun group of the surface prepositional phrase contains a trigger, this phrase constitutes a plane environment and "CONFER" introduces the plane created.

II.22 **Heuristic Rules.** The process I have outlined so far requires a corpus of heuristic rules - associated with the predicative patterns of RESEDA' metalanguage - which will enable the slots in these patterns to be filled using the surface information in accordance with the predictions which characterize the slots. In the case of the pattern in figure 4, this filling-in poses no real problems, since the surface elements "Robert de Bonnay", "bailli", "King's council" and "27th September 1413" - standardized according to RESEDA's conventions, see figure 1 - will match the slots "SUBJECT", "OBJECT", "SOURCE" and "date1" directly. The filling-in operations are usually much more complicated and may require the use of complex inference rules, especially for solving the ambiguities caused by different types of anaphorical references (Grosz 1977; Webber 1978; etc.).

The strategy which we have adopted, at least for the time being, to solve the problem of anaphora is inspired from the work of Candace Sidner (1978; 1981). Her PAL system is a top-down anaphora resolution method which makes use of the notion of "focus" (likened to the theme of the discourse). By searching in the text for focuses which refer to a system of knowledge representation organized as a series of "frames", it is able to solve references. The relevance of this work to our study lies in the fact that the corpus of domain specific knowledge, that Sidner's approach pre-supposes, can be provided - represented, as we have seen, in a form very similar to a system of frames - by RESEDA itself used in its normal role as an intelligent information retrieval system. Thus, in our example, the nomination of Robert de Bonnay refers to the context of the "civil war at the beginning of the 15th century", which is a notion that already exists in the knowledge base of the "historical" RESEDA under a number of forms, see III.22 for example. It isn't possible here to say more about our interpretation of Sidner's ideas ; for further information, see Faribault **et al.** (1984).

III. QUERYING THE SYSTEM

RESEDA enables a number of "levels" of inference procedures, ranging from simple generalization operations using the tree structure of the lexicon, via inferences based on temporal data, to highly complex operations which involve restructuring the "search patterns" that one attempts to match against the fact database or the automatic generation of new logical links between events recorded in the base.

These different inference procedures have the following characteristics :

- They are all based on the same "kernel" of elementary functions from RESEDA's interpreter ; this kernel is the system's "match machine". Thus, the match machine forms the inner core of the Knowledge Processing Unit (KPU) of RESEDA.

- Only high level inferences require the recourse to real "inference engines" of the type encountered in MYCIN or PROLOG, which necessarily make use of the complex information in the rule base. The low level ("level zero") does not require access to data in this base and is provided by using the "match machine" alone.

III.1 **"Level zero" or RESEDA's inference procedures.**

The example in figure 5 should make it clear what we mean by "level zero inference". The question at the top of the figure - which we assume to have been asked by the user in a traditional "information retrieval" context - corresponds to the following natural language formulation : "Give me any information existing in the fact database concerning the posts that Robert de Bonnay may have had during 1414". The original question is thus reduced to a "search pattern", which is one of RESEDA's fundamental concepts : a "search pattern" carries the essential elements, expressed in terms of RESEDA's metalanguage, which it is necessary to search for in the fact database ; the aim is to deduce from this base all the planes which fit the pattern. A search pattern may originate from outside RESEDA, if it is a direct, system assisted, translation of a query posed by the user. On the other hand, it may be automatically generated from inside RESEDA, as will be clarified later, during the execution of a high-level inference procedure.

To recover information from the fact database, a search pattern, whether it originates internally or externally, calls upon the modules of the match machine in the KPU. The "match machine" is made up of three main modules ; all three have a search pattern as starting point :

- The "PLANE-SELECTOR" has no other input, and produces a first list of labels (addresses) of planes contained in the fact database (see the list of eight addresses indicated in figure 5).

- The "PARSER" receives as input the search pattern and a plane (the address of which is in the list produced by the plane selector). It compares the two to decide whether the plane matches the pattern or not. (In the case of figure 5, only planes 114 and 115 were retained by the module as truly corresponding to the entry pattern).

- The "VARIABLE-ASSIGNER" shares with the PARSER the inner core of the match machine routines ; it has been developed in relation to the needs of the high level inference procedures - and thus does not come into play at level zero.

The reason for using a preselection module ("PLANE-SELECTOR") working with the match module itself ("PARSER") is mainly linked to the fact that the syntactic structure of the planes is normally far more complex than it appears at a first glance when examining the very simple examples given in figure 5 (planes 114 and 115). Thus, it is an advantage to delay the match with the patterns until it is reasonably certain that a group of planes **a priori** relevant has been isolated (the eight "selected planes" in figure 5).

---

query (search pattern)

```
[1-january-1414,31-december-1414]
          BE-AFFECTED-BY   SUBJ    Robert-de-Bonnay
                           OBJ     post
```

answer

```
selected planes : 8
114 115 116 117 143 144 145 159

matched planes : 2
114 115

114) begin+soc+BE-AFFECTED-BY    SUBJ      Robert-de-Bonnay
                                 OBJ       bailli:Mâcon
                                 SOURCE    king's-council
                                 date1 :   27-september-1413
                                 date2 :
                                 bibl. :   Demurger1,234

115) begin+soc+BE-AFFECTED-BY    SUBJ      Robert-de-Bonnay
                                 OBJ       seneschal:Lyon
                                 SOURCE    king's-council
                                 date1 :   27-september-1413
                                 date2 :
                                 bibl. :   Demurger1,234
```

Do you wish to transform the pattern (.yes/.no)
.no

figure 5

The criteria used in establishing this first sub-group are, in order, the following :

- Select the planes built around the same predicate appearing in the search pattern.

- Select the planes where "personages" named in the search pattern appear.

- Select the planes where there is a correspondence between the temporal information encoded in the "search interval" of the pattern and the dates indicated in the planes. The search interval - see the information between square brackets associated with the pattern in figure 5 - is employed to limit the search to the slice of time which it is considered appropriate to explore in the fact database.

The search for a correspondence between search interval and dates is particularly complex, see Zarri (1983b : 100-106). There is no question of going into more detail here, and we must limit ourselves to a few remarks concerning the results of figure 5. The answer to the question asked, which concerned the posts held by Robert de Bonnay in 1414, is provided in the form "On the 27th of September 1413 (i.e. the year before), Robert de Bonnay was appointed (**begin**+BE-AFFECTED-BY) **bailli** of Mâcon and seneschal of Lyon" ; in the absence of any information to the contrary explicitly included in the base, the preselection algorithms were able to infer, despite the fact that the dates in the plane and the search interval do not coincide, that it is **possible** that in 1414 Robert de Bonnay still occupied those posts. These simple temporal data level inferences are amongst the most interesting of RESEDA's level zero inference system.

The kind of match performed by the PARSER has certain characteristics which differentiate it from a normal unification even if the basic mechanism is, as in PROLOG (Colmerauer 1983), a comparison of labelled trees. I will here point out only that any element which can be used in a well-formed expression in RESEDA's metalanguage is a "tagged" element : in its internal representation, seven bits are reserved to specify the "type", that is the category of the metalanguage to which it belongs (temporal information, location, predicates, modulators, cases, classes and sub-classes of the lexicon, variables, etc.). The advantages are obvious from the point of view of the simplification of coherence checks and, in particular, of being able to build a fast data type checking mechanism to speed up the match process.

III.2 **Informal introduction to the high level inference procedures**.

III.21 **Transformations**. Let us suppose that, when asking the system the question that corresponds to the search pattern in figure 5, we obtain no answer ; or that having recovered planes 114 and 115, we would like to know more. It is then possible (by answering "yes" to RESEDA's question) to allow the system to automatically "transform" the initial search pattern by substituting it with another "semantically equivalent" pattern, if such a thing exists, and then executing the corresponding program. "Semantically equivalent" means that the information eventually obtained with the new pattern should "imply" the information that we did obtain or would have obtained with the original pattern.

To keep to an extremely simple example, consider the transformation of figure 6, allowing us to change a search pattern formulated in terms of "end+BE-PRESENT" into a new one in terms of "MOVE", which can be submitted, in turn, to the usual preselection and match procedures. This formal rule translates the common sense rule "If someone goes from one place to another, he has certainly left his starting point" : the justification of the use of substitution in figure 6 lies in the fact that any information about some personage **x** having moved from **k** to **l** is at the same time a response to any query about the possibility of his no longer being at place **k**. Note that, in the terms of RESEDA's metalanguage, the movements of a personage are always expressed in the form of a subject **x** which moves itself as an object.

On a conceptual level, it is worthwhile noting that the explicit "variables" which appear in the original search pattern (**x** and **k** in figure 6) must appear in the transformed pattern and/or in the "restrictions" associated with the new variables (**l** in figure 6) introduced at the level of this transformed pattern, see rule t1. This ensures the logical coherence between the two parts of the transformation; as we said, the pattern on the right hand side must indeed "imply" the one on the left. The values which replace the variables in the retrieved plane (or planes) using the transformed pattern must obviously respect the restrictions associated with all the explicit variables which appear in the transformation.

For more examples of transformations, see Zarri (1981 ; 1984a).

```
t1) end+BE-PRESENT  SUBJ x : k ——▶ MOVE  SUBJ x : k
                                          OBJ  x : l
x = <personage>
k,l = <location>
k ≠ l
```

figure 6

III.22 **Hypotheses**. A second category of inference rules makes it possible to search for the hidden "causes", in the widest sense of the word, of an attested fact in the database. For example, after retrieving planes 114 and 115 in response to the question in figure 5, and if we assume that the "reasons" for the nominations are not explicitly recorded in the fact database, the user will now be able to ask the system to automatically produce a **plausible** explanation of these facts by using a second category of inference rules, the "hypotheses".

In order to give an idea, on an intuitive level, of the functioning of the hypotheses, figure 7 shows the formulation in natural language of two characteristic hypotheses of the RESEDA system. The first part of each of these rules corresponds to a particular class of confirmed facts (planes) for which one asks the "causes". For example, the planes in figure 5 are clearly an exemplification of the first part of the second hypothesis in figure 7. In RESEDA's terminology, the formal drafting of this first part is called a "premise". The second part (the "condition") gives instructions for searching the database for information which would be able to justify the fact which has been matched with the premise. That is, if planes matching the particular search patterns which can be obtained from the "condition" part of the hypothesis can be found in the database, it is considered that the facts represented by these planes **could** constitute the justification for the plane-premise and are then returned as the response to the user's query.

h1) ... one might take a particular attitude in an argument

BECAUSE

one has close links with one of the parties in a conflicting situation

h2) ... one might be chosen for a (official) post

BECAUSE

one is attached to a very important personage who has just taken power

figure 7

Let us now look in some detail at the hypothesis h2 in figure 7. A whole family of inference rules expressed in RESEDA's metalanguage corresponds in reality to the natural language formulation given in h2 ; one of these realizations is shown in figure 8. A description of the procedure followed to isolate the elements of these families can be found in Zarri (1981).

The meaning, in clear, of the formalism in figure 8 is as follows (see also h2 in figure 7). To explain what brought the administration n to give post m to x, the hypothesis suggests we check in the system's database for the following two facts, which must be verified simultaneously (operator "Λ", "and") :

A) At a date that is previous, but sufficiently close to the date of nomination d1, the administration n comes under the leadership of y (n starts to have y for chief (lid = leader)). The information associated with b1 and b2 allow the system to automatically construct the two limits (bound1, bound2) of the search interval, using the date of nomination d1 which is retrieved by the premise from the plane that is being explained. These limits will be associated with the search pattern to be extracted from condition schema A.

B) x was permanently employed by an important person y (the seigniorial administration p specific to y was "augmented" by x) during a sufficiently long period around the date of nomination.

Note also, in the formulation of the premise α , the introduction of a modulator variable "a" to explicitly exclude from the planes which will be explained by the hypothesis all those planes which involve the take-over of some organization (a = lid), or which relate an aborted nomination (a = neg).

```
premise : α

α) begin+soc+a+BE-AFFECTED-BY    SUBJ     x
                                 OBJ      m
                                 SOURCE   n
                                 date1 :  d1
                                 date2 :

restrictions on the variables of the premise schemata :

   a ≠ neg,lid
   x = <personage>
   m = <monarchic-post>|<seigniorial-post>
   n = king's-council | lord's-council
if m = <monarchic-post> then n = king's-council
if m = <seigniorial-post> then n = lord's-council

condition : A Λ B

A) begin+lid+BE-AFFECTED-BY     SUBJ       n
                                OBJ        y
                                bound1 :   b1
                                bound2 :   b2

B) BE-AFFECTED-BY     SUBJ       p (SPECIF y)
                      OBJ        x (SPECIF r)
                      bound1 :   b3
                      bound2 :   b4

restrictions on the variables of the condition schemata :

   y = <personage>
   x ≠ y
   p = <seigniorial-organization>
   r = <permanent-post>

information for creating a search interval :

   b1 = d1 - 1 month
   b2 = d1
   b3 = d1 - 2 years
   b4 = d1
```

figure 8

Figure 9 shows natural language redaction of planes (150 and 145) obtained by means of the formal rule of figure 8 in the case of a query about the possible causes of the events related in planes 114 or 115 (Robert de Bonnay's nomination). The two planes are thus obtained using the search patterns automatically derived from the two condition schemata A and B which constitute the condition part of this formal structure.

150) "On the 1st september 1413, the leaders (Louis d'Anjou, Jean de Bourbon, Jean de Berry, Charles d'Orléans, etc.) of the faction favourable to the Duc d'Orléans took control of the administration of the state"

145) "Robert de Bonnay held the post of chamberlain to the Duc d'Orléans from 8 april 1409 until 1415"

figure 9

Let me finish by emphasizing that the system does not restrict itself to displaying at the terminal the planes recovered from the fact database, but also explicitly displays to the user the new "causality" relationships found in the form of a parenthetical plane; this second type of high-level inferences, the hypotheses, provides the system with an, albeit elementary, **learning capability**.

III.3 The computational structure of RESEDA's inference engine.

The high level inferences introduced in III.2 are executed by an inference engine. The behaviour of this engine is defined by two machines in RESEDA's interpreter, the "transformation" and the "hypothesis" machines, which are part of the Knowledge Processing Unit and which make use of the match machine. They can function independently, or in an integrated fashion, with the transformation machine being called in the context of the hypothesis machine. This means that - whenever all the possibilities of matching associated with a search pattern extracted from the condition schema "i" of a hypothesis have been exploited - the pattern can still be used by transforming it before "backtracking" to level **i-1**, thus retrieving new values for the variables which permit the "forward" processing of the hypothesis to continue.

The "hypothesis machine" consists of two main modules :

- an "H-SELECTION" module which, from a plane P existing in the base, provides a list of addresses of hypotheses liable to explain P ;

- an "H-EXECUTION" module which, given a plane P and the address of an hypothesis H, displays all the planes offered by H as an explanation of P.

The execution module in turn consists of three sub-modules : a premise schema is processed by a sub-module EXECPREM ; a condition schema is processed by a sub-module EXECCOND ; EXECPREM and EXECCOND ensure the "forward traversal" in the "choice tree" ; the "backtracking" is ensured, on the other hand, by the sole sub-module REEXEC.

In the same way, the "transformation machine" consists of two main modules, a "T-SELECTION" module which, from a search pattern R, provides a list of addresses of transformations liable to operate on R, and a "T-EXECUTION" module which, from a search pattern R and a transformation T, provides the pattern transformed from R by T.

This way of structuring the two machines is linked to the particular way in which a high-level inference rule is executed and which includes two distinct steps :

- a "bottom-up" phase which involves going from a **particular** expression compatible with RESEDA's metalanguage (a plane which is to be explained in the case of a hypothesis or a pattern for which a substitute must be found in the case of a transformation) and selecting in the **rule base** one or more "rule heads" (premises or left hand sides of a transformation) which define a **general** class encompassing the expression in question : this is the **selection phase** ;

- a "top-down" phase, corresponding to the top-down functioning of PROLOG interpreters (Kowalski 1982 ; Colmerauer 1983), during which the program that corresponds to the rule or rules selected is executed generating **particular** search patterns with which to explore the fact database (**execution phase**). Note that, in the long run, the execution phase of RESEDA's high level inference rules has identical characteristics whether in an "hypothesis" or "transformation" framework : only at the end of execution will the planes retrieved be interpreted as events explaining a certain fact (hypotheses) or as an indirect response to a question put to the system (transformations). This explains how the same blocks in the interpreter can be used in contexts which seem **a priori** quite different.

Let us take a look now at some technical details of the execution modules, limiting ourselves to a "hypothesis" context; for more on this, see Zarri (1984b).

The search for solutions within the fact database by means of high-level inference rules of the "hypothesis" type amounts to the exploration of a "choice tree" ; this exploration is carried out by the sub-modules EXECPREM, EXECCOND and REEXEC. EXECCOND is called each time there exist conditions favourable for advancing in the hypothesis, in other words, for being able to process a new condition schema ; its function is to find - using the PLANE-SELECTOR and VARIABLE-ASSIGNER modules of the match machine - a series of values which could be "acceptable" bindings for the variables introduced by the schema in question. "Acceptable" means that these bindings were retrieved from planes in the base which were syntactically comparable with the search patterns extracted from the condition schema, and that they satisfy the constraints associated with the variables. EXECPREM processes the premise schema with the same aims as EXECCOND, but is called in a situation where no bindings for the variables of the hypotheses exist so far ; to reach their goals, EXECCOND and EXECPREM must carry out a fairly complex sequence of operations (instantiating the variables of the schema being processed with the values which may already have been retrieved from previous schemata, constructing search patterns, determining the combinations of binding variables, etc.). EXECPREM and EXECCOND perform the forward traversal of the choice tree ; if the attempt to find a combination of values valid for the variables of a new condition schema fails, or if it succeeds, and the condition schema examined was the last one in the hypothesis, then the inference engine is forced to backtrack. This is done by the REEXEC sub-module, which backs up to the level of the schema **Si-1** preceeding the one, **Si**, were the dead-end was found ; an attempt by REEXEC to reach a level higher than the premise indicates that the traversal of the choice tree is finished. REEXEC would not function correctly if, at every level "i" encountered during a hypothesis, the "environment" of the process was not stored ; the information which defines the environment is contained in a "Hypothesis Structure".

It should be obvious from the above that, in the execution modules of RESEDA's inference engine, the forward traversing of the choice tree is of the depth-first type : the backtracking, at least in the present prototype, is systematic however. In other words, REEXEC is called even if the exploration of a branch of the tree is terminated and an acceptable solution is found. This method enables us to have a full panorama of the successes and failures associated with the different branches of the choice tree ; obviously, this can be computationally expensive, see, for example, the criticisms of Charniak **et al.** (1980 : 140-161).

In PROLOG, expensive tree searches can be controlled either at the meta-level, or by using the "cut" operator. In RESEDA, we are able to maintain full backtracking and gain efficiency thanks to the following characteristics of its architecture :

- the use of the PLANE-SELECTOR module of the match machine within the inference engine, which allows inferencing to be carried out on a much-reduced sub-set of the fact database ;

- the notion of "type" mentioned in III.1, which speeds up considerably the match operations themselves (VARIABLE-ASSIGNER module).

This obviously does not mean that we refuse to consider the possibility of adding to RESEDA the option of superposing, when necessary, a "best first" approach onto the basic "depth first" mechanism. Studies are being carried out at the moment which may lead to the introduction in RESEDA of an "intelligent" control option of the kind described in Gallaire and Lasserre (1979) or Pereira and Porto (1983).

IV. CONCLUSION

The aims of this article were :

- to provide a glimpse into the possibilities of "intelligent" searching within a "fact database" which are easily obtained by coding the base using the same advanced knowledge representation language which is needed to represent the inference procedures of the "rule base" (section III, III.1 and III.2) ;

- to show that the building of inference engines which are capable of operating on a "knowledge base" (fact database + rule base) constructed according to this "integrated approach" is fairly easy and comes down to the use of techniques well known in the field of "Knowledge Engineering" (section III, III.3) ;

- to describe, briefly, a possible methodology for enabling, at least partly, the automatic generation of the fact database, thus avoiding the inconvenience of constructing this base "manually" (section II).

The RESEDA project may provide a not unreasonable approach to the problem of the construction and use of large knowledge bases.

ACKNOWLEDGMENTS

The work described in this paper was accomplished while the author was at the Centre National de la Recherche Scientifique in Paris, France. The preliminary study concerning the automatic or semi-automatic construction of the fact database was jointly financed by the "Agence De l'Informatique - A.D.I." (CNRS-ADI contract n° 507568) and the "Centre National de la Recherche Scientifique - C.N.R.S." (ATP n° 955045). The construction of the RESEDA's Knowledge Processing Unit has been achieved thanks to grants from the "Délégation Générale à la Recherche Scientifique et Technique - D.G.R.S.T." (CNRS-DGRST contract n° 75.7.0456) and the "Institut de Recherche d'Informatique et d'Automatique - I.R.I.A." (CNRS-IRIA contract n° 78.206).

REFERENCES

BOBROW, D.G., and STEFIK, M. (1981) The LOOPS Manual (Tech. Rep. KB-VLSI-81-13). Palo Alto: Xerox Palo Alto Research Center.

BOBROW, D.G., and WINOGRAD, T. (1977) "An Overview of KRL, a Knowledge Representation Language", Cognitive Science, I, 3-46.

BRUCE, B. (1975) "Case Systems for Natural Language", Artificial Intelligence, VI, 327-360.

CECCATO, S., ed. (1961) Linguistics Analysis and Programming for Mechanical Translation. New York: Gordon and Breach.

CHARNIAK, E. (1981) "The Case-Slot Identity Theory", Cognitive Science, V, 285-292.

CHARNIAK, E., RIESBECK, C.K., and McDERMOTT, D. (1980) Artificial Intelligence Programming. Hillsdale: Lawrence Erlbaum Associates.

COLMERAUER, A. (1983) "PROLOG in 10 Figures", in Proceedings of the 8th International Joint Conference on Artificial Intelligence - IJCAI/83. Los Altos: William Kaufmann.

DeJONG, G. (1979) "Prediction and Substantiation: A New Approach to Natural Language Processing", Cognitive Science, III, 251-273.

DYER, M.G. (1983) In-Depth Understanding - A Computer Model of Integrated Processing for Narrative Comprehension. Cambridge (Mass.): The MIT Press.

FARIBAULT, Marthe, LEON, Jacqueline, MEISSONNIER, V., MEMMI, D., and ZARRI, G.P. (1984) "From Natural Language to a Canonical Representation of the Corresponding Semantic Relationships", in Cybernetics and Systems Research II, Trappl, R., ed. Amsterdam: North-Holland.

FEIGENBAUM, E.A. (1977) "The Art of Artificial Intelligence : Themes and Case Studies of Knowledge Engineering", in Proceedings of the 5th International Joint Conference on Artificial Intelligence - IJCAI/77. Los Altos: William Kaufmann.

GALLAIRE, H., and LASSERRE, Claudine (1979) "Controlling Knowledge Deduction in a Declarative Approach", in Proceedings of the 6th International Joint Conference on Artificial Intelligence - IJCAI/79. Los Altos: William Kaufmann.

GOLDBERG, Adele, and ROBSON, D. (1983) SMALLTALK-80: The Language and its Implementation. Reading (Mass.): Addison-Wesley.

GROSZ, Barbara J. (1977) "The Representation and Use of Focus in a System for Understanding Dialogs", in Proceedings of the 5th International Joint Conference on Artificial Intelligence - IJCAI/77. Los Altos: William Kaufmann.

INTELLICORP (1984) KEE Software Development System - User's Manual (Fifth Edition). Menlo Park: Intellicorp.

KELLOG, C. (1982) "Knowledge Management ; A Practical Amalgam of Knowledge and Data Base Techniques", in Proceedings of the 1982 National Conference on Artificial Intelligence - AAAI/82. Los Altos: William Kaufmann.

KOWALSKI, R. (1982) "Logic as a Computer Language", in Logic Programming, Clark, K.L., and Tärnlund, S.A., eds. New York: Academic Press.

LAFUE, G.M.E., and SMITH, R.G. (1984) "Implementation of a Semantic Integrity Manager with a Knowledge Representation System", in Proceedings of the First International Workshop on Expert Database Systems, Kerschberg, L., ed. Columbia (S.C.): University of South Carolina College of Business Administration.

MIZOGUCHI, F., OHWADA, H., and KATAYAMA, Y. (1984) "LOOKS: Knowledge Representation System for Designing Expert Systems in a Logic Programming Framework", in Proceedings of the International Conference on Fifth Generation Computer Systems 1984. Tokyo: Institute for New Generation Technology.

PEREIRA, L.M., and PORTO, A. (1982) "Selective Backtracking", in Logic Programming, Clark, K.L., and Tärnlund, S.A., eds. New York: Academic Press.

PLANTE, P. (1980a) DEREDEC - Logiciel pour le traitement linguistique et l'analyse de contenu des textes (Manuel de l'usager). Montréal: Université du Québec à Montréal.

PLANTE, P. (1980b) Une grammaire DEREDEC des structures de surface du Français, appliquée à l'analyse de contenu des textes. Montréal: Université du Québec à Montréal.

SCHANK, R.C. (1973) "Identification of Conceptualizations Underlying Natural Language", in Computer Models of Thought and Language, Schank, R.C., and Colby, K.M., eds. San Francisco: Freeman.

SCHANK, R.C., ed. (1975) Conceptual Information Processing. Amsterdam: North-Holland.

SCHANK, R.C., and ABELSON, R. (1977) Scripts, Plans, Goals and Understanding. Hillsdale: Lawrence Erlbaum Associates.

SIDNER, Candace L. (1979) Towards a Computational Theory of Definite Anaphora Comprehension in English Discourse (Ph.D. thesis). Cambridge: MIT Artificial Intelligence Laboratory.

SIDNER, Candace L. (1981) "Focusing for Interpretation of Pronouns", American Journal of Computational Linguistics, VII, 217-231.

SMITH, R.G. (1983) "STROBE : Support for Structured Object Knowledge Representation", in Proceedings of the 8th International Joint Conference on Artificial Intelligence - IJCAI/83. Los Altos: William Kaufmann.

STONEBRAKER, M. (1984) "Adding Semantic Knowledge to a Relational Database", in On Conceptual Modelling - Perspectives from Artificial Intelligence, Databases and Programming Languages, Brodie, M.L., et al., eds. New York: Springer-Verlag.

TSUR, S., and ZANIOLO, C. (1984) "An Implementation of GEM - Supporting a Semantic Data Model on a Relational Back-end", in SIGMOG '84 - Proceedings of Annual Meeting, Yormark, Beatrice, ed. ACM Sigmod Record, XIV, n° 2.

WEBBER, Bonnie L. (1978) A Formal Approach to Discourse Anaphora (Report n° 3761). Cambridge (Mass.): Bolt, Beranek and Newman.

WILENSKY, R., and ARENS, Y. (1980) PHRAN: A Knowledge Approach to Natural Language Analysis (Memo VCB/ERL M80/4). Berkeley: Electronics Research Laboratory.

ZARRI, G.P. (1981) "Building the Inference Component of an Historical Information Retrieval System", in Proceedings of the 7th International Joint Conference on Artificial Intelligence - IJCAI/81. Los Altos: William Kaufmann.

ZARRI, G.P. (1983a) "Automatic Representation of the Semantic Relationships Corresponding to a French Surface Expression", in Proceedings of the Conference on Applied Natural Language Processing. Menlo Park: Association for Computational Linguistics.

ZARRI, G.P. (1983b) "An Outline of the Representation and Use of Temporal Data in the RESEDA System", Information Technology : Research and Development, II, 89-108.

ZARRI, G.P. (1984a) "Expert Systems and Information Retrieval : An Experiment in the Domain of Biographical Data Management", International Journal of Man-Machine Studies - Special Issue on Developments in Expert Systems, XX, 87-106.

ZARRI, G.P. (1984b) "Intelligent Information Retrieval: An Interesting Application Area for the New Generation Computer Systems", in **Proceedings of the International Conference on Fifth Generation Computer Systems 1984**. Tokyo: Institute for New Generation Technology.

Experiences with SRL: An Analysis of a Frame-based Knowledge Representation

Mark S. Fox
*J. Mark Wright**
David Adam

Intelligent Systems Laboratory
Robotics Institute
Carnegie-Mellon University
Pittsburgh, Pennsylvania 15213

1. Introduction

During the latter half of the 70's the field of AI experienced a proliferation of semantic network and frame-based knowledge representation languages: Concepts (Lenat, 1976), FRL (Roberts & Goldstein, 1977), KLONE (Brachman, 1977), NETL (Fahlman, 1977), Scripts (Schank & Abelson, 1977), Units (Stefik, 1979), and SRL (Fox, 1979). With the advent of AI techniques as marketable products, we are beginning to see a similar surge of vendor supported knowledge representation languages in the market place: KEE (Intelligenetics, 1984), LOOPS (Bobrow & Stefik, 1983), and ART (Williams, 1983).

One would think that before an idea is "productized" a clear understanding of it and its use would have emerged. Yet the majority of the applications of knowledge representation languages have been experimental, and have yet to move into production use. A survey of systems in field test or production use are either rule-based, e.g., R1 (McDermott, 1980), ACE (Stolfo, 1982), XSEL (McDermott, 1983), and CATS-1 (GE, 1983), or utilize an ad hoc representation. In the case of knowledge representation languages, though the size of the intersection of frame-based languages has grown larger, no clear subset has yet to emerge; and the field continues to evolve as new ideas are explored, e.g., RLL-1 (Greiner, 1980), and MRS (Genesereth, 1980).

The goal of this paper is to examine a single representation language, SRL, and its applications to determine utility of its ideas. Post mortems have been performed before (Bobrow et al., 1977), but have the appearance of a massive "weeding" due to the plethora of ideas included in the initial version of the language. What distinguishes SRL is its *evolution* from a research engine to a "production level" language. Its evolution has been hastened by its application to "real" problems, and its transition to industrial use.

In the rest of this paper, the SRL system and its applications are described, followed by a description of our experiences and what may be concluded from them.

2. What is SRL

2.1. Language Overview

SRL is a frame-based language with the "schema" as its primitive. A schema is a symbolic representation of a concept. Its definition is the summation of its slots and values. Slots are used to represent attributive, structural and relational information about

* Current address: Inference Corp., Los Angeles CA.

† This research was sponsored in part by Digital Equipment Corp., and the CMU Robotics Institute.

a concept. A schema is composed of a schema name (printed in the bold font), a set of slots (printed in small caps) and the slot's values (lisp printing conventions are observed). Values can be any lisp expression and reference schemata when they are strings. When printed, a schema is always enclosed by double braces with the schema name appearing at the top. The **hl-spec** schema (figure 2-1) contains six slots, each of which contains a value.

{{ **hl-spec**
IS-A: "engineering-activity"
SUB-ACTIVITY-OF: "develop-board-hl"
INITIAL-ACTIVITY-OF: "develop-board-hl"
ENABLED-BY: "TRUE"
CAUSE: "hl-spec-complete"
DESCRIPTION: "Develop specifications for the cpu board" }}

Figure 2-1: hl-spec Schema

Many of the ideas found in other representation systems have been incorporated into SRL. These include meta-information, demons, restrictions on legal slot value and a context facility.

Meta-information may be associated with schemata, their slots, and values in the slots. It is represented by another schema, called a meta-schema, that is attached to the schema, slot, or value. Representing meta-information as schemata provides a uniform approach to representation. The user is provided with access functions for retrieving meta-schemata. Once retrieved, they are manipulated just as any other schema. The meta-information is printed in italics beneath schema, slot or value to which it is attached.

{{ **hl-spec**
Creator: "mark fox"
To-Create:: schemac

IS-A: "engineering-activity"
SUB-ACTIVITY-OF: "develop-board-hl"
range: (type "instance" "activity")
INITIAL-ACTIVITY-OF: "develop-board-hl"
ENABLED-BY: "TRUE"
CAUSE: "hl-spec-complete"
DESCRIPTION: "Develop specifications for the cpu board" }}

Figure 2-2: hl-spec Schema

Any slot may have *facets* associated with it. Four facets are defined in SRL: DEMON, DOMAIN, RANGE, and CARDINALITY. The DEMON facet allows lisp procedures to be associated with a slot. The execution of demons is keyed to particular SRL access functions, such as filling or retrieving the value of a slot. RANGE and DOMAIN facets are used to restrict the values that may fill a slot and the schemata in which a slot may be placed, respectively. The CARDINALITY is used to restrict the number of values that a slot may contain. Values for each facet may be inherited from slots in other schemata.

As in other representation languages, a standard set of relations are provided to the user to form taxonomic and part hierarchies. Slots and values may be inherited automatically between schemata along these relations. One of the novel representational ideas introduced by SRL is *user-defined inheritance relations* (Fox, 1979). In most other knowledge representation systems, several relations for inheriting slots and values are defined as part of the representation (eg. AKO, is-a, virtual-copy). In contrast, SRL offers a facility by which users can define their own inheritance relations, allowing only slots and values of the user's choice to be inherited. In addition, slot structures can be elaborated between schemata, and slots and their values mapped arbitrarily between schemata, as need demands. Inheritance relations are represented by additional slots in a schema. A *dependency mechanism* is integrated into the inheritance facility that notes as meta-information the source of inherited slots and values. Here again, the user can define the dependency relations that are put into place.

Another novel feature provided by SRL is a means of *controlling the search* performed by the inheritance process. Any query of the model may optionally use a *path* to restrict which relations may be traversed while searching for a suitable value to inherit. Paths may also be used to specify the *transitivity* properties of relations. For example, a **PART-OF** hierarchy for describing a car might represent the **battery** as **PART-OF** the **electrical system**, and the **electrical system** is **PART-OF** the **car**. The implicit notion that the **battery** is **PART-OF** the **car** (ie., that **PART-OF** is transitive with itself) is represented using paths.

Contexts in SRL act as virtual copies of databases in which schemata are stored. In the copy, schemata can be created, modified and destroyed without altering the original context. Contexts are structured as trees where each context may inherit the schemata present in its parent context. Hence, only schemata that are used in a context need be explicitly represented there. This avoids copying schemata that will never be used in the context. The context provides for version management and alternate worlds reasoning with SRL models.

Error handling is also schema based. An instance of the **error** schema is created to describe each error encountered by the system. **error-spec** schemata may be defined that specify how to recover from each kind of error.

In order to support large applications, a database system is integrated into SRL. Schemata are stored in a database until they are accessed, at which time they are brought into lisp. A *cache* of the most recently accessed schemata are kept in lisp for quick access. When the cache becomes too large, schemata are swapped back to the database using recency algorithm.

2.2. Extensions to the Language

SRL serves as the core of a knowledge engineering environment called Islisp (ISL, 1984). It offers a number of inference tools that operate on schemata: HSRL, PSRL, OSRL, ESRL, and KBS. HSRL (Allen & Wright, 83) takes HCPRVR, (Chester, 80) a *logic program interpreter*, and alters it to use SRL models as its axioms. The system combines the modus ponens inference of logic programming systems with the representation power of SRL. In addition, the inheritance mechanism provides default reasoning, not available in logic programming environments.

Similarly, PSRL is a *production rule interpreter* that operates on SRL models (Rychener et al., 1984). Production rules and their parts are represented by schemata. A subset of PSRL provides the form and execution pattern of OPS5 rules (Forgy, 81). OSRL provides a schema-based object programming facility similar to Flavors (Weinreb & Moon, 1981). ESRL (ISL, 1984) provides an event mechanism which enables the user to schedule events to occur either in a simulated or normal operating mode. KBS, a knowledge-based simulation system (Reddy & Fox, 1982) uses ESRL to perform discrete simulations of systems modeled in SRL. Simulation objects are represented as schemata. An object's associated events and behaviors are represented as slots and values in the schema. An object's event behavior may be inherited along relations which link it to other schemata.

In addition to inference tools, system building tools are provided. RETINAS (Greenberg, 1983) is a schema based *window system*. Schemata for windows, displays, and canvases are instantiated to build an interface. Default specifications for windows, etc., may be inherited from the prototype schemata. KBCI (ISL, 1984) is a schema based *command system*. Again, the **command** schema is instantiated to create commands. A command interface is defined by a collection of command schemata organized in a **SUB-COMMAND-OF** hierarchy. CPAK (ISL, 1984) is a 2D graphics package based on the CORE definition. A business graphics facility is provided on top of CPAK.

2.3. Applications

Each of the following applications are supported by one or more corporations with the goal of transferring the technology for internal use. Each system uses SRL as its modeling language and makes extensive use of the RETINAS, KBCI, and graphics package for user interfacing.

- **Callisto**: A project management system which focuses on the semantic representation of activities and product configurations (Fox, Sathi, & Greenberg, 1984). Callisto makes extensive use of the SRL's meta-information, search specifications, user-defined relations, and context. In addition, it uses PSRL for representing managerial project management heuristics, and ESRL for project scheduling. Portions of Callisto are in field test.
- **INET** tm: A corporate distribution analysis system which models and simulates a corporation's manufacturing, distribution, and sales organization (Reddy & Fox, 1983). INET uses SRL's meta-information and context mechanism. OSRL is the simulation vehicle, and PSRL is used to represent post-analysis heuristics. INET is now being transferred to the sponsor.
- **ISIS**: A production management system which models, schedules, and monitors activities (Fox, 1983; Fox & Smith, 1984). ISIS utilizes all of SRL's facilities, with the majority of the search algorithm implemented in lisp. ISIS is now being transferred to the sponsor.
- **PDS**: A rule-based architecture for the sensor-based diagnosis of physical processes (Fox et al., 1983). PDS utilizes the basic schema representation only. PDS is in production use.
- **Rome**: A quantitative reasoning system for long range planning (Kosy et al., 1983; Kosy & Wise, 1984). Rome utilizes SRL's meta-information, context mechanism, and user-defined relations. HSRL is a primary inference mechanism.

What are some of the characteristics of the applications to which SRL has been applied?

- **Size**: The number of schemata in a system are large enough to exceed their practical storage directly in memory.
- **Complexity**: The complexity of decision making required by an application requires the incorporation of many of the types of semantic primitives that have evolved in the field, including time, causality, states, actions, etc., and corresponding inference techniques.
- **Efficiency**: The efficiency of the language is important. Response must be provided in a reasonable amount of time, whether for realtime control or interactive support.

3. Experiences

This section discusses the experiences we have had building knowledge based systems in SRL. Our results have been mixed. Some facilities have proven surprising useful, while others remain almost entirely unused. The discussion is organized by facility.

3.1. User-Defined Relations

Definition. User defined relations allow the user to tailor the inheritance definition of their relations to the needs of their application. Each relation is represented by a schema. The inheritance semantics of a relation are specified using inheritance specs. There are five kinds of inheritance specs that allow the user to finely tailor the inheritance of their relations.

inclusion — Specifies slots and values that should be inherited unchanged.

exclusion — Specifies slots and values that are specifically excluded.

elaboration — Specifies a one to many mapping of slots. Values may not be inherited along an elaboration.

map — Specifies one to one mappings of slots and values

introduction — Specifies slots and values that are introduced when the relation is created.

Relations may also specify their inverse, which is used to perform automatic inverse linking.

The **previous-activity** relation embodies some of this functionality.

```
{{ previous-activity
   IS-A: "relation"
   DOMAIN: (type "is-a" "activity")
   RANGE: (type "is-a" "activity")
   MAP: "previous-activity-map"
   INCLUSION: "previous-activity-inclusion"
   INVERSE: "next-activity"
   TRANSITIVITY: (repeat (step "previous-activity" all) 1 inf)  }}

{{ previous-activity-map
   comment: "the finish-time slot in the range schema of the relation is
      mapped onto the start-time slot of the domain schema.
      Hence, the finish time of the preceding activity
      becomes the start time of the following activity."
   IS-A: "map-spec"
   DOMAIN: "start-time"
   RANGE: "finish-time"  }}

{{ previous-activity-inclusion
   IS-A: "inclusion-spec"
   SLOT: "sub-activity-of"
   comment: "the slot which may be inherited from the range
         of the relation to the domain"
   VALUE: all   }}
```

The **previous-activity** relation allows two kinds of inheritance. First, it maps the previous activity's finish time to the next-activity's start time. Second, it allows the inheritance of the SUB-ACTIVITY-OF slot and its values along the relation.

Reflections. User defined relations have proven to be one of the most extensively used features of SRL. They have been exploited by most of the applications yet built using the language. We have several theories as to their usefulness. First, their use has enabled more inference to take place automatically in the systems. In many applications, relations peculiar to a domain (e.g., next-activity, child-of, etc.) will be used often. Inheritance along these relations could not be supported by other languages since only a few relations (e.g., is-a, instance, part-of) would be provided. To overcome this deficiency, the user would have to provide code in their inference engine to deduce what information could have been inherited. But in SRL, the user may define their own relations and their inheritance semantics, and use them where needed.

Second, they allow the terminology of the models to resemble more closely that of the model builder. Separate relations might be constructed for SUB-CLASS, IS-A and KIND-OF which have the same inheritance properties to make models more understandable.

A third point is perspicuity. A relation incapsulates all the information required to use it, including restrictions on its domain and range of use, its inheritance semantics, and its transitivity. Even local overrides to its general definition are defined in the schema (e.g., a platypus is-a mammal but does not lay eggs).

Making the user defined relations work with reasonable speed took a number of iterations. In the first implementation, inheritance specs could be inherited along the relation type hierarchy (i.e., relations could form type hierarchies of arbitrary depth). This was far to slow. The second implementation restricted the definition of relations to avoid excessive searching. That is, a new relation had to be related directly to the "relation" schema via an "is-a" relation. Speed was obtained, but the restriction on the definition of the facility was too great. The third implementation introduced a compiler for relations. This allowed a return to the more general definition of relations. Compiling relations combines the best of both worlds. It has the speed of the limited representation, and the power of the general representation. The only sacrifice is that relations cannot be altered dynamically. This compromise yields a powerful and usable system.

3.2. Demons

Definition. Demons provide a facility for reactive processing within SRL. They may be placed in any slot's meta-schema and are executed based on the SRL function used to access the slot. Demons may be inherited from other schemata in a manner similar to that of values. Each demon specifies what slot access functions causes it to fire. Each demon has an action slot that contains any number of lisp functions. They are executed either before or after the slot access is performed. There are three kinds of demons. First, the "side-effect" demon has no direct effect on the slot access. Second, the "alter-value" demon alters the values that the access function is using. Third the "block" demon stops the slot access function from executing. They are only valid before the function is performed. The ACCESSOR, ACCESS-VALUE, and CURRENT-VALUE hold information about the call for use by the ACTION functions. The demon schema is defined as follows.

{{ **demon**
ACCESS: <access> +
range: (type "is-a" "SRL-access-fn")
ACCESSOR:
ACCESS-VALUE:
CURRENT-VALUE:
WHEN:
range: (or before after)
ACTION:
range: <Must be a function definition>
EFFECT:
range: (or alter-value block side-effect) }}

Reflections. Demons have fallen into disuse, because they are very expensive. When the facility is enabled, SRL must attempt to inherit demons on every slot access. *This slows the system down by an order of magnitude*, as often many slot access functions are performed internally, for each call to SRL.

All attempts to use demons have used them sparsely. The user found a way to avoid demons eventually, to speed up their program. There are two reasonable approaches to using demons within SRL. The first is to limit their functionality. This would entail restricting inheritance of demons, or the SRL functions that check for demons. For instance if only a subset of the slot access functions of SRL checked for demons, then the system might run at a reasonable speed. The second approach is to use demons extensively. For instance, if most slots had demons for most slot access functions, then the user would not be paying for a facility they were not using.

3.3. Restrictions

Definition. SRL provides a mechanism, for restricting the domain and range of a slot. It is possible to restrict the domain of the slot, the range of the slot, and the number of values in the range. Domain, range and cardinality restrictions are placed in the meta-schema associated with a slot. Also like demons the values of the various restrictions may be inherited along a meta-schema's relational network.

Reflections. Automatic restriction checking is not used, for the same reasons that demons are not used. On every attempt to alter the contents of a slot, SRL must attempt to inherit each facet used for restriction. Restrictions do not merit the associated cost. Restriction checking slows the system down by an order of magnitude.

A facility for manually checking restrictions is used, particularly to check user input. Manual restriction checking gives users the benefit of restriction checking, when they need it, but avoids the excessive overhead. Full restriction testing is usually turned on during the debugging phase of a system only, much like array bound checking is provided in a compiler.

3.4. Paths for Transitivity

Definition. Transitivities are an important part of SRL, as they allow the user to test if two schemata are related by a particular relation. For example the transitivity for the **instance** relation is:

(list (step "instance" all) (repeat (step "is-a" all) 0 inf))

This path specifies to step one INSTANCE relation, and any number of IS-A relations. Using this path it is possible to determine if one schema is an instance of another. It is also possible to find all the schemata which are related to a particular schema by a relation.

Reflections. Transitivities are used by all SRL applications, some extensively. Both types of transitivities are used. Two factors combine to make transitivities an important addition to SRL. First they are a very expressive and powerful for model definition. Second, they do not add any fixed cost to other SRL accesses. Therefore transitivities are expressive and economical.

3.5. Paths for Search

Definition. Paths are of the same form as transitivity paths, and are used as an added parameter to slot-value access functions in SRL. A path specification can be used to restrict the relations along which inheritance is to be performed for the particular slot access.

Reflections. Search paths have been gradually introduced to most projects. There are two reasons for restricting the search. The first is selective inheritance. For instance if one path for inheritance is correct at the current state of the user's program, this may be specified by a path argument. Consider the situation where a "dog" schema is related to both "pet" and "guard" via an "is-a" relation.

```
{{ dog
IS-A: "pet" "guard"     }}

{{ pet
DISPOSITION: docile     }}

{{ guard
DISPOSITION: mean       }}
```

Figure 3-1: Search Paths

Depending on what role the dog is playing, the value of its DISPOSITION slot differs. Search paths enable the user to specify along which relations inheritance is to be performed.

The second reason for focusing the search is to avoid searching branches which the user knows are irrelevant. This is used to improve performance by avoiding an exhaustive search. The user community views paths first as a method for improving efficiency, and second as a tool for selective inheritance. Only one project has ever used search paths for selective inheritance, while most projects use them to speed up their programs.

3.6. Meta-information

Definition. Each schema, slot and value may have a schema attached to it in which "meta-information" is placed. These schemata are manipulated in the same manner as other schemata. Meta-schemata enable to user to embed a wide variety of information in a model. Using meta-information it is easy for a user to associate semantics with the elements of a model. Meta-information is used to maintain dependencies of slots and values, when they are inherited. It is also used to define facets like DEMON and RANGE.

Reflections. Meta-information is used by all applications, some more extensively than others. Usage falls into three categories: restrictions, documentation, and dependencies. Meta-schemata attached to slots provide information restricting the domain and range of the slot (see section 3.3). Meta-schemata also document who created the schema, slot or value, when and why. Meta-schemata attached to values usually provide dependency information, which describes how the value was derived. The BRUTUS facility (Adam et al., 1984) which was just implemented, uses dependencies to provide both truth (Doyle, 1979) and belief (van Melle, 1980) maintenance at the meta-level.

There have been divided opinions on the efficiency of meta-information. Using it adds a fixed cost to some kinds of inheritance. But it adds a great deal of power to SRL. The result is that automatic generation of meta-information has been separated from maintaining dependencies. This means that users can now use meta-information without increasing the cost of inheritance. This compromise will make meta-information cheap to use, as there is no overhead unless a user wants to maintain dependencies for inherited information.

3.7. Contexts

Definition. SRL has a context facility, which allows the user to have different data spaces for schemata. Contexts are defined in 2.1.

Reflections. The primary use of contexts has been to support version management of knowledge bases, and "what-if" reasoning. In the former, new contexts are sprouted, in a hierarchical fashion, as alternative or successive versions of the knowledge base are created. This has been quite useful during model building and testing in INET and KBS in general. Other systems such as ROME use it to support reasoning about alternative scenarios. In this role, the use of contexts is limited, since there does not exist the ability to relate schemata in two different contexts.

3.8. Database Interaction

Definition. SRL uses a database in order to deal with very large knowledge bases. This allows models which are larger than the memory available to Lisp. It also provides a convenient facility for saving knowledge bases. SRL uses a cache for fast access of the most recently used schemata. The database system greatly extends the upper limit on the size of a knowledge base.

Reflections. There are two performance problems with using a database. First, schemata must be copied in and out of the database. This is a reasonably expensive operation. In addition to copying schemata, there is added expense to determine that a schema is not in the knowledge base, as the database must be checked. This was a problem when determining whether a slot was a relation involved looking at the possibly nonexistent schema which represents the slot. Second, users can not have pointers to schemata, because not all schemata are resident in memory. This means that a users reference to a schema must be converted into a schema every time the user calls SRL. Never the less, without the database, the large applications to which SRL has been applied would not be "doable".

3.9. Efficiency

Definition. Efficiency, as defined by the speed with which information may be created and accessed, has became increasingly important as the complexity of the models in SRL increased.

Reflections. As soon as people started writing real programs in SRL speed became a constant issue. Some projects push SRL to be as fast as possible. Many design decisions balance efficiency versus functionality. To increase the speed of SRL, the decision was made to compile relations, and make many of SRL's features selectable via user switches. For example, value caching, restriction checking, demon execution, meta-information creation, dependency maintenance and other facilities are user selectable. This has provided a good balance between those who require speed and those who require power.

4. Conclusion

A number of features have proven useful in most of our applications. In particular, user-defined relations for adapting the representation to the user's domain, meta-knowledge such as dependencies and facets, relational path specifications for both transitivity checking and search restrictions, contexts for knowledge-base version control, and the caching system for managing large schema bases.

Efficiency has been the overriding concern governing the acceptability of a particular feature in SRL. Both demons and restriction checking have fallen into disuse (except the latter for debugging) because they "overload" schema access functions. While such concerns may be ignored in lieu of faster machines, the inherent complexity of relational search (when information is non-local) in large knowledge bases invalidates such approaches. Two solutions present themselves. The first is an interim solution. Current technology enables the creation of an "SRL machine". It would be a micro-programmed multi-processor database machine which performs schema accesses and search. The longer term solution lies in the work of connection machines as proposed by Fahlman et al. (1983) and Hillis (1981).

5. References

Adam D., B. Allen, M. Fox, and P. Spirtes, (1984), "BRUTUS: A System for Dependency and Belief Maintenance," Technical Report, Robotics Institute, Carnegie-Mellon University, Pittsburgh PA, in preparation.

Allen, B.P., and Wright, J.M., (1983),"Integrating Logic Programs and Schemata." *Proceedings of the 8th International Joint Conference on Artificial Intelligence*, Karlsruhe, West Germany, 1983.

Bartlett F.C., (1932), *Remembering*, Cambridge: Cambridge University Press.

Bobrow D.G. and M. Stefik, (1983), "The LOOPS Manual," Xerox PARC, Palo Alto CA.

Bobrow D., and T. Winograd, (1977), "KRL: Knowledge Representation Language," *Cognitive Science*. Vol 1, No. 1, 1977.

Bobrow D., and T. Winograd, (1977), "Experience with KRL-0, One Cycle of a Knowledge Representation Language," *Proceedings of the Fifth International Joint Conference on Artificial Intelligence*, pp. 213-222, Cambridge MA.

Brachman R.J., (1977), "A Structural Paradigm for Representing Knowledge," (Ph.D. Thesis), Harvard University, May 1977.

Chester, D., (1980), "HCPRVR: an Interpreter for Logic Programs," *Proceedings of the National Conference on Artificial Intelligence), 1980.*

Fahlman S.E., (1977), "A System for Representing and Using Real-World Knowledge," (Ph.D. Thesis), Artificial Intelligence Laboratory, MIT, AI-TR-450.

Fahlman S.E., G.E. Hinton, and T.J. Sejnowski, (1983), "Massively Parallel Architectures for AI: NETL, Thistle, and Boltzmann Machines," *Proceedings of AAAI-83*, pp. 109-113, Washington DC.

Weinreb D., and D. Moon, (1981), "Lisp Machine Manual," Fourth Edition, Symbolics Inc., Cambridge MA.

Forgy, C.L., "OPS5 User's Manual, Department of Computer Science, Carnegie-Mellon University, 1981.

Fox M.S., (1979), "On Inheritance in Knowledge Representation," *Proceedings of the Sixth International Joint Conference on Artificial Intelligence*, pp. 282-284, Tokyo

Japan.

Fox M.S., (1983), "Constraint-Directed Search: A Case Study of Job-Shop Scheduling," (PhD Thesis), Technical Report, Robotics Institute, Carnegie-Mellon University, Pittsburgh PA.

Fox M., A. Sathi, and M. Greenberg, (1984), "The Application of Knowledge Representation Techniques to Project Management," *Proceedings of the IEEE Workshop on Principles of Knowledge-Based Systems*, Colorado.

Fox M.S., S. Lowenfeld, and P. Kleinosky, (1983), "Techniques for Sensor-Based Diagnosis," *Proceedings of the International Joint Conference on Artificial Intelligence*, Karlsruhe, West Germany, August 1983.

Fox M., and S. Smith, (1984), "ISIS: A Knowledge-Based System for Factory Scheduling," *International Journal of Expert Systems*, Vol. 1, No. 1.

General Electric, (1983), "Delta/CATS-1," *Artificial Intelligence Report.*

Genesereth M.R., R. Greiner, and D. Smith, (1980), "MRS Manual," Computer Science Dept., Stanford University, Stanford CA.

Greenberg M., (1983), "RETINAS User's Manual," Internal report, Robotics Institute, Carnegie-Mellon University, Pittsburgh PA.

Greiner R., (1980), "RLL-1: A Representation Language Language," HPP-80-0, Computer Science Dept., Stanford University, Stanford CA.

Hillis W.D., (1981), "The Connection Machine," Technical Report 646, MIT AI Lab., Cambridge MA.

Intelligenetics, (1984), "KEE tm User's Manual," Third Edition, IntelliGenetics Inc., Palo Alto CA.

ISL, (1984), "Intelligent Systems Laboratory Software Systems Manual," Internal report, Robotics Institute, Carnegie-Mellon University, Pittsburgh PA.

Kosy D.and V. S. Dhar, (1983), "Knowledge-Based Support System for Long Range Planning," Technical Report, Robotics Institute, Carnegie-Mellon University, Pittsburgh, Pennsylvania, December, 1983.

Kosy D., and B. Wise, (1984), "Self-Explanatory Financial Planning Models," *Proceedings of the American Association for Artificial Intelligence*, Austin, Texas.

Lenat, D., (1976), "AM: An Artificial Intelligence Approach to Discovery in Mathematics as Heuristic Search," (Ph.D. Thesis) Computer Science Dept., Stanford University.

McDermott J., (1980), "R1: an Expert in the Computer Systems Domain," *Proceedings of the First Annual National Conference on Artificial Intelligence*, Stanford University, Aug. 1980, pp. 269-271.

Minsky M., (1975), "A Framework for Representing Knowledge," In *The Psychology of Computer Vision*, P. Winston (Ed.), New York: McGraw-Hill.

Reddy Y.V. and M.S. Fox, (1982), "KBS: An Artificial Intelligence Approach to Flexible Simulation," CMU-RI-TR-82-1, Robotics Institute, Carnegie-Mellon University, Pittsburgh PA.

Reddy Y.V., and M.S. Fox, (1983), "INET: A Knowledge-Based Simulation Approach to Distribution Analysis," *Proceedings of the IEEE Computer Society Trends and Applications*, National Bureau of Standards, Washington DC.

Roberts R.B., and I.P. Goldstein, (1977), "The FRL Manual," MIT AI Lab Memo 409, MIT, Cambridge MA.

Rychener M., (1984), "PSRL User's Manual," Technical Report, Robotics Institute, Carnegie-Mellon University, Internal Report.

Schank R., and R. Abelson, (1977), *Scripts, Plans and Understanding*, Hillsdale NJ: Lawrence Erlbam Ass. Inc.

Stefik M., (1979), "An Examination of a Frame-Structured Representation System," *Proceedings of the Sixth International Joint Conference on Artificial Intelligence*, Tokyo, August 1979.

Stolfo A., (1982), "ACE: An Expert System Supporting Analysis and Management Decision Making," Technical Report, Computer Science Dept., Columbia University.

van Melle W., (1980), "A Domain Independent System that aids in Constructing Knowledge-based Consultation Programs," Ph.D. Thesis, STAN-CS-80-820, Computer Science Dept., Stanford University, Stanford CA.

William C., (1983), "Advanced Reasoning Tool: Conceptual Overview," Inference Corp., Los Angeles CA.

Wright J.M., M.S. Fox and D. Adam, (1984), "SRL/1.5 Users Manual," Technical Report, Robotics Institute, Carnegie-Mellon University, Pittsburgh PA.

A System-Controlled Multi-Type Specialization Hierarchy

Ulrich Reimer

Universitaet Konstanz
Informationswissenschaft
Postfach 5560
D-7750 Konstanz, W. Germany

Abstract

A formal specification of a specialization hierarchy upon frames which consists of three types of specialization relations (is-a, instance-of, reference-of) is presented. Each relation is defined by properties which hold for two frames if and only if a relation link exists between them. The specification of necessary and sufficient conditions for relation links makes possible the automatic maintenance and control of the specialization hierarchy by the knowledge base system. This way, the semantic integrity of the knowledge base (with respect to these relations) is always guaranteed.

1. Introduction

A frame-based knowledge representation model is being developed (and implemented by a knowledge base system) as part of the TOPIC project, an experimental text understanding and abstracting system (for an overview see TOPIC 1983 and KUHLEN 1984). The semantics of the representation structures is based on integrity rules which control their generation and modification. The semantics of the frame data model* can then be given by the specification of its operations which take these integrity rules into account (not part of this paper). This way, the well-defined behaviour of the knowledge base system which realizes the data model is guaranteed.

Other knowledge representation languages which employ the frame idea, like KRL (BOBROW/WINOGRAD 1977) and FRL (ROBERTS/GOLDSTEIN 1977), have already become standard representation languages in artificial intelligence. However, no formal definition of their semantics has ever been given. The translation of a subset of KRL (KRL-0) into first-order predicate logic in (HAYES 1979) remains on a pure representational level and says little about its semantics: frame-specific inference rules or operations are missing although they are essential because they determine the interpretation of the frame structures. In (CERNY/KELEMEN 1980) some of such frame-specific operations are defined by an algebraic specification of their semantics, thus providing an abstract data type view on frames. With the development of the frame data model in TOPIC an attempt is made to exhaustively specify the semantics of an entire frame-based knowledge representation model.

---

* The terms knowledge representation model and data model are used as synonyms, less to express a commonly true fact than to express that they need not necessarily refer to different things.

The emphasis of this paper lies on the specialization hierarchy of TOPIC's frame data model which is given by three different types of specialization relations. Their maintenance (creation and deletion) is strictly system-controlled by giving necessary and sufficient conditions for their existence, thus leading to a knowledge base system capable of guaranteeing the semantic integrity of the specialization hierarchy in its knowledge base (integrity maintenance with respect to the entire TOPIC representation model is described in REIMER/HAHN 1985). Aspects of integrity management in general are dealt with in the chapters by Lafue/Smith, Morgenstern, Adiba/Nguyen, Cammarata/Melkanoff, Shepherd/Kerschberg and Roussopoulos/Mark/Chu. Closely related to the current chapter is the one by Finin/Silverman where an interactive facility which supports augmenting a concept hierarchy and keeps control of its integrity is described. Closely related is also the chapter by Ait-Kaci where a programming language based on type (or concept) specialization is defined. A program in this language can be regarded as being a knowledge base that consists of the types (concepts) defined.

Section 2 contains a short introduction to the basic concepts of the frame data model of TOPIC so that in section 3 the description of its specialization hierarchy can be given.

2. The Basic Concepts of the Frame Data Model

TOPIC's frame data model (REIMER/HAHN 1983, REIMER/HAHN 1985) basically consists of relationally connected frames (MINSKY 1975). A frame is an object which is structured by a set of closely associated concepts, called slots. A slot may be filled with objects which either are simple strings or which are frames again. Semantic relations (e.g. specialization, part-of) are used to connect frames with each other. Each knowledge concept can be denoted by a name. Naming conventions, treatment of synonyms, homonyms, etc. are dealt with on a significational level which is separated from the structural level (similarly suggested in KENT 1978 and BUBENKO 1980).

In the following, a formal specification of the frame notion is given together with several integrity constraints which will be needed for the description of the specialization hierarchy. The notational presentation refers to the META-IV-Language (as illustrated in BJORNER 1980).

A frame is defined as a sequence of three mappings. The first one maps a frame identifier to a mapping which is defined upon the set of slot identifiers for that frame and maps each of them to another mapping which finally gives the entries of the selected slot.

The set of all mappings which start from a set of frame identifiers is given by FRAMES:

FRAMES = Fname --> SLOTS

Fname denotes the set of frame identifiers and SLOTS denotes the set of mappings which specify the slots of a frame:

SLOTS = Sname --> SENTRY

Sname denotes the set of slot identifiers and SENTRY denotes the set of mappings which yield the actual and permitted entries of a slot (see integrity constraint (1) below) as well as the obligatory and not-obligatory ones (see integrity constraints (3) and (6) (in sec. 3.) below):

$$\underline{\text{SENTRY}} = \{\ \underline{\text{act}},\ \underline{\text{perm}},\ \underline{\text{obl}},\ \underline{\text{not-obl}}\ \} \dashrightarrow 2^{\text{Entries}}$$

Since the elements of the sets FRAMES and SLOTS are mappings two frames or two slots of a frame with identical names cannot occur. The three mappings above exhaustively characterize the formal syntax of the frame data model.

In the rest of the paper an arbitrary element of the set FRAMES is considered, thereby selecting an arbitrary but specific knowledge base. With dom f denoting the domain of the mapping f

dom FRAMES	means the set of all frame identifiers
dom FRAMES(f)	means the set of all slot identifiers of frame f
FRAMES(f)(s)(act)	denotes the set of all actual entries of slot s of frame f; applying perm in place of act yields the set of permitted entries, obl yields the set of permitted obligatory entries and not-obl the permitted not-obligatory ones.

Two basic kinds of integrity constraints are distinguished in the frame data model. Model dependent integrity constraints are an integral part of the data model. Only knowledge structures which satisfy all model dependent integrity constraints are (legal) knowledge structures in view of the data model. World dependent integrity constraints are not predefined but may dynamically be included and deleted in dependence on the semantics of the world represented in the knowledge base, thus additionally restraining the set of legal knowledge structures (the problems which arise with this point are not deeply examined yet but will be one of the next subjects of consideration). Via some integrity constraints the still unspecified meaning of the different kinds of slot entries will now be given:

(1) Actual slot entries must also be element of the set of permitted slot entries, employing the set of permitted slot entries for controlling slot filling:

$$\forall f \in \underline{\text{dom}}\ \text{FRAMES}: \forall s \in \underline{\text{dom}}\ \text{FRAMES}(f): \text{FRAMES}(f)(s)(\underline{\text{act}}) \subseteq \text{FRAMES}(f)(s)(\underline{\text{perm}})$$

(2) Distinguishing two types of slots allows for a more stringent control of slot filling:

A slot (s --> SENTRY) ∈ SLOTS (with SLOTS ∈ SLOTS and SENTRY ∈ SENTRY) is called non-terminal, iff s ∈ dom FRAMES. All other slots are called terminal (in the rest of the paper slots and frames are referred to by their identifiers):

is-non-terminal(s) :<==> s ∈ dom FRAMES
is-terminal(s) :<==> ~ is-nonterminal(s)

The mapping SENTRY gives for each slot the set of actual and the set of permitted slot entries. The permitted slot entries for terminal slots are not predefined in the data model and must be specified when setting up a knowledge base (being dependent on the domain of discourse) whereas the permitted slot entries for non-terminal slots are given by the following model dependent integrity constraint which states that permitted slot entries of a non-terminal slot s are subordinates of the frame with the identifier s (indicated by the E-is-a specialization relation which will be introduced in sec. 3.):

$$\forall f \in \underline{\text{dom}}\ \text{FRAMES}: \forall s \in \underline{\text{dom}}\ \text{FRAMES}(f): \text{is-non-terminal}(s) \Longrightarrow$$
$$\Longrightarrow \text{FRAMES}(f)(s)(\underline{\text{perm}}) := \{\ f' \mid f' \in \underline{\text{dom}}\ \text{FRAMES} \wedge \langle f',s\rangle \in \text{E-is-a}\ \}$$

(3) Obligatory slot entries are entries that cannot be omitted while descending the specialization hierarchy (see integrity constraint (6) in sec. 3.). Entries of terminal slots are by definition always obligatory while non-terminal slots must be marked from external (e.g. by a knowledge engineer) as being obligatory. A slot is specified as either to be filled only with obligatory entries or only with not-obligatory ones:

$$\text{FRAMES}(f)(s)(\underline{\text{perm}}) = \text{FRAMES}(f)(s)(\underline{\text{obl}}) \cup \text{FRAMES}(f)(s)(\underline{\text{not-obl}})$$

$$\forall f \in \underline{\text{dom}}\ \text{FRAMES}: \forall s \in \underline{\text{dom}}\ \text{FRAMES}(f):$$
$$[\ [\ \text{is-terminal}(s) \Longrightarrow \text{FRAMES}(f)(s)(\underline{\text{perm}}) = \text{FRAMES}(f)(s)(\underline{\text{obl}})\ ] \wedge$$
$$\wedge [\ \text{is-non-terminal}(s) \Longrightarrow (\ \text{FRAMES}(f)(s)(\underline{\text{perm}}) = \text{FRAMES}(f)(s)(\underline{\text{obl}}) \vee$$
$$\vee\ \text{FRAMES}(f)(s)(\underline{\text{perm}}) = \text{FRAMES}(f)(s)(\underline{\text{not-obl}})\ )\ ]\ ]$$

$$\text{is-obl}(f,s) \quad :\Longleftrightarrow \text{FRAMES}(f)(s)(\underline{\text{perm}}) = \text{FRAMES}(f)(s)(\underline{\text{obl}})$$
$$\text{is-not-obl}(f,s) :\Longleftrightarrow \text{FRAMES}(f)(s)(\underline{\text{perm}}) = \text{FRAMES}(f)(s)(\underline{\text{not-obl}})$$

Note, that with integrity constraint (1) the following statement can be derived for obligatory slots (correspondingly for not-obligatory ones):

$$\text{FRAMES}(f)(s)(\underline{\text{act}}) \subseteq \text{FRAMES}(f)(s)(\underline{\text{obl}})$$

The concept of obligatory slots is intended to be a tool to make explicit the existence of two possible meanings of a slot entry. In certain slots an entry carries the meaning of describing an actual property of the corresponding frame whereas in certain other slots an entry describes a property which can be true but not at all need to be true. As an example, take the cpu slot of a microcomputer frame. Its entry specifies which microprocessor is built in as the cpu of the micro. Entries of a slot 'peripheral devices' of the same frame specify which kinds of peripheral devices are available for the micro but do not mean that a specific micro has all of them installed (this statement does not hold for reference frames: see sec. 3.). The task of a knowledge engineer who maintains the knowledge base is to take care that a frame does not have a slot which is marked as being obligatory or not obligatory but which may conceptually (i.e. corresponding to the semantics of the world represented in the knowledge base) have both kinds of entries. He must appropriately specify the slots and if necessary split up a non-terminal slot into several slots which are subordinates of the splitted one, thereby reducing the size of the set of permitted entries (e.g. splitting 'peripheral devices' into the obligatory slots 'display' and 'keyboard' and into the not-obligatory slots 'printer' and 'external storage').

Now restricting the view to the subset of the frame data model as given above, the relations which build up a specialization hierarchy can be introduced.

3. The Specialization Hierarchy

The idea of representing knowledge about objects as specializations of one another was applied first in (QUILLIAN 1968) for the purpose of modelling human memory. Being a standard in artificial intelligence for knowledge representation the concept of specialization hierarchies was adopted by data base researchers, besides other semantic relations, to extend data models such that more information about the application environment could be represented. Some important advantages of these extensions are a better support of different user views by appropriate abstractions which conceal irrelevant aspects by ascending the is-a hierarchy, more support of query formulation and user interfaces and the formulation of semantic integrity constraints which help to keep a data base in well-defined states. An extension of the relational model by a combination of a specialization and an aggregation hierarchy was first given in (SMITH/SMITH 1977), where adding attributes to a relation results in its specialization. Relations and their attributes correspond to frames and slots in the frame data model. In TAXIS (WONG 1981) a subordinate class inherits the properties of its superordinate one but need not have additional properties. The specialization is constrained by the requirement that the property values of a subordinate class are a specialization of those of the superordinate class, given e.g. by set inclusion. As the value of a property of a class is the domain of possible values an instance may have, this kind of specialization resembles the idea of restraining the set of permitted slot entries in the frame data model below. Inheritance rules that take into account the distinction of an is-a and an instance relation as well as the distinction of the inheritance of properties and property values which corresponds to the inheritance of slots and slot entries in the frame data model are given in (LEVESQUE/MYLOPOULOS 1979). A procedural interpretation of concept specialization can be found in some programming languages. SIMULA incorporates a facility for defining an object class as a specialization of an already existing one, inheriting its attributes (DAHL/HOARE 1972). In more recent, object-oriented programming languages like Smalltalk (GOLDBERG/ROBSON 1983) and Flavors (WEINREB/MOON 1980) similar facilities are realized. A detailed comparison of different approaches to specialization of procedures can be found in (BORGIDA 1981).

All current approaches to concept specialization, however, lack of a sufficiently formal treatment, i.e. they do not present a characterization of the properties of their specialization relations stringent enough to be sufficient and necessary so that insertion and deletion of relation links can be fully system-controlled. The explicit specification of an object as being subordinate to another one easily gives rise to the appropriate property inheritance but the other way round, relating or unrelating two objects in view of their properties requires an exhaustive definition of the specialization relations. Concerning programming languages, resp. procedural knowledge representation languages, which specify an object by a set of procedures which determine its behaviour, this argument demands a compiler or interpreter which detects if for two given objects the conditions of specialization are fulfilled and explicitly states the specialization relation between them. As it is in general not decidable if two programs are computationally equivalent such a facility can only be realized for appropriately restricted cases. Specialization concerning procedural knowledge representation is not dealt with further in this paper which focuses on declarative knowledge representation although the fundamental idea given here is relevant for both. Considering declarative knowledge representation languages, only KL-ONE includes an algorithm for automatic insertion of new concepts into the specialization hierarchy in virtue of their structure (SCHMOLZE/LIPKIS 1983). This algorithm comes closest to a system-controlled maintenance of the specialization hierarchy. The constraints of a specialization link, however, are incorporated in a decision procedure which suffers from not being proven to be complete. In the approach as given below this problem cannot arise since the existence of a specialization link is by definition synonym to the accomplishment of all required properties.

The definition of the specialization relations was guided by the intention to have a distinction of three types of frames. As it is common practice, <u>prototype objects</u> which act as representatives of a set of instance objects with some common properties are distinguished from these <u>instance objects</u>. This may be illustrated by a microprocessor frame which represents as a prototype the set of all microprocessor instances, like Z8Ø, M68ØØØ, etc. A third object type comes into consideration if a referential level is added which consists of <u>referential objects</u> as members of classes whose representatives are given by instance frames. A referential frame stands for a physically existent world concept, e.g. "the terminal in room 348". Although in the TOPIC system a referential level is not needed yet the description of a referential relation is included to give a closed view. The three object types are formally defined as follows, presupposing the definitions of the specialization relations (see below).

$$\begin{aligned}
&\text{is-prototype}(f) &&:\Longleftrightarrow f \in \underline{\text{dom}}\ \text{FRAMES} \wedge \forall s \in \underline{\text{dom}}\ \text{FRAMES}(f): \text{FRAMES}(f)(s)(\underline{\text{act}}) = \emptyset \\
&\text{is-instance}(f) &&:\Longleftrightarrow f \in \underline{\text{dom}}\ \text{FRAMES} \wedge \exists f' \in \underline{\text{dom}}\ \text{FRAMES}: \langle f,f' \rangle \in \text{Inst} \\
&\text{is-refobject}(f) &&:\Longleftrightarrow f \in \underline{\text{dom}}\ \text{FRAMES} \wedge \exists f' \in \underline{\text{dom}}\ \text{FRAMES}: \langle f,f' \rangle \in \text{Ref}
\end{aligned}$$

The <u>Is-a relation</u> may hold between two prototype frames describing one of them as the <u>subordinate</u> of the other one. The semantics of Is-a is given by the properties of the corresponding frames which hold iff the Is-a relation holds between them. With the idea that the subordinate is in a way more specific than its superordinate Is-a incorporates facilities to make a frame more specific:

- Adding a slot to a frame creates a subordinate of it, e.g.

  <figure 1>

- Restricting the set of permitted entries of a slot, either explicitly for terminal slots or implicitly by specialization of a non-terminal slot (due to integrity constraint (2) as given in sec. 2.), also creates a subordinate frame:

  <figure 2>

More than one of these conditions may hold but at least one is required. The formal specification of Is-a is given by

$$\begin{aligned}
\text{Is-a} = \{ \langle f,f' \rangle \mid\ & f, f' \in \underline{\text{dom}}\ \text{FRAMES} \wedge \text{is-prototype}(f) \wedge \text{is-prototype}(f') \wedge \\
& \wedge \forall s' \in \underline{\text{dom}}\ \text{FRAMES}(f'): \exists s \in \underline{\text{dom}}\ \text{FRAMES}(f): \\
& \qquad (s = s' \vee \text{is-non-terminal}(s) \wedge \text{is-non-terminal}(s') \wedge \langle s,s' \rangle \in \text{Is-a}) \wedge \\
& \wedge \forall s \in \underline{\text{dom}}\ \text{FRAMES}(f) \cap \underline{\text{dom}}\ \text{FRAMES}(f'): \\
& \qquad \text{FRAMES}(f)(s)(\underline{\text{perm}}) \subseteq \text{FRAMES}(f')(s)(\underline{\text{perm}}) \wedge \\
& \wedge \exists s \in \underline{\text{dom}}\ \text{FRAMES}(f): (s \notin \underline{\text{dom}}\ \text{FRAMES}(f') \vee s \in \underline{\text{dom}}\ \text{FRAMES}(f') \wedge \\
& \qquad\qquad \wedge \text{FRAMES}(f)(s)(\underline{\text{perm}}) \subset \text{FRAMES}(f')(s)(\underline{\text{perm}})) \}
\end{aligned}$$

The Inst relation is intended to introduce the concept of an instance frame. The definition of Inst is divided into two parts distinguishing a first layer from the subsequent ones. On its first layer Inst holds between a prototype and an instance frame whereas on deeper layers it further specializes instances, so holding between two instance frames. Accordingly, the definition of Inst is slightly different for both cases, however, preserving as the common characteristic property the consideration of slot entries:

- A frame becomes as an instance frame subordinate of a prototype by adding an (arbitrary) slot entry (remember that prototypes are defined as having no slot entries):

  <figure 3>

- Specialization of an instance frame is possible by adding an obligatory entry (cf. integrity rule (3) in sec. 2.) or by specialization of an obligatory entry of the superordinate frame:

  <figure 4>

Distinguishing two levels and loosening the conditions on the first one by considering arbitrary slot entries instead of only obligatory ones is necessary because otherwise a frame with only not-obligatory entries would not be part of the specialization hierarchy as Inst essentially considers only obligatory entries. Inst is restricted to changes on the slot entry level, requiring that everything else is kept constant. This way, it accomplishes the intuitively desired similarity between subordinate and superordinate and avoids interference with the Is-a relation. Entries of obligatory slots of the superordinate frame which are not specialized are passed to the subordinate frame. The superordinate frame must be either prototype or instance. Without this condition a referential frame as superordinate would by-pass the intention of the Inst definition (leaving out the implications in the definition below); the specialization relation E-is-a' (extended Is-a) used in the following definition is given subsequently.

$$
\begin{aligned}
\text{Inst} = \{ \langle f,f'\rangle \mid\ & f, f' \in \underline{\text{dom}}\ \text{FRAMES} \wedge (\text{is-prototype}(f') \vee \text{is-instance}(f')) \wedge \\
& \wedge [\ \text{is-prototype}(f') \Longrightarrow \\
& \quad \Longrightarrow \exists s \in \underline{\text{dom}}\ \text{FRAMES}(f) : \text{FRAMES}(f)(s)(\underline{\text{act}}) \neq \emptyset\ ] \wedge \\
& \wedge [\ \text{is-instance}(f') \Longrightarrow \\
& \quad \Longrightarrow [\ \exists s \in \underline{\text{dom}}\ \text{FRAMES}(f) : (\ \text{is-obl}(f',s) \wedge \\
& \qquad\qquad \wedge \exists e \in \underline{\text{dom}}\ \text{FRAMES}(f)(s)(\underline{\text{act}}) : e \notin \text{FRAMES}(f')(s)(\underline{\text{act}})\ ) \wedge \\
& \qquad\qquad \wedge \forall s \in \underline{\text{dom}}\ \text{FRAMES}(f) : [\ \text{is-not-obl}(f',s) \Longrightarrow \\
& \qquad\qquad\quad \Longrightarrow \text{FRAMES}(f)(s)(\underline{\text{act}}) = \text{FRAMES}(f')(s)(\underline{\text{act}})\ ]\ ]\ ] \wedge \\
& \wedge \forall s \in \underline{\text{dom}}\ \text{FRAMES}(f') : [\ \text{is-obl}(f',s) \Longrightarrow \forall e' \in \text{FRAMES}(f')(s)(\underline{\text{act}}) : \\
& \qquad\qquad (\ e' \in \text{FRAMES}(f)(s)(\underline{\text{act}}) \vee \text{is-non-terminal}(s) \wedge \\
& \qquad\qquad\quad \wedge \exists e \in \text{FRAMES}(f)(s)(\underline{\text{act}}) : \langle e,e'\rangle \in \text{E-is-a}'\ )\ ] \wedge \\
& \wedge \underline{\text{dom}}\ \text{FRAMES}(f) = \underline{\text{dom}}\ \text{FRAMES}(f') \wedge \\
& \wedge \forall s \in \underline{\text{dom}}\ \text{FRAMES}(f) : \text{FRAMES}(f)(s)(\underline{\text{perm}}) = \text{FRAMES}(f')(s)(\underline{\text{perm}})\ \}
\end{aligned}
$$

A subordinate frame of the Ref relation is defined to be a referential frame. Like Inst the Ref relation relies upon the concept of (not-)obligatory slot entries, but whereas Inst achieves specialization by adding obligatory entries Ref specializes by discarding those not-obligatory entries that do not hold true for the reference frame.

- An instance frame is specialized by selecting from slots that contain not-obligatory entries (which specify potential properties of the corresponding frame) those entries which actually hold for the referential frame (below, the postfix '-i' of a frame name indicates an instance frame, the postfix '-r' indicates referential frames):

  <figure 5>

- Not-obligatory entries which are prototypes or instances are representatives of all their subordinates. Therefore, they may be substituted by one or more of them, omitting the other ones:

  <figure 6>

- Obligatory entries of non-terminal slots may be specialized to referential frames:

  <figure 7>

  Note, that the restriction to referential frames as subordinates of obligatory entries avoids any interference with the Inst relation which also specializes obligatory entries, but not down to the referential level.

Again, conditions may be combined. It is required that selection and substitution leaves no prototype as a slot entry in the reference frame. All other frame properties are the same for the reference subordinate and its superordinate. The superordinate of a reference frame must be an instance frame so that slot entries exist upon which specialization can be performed. As a conclusion, a referential frame cannot be superordinate of any other frame and thus is a leaf node of the specialization hierarchy. For all slots it is excluded that the subordinate has entries which its superordinate does not have, except those which are a specialization of one of the superordinate entries. It is further required that all entries of obligatory slots are passed from the superordinate to the subordinate, again possibly accompanied by specialization.

$$
\begin{array}{l}
\text{Ref} = \{ \langle f,f' \rangle \mid f, f' \in \underline{\text{dom}}\ \text{FRAMES} \wedge \text{is-instance}(f') \wedge \\
\quad \wedge [\ \exists s \in \underline{\text{dom}}\ \text{FRAMES}(f') : [\ \text{is-not-obl}(f',s) \wedge \exists e' \in \text{FRAMES}(f')(s)(\underline{\text{act}}) : \\
\qquad\quad e' \notin \text{FRAMES}(f)(s)(\underline{\text{act}})\ ] \vee \\
\qquad \vee \exists s \in \underline{\text{dom}}\ \text{FRAMES}(f') : [\ \text{is-obl}(f',s) \wedge \text{is-non-terminal}(s) \wedge \\
\qquad\quad \wedge \exists e' \in \text{FRAMES}(f')(s)(\underline{\text{act}}) : \exists e \in \text{FRAMES}(f)(s)(\underline{\text{act}}) : \langle e,e' \rangle \in \text{Ref}\ ]\ ] \wedge \\
\quad \wedge \forall s \in \underline{\text{dom}}\ \text{FRAMES}(f) : \forall e \in \text{FRAMES}(f)(s)(\underline{\text{act}}) : \\
\qquad (\ e \in \text{FRAMES}(f')(s)(\underline{\text{act}}) \vee \text{is-non-terminal}(s) \wedge \\
\qquad\quad \wedge \exists e' \in \text{FRAMES}(f')(s)(\underline{\text{act}}) : \langle e,e' \rangle \in \text{E-is-a}\ ) \wedge \\
\quad \wedge \forall s \in \underline{\text{dom}}\ \text{FRAMES}(f') : [\ \text{is-obl}(f',s) \Longrightarrow \forall e' \in \text{FRAMES}(f')(s)(\underline{\text{act}}) : \\
\qquad (\ e' \in \text{FRAMES}(f)(s)(\underline{\text{act}}) \vee \text{is-non-terminal}(s) \wedge \\
\qquad\quad \wedge \exists e \in \text{FRAMES}(f)(s)(\underline{\text{act}}) : \langle e,e' \rangle \in \text{Ref}\ )\ ] \wedge \\
\quad \wedge \underline{\text{dom}}\ \text{FRAMES}(f) = \underline{\text{dom}}\ \text{FRAMES}(f') \wedge \\
\quad \wedge \forall s \in \underline{\text{dom}}\ \text{FRAMES}(f) : \text{FRAMES}(f)(s)(\underline{\text{perm}}) = \text{FRAMES}(f')(s)(\underline{\text{perm}}) \wedge \\
\quad \wedge \sim \exists s \in \underline{\text{dom}}\ \text{FRAMES}(f) : \exists e \in \text{FRAMES}(f)(s)(\underline{\text{act}}) : \text{is-prototype}(e)\ \}
\end{array}
$$

Pathological, but rare, is the occurrence of a reference frame without any slot entries. It seems improper to explicitly exclude such cases in the definition of Ref but in order to avoid such reference frames also being a prototype the definition of a prototype frame must be augmented:

$$\text{is-prototype}(f) :\Longleftrightarrow f \in \underline{\text{dom}}\ \text{FRAMES} \wedge \forall s \in \underline{\text{dom}}\ \text{FRAMES}(f): \text{FRAMES}(f)(s)(\underline{\text{act}}) = \emptyset \wedge \wedge \sim \overline{\text{is-refobject}}(f)$$

Finally, the E-is-a' relation combines Is-a and Inst while E-is-a collects all the above relations into one:

$$\text{E-is-a}' = \text{Is-a} \cup \text{Inst} \qquad \text{E-is-a} = \text{Is-a} \cup \text{Inst} \cup \text{Ref}$$

Note, that Is-a and Inst are irreflexive, anti-symmetric and transitive. Ref, E-is-a' and E-is-a are only irreflexive and anti-symmetric.

All three relation types are clearly distinguished from each other. Is-a considers the slot level, Inst and Ref both the slot entry level, Inst (on its deeper layers) restricted to obligatory entries and Ref to not-obligatory ones (except of specializations to referential frames). Their different features correspond with their different usage. While Ref is currently not used by the TOPIC system the distinction of Is-a and Inst is e.g. of importance for anaphora resolution and for the computation of dominant concepts in a text passage.

All the relations are defined in a way such that the specialization hierarchy can strictly be divided into three layers. The top layer consists of Is-a links only, the next layer consists of Inst links only which finally may be followed by a Ref link. Of course, the second and third layer need not be present at all places in the hierarchy.

The specialization relations can now be applied to the specification of additional (model dependent) integrity constraints which exclude further ill-formed representation structures from the data model:

(4) A frame must not have a slot with a name identical to the frame name and no slot whose name is the name of a subordinate or superordinate of the frame, thus excluding the frame itself and all its subordinates of being permitted entries of one of its slots:

$$\forall f \in \underline{\text{dom}}\ \text{FRAMES}: \sim\exists f'' \in \underline{\text{dom}}\ \text{FRAMES}: (f'' \in \underline{\text{dom}}\ \text{FRAMES}(f) \wedge \wedge (\overline{f} = f'' \vee \langle f,f''\rangle \in \text{E-}\overline{\text{is}}\text{-a} \vee \langle f'',f\rangle \in \text{E-}\overline{\text{is}}\text{-a}))$$

(5) A non-terminal slot must not refer to a referential frame because no slot filling would be possible due to integrity constraint (2) and the definition of Ref:

$$\forall f \in \underline{\text{dom}}\ \text{FRAMES}: \forall s \in \underline{\text{dom}}\ \text{FRAMES}(f): \sim\text{is-refobject}(s)$$

(6) As an extension of integrity constraint (3) the treatment of obligatory and not-obligatory slots with concern to frame specialization is given by two conditions. The first one which states that an obligatory entry must not be omitted while descending a specialization link can be derived from the definition of the specialization relations:

$\forall$ <f,f'> $\in$ E-is-a: $\forall$ s $\in$ dom FRAMES(f'): [is-obl(f',s) ==>
==> $\forall$ e' $\in$ FRAMES(f')(s)(act): $\exists$ e $\in$ FRAMES(f)(s)(act):
(e = e' $\vee$ is-non-terminal(s) $\wedge$ <e,e'> $\in$ E-is-a)]

The second condition states that a (not-)obligatory slot keeps being (not-)obligatory while passing a specialization link:

$\forall$<f,f'> $\in$ E-is-a: $\forall$ s' $\in$ dom FRAMES(f'): $\forall$ P $\in$ { is-obl, is-not-obl }:
[P(f',s') ==> (s' $\in$ dom FRAMES(f) $\wedge$ P(f,s') $\vee$ is-non-terminal(s') $\wedge$
$\wedge$ $\exists$ s $\in$ dom FRAMES(f): (<s,s'> $\in$ Is-a $\wedge$ P(f,s)))]

4. Conclusions

A formal specification of a specialization hierarchy upon frames which consists of three types of specialization relations has been presented. Each relation is defined by properties which hold between two frames if and only if the relation link exists between them. The specification of necessary and sufficient conditions for relation links makes possible the automatic maintenance and control of the specialization hierarchy by the knowledge base system: the creation and deletion of relation links cannot be performed directly by an operation but only by changing the structure of the corresponding frames so that they accomplish the required properties.

In practice difficulties may arise always to find a specialization criterion by which a link between two frames becomes established, especially if the Is-a relation is concerned. As an example imagine the frame 'application software' as a subordinate of the frame 'software'. An Is-a link between them, which clearly is appropriate, requires an additional slot or the restriction of the set of permitted entries of a slot for the application software frame. If a meaningful specialization by one of these constraints (i.e. one that does not require to represent large amounts of knowledge outside the application domain) cannot be found a knowledge engineer who edits the knowledge base would need to add a meaningless dummy slot in order to accomplish the formal requirements. The knowledge base system would not know about this conceptually inadequate representation structure. In order to avoid such situations it is intended to design a knowledge engineering layer (to be presented in a forthcoming paper) which will be positioned above the frame data model. On this layer the establishment of a link between two frames can be enforced even if an integrity constraint is violated. From the knowledge engineering layer (possibly invalid) structures are mapped into the knowledge base kernel which corresponds to the frame data model. Since no integrity violation is tolerated in the kernel the mapping has to correct invalid structures, e.g. by adding a dummy slot just as the knowledge engineer would have done. However, the advantage is now that the knowledge base system has knowledge of all conceptual integrity violations (i.e. violations that are only seen on the knowledge engineering layer). If requested it can call the attention of the knowledge engineer to them in order to check for their removal. An integrity violation, however, must explicitly be enforced by the knowledge engineer, the standard case being the restriction and guidance of the knowledge engineer by the integrity constraints which guarantee a proper knowledge base and help him to cope with possibly large knowledge bases consisting of highly interconnected, complex representation structures. The result is a sound knowledge base with a correspondingly positive effect on the application programs which make use of it.

Acknowledgements

I would like to thank my colleagues U. Hahn, R. Hammwoehner, R. Kuhlen and U. Thiel for the many discussions which helped clarifying my ideas and which gave many valuable hints for improvement. Thanks also to the referee of an earlier version of this paper for his comments.

References

BJORNER, D.:
Formalization of Data Base Models. In: D. Bjorner (ed.): Abstract Software Specifications. Berlin: Springer, 1980, pp.144-215.

BOBROW, D.G. / WINOGRAD, T.:
An Overview of KRL, a Knowledge Representation Language. In: Cognitive Science, Vol.1, No.1, 1977, pp.3-46.

BORGIDA, A.:
On the Definition of Specialization Hierarchies for Procedures. In: Proc. of the 7th Int. Joint Conf. on Artificial Intelligence, 1981, pp.254-256.

BUBENKO, J.A.:
Data Models and their Semantics. In: Data Design. Infotech State of the Art Report, Series 8, No.4, 1980, pp.107-136.

CERNY, A. / KELEMEN, J.:
FDT - An Approximation of an Abstract Frame-Like Data Type. In: Proc. of the 2nd Meeting on Artificial Intelligence, Repino (USSR), Oct.12-19, 1980.

DAHL, O.-J. / HOARE, C.A.R.:
Hierarchical Program Structures. In: O.-J. Dahl, E.W. Dijkstra, C.A.R. Hoare (eds.): Structured Programming. Academic Press, 1972.

GOLDBERG, A. / ROBSON, D.:
SMALLTALK-80: The Language and its Implementation. Addison-Wesley, 1983.

HAYES, P.J.:
The Logic of Frames. In: D. Metzing (ed.): Frame Conceptions and Text Understanding. Berlin, New York: de Gruyter, 1979, pp.46-61.

KENT, W.:
Data and Reality. North-Holland, 1978.

KUHLEN, R.:
A Knowledge-Based Text Analysis System for the Graphically Supported Production of Cascaded Text Condensates. Technical Report TOPIC-9. Universitaet Konstanz, Informationswissenschaft, 1984.

LEVESQUE, H. / MYLOPOULOS, J.:
A Procedural Semantics for Semantic Networks. In: N.V. Findler (ed.): Associative Networks. Academic Press, 1979, pp.93-120.

MINSKY, M.:
A Framework for Representing Knowledge. In: P.H. Winston (ed.): The Psychology of Computer Vision. Mc Graw-Hill, 1975, pp.211-277.

QUILLIAN, M.R.:
Semantic Memory. In: M. Minsky (ed.): Semantic Information Processing. MIT Press, 1968.

REIMER, U. / HAHN, U.:
A Formal Approach to the Semantics of a Frame Data Model. In: Proc. of the 8th Int. Joint Conf. on Artificial Intelligence, 1983, pp.337-339. (An extended version appeared as internal report TOPIC-3).

REIMER, U. / HAHN, U.:
On Formal Semantic Properties of a Frame Data Model. Submitted for publication.

ROBERTS, R.B. / GOLDSTEIN, I.P.:
The FRL Manual. MIT AI-Lab., 1977.

SCHMOLZE, J.G. / LIPKIS, T.A.:
Classification in the KL-ONE Knowledge Representation System. In: Proc. of the 8th Int. Joint Conf. on Artificial Intelligence, 1983, pp.330-332.

SMITH, J.M. / SMITH, D.C.P.:
Database Abstractions: Aggregation and Generalization. In: ACM Transactions on Database Systems, Vol.2, No.2, 1977, pp.105-133.

TOPIC:
A System for Automatic Text Condensation. In: ACM SIGART Newsletter #83, 1983, pp.20-21.

WEINREB, D. / MOON, D.:
Flavors: Message Passing in the Lisp Machine. MIT AI Memo No.602, 1980.

WONG, H.K.T.:
Design and Verification of Interactive Information Systems Using TAXIS. Technical Report CSRG-129. Computer Systems Research Group, University of Toronto, 1981.

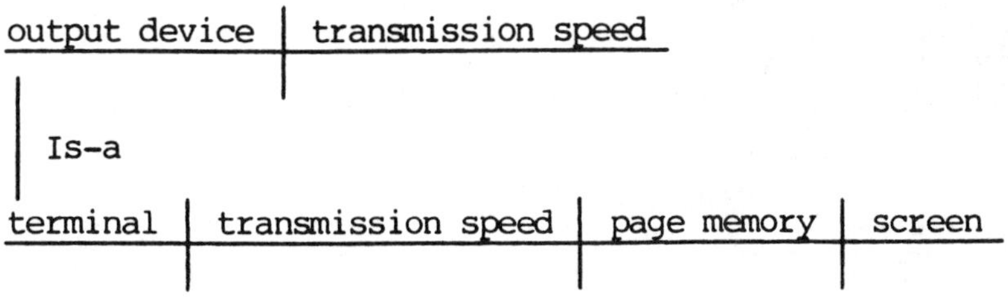

output device	transmission speed

Is-a

terminal	transmission speed	page memory	screen

<figure 1>, Reimer

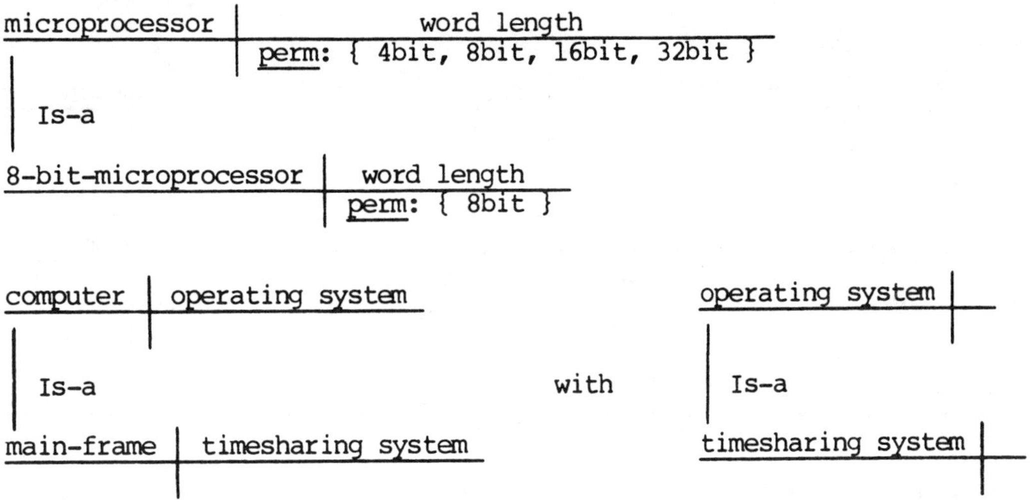

microprocessor	word length
	perm: { 4bit, 8bit, 16bit, 32bit }

Is-a

8-bit-microprocessor	word length
	perm: { 8bit }

computer	operating system

Is-a

main-frame	timesharing system

with

operating system	

Is-a

timesharing system	

<figure 2>, Reimer

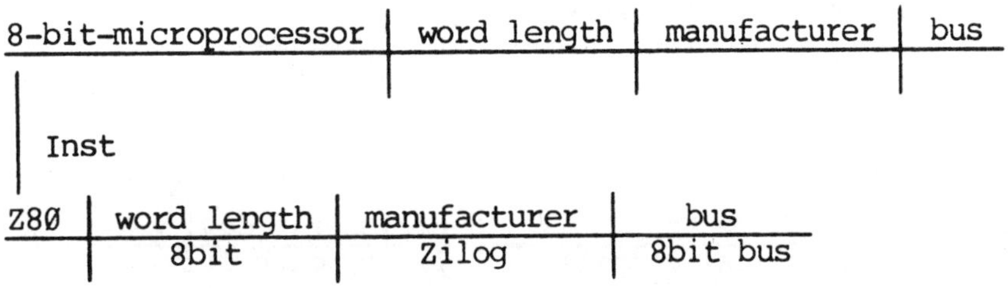

8-bit-microprocessor	word length	manufacturer	bus

Inst

Z80	word length	manufacturer	bus
	8bit	Zilog	8bit bus

<figure 3>, Reimer

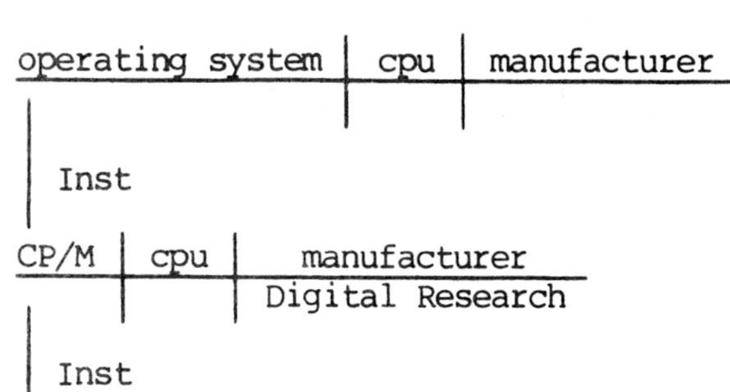


```
CP/M 86 | cpu  | manufacturer
        | 8Ø86 | Digital Research
```

```
compiler | programming language | cpu                         programming language |
   |
   Inst                                                           Inst
   |
pascal-compiler | programming language | cpu        with      Pascal |
                |        Pascal        |
   |
   Inst                                                           Inst
   |
UCSD-pascal-compiler | programming language | cpu             UCSD-Pascal |
                     |     UCSD-Pascal      |
```

<figure 4>, Reimer

```
microcomputer-i | cpu | software             | peripheral devices
                | Z8Ø | pascal compiler-i    | printer
                |     | basic interpreter    | floppy disk drive-i
                |     | editor               | hard disk drive
   |
   Ref
   |
microcomputer-r | cpu | software             | peripheral devices
                | Z8Ø | pascal compiler-i    | floppy disk drive-i
```

<figure 5>, Reimer

microcomputer-i	cpu	software	peripheral devices
	Z80	pascal compiler-i basic interpreter editor	printer floppy disk drive-i hard disk drive

Ref

microcomputer-r	cpu	software	peripheral devices
	Z80	basic interpreter-i screen editor-i	hard disk drive-i daisy wheel printer-i matrix printer-i

<figure 6>, Reimer

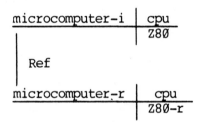

microcomputer-i	cpu
	Z80

Ref

microcomputer-r	cpu
	Z80-r

<figure 7>, Reimer

PART IV:

Logic Programming and Databases

On Integrating Logic Programming and Databases

Michael L. Brodie

Computer Corporation of America
Four Cambridge Center
Cambridge, Massachusetts 02142

Matthias Jarke

Computer Applications and Information Systems
Graduate School of Business Administration
New York University

ABSTRACT

Researchers are currently challenged to provide data management support for large-scale Knowledge Base Management Systems (KBMSs). This requires both a powerful knowledge representation scheme and efficient support for processing large amounts of complex knowledge. First-order logic frequently is proposed as a candidate for solving these problems in a uniform framework. However, logic programming and databases have fundamental differences in their respective treatment of databases. This chapter critically evaluates logic, logic programming, and, in particular, Prolog with respect to conventional database paradigms. The differences that must be resolved for the successful integration of logic programming and databases are identified.

1. Introduction

Logic programming and databases have fundamental differences in their respective treatment of databases. While some issues (e.g., systems issues) can be readily resolved, more fundamental issues are based on theoretical differences such as the model theory versus proof theory.

Logic provided a basis for relational databases and database theory, especially for expressing queries and for the definition of views and integrity constraints. However, the traditional view of databases is *model-theoretic*: a time-invariant definition of a database schema (a theory) is provided by defining data structures and integrity constraints. A database state at any given time is an interpretation (which must be a model) of the theory. Hence, query evaluation constitutes the computation of a truth value for the query predicate over the current model (database state). Updates change the model but not the underlying theory (database schema); consequently, update transactions must preserve database integrity such that the new database will be a model of the theory.

In contrast, the logic programming community has preferred a *proof-theoretic* view of databases. Facts and deduction rules (which are more general than view definitions in databases) constitute the theory itself rather than a model of the more general underlying theory. Queries constitute theorems that have to be proven from the theory by using a small number of well-founded proof techniques (e.g., resolution [Robinson 1982]) whose correctness is generally accepted. A time-invariant schema in the model-theoretic sense of database theory does not exist. Consequently, update operations change the theory. Enforcing constraints on updates (i.e., integrity preservation [Miyachi, et al., 1984]) therefore requires "stepping out of the system" and controlling the updates from the viewpoint of a meta-theory in which the database state constitutes a model. Hence, it seems that updates require a model-theoretic approach, albeit on a metalevel.

How can these two perceptions of logic in databases be reconciled for the benefit of efficient and intelligent knowledge base management? This chapter attempts to stimulate discussion of this question by contrasting the needs of database management with the capabilities of logic in general and of current logic programming concepts in particular.

Based on experience with building Prolog-based "expert systems" for physical database design [Brodie 1984] and semantic query optimization [Jarke, et al., 1984; also the chapter "External Semantic Query Simplification" by M. Jarke], we critically review knowledge representation in logic, the application of logic programming in databases, and various options for using Prolog as a language for database manipulation, database implementation, and database design. Some practical, short-term solutions are listed. The chapter concludes with open research problems that must be resolved for the successful integration of logic programming and large scale knowledge bases.

The chapter "Logic Programming and Databases" by Scott Parker, et al. (in this volume) addresses additional issues that also must be resolved for the successful integration of logic programming and databases. This chapter presents a decidedly optimistic view of the problems and of potential logic programming extensions. Although many benefits of the integration are clear and many potential benefits have been proposed, most problems raised in both chapters require significant research. The most likely outcome of this research will be individual KBMSs which integrate aspects of logic programming and databases as well as basic improvements in both DBMSs and logic programming systems.

2. Logic as a Knowledge Representation Scheme

In first order logic, facts and relations between facts are represented as logical formulae in a knowledge base. The benefits of logic as a knowledge representation scheme include [Reiter 1984]:

* Well-Defined Semantics

  The semantics of first order logic is formally well-defined.

* Simple Notation

  The syntax of first order logic is simple and well-understood.

* Conceptual Economy

  Each formula (i.e., fact or deduction rule) is represented once, independently of its different uses.

* Representational Uniformity

  Facts, hypotheses, implications, queries, and views are all expressed in the same first-order language. Even metalevel assertions to be enforced in the knowledge base (e.g., integrity constraints) can be programmed (though not directly asserted) in logic.

* Operational Uniformity

  First order proof theory is the sole mechanism for query evaluation. As a result of representational and operational uniformity, inference rules can be directly applied to facts.

* Standard Representation Scheme

Logic provides a common basis for defining and comparing other knowledge representation schemes.

* Generality of Inference and Proof Procedures

  Inference and proof procedures can be used for querying, deduction of new facts, retrieval, problem solving, and theorem proving.

* Defining New Logics

  Once the semantics of a new logic (e.g., incomplete information, time, space) is well-understood, the semantics can be formally defined using first order logic. The definitions then extend the expressive power of the logical system.

There are three distinct disadvantages of logic as a representation scheme. (The chapter by Stott Parker, et al., looks largely at the advantages of the logic as a representation scheme.) Some disadvantages can be overcome by defining, in logic, the precise semantics desired. However, this may mean defining the semantics from first principles.

First, the representation power of logic is powerful but limited with respect to basic knowledge representation requirements. Standard first-order logic cannot easily be used to represent such real world knowledge as beliefs, defaults, incomplete knowledge, and self-knowledge, although aspects of this knowledge can be represented. For example, it is possible to express knowledge about knowledge-base contents (corresponding to a data dictionary in a DBMS). Even if a certain kind of knowledge can be expressed in logic, the formalization process required may be difficult to carry out and more natural forms of knowledge representation may exist.

Second, procedural and heuristic knowledge is difficult to represent in logic. Procedural knowledge is critical for any integration of knowledge and data, particularly for knowledge acquisition and manipulation. First-order logic tends to deal with static collections of facts. For example, it provides a logical query facility over a set of clauses. Logic does not provide clean semantics for updating a collection of facts while preserving integrity (this also is discussed in the chapter by Stott Parker, et al.). The inability to represent procedural knowledge is a limitation not only for knowledge representation but also for logic programming.

Third, logic lacks organizational principles that for large or complex knowledge bases are essential for logical design, performance, and software engineering. In a logic knowledge base, all formulae are independent. Any structure or relationship between them is established operationally via inference procedures. This extreme modularity is an advantage in small to medium-sized systems since it permits multiple uses of facts. However, there are no higher-level concepts that provide modularity of larger chunks of knowledge. In our experience with moderate sized applications, the lack of structure has proven a substantial burden (e.g., object oriented knowledge organization, maintaining uniqueness of predicate names, understanding knowledge organization, debugging).

3. Logic and Databases

First order languages can be used in databases for the definition, analysis, and evaluation of queries, views, and integrity constraints. In particular, the relational data model and database theory are based on a model theoretic view of first order logic with extensions that address some of the above disadvantages of logic.

The logic programming community generally takes a proof theoretic view of databases. The proof theoretic approach views a database schema and a database state as a theory with a single model. Proof theory provides means for reasoning over the theory while model theory provides means for dealing with a database state alone.

Potential benefits of the proof theoretic approach for databases include uniform means to:

* Apply deduction rules and retrieve facts. Logic can be used to derive all facts that can be deduced from stored facts. For this purpose, conventional databases require special view processing capabilities.
* Formally define the semantics of nonlogical data models.
* Compare data models (expressed in logic).
* Investigate, define, and support special or extended data model semantics (e.g., disjunctive information, null values, semantic data model concepts).
* Investigate and analyze the semantics of applications (expressed in logic).
* Evaluate queries over incomplete information.
* Express, analyze for satisfiability, and enforce integrity constraints.
* Prove the correctness of nonproof theoretic query evaluation algorithms with respect to the logical semantics of queries.
* Prove the correctness of integrity maintenance algorithms with respect to the proof theoretic definition of constraint satisfaction.

Due to efficiency issues involved in implementing theorem proving, the proof theoretic approach may not be appropriate for implementing retrieval algorithms over large databases. Rather, it could be used as a theory for definition and analysis of data model semantics and to augment query evaluation outside the DBMS.

4. Logic Programming and Databases

Logic programming provides a computational language for logic. Basically, it provides a question-answering system [Robinson 1983] in which axioms and facts form the premises of deductive inference for queries. You state or assert what is true and ask the system to draw conclusions. Logic programming is based on first order predicate calculus, usually on the Horn clause subset. Query expression and definitions of views and constraints in databases are similar to expressions in logic programming; they are both based on the syntax and semantics of first order languages.

A major issue for a logic programming implementation is how resolution (e.g., unification in the case of Prolog) is done both correctly and efficiently. Resolution theorem proving can result in combinatorial explosions for two main reasons. First, all clauses and facts are stored in an unstructured, homogeneous database. Second, all clauses are treated by the theorem prover without regard for their semantics. To reduce these problems, some logic programming systems provide means for expressing control or procedural knowledge (e.g., cut and annotations [Clark, et al., 1982]).

Logic programming provides both a potential knowledge representation scheme and a computational model for intelligent databases or knowledge bases. It provides means for expressing first order formulae and for executing queries (i.e., testing hypotheses) over databases. Some logic programming languages also provide limited means for storing and updating clauses in a knowledge base.

Query facilities equivalent to those of logic programming can be added to relational algebra by the addition of the fixed point operator to the algebra [Aho and Ullman 1979]. It has been shown that the positive Horn clause subset of logic is equivalent to a relational algebra consisting of selection, join, and projection (SJP), plus single applications of the least fixed point operator [Chandra and Harel 1980, 1982]. This subset can be implemented as the relational algebra plus iterative algorithms for applications of the least fixed point operator [Aho and Ullman 1979]. A major concern for the extended language is the efficiency of algorithms for the least fixed point operator.

Further disadvantages of logic programming (and its implementations) for databases concern its limited knowledge representation power, the inapplicability of the logic programming paradigm to database applications (e.g., those involving updates and procedurality), efficient processing of logical formulae, and efficient DBMS support of the knowledge base. For approaches to some of the database and efficiency issues, see [Chomicki and Grundzinski 1983], [Gallaire 1983] [Kunifuji and Yokota 1982], [Lloyd 1980, 1982].

5. Prolog as an Implementation of Logic Programming

Prolog is a class of implementations of the positive Horn clause subset of logic programming. Prolog programs correspond to hypotheses. Queries correspond to theorems to be proven by the theorem prover which uses unification. Prolog is based on a procedural interpretation of positive Horn clauses in which the implication:

B1 AND B2 AND ... AND BN IMPLIES A

is interpreted as a procedure that reduces the problems of the form A to subproblems B1 and B2 and ... and Bn. Each subproblem in turn is interpreted as a procedure call to other implications. Assertions of the form P are interpreted as "P if true" with the empty collection of subproblems.

Standard Prolog differs from pure logic programming in several ways. First, Prolog introduces four types of extra-logical features. For input and output, Prolog provides built-in predicates that permit clauses to be read and written to and from terminals and the database. For control of the search mechanism (i.e., depth first search with backtracking), Prolog provides built-in predicates and other features (i.e., cut, fail, order of predicates in database, order of terms in predicates). For data, Prolog provides limited data structures (e.g., lists, trees), means for dealing with variables (e.g., isvar, real, integer), and limited arithmetic. Finally, for the support of program development, Prolog provides a few utilities for debugging and tracing programs. While some of these features could be expressed in first order logic (though less efficiently), others have no logical equivalent.

Second, Prolog's proof theoretic resolution is incomplete for the positive Horn clause subset of logic programming. Prolog matching differs in two ways from unification used in resolution. First, Prolog's resolution uses left to right and top to bottom matching. Second, resolution requires that a variable cannot be instantiated to something containing itself, as in the Prolog expressions:

```
equal(X,X).
?- equal(foo(Y), Y).
```

To detect and avoid such cases (which produce infinite terms), Prolog should execute an "occurs" check. This check would seldom be needed but if implemented would make all resolutions much less efficient. Hence, it is offered as an option in some Prologs. Without the occurs check, Prolog misses some valid models and does not give a complete proof.

Third, Prolog provides model theoretic evaluation of predicates as a side effect of proof theoretic evaluation. Unification proceeds by matching terms in clauses. Since Prolog does not distinguish facts from predicates all possible matches are made and printed. Hence, model theoretic answers are obtained simultaneously with proof theoretic answers.

Fourth, most implementations of Prolog do not provide complete logical negation. For example, not(P) is false if P(X) is not instantiated in the database. Hence, it does not support the closed world assumption. In the following Prolog fragment, the fact "likes(bill, mary)" is asserted into the database, whereas the fact "likes(sally, fred)" is not. Hence, the first two queries (preceded with "-?"), which ask if the facts are true (known to the database), result in "true" and "false" respectively. Under the closed world assumption, we assume "likes(sally, fred)" to be "false", hence "not(likes(sally, fred)" to be "true." However, Prolog returns "false."

```
asserta( likes(bill, mary)).

-? likes(bill, mary)
true
-? likes(sally, fred)
false
-? not(likes(bill, mary))
false
-? not(likes(sally, fred))
false
```

There also may be problems with universal quantification since it can be expressed by negation and existential quantification.

A number of implementations of logic programming have been developed to address some of the above issues (see [Clark, et al., 1982], [Chomicki and Grundsinski 1983], [Naish 1983]). IC-Prolog [Clark, et al., 1982] does not use the extra-logical features introduced in Prolog. IC-Prolog provides a set of control structures that are expressed independently of the logical implications, thereby not affecting the pure logical semantics [Clark and McCabe 1979]. This avoids the need for the extra-logical features for purposes of control. IC-Prolog does not permit assert and retract operations during query evaluation and does not provide the "isvar" predicate. Pseudo parallelism and co-routining can be invoked with communication provided via shared variables. Finally, logical negation (hence, the closed world assumption) and set expressions are IC-Prolog primitives [Clark 1978].

6. Prolog as a Programming Language

Prolog often is proposed as a complete programming language. However, many features of modern programming languages and their environments are missing from most Prolog implementations. Important missing features include:

* Avoidance of Implicit Side Effects

  Side effects frequently are required in Prolog programs. For example, most database operations and other I/O are accomplished via side effects to the logic programming paradigm.

* Knowledge Base Structure

  The lack of structure on facts and predicates poses problems in program design and development. For example, Prolog does not provide the concept of a module with which to group clauses (either facts or predicates) to form abstractions for structuring program and knowledge base development. Although this gives the programmer freedom to manipulate arbitrary data structures in multiple ways (i.e., multiple uses of facts similar to the blackboard concept [Erman, et al., 1980]), this freedom is exchanged for a lack of support in error checking.

* Functions and Procedures

  Prolog does not support functions or procedures either as abstraction mechanisms or as computational tools. Functions can be integrated with logic (e.g., as proposed by Frege) and with logic programming languages. FOL [WEHY80] combines inference and procedures. LOGLISP [Robinson and Sibert 1981] combines functional and logic programming by adding functions to logic (in addition to relations).

* Type Concept

Prolog does not provide a built-in type mechanism. Types can be defined using predicates that must be invoked explicitly by the programmer. Hence, typing must be imposed by programmer discipline (i.e., by predicates that must be explicitly invoked). In our experience, this kind of type checking has proven inefficient.

* Programming Tools

There is no programming environment for Prolog.

* Efficiency

Most computation in Prolog is done via unification that is implemented by using depth first search with backtracking (augmented by some programmer control). Minimal indexing is provided. Processing in Prolog can be inefficient even over small knowledge bases if the computational task (e.g., inequality comparisons) does not lend itself to a representation that exploits the unification technique.

* Program Communication

Most implementations of Prolog do not allow effective communication with other programming languages and systems. This is particularly inconvenient when one needs features not provided by Prolog itself. For example, in building an actuarial expert system [Sivasankaran and Jarke 1984], there was a need for advanced statistical methods of using double-precision floating point numbers that are not available on Prolog. There were two choices, implementing an extension to Prolog (which proved awkward and inefficient) and programming in machine language. The design expert required communication with a number of existing systems.

* Control Structure

Prolog provides one control structure: the search mechanism (depth first search with backtracking). If other control structures are required, they must be constructed using the extra-logical features mentioned above. Forcing the Prolog control structure to operate differently (e.g., breadth-first search) may decrease the performance of Prolog substantially.

IC-Prolog avoids extra-logical control (as mentioned above). Several parallel Prologs are being developed [Conery and Kibler 1981], [Khabaza 1984], [Taylor, et al., 1984] in which the search structure is hidden; hence extra-logical control mechanisms are not required.

* Programming Methodologies

The Prolog programming paradigm is unconventional. Methodologies that guide design, programming, or debugging of Prolog programs have yet to be developed. Due to the unification algorithm and the lack of control structures, these activities can be very complex.

An important open question remains: What class of problems are well-suited to programming in logic and to Prolog in particular? In developing the physical database design expert, the logical rules were ideally represented as logic programs. The logical representation was ideal for analyzing and querying the large knowledge base. However, Prolog's backtracking, control structure, and lack of procedures and functions made it unsuitable to the basic program. For example, backtracking was essential; however for 12 binary decisions to be coded to accommodate all backtracking possibilities, 2**12 rules would be required. In addition, most of the disadvantages raised in previous sections (e.g., database inconsistency, no logical negation) proved to be real problems. In another case, Prolog has proven to be an excellent tool for implementing semantic query optimization strategies for all cases where its pattern matching capabilities can be utilized. However, it was inferior to procedural programming languages when inequality comparisons or mathematical computations were required.

7. Prolog as a Database Language

There is a rough analogy between database and Prolog concepts, as follows:

DATABASE	PROLOG
base relation tuple	ground clause (fact)
attribute	predicate argument
view definition	Horn clause
query	theorem
program	hypothesis
insert/delete	assert/retract
assertion (constraint)	query (returning true)
trigger	predicate
set valued query result	set of facts with which to prove a theorem

The correspondence is not exact, since the semantics of corresponding concepts differ as the following comparisons indicate:

* Base Relations versus Facts

In Prolog, there is no concept of a relation type that has a defined record structure and related integrity constraints (e.g., keys). A Prolog "base relation" is simply defined as a set of ground clauses (facts) that have the same predicate name and an identical number of parameters. The same predicate (relation) name can appear with a different number of attributes. Moreover, a relation can be defined partially by ground clauses and partially by Horn clauses with the predicate as its left-hand side. Thus, there is no clear distinction between base relations and derived relations (i.e., concrete views) in Prolog.

* View versus Predicate Semantics

A database view can be defined as the value of a relational expression over existing base relations and other views. Typically in databases, views can be updated only when the update satisfies the view definition and there is a well-defined (e.g., one to one) mapping between the view and the underlying base relations. That is, views are updatable only when the underlying base relations can be correspondingly updated.

In Prolog, a knowledge base contains both relations and view definitions. For example, both

grandfather(fred, bill)
and
grandfather(X,Y) :- father(X,Z), father(Z,Y)

can be stored in the knowledge base. Prolog does not distinguish the schema (theory) from the database (model). Relations, views, and view definitions in the knowledge base can be modified directly by means of "assert" and "retract" operations. Prolog does not ensure that the modifications satisfy any conditions. In database terms, this corresponds to updating the view without concern for the view definition. Such view update semantics also have been considered for databases [Furtado, et al., 1979]

* Queries versus Theorems

  In databases, queries are evaluated over a fixed interpretation. In Prolog, queries correspond to theorems that are evaluated according to proof theory (model theoretic evaluations are obtained as side-effects). On the one hand, the uniform approach of Prolog to query evaluation makes its basic algorithm very simple. Efficiency can be enhanced using cuts and clause reordering [Warren 1981]. On the other hand, uniformity also can be a disadvantage: set-oriented query processing (in particular the multiple use of intermediate results) is difficult to support unless special-purpose predicates are introduced (thus destroying uniformity).

* Insert/Delete versus Assert/Retract

  In databases, the semantics of insert and delete operations to manipulate relations (facts) are part of the semantics of the data model. Additional operations (e.g., create and drop) are required to manipulate relation definitions. Typically, data models include a concept of consistency that the operations maintain (e.g., uniqueness of keys). In Prolog assert and retract operations are extra-logical and apply to both facts and predicates. The operations do not maintain consistency of the facts with respect to existing predicates (the theory).

* Assertions versus Query (returning true)

  Assertions in a database are (typically) first order predicates that require that any database modification must satisfy the constraints or be rejected. Such assertions do not exist in Prolog although they can be implemented [Kitakami, et al., 1984]. Implementing such basic operations in Prolog, rather than in the underlying system, is likely to be very inefficient and to rely on programmer discipline.

* Triggers versus Predicates

  Triggers are similar to Prolog deduction rules because a pattern (or condition) causes a predefined program to be executed. Database triggers are fired whenever the pattern or condition is detected. This is similar to the AI concept of a daemon. Triggers are a particular implementation mechanism used sparingly in databases (due to the their cost). In Prolog, predicates are invoked by pattern matching within the execution of a Prolog program rather than by a daemon mechanism. All Prolog programming is done via pattern matching.

There are a number of additional differences between Prolog and databases. The following is a list of database features missing from Prolog:

* Control Structures and Declarative Query Expression

A major difference between Prolog and relational query languages concerns the declarative expression of queries. Relational query languages are declarative, set-oriented languages that do not require explicit control structures. Control structures may be implied (e.g., by quantification, GROUP BY clauses, nesting, and set oriented operations). Optimal control structures are determined by query optimizers and evaluation algorithms. For update transactions, database languages (or the host languages) provide explicit control structures (i.e., sequence, iteration, and choice). Hence, queries are expressed declaratively and updates are expressed procedurally.

For Prolog programs (queries), the execution must be considered and in some cases (e.g., for efficiency and recursions that would not terminate) explicit control must be introduced. Once again, by using metalevel predicates, the system can take over part of the necessary transformations [Warren 1981]. Explicit control defeats one of the main goals of logic programming and would be very inefficient over large scale databases. Other logic programming languages (e.g., IC-Prolog and parallel Prologs) do not force the concern for efficiency; however, they address these issues only over in-core knowledge bases.

* Backtracking over the Database

It is frequently desirable to construct a model in the knowledge base during the execution of a Prolog program. Examples of models are the translation of a natural language sentence for a natural language processor, the result of applying rewrite rules for an intelligent parser, and the result of design decisions for an design expert. Models are constructed in the database by means of "assert" and "retract" predicates. However, changes to the model (knowledge base) are not automatically undone when the predicates that invoked the changes are backtracked.

This corresponds, in part, to the database concept of transaction which ensures that the entire transaction is completed successfully before the database modifications are committed to the database. There is no corresponding concept in Prolog.

Kowalski has proposed backtrackable "assert" and "retract", which get backtracked whenever the clause in which they were invoked is backtracked. This solution is not generally applicable. First, extra-logical features (such as cut) are used to control backtracking for efficiency and semantic reasons. In certain cases, assert and retract operations should not be backtracked. Second, all asserts and retracts that would potentially require undoing within a program (i.e., within the scope of the transaction) would have to be programmed so that they would be backtracked. As mentioned earlier for the physical database design expert, complete backtracking would require a vast programming effort.

More powerful truth maintenance [Doyle 1979] [McAllester 1980] may be required so that programming is independent of the concern for backtracking the database. Truth maintenance also would provide means to investigate the logical support for any logical consequence for purposes of explanation, consistent modification, and efficiency (i.e., inferences need only be evaluated once and the results saved). It remains to be seen whether extensions of logic to cover default reasoning [Reiter 1980] can be applied to support transaction processing in logic.

* Three Assumptions about Database

Relational databases make three assumptions not fully supported by Prolog: closed world assumption (incomplete logical negation), domain closure, and the unique name assumption [Reiter 1984].

* Data Types

DBMSs make extensive use of data types (e.g., to ensure semantic integrity and to ensure data validation). Considerable effort is made to implement data type facilities efficiently. Prolog is a typeless language. It does not directly support the data type concept; however, predicates could be used to define types. This support of types is far less efficient than mechanisms used in programming languages and databases.

* Consistency

Databases typically support some form of consistency of the database with respect to the schema. For example, tuples in a relational database are unique (i.e., there cannot be more than one set of attribute values for each entity), and views must be updated consistently with their definitions (as mentioned earlier). Prolog does not have the concept of a schema nor update semantics that include consistency. Prolog does not ensure that facts asserted into the knowledge base are consistent with the associated predicate. Facts for the same predicate can be inconsistent (e.g., p(a) and not(p(a)) can both be in the same knowledge base). Prolog complicates the problem of inconsistent clauses by ordering, in the knowledge base, clauses that determine which clause is retrieved first in unification.

For example, when constructing the external semantic query simplifier, database schema information (relation types and integrity constraint) had to be provided in the Prolog knowledge base. Moreover, one has to assume that the integrity constraints used for query optimization were actually enforced in the DBMS.

It may be desirable to store inconsistent facts in a database in which case the conventional database semantics would have to be modified. Prolog could be used to detect, and avoid, inconsistent facts [Kitakami, et al., 1984]. To interface Prolog with a database, the two systems would have to agree.

* Database Facilities

Prolog implementations do not have a DBMS facility to manage a knowledge base. A file system is used to manage data in secondary storage. The following DBMS facilities missing from Prolog distinguish Prolog from DBMSs and would be needed for logic-based KBMSs:

- Efficient access to large fact bases. This is the traditional domain of DBMSs that have a small number of types but a large number of instances [Vassiliou, et al., 1984].
- Multiple users. Prolog is a single user system. For multiple users to share a Prolog database, concurrency control must be provided. This would provide substantial opportunity for multiple query optimization.
- Multiple views. Prolog supports multiple views of facts through its deduction rules, but their interplay with consistency constraints is not well-understood.
- Database structure. Efficient management and programming of large databases benefits from structuring (e.g., entities and relationships, hierarchies, etc.).

- Set-oriented query optimization with management of permanent access paths and intermediate results.
- Data management including recovery and security.
- Transactions. A database transaction can include any number of actions over objects in the database and provide transaction consistency. In Prolog, there is only one goal predicate per deduction rule (e.g., it is difficult to state "If B1 and B2, and ... and Bn then do A1 and A2 and ... and Ak"). Prolog provides no concept of update or transaction consistency.

* Prolog Facilities

Prolog supports many facilities not provided by databases.

- Inference

  Prolog provides a proof theoretic evaluation of Horn clauses whereas databases provide only model theoretic query evaluation (without recursion). Recursion currently is being added to some database query systems (see the chapter "Expert Database Systems: A Database Perspective" by J.M. Smith).

- Dynamic Type Definition

  Typically, DBMSs do not support the dynamic definition of types (e.g., entity or relationship types). However, some DBMSs permit views to be defined dynamically. Prolog does not distinguish between the assertion of new predicate types and existing ones (i.e., it does not have a type concept); there is no distinction between defining a new relation type and creating a new relation. Therefore, data of new types can be inserted into the knowledge base at any time.

- Partial Knowledge, Axioms, and Partial Match

  Prolog provides means to express nonground formulae and facts with incomplete knowledge (e.g., don't care values "_"). Correspondingly, Prolog also permits queries that contain partial information. Relational algebra supports some partial information and partial match.

- Recursion

  Prolog permits recursively defined predicates. Recursion is not currently supported in databases but could be applied to both data structures and queries.

- Negative Clauses

  Prolog permits negative clauses to be stored in the knowledge base (e.g., not(p(a)) and not(p(X))).

- Backtracking and Tracing

  Prolog backtracks whenever a match fails in unification and maintains a trace of all steps taken during the unification process. Traces are necessary for understanding the execution of programs (e.g., for debugging).

- Functors

  Prolog permits functors (i.e., nonground predicates as arguments of predicates) whereas database query languages do not. Relational databases in first normal form strictly prohibit relations within relations.

- Database Order

  In Prolog, order of clauses in the database and of terms within clauses is significant. In relational databases, order of tuples in relations, and of attributes in tuples, is not significant.

8. Integrating Prolog and Databases

Large scale knowledge Bases will require more intelligent processing than current DBMSs offer as well as more efficient and more intelligent access to large scale databases than current AI systems offer. Integrating logic programming and databases may meet the requirements of KBMSs (as far as they are currently understood). The benefits of integration for databases (given above) include extensions due to the knowledge representation power of logic, the proof theoretic approach of logic programming, and the facilities of Prolog. The benefits of integration for logic programming (given above) include efficient access to and data management of large scale databases, data sharing, extended knowledge representation power (e.g., procedural and update semantics), and knowledge organization. This chapter has identified key problems to be resolved to achieve the integration. An open question is the nature of the integration: Within what framework should logic programming be integrated with databases?

Four basic architectural frameworks have been identified for integrating logic programming and databases [Gallaire 1983], [Jarke and Vassiliou 1984]: loose coupling of two independent systems, extension of Prolog to a logic database system, enhancement of a DBMS by deductive capabilities in interface and operation, and the tight integration of a logic programming system with a DBMS. Although the first three approaches have the advantages of conceptual purity, the integrated approach reflects the belief that no single system has all the advantages on its side.

Loose coupling suggests a logic programming facility for query and a DBMS facility for update. On the one hand, the proof-theoretic approach of Prolog is particularly suitable for "intelligent" querying. Relatively simple metalevel concepts could be used for logical-level query optimization to make Prolog an efficient, declarative, and "intelligent" query language. On the other hand, database updates appear to require the model-theoretic approach of databases to ensure consistency between base relations and views. However, knowledge base management may require more complex integrity maintenance than can be handled by a conventional DBMS. In this case, the increased effort for metalevel logic programming required for the proof theoretic approach may be justified.

Augmenting Prolog with a DBMS facility or a DBMS with a deductive front-end are partial solutions. This approach raises most of the problems of the tight integration approach with potentially less system capability as a result. For example, many features missing from Prolog for which the semantics is well-understood can be expressed as predicates in Prolog (e.g., database keys consistency, data types, logical negation). However, this requires programmer discipline and is likely to be much less efficient than having the semantics implemented directly in the underlying system.

For knowledge representation, software engineering and performance, a tight integration is desirable. This can be seen when considering language and knowledge representation. One programming paradigm is not ideal for all programming applications. Rather, special purpose paradigms (such as logic programming) are best suited to specific types of problems. A challenge is to integrate the desired paradigms into a programming facility ideal for the class of applications of interest. A programming language for Large Scale Knowledge Based Systems might have components from logic, databases, and programming languages. For example, a logic programming component could be added to PASCAL/R [Schmidt and Mall 1980] that integrates database and programming language concepts as found in Pascal.

For the tight integration approach, all of the problems raised above must be addressed. An additional class of issues concerns the best division of labor between a DBMS and logic programming. In many cases, the division of labour is obvious. However, there are a few areas where the assignment of tasks remains to be investigated, including:

* How should inference be divided between the DBMS and a theorem prover? Should DBMS do all model theoretic inference or query evaluation and the theorem prover do all proof-theoretic inference? Could the theorem prover make use of the DBMS query/view processor and data dictionary of the DBMS? When is proof theory more efficient than model theory (e.g., in evaluating satisfiability of queries)?
* Which usage patterns require a deductive front-end at all? A simple menu-base transaction environment may not require any of the sophisticated view processing capabilities of a logic programming interface, nor the sophisticated logical optimization strategies that are provided by such a system.
* Is it more efficient to distribute the processing of recursion (i.e., issue a sequence of database calls from the logic programming front-end), should one incorporate a least-fixpoint operator into the DBMS query language, or should one incorporate a setof operator [Kunifuji and Yokota 1982] into logic programming and handle the complete recursive query in virtual memory? More generally, how can recursive query processing be implemented with maximum efficiency?
* For which operations are data types a necessity? Should one expand logic programming into a typed logic, leave type checking to the DBMS, or leave type checking as a responsibility to the programmer?
* What are the relative merits of having multiple users share one logic programming front-end? Having multiple front-ends share a database? Constructing general-purpose or special-purpose (e.g., query only) front-ends?

Acknowledgement

The authors would like to thank Frank Manola for his useful comments on a previous version of this chapter.

9. Bibliography

Aho, A.V., and J.D. Ullman [1979]. "Universality of data retrieval languages," *Proc. ACM POPL*, San Antonio, Texas, January 1979.

Apt, K. R., and M. H. van Emden [1982]. "Contributions to the theory of logic programming," *J. ACM 29,*, No. 3.

Brodie, M. L. [1984]. "An expert for physical database design," Computer Corporation of America, July 1984, (internal report).

Chandra, A. K., and D. Harel [1980]. "Structure and complexity of relational queries," *Proc. Twenty-First Annual IEEE Symposium on Foundations of Computer Science*, pp. 333-347.

Chandra, A. K., and D. Harel [1982]. "Horn clauses and fixpoint query hierarchy," *Proc.*

ACM Symposium on Principles of Database Systems.

Chomicki, J., and W. Grundzinski [1983]. "A database support system for PROLOG," *Proc. Logic Programming Conference*, Portugal, June 1983.

Clark, K. L. [1978]. "Negation as failure," in [Gallaire and Minker 1978], pp. 293-323.

Clark, K. L., and F. G. McCabe [1979]. "The control facilities of IC-PROLOG," in Michie (ed.), *Expert Systems in the Micro Electronic Age*, Edinburgh University Press.

Clark, K. L., F. G. McCabe, and S. Gregory [1982]. "IC-Prolog language features," in [Clark and Tarnlund 1982].

Clark, K. L., and S.-A. Tarnlund [1982]. *Logic programming*, Academic Press, New York.

Clocksin, W. F., and C. S. Mellish [1981]. *Programming in Prolog*, Springer-Verlag.

Conery, J. S., and D. F. Kibler [1981]. "Parallel interpretation of logic programs," *1981 Conf. on Functional Programming Languages and Computer Architecture.*

Domolki, B., and P. Szeredi [1983]. "Prolog in practice," *Proc. 1983 IFIP Congress*, North Holland, Amsterdam.

Doyle, J. [1979]. "A truth maintenance system," *Artificial Intelligence 12* (1979).

Erman, L. D., F. Hays-Roth, V. Lesser, and D. Reddy [1980]. "The HEARSAY-III speech-understanding system," *Computing Surveys 12*, No. 2. (1980).

Furtado, A. L., K. C. Sevcik, and C. S. dos Santos [1979]. "Permitting updates through views of data bases," *Information Systems 4* (1979).

Futo, I., F. Darvas, and P. Szeredi [1978]. "The application of PROLOG to the development of QA and DBM systems," in [Gallaire and Minker 1978].

Gallaire, H. [1983]. "Logic data bases vs deductive data bases," Working Paper presented at the Logic Programming Workshop 1983, Albufeira, Portugal.

Gallaire, H., and J. Minker, (eds.) [1978]. *Logic and databases*, Plenum Press, New York.

Henschen, L. J., and S. A. Naqvi [1984]. "On compiling queries in recursive first-order databases," *J. ACM 31,* No. 1.

Jarke, M. [1984]. "External semantic query simplification: a graph-theoretic approach and its implementation in Prolog" (in this volume).

Jarke, M., J. Clifford, and Y. Vassiliou [1984]. "An optimizing Prolog front-end to a relational query system," *Proc. ACM-SIGMOD Conference,* Boston.

Jarke, M., and Y. Vassiliou [1984]. "Coupling expert systems and database management systems," in W. Reitman (ed.), *Artificial Intelligence Applications for Business,* Ablex, Norwood, N.J..

Khabaza, T. [1984]. "Negation as failure and parallelism," *1984 Intl. Symp. on Logic Programming.*

Kitakami, H., S. Kunifuji, T. Miyachi, and K. Furukawa [1984]. "A methodology for implementation of a knowledge acquisition system," *Proc. International Symposium on Logic Programming*, Atlantic City.

Kowalski, R. [1974]. "Predicate logic as a programming language," *Proc. 1974 IFIP Congress*, North Holland, Amsterdam.

Kowalski, R. [1975]. "A proof procedure using connection graphs," *J. ACM 22*, No. 4, 1975.

Kowalski, R. [1982]. "Logic as a programming language," in [Clark and Tarnlund 1982].

Kowalski, R. [1983]. "Logic programming," *Proc. 1983 IFIP Congress*, North Holland, Amsterdam.

Kowalski, R. A. [1979]. *Logic for problem solving*, North Holland Press.

Kunifuji, S., and H. Yokota, [1982]. "PROLOG and relational databases for fifth-generation computer systems," *Logical Bases for Data Bases*, Toulouse, December, 1982.

Lloyd, J. W. [1980]. "Optimal partial-match retrieval," *BIT 20*, 1980.

Lloyd, J. M. [1982]. "An introduction to deductive database systems," TR 81/3, Dept. of Computer Science, Univ. of Melbourne, revised 1982.

McAllester, D. A. [1980] "An outlook on truth maintenance," MIT AI Memo No. 551, April 1980.

Minker, J. [1978a]. "An experimental relational database system based on logic," in [Gallaire and Minker 1978].

Minker, J. [1978b]. "Search strategy and selection function for an inferential relational system," *ACM Transactions on Database Systems 3,* No. 1, 1978.

Naish, L. [1983]. "Introduction to MU-PROLOG," TR 82/2, Dept. of Computer Science, Univ. of Melbourne, revised 1983.

Miyachi, T., S. Kunifuji, H. Kitakami, K. Furukawa, A. Takeuchi, and H. Yokota [1984]. "A knowledge assimilation method for logic databases," *Proc. International Symposium on Logic Programming*, Atlantic City, pp. 118-125.

Nicolas, J.-M., and K. Yazdanian [1978]. "Integrity checking in deductive databases," in [Gallaire and Minker 1978].

Nicolas, J.-M. [1982]. *Logical bases for data bases*, workshop preprints, Toulouse, December 1982.

Parsaye, K. [1984]. "Logic programming and relational databases," *Proc. International Symposium on Logic Programming,* Atlantic City.

Reiter, R. [1984]. "Towards a logical reconstruction of relational database theory," in Brodie, M. L., J. Mylopoulos, and J.W. Schmidt (eds.), *On Conceptual Modelling*, Springer-Verlag, New York, 1984.

Reiter, R. [1980]. "A logic for default reasoning," *Artificial Intelligence 13*, 1980.

Robinson, J. A. [1983]. "Logic programming: past, present, and future," *New Generation Computing 1*, (1983) OHMSHA and Springer-Verlag.

Robinson, J. A. [1982]. "Fundamentals of machine-oriented deductive logic," in D. Michie (ed.), *Introductory Readings in Expert Logic,* Gordon and Breach Publishers, New York.

Robinson, J. A., and E. E. Sibert [1982]. "LOGLISP: motivation, design and implementation," in [Clark and Tarnlund 1982].

Schmidt, J.W., and M. Mall [1980]. "PASCAL/R report," Bericht Nr. 66, Fachbereich Informatik, University of Hamburg, January 1980.

Siklossy, L. [1982]. "Updating views: a constructive approach," in *Preprints, Workshop on Logical Bases for Databases*, Toulouse, France, December 1982.

Sivasankaran, T., and M. Jarke [1984]. "Formula management strategies in an actuarial consulting system," submitted for publication, extended abstract to appear in *Proc. 6th European Conference on Artificial Intelligence,* Pisa, September, 1984, NYU Working Paper Series CRIS #69, GBA 84-44 (CR).

Stickel, M. E. [1984]. "A Prolog theorem prover," *Proc. International Symposium on Logic Programming,* Atlantic City.

Taylor, S., et al. [1984]. "Logic programming using parallel associative operations," *1984 Intl. Symp. on Logic Programming.*

Vassiliou, Y., J. Clifford, M. Jarke [1984]. "Access to specific declarative knowledge in expert systems: the impact of logic programming," forthcoming in *Decision Support Systems.*

Warren, D. H. D. [1981]. "Efficient processing of interactive relational database queries expressed in logic," *Proc. 7th Intl. Conf. on Very Large Data Bases*, Cannes, France, Sept. 1981.

LOGIC PROGRAMMING FOR CONSTRUCTIVE EXPERT DATABASE SYSTEMS

Veronica Dahl

Computing Sciences Dept.
Simon Fraser University
Burnaby, B.C. V5A 1S6
Canada

ABSTRACT

We discuss expert data base systems that can be viewed as sets of specifications for combining different components into desired configurations or structures. These are constructed on demand, according to the combination rules stored and the particular requirements in a user's query. We emphasize intelligent synchronization of constructive processes, and relate our proposal to recent developments on concurrent logic programming.

1. INTRODUCTION

The uses of logic programming for data base applications (cf. Gallaire 1978) are being investigated since 1976. Most of the research in this direction concerns typical relational data bases. The first data base system implemented in Prolog, however, already included several features we could sum up in the term "constructive": it was an expert system that could build up the description of a computer configuration for the SOLAR 16 series of French computers, out of several combination rules stored and the particular requests in a user's query (Dahl et.al., 1976).

Some of the techniques used in this system (namely, query reordering, negation as failure and set-constructing primitives) have since been used, with some variations, by other researchers (cf. Warren 1980a, Warren 1980b, Clark et.al. 1980).

However, other details (namely, those related to the combination of modules into dynamically constrained configurations) have not been adequately described in accessible publications.

This article reviews such features, focusing on intelligent synchronization of constructive processes, and presents the general lines of an alternative, more general approach, inspired by recent developments on concurrent logic programming (e.g., Hogger 1980, Monteiro 1981 Shapiro 1983). Some implementation considerations are illustrated by using L. Monteiro's concurrent programming formalism — for which a minor extension is suggested — but there is no attempt at comprehensive or definite conclusions, our main goal being to stimulate interest in the problems discussed.

While the term "constructive" should not be taken in a too exclusive sense, we argue that expert data bases that can be viewed as such have specific characteristics deserving a peculiar treatment.

Another approach to configuring computer systems automatically was taken in the R1 system (McDermott 1982), using production rules plus extensive specialized knowledge that result in a deterministic, bottom-up system. It seems to us that generalizing the constructive R1 System into an expert configurer of arbitrary constructive worlds would be very hard indeed. Achieving determinism for an arbitrary such world would probably require the user to get into the operational details of the extensive specialized knowledge needed, thus destroying data independence. In this paper we try to show that logic programming might provide a more natural, and easier-to-generalize setting for this attempt.

Familiarity with Prolog (Colmerauer et al. 1973, Roussel 1975, Warren et al. 1977) is assumed, and we do not go into the basic arguments of its fitness for traditional data base applications, which we have given elsewhere (Dahl 1979, 1981, 1983)

2. BRIEF OVERVIEW OF SOLAR 16

The SOLAR 16 system (Dahl et al., 1976) was designed to do the job of a computer salesman: it provides a potential buyer with a description of a (SOLAR 16) computer configuration suited to his/her needs, and can also answer questions about individual components.

It communicates with the user through written, isolated questions and answers in a small subset of French, e.g.,:

Q) Quel est le systeme qui possede le module Fortran et dont la taille memoire est 48 K mots? (Which is the system having the Fortran module and a memory size of 48 K words?)

A) Caracteristiques du system demande:

- Configuration de base: BCD40/0.
- Taille de la memoire centrale: 48 K mots.
- Structure des modules de memoire: 3FCM16/0.
- Liste de peripheriques: 1 ASR33/0.
- Software: 1 BOSD/0.
- Langages: 1 FOR16/0.
- Modules optionnels: 1 MTS40/0, 1 DRP40/0.

Q) Quelle est la designation de 'DRP40/0'? (what does 'DRP40/0' designate?)

A) Protection reallocation mem. sur 16-40.

Q) Quel est le prix du module 'DRP40/0'? (What is the price of module DRP40/0?)

A) 8000 francs.

Q) Que necessite 'BOSD/0'? (What does 'BOSD/0' need?)

A) 16 K mots, processeur 16/40, 1 MTS40/0, 1 ASR33/0.

Q) Quel est le prix d'un disque a tetes fixes dont la capacite est 512 K mots? (What is the price of a fixed headed disk the capacity of which is 512 K words?)

A) 51000 francs.

Most of these questions are typically handled by contemporary data base systems. The first one, however, involves several less usual problems which the following section attempts to identify. Some are typical of data bases that can be viewed as constructive. Others, while present in ordinary data bases, acquire peculiar characteristics within constructive ones.

3. THE MAIN PROBLEMS ENCOUNTERED

3.1. Combining Modules into Configurations

How can one go about describing the alternative ways of combining computer modules into desired configurations? Because the user's requirements can not be foreseen, it is clear that all possible configurations must be contemplated. Because the possibilities are usually combinatorially explosive (and may be even infinite in number), the most convenient course seems to be to describe them modularly — i.e., to start by describing non-decomposable elements, and then use general rules for describing all alternative realizations of each remaining module in terms of its constituents, until an arbitrary configuration has been thus described.

This, however, cannot be done in a standard, routine way, as the user's requirements may influence the task of producing a given configuration in a variety of ways: they may require subtasks that are redundant with those already present in the configuration-building process, subtasks that had better be carried out before such process, or after, or intermingled, etc.

For instance, if a user asks for a Fortran compiler, its inclusion prior to the remaining building up, rules out the useless generation of configurations without Fortran. It should also have the further side effect of enforcing all constraints that depend upon the presence of Fortran (e.g., a minimal memory size). Constraints as the latter shall be called *implicit requests*, as opposed to those explicit in a user's query.

The order in which the various components of a configuration should be built up, then, crucially depends upon the explicit and implicit requests in a given query. Notice, moreover, that a convenient top-level task ordering may result in generating inconveniently ordered subtasks. For instance, if Fortran requires that the central unit be different from the one named '05', the top-level task: "Add Fortran into configuration x and then construct the remaining modules of x," could become, after Fortran's inclusion into x: "Check that the central unit in x is different for '05' and then construct the remaining modules of x."

Because of this kind of problem, relying on the user to state a "conveniently" ordered task would be of no use (besides destroying data independence). A general enough constructive expert system must include a dynamic analysis of the form of each problem and of the subproblems its solution entails.

SOLAR 16 included such an analysis, but in a too problem-dependent manner. A more recent proposal (Giraud, 1980) achieves greater generality by describing modules through a special language based on lists of properties, but lacks a temporal coordination of the search-space reducing operations (called "simplifications"), and does therefore not seem suitable for domains with complex constraints.

3.2. Query Reordering

In logic programs, task reordering amounts to query (i.e., goal) reordering in order to correct the strict left-to-right goal execution order imposed in standard Prolog versions.

Query reordering has become part of the folklore of logic programming. It is necessary for all those problem domains in which, for some reason or other, the programmer cannot be expected to exercise full control over the way in which a query is stated. These typically include two areas that concern our subject matter:

- natural language driven queries, as their translation into whatever formalism should not be always expected to directly produce operationally efficient code, and
- data base applications, as the user need not know how to program and should therefore be spared as many operational concerns as possible.

SOLAR 16 achieves query reordering through a user-invisible coroutine extension to Prolog, implemented in Prolog itself, which examines each successive goal statement and reorders it according to run-time tested conditions.

It assumes numeric delay values associated to each predicate and each state of intantiation of its arguments. For instance, "price(x,y)" (i.e., calculate the price y of a configuration x) is assigned and "infinite" (i.e., prohibitively big) delay whenever x is not fully instantiated, and a zero delay otherwise.

An interesting variation of this idea has been exploited in Chat80 (Warren, 1980), where delay values depend upon the size of the relations in the data base, and of the domains over which their arguments range. This gives a useful measure for minimizing search spaces in relational data bases, but other factors must be taken into account where constructive data bases are concerned (e.g., the size of the "price" relation seems less important than the fact that it involves a complex term that might not be fully instantiated).

Further gains in efficiency are obtained in Chat-80 by distinguishing dependent from independent sets of subgoals, but here again, this technique seems inadequate for the constructive case, as it relies on the assumption that the solution of any subgoal is ground.

A recent Prolog version, MU PROLOG, also incorporates a delaying mechanism in the form of "wait" declarations (Naish 1983).

3.3. Representing Negative Information

In SOLAR 16, facts are assumed to be false when their truth cannot be proved — the *closed world* assumption (Reiter, 1978).

However, the constructive nature of our database requires some special cases to be considered. For instance, if a user requires a configuration which does *not* have Fortran, it is no use checking the constraint before the list of languages has been constructed. The requirement must be appropriately coroutined with the building up of the different modules, always taking implicit requirements into account.

Notice that this can be easily achieved by attaching an "infinite" delay to the "not-has" predicate whenever its first argument is not sufficiently known.

Negative requirements, however, often provide useful information that can be exploited in order to further reduce the search space. The above one, for instance, could be used to somehow register the mandatory absence of Fortran within the configuration-representing term, so that those irrelevant configurations having Fortran would be blocked to begin with. SOLAR 16's negation treatment includes this feature.

Another characteristic of SOLAR 16's treatment of negation follows from the fact that a query is internally expressed as a Predicate Calculus-like formula instead of in the Horn-clause subset. The coroutine demonstrator takes care of translating such queries into reordered lists of goals. In particular, the scope of a negation is not limited to single atomic predicates, but may be any arbitrary formula.

For reasons having been examined elsewhere (Dahl 1980), only "safe" negated formulas — i.e., those which do not contain uninstantiated free variables — can be executed. In SOLAR 16, this is ensured simply by attaching a zero delay value to any safe negated expression, whereas those containing uninstantiated free variables are associated an "infinite" delay.

Primitives implementing safe negation as failure have since been incorporated directly into Prolog versions. Notably, the one used in IC-Prolog (Clark et al., 1980) reports a control error for each attempt to execute an unsafe negated expression. It seems however more intelligent to postpone its execution in the hope of its becoming safe, and only report an error when this has proved impossible. This is the course taken in SOLAR 16, as well as in the latest Marseille Prolog version (van Caneghem, 1982).

Chat-80 (Warren, 1980b) also treats negation similarly, although the negated formulas allowed are more restricted. MU-PROLOG (Naish, 1983) also includes safe negation by failure though automatic delaying of negated goals that are not sufficiently instantiated.

3.4. Avoiding Blind Backtracking

Note that an intelligent analysis of the meaning of various central predicates like "has" provides us, in some cases, with a useful while non-expressive alternative to intelligent backtracking: in the example above (a system not having Fortran), if one allowed the constraint to serve only as a verifier once a given configuration is constructed, it would also be necessary to provide a means for backtracking only upon the language-constructing predicate. The brute force approach of backtracking upon successive (and possibly infinite) configurations would be entirely out of the question.

3.5. Set Handling

Another major drawback, with respect to data bases, in standard Prolog, is the lack of set-manipulating primitives. SOLAR 16 includes a means for expressing and calculating a list of all those modules satisfying a given property. A similar facility has become a part of Edinburgh Prolog (Warren, 1980a).

Constructive data bases, however, call for manipulation, rather than evaluation, of intensionally represented sets, as they often refer to abstract concepts (e.g., "two teletypes"), regardless of the concrete individuals they may denote (e.g., "Teletypel, Teletype2").

SOLAR 16 allows those intensional representations involving semantic categories plus cardinality constraints, and provides the corresponding set operations. This feature needs further generalizing for arbitrary constructive domains, but we shall not go into the details here.

4. MORE GENERAL SOLUTIONS

The preceding section has shown some of the peculiar features of constructive data bases that can be exploited in a system dealing with them in general.

In this section we describe the main lines of a more comprehensive approach to the temporal synchronization of building-up primitives, and illustrate it by sketching a possible implementation using the concurrent programming formalism proposed by L. Monteiro (Monteiro, 1981). We also motivate a minor extension to this formalism in connection with our treatment of negation.

4.1. Concurrent Programming

Our SOLAR 16 demonstrator can be viewed as a process synchronizer, where some processes could be performed concurrently (those having the same current delay value), whereas others must be kept sequential (those currently ordered by successive delays). Several Prolog proposals in this sense have been forwarded (e.g., Hogger 1980, Monteiro 1981), including the idea of multiple processors (Coery et al., 1981).

We now describe L. Monteiro's approach, which we have chosen to illustrate implementation considerations in view of its simplicity and power.

Briefly and informally stated, this proposal amounts to allowing processes to be performed concurrently by annotating "+" instead of "," between the subgoals representing them, and enforcing sequentiality through the annotation "." instead. For instance, the query:

```
<- (has(x,Fortran) + has(x,l-teletype)) . configuration(x) . print(x)
```

indicates that the addition of Fortran and of a teletype can be made in parallel, but must both precede the completion and successive printing of configuration x.

To ensure this, only atoms in what is called the "front" of a goal statement are allowed to be resolved upon, the *front* of a goal statement G being defined by:

front(G)=G if G is either ^ or an atom
front(G1+G2)=front(G1)+front(G2)
front(G1.G2)=front(G1).

(this corresponds roughly to the set of atoms having our demonstrator's current delay value).

Moreover, processes can be synchronized through so-called "generalized clauses" — i.e., the collapsing of a set of clauses of the form:

A1 <- B1
A2 <- B2
⋮
An <- Bn

into the form:

A1,A2, · · · ,An <- B1,B2, · · · Bn

taken to indicate that these clauses can only be used simultaneously — i.e., when the front of the goal contains atoms to match all atoms A1,...,An (the ordering implied by the indices being irrelevant).

Notice that these conventions allow us to manipulate selected subgoals in a query, regardless of what the rest of the query looks like. The liberty gained can be paralleled to the one extraposition grammars (F. Pereira, 1980) or, more generally, gapping grammars (Dahl and Abramson 1984, Dahl 1984) achieve with respect to metamorphosis grammars (Colmerauer, 1978) — namely, the ability for singling out selected symbols in a given chain while disregarding the precise form of those in between.

Concurrent programming, moreover, includes the two following facilities :

- "passive predicates" can be defined, serving basically for global data sharing. Unlike ordinary predicates, they are not required to be canceled in order for a proof to succeed. They provide an interesting alternative to the "add-delete" facilities of standard Prolog — any process can consult and update its arguments through "generalized clauses".
- conditions upon rule application. These are goal statements appended to the right of a clause, e.g.,:

  Head <- Body if Condition

  meaning that the-clause "Head <- Body" can only be applied if Condition can be proved.

4.2. Coordination Between Building Processes

In SOLAR 16, implicit requests were expressed through the definitions of each module, in an ad-hoc manner. A more general way of dealing with them should provide a uniform representation of all constraints through system-defined predicates in charge of enforcing them, in such a way as to ensure temporal coordination. This should be a part of a set of primitives allowing easy, operation-independent descriptions of arbitrary data bases.

Because the building up of a given module may affect any other module in the superstructure involved, our system primitives shall carry the (outermost) superstructure's representation into all the primitives in charge of building up its components. Thus, data communication between concurrent processes is ensured.

In terms of concurrent programming, let us suppose that a user's description of a computer configuration gets translated into something like:

configuration(Computer,s) <- component(Central-unit,c,s) +
component(Languages,l,s) + · · · + component(optional-modules,o,s)

where s represents the assembly of all the components in question. Now it is easy to synchronize the actual building up of each module with, for instance, those constraints that must precede its construction — represented through the predicate "constraint" — , as follows:

component(n,m,s),constraint(n,c) <- enforce-constraint(n,c,s).component(n,m,s),^

This rule ensures that, independently of the point in the derivation in which a given constraint is generated, it will have precedence over the predicate defining the concerned component. The question now is when to actually build it up.

4.3. Analyzing Dependencies

In order to determine how the actual building up of components should be sequenced, and assuming that all module interdependencies have been reduced to constraint specifications, we now need a dynamic analysis of the *dependency* relation, defined as follows:.

We shall say that a module named n2 depends upon a module named n1 whenever n1's construction imposes a constraint over n2 that has not yet been enforced. Assuming such a relation, the dynamically convenient order in which to build up modules can be defined through rules such as:

component(n,m,s) <- construct(n,m,s) if independent(n)

which triggers the actual construction of a module m named n only when it has become independent (i.e., depends upon no other module).

A thorough analysis of dependencies for the general case falls outside the scope of this paper, but we shall illustrate the idea that it can be system-deduced for the special case in which no pair of modules can constrain each other.

Under this simplifying assumption, one possible course (though not the most intelligent) is simply to keep a history of modules already constructed and use it to calculate dynamic dependencies from static ones (i.e., those that can be deduced from a data base's definition).

In Monteiro's formalism, this information can be readily carried in a passive predicate (say with initial form : history(nil)), which is consulted and updated when building up any module, e.g.,:

construct(n,m,s), history(l) <- build(n,m,s), history(n.1)

where "build" defines the actual building up.

A realistic analysis of dependencies, however, should involve a study of the *cases* in which a module's construction imposes a constraint upon another, of possible deadlocks, etc.

4.4. Negation

We now insert our treatment of negation, as described in 3.3, into the concurrent programming approach.

Basically, a subgoal of the form not(p) shall be processed concurrently with the rest of the query where it appears. If it contains uninstantiated free variables it just remains as it stands (i.e., is replaced by itself). Else if p can be proved it is replaced by a predicate indicating failure. Else it is erased (i.e., considered solved). In concurrent programming terms, this can be defined in just three clauses provided that a further extension — the controversial "cut" operator, or "slash", is allowed within the new conditional part of a clause:

```
not(p) <- not(p) if unist-free-vars(p)./
not(p) <- fail   if p./
not(p) <- ^
```

These definitions are in turn preceded by the definitions of those negated requirements that serve to minimize the search space (e.g., not(has(x,y))). The transformation of a Predicate Calculus-like formula into a list of queries can be similarly defined, e.g.,:

```
not(every(x,p)) <- exists(x,not(p)) /
```

5. SUMMARY

We have discussed a few problems that are typical of expert databases that can be regarded as constructive or that, while shared with conventional data bases, call for peculiar solutions in the constructive case. Starting from a previous, less general solution, we have proposed a process-synchronization approach to the main problems, based upon the following features:

- a concurrent programming facility,
- intelligent synchronization of various central processes through system primitives,
- data sharing of superstructures by concurrent processes concerning them,
- a dynamic study of the underlying dependencies imposed by compatibility constraints,
- global data sharing to aid such an analysis, and
- intelligent specification to negation as failure.

Neither the approach suggested here nor the formalism through which we illustrate it are definitely settled, our main objective being that of stimulating further research into these problems.

ACKNOWLEDGEMENT

The SOLAR 16 system was developed at the Aix-Marseille University, under the supervision of Alain Colmerauer.

6. REFERENCES

Colmerauer A. et al (1973) Un systeme de communication homme-machine en Francais. Univ. d'Aix-Marseille, France.

Colmerauer A. (1978) Metamorphosis grammars. In: *Natural language communication with computers*, vol. I. Springer-Verlag, 1978, pp. 133-189.

Clark K. L. et al. (1980) IC Prolog — language features. In: *Logic Programming Workshop*, Debrecen, Hungary.

Coery J. S. et al. (1981) Summary of "Efficient logic programs: a research proposal". Short communication, Logic Programming Newsletter.

Dahl V. (1979) Logical design of deductive, natural language consultable data bases. *Proc. International Conference on Very Large Data Bases*, Rio de Janeiro, Brazil.

Dahl V. (1980) Two solutions for the negation problem. *Logic Programming Workshop*, Debrecen, Hungary.

Dahl V. (1982) On data base systems development through logic. *Transactions on Data Base Systems*, ACM.

Dahl V. (1983) On logic programming as a representation of knowledge. *IEEE Computer*, vol. 16, No 10, pp. 106-111.

Dahl V. and Abramson H. (1984) On gapping grammars. *Proc. II International Conference on Logic Programming*, Sweden.

Dahl. V. More on gapping grammars. SFU TR84-7

Gallaire H. et al. (eds) (1978) *Logic and data bases*. Plenum Publishing Co.

Giraud C. (1980) Logique et conception assistee par ordinateur. These de troisieme cycle, Univ. d'Aix-Marseille, France.

Hogger C. J. (1980) Logic representation of a concurrent algorithm. Logic

McDermott J. (1982) R1: A rule based configurer of computer systems. In: *Artificial Intelligence*, No. 19, pp. 39-88.

Monteiro L. (1981) A new proposal for concurrent programming in logic. Short communication, Logic Programming Newsletter.

Naish L. (1983) MU-PROLOG 3.0 reference manual. Melbourne University, Australia.

Pereira F. (1981) Extraposition grammars. *American Journal of Computational Linguistics* 7, pp. 243-256.

Reiter R. (1978) On closed world data bases. In: Gallaire et al.

Roussel Ph. (1975) Prolog: manuel de reference et d'utilisation. Univ. d'Aix-Marseille, France.

Shapiro E.Y. (1983) A subset of concurrent Prolog and its interpreter. ICOT Technical Report TR-003.

Van Caneghem M. (1982) Prolog II - Manuel d'utilisation. Universite d'Aix-Marseille, France.

Warren D.H.D. (1980a) Higher order extensions to Prolog — are they needed? Report n 154, Univ. of Edinburgh, Scotland.

Warren D.H.D. (1981) Efficient processing of interactive relational database queries expressed in logic. DAI Research Paper No. 156, Univ. of Edinburgh.

Prolog: A Database Query Language for All Seasons

Carlo Zaniolo

Microelectronics and Computer Technology Corporation
Austin, Texas

ABSTRACT

This paper elucidates the deep affinity that exists between Logic Programming languages, and database query languages. Relational query languages and Logic Programming are related by their common ancestry of mathematical logic. The first part of the paper discusses this relationship, focusing on the problem of interfacing Prolog with relational databases. The main enphasis of the paper is on the navigational nature of Prolog and on its resulting suitability as a query language for navigational DBMSs, such as Codasyl-compliant and Entity-Relationship oriented DBMSs. The second part of the paper shows that Prolog with simple object-oriented extensions becomes an attractive and very powerful high-level navigational query language for these systems. This paper suggests that a convergence of Logic Programming and Database techniques will provide the technology for building powerful new systems for knowledge representation and management, and outline the research problems that must be solved for the realization of such goal.

1. Introduction

Logic was never a strange in database field; as described in excellent surveys [Gall,GaMN], Logic has been used as a formal tool in the study of various database problems, including query language definition, integrity constraint and dependency theory, null values, proving consistency of transactions and deductive databases. But the impact of Logic on databases had in the past been predominantly in the theoretical domain.

Lately however, the field of Logic Programming is having a growing impact upon database technology. This new trend represents a marked departure from what happened in the 70's when the two fields followed parallel lines of development, and largely ignored one another from a technological standpoint. Thus, for instance, Prolog implementations are designed for main memory while databases' main concern is with secondary storage management. In the last few years, however, a strong interest is emerging in combining the *functionality and techniques* of the two fields and, in the process, Logic Programming is having a strong impact in shaping the future of database systems.

The main motivations for combining the two technologies are [Smit2]:

- **(Performance:)** Expert systems and similar knowledge-based systems will be widely used in the future. Many of them will need to store, manage and draw inferences upon large databases of facts and rules (e.g. 100 million of facts and 100 thousand rules). This suggests the use of secondary store, storage organizations and a parallel search techniques similar to those of database systems.
- **(Knowledge Sharing and Control:)** Large knowledge bases are important and expensive and will have to be shared and protected. Concurrency control, integrity constraint management and security enforcement will be needed — much as in DBMSs today.

- **(New Functionality:)** Advanced applications, such as CAD, have revealed various shortcomings of current database systems (e.g., their inability to handle complex objects, closures and metadata) and suffered from an "impedance mismatch" when interfacing the database to procedural Programming Languages [CoMa, MaPr].

Logic Programming lies at the confluence of Knowledge Based Systems, Databases and Programming Languages [Parker] and suggests itself as a natural vehicle for addressing these requirements. Databases will benefit greatly from a closer relationship with Logic Programming, which provides an elegant extension of Relational Databases with deduction and procedural objects, storage of general information structures — not only records — and 'amalgamation' of intentional information with extensional information (i.e., one can freely combine schema or metadata, constraints, etc. with typical database facts).

This paper adopts the viewpoint that a closer integration of Logic Programming and Databases is highly desirable and contributes to this goal in the following ways:

(1) It presents an overview and critique of the various approaches previously proposed for coupling Logic Programming and Databases,

(2) It introduces a novel approach — coupling Prolog with a navigational database — which is of superior practicability as a short-to-medium term solution,

(3) It identifies two key research problems that must be solved for a truly synergistic merge of the two technologies to occur, in the longer term future.

This paper is organized as follows. In the next section we compare today's main Logic Programming Language, Prolog, with relational query languages, and show that, whereas they share the same theoretical foundations, the navigational nature of the former and the non-navigational one of the latter yield different programming practices and implementation techniques. The many current attempts to connect a Prolog front-end with a relational back-end, suffer from this impedance mismatch, discussed in Section 3.

Because of these problems, this paper claims that Prolog is a better interface to DBMSs that support high-level navigational queries. These DBMSs include those based on the Entity-Relationship model [Chen], and those supporting database aggregation [SmSm], including the Codasyl-compliant ones [Coda] (after cosmetic corrections). Therefore, Section 4 of the paper discusses these non-relational data models and Section 5 presents simple extensions that turn Prolog into a simple query language for these systems.

The final section of the paper considers the longer term outlook, and suggests that the ultimate combination of the two technologies will feature a non-navigational Logic-based language and relational DBMS-like query optimization techniques.

2. Prolog and Relational DBMSs

Prolog constitutes an attractive domain-oriented query language for relational databases [Ullm1], syntactically resembling an in-line version of QBE [Zloo], where the specification of joins is is easier than in tuple-oriented languages. The power of Prolog as a pure logic language (Horn Clauses only) surpasses that of relational calculus, since it is *relationally complete* [Codd], and, through recursion, it also handles least fixed point queries that exceed the power of relational calculus. Actually, pure Prolog can express queries in the set known as YE+ (all queries representable by a fixpoint applied to a positive existential query [ChHa]).

However, Prolog is more than just a logic language, since it offers features and embodies an execution model that turns it into a general-purpose PL. This generality adds to Prolog's desirability as a practical database language, since complete applications can now be developed in it. This contrasts with the current approach to the development of database-intensive applications that uses a general purpose PL with embedded database query statements [SQL, Adplx].

Therefore, a system which combines a Prolog front-end with a database back-end appears to be a very promising vehicle for developing database and knowledge-based applications. However, connecting Prolog to a DBMS poses some challenging technical problems; the examples which follow are intended to clarify these problems and the navigational nature of Prolog.

Suppose that we have the database of Figure 1, consisting of employees, departments, items and sales, described by the following set of Prolog facts.

```
% dept has arguments Dept_Name, Floor
dept(sport, 1).
dept(management, 2).

% item has arguments  Name and Price
item(skis, 260).
item(basketball, 21).

% sales has as arguments Item_name, Dept_name and Volume.
sales(skis, sport, 12).
sales(basketball, sport, 48).

% the empl relation has arguments Name, Dept_name, Salary and Supervisor_name
empl(smith, sport, 23000, jones).
empl(green, sport, 26000, jones).
empl(jones, sport, 36000, dimaggio).
empl(dimaggio, management, 120000, none).
```

Figure 1. An example database.

A simple query such as "Find all employees in departments on the first floor" can be formulated via the following rule:

```
first_fl_emp(Name) :-      dept(D_name, 1),
                           empl(Name, D_name, _ , _ ).
```

Figure 2. Employees working for a department on the first floor.

Thus the setting of the goal:

```
?- first_fl_emp(X).
```

Will return all the X's that make this rule true, i.e

```
X = smith
X = green
X = jones.
```

The obvious similarity between the Prolog query above and a domain-based relational calculus, such as QBE, hides the deep differences in the underlying execution models; unlike in most relational databases, Prolog's goals are executed in the very order in which they are specified. Thus, the above rule is executed as in a nested iteration where the tuples of **dept** are searched in the outer loop and the tuples of **empl** are visited in the inner loop. In order to ensure efficient execution therefore, Prolog programmers order their goals so that the more selective ones appear first. We will refer to this discipline as (physical) *navigation.*

To illustrate the impact of goal order, for instance, consider reordering the goals for the rule of Figure 2. Then the **empl** predicates will be searched first, and the qualification that their department must be at the first floor will be used only later. On the average, if one out of k departments is at the first floor, this second navigation will visit k times more records than the former.

Recursive predicates supply another good example, as in the following rule that defines the relationship between employees and their immediate or remote managers:

```
manager_star(Emp, Mg) :-    empl(Emp, _, _, Mg).
manager_star(Emp, Mg) :-    empl(Emp, _, _, Middle_mg),
                            manager_star(Middle_mg, Mg).
```

Figure 3. Employees and all their managers.

This example illustrates Prolog's ability of computing closures via recursion, that is not supported by the Relational Calculus [Codd].

While the rule of Figure 3 can be used to compute both the managers of a given employee and the subordinates of a given manager, it works efficiently only in the first case. In the second case it will systematically enumerate all the employees with all their managers, until the given manager is found. Thus a programmer must use a rule embodying the inverse navigation (i.e. starting from a manager and proceeding to his subordinates) for the second case.

The navigational nature of Prolog becomes even more obvious when the metapredicates, the cut and, in most implementations, arithmetic and comparison predicates are considered. When these are present, a change in the order of goal execution, may compromise the correctness of the program. For example, suppose that management employees receive an extra month of pay each year. Then to compute the annual salary of an employee we can write

```
sal(Emp, Ansal) :-   empl(Emp, Dept, Msal, _),
                              compsal(Dept, Msal, Ansal).

compsal(management, Msal, Ansal) :-    !, Ansal is Msal * 13.
compsal( _          , Msal, Ansal) :-    Ansal is Msal * 12.
```

Figure 4. A computation of employee salaries.

In the first rule of Figure 4, **empl** must precede **compsal**, to ensure that **Dept** and **Msal** are instantiated as required by the arithmetic predicate **is**. The cut ought to precede the **is** predicate in the second rule, and the second rule must precede the third. Thus, even in this simple example the order of goals is essential.

In contrast to Prolog, most relational DBMSs are non-navigational, since the order of clauses in a query conjunction is immaterial because the responsibility for efficient execution lies with the system's optimizer and not the user.

These differences between Prolog and relational DBMSs complicate the task of connecting them.

3. Coupling Prolog with a Relational DBMS

This is the first and easier step towards the benefits of an integrated system [KuYo, Naqv, JaCV, ChWa, MPMJ]. A first benefit expected is faster execution of Prolog programs, since database predicates can be off-loaded to the database system for more efficient, and possibly parallel, execution. This is particularly useful, when the ability is needed of making inferences on large volumes of data, such as in data-intensive expert systems. A second benefit consists in the enhanced functionality of the database system, due to the newly accrued inferential capability. Also in such a system, programmers will be able to develop the entire application in Prolog (a complete PL) whereas presently they must resort to a conventional PL with an embedded query language.

To evaluate this solution, assume that all facts are stored in the DBMS as relations and all rules are kept within the Prolog front-end processor. (This is only a simplification of convenience; in general, there are facts that one may want to keep in the Prolog front-end, and rules that one may want to support in the DBMS using its view support primitives.) Then the Prolog database of Figure 1, will be replaced by the relational database of Figure 5, and the following technical problems must be addressed:

(1) When should the database goals be executed (i.e. as they are encountered or after the Prolog goals)?

dept	(dp_name,	floor)
	sport	1
	management	2

item	(it_name,	price)
	skis	260
	basketball	21

sales	(dp_name,	it_name,	vol)
	skis	sport	12
	basketball	sport	48

empl	(name,	dp_name,	sal,	spv)
	smith	sport	23000	jones
	green	sport	26000	jones
	jones	sport	36000	dimaggio
	dimaggio	management	120000	none

Figure 5. The relational database equivalent to that of Figure 1.

(2) How should data be exchanged to and from Prolog and the DBMS?

(3) How can the translation of database goals be optimized?

(4) How should recursive database calls be supported (such as in **manager_star**)?

A solution to the last problem has been proposed in [Naqv]. This solution consists in the compilation of recursive database queries into iterative queries that are to be run in the DBMS. The solution proposed in [JaCV] addresses point 3 above by taking advantage of integrity constraints, such as functional dependencies and inferential integrity, to optimize the translation of Prolog statements into SQL queries. (Note however that efficient execution of these queries on the basis of the available storage structures still falls on the DBMS).

Since Prolog basically operates on one tuple at a time, while relational DBMSs tend to return sets of tuples, streaming data between the two systems faces problems similar to those found in interfacing relational languages to PLs. Say for instance that in a clause we have the sequence of goals A, B1, B2, ... where A is a database goal while B1, B2, ... are Prolog goals. Then, if these goals are executed in the order in which they are written, the DBMS may run ahead of Prolog by computing and returning all tuples that satisfy A, even though only one is needed at first, and the others may not be needed even later (e.g. if B2 is the cut). Therefore, most workers follow the approach of [KuYo] and execute the database goals after the Prolog goals. In other words, database goals are moved to the end of each rule (A will follow all the B's). The supporters of this approach note that since all database goals are concentrated at the end of the rules, then communication between Prolog and the DBMS is reduced, and the search in the DBMS's large data space is more efficient since the execution of Prolog goals has narrowed the search space.

However, this solution disregards the navigational nature of Prolog and is bound to create confusion and errors. For instance, in Figure 4, if the goal **empl** is executed after **compsal**, the salary of all employees is computed on a thirteen months per year basis (an outcome that may be palatable to the populace but is definitely incorrect). A programmer will not be able to develop an application program using a sample Prolog database and then apply it to a real DBMS database. For all these reasons, we claim that it is preferable to evaluate *all* goals in the order in which they are listed. A programmer is then free to order his goals so that they will be executed most efficiently — possibly by collecting all database goals at the end of the rules. (Any good Prolog programmer has already plenty of experience at such a task.) Groups of adjacent database goals can still be translated into a single query and the improvements of [JaCV] and [Naqv] are still applicable. The problem of the DBMS running ahead of Prolog can be controlled by appropriate buffer management during inter-process communication. This solution preserves both the navigational nature of Prolog and the non-navigational nature of the relational DBMS.

A third approach is also possible: assign a navigational interpretation to both Prolog goals and the database goals. Here the programmer orders the database goals to ensure efficient execution, and the DBMS follows the given navigation in a *nested loop join* strategy; the DBMS's responsibility is now limited to an effective use of available indexes in performing selection operations. This strategy is obviously the most suitable when one wants to build DBMS capabilities within Prolog. It is also particularly attractive when the DBMS is based upon a data model where a navigational language is the query language of choice. The next two sections of the paper are devoted to this novel approach.

4. Data Models and Navigational Query Languages

Navigational languages constitute the query languages of choice for a broad range of DBMSs that can be described as having a data model supporting the notion of entities and a graph-like representation for relationships between entities. While this purposely general description covers a wide spectrum of data models, we will concentrate on a few of them for the sake of specificity.

All these models, support the concept of an entity with its unique identifier, often called a surrogate, that distinguishes an entity occurrence from any other; the value of the surrogate is immaterial and normally inaccessible to users. The representation of relationships used by the various models is much less uniform, as discussed next.

Entity-Relationship diagrams represent entities as rectangles and relationships as diamonds, as described in Figure 5.

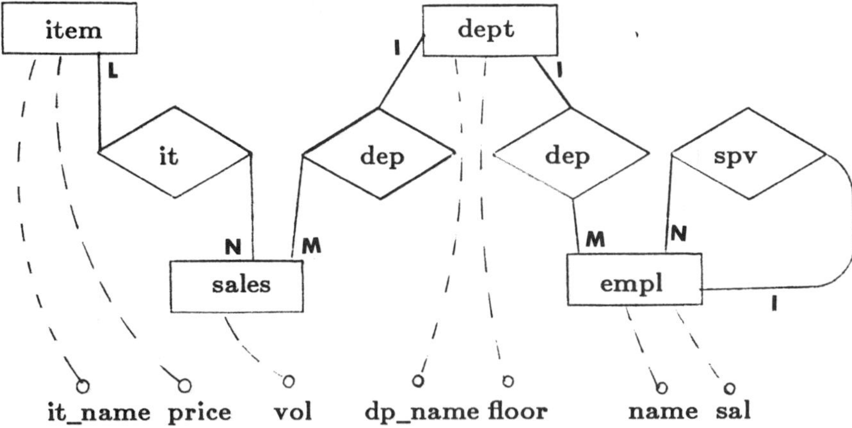

Figure 6. An E-R diagram for the example of Figure 1.

While the original E-R proposal also contemplates the direct representation of many-to-many relationships [Chen], the problem of having attributes attached to relationships and considerations of uniformity and query convenience have suggested their elimination via a technique called *aggregation* [SmSm]. With this technique, a relationship is modeled as an entity incorporating the entities participating in the relationship. Aggregation is illustrated by Figure 6 where a many-to-many sales relationship between departments and items is represented by the the entity **sales** with a many-to-one edges to **dept** and another to **item**; thus, the attribute **vol** describing the relationship is conveniently attached to the new aggregate entity **sales**.

Two benefits of the data modeling approach exemplified by the schema of Figure 6 are that schemas can be recast into a wide spectrum of seemingly different, but basically equivalent, representations and many query languages of various flavors will work well with these schemas. The in-line representation used by GEM [Zani1, TsZa], for instance is given in Figure 7. This is designed as an extension of relational DDL. In addition to the basic data types (e.g. character, integer, etc.)

attributes can also be assigned to be of a certain entity-type. For instance in Figure 7, **spv** of **empl** is of type **empl** while **dep** in **sales** is of type **dept**.

item (it_name, price)
dept (dp_name, floor)
sales (it:item, dep:dept, vol)
empl(name, dep:dept, sal, spv:empl).

Figure 7. The in-line representation for the schema of Figure 6.

A graphical representation derived from that of Figure 7 is given in Figure 8. The arrows in Figure 8 suggest that attributes of type entity can be viewed as logical pointers to these entities. No dangling pointer is allowed (referential integrity), except for null pointers, that may, for instance, be used in **empl** to represent employees without supervisors. A second interpretation of these arrows is as functions; for instance **dep** defines a function from **sales** to **dept**.

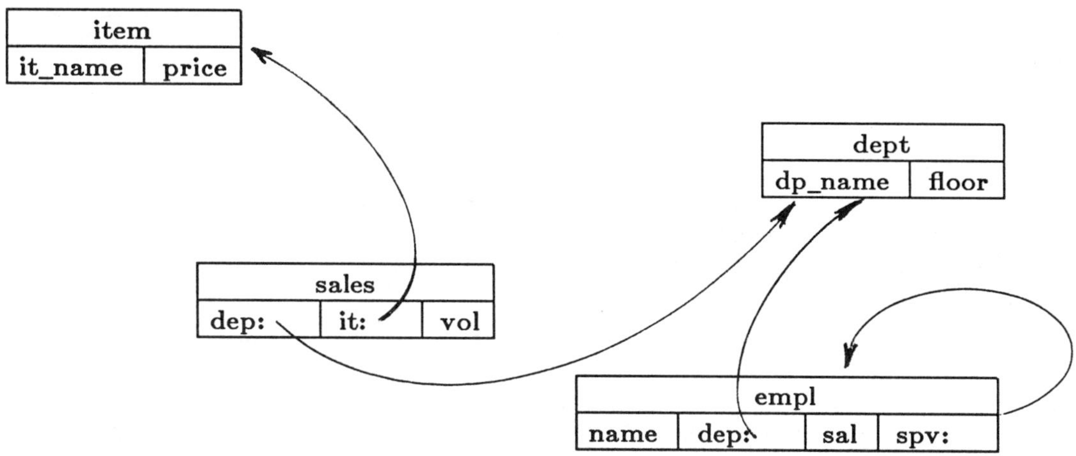

Figure 8. A graphical representation of the in-line schema above.

Before we discuss query languages for these data models, let us consider yet another transformation on the diagrams of Figure 8. Suppose that we reverse the directions of all arrows and move the entity attributes out of the boxes, appending them as labels to these arrows. Then, we obtain the data-structure diagram [Coda] shown in Figure 9; here edges denote owner-coupled sets and rectangles denote record-types with the simple data-items describing the records. Thus Codasyl-compliant systems can also be handled with this approach (but repeating groups and multimember sets require further elaboration).

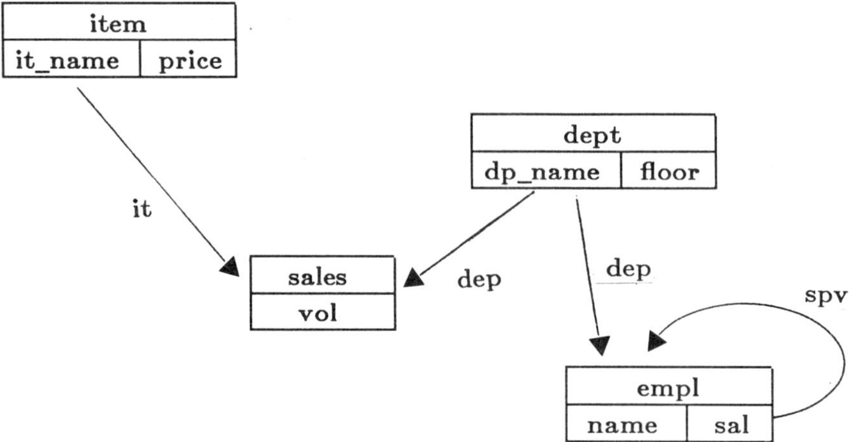

Figure 9. A data structure diagram for the example at hand.

As previously mentioned, these types of data models are supportive of navigational query languages, both at the logical and the physical levels.

(1) At the logical level, by providing primitives to express graph-traversal or functional composition, they relieve users from the burden of specifying joins explicitly.

(2) Systems based upon these models tend to provide some physical support for relationships between entities — for instance, links and other storage organizations implemented to support the owner-coupled set concept [Coda]. Similar storage structures, may or may not be available for relational systems.

A distinction between the logical level and the physical one is also fundamental to understand query languages for these models. It is possible to have a system where the query language is navigational in style, while the underlying implementation is not. GEM supplies an excellent example of such a language. For the purpose of making queries more expressive and concise, GEM supports a generalization of QUEL's dot-notation. If **empl** denotes a variable occurrence of entity type **empl**, then **empl.dep** is the department of that employee and **empl.dep.floor** denotes the floor of that employee's department. Therefore the query of Figure 2 can be expressed in GEM as follows:

retrieve (empl.name)
where empl.dep.floor = 1

Figure 10. "Find all employees of departments at the first floor" in GEM.

The valued-based join of QUEL was replaced in Figure 10, by the extended dot-notation which can be viewed as functional composition. Since functional composition is always unidirectional, it follows the arrows, GEM should not be interpreted as a navigational language in the physical sense, since that would lead to a very inefficient implementation. Take for example Figure 10: the path there embodied states that **empl** is visited first, and **dept** next. An efficient navigation should instead begin from **dept** and progress to **empl**; such navigation cannot be expressed in GEM. Thus navigation in GEM queries is only a device of notational convenience and not the script for its physical implementation. It is no surprise therefore that GEM's proposed implementation maps back into relational queries [TsZa]; and indeed interfacing Prolog with GEM would require implementation techniques similar to those used for relational DBMSs.

The language DAPLEX [Ship] supplies an excellent example of a query language that can be used to express physical navigation. In DAPLEX, that is totally committed to the functional data model [SiKe], both the relationship from an entity occurrence to another and that from an entity occurrence to its attribute values are modeled as functions. Functional composition is then represented using the usual nested parenthesis notation. Thus the previous query can be expressed as follows:

FOR EACH X IN empl()
SUCH THAT floor(dept(X)) = 1
PRINT name(X)

Figure 11. A DAPLEX expression of the same query.

Unlike GEM however, DAPLEX supports the use of inverse functions. Thus after writing

DEFINE emp_of_dep(dept) =>>
INVERSE OF dep(empl)

the previous query can also be expressed as follows:

FOR EACH Y IN dept
SUCH THAT floor(Y) = 1
PRINT name(emp_of_dep(Y))

Figure 12. A logically equivalent formulation for the same query.

The query in Figure 12 is *logically* equivalent to that of Figure 11, but unlike figure 10 it embodies a navigation path that leads to efficient implementation (i.e. it first selects departments at the first floor and then find the employees working there). Thus DAPLEX, unlike GEM, can be implemented as a navigational language in the physical sense. As described in the last section, navigational languages are very compatible with Prolog. But in spite of its navigational nature, and its suitability for use with any data model described so far, DAPLEX does not provide a desirable interface to Prolog. The problem is that DAPLEX is a language based upon the concept of functional evaluation, while Prolog as a logic programming language is based on unification.

In the next section we present a new solution that is totally compatible with Prolog and expresses navigation without requiring the definition of inverse functions.

5. Prolog as a Navigational Query Language

In Prolog, there is no notion of predicate occurrence, in the same way as, in relational databases, there is no notion of an entity occurrence independent of attribute values. To interface with our data models that support the concept of entity occurrence via unique surrogate values, we need to introduce the notion of predicate occurrence in Prolog. Some Prolog implementations already support the concept of unique references to predicates [CProl], as a means to a faster and more effective execution. Here we need syntactic constructs that are easy to use, expressive and support navigational queries on the data models described in the last section.

Suppose that, via some special declaration, we include a schema such as that of Figure 8 in our Prolog front-end. Then the programmer can call as goals predicates of the same name and arity as the entities in Figure 7. Thus, for instance the simple rule,

dep_on_2_3(Name) :- dept(Name, 2).
dep_on_2_3(Name) :- dept(Name, 3).

defines the names of all departments on the second and third floor.

To implement navigational queries we need the capability of referring to entity occurrences as values. Therefore we introduce the infix predicate "@" which takes a predicate as its left argument and a predicate reference as the right one and succeeds when the right argument does in fact refer to the left one. (At least one argument must be instantiated for the predicate to succeed.) For instance the rule:

dep_on_2(Name) :- dept(_ , 2) @ X, dept(Name, _) @ X.

will produce all departments on the second floor, since **dept(_ , 2) @ X** leaves **X** pointing to a department on the second floor, and the second rule **dept(Name, _) @ X** retrieves that department again. In this example the new infix operator "@" is not really necessary, since one can express the same query by:

```
?-dept(Name, 2).
```

But consider now aggregation. The query of Figure 1 must be expressed as follows:

```
first_fl_emp(Name) :-    dept(_ , 1) @ X,
                         empl(Name, X, _ , _ ).
```

Figure 13. The query of Figure 2 on a schema of Figure 8.

Execution of the first goal, **dept(_ , 1)@X**, finds all occurrences of departments on the first floor and leaves **X** pointing at them. Thus, **empl(Name, X, _ , _)** finds all the employees working in those departments. Thus our query is specified as a navigation from **dept** to **empl**, using our new predicate "@"; without it, this query could not be expressed on the schema of Figure 8.

More complex queries may demand more elaborate navigations. The predicate of Figure 14 shows a navigation that goes from **sales** to **item**, and then again from **sales** to **dept** and finally to **empl** twice.

```
sales(Iname, Dname, Sname) :-    sales(Dep, It, 0),
                                 item(Iname, Price)@It, Price<500,
                                 dept(Dname, _ )@Dep,
                                 empl(_ , Dep, _ , Spv)
                                 empl(Sname, _ , _ , _ )@Spv.
```

Figure 14. Find the names of items, departments and supervisors of employees working there, for items with zero sales and price less than $500.

Recursive queries are important in engineering applications requiring the computation of closures [MaPr, Smit1]. Figure 15 shows how to formulate a query similar to that of Figure 3 without having to depend on the presence of user-supplied entity identifiers.

```
mgr_star(Emp, Mgr) :-  empl(_ , _ , _ , Mgr) @ Emp.
mgr_star(Emp, Mgr) :-  empl(_ , _ , _ , Mdmgr) @ Emp,
                       mgr_star(Mdmgr, Mgr).
```

Figure 15. All managers of a given employee occurrence.

In order to derive the managers' names of an employee with a given name we can write:

```
manager_star(Emp_name, Mgr_name):- empl(Emp_name, _ , _ , _ ) @ X,
                                   mgr_star(X, Y),
                                   empl(Mgr_name, _ , _ , _ ) @ Y.
```

This last query is then equivalent to that of Figure 3.

The approach just proposed obtains the desired effect with minimal extensions to Prolog. But other solutions exist and may be preferable in certain situations. An interesting one is to use an object-oriented approach to Prolog [Zani2]. With this approach methods can be associated with objects and a message of the form:

object : method

can be used to specify the application of a method to an object. Then we can assume that the boxes in Figures 9 or 10 defines objects, while the edges define methods applicable to them. For instance we now have an object **empl** with two arguments (name and salary) with the following associated methods:

```
dep(X)
spv(X)
self(X)
```

The argument of **dep** unifies with the department of the given employee, the argument of **spv** with his manager. Thus for instance, the goal

empl(jones):dept(X)

instantiates **X** to the department occurrence of employee jones. The system defined method **self** is available for every entity type and its argument unifies with the occurrence of the given predicate(same as the right argument of @). We can now reformulate the query of Figure 2 as follows:

```
first_fl_emp(Name) :-    dept(_ , 1):self(X),
                         empl(Name, _ ):dep(X).
```

Figure 16. All the employees in departments at the first floor.

The recursive query of Figure 15 can be expressed as follows:

```
mg_star(Emp, Mgr) :-    empl(_ , _ ):self(Emp):spv(Mgr).
mg_star(Emp, Mgr) :-    empl(_ , _ ):self(Emp):spv(Mdmgr),
                        mgr_star(Mdmgr, Mgr).
```

Figure 17. Same query as that of Figure 15.

Figure 17 illustrates the capability of having more than one method applied to same object.

This second approach is preferable to the first one when the user wants to deal with graphic schemas directly, without going through an in-line representation such as that of Figure 7. Also, it provides a better interface to DBMS supporting the notion of *generalization* [SmSm], a topic of future reports.

Finally, it is important to remember that if one wants either to adopt a parallel execution strategy for Prolog, or to work in a pure logic framework (no navigational interpretation of clause order), the syntactic constructs introduced here retain their full validity. The notion of objects supplies the needed link between Logic Programming and structured database schemas.

6. Discussion

Prolog is a powerful and flexible language that can be used in conjunction with different data models and database systems. While, previous work has considered interfaces between Prolog and relational databases, this paper has shown that connecting Prolog with navigational DBMSs is feasible and often preferable. This conclusion also emerges from the works presented in [Fran] and [Gray]. The approach proposed here also suplies a natural solution to the problem of extending Prolog with database primitives — a problem considered in [CaDG, EgPP, ScWa]. Its main strength is as a short-to-medium term solution, since it outlines how to build a completely integrated system using only available technology.

Considering the longer-term outlook, we can see how the elimination of navigation can yield considerable advantages in terms of ease-of-use, data independence and better suitability for parallel implementation. Even in the case of serial implementation, there are situations where performance gains can be achieved by by replacing Prolog's looping join by computationally more efficient joins. Thus, in analogy with the current trend in databases, we can envision a future evolution of logic programming away from the navigational paradigm. It is also probable that the two fields will eventually merge. For instance, the decreasing cost of main memory may lead to main memory databases [DeWi], thus eliminating the main difference in underlying technology of the two fields. But difficult research problems must be solved before such scenario can become a reality. These are the main problems:

- The design of a Logic-Based Language that retains the power of Prolog without relying on a sequential execution model. Research is currently being developed towards this goal [Robi] with functional languages [Turn] proposing interesting alternatives to such an effort.
- The extension of relational query optimization and compilation techniques based on aggregate operators (select, join, union, etc.) to Logic Programming. To accomplish this goal, efficient mechanisms must be devised to support recursion and unification. This represents a difficult problem for which only partial solutions have been proposed so far [HeNa, Li,

McSh, Ullm2, Zani3].

Acknowledgments

The author is grateful to Gene Lowenthal, Dewayne Perry and Won Kim for their comments and suggested improvements.

References

[Adplx] Smith, J.M., S. Fox, T. Landers, "ADAPLEX: The integration of the DAPLEX Language with the Ada Programming Language," Technical Report, Computer Corporation of America, 1982.

[CaDG] Carey, M., D.J. DeWitt and G. Graefe "Mechanisms for Concurrency Control and Recovery in Prolog" *Proc. First Int. Workshop on Expert Database Systems,* 1984.

[ChHa] Chandra A., D. Harel, "Horn Clauses and the Fixpoint Query Hierarchy," *ACM Conference on Principles of Database Systems,* 1982.

[ChWa] Chang C.L. and A. Walker, "PROSQL: A Prolog Programming Interface with SQL/DS," *Proc. First Int. Workshop on Expert Database Systems,* 1984.

[Chen] Chen, P.P., "The Entity-Relationship Model — Toward an Unified View of Data," *ACM Trans. Database Syst.,* 1, 1, pp. 9-36, 1976.

[ClMe] Clocksin, W.F. and Mellish, *Programming in Prolog,* Springer-Verlag, 1981.

[CProl] Pereira F., et al, "C-Prolog User's Manual, version 1.4", Dept. of Architecture, University of Edinburgh.

[Coda] "CODASYL Data Description Language Journal of Development," Material Data Management Branch, Dept. of Supplies and Services, Ottawa, 1978.

[Codd] Codd E. F., "Relational Completeness of Data Base Sublanguages," *Courant Computer Science Symp.,* Prentice Hall, 1972.

[CoMa] Copeland, G. and D. Maier, "Making Smalltalk a Database System," *Proc. ACM SIGMOD Conference,* 1984.

[DeWi] DeWitt, D.J. et al., "Implementation Techniques for Main Memory Databases," *Proc. ACM SIGMOD Conference,* 1984.

[EgPP] Eggert, S. Parker and K. Parsaye, "Prototyping in Prolog: Experiences and Lessons'" unpublished manuscript, 1983.

[Fran] Frank A.U., "Extending a Network Database with Prolog," *Proc. First Int. Workshop on Expert Database Systems,* 1984.

[HeNa] Henschen, L.J. and S. A. Naqvi, "On Compiling Queries in Recursive First-Order Databases," *JACM,* Vol. 31, No. 1, pp. 47-85, 1984.

[HeSW] Held, G.D., M.R. Stonebraker and E. Wong, "INGRES: a Relational Data Base System," *AFIPS Nat. Computer Conf.,* Vol. 44, pp. 409-416, 1975.

[KuYo] Shybayama, S. et al "Query Processing Flow On RDBM DELTA's ..." *Proc. of Int. Conference on Fifth Generation Computer Systems,* 1984.

[Gall] Gallaire, H., "The Impacts of Logic on Data Bases," *Proc. 7th Int. Conference on Very Large Data Bases,* IEEE, New York, N.Y., pp.248-259, 1981.

[GaMN] Gallaire, H., J. Minker and J.M. Nicolas, " Logic and Databases: A deductive Approach," *ACM Computing Surveys,* Vol. 16, No. 2, 1984.

[Gray] Gray, Peter M.D., "Efficient Prolog Access to Codasyl and FDM Databases,"

[KuYo] Kunifuji S., H. Yokota, "Prolog and Relational Databases for 5th Generation Computer Systems," Proc. Logical Workshop on Logical Basis for Databases, Toulose,

1982.

[JaCV] Jarke M., J. Clifford and Y. Vassiliou, "An Optimizing Prolog Front-end to a Relational Query," *Proc. ACM SIGMOD Conference on Management of Data,* pp. 437-444, 1985.

[Li] Li D., "*A Prolog Database System,*" *Research Institute Press,* Letchworth, Hertfordshire, England, 1984.

[MaPr] Maier D. and Price D., "Data Model Requirements for Engineering Applications," *Proc. First Int. Workshop on Expert Database Systems,* 1984.

[McSh] McKay, D. and S. Shapiro, "Using Active Connection Graphs for Reasoning with Recursive Rules," *Proc. 7th IJCAI,* pp. 368-374, 1981.

[MPMJ] Marque-Pucheu, G., J. Martin-Gallausiaux an G. Jomier, "Interfacing Prolog and Relational Database Management Systems," in *New applications of Databases,* G. Gardarin and E. Gelembe (eds.), Academic Press, 1984.

[Naqv] Naqvi, S. A., "Prolog and Relational Databases: A road to Data intensive expert Systems," *Proc. First Int. Workshop on Expert Database Systems,* 1984.

[Park] Parker D. S. "Logic Programming and Databases — Panel Session" *Proc. First Int. Workshop on Expert Database Systems,* 1984.

[Robi] Robinson, J.A., Logic Programming — Past, Present and Future," *New Generation Computing,* Vol. 1, No. 1, 1983.

[SQL] I.B.M. "SQL/Data System Application Programming Manual," Order No. SH24-5018-0, First Edition, August 1981.

[ScWa] Sciore, E. and D.S. Warren, "Towards an Integrated Database-Prolog System," *Proc. First Int. Workshop on Expert Database Systems,* 1984.

[Ship] Shipman, D.W., "The Functional Model and the Data Language DAPLEX," *ACM Trans. Data Base Syst.,* 6,1, pp. 140-173, 1982.

[SiKe] Sibley, E. H., and Kerschberg, L. "Data Architecture and Data Model Considerations," *Proc. AFIPS Nat. Computer Conf.,* Dallas, Tex, June 1977, pp. 85-86.

[Smit1] Smith, J.M., "Multiple Data Types and Inferencing in Database Models," Database Extravaganza, Boston, August 1984.

[Smit2] Smith J.M. Expert Database Systems: A Database Perspective," *Proc. First Int. Workshop on Expert Database Systems,* 1984.

[SmSm] Smith, J.M. and D.C.P. Smith, "Database Abstractions: Aggregation and Generalization," *ACM Trans. Database Syst.,* 2, 2, pp. 105-133, 1977.

[TsZa] Tsur S. and C. Zaniolo, "On the Implementation of GEM: supporting a semantic data model on a relational back-end," *Proc. ACM SIGMOD Conference on Management of Data,* 1984.

[Turn] Turner, D.A., "A New Implementation Technique for Applicative Languages," *Software Practice and Experience,* Vol 9, pp. 31-49, September 1979.

[Ullm1] Ullman, J., "*Principles of Database Systems,*" Computer Science Press, 1980.

[Ullm2] Ullman, J.D., "Implementation of Logical Query Languages for Databases," *TODS,* to appear.

[Warr] Warren, D.H.D. "Efficient Processing of Interactive Relational Database Queries Expressed in Logic," *Proc. 7th Int. Conference on Very Large Data Bases,* pp. 272-281, 1981.

[Wrig] Wright D., "Prolog as a Relationally Complete Database Query Language that can Handle Least Fixed Point Operators," University of Kentucky tech. report no. 73-80.

[Zani1] Zaniolo, C., "The Database Language GEM," *ACM SIGMOD Conference, May 1983.*

[Zani2] Zaniolo C., "Object-Oriented Programming in Prolog," *Int. Logic Programming Symposium, 1984.*

[Zani3] Zaniolo, C., "The Representation and Deductive Retrieval of Complex Objects," *Proc. 11th Int. Conference on Very Large Data Bases,* 1985.

[Zloo] Zloof M.M., "Query by Example," *Proc. AFIPS NCC 44,* pp. 431-438, 1975.

PROSQL: A PROLOG PROGRAMMING INTERFACE WITH SQL/DS

C. L. Chang
A. Walker

IBM T. J. Watson Research Laboratory
Yorktown Heights, New York

ABSTRACT

SQL/DS (SQL/Data System) is an IBM relational data base system. It has the full functions of a data management system, including access paths (e.g., indexing), query optimization, data sharing, recovery, concurrency control and protection, and so on. It supports efficient retrieval from a large data base in secondary storage.

PROLOG is a language suitable for constructing knowledge based systems. A PROLOG program consists of facts, (i.e assertions), and rules. A fact in PROLOG can be used to represent a tuple in a relational data base. A rule can be used to specify a view in a relational data base, or to represent knowledge about how to use the facts.

Used as a query language, PROLOG is formally as powerful as an application program running over a SQL/DS data base. However, existing versions of PROLOG do not have the full data management functions of SQL/DS. Since re-implementing these functions in PROLOG would be expensive, this paper will describe an approach of coupling PROLOG to SQL/DS. This gives a user the advantages of both PROLOG and SQL/DS. The coupling consists of a method of calling SQL statements from PROLOG. It is flexible, because it allows either loose coupling or tight coupling between PROLOG and SQL/DS. We call our interface PROSQL.

1. INTRODUCTION

PROLOG [Battani and Meloni 1973, Colmerauer et al. 1973, Kowalski 1979, Roberts 1977, Roussel 1975, Sowa 1981, Warren et al. 1977] is a logic programming language which is convenient and powerful for representing both data, and knowledge about how to use data. Basically, a PROLOG program is a set of Horn clauses having one of the following forms:

A	(assertion)
B <- C1 & ... & Cm	(rule)
G1 & ... & Gn ?	(goal)

where A, B, C1,...,Cm, G1,...,Gn are atomic formulas. We note that a tuple in a relational data base is an assertion. The PROLOG language is modular and flexible. Clauses in a program can be added and deleted as desired. Usually, the cost of writing a program in PROLOG is considerably less than in a procedural programming language such as PASCAL.

In many applications such as expert systems [Chang 1983, Pereira et al. 1982, Pereira and Porto 1982, Walker 1983a, Santane-Toth and Szeredi 1982, Wilson and John 1983], and natural language processing [Walker 1983b, Walker and Porto 1983 Warren 1981, McCord 1982], it is desirable that a PROLOG program support a large number of assertions efficiently. In very large applications, there may be system limits on main memory, which can force an extensive swapping of assertions. To avoid extra support programming in PROLOG, or in another language as in [Chomicki and Grudzinski 1983], we propose to use the relational data base system, SQL/DS [IBM 1981], to store the assertions, and to have PROLOG couple with it. We call our PROLOG programming interface PROSQL. In addition there are cases where we have data already in SQL/DS, and we wish to build an application program (e.g. an expert system) in PROLOG. In these cases, PROSQL can be useful.

Basically, a PROSQL program is a PROLOG program that contains SQL statements. In this paper, we shall describe the PROSQL interface, and some experiments in which it is used to couple a PROLOG package and SQL/DS [IBM 1981].

Linking a deductive system, (e.g. PROLOG, DEDUCE, SYLLOG) with a relational data base is also considered in [Chang 1976, 1978, 1979], [Kunifuji and Yokota 1982], [Vassiliou et al. 1983], and [Walker 1981, 1983b]. In these papers, essentially, a query is represented by a logic goal. Then, using rules in a logic program, the query is transformed into queries containing only base relations in the relational data base. The transformed queries are still in logic clausal form. We note that Chang transforms the query into a "recursive" query graph which is then compiled into an iterative program. Kunifuji et al. and Vassiliou et al. transform the query into a "sequence" of queries, each of which is then evaluated "independently" by the relational data base management system. Walker constructs "program trees" which are executed iteratively over the data base.

The PROSQL system proposed here is more flexible than the above approaches. By writing an appropriate PROSQL program, the user can choose whether she wants an evaluational or non-evaluational method, an interpreter or compiler approach, loose or tight coupling, or whether she wants to store all tuples of a relation in PROLOG or SQL/DS, or split them between PROLOG and SQL/DS.

2. STRUCTURE OF PROSQL PROGRAMS

We assume that PROSQL programs will be written by persons who are familiar with both the PROLOG and SQL languages. A PROSQL program is a PROLOG program that uses the special predicate SQL. SQL is a one-place predicate. It is used to create tables or views, insert tuples into SQL/DS, or to retrieve tuples from SQL/DS.

We now describe the SQL predicate as follows:

DATA DEFINITION

```
Format:
                     SQL( <SQL-definition-statement> ).

Examples:

                     SQL( 'CREATE TABLE EMP( NAME VARCHAR(20),
                                   MGR VARCHAR(20),
                                   SAL INTEGER) IN DBSP' ).

                     SQL( 'CREATE INDEX INAME ON EMP (NAME ASC)' ).

                     SQL( 'DROP TABLE INVENTORY' ).

                     SQL( 'CREATE VIEW T AS SELECT * FROM P' ).
```

For data definition, an argument of the SQL predicate must be a string representing a SQL data definition statement. It may be used to create or drop a table or a view. Once a table or view is defined, PROLOG can get tuples from the table or view from SQL/DS, or insert tuples into a table in SQL/DS. To improve the performance, indexes on columns of a table can be specified.

DATA INSERTION

```
Format:
                     SQL( <SQL-INSERTION-statement> ).

Examples:

                     SQL( 'INSERT INTO EMP VALUES (*x, JONES, *y)' ).

                     SQL( 'INSERT INTO EMP VALUES (*x,*y,*z)' ).
```

For insertion, an argument of the SQL predicate is a string representing a SQL Format 1 INSERT statement. Table names appearing in the INSERT statement must be first defined either by PROSQL, or separately on SQL/DS. A list of data items in the INSERT statement is a list of variables and constants. In the above examples, *x, *y, and *z are variables, while JONES is a constant. A PROSQL program is written so that each variable in an INSERT statement is bound to a constant before the INSERT statement is executed.

DATA RETRIEVAL

Format:	
	SQL(<SQL-SELECT-statement>).
Examples:	
	SQL('SELECT * FROM EMP'). SQL('SELECT * FROM EMP WHERE SAL > 50000'). SQL('SELECT NAME, SAL INTO *x, *y FROM EMP WHERE MGR=JONES').

For data retrieving, an argument of the SQL predicate must be a string representing a SQL SELECT statement. Table or view names appearing in the SELECT statement must be first defined either by a PROSQL program, or separately on SQL/DS.

Our logical database design consists of a representation of some of the predicates of a Prolog program in SQL/DS. For example, if p(X, Y) and q(Y, Z) are predicates in our Prolog/Prosql program, and we wish to store tuples for p and for q in SQL/DS, then the SQL/DS system catalog will contain entries for the binary relations p and q.

A SELECT statement in an SQL clause need not contain an INTO clause. If it does not contain an INTO clause, then it causes SQL/DS to retrieve a set of tuples. These tuples are deposited in the PROLOG workspace as assertions about the predicate with the same name as the *first* table (or view) mentioned in the FROM clause. For example, 'SQL(select * from p)' causes the entire relation p to be copied from SQL/DS to the Prolog work space. (We note that we can have any predicate name in the assertions by using the view facility of SQL/DS.) We call this kind of interaction between PROLOG and SQL/DS a *loose coupling.*

However, if the SELECT statement contains an INTO clause, as soon as a tuple that satisfies the SELECT query is generated, it is sent to PROLOG. When PROLOG receives the tuple, it will both load the tuple as an assertion into its work space, and bind the components of the tuple to the variables in the INTO clause. In the meantime, if it is necessary, SQL/DS could asynchronously continue to generate other tuples to satisfy the SELECT query, preparing for another "possible" call of the same SELECT query from PROLOG. We note that by using an INTO clause, we can achieve a *tight coupling* between PROLOG and SQL/DS.

To illustrate tight coupling, consider

SQL('SELECT NAME, SAL INTO *x, *y FROM EMP WHERE MGR=JONES').

Assume that when SQL/DS evaluates the SELECT statement it finds the employee Bruce and his salary $30000. The PROSQL system will load the assertion EMP(Bruce, 30000) into the PROLOG workspace. In addition, since the variables in the INTO clause are *x and *y, it will bind the variables *x and *y to Bruce and 30000, respectively.

At present, SELECT without INTO is implemented. SELECT with INTO is designed but not implemented.

AUTOCOMMIT OFF

Format:	
	SQL('AUTOCOMMIT OFF').

COMMIT WORK

Format:	
	SQL ('COMMIT WORK')

SQL('AUTOCOMMIT OFF') and SQL('COMMIT WORK') are the statements that allow us to begin a transaction and to end a transaction, respectively. If we have a collection of SQL statements to be executed as a single transaction, we can so indicate by using SQL('AUTOCOMMIT OFF') and SQL('COMMIT WORK'). Otherwise, every SQL statement will be treated as a single transaction.

3. EXAMPLES OF PROSQL PROGRAMS

In this section, we shall consider the following examples to illustrate how PROSQL programs can be written.

Example 1.

Consider the PROLOG program:

```
p(1).          |
p(2).          |
p(3).          |
q(1,3).        |
q(1,2).        |    (assertions)
q(2,2).        |
q(3,4).        |
r(3).          |
r(1).          |
r(4).          |

t(*x,*y) <- p(*x) & q(*x,*y) & r(*y).      (rule)

t(*x,*y) ?                                  (goal)
```

Now, suppose we store the assertions in SQL/DS. That is, we create tables p, q and r, and insert the assertions into the tables. Let us assume that p1 is the column name of p, q1 and q2 are the first and second column names of q, and r1 is the column name of r. Then, there are many ways to write PROSQL programs to retrieve t:

CASE 1.

```
(1)  SQL( 'SELECT * FROM p' ) ?     |
                                    |  for getting
(2)  SQL( 'SELECT * FROM q' ) ?     |  the assertions
                                    |  from SQL/DS
(3)  SQL( 'SELECT * FROM r' ) ?     |

(4)  t(*x,*y) <- p(*x) & q(*x,*y) & r(*y).

(5)  t(*x,*y) ?
```

In this PROSQL program, statements (1)-(3) are requests from PROLOG to the SQL/DS data server. Each is treated as a distinct transaction by SQL/DS. (We note that clauses ending with the question mark "?" are treated as goals.) SQL/DS executes the SQL calls in (1)-(3) and sends the results to PROLOG which stores them as assertions in its work space. Statement (4) is a clause which is used by PROLOG in executing the goal (5). In statement (4), the *x in p(*x) refers to a whole record in the unary SQL relation p. The *x and *y in q(*x, *y) refer to the first and second columns, respectively, of the binary SQL relation q. Note that the conjunction p(*x) & q(*x,*y) in Prolog corresponds to a join of p and q in SQL with a 'where' clause p.p1=q.q1. Since (1)-(3) are executed before (5), the data needed for the right side of (4) are in the PROLOG work space by the time they are needed.

CASE 2.

If the assertions for predicates p, q and r are concurrently shared and updated by many users, then the three SQL statements in the above PROSQL program can not be treated as three independent transactions, because the assertions of p obtained in one transaction may be inconsistent with the assertions of q or r obtained in another transaction. To avoid this problem, we can use SQL('AUTOCOMMIT OFF') and SQL('COMMIT WORK') for the following PROSQL program, where the three SQL statements appear in a single transaction:

```
pqr  <-  SQL( 'COMMIT WORK' ) &          /* ends any prior transaction */
         SQL( 'AUTOCOMMIT OFF' ) &       /* prosql now controls commit */
         SQL( 'SELECT * FROM p' ) &
         SQL( 'SELECT * FROM q' ) &
         SQL( 'SELECT * FROM r' ) &
         SQL( 'COMMIT WORK' ).

pqr ?

t(*x,*y) <- p(*x) & q(*x,*y) & r(*y).

t(*x,*y) ?
```

CASE 3.

If there are too many tuples for tables p, q and r, to be held in the PROLOG work space, then we compute t(*x,*y) on SQL/DS. This is done through the following PROSQL program:

```
SQL( 'CREATE VIEW T (q1, q2) AS
     SELECT q1, q2 from p,q,r
     WHERE p1=q1
     AND  q2=r1' ) ?

SQL( 'SELECT * FROM t' ) ?

t(*x,*y) ?
```

The first SQL statement defines view T. This definition corresponds to the PROLOG rule

```
t(*x,*y) <- p(*x) & q(*x,*y) & r(*y).
```

The second SQL statement causes the join of p, q, and r to be computed by SQL/DS, and then loaded into the PROLOG work space. Once there, it can be queried in the usual PROLOG manner. We note that the view facility of SQL/DS can be used only for non-recursive PROLOG rules.

Example 2.

Consider a PROLOG program:

```
s(*y,*z) <- p(*x) & q(*x,*y) & t(*y,*z).

p(*x) <- L1 & ... & Ln.
  .
  .
  .

s(*y,*z) ?
```

Assume that q is a relation we store in SQL/DS. As in Example 1, we could first get all the tuples of table q from SQL/DS and then load them into PROLOG. However, the table q could be very big. In this case, it may be more efficient to have PROLOG execute the subgoal, p(*x), and find all values for *x that satisfy p(*x), send them to SQL/DS to join with q(*x,*y), and then finally send the result of the join back to PROLOG. To do all these, we need to write the following PROSQL program:

```
SQL( 'CREATE TABLE p (p1 CHAR(1)) IN DBSP' ) ?   (1)
p(*x) <- L1 & ... & Ln.                           (2)
.
.
.

ins <- p(*x) &
       SQL( 'INSERT INTO p VALUES (*x)' ) &
       fail.                                      (3)

ins ?                                             (4)

SQL( 'CREATE VIEW r (q2) AS
       SELECT q2 FROM p,q
       WHERE p1=q1' ) ?                           (5)

SQL( 'SELECT * FROM r' ) ?                        (6)

s(*y,*z) <- r(*y) & t(*y,*z).                     (7)

s(*y,*z) ?                                        (8)
```

In this PROSQL program, Clause (1) first creates table p in SQL/DS. Clause (4) is a goal that causes PROLOG to compute the tuples of table p and then send them to SQL/DS for insertion. Then, Clause (5) defines view r(*y)=(p(*x) & q(*x,*y)). Clause (6) causes SQL/DS to compute all the tuples of view r and send them to PROLOG. We note that the rule

s(*y,*z) <- r(*y) & t(*y,*z)

in the PROSQL program corresponds to the rule

s(*y,*z) <- p(*x) & q(*x,*y) & t(*y,*z)

in the previous PROLOG program.

4. RECURSIVE RULES

In [Chang 1976,1978,1979, Walker 1981, 1983b], some examples of relations that are recursively defined are given. In this section, we shall discuss how recursively defined relations could be handled in PROSQL.

Let us consider a base relation, father(*x,*y), which denotes that *y is the father of *x. Now, suppose one wants to know who is an ancestor of whom. This type of question can be answered by introducing a new concept, ancestor(*x,*y), which denotes that *y is an ancestor of *x. To find a John's ancestor who was born in 1926, we can write the following PROLOG program:

```
person(Richard, 1950).      |
   .                        |   assertions
   .                        |   for "person"
   .                        |

father(John, Allen).        |
   .                        |   assertions
   .                        |   for "father"
   .                        |

ancestor(*x,*y) <- father(*x,*y).

ancestor(*x,*z) <- father(*x,*y) & ancestor(*y,*z).

ancestor(John, *x) & person(*x, 1926) ?
```

Now, suppose that the assertions for father are stored in SQL/DS. Then, we can write PROSQL programs for the following cases:

CASE 1.

Let us assume that the father relation is static. That is, the father relation is not changed during the searching of John's ancestors. We may write the following PROSQL program, where the first and second attributes of the "father" relation in SQL/DS are CHILD and NAME, respectively.

```
person(Richard, 1950).
   .
   .
   .

ancestor(*x, *y) <- SQL( 'SELECT CHILD, NAME
                        INTO *x, *y
                        FROM father
                        WHERE CHILD=*x' ).

ancestor(*x,*z) <- father(*x,*y) & ancestor(*y,*z).

ancestor(John, *x) & person(*x, 1926) ?
```

Since the first clause for 'ancestor' contains an INTO clause, it uses tight coupling. That is, when the SQL statement is executed, a 'father' assertion is loaded into the PROLOG workspace, and in the meantime the variables *x and *y are bound to the arguments of the 'father' assertion.

The program executes as follows. First it gets John's father and tests if he was born in 1926. If he was not born in 1926, PROLOG will get the father of John's father, and so on. Every execution of the SQL statement is a single transaction. Therefore, there may be many transactions executed before an answer is found. The answer will be consistent if none of John's ancestors are changed during the execution of the PROSQL program. Note that we use the variables in the SQL statement to pass parameters (values) between PROLOG and SQL/DS.

CASE 2.

If the father relation is dynamically changed, then we can not use the above PROSQL program, because the answer we get may be inconsistent. Therefore, in this case, we should use SQL('AUTOCOMMIT OFF') and SQL('COMMIT WORK') to lock the 'father' relation as shown in the following PROSQL program:

```
person(Richard, 1950).
  .
  .
  .

ancestor(*x, *y) <- SQL( 'SELECT CHILD, NAME
                          INTO *x, *y
                          FROM father
                          WHERE CHILD=*x' ).

ancestor(*x,*z) <- father(*x,*y) & ancestor(*y,*z).

SQL( 'COMMIT WORK' ) & SQL( 'AUTOCOMMIT OFF' ) &
   ancestor(John, *x) & person(*x, 1926) &
SQL( 'COMMIT WORK' ) ?
```

This PROSQL program is similar to the previous PROSQL program except we add the SQL('AUTOCOMMIT OFF') and SQL('COMMIT WORK') in the goal statement. We use SQL('AUTOCOMMIT OFF') and SQL('COMMIT WORK') to lock the 'father' relation during the execution of the goal.

CASE 3.

In each of the above cases, each SQL request gets an ancestor of John. However, if John has many ancestors, then the PROSQL program may have to send out many SQL requests, and the total communication cost may be high. Therefore, in this case, we can use a compiler approach. Essentially, the idea is to compile recursive rules in a PROSQL program into an iterative program that can be executed by SQL/DS. A PROSQL program for this case can be written as follows:

```
person(Richard, 1950).                                  |
  .                                                     |  assertions
  .                                                     |  for "person"
  .                                                     |

ancestor(*x,*y) <- father(*x,*y).                       |  rules to
                                                        |  define
ancestor(*x,*z) <- father(*x,*y) & ancestor(*y,*z).     |  "ancestor"

SQL( 'SELECT * FROM ancestor WHERE CHILD=John' ) ?

ancestor(John, *x) & person(*x, 1926) ?
```

For this program, the PROSQL system will take the SQL request and the rules that define "ancestor," and compile the SQL request into an iterative program. The iterative program will then be sent to SQL/DS for execution. The SQL/DS system will produce all John's ancestors, which are then sent to and loaded in PROLOG. Therefore, when the goal, ancestor(John,*x), is executed, tuples for John's ancestors will be there.

We note that compiling recursive rules into an iterative program is a non-trivial problem. In this paper, we shall not discuss compilation techniques, beyond noting that PROSQL provides a framework for compilation experiments. The interested reader should see [Chang 1978,1979, Henschen and Naqvi 1983, Walker 1981,1983b].

5. IMPLEMENTATION OF PROSQL

Most of the PROSQL language features, apart from compilation, have been implemented using the following architecture:

In this architecture, PROLOG and SQL/DS run on two independent machines. In the present implementation they occupy different virtual machines on the same physical machine, running under the VM/CMS operating system. Communication consists of sending messages in files. It is expected that other communication mechanisms could also be used.

SQL/DS acts as a database server to PROLOG. Each invocation of the SQL predicate in a PROSQL program is a request to SQL/DS. After the request is sent out to SQL/DS, PROLOG will wait for the answer to come back. We do not allow PROLOG to execute other goals while the request is still being processed by SQL/DS, because these other goals may depend upon the answer to the request.

To implement PROSQL, we take the approach of transforming a PROSQL program into a PROLOG program. This is done by transforming SQL statements

SQL(<SQL-definition-statement>), and
SQL(<SQL-insertion-statement>),

into the statements

SQL-DEF(*list, <SQL-definition-statement>), and
SQL-PUT(*list, <SQL-insertion-statement>), respectively,

where the first argument of SQL-DEF is a list of variables obtained by scanning <SQL-definition-statement>, and the first argument of SQL-PUT is a list of variables occurring in <SQL-insertion-statement>.

For a SELECT statement, to allow parameter passing between PROLOG and SQL/DS, the transformation will be done differently. For example, in the statement,

SQL('SELECT * FROM father WHERE CHILD=*x'),

there is a variable *x. Variable *x is used to pass a value from PROLOG to SQL/DS. That is, variable *x must be replaced by a constant before the SQL statement is sent to SQL/DS. To implement this kind of parameter passing, the PROSQL system will transform the above statement into the following statement:

SQL-GET(*x.nil, 'SELECT * FROM father WHERE CHILD=*x'),

where the first argument of SQL-GET is a list of variables obtained by scanning the WHERE clause of the SELECT statement. Since SQL-GET will be implemented in PROLOG, the variables in the list will get bound. If any variable in the list can not be bound to a constant, an error will be issued. When all the variables in the WHERE clause of a SELECT statement are replaced by constants, PROLOG will use the built-in SYSTEM predicate to call the communication facility to send the SELECT statement to SQL/DS. We note that the SYSTEM predicate is an escape mechanism that allows us to call other systems from PROLOG. The above variable-substitution method does not require that variables represent values of attributes of relations, so long they are bound to strings of symbols. In fact, a variable may represent a relation or an attribute name. This is how the parameters are passed from PROLOG to SQL/DS.

On the other hand, if we have the following SQL statement containing an INTO clause,

SQL('SELECT * INTO *x,*y FROM father WHERE CHILD=*x'),

then the PROSQL system will transform it into the following statement:

SQL-GET(*x.nil, 'SELECT * INTO *x,*y FROM father WHERE CHILD=*x') &
father(*x,*y),

where the variables in the INTO clause are made to be the arguments of the "father" predicate. When the result is sent back from SQL/DS, the goal, father(*x,*y), will be executed so that variables *x and *y can be bound to components of the result that has just been placed in the PROLOG work space. Therefore, by this way, we can also pass parameters from SQL/DS to PROLOG.

When a SQL request is sent from PROLOG to SQL/DS, we need to use the "dynamically defined query facility" of SQL/DS for executing a SELECT statement. Usually a SELECT statement (query) returns the result into one or more variables. When the query is received from PROLOG at run-time, SQL/DS does not know in advance how many and what type of variables to allocate to hold the query result.

Fortunately, SQL/DS provides a facility to dynamically allocate a data area to hold the result of the query. This is done through the combination of a PREPARE and a DESCRIBE statement. When the query is executed, the result will be put into the data area. Eventually, a module will be invoked to take the result from the data area, and format it into assertions. These assertions are then sent to PROLOG.

6. CONCLUDING REMARKS

We have introduced the special predicate SQL. The syntax of an argument of the predicate is the same as the syntax of the SQL language. The advantage of using the SQL language directly is that tools for managing data bases are already available in SQL/DS, and therefore we do not need to rebuild them.

We have also introduced SQL('AUTOCOMMIT OFF') and SQL('COMMIT WORK'). They are used to signal the beginning and end of a transaction.

By judicial uses of the SQL predicate in a PROSQL program, we can handle many different problems that involve recursive or non-recursive views, transactions, or different data distributions among PROLOG and SQL/DS, etc.

We are currently implementing a PROSQL system. The implementation consists of the following parts:

(1) Set up a communication link between PROLOG and SQL/DS,

(2) Write programs for transforming SQL statements,

(3) Write programs to process SQL statements in SQL/DS,

(4) Write programs for loading assertions (sent by SQL/DS) into PROLOG, and

(5) Write programs for compiling recursive rules into programs.

The PROSQL design described in this paper is largely independent of any communication system. Parts (1)-(4) are running at the time of writing, apart from SELECT with INTO. The major task that remains to be implemented is part (5), which is non-trivial because it requires analyzing queries and recursive rules.

Since the PROSQL system is flexible, we can now make practical experiments to test various methods such as a non-evaluation (interpreter) versus evaluation (compiler) method, loose versus tight coupling, and various distributions of tuples of relations among the PROLOG and SQL/DS systems.

ACKNOWLEDGMENTS

The authors would like to thank Pat Selinger and Dick Mattson for their comments on a draft of this paper.

7. REFERENCES

Battani, G., and Meloni, H. [1973] Interpreteur du Langage de Programmation PROLOG, Groupe d'Intelligence Artificielle, Marseille-Luminy, Manual for the first implementation of PROLOG.

Chang, C. L. [1976] DEDUCE — A Deductive Query Language for Relational Data Bases, In: *Pattern Recognition and Artificial Intelligence,* (C. H. Chen, Ed.), Academic Press, Inc., New York, 1976, 108-134.

Chang, C. L. [1978] DEDUCE 2: Further Investigations of Deduction in Relational Data Bases, In: *Logic and Data Bases,* (H. Gallaire and J. Minker, Eds.), Plenum Publishing Corp., New York, N. Y., 1978, 201-236.

Chang, C. L. [1979] On Evaluation of Queries Containing Derived Relations in a Relational Data Base, IBM Research Report RJ2667, IBM Research Laboratory, San Jose, Ca, 95193, October 1979. Also In: *Advances in Data Base Theory,* Vol. 1 (H. Gallaire, J. Minker and J-M. Nicolas, Eds.), Plenum Publishing Corp., New York, N. Y., 1981, 235-260.

Chang, C.L. [1983] An Experience of Building An Expert System with PROLOG, IBM Research Report RJ3925, IBM Research Laboratory, San Jose, Ca, June 20, 1983.

Chomicki, J., and Grudzinski, W. [1983] A Database Support System PROLOG, Proc. of Logic Programming Workshop 1983, University of Lisbon, Portugal, 1983, 290-303.

Colmerauer, A., Kanoui, H., Pasero, R., and Roussell, P. [1973] Un Systeme de Communication Homme-machine en Francais, Groupe d'Intelligence Artificielle, Univ. d' Aix Marseille, Luminy.

Colmerauer, A., et al. [1973] Etude et Realisation d'un Systeme PROLOG, Convention de Research IRIA-Sesori No. 77030.

Henschen, L.J., and Naqvi, S. A. [1983] On compiling queries in recursive first-order databases, To appear in JACM.

IBM SQL/Data System Application Programming Manual, Order No. SH24-5018-0, First Edition (August 1981).

Jarke, M., and Vassiliou, Y. [1983] Coupling Expert Systems with Database Management Systems. In: *Artificial Intelligence Applications for Business,* W. Reitman (ed.), Ablex, 1983 (in press).

Kowalski, R. [1979] *Logic for Problem Solving,* North-Holland Publishing Co., New York.

Kunifuji, S. and Yokota H. [1982] PROLOG and relational data bases for Fifth generation Computer Systems. Proc. Workshop on Logical Bases for Data Bases, Toulouse, 1982.

McCord, M. [1982] Using slots and modifiers in logic grammars for natural language. Artificial Intelligence 18, 327-367, 1982.

Pereira, L. M., P. Sabatier and E. Oliveira. [1982] Orbi: an expert system for environmental resources evaluation through natural language. Proc. 1st Int. Logic Programming Conference, University of Marseilles, France, 1982, 200-209.

Pereira, L. M. and A. Porto. [1982] A Prolog implementation of a large system on a small machine. Proc. 1st Int. Logic Programming Conference, University of Marseilles, France, 1982, 255-230.

Roberts, G.M. [1977] An implementation of PROLOG, MS Thesis, Department of Computer Science, University of Waterloo.

Roussel, P [1975] PROLOG: Manuel de Reference et d'Utilisation, Groupe d'Intelligence Artificielle, U.E.R., de Luminy, Universite d'Aix-Marseille, September 1975.

Santane-Toth, E. and P. Szeredi [1982] Prolog applications in Hungary. In: *Logic Programming,* K.L. Clark and S.-A. Tarnlund (Eds.), Academic Press, 1982.

Sowa, J.F. [1981] A PROLOG TO PROLOG, IBM Systems Research Institute, 205 East 42nd Street, New York, NY 10017.

Vassiliou, Y., Clifford,J., and Jarke, M. [1983] How does an Expert System get its Data ? To appear in Proc. VLDB, 1983.

Walker, A. [1981] Syllog: A Knowledge Based Data Management System, Report No. 034, Computer Science Department, New York University, 1981.

Walker, A. [1983a] Databases, Expert Systems, and PROLOG. In: *Artificial Intelligence Applications for Business,* W. Reitman (ed.), Ablex, 1984.

Walker, A. [1983b] Syllog: An Approach to PROLOG for Non-Programmers, In *Logic Programming and its Applications,* M. van Caneghem and D. H. Warren (Eds.), Ablex, 1985 (in press).

Walker, A., and Porto, A. [1983] KB01 — A Knowledge Based Garden Store Assistant, Report RJ3928, IBM Research Laboratory, San Jose, Ca, 1983.

Warren D. H. D. and F. C. N. Pereira. [1981] An efficient easily adaptable system for interpreting natural language queries. DAI Research Paper No. 155, Department of Artificial Intelligence, University of Edinburgh, 1981.

Warren, D.H.D., Pereira, L.M., and Pereira, F. [1977] "PROLOG — the language and its implementation compared with LISP," SIGART/SIGPLAN Notices, August 1977, pp.109-115.

Wilson, W. and C. John. [1983] Semantic code analysis. Proc. 8th Int. Joint Conf. on Artificial Intelligence, Karlsruhe, 1983, 520-525.

RULE SUPPORT IN PROLOG

Oded Shmueli[1]
Shalom Tsur[2]
Hana Zfira[3]

In this paper we propose the idea of *rule support* - a method which improves the performance of goal-proof processes in PROLOG by augmenting the rules in the rule-base with additional support knowledge. This method is especially appropriate when a PROLOG program contains a large internal database. We discuss the idea in general and show two variants of its implementation: a_priori and dynamic support. For a_priori support, the supporting knowledge is collected for all feasible cases prior to using the rule. For dynamic support, the supporting knowledge is accumulated incrementally as the rule is used.

1. INTRODUCTION

One of the most promising developments of logic programming appears to be the application of the method to problems in the database area. The main attraction of the method is in its ability to address the problems of data organization and the operations on data in terms of first order logic. In database terms this means that the problems of data modeling and query languages are treated in a uniform way in which no formal distinction between data objects and the operations on these objects is made. An additional advantage of this method is that the formalism enables the specification of powerful queries, e.g. recursive queries which are often beyond the limits of expression of traditional query languages.

Whereas it is clear that logic programming is a potent tool of expression in the database area, other aspects, notably those that are performance related, must be examined. Many traditional database problems such as query optimization (see e.g. [Ull]) have their counterparts in the context of logic programming. These problems have received some attention [War, KY, Ull1, JCV, Kel] but more is required.

In this paper we address one of these problems. We have chosen to call it "rule support" and, in concept, it is akin to the view maintenance problem of database systems. We describe the problem in terms of PROLOG [CM] and assume some familiarity on behalf of the reader with this language. Although we have chosen this specific language to illustrate the problem, it is by no means restricted by this particular context and should be regarded as a general problem of logic programming and databases.

Many applications, e.g. expert systems, maintain a *knowledge base* - a large, almost static set of rules which is used by the inference mechanism to prove submitted hypotheses (or goals). In PROLOG like systems, proofs are executed as a rule-directed depth first search through a solution

[1] Computer Science Department, Technion - Israel Institute of Technology, Haifa, Israel.

[2] Microelectronics and Computer Technology Corporation, Austin, Texas.

[3] Computer Science Department, Technion - Israel Institute of Technology, Haifa, Israel.

space and are terminated when data can be found to satisfy all goals and their subgoals in the search tree. This process is sequential and often requires backtracking in order to satisfy a subgoal with a new candidate for a solution.

During the proof process, a significant amount of additional knowledge is created which is immediately discarded and hence, is nonexistent when the same proof is attempted at a future time. The idea of rule support is to save this knowledge in suitable structures so as to shorten the required time when the same proof is repeated. We propose thus to trade time for space in these proof processes.

Consider the following trivial example:

```
girl(mary).
girl(sue).
boy(john).
boy(jack).

pair(X, Y) :- boy(X), girl(Y).
```

To generate all possible pairs of girls and boys we specify the query:

```
:-pair(X, Y), write(X,Y), nl, fail.
```

During execution the fact base is scanned over and over again to produce the set of possible results. Ordinarily, these results are lost and must be reproduced when the query is specified again. Instead, we could augment the fact base and retain these results for future use in the form of:

```
pair(john, mary).
pair(john, sue ).
pair(jack, mary).
pair(jack, sue ).
```

We say that in this form the rule 'pair(X, Y)' is ***supported.*** We call the facts 'boy' and 'girl' ***base facts*** and the retained 'pair' information ***derived facts.*** Intuitively, a rule is supportable if in all its appearances it is either immediatly resolvable or all of its right hand goals are supported. Precise definitions will be given in the sequel.

So far it was implicitly assumed that the knowledge base is static i.e. the information contained in it never changes. In practice this is of course seldom true, although as mentioned, in many cases changes are infrequent. We must therefore consider the potential effect of changes in the knowledge base on the supported rules. In this respect we must address the following questions:

(1) Which rules can be supported? np If a rule is supportable - how do we support it?

(2) For which of the supportable rules does it pay off to lend the support?

Another aspect of the problem is the time of support. Rules can be supported a priori - they are evaluated ***before*** their actual use in a proof and only updated when changes occur. We will refer to this method as ***a_priori support.*** Alternatively, support can be generated for rules during their actual use in proofs. The resulting support will be built incrementally and no distinction will be made between the buildup phase and the update phase. We call this method ***dynamic support.*** Some hybrid methods are also possible. A_priori rule support is similar to the generation approach in [NY].

In this paper we present versions of the a_priori support method and the dynamic support method. We assume for the time being that the user, who knows the most about the problem to be solved, will indicate to the system which of the rules he wants supported. Obviously, an operational analysis which accounts for such factors as the frequency of use of the various rules, the available memory space and other statistics would be most useful in this respect. Such an analysis, which would be within the realm of the third question that we have posed, is still an open problem.

In supporting PROLOG rules the concept of *tree database* [GS1] (also called *acyclic database* [BFMMUY, Ull]) is utilized. Acyclicity is a property of the database schema which has wide implications in query processing, dependency theory and schema design (see [SI] for references). It has been shown [BC, BG, GS1, Yan] that certain queries which imply acyclic databases, called *tree queries*, appear easier to process than queries which imply cyclic databases (called *cyclic queries*); and that the crux of join based query processing is constructing a tree (actually an "embedded tree") [GS2].

In [SI] a mechanism was proposed for maintaining results of queries over time; it consists of maintaining an acyclic database (which is derived from the the original database and the query) together with information that may be useful for future maintenance following additions and deletions of tuples. If the derived database is cyclic, then it is made acyclic by adding relations. The added relations are called *templates*. During additions (or deletions) base and template relations undergo modifications to reflect changes to base relations. Changes propagate towards the *database root* where relations are viewed as tree nodes.

In this paper the query maintenance mechanism is modified, extended and adapted for supporting PROLOG rules. Relational databases are "built into" PROLOG, one can think about tuples as base facts, relations as a collection of base facts for the same rules and queries as PROLOG procedures. Hence, the query maintenance mechanism lends itself (with certain modifications) to the support of PROLOG rules.

The paper is organized as follows. Section 2 defines basic concepts and relates these to the more traditional concepts of relational databases. Section 3 discusses the transformation of the original PROLOG program and the construction of the support structure. Sections 4 and 5 discuss two variants of the idea which we have called "a_priori support" and "dynamic support". We conclude this work in section 6 with some suggestions for further research.

2. BASIC CONCEPTS

2.1. Classification of PROLOG Rules

A fundamental unit of a PROLOG program is the *literal.* For example: father(jacob,joseph), q(X,Y,Z), A<B. The literal's predicate name corresponds to a procedure name in a conventional programming language. A PROLOG program consists of a sequence of statements called *clauses.* A clause comprises a *head* - the left hand side of the clause, and a *body* - the right hand side of the clause. The head either consists of a single literal or is empty. The body consists of a sequence of zero or more literals. The body literals are called *goals* or *procedure calls.* We say that procedure p *calls* procedure q if a rule for p contains a goal whose predicate name is q. Procedure p *references* procedure q if either p calls q or p calls some procedure h and h references q.

A clause with an empty head is called a *query.* It represents a command to the interpreter to prove the goals in its body. The form of a query is: :- $p_1,\ldots,p_k$. The goals in the body of a clause are linked by the operator ',' which can be interpreted as a conjunction.[4] A clause with an empty body is called a *unit clause* or a *fact.*

A PROLOG *rule* is a non-unit clause. A PROLOG *procedure* is a collection of PROLOG rules all having the same predicate name in their head. We shall restrict attention to *simple* variables, no functions are allowed. A variable appearing only once in a rule need not be named and

[4]We assume that prior to processing, all PROLOG clauses have been normalized to conjunctions of goals.

may be written as an *anonymous* variable, denoted by the underline character "_". A literal containing no variables is called a *ground* literal; similarly, a clause containing no variables is called a *ground clause.* A *base fact* is a ground unit clause (an assertion, or a tuple in the relational database sense). A collection of base facts all having the same head predicate. is called a *base relation.*

We treat unit clauses containing variables as rules. For example, the fact a(X) is treated as the rule a(X) :- X = X. From now on we distinguish between "rules" and "facts", and assume that there is no rule having the same predicate name as that of a base relation. Also, rules are assumed to have no constant elements within the rule head. (Observe that the rule a(X,3,1) :- X < 80 is equivalent to the rule a(X,Y,Z) :- X<80, Y=3, Z=1.) We shall further restrict rules so that any variable appearing at the head of a rule must also non-trivially appear in the body of the rule. This restriction prevents the creation of infinite relations from finite ones.

There are several assumptions we make about the user's program. First, the program must ensure that the arguments of comparison operators (e.g. X < Y), are always instantiated. Another assumption concerns negative literals within PROLOG rules. PROLOG operates under the 'negation as failure' approach [Cla]; i.e. if the proof of a positive literal fails, then the negation of that literal is assumed true. There are some well known problems in PROLOG's treatment of negative goals containing variables. We impose some constraints on the use of negation. All non-anonymous variables appearing in a negative goal must be bound along any syntactically feasible program path through which the goal is reachable. A similar restriction, called the 'safe computation rule', appears in [Llo]. Note that under this approach, bindings are only made by successful calls of positive goals. Negative literal calls never create new bindings; they either succeed or fail and thus may be considered as tests.

As will be explained later, we can only maintain special cases of rules containing the *cut* operator. Instead, an additional backtracking limiting operator called *braces,* denoted {}, is used [War]. The interpretation of this operator is as follows. The left bracket '{' always succeeds. When the right bracket '}' is reached during backtracking, the backtracking continues at the goal immediately to the left of the left bracket '{'. The braces operator may be nested.

example:

The rule: q :- {x, {y}, z}, w, {t, u}, v.

is equivalent to the following sequence of rules:

```
q :- q1, w, q2, v.

q1 :- x, q3, z, !.

q2 :- t, u, !.

q3 :- y,!.
```

The semantics of the {} operator is reminiscent of the concept of *Functional Dependency (FD)* in relational databases. Relation R satisfies the functional dependency X -> Y, provided for every two tuples t1 and t2 in R, if t1[X] = t2[X] then t1[Y] = t2[Y].[5] As an example consider the rule: q(Q) :- p(P),{r(R)}, where Q,P and R are the sets of variables appearing within the goals q,p and r, respectively. We claim that the result relation q is a projection of a relation over P ∪ R which satisfies the FD P∩R -> R. Consider values $x_1,...,x_k$ for variables in P ∩ R at the point of evaluation when '{' is encountered, and values $y_1,...,y_m$ which are assigned to variables in R when '}' is encountered. This is the only set of values possible for variables in R, because backtracking leads to the left of '{'. Thus, entering '{' with values $x_1,...,x_k$, for variables in P∩R always yields the same result $y_1,...,y_m$. Observe that this holds even if some of the variables remain

[5] t[X] is the projection of tuple t onto attributes X.

uninstantiated.

2.2. Defining Correct Support

Let p(X_1,...,X_n) be a PROLOG procedure, and let Y_1,...,Y_n be either constants or uninstantiated variables. The set S *returned* by p with *parameters* Y_1,...,Y_n is the (possibly infinite) set of s facts installed by:

:- p(Y_1,...,Y_n), asserta(s(Y_1,...,Y_n)), fail.

(Where the goal 'asserta(C)' adds the clause C to the database as the first clause for its procedure).

Procedure p' *maintains* procedure p if for all parameters Y_1,...,Y_n, if S is returned by p' then for each occurrence of a base relation R in p, there exists an ordering of the facts in R such that S is returned by p. Basically, the above states that p' maintains p if p' returns the same set of results as p, although each is allowed to look at a different permutation of the facts in the database. (This is consistent with a point of view in which base relations are considered as sets and scanning them returns the tuples in some order.)

2.3. Definitions

Definition - Immediate Goals

Goals that are not unified (in the PROLOG sense) are called *immediate goals,* e.g. negation ('not'), 'fail', X Θ C, X Θ Y, where X,Y are variables, C is a constant and Θ is a comparison operator.

Variables which appear for the first time in a rule inside 'not(...)' are treated as anonymous variables. For example, the rule

p(X,Y) :- q(Y), not p(X,Z), r(Z).

is equivalent to the rule

p(X,Y) :- q(Y), not p(X,_), r(Z).

Definition - Semi Elementary Goal.

A goal in a body of a rule is *semi elementary* in exactly one of the following cases:

(1) The goal's predicate is the name of a base relation.

(2) It is of the form X = C where X is a variable and C is a constant.

(3) It is of the form X = Y where X or Y appear in a semi elementary goal written prior to this one.

(4) It is of the form X Θ C where X appears in a semi elementary goal written prior to this one, and Θ is a comparison operator.

(5) It is of the form X Θ Y where both X and Y appear in semi elementary goals written prior to this one, and Θ is a comparison operator.

(6) All rules whose head predicate is the same as the goal's predicate are semi elementary (see below).

Definition - Semi Elementary Rule.

A rule is *semi elementary* exactly when it satisfies all of the following requirements:

(1) Every head variable of the rule appears in a semi elementary goal in the body of the rule.

(2) Each of its goals is either semi elementary or a negative goal of the form 'not(p(...))' where p matches a semi elementary procedure. (A procedure is semi elementary if all its rules are

semi elementary.)

(3) Every head variable appearing within a negative goal must appear previously in a semi elementary goal.

Definition - Loose Constraints

An immediate goal is a *loose constraint* in exactly the following cases:

(1) It is an inequality which involves a variable not appearing in any semi elementary goal of the rule written prior to this inequality.

(2) It is the PROLOG axiom 'fail'.

(3) It is the predicate {}.

(4) It is a negative goal which involves head variables not appearing in any semi elementary goal of the rule written prior to the negation.

(5) It is of the form 'not(p(...))' where p is not a semi elementary procedure.

Definition - Serviceable Rules and Procedures.

A rule is *serviceable* if after syntactically erasing from it all '{' and '}' symbols and then discarding from it all cuts and loose constraints, the result is a semi elementary rule. A procedure is *serviceable* if all its rules are serviceable.

2.4. Graph Representation of Rules

In this subsection we will relate the above concepts with known relational database concepts [Ull]. Consider a PROLOG rule of the form:

$$q(X_1,...,X_n) \text{ :- } \wedge_{i=1}^{j} p_i(Y_{i1},..., Y_{in_i}).$$

where $(X_1,...,X_n)$ is the set of *target variables* and the literals on the right hand (r.h.) side are called the *qualification*. The X_i's are variables and the Y_i's may be X_i's, constants or variables.

We need to encode the way in which literals interact in rules. With each variable in the rule we associate a unique new constant - the *attribute* for this variable. Each goal is associated with a *goal schema* which is composed of a unique constant corresponding to the goal's predicate, which we call a *relation name,* and the list of attributes appearing in the goal. The collection of goal schemas for a rule, together with the schema containing the attributes corresponding to the target variables (called the *target schema),* is called a *rule schema*. Note that a goal (resp. rule) schema corresponds to a relation (resp. database) schema in relational databases terminology. In fact, we shall use goal schemas as *relation schemas* for relations (in the database sense).

A *qual graph* for a rule is an undirected graph whose nodes are in one-to-one correspondence with the goal schemas of the qualification and the target schema. It must satisfy the following *attribute connectivity* constraint: for each attribute A, the subgraph induced by the nodes whose corresponding literals contain A must be connected [BG]. A rule is a *tree rule* if *some* qual graph for it is a tree; otherwise it is a *cyclic rule*.

example:

Consider the rule:

q(A,B,X) :- p(A,B,C,X), s(A,C), t(A,B,D), r(B,D).

The rule schema is:
(q,[a,b,x]), (p,[a,b,c,x]), (s,[a,c]), (t,[a,b,d]), (r,[b,d]).

This is a tree rule as depicted by the following qual graph:

```
abx-----abcx----ac
          |
        abd-----bd
```

example:

Consider the rule:

q(A,X) :- p(A,B), r(A,C), s(B,C,D), t(B,D).

This is a cyclic rule, in fact any qual graph for it contains the following cyclic graph:

```
ab-----ac
  \   /
   bcd
```

Intuitively, all equality constraints among goal and head variables are represented in the qual graph via attribute connectivity. The graph structure, tree or cyclic, indicates how complex the rule is. In a sense that could be formalized, tree rules correspond to simpler queries than those implied by cyclic rules. A simple procedure, discovered independently by [Gra] and [YO], recognizes tree rules. The procedure applies the following two steps until neither is applicable. For tree rules it also constructs T, the edge set of a qual tree for the rule (T is initially empty).

Step 1: Delete any attribute which appears only in one goal schema or only in the target schema.

Step 2: Find a goal schema (r_1,A) such that either the attributes appearing in A are a subset of the target attributes, or there is another goal schema (r_2,B) such that $A \subseteq B$. Delete (r_1,A) from the rule schema and add the edge $\{r_1,r_2\}$ to T.

It can be shown that the original rule is a tree rule iff upon termination of the above procedure all goal schemas and the target schema are eliminated. If the input rule is in fact a tree rule then T is a qual tree for the rule.

2.5. Support Structure Components

The ***support structure*** for a rule contains the following information:

(1) A ***set of facts*** which replaces the rule and is used in the resolution of any goal that can be unified with the head of the rule.

(2) An ***update structure*** which is used to modify the set of facts when a change occurs in any of the underlying rules.

(3) A ***service program*** which is used to access the serviced rule.

The update structure is hierarchical, induced by the qual trees defined previously. Changes in any of the underlying rules may affect the validity of their associated fact-sets. These changes may in turn propagate upwards and affect the facts of rules at higher levels. Whereas updates may propagate upwards in the support structure, we require that goal resolution be performed from the ***top level*** of the structure, i.e. that we will not have to descend to its lower levels for this purpose. It may be necessary to transform the original PROLOG program in order to satisfy this requirement. The transformation is described in the next section.

3. CONSTRUCTING AN A_PRIORI SUPPORT STRUCTURE

An a_priori support structure, for a procedure p that need be serviced, is created in three steps:

(1) Transforming p into a serviceable procedure.

(2) Creation of rule schemas for all the rules in p and those which are referenced by P.

(3) Creation of qual trees for each of the rule schemas created above.

3.1. Transformation into a Serviceable Procedure

Ordinarily, all semi elementary (s.e.) rules are serviceable. In certain cases a procedure p which is not serviceable due to some non serviceable rules may be transformed into a correctly maintained procedure. This transformation may affect other procedures which take part, directly or indirectly, in the definition of the procedure that need be serviced. The transformation described in this section terminates precisely when there is no procedure p, for which a 'maint(p)' directive is present, such that p references itself or p references another procedure q and q references itself.

The transformation uses the following operations:

(1) partition and duplicate (pad)

Let the rules for a procedure g appear in the program in the order $g_1, \ldots, g_n$. The sequence $g_1, \ldots, g_n$ is partitioned into m subsequences, called ***groups***, $G_1, \ldots, G_m$ in such a way that each group is made either of rules which are all s.e. or of rules which are all non s.e. The rules in each group are uniquely renamed to form a new procedure; let $g'_1, \ldots, g'_m$ be the names of these new procedures. Next, each program rule p calling procedure g is duplicated m times; in the i'th copy g is replaced by g'_i.

(2) duplicate and subsume (das)

Let the rules for a procedure g appear in the order $g_1, \ldots, g_n$. Each program rule p calling procedure g is duplicated n times; the i'th copy incorporates rule g_i. This is performed by substituting the r.h. side of g_i, with appropriate variables renamed, for the call to g.

If neither p nor g contains cuts or references a procedure containing cuts, then the pad and das operations preserve the semantic of the original program [Zfi].

The transformation is done "bottom up" reflecting the directed acyclic graph nature of the s.e. definition. The pad operation partitions a procedure into s.e. and non s.e. procedures; the duplication ensures that all these procedures will be used in a derivation. The das operation is useful in treating non s.e. procedures. Essentially, rules for such procedures are percolated "upwards" to rules referencing them.

The transformation does not always succeed, because both pad and das may alter the program's semantics and lead to in incorrect maintenance. The transformation must not apply pad or das to procedures containing the cut operator. (Still, procedures containing cuts may be serviceable as discussed below.) Similarly, the transformation should not apply pad or das to a procedure called by a goal appearing *within* braces.

example:

Consider the program fragment:

(1) p(X,Y) :- a(Y,Z), b(Z,Y), Y > 90, g(X,Y,Z).

(2) b(X,Y) :- c(Y,Z), f(Z), X < 100.

(3) c(X,Y) :- d(X,Z), { k(Z,W) }, l(W,Y).

(4) c(X,Y) :- not h(X,Y).

(5) c(X,Y) :- e(X,Y), e1(Y).

(6) g(K,L,M) :- h(K,L), i(L,M), j(M).

(7) g(K,L,M) :- h(K,L), j(M).

Goals that do not appear in the left hand side of any rule correspond to base relations. In order to service procedure 'p' an equivalent serviceable program is generated in three steps:

Step 1 :

Apply pad by partitioning procedure 'c'.

(3') c1(X,Y) :- d(X,Z), { k(Z,W) }, l(W,Y).

(4') c1(X,Y) :- not h(X,Y).

(5') c2(X,Y) :- e(X,Y), e1(Y).

(2') b(X,Y) :- c1(Y,Z), f(Z), X < 100.

(2'') b(X,Y) :- c2(Y,Z), f(Z), X < 100.

step 2 :

Apply das by subsuming procedure 'c1'.

(2'.1) b(X,Y) :- d(Y,T), { k(T,W) }, l(W,Z), f(Z), X < 100.

(2'.2) b(X,Y) :- not h(Y,_), f(Z), X < 100.

Step 3 :

Apply das by subsuming procedure 'b'.

(1') p(X,Y) :- a(Y,Z), d(Y,T), { k(T,W) }, l(W,M), f(M), Z < 100,
Y > 90, g(X,Y,Z).

(1'') p(X,Y) :- a(Y,Z), not h(Y,_), f(_), Z < 100, Y > 90,
g(X,Y,Z).

(1''') p(X,Y) :- a(Y,Z), c2(Y,N), f(N), Z < 100, Y > 90, g(X,Y,Z).

3.1.1. The Problematic Cut

There are difficulties in properly supporting a rule referencing a procedure containing cuts. The effect of a cut in rule r of procedure p is as follows. When first encountered as a goal of r, the cut succeeds immediately. If backtracking should later return to the cut, the effect is to fail the *parent goal,* i.e. the goal that called r. In other words, the cut commits the system to all choices made since the parent goal was invoked and causes other alternative rules in p to be discarded. Leaving cuts within rules that match a goal in a supported rule contradicts the basic idea of the a_priori support, which is to keep all the information needed to service the rule in one relation corresponding to the *root* of the qual tree. On the other hand, "percolating" the cuts upwards (as done by the das operator) does not preserve program equivalence, as illustrated by the following example.

example:

consider the following program:

```
(1) p :- q, r.

(2) p :- s.

(3) r :- x, !, y.

(4) r :- t.
```

When given the query ':- p.' the system first attempts to prove the goal q. If this succeeds, the system will proceed to prove the goal r by trying to prove the goals x and y (rule no. 3). Assume that x succeeds and y fails. The cut causes goal r to fail (without trying to use rule no. 4). The backtracking process now re-tries goal q (in rule no. 1). The following program would be created if the transformation were applied to the above program (assuming the cut is treated as a loose constraint).

```
(1) p :- q, x, !, y.

(2) p :- q, r2.

(3) p :- s.

(4) r1 :- x, !, y.

(5) r2 :- t.
```

In the new program, failure in y causes goal p to fail without trying new alternatives in goal q (rule no. 2) or trying to use rule no. 3. It is clear that moving the cut from its original rule, as the transformation program would have done, does not preserve equivalence.

3.2. Creation of a Rule Schema

A goal schema has the form:

relation(schema_name,relation_name,[$a_1,a_2,\ldots,a_n$]).

The 'schema_name' identifies the rule schema, relation_name is the name of the goal schema and the a_i's are the attributes corresponding to the variables in the goal (see section 2.4). In order to service a procedure, a rule schema is created for each rule in the procedure. A Goal that matches a semi elementary procedure p is associated with distinct rule schemas, which are used to maintain the rules of p. An extra node called a ***union node*** is created. This node is the parent node of all the subtrees constructed for the rules in p. Each rule schema in the database is assigned a unique 'schema_name'.

For an immediate goal a special axiom is added to the rule base indicating the extra work necessary in later steps. The format used for such an axiom is:

constraint(schema_name,predicate_name,[a_1,a_2]).

Where predicate_name is the operator name (e.g. '>'), and the a_i's are the attributes associated with the goal.

Negative goals are specially treated. If the 'not' operator negates a conjunction of goals then a new rule is added to the program, whose right hand side is the same conjunction of goals. The variables in its head are the non-anonymous variables that appear within the negation. The conjunction of goals is replaced by a new goal that matches the new rule. A rule schema for the new rule is also created.

In case the rule contains either {} or cut, the target schema is enlarged in order to maintain information which is necessary for correctly preserving the semantics of the original procedure. Only the last occurrence of the cut operator, which is not enclosed in braces, is of interest. Let the set of variables appearing in a rule containing cuts be classified as follows:

X - The target variables.

Y - The variables appearing in the body before the last cut.

Z - The variables appearing after the last cut.

The target schema is augmented with the set T where if $(Z \cap X) - (Y \cap X) \neq \emptyset$ then $T = (Z \cap Y)$ and otherwise $T = \emptyset$. Our intention is to maintain results for the rule as if no cuts appeared at all. When providing result tuples, the added variables in T enable us to preserve equivalence to the original program. The set of derived facts one can expect to get when executing a rule containing cuts satisfies the following: all the tuples in that set have the same values for the variables that appear before the last cut. They may have different values only for the attributes which appear after the last cut.

Consider an occurrence of the {} operator within a rule. Let the set of variables appearing in the rule be classified thus:

X - The target variables.

Y - The variables appearing in the body before the '{'.

Z - The variables appearing within the '{...}'.

L - The variables appearing after the '}'.

The target schema is augmented with the set T where if $(Y \cap X) \neq X$ then $T = Z \cap (Y \cup L)$ and otherwise $T = \emptyset$. Again, we maintain results for the rule as if no {} appeared at all. When providing result tuples, the added variables in T enable us to preserve equivalence to the original rule, i.e. to obtain a set of tuples which is a projection of a relation satisfying the set of FD's implied by {}. Note that each occurrence of {} independently contributes attributes to the target.

The following example illustrates the rule schemas created for "simple" rules.

example :

query(A,B) :- r1(A,B), r2(A,C), r3(D,B), r4(D,E), r5(D,F,'sf'), E > 100.

question(A) :- r1(B,A), not r6(B).

r1(5,8). r1(5,15). r1(9,17). r1(19,55). r1(13,55).

r2(1,h). r2(3,l). r2(7,m). r2(9,l). r2(19,m).

r3(33,15). r3(47,8). r3(55,8). r3(99,17). r3(90,55).

r4(1,101). r4(3,90). r4(47,95). r4(55,600). r4(90,400). r4(99,500).

r5(33,jones,sf). r5(47,white,sf). r5(55,brown,sf). r5(90,smith,sf).

r5(99,white,ny).

r6(5). r6(19). r6(21).

Variables begin with capital letters. Each r_i is a base relation.

The goal schemas for the rule 'query' are:

relation_name	**attributes**
r_1	(a_1, a_2)
r_2	(a_1, a_3)
r_3	(a_4, a_2)
r_4	(a_4, a_5)
r_5	(a_4, a_6, a_7).

constraint: a7 = 'sf'.
constraint: a5 > 100.
target_attributes: (a1,a2).
target_name : query.

This information is represented in PROLOG as:

```
relation(s1,r1,[a1,a2]).
relation(s1,r2,[a1,a3]).
relation(s1,r3,[a4,a2]).
relation(s1,r4,[a4,a5]).
relation(s1,r5,[a4,a6,a7])

target(s1,query,[a1,a2]).

constraint(s1,[r4],'>',[a5,100]).
constraint(s1,[r5],'=',[a7,'sf']).
```

Similarly, rule 'question' is represented in PROLOG as:

```
relation(s2,r1,[a1,a2]).

negation(s2,r6,[a1]).

target(s2,question,[a2]).
```

3.3. Qual Tree

Following the transformation sketched in the previous section, the rule schemas associated with maintained procedures are the input to this stage. For each rule schema t, a corresponding qual tree is created. The qual tree determines the logical structure for maintaining facts. The algorithm for constructing a tree is described below. Its goal is to build a qual tree in which each inequality either involves attributes appearing within some relation or in adjacent relations (via an edge).

(1) Consider a schema for a negative literal (negative schema) over variables X. Let Y $\subseteq$ X be those variables which also appear in other goal schemas in the rule schema. If there is no positive goal schema containing Y, then add Y as the attributes of a new goal schema p, p(Y) is called a ***template literal.*** Do the above, in turn, for each negative schema.

(2) If the rule is cyclic then transform it into an acyclic one by adding templates. Several heuristic methods for choosing templates are given in section 3.3.2.1. Add a new rule p to the database whose target variables are the template attributes Y, with the template's generators (i.e. literals whose attributes contain Y) on its r.h. side. Rule p is supported according to its own qual tree.

(3) Construct a qual tree (e.g. by using an algorithm similar to that given in section 2.4). Force the negative literals in the rule schema to be leaves in the tree; this is made possible by (1). The reasons for forcing negative literals to be leaves are given in section 4.1.1.

(4) Check inequality constraints; each inequality associated with two attributes is treated as follows:

[4.1] If the inequality attributes appear within a single relation schema then treat this inequality as a selector on that relation.

[4.2] Else, if there already exists an edge between two relations (nodes) in the tree, each containing one of the inequality attributes, or this inequality can be derived from existing tree edges and constraints, then do nothing. A simple algorithm for checking whether an inequality can be derived from other inequalities is given in [Ull].

[4.3] Otherwise, arbitrarily choose two relations, each containing one of the inequality attributes. To each of them, temporarily, add the other's attribute.

(5) If this results in a cyclic schema then add templates, as in (2), and transform it into an acyclic schema. Finally, produce a qual tree for the resulting schema and discard the attributes added in [4.3].

We keep the information about the tree edges as follows:

$$\text{edge}(s_n, r_i, [r_j, \ldots, r_k]).$$

Where $r_j, \ldots, r_k$ are the children of r_i in the tree, in rule schema s_n. We differentiate between ordinary relations and templates by adding the clause:

template(schema_name,relation_name)

for each template created by the above algorithm.

example :

The tree for the rule schema 'query' is:

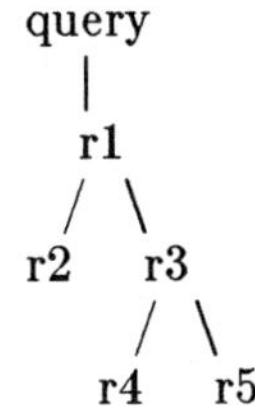

in PROLOG this tree is kept as :

```
edge(s1,query,[r1]).
edge(s1,r1,[r2,r3]).
edge(s1,r3,[r4,r5]).
```

root(s1,query).

3.3.1. Templates

As mentioned before, a template is created in order to transform a cyclic schema into an acyclic one. It is always possible to add a new relation (i.e. a template) which contains all the attributes in the original schema. The new schema is an acyclic schema with the template as the root and all the original relations as leaves. Unfortunately, this template may be too big and contain redundant information; therefore supporting it is expensive.

example:

Consider the rule :

q(X,Y) :- p(X,Z), r(Y,Z,W), s(W,A,B), t(B,C), u(C,A).

The minimal qual graph for this rule is:

```
      xy
     / \
   xz---yzw---wab
               / \
             bc---ca
```

A bad choice of a template is :

template(A,B,C,W,X,Y,Z).

A better choice of templates is as follow:

template1(A,B,C).

template2(X,Y,Z).

The qual graph for the rule schema containing the two templates is:

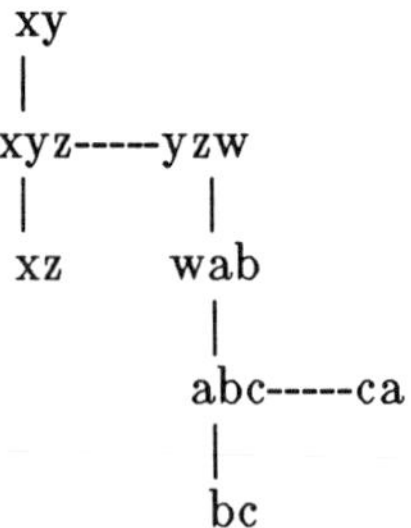

There are several possible heuristics for choosing "good" templates. Here are some alternatives:

(1) When sizes of base relations are known, try to generate the templates from "small" relations.

(2) When domain sizes are known, try to choose template attributes for which the maximum possible number of tuples for the template is as small as possible.

(3) Choose templates as "thin" as possible (i.e. with few attributes).

(4) Choose templates that can be formed by using project and join operations from base relations in such a way that a cartesian product is not formed; if this is not possible give preference to templates which induce as few cartesian products as possible.

Following is a simple algorithm implementing some of the above ideas:

(1) Execute the Graham reduction (see 2.4).

(2) If the reduction terminates with a non-empty rule schema (i.e. a cyclic schema) then proceed, else stop.

(3) Find as small a set of attributes T as possible whose addition to the rule schema will enable the Graham reduction to continue. T must satisfy the following: There are as many as possible pairs of relations R1,R2 such that $(R1 \cap U) \subseteq T$, $(R2 \cap U) \subseteq T$, and $(R1 \cap R2 \cap U) \neq \emptyset$ where U is the set of all attributes appearing in more than one relation schema.

(4) Add T to the schema and go to step 1.

4. A_PRIORI RULE SUPPORT

The main purpose of a_priori rule support is to replace, in advance, the original rule by a simple support structure which contains all the information needed in order to serve calling goals. This is done by utilizing the empty structure constructed in section 3. We show how to populate this structure, update it and use it to service goals which unify with the rule.

4.1. Populating the Support Structure

To insert the relevant knowledge into the (until now empty) support structure, we insert *all* the facts (base facts or derived facts, depending on the node), into the tree relations, starting at the leaves and progressing towards the root. We distinguish between two types of facts which we respectively denote by "good" and "bad". Intuitively, a good fact may contribute to the proof of a goal. Bad facts, on the other hand, will not contribute but may do so in the future when changes in the underlying rule base occur. For a detailed discussion of those concepts see [SI]. The status of a fact is recorded in its *marks* which we denote by a list in PROLOG. If the list is empty the fact is good, else it is bad. We will elaborate on these notions in the sequel.

The node contents in the populated tree corresponding to the rule 'query' in our previous example are as follows:

r1:	**a1**	**a2**	**marks**
	5	8	$[r_2]$
	5	15	$[r_2,r_3]$
	9	17	$[r_3]$
	19	55	[ ]
	13	55	$[r_2]$

r2:	**a1**	**a3**	**marks**
	1	h	[ ]
	3	l	[ ]
	7	m	[ ]

9	l	[ ]
19	m	[ ]

r3:

a4	a2	marks
33	15	[r4]
47	8	[r4]
55	8	[ ]
99	17	[r5]
90	55	[ ]

r4:

a4	a5	marks
1	100	[ ]
55	600	[ ]
90	400	[ ]
99	500	[ ]

r5:

a4	a6	a7	marks
33	Jones	sf	[ ]
47	White	sf	[ ]
55	Brown	sf	[ ]
90	Smith	sf	[ ]

Only those facts that satisfy selector constraints are inserted into the structure (see e.g. r_4,r_5 in the example). Facts that belong to a leaf relation are marked as good. A fact that belongs to a node is *represented* in a positive child of that node if each of its components have either the same value (for the same attributes) in some fact in the child node, and, in the case of constraints, also have values that satisfy the constraints. Facts that belong to an internal node are checked for representation in every child of that node. If so - the fact is added to the node as a good one. Else, the fact is marked as a bad one and its marks list includes those children that do not represent the fact. Information about a fact is represented in PROLOG as:

$$\text{fact}(s_m, r_i, [d_1, \ldots, d_n], [r_j, \ldots, r_k]).$$

Where r_i denotes the relation to which the fact belongs. $[d_1, \ldots, d_n]$ is the list of values contained in the fact, and $[r_j, \ldots, r_k]$ is the marks list. Notice that a relation r_k can appear in more than one schema, or even more than one time in the same schema. A certain tuple of r_k may be 'good' in one schema and 'bad' in another, so, we treat every occurrence of a relation as a unique relation and duplicate the contents of the relation as many times as it appears in supported rules. (Another alternative is to keep $[d_1, \ldots, d_n]$ once and a mark list for each rule schema and occurrence in that rule schema in which the relation appears).

4.1.1. Populating a Support Structure Containing Negative Goals

As already mentioned, a negative goal is forced to be a leaf in the qual tree corresponding to the rule schema. Let R be the parent of a negative goal S in the qual tree, and let t be one of R's tuples. The tuple t is represented in S if S contains no good tuple t1 such that t[X]=t1[X], where

X is the set of attributes common to R and S.

It is important that negative goals should be leaves. Consider the following example :

query(X) :- q(X,Y), r(X,W), p(Y,T,Z), not s(Y,Z).

If s(Y,Z) were treated as other relations, then the following qual tree might be obtained:

```
x----xy-----yz
     |      |
     xw     ytz
```

Observe that the negative goal s(Y,Z) appears as an internal node of the tree. In order to check the status ('good' or 'bad') of a tuple q(x1,y1) one should check if there exists a good tuple r(x1,_) and there is no tuple s(y1,_) that is represented in p. To do so, one has to check all the tuples that do not exist (i.e. ***phantom tuples***) in s in order to verify representation. Those phantom tuples cannot be realistically maintained.

On the other hand, consider the following tree (which is also a qual tree for the same rule schema).

```
x----xy-----ytz
     |      |
     xw     yz
```

Here the negative goal s is a leaf. Apparently, the tuple p(y1,t1,z1) should be marked as 'good' if there is no 'good' tuple s(y1,z1). This can be easily checked. Therefore, what is actually checked is the absence of a representation in s.

4.1.2. Populating a Support Structure Containing Templates

An internal node may correspond to a template. Such a node is populated by joining already populated relations, called ***generators,*** such that the union of their attributes spans the template attributes. A negative goal cannot be a generator. Two possible ways for populating a template are:

(1) Method 1: Use only good facts from the generators.

(2) Method 2: All the facts from generators are joined.

In method 1 the template contains only good facts and is therefore smaller than the template created by method 2. On the other hand, method 1 has a higher overhead when changes occur.

4.1.3. Populating a Union Node

The population of union nodes is different than that of other nodes. A union node is populated by good facts from already populated root nodes of the rule schemas for which the union node was created. A fact appears in the union node only once, and the marks associated with that fact indicate in which descendent nodes the fact appears marked as 'good'. This method saves time when looking for maintained information for the procedure; the marks help when changes occur in descendent nodes. (A union node is similar to an "OR" node, while the other nodes in a qual tree are similar to "AND" nodes in "AND/OR" tree.)

4.2. Changes in the Underlying Rules

For simplicity, we analyze insertions and deletions into positive programs that include no negative literals. When the support structure is populated, the good facts at the root determine the answer for each serviceable goal that can be unified with the rule. Changes in the underlying rule base may affect the status of facts at the root, good ones may become bad and vice verse.

We allow changes (insertions and deletions) only in the base relations (see section 2.1). Upon insertion of a fact, bad facts at upper tree levels may turn into good ones. This transformation of bad facts into good ones may propagate up to the root (and to other trees in the support structure if the relation represented by the root appears as an internal node in other trees). Facts that were previously good remain so. Upon deletions, facts that were previously good may now turn into bad ones and, as in the insertion case, the changes may propagate.

The following is a PROLOG procedure skeleton for insertion of one tuple into a base relation.

```
insert(Fact,Relation) :- relation(Schema,Relation,_ ),
                         check_below(Fact,Relation,Mark_list),
                         asserta(fact(Schema,Relation,Fact,Mark_list)),
                         empty(Mark_list),
                         check_insert_above(Fact,Relation,Schema),
                         fail.
insert(Fact,Relation).
```

This program illustrates how a fact Fact can be inserted into a base relation, named Relation, in every rule schema in which Relation appears. The procedure 'check_below' checks the status of Fact: if it is a good fact then Mark_list is empty, else Mark_list contains the list of children that do not represent Fact. Procedure 'check_insert_above' is invoked when Fact is determined to be good. It propagates the changes (recursively) upwards to the parent of Relation. The 'fail' causes the procedure to continue the process for every rule schema in which relation Relation appears.

The following is a PROLOG program for handling deletion of a tuple from a base relation.

```
(1) delete(Fact,Relation) :- relation(Schema,Relation,_ )
                             delete_fact(Schema,Fact,Relation),
                             fail.
    delete(Fact,Relation).

(2) delete_fact(Schema,Fact,Relation) :-
                             fact(Schema,Relation,Fact,[]),!,
                             retract(fact(Schema,Relation,Fact,[])),
                             check_delete_above(Fact,Relation,Schema).

(3) delete_fact(Schema,Fact,Relation) :-
                             fact(Schema,Relation,Fact,[_ |_ ]),!,
                             retract(fact(Schema,Relation,Fact,_ )).
```

The fact Fact is deleted from base relation Relation; possible propagation effects are checked for in every rule schema in which Relation appears. Procedure 'delete' invokes procedure 'delete_fact' for each appearance of Relation in the support structure. Procedure 'delete_fact' handles the deletion of a single fact from one appearance of Relation. Rule no. 2 handles the deletion of a good fact which may have propagation effects. Rule no. 3 handles the deletion of a bad fact for which there are no propagation effects.

We now consider programs containing negative literals. Observe that an insertion into a negated base relation has the same effect as a deletion from an ordinary relation. For the same reasons, a deletion from a negated relation has the same effect as an insertion into ordinary relation.

4.3. A Service Program

If there are no special operators in a serviced rule, i.e. !, or loose constraints, then service is relatively simple. The service rule for the rule 'query' in the previous example is:

query(X,Y):- fact(s1,query,[X,Y],[]).

Where 's1' is the rule schema and 'query' is the name of the root structure.

4.3.1. Service for a Rule Containing a Cut

The general form of service for rules containing cuts is:

$$q(X) :- fact(S,q,[(T \cup X) \cap Y,\_],[]), !, fact(S,q,[T \cup X],[]).$$

The corresponding schema is indicated by S, q is the name of the rule and X is the set of target variables. $T \cup X$ is the augmented set of attributes as explained in 3.2, and Y is the set of variables appearing before the last cut. All the tuples returned by a call to q have the same values for the attributes in $(T \cup X) \cap Y$. The attributes in $(T \cup X) - Y$ can receive different values.

We demonstrate the service program in the presence of a cut and an inequality loose constraint (b, c, d and e are base relations):

a(X,Y,Z) :- b(X,Y,W), !, c(Y,Z,W).

a(X,Y,Z) :- d(X,X), e(Z,Z), Y > 50.

The service program is:

a(X,Y,Z) :- fact(s1,a,[X,Y,_ ,W],[]), !, fact(s1,a,[X,Y,Z,W],[]).

a(X,Y,Z) :- fact(s2,a,[X,_ ,Z],[]), Y > 50.

4.3.2. Service for a Rule Containing {}

Tuples are serviced until no more tuples which satisfy the calling goal also satisfy the FD's implied by the appearances of {}. Thus, on a per call basis, served tuples are collected in a list and a candidate answer tuple (taken from the root of the qual tree) is served and added to the list only if it does not violate any such FD.

5. DYNAMIC RULE SUPPORT

The idea behind dynamic rule support is to incrementally maintain support structures. The amount of work invested in maintaining the support structures is related to the number of activations of the rule. The dynamic support mechanism relies on structures similar to those constructed in section 3. We illustrate the dynamic rule support concept with a simple example. Consider the rule:

q(X) :- b(A,B,C,X), c(A,B,D), d(A,C), e(B,D,E).

Suppose b,c,d and e are base relations. Rule q(X) is a tree rule as depicted by the following qual graph:

```
x-----abcx-----ac
        |
      abd-----bde
```

The support structure will consist of two new relations bb and cc corresponding to the internal tree nodes 'abcx' and 'abd', respectively. Essentially, facts maintained in cc will be represented in e and those in bb will be represented in relations c,d and e. Initially both bb and cc are empty; as q(X) is activated, facts may migrate from c to cc and from b to bb. When facts are deleted, some facts may migrate from cc to c or from bb to b.

The original rule is transformed to allow for dynamic support. The result of this transformation on q(X) is:

```
(1)  q(X) :- bb(A,B,C,X).
(2)  q(X) :- b(A,B,C,X) ,{ okc(A,B,_ ) }, { d(A,C) },
             retract(b(A,B,C,X)), uniqueasserta(bb(A,B,C,X)).
(3)  okc(A,B,D) :- cc(A,B,D).
(4)  okc(A,B,D) :- c(A,B,D), { e(B,D,_ ) },
                   retract(c(A,B,D)), uniqueasserta(cc(A,B,D)).
```

The first rule attempts to satisfy q(X) by stepping through all known bb facts which contain all the answers deduced thus far. Observe that no real attempt is made to prevent duplicate satisfaction of q(X) (although this could be done with some extra work). Once all known results in bb are exhausted, a search for new answers commences in rule 2. A fact (a1,b1,c1,x1) is drawn out of b using b(A,B,C,X) and okc is called to verify that (a1,b1,c1,x1) is represented in c; if it is, then representation from d is checked as well. The {} is used to eliminate the search for additional redundant evidence for representation. In case fact (a1,b1,c1,x1) is represented in c,d and e this fact is moved from b to bb. The predicate uniqueasserta prevents the installment of duplicate facts. It is defined by the following PROLOG procedure:

```
uniqueasserta(A) :- not(A), !, assertz(A).
uniqueasserta(A) :- !.
```

So, if clause A is not in the database, then it is added to the database and becomes the last clause of its procedure; otherwise nothing is done.

Rule 3 indicates that okc(a1,b1,d1) is satisfied if it has been previously derived and put into cc. Rule 4 presents another way to satisfy okc(a1,b1,d1) by locating a fact (a1,b1,d1) in c and a representing fact (b1,d1,e1) in e. Again, once representation for a fact (a1,b1,d1) in c has been derived, this fact is moved from c to cc. The {} prevents useless scanning of e facts.

The above rules use previously derived knowledge instead of deriving facts anew. When the database is stable, i.e. no facts are inserted or deleted, as the rule q(X) is activated, more and more knowledge is accumulated in the form of bb and cc facts. Thus a new procedure call q(X) may use already derived knowledge. When this knowledge is exhausted, new derivations are attempted which may lead to yet more stored knowledge. The problem is that few databases are that stable and hence we must specify how new facts are inserted and how database facts are deleted.

Insertions are simply performed into the original relations, i.e. b,c,d and e. We assume that a deletion implies the removal of at most one qualifying tuple. Deletions may invalidate derived facts, as illustrated in a continuation of the example.

```
(5) detractx(b(A,B,C,X)) :- retract(bb(A,B,C,X)), !.

(6) detractx(b(A,B,C,X)) :- retract(b(A,B,C,X)), !.
```

```
(7) detmove(b(A,B,C,X)) :- bb(A,B,C,X),
                    retract(bb(A,B,C,X)), asserta(b(A,B,C,X)), fail.
    detmove(b(A,B,C,X)).

(8) detractx(c(A,B,D)) :- retract(cc(A,B,D)), !, (not(cc(A,B,_ )),
                    detmove(b(A,B,_ ,_ )); true).

(9) detractx(c(A,B,D)) :- retract(c(A,B,D)) ,!.

(10) detmove(c(A,B,D)) :- cc(A,B,D),
                    retract(cc(A,B,D)), asserta(c(A,B,D)),
                    not(cc(A,B,_ )), detmove(b(A,B,_ ,_ )), fail.
    detmove(c(A,B,D)).

(11) detractx(e(B,D,E)) :- retract(e(B,D,E)), !, (not(e(B,D,_ )),
                    detmove(c(_ ,B,D)); true).

(12) detractx(d(A,C)) :- retract(d(A,C)), !, (not(d(A,C)),
                    detmove(b(A,_ ,C,_ )); true).
```

Deletions are performed using the rule detractx and are reflected in both original and derived relations. Rule 5 states that if a fact (a1,b1,c1,x1) is deleted, it is first searched for in bb and removed if found. Otherwise, by rule 6, deletion is performed from b. Rule 8 states that deletion of a fact (a1,b1,d1) is first attempted from cc. In case the fact was in cc it is deleted and if no other fact in cc has the same A,B components some facts in bb may be invalidated. This is checked for by the first alternative for procedure 7; bb facts which are no longer represented are located and moved from bb to b. In case (a1,b1,d1) is not found in cc, the deletion is carried out from c (rule 9). Deletion of a fact (b1,d1,e1) is performed on e (rule 11). This may invalidate cc facts which are handled in procedure 10. Observe that once facts are moved from cc to c in procedure 10 and there may be unrepresented facts in bb, procedure 7 is invoked. Rule 12 handles deletions from d.

There is a high cost which may be associated with a *single* deletion. For example, a fact deleted out of relation e in our example could affect the migration of many facts from cc to c or from bb to b. However, we may "charge" the cost of this motion to the derivation which has installed that derived fact which is now migrating. As each fact is installed once and migrates back at most once for each installment, the overall cost is bounded by a constant times the cost PROLOG would have "normally" invested (assuming a hash based O(1) fact locating method). In other words, the worst case complexity of a sequence of operations in the transformed program is the same as that of the original program. Of course, substantial savings may be realized when the number of insertions and deletions is relatively small, or when there are many "independent" procedure invocations each starting from "scratch". The worst case behavior is a manifestation of non-monotonicity which may convert the support mechanism into pure overhead.

6. CONCLUSION

In this paper we have proposed a program transformation method aiming at improving the efficiency of proof processes in PROLOG. The basic idea is trading time for space. In our approach the program is augmented with additional support knowledge and, with this additional knowledge, we show how to improve the efficiency of proof processes. As in many knowledge organization methods, the price to be paid for this improved service is the additional overhead in maintaining an up-to-date support structure when changes occur.

We have demonstrated the method and have shown two variants of its implementation: the a_priori and dynamic methods. We have shown that the techniques of view maintenance, originally developed in the context of relational databases, readily carry over to the area of logic programming. In the development we have borrowed and adapted other relational database concepts, notably the graph representation of queries. The ease with which we were able to adopt these concepts supports our opening contention that logic programming is indeed a suitable tool for a unified treatment of problems in the database area. We believe that the ideas presented herein are indeed feasible.

An important issue concerns the semantics of PROLOG. A program produced by our transformation methods does not always exhibit a behavior which is identical to the original program. First, duplicates are not supported and secondly, the order in which facts are derived may differ from the source program. It is our contention that these issues are not critical in most database oriented PROLOG applications.

More work remains to be done. The methods that we have proposed are two isolated cases from a spectrum of "hybrid methods" which combine these ideas in different ways. In this paper we have not touched upon the operational aspects of the methods and the performance gains that are to be expected. We hope to discuss these problems in our future work.

REFERENCES

[BC] Bernstein, P.A., and D.W. Chiu, "Using Semi-Joins to Solve Relational Queries", J. ACM 28 (1): 25-40, January 1981.

[BFMMUY]
Beeri, C., R. Fagin, D. Maier, A. Mendelzon, J.D. Ullman, and M. Yannakakis, "Properties of Acyclic Database Schemas", in Thirteenth Annual ACM Symp. on Theory of Computing, 355-362. Association for Computing Machinery, New York, N.Y., May 1981.

[BG] Bernstein, P.A., and N. Goodman, "The Power of Natural Semijoins", SIAM J. of Comput., 10 (4), November 1981.

[Cla] Clark, K.L., "Negation as Failure", in: H. Gallaire and J. Minker (eds.), Logic and Data Bases (Plenum Press, New York, 1978).

[CM] Cloksin, W.F., and C.S. Mellish, *Programming in Prolog,* Springer-Verlag, 1981.

[Gra] Graham, M.H., "On the Universal Relation", Technical Report, University of Toronto, September 1979.

[GS1] Goodman, N., and O. Shmueli, "Tree Queries: A Simple Class of Queries", ACM Transactions on Database Systems, 7,4, 653-677, December 1982.

[GS2] Goodman, N., and O. Shmueli, "The Tree Property is Fundamental for Query Processing", in Proc. ACM SIGACT- SIGMOD Conference on Principles of Database Systems, 40-48, Los Angeles, CA, March 1982.

[JCV] Jarke, M., J. Clifford, and Y. Vassiliou, "An Optimizing PROLOG Front-End to a Relational Query System", in Proc. ACM SIGMOD '84 Conference, 296-306, Boston , MA, June 1984. SIGMOD Record 14,2.

[Kel] Kelogg, C., "Knowledge Management: A Practical Amalgam of Knowledge and Database Technology", Proceedings AAAI 1982, 306-308.

[KY] Kunifuji, S., and H. Yokota, "Prolog and Relational Databases for Fifth Generation Computer Systems", Tech. Rep. No. TR002, ICOT, Tokyo, Japan, October 1982.

[Llo] Lloyd, J.W., "Foundations of Logic Programming" (Springer-Verlag,1984).

[NY] Nicolas, J.M. and Yazdanian, K., "An outline of BDGEN: A Deductive DBMS", in: Proc. of IFIP congress 83 (North-Holland, 1983).

[SI] Shmueli, O., and A. Itai, "Maintenance of views", in Proc. ACM SIGMOD '84 Conference, 240-255, Boston , MA, June 1984. SIGMOD Record 14,2.

[Ull1] Ullman, J.D., "Implementation of Logical Query Languages for Databases", unpublished manuscript, 1984.

[Ull] Ullman, J.D., *Principles of Database Systems,* Computer Science Press, 1982 (second edition).

[War] Warren, D.H.D., "Efficient Processing of Interactive Relational Database Queries Expressed in Prolog" Proc. 7'th VLDB Conf.,272-282 Cannes, France, 1981.

[Yan] Yannakakis, M., "Algorithms for Acyclic Database Schemes", in Proc. VLDB, 82-94, Cannes, France, September 1981.

[YO] Yu, C.T., and M.Z. Ozsoyoglu, "An Algorithm for Tree-Query Membership of a Distributed Query," in Proc. COMPSAC79, IEEE Comp. Society, November 1979.

[Zfi] Zfira, H., "Speeding up Prolog-Database Interactions", M.Sc. thesis, Technion-Israel Institute of Technology, Haifa, Israel (1985).

Mechanisms for Concurrency Control and Recovery in Prolog — A Proposal

Michael J. Carey
David J. DeWitt
Goetz Graefe

Computer Sciences Department
University of Wisconsin
Madison, WI 53706

ABSTRACT

Prolog is beginning to receive a great deal of attention as a vehicle for creating intelligent database management systems. This paper proposes concurrency control and recovery mechanisms which are particularly well-suited to a Prolog environment. The proposed concurrency control mechanism, query-fact locking, is based on a database concurrency control algorithm known as precision locking. The proposed recovery mechanism is based on a differential file scheme known as hypothetical databases. The combined effect of the proposed algorithms for concurrency control and recovery is a mechanism for correctly and reliably executing sequential Prolog programs and Concurrent Prolog programs in a multiuser environment with a shared knowledge base.

1. INTRODUCTION

During the past few years, researchers have begun to address the task of adding deductive capabilities to database management systems [Gall79, Gall81a, Gall81b, Kowa81, Dahl82, DBE83, Pars83, Jark82]. Prolog [Cloc81] is frequently mentioned as a suitable implementation language for such systems. First, however, Prolog must be extended in a number of ways before it can used to process large databases in a multiuser environment [Park85, Scio85]. One extension is to augment Prolog to include some notion of file input and output. Second, concurrency control and recovery mechanisms need to be added. In this paper, we propose concurrency control and recovery mechanisms which are well-suited for a Prolog environment.

There are several forms of concurrency that must be controlled in a Prolog-based intelligent database management system, as Prolog semantics allow queries that update the facts and/or rules in the knowledge base (via the *assert* and *retract* operators). The first form of concurrency occurs in a Concurrent Prolog environment when a user initiates a query whose subqueries can be executed concurrently [Shap83]. This form of concurrency can occur only with subqueries whose variables are either already instantiated or will be instantiated by the subquery itself. For example, the subqueries of the rule:

```
parent(X,Y) :- father(X,Y); mother(X,Y).
```

can be executed concurrently. On the other hand, the subqueries of the rule:

```
grandfather(X,Z) :- father(X,Y), parent(Y,Z).
```

cannot be run concurrently, as father(X,Y) must instantiate Y before parent(Y,Z) can be executed. While one might control this form of concurrency with a formal mechanism, for the present time we have decided to resolve conflicts among concurrently executing subqueries by adopting before-image semantics and a differential-file based recovery mechanism. These will be addressed in more detail below.

The second form of concurrency that must be controlled in a Prolog-based intelligent database management system is the concurrent execution of queries initiated by different users. The queries themselves may or may not display the type of concurrency discussed above. The following example illustrates the need for a concurrency control mechanism in a multiuser Prolog environment. Assume that the database consists of facts of the form child(x,y) indicating that x is a child of y:

```
child(sue,larry).
child(carol,larry).
child(fred,larry).
child(joe,larry).
```

the rule:

```
grandchild(X,Y) :- child(Z,Y), child (X,Z).
```

and the two queries:

Q_1: grandchild(X,larry).
Q_2: assert(child(john,sue)), assert(child(alice,joe)).

If Q_2 is run after Q_1 finishes, Q_1 will find that larry has no grandchildren. If Q_2 is run before Q_1 starts, Q_1 will produce the result set {john, alice}. The objective of *all* database concurrency control algorithms is to permit the concurrent execution of operations from different queries while insuring that the final state of the database corresponds to *some* serial schedule of the transactions [Eswa76]. Thus either of the above results is correct.

Execution of Q_1 consists of a number of subqueries. First, Prolog will instantiate Z with the value "sue" and attempt to prove the subgoal child(X,sue). Following the outcome of this goal, Z will be instantiated with "carol". Execution proceeds until all of larry's children are tested. Assume rather than Q_2 being executed completely before or after Q_1, that it is instead executed after execution of the subgoal child(X,sue) and before instantiating Z with carol. The outcome of Q_1 in this case is that alice is the only grandchild of larry. Since this result is not equivalent to any serial schedule of Q_1 and Q_2, it is not correct.

In addition to illustrating the need for a concurrency control mechanism in a multiuser Prolog-based database system, this example illustrates a classical concurrency control problem known as *phantoms* [Eswa76]. When Q_1 began executing larry had no grandchildren. If Q_2 had added grandchildren for anybody other than larry, running Q_2 in the middle of Q_1 would not have caused any problems. It is interesting to note that concurrency control in Prolog is different than concurrency control in conventional database management systems as Prolog provides no vehicle for modifying facts already in the database. Thus, while conventional concurrency control mechanisms deal primarily with controlling access to the partial updates by a query and pay little or no attention to the problems of phantoms, a concurrency control mechanism for Prolog must deal exclusively with the problem of phantom facts. In Section 2 we present a concurrency control mechanism that solves the problem of phantom facts.

The job of the database system recovery mechanism is twofold. First, it must insure that all updates made by queries which commit (terminate normally) are durable. By durable one means that the changes made by the query will persist in spite of subsequent hardware and/or software failures. The second task of the recovery mechanism is to undo any changes to the database made by queries which partially execute before being terminated by the system (as the result of deadlock, for example) or aborting themselves (due to erroneous input data or the user hitting the delete key).

As discussed earlier, subgoals of Prolog queries may assert or retract database facts. When such a subgoal fails two options exist. The first is to undo its effects by removing the set of facts asserted by the query and replacing the set of facts retracted by it. The second option is to simply ignore the problem. This is the approach used by most Prolog implementations. We feel that this approach is unacceptable if Prolog is to be used to implement intelligent database systems. In Section 3, we present a recovery mechanism for Prolog based on the ideas of differential files [Seve76] and hypothetical relations [Ston80, Ston81, Wood83, Agra83b]. In addition to providing a mechanism for undoing the effects of subqueries that fail, this mechanism facilitates implementation of before-image semantics for parallel subqueries and insures that the updates made by a query are durable.

We have made the following assumptions in developing our proposed concurrency control and recovery mechanisms:

(1) *undo semantics for subqueries that fail* - The effects of a subquery that fails will be undone. Since a subquery that fails may use the assert and/or retract operators to cause a side effect, we will also present a mechanism which permits delaying undoing the effects of such subqueries until the query terminates.

(2) *before-image semantics for parallel subqueries* - Facts asserted and retracted by subqueries executed concurrently are not visible to one another.

(3) *'all' semantics for goals connected with conjuncts* - These are the standard Prolog semantics. Our approach assumes that updates made by the subqueries are applied in the sequence corresponding to the left to right ordering of the goals in the rule.

(4) *'any' semantics for goals connected with disjuncts* - While sequential Prolog specifies that disjuncts are to be evaluated in a left to right order, we have assumed that a goal is satisfied by the first successful subquery in a concurrent Prolog environment. Furthermore, once one subquery succeeds the remaining active subqueries are terminated.

(5) *fixed rule base* - For the present time we have assumed that queries do not assert new rules or retract existing ones. At the end of the paper we briefly outline the changes that would be required to handle subqueries that update the rule base.

2. CONCURRENCY CONTROL

In this section we propose a concurrency control mechanism for Prolog. We begin with a discussion of the concurrency control problems posed by Prolog, and then we describe the proposed concurrency control mechanism. After examining our proposal in detail, we reflect on why we prefer our mechanism over several alternatives that were also considered. We conclude this section with a summary of the salient features of our concurrency control proposal.

2.1. The Problem

As described in Section 1, Prolog transactions are user queries which access *facts* (or unit clauses) and *rules*, possibly also *asserting* or *retracting* facts during their execution. The job of the concurrency control mechanism is to prevent transactions submitted by multiple users from interfering with one another. In particular, it should make transactions *serializable* [Eswa76] — the effect of the concurrent execution of a set of transactions should be equivalent to some serial execution of the transactions. There are several ways in which Prolog transactions can conflict and produce behavior which is non-serializable:

Fact – Fact Conflicts. This problem arises when two concurrent transactions attempt to perform updates involving the same fact(s). For instance, consider the following pair of transactions:

T_1 :- assert(foo(a,b)), retract(foo(a,c)).
T_2 :- assert(foo(a,c)), retract(foo(a,b)).

The outcome of serially executing T_1 and then T_2 is that foo(a,b) is false and foo(a,c) is true. The outcome of executing the transactions serially in the opposite order is that foo(a,b) is true and foo(a,c) is false. However, if the two transactions are interleaved, executing their assert steps and then their retract steps, the outcome is non-serializable — both foo(a,c) and foo(a,b) are false.

Query – Fact Conflicts. This problem arises when one transaction asserts or retracts a fact used by another concurrent transaction. For example, suppose that the queries Q_1 and Q_2 from Section 1 are run concurrently without concurrency control. We saw that it is possible for Q_1 to see one, but not both, of Q_2's updates to the Prolog knowledge base, leading to non-serializable behavior. In this example, the problem is due to the concurrent execution of a read-only query (Q_1) and a query that asserts new facts (Q_2), but a similar problem would arise if Q_2 were to retract facts used by Q_1.

Query – Rule Conflicts. This problem arises when one transaction asserts or retracts a rule used by another concurrent transaction. Since we do not address queries which assert or retract rules in this paper, we need not concern ourselves with this type of conflict for now. We will return to this issue when we discuss future work at the end of the paper.

The problem at hand, then, is to prevent fact-fact conflicts and query-fact conflicts through the use of an appropriate concurrency control mechanism. Readers familiar with the concurrency control literature will recognize that these conflicts are similar to the write-write and read-write conflicts of database concurrency control. However, there are some differences as well. The main salient features of the Prolog concurrency control problem have to do with *phantoms* and *parallel subqueries*.

We focus first on the issue of phantoms. All updates to the knowledge base in Prolog occur through the built-in *assert* and *retract* predicates. Thus, in database terms, Prolog programs can insert and delete facts, but they cannot modify existing facts.[1] As a result, all conflicts in Prolog are instances of the problem known as the *phantom tuple* problem (illustrated in the example in Section 1). As described in [Eswa76] and [Jord81], this problem arises when one transaction calls for a fact, or a tuple in database terminology, which does not (does) exist at the time of the request, but which is later created (deleted) due to the action of another transaction.

We next consider the second difference between database concurrency control and Prolog concurrency control, the issue of parallel subqueries. Consider the following Prolog rule:

sibling(X,Y) :- brother(X,Y); sister(X,Y).

This rule says that X is the sibling of Y if X is the brother or sister of Y. Suppose we now present the system with the query sibling(john,martha) in order to find out if john is a sibling of martha's. In a Concurrent Prolog implementation, the two sub-queries in the disjunction, brother(john,martha) and sister(john,martha), can be executed concurrently. The same is true for similar conjunctive queries. As we shall see, the possibility of concurrent subqueries will complicate the concurrency

[1] To modify a fact, a Prolog program must retract the old version of the fact and then assert a modified version

control problem somewhat.

2.2. A Solution: Query-Fact Locking

The Prolog concurrency control problem can be dealt with by an algorithm that we call *query – fact locking*. This algorithm is a Prolog-oriented variant of a database concurrency control algorithm known as *precision locking* [Jord81]. Precision locking is based on the popular notion of two-phase locking [Eswa76, Gray79], where transactions set read locks and write locks on the data items that they read and write (respectively) and hold locks until end of transaction. Most database systems apply locks to *physical* objects such as files, pages, or records. Precision locking, on the other hand, sets read locks on groups of *logical* objects, which are specified by predicates, and it applies write locks to physical objects (tuples or records). The algorithm is related to the predicate locking scheme proposed by Eswaren et al [Eswa76], but it is much more efficient (and thus practical) because it avoids the problem of having to decide whether or not a pair of predicates are jointly satisfiable. We will describe the reasoning that led to our selection of precision locking later on, but the basic reason is that the mechanism effectively and efficiently handles the concurrency control problems of interest, including phantoms. Physical locking algorithms do not correctly deal with phantoms [Jord81].

2.2.1. The Basic Algorithm

In query-fact locking, each transaction T_i maintains two sets: a set of queries $\mathbf{Q_i}$, and a set of facts $\mathbf{F_i}$. The set $\mathbf{Q_i}$ is the set of queries $\{Q_{ij}\}$ that the transaction has executed, specifying the read-set of the transaction. Read locks will be set on each query in this set, as we will see shortly. The set $\mathbf{F_i}$ is the set of facts $\{f_{ij}\}$ that the query has asserted or retracted, specifying the writeset of the transaction. Write locks will be set on each fact in this set. In addition, the concurrency control algorithm will maintain two global sets, $\mathbf{Q_L}$ and $\mathbf{F_L}$. $\mathbf{Q_L}$ is the global set of queries for which read locks have been granted and not yet released, and $\mathbf{F_L}$ is the set of facts for which write locks have been granted and not yet released. Entries in $\mathbf{Q_L}$ are of the form (Q_{ij}, T_i), where Q_{ij} is the locked query and T_i is the locking transaction. Similarly, entries in $\mathbf{F_L}$ are of the form (f_{ij}, T_i), where f_{ij} is the locked fact. These sets are equivalent to the sets of predicates and tuples in the precision locking algorithm [Jord81], and the union of the global sets $\mathbf{Q_L}$ and $\mathbf{F_L}$ is the equivalent of a lock table.

We are now almost ready for the details of the query-fact locking algorithm. First, though, we need one definition: We will say that one Prolog query Q_p *covers* another Prolog query Q_c if (1) they have identical predicate names, and (2) every constant or instantiated variable in the ith argument position of Q_c has the same value as the corresponding argument of Q_p if Q_p's i^{th} argument is a constant or an instantiated variable. For instance, child(X,larry) covers child(bob,larry) and child(Y,larry), but it does not cover child(bob,X). Intuitively, Q_p covers Q_c if Q_c could arise as a subquery of Q_p through variable instantiation during the execution of Q_p (or if Q_p and Q_c are the same query). Note that a special case of this definition is a query covering a fact. We are now ready to proceed with the specification of the query-fact locking algorithm.

2.2.1.1. Fact Assertion or Retraction

Before a transaction T_i can assert or retract a fact f_{ij}, it must do the following:

(1) Add the fact f_{ij} to its fact set $\mathbf{F_i}$.

(2) Check to see if there exists a fact f_{km} in the set of locked facts $\mathbf{F_L}$ such that $f_{ij} = f_{km}$, or if f_{ij} is covered by any query Q_{kn} in the set of locked queries $\mathbf{Q_L}$, where $i \neq k$. If so, Ti must block until f_{km} or Q_{kn} is unlocked.

(3) Add f_{ij} to $\mathbf{F_L}$ and proceed.

Step (1) serves to provide T_i with a list of the facts that it has locked so that they can be unlocked easily at end of transaction. Step (2) checks for fact-fact and query-fact conflicts, with T_i being blocked if either type of conflict is found. Step (3) records T_i's newly granted lock in the global list of locked facts. Steps (2) and (3) must be executed together as an atomic action (i.e., in a critical section).

2.2.1.2. Subquery Execution

Before a transaction T_i can execute a subquery Q_{ij}, it must do the following:

(1) Check to see if there exists a query Q_{im} in its query set $\mathbf{Q_i}$ such that Q_{im} covers Q_{ij}. If so, T_i can skip the remaining steps and simply execute Q_{ij}.

(2) Add the query Q_{ij} to its query set $\mathbf{Q_i}$.

(3) Check to see if there exists any fact f_{kn} in the list of locked facts $\mathbf{F_L}$ such that Q_{ij} covers f_{kn} and $i \neq k$. If so, T_i must block until all such facts f_{kn} are unlocked.

(4) Add Q_{ij} to $\mathbf{Q_L}$ and proceed.

Step (1) checks to see if T_i already has a lock which covers the facts to be dealt with by subquery Q_{ij}. If so, there is no need to lock a subset of these facts. This is an important performance optimization, as a query can lead to potentially many subqueries through variable instantiation. If each such subquery led to an entry in the set of locked queries, query-fact conflict testing could become overly expensive. Step (2) adds Q_{ij} to the list of locked queries for T_i for use at end of transaction. Step (3) checks for query-fact conflicts, blocking T_i if such a conflict is found. Step (4) records Q_{ij} in the global set of locked queries. Steps (3) and (4) must be executed together as an atomic action.

2.2.1.3. End of Transaction

When a transaction T_i terminates, it applies its knowledge base updates (as will be described in Section 3 of the paper), and then releases its locks as follows using the information in $\mathbf{F_i}$ and $\mathbf{Q_i}$:

(1) $\mathbf{F_L} = \mathbf{F_L} - \{T_i, F_{ij}\}$.
(2) $\mathbf{Q_L} = \mathbf{Q_L} - \{T_i, Q_{ij}\}$.

2.2.2. Blocking and Deadlocks

As described above, conflicts are handled by blocking transactions until the conflicts disappear. Thus, in addition to the global query and fact lock sets $\mathbf{Q_L}$ and $\mathbf{F_L}$, the concurrency control mechanism will have to manage queues of waiting transactions, as does the lock manager in a typical database system [Gray79]. Also, as with most dynamic two-phase locking algorithms, query-fact locking may lead to occasional deadlocks. For example, it is possible for two transactions each to set query locks which cover a set of common facts, and then for each to try to assert or retract a fact included in their joint coverage. Deadlocks can be handled by maintaining a waits-for graph and checking for cycles in the usual way [Gray79, Agra83a].

2.2.3. Query-Fact Locking in Action: An Example

Let us now see how the query-fact locking algorithm solves the problem illustrated by the example in Section 1. As a refresher, the example involved the following collection of facts:

```
child(sue,larry).
child(carol,larry).
child(fred,larry).
child(joe,larry).
```

The set of rules for the example consisted of a single rule:

```
grandchild(X,Y) :- child(Z,Y), child(X,Z).
```

Finally, the two conflicting queries were as follows:

Q_1: grandchild(X,larry).
Q_2: assert(child(john,sue)), assert(child(alice,joe)).

When query Q_1 is executed, the following subqueries and associated query locks will be set (assuming only the facts given above are in the knowledge base):

	Subquery	Query Locked
1.	child(X,larry)	child(X,larry)
2.	child (sue,larry)	
3.	child(X,sue)	child(X,sue)
4.	child(carol,larry)	
5.	child(X,carol)	child(X,carol)
6.	child(fred,larry)	
7.	child(X,fred)	child(X,fred)
8.	child(joe,larry)	
9.	child(X,joe)	child(X,joe)

Steps 2, 4, 6, and 8 illustrate the benefit of the optimization included in the query locking algorithm: If a new query lock is set *every* time a subquery begins to execute, regardless of whether or not the transaction already holds a covering lock, locks would have been set at each of these steps as well. The result would have been that nearly twice as many locks would have been set as are really needed to achieve the desired concurrency control effect in this example.

When query Q_2 is executed, the following subqueries and associated fact locks will be set:

	Subquery	Fact Locked
1.	assert(child(john,sue))	child(john,sue)
2.	assert(child(alice,joe))	child(alice,joe)

Now let us examine what would happen if the two queries are run concurrently. Suppose that steps 1-3 of Q_1 have completed and now Q_2 begins running. When Q_2 attempts to execute its first step, it will first try to lock the fact child(john,sue). Since Q_1 has already locked child(X,sue), which covers child(john,sue), Q_2 will be blocked until Q_1 completes and releases its locks. What if Q_2 had begun first instead? Q_2 will lock the fact child(john,sue) in its first step, causing Q_1 to block at its step 3 because child(X,sue) covers child(john,sue). Thus, in this case, Q_1 will wait until Q_2 completes and releases its locks. Regardless of the attempted execution order, the query-fact locking algorithm prevents non-serializable behavior by blocking one of the two conflicting queries until the other has finished.

2.2.4. Concurrent Subqueries: A Complication

The execution of a Concurrent Prolog program forms an and-or tree of concurrent conjunctive and disjunctive subqueries. This permits us to optimize our locking protocol a bit, releasing some locks earlier than end of transaction without compromising serializability. Consider the following set of disjunctive subqueries:

$$f(X,Y,Z) :- f_1(X,Y,Z); f_2(X,Y,Z); f_3(X,Y,Z).$$

Under the Concurrent Prolog semantics discussed in Section 1, f(X,Y,Z) will be evaluated in a way such that if any of the subqueries are true, the entire query will be true. Beyond this, however, no guarantees are provided. In particular, each subquery sees the knowledge base state prior to the execution of all concurrent subqueries, and only the results of one of the successful (true) subqueries are guaranteed to be applied to the knowledge base. Given these conditions, then, we can allow failed subqueries in a set of disjunctive subqueries to release their locks. In addition, we can discard the results of all but one of the successful subqueries, and each of the discarded subqueries can also release its locks. We refer to the selected successful subquery as the *selected disjunct*, and the other queries in the disjunction are referred to as *insignificant disjuncts*. All queries which are not insignificant disjuncts (i.e., either conjuncts or selected disjuncts) are referred to as *significant queries*.

These observations lead to the following algorithmic changes: Each subquery Q in a set of concurrent subqueries inherits a copy of the lock sets $\mathbf{F_i}$ and $\mathbf{Q_i}$ from its parent query at the time of the subquery's initiation. It then proceeds to apply the query-fact locking algorithm as described in the previous section. When the subquery completes, if it turns out to be an insignificant disjunct, the recovery manager can discard its results (as long as some other disjunct is successful); all of the locks added to $\mathbf{F_i}$ and $\mathbf{Q_i}$ by this insignificant disjunct may be released. Otherwise, the parent query's lock sets $\mathbf{F_i}$ and $\mathbf{Q_i}$ must be augmented with any new locks set by the subquery, as these locks must remain set until end of transaction (i.e., the parent query inherits locks from its significant child queries). Readers familiar with the concurrency control literature may notice that our mechanism has a flavor somewhat similar to that of nested transactions [Reed78, Moss81]. A difference is that our subqueries are not required to be serializable with respect to one another, with before-image semantics for concurrent subqueries being provided by the recovery mechanism (see Section 3).

2.2.5. Concurrent Rules

As discussed earlier, concurrent queries that satisfy the same goal can be regarded as a disjunct with an order imposed. Consider, for example, the following predicate specification:

```
p(X) :- s1(X).
   . . .
p(X) :- si-1(X).
p(X) :- si(X).
p(X) :- si+1(X).
   . . .
p(X) :- sn(X).
```

To evaluate p(X), all s_k(X) are evaluated concurrently. If one of them returns with a success, say s_i, then the subqueries s_{i+1} to s_n are treated as insignificant disjuncts, whether or not they have already produced a result, but the subqueries s_1 to s_{i-1} must be continued. If the result of s_i is a failure, then this subquery is treated as an insignificant disjunct. In terms of subquery completion, this means that the first rule is always completely evaluated and the other ones are evaluated only if all preceding ones failed or a preceding one took longer to execute.

2.2.6. Backtracking

During backtracking the effects of backtracked subqueries must be undone. However, locks are not released during backtracking. The reason for not releasing locks is that the database conditions that caused the query to backtrack must still hold at end-of-transaction to ensure serializability.

2.3. Other Solutions Considered

In the process of designing the Prolog concurrency control mechanism just described, we considered and ruled out a number of other alternatives. In this section we briefly consider each such alternative in turn, explaining what led us to eliminate it. The alternatives considered include locking facts, locking predicate names, or using a non-locking-based algorithm such as optimistic concurrency control [Kung81].

Our first inclination was to set locks on individual facts. However, we quickly realized that this would not work, as this would not solve the phantom fact problem. In particular, having transactions lock facts read and written would not prevent the transactions in the example from Section 1 from interleaving in a non-serializable way — Q_1 can lock the facts that it reads, but it cannot possibly set read locks on facts before they are asserted.

Our second inclination was to set locks on predicate names, such as child in the example. This will work, but it has terrible performance implications: This solution is equivalent to locking entire relations in a relational database system, which is an unacceptably coarse granularity for locking. As an illustration, suppose that the set of child facts included information about 10,000 children, yet the only child facts relevant to queries Q_1 and Q_2 are the six facts that they deal with. Since transactions hold locks until end of transaction (with a few possible exceptions as outlined in the previous section), other transactions would have to block for potentially long periods of time. In the example, *no* other transactions would be able to access *any* of the child facts while Q_1 or Q_2 execute.

Having considered these two possibilities, we came to the realization that some form of predicate-like locking would be necessary. A desire for a practical mechanism led us to select precision locking [Jord81] rather than true predicate locking [Eswa76] as a starting point.

We also considered other forms of concurrency control, such as optimistic algorithms [Kung81] or timestamp-based algorithms [Bern81]. Using either type of algorithm on physical objects, such as facts or predicate names, leads to the same sorts of problems as the rejected locking algorithms that we considered. However, it would be possible to use such algorithms in conjunction with queries and facts, as is done in query-fact locking. For example, if one wished to use the serial validation algorithm for optimistic concurrency control [Kung81], one could use $\mathbf{Q_i}$ as the readset for a transaction T_i, use $\mathbf{F_i}$ as its writeset, and validate T_i at commit time by checking that no recently committed transaction T_j had a writeset of facts $\mathbf{F_j}$ which is covered by any query in $\mathbf{Q_i}$. If T_i passed this validation test, it would be committed, its updates would be applied to the knowledge base, and $\mathbf{F_i}$ would be saved for use in validating future completing transactions. If not, it would be restarted. Thus, an optimistic algorithm would work equally well, at least in a logical sense. However, we chose locking over alternative mechanisms for performance reasons: A recent study has indicated that it is better to use locking algorithms instead of restart-oriented algorithms if conflicts are fairly likely, and that it does not matter what sort of mechanism is employed if conflicts are rare [Care84].

2.4. Summary

We have outlined a concurrency control mechanism which seems to nicely fit the concurrency control needs of Prolog. The mechanism, query-fact locking, is a form of two-phase locking in which transactions set read locks on queries and set write locks on facts. We expect that this mechanism can be implemented efficiently, as it is based on a notion of covering which is efficiently testable. The mechanism seems likely to perform at least as well as a physical locking mechanism would, as argued in the original precision locking paper [Jord81], and physical locking would not handle phantoms correctly. Since all conflicts in Prolog are instances of the phantom problem, and since query-fact locking correctly deals with this problem, we believe that our proposal is a promising one.

3. RECOVERY

In this section we propose a recovery mechanism for Prolog. The section begins with a discussion of the recovery problems posed by Prolog. Next we describe the operation of our proposed recovery mechanism. Finally, we discuss why we feel that it is the most appropriate recovery mechanism for the Prolog environment.

3.1. The Problem

A recovery mechanism for Prolog must provide three fundamental services. First it must make the effects of Prolog queries that update the database durable. By durable we mean that once a query commits its changes to the database they will not be affected by subsequent hardware and/or software failures. The second service is to undo any changes to the database that are made by aborted queries. While both of these services are found in conventional database systems, the recovery manager for Prolog must additionally provide a mechanism for undoing the effects of subqueries that fail in the process of answering a query. In the following section we will propose a mechanism that provides these three services.

3.2. Recovery Using Differential Files

With the differential file scheme proposed in [Seve76], each logical file consists of two physical files: a read-only *base file* and a read-write *differential file* containing all changes to the file. The base file remains unchanged until reorganization. All updates are confined to the differential file. In [Ston80, Ston81, Wood83], Stonebraker extended the differential file idea to introduce the notion of hypothetical relations. Each relation R in the database consists of three parts: B, a read-only base portion of R, A, a file containing all additions to R, and D, a file containing all tuples deleted from R. From the point of view of a query, R is equal to $(B \cup A) - D$. Recovery from software and/or hardware failures is simplified, as A and D are both append-only files. A and D are merged with R only during database reorganization.

3.3. A Recovery Mechanism for Prolog

We propose to use the notion of hypothetical relations as a basis for a recovery mechanism for Prolog. For the duration of a query (or a group of queries designated as a transaction), the knowledge base, KB, is treated as a read-only file. Whereas the A and D files in Stonebraker's hypothetical relation mechanism are permanently associated with a relation R, we propose to instead associate A and D files[2] with each query and to merge A and D with KB when the query commits. The A file is used to hold facts (and rules) asserted by the query and the D file is used to hold facts (and rules) which the query proposes to retract from the knowledge base.

Execution of a query may actually cause a number of A and D files to be created. Empty A and D files are created when a query first begins execution. In addition, whenever a subgoal is executed which asserts or retracts one or more facts, an additional pair of A and D files are created. This is illustrated by the example of Figure 1. In this example, queries Q_1, Q_2, and Q_5 assert or retract one or more facts that are stored in the A and D files local to the corresponding goal. From the viewpoint of goal Q_4, the knowledge base corresponds to $((((KB \cup A_1) - D_1) \cup A_2) - D_2)$. For Q_5, it is $((((KB \cup A_1) - D_1) \cup A_5) - D_5)$. A_5 and D_5 are empty until the goal asserts or retracts a

[2] A and D are probably more properly referred to as storage structures since they generally will reside in main memory.

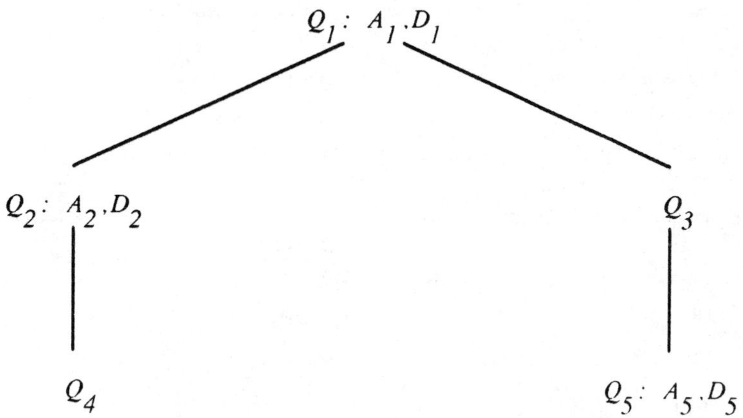

Figure 1: Recovery Example.

fact. This approach quite obviously generalizes to queries at arbitrary depths.

When a subgoal succeeds, its associated A and D files, if any, are appended to those of its parent. If the parent does not have A and D files associated with it, it inherits those of the first child to succeed.

When a subgoal fails, two alternative courses of action are possible. The first is to delete its associated A and D files. This strategy preserves the undo semantics for subqueries that fail as assumed in Section 1. If this is not acceptable, the following alternative is feasible. First, a second set of files, *Undo_A* and *Undo_D*, is created whenever a set of A and D files is created. Whenever a goal fails, the union of the A file is formed with the A and *Undo_A* files of its parent. The D file is processed in the same manner. In addition, the *Undo_A* and *Undo_D* files of the goal are combined with the *Undo_A* and *Undo_D* files of its parent. In this way, all assertions and retractions are visible for the duration of the query. However, before committing the effects of the query we form $A = A - Undo\_A$ and $D = D - Undo\_D$ in order to undo the effects of those subqueries which failed during the execution of the query.

When a query backtracks, the effects of its subqueries are undone by truncating those portions of its A and D files that were appended when its subqueries terminated.

Committing the effects of a transaction (query) requires updating the knowledge base by forming $KB = (KB \cup A) - D$ in such a manner that either all of the changes made by the query are reflected in KB or none are. The following algorithm can be used:

(1) Write A and D to stable storage [Gray79, Lamp79].

(2) Write a pre-commit record to stable storage. This record should contain the id of the query and pointers to the A and D files.

(3) Update the copy of KB on disk using the copies of A and D still in primary memory.

(4) Write a commit record to stable storage. This record contains the id of the query.

Once step 2 has been completed, the recovery software insures that the updates made by the query will eventually be applied to the knowledge base. If the system crashes during step 3, then the fact that the commit record for the query does not appear in stable storage will be noted during system restart and step 3 will be repeated.[3]

Finally, if a transaction is aborted by the user or the system, undoing its effects can be accomplished by simply deleting all of its A and D files.

3.4. Discussion

Our proposed mechanism appears to provide a robust yet efficient recovery mechanism for Prolog. By structuring the A and D files in the same way as the KB, existing software can be used. Furthermore, $KB \cup A$ and $(KB \cup A) - D$ do not ever have to actually be materialized.

Generally, the proposed recovery mechanism preserves the semantics for use in a sequential Prolog system, while providing a reasonable set of semantics for a Concurrent Prolog environment. In particular, by utilizing before-image semantics for parallel subqueries, we can eliminate concurrency problems having to do with parallel subqueries. (It is important to note that we do *not* demand or provide serializability for these subqueries, as our before-image semantics prohibit it.)

---

[3] See [Gray79] for a discussion on how idempotence can be achieved.

If queries instead used in-place updates and logging [Gray79] as the recovery mechanism, updates by parallel subqueries would be visible to one another, leading to nondeterministic results. Furthermore, since subqueries frequently fail, the cost of undoing updates made by these subqueries by reading the log from stable storage would be prohibitively high.

4. CONCLUSIONS

This paper has proposed concurrency control and recovery mechanisms which are designed specifically for use in a Prolog environment. The proposed concurrency control mechanism, query-fact locking, handles fact-fact and query-fact conflicts that can arise when concurrently executed Prolog transactions share a knowledge base. The mechanism requires transactions to set read locks on queries and write locks on facts to guarantee serializable behavior. In addition, a lock inheritance mechanism was outlined for dealing with concurrent subqueries in Concurrent Prolog programs. We expect that our algorithm will be reasonably efficient, as it is based on an easily-testable notion of queries covering other queries and facts.

The proposed recovery mechanism is based on a differential file scheme known as hypothetical databases. The scheme can handle normal sequential Prolog programs, sequential Prolog programs where the results of failed subqueries are to be backed out, and Concurrent Prolog programs where before-image semantics are desired for concurrent subqueries. The proposed scheme uses multiple levels of hypothetical relations to handle subqueries in Prolog programs, though a single set of hypothetical relations would be sufficient to handle the case of normal sequential Prolog programs.

One way in which this work can be extended is to handle rule updates as well as fact updates on a dynamic basis. This appears to be a simple extension: Rule assertions and retractions lead to two new types of conflicts, *rule − rule* conflicts and *query − rule* conflicts. Prolog transactions can be augmented with sets of updated rules, $\mathbf{R_i}$, analogous to their sets of updated facts. The global concurrency control information can be augmented with a set of locked rules, $\mathbf{R_L}$, analogous to the set of locked facts. These sets can then be used to check for conflicts when subqueries are executed and when rules are asserted or retracted. The conflict-checking algorithm will be similar to the algorithms for checking for fact-fact and query-fact conflicts, except that the covering tests can be replaced by a simple test for matching predicate names in this case. As for recovery, rule updates can be recorded in the same files as the fact updates in the current scheme.

In summary, this paper has presented a fairly detailed proposal for adding concurrency control and recovery facilities to Prolog. These additions are necessary if Prolog is to someday be truly useful as a vehicle for the creation of practical, commercial, intelligent database management systems. The combined effect of our proposed algorithms for concurrency control and recovery is a mechanism for correctly and reliably executing either sequential Prolog programs or Concurrent Prolog programs in a multi-user environment with a shared knowledge base.

ACKNOWLEDGEMENTS

This research was partially supported by the National Science Foundation under grant MCS82-01870, by the IBM Corporation through an IBM Faculty Development Award, and by the Wisconsin Alumni Research Foundation.

REFERENCES

[Agra83a] Agrawal, R., Carey, M., and DeWitt, D., "Deadlock Detection is Cheap", *ACM SIGMOD Record* 13(2), January 1983.

[Agra83b] Agrawal, R., and DeWitt, D., "Updating Hypothetical Databases", *Information Processing Letters* 16(3), April 1983.

[Bern81] Bernstein, P., and Goodman, N., "Concurrency Control in Distributed Database Systems", *ACM Computing Surveys* 13(2), June 1981.

[Care84] Carey, M., and Stonebraker, M., "The Performance of Concurrency Control Algorithms for Database Management Systems", *Proceedings of the Tenth International Conference on Very Large Data Bases*, August 1984.

[Cloc81] Clocksin, W., and Mellish, C., *Programming in Prolog*, Springer-Verlag, 1981.

[Dahl82] Dahl, V., "On Database Systems Development Through Logic", *ACM Transactions on Database Systems* 7(1), March 1982.

[DBE83] *Database Engineering* 6(4), Special Issue on Expert Systems and Database Systems, December 1983.

[Eswa76] Eswaran, K., Gray, J., Lorie, R., and Traiger, I., "The Notions of Consistency and Predicate Locks in a Database System", *Communications of the ACM* 19(11), November 1976.

[Gall79] Gallaire, H., and Minker, J., eds., *Logic and Data Bases*, Plenum Press, 1978.

[Gall81a] Gallaire, H., "Impacts of Logic on Databases", *Proceedings of the Seventh International Conference on Very Large Data Bases*, 1981.

[Gall81b] Gallaire, H., Minker, J., and Nicolas, J-M., *Logic and Data Bases*, Plenum Press, 1981.

[Gray79] Gray, J., "Notes On Database Operating Systems", in *Operating Systems: An Advanced Course*, Springer-Verlag, 1979.

[Jark84] Jarke, M., Clifford, J., and Vassiliou, Y., "An Optimizing Prolog Front-End to a Relational Query System", *Proceedings of the 1984 ACM-SIGMOD International Conference on Management of Data*, June 1984.

[Jord81] Jordan, J., Banerjee, J., and Batman, R., "Precision Locks", *Proceedings of the 1981 ACM-SIGMOD International Conference on Management of Data*, May 1981.

[Kowa81] Kowalski, R., *Logic as a Database Language*, Technical Report, Imperial College, London, July 1981.

[Kung81] Kung, H., and Robinson, J., "On Optimistic Methods for Concurrency Control", *ACM Transactions on Database Systems* 6(2), June 1981.

[Lamp79] Lampson, B., and Sturgis, H., *Crash Recovery in a Distributed Data Storage System*, Research Report, Xerox PARC, 1979.

[Moss81] Moss, E., *Nested Transactions: An Approach to Reliable Distributed Computing*, Ph.D. Thesis, Department of Electrical Engineering and Computer Science, Massachusetts Institute of Technology, 1981.

[Park85] Parker, D., et al, "Logic Programming and Databases", in this book.

[Pars83a] Parsaye, K., "Database Management, Knowledge Base Management, and Expert System Development in Prolog", *Proceedings of the ACM-SIGMOD Database Week Conference (Databases for Business and Office Applications)*, May 1983.

[Reed78] Reed, D., *Naming and Synchronization in a Decentralized Computer System*, Ph.D. Thesis, Department of Electrical Engineering and Computer Science, Massachusetts Institute of Technology, 1978.

[Scio85] Sciore, E., and Warren, D., "Towards an Integrated Database-Prolog System", in this book.

[Seve76] Severence, D., and Lohman, G., "Differential Files: Their Application to the Maintenance of Large Databases", *ACM Transactions on Database Systems* 1(3), September 1976.

[Shap83] Shapiro, E., *A Subset of Concurrent Prolog and Its Interpreter*, Technical Report TR-003, ICOT, January 1983.

[Ston80] Stonebraker, M., and Keller, K., "Embedding Expert Knowledge and Hypothetical Data Bases into a Data Base System", *Proceedings of the 1980 ACM-SIGMOD International Conference on Management of Data*, May 1980.

[Ston81] Stonebraker, M., "Hypothetical Data Bases as Views", *Proceedings of the 1981 ACM-SIGMOD International Conference on Management of Data*, May 1981.

[Wood83] Woodfill, J., and Stonebraker, M., "An Implementation of Hypothetical Relations", *Proceedings of the Ninth International Conference on Very Large Data Bases*, August 1983.

TOWARDS AN INTEGRATED DATABASE-PROLOG SYSTEM

Edward Sciore
David Scott Warren

Computer Science Department
SUNY at Stony Brook
Stony Brook, NY 11794

ABSTRACT

One way to expand the power and flexibility of a database system is to include an inference mechanism such as the logic programming language Prolog. A common approach to combining Prolog and relational databases is to have a Prolog system use an existing database system as a backend server. In this paper we argue that such a composite system has a poor division of labor, and results in redundancy and inefficiency. A better approach is to construct a single integrated system that combines both inferencing and data retrieval. Designing such a system involves generalizing some of the components of a database system and adding them to a Prolog system. In this paper we give examples that show how this can be done. The purpose of the paper to show that this approach is promising and can be expected to result in a more general system that is at least as efficient as current relational database systems.

1. Introduction

Prolog is a programming language based on logic. It was invented and developed in the Artificial Intelligence community [CKP73, Kow79, WPP77], and its ability to traverse a search space efficiently and automatically has proven to be very useful there. It is becoming increasingly clear that there is a close and fundamental relationship between Prolog and relational databases. Consider the Prolog clause:

$$p(X,Z) \text{:-} q(X,Y), r(Y,Z).$$

This clause is understood declaratively by a Prolog programmer as saying that p is true of individuals X and Z if there is some Y such that q is true of X and Y and r is true of Y and Z. It can be understood procedurally as saying that one way to execute the procedure p with parameters X and Z is to call procedures q and r with the appropriate parameters. But this clause can also be understood as a statement in a relational database language: that the relation p is the *join* of the relations q and r. Other relational operations are easily and naturally expressed as Prolog clauses. The point we wish to make is not that relational databases are easy to program in the Prolog language, but that the Prolog language itself *is* a relational database language.

The relationship between Prolog and relational databases is deep and fundamental. Prolog is more general than relational databases in that it allows recursion, both in rules and in its data objects. Relational databases are more developed in their management of large amounts of data, their treatment of updates, and their handling of concurrent users and shared data. There is a well-recognized need to extend logic programming systems to include more sophisticated database facilities; in this paper, we discuss our approach to the problem.

Many researchers have noticed the close relationship between Prolog and relational databases [GaM78, Kow81, Par83, War81], and several research projects have attempted to implement a combined system [EPP83, VCJ83, YKK84]. However, that research is focused on using an existing relational database system as a backend to a Prolog language processor. The idea is to modify the processing of a Prolog program so that it collects together, unevaluated, the subqueries that access data stored in the relational database. These subqueries are then translated into the query language of the backend database system and sent to it for processing.

Connecting existing Prolog and database systems is attractive, and may prove to be a good short term solution to the problem. For example, a database system is considerably larger than a Prolog interpreter, so it is much easier to use an existing system than to write a new one. In addition, existing database files can be accessed by the system without any conversion problems. However, we think that there are several problems inherent in this approach. Such a composite system duplicates many functions in each component, resulting in inelegance and inefficiency. It requires a conversion between a database source language and Prolog, which means unnecessary overhead. By separating the database component from a Prolog program, optimization possibilities are reduced. Finally, a significant portion of the database management system, such as the view definition mechanism, is not used at all.

As a concrete example of a situation in which this composite approach does rather poorly, consider a database with a relation that stores employees and their managers. Consider a query which, given a single employee, asks who is the highest boss over that employee. This is a standard transitive closure example and, since it cannot be answered by a simple relational calculus query, is often cited as evidence for the need for the Prolog component. Consider how a composite system (such as described in [YKK84]) would evaluate this query. The Prolog component would construct a database query to retrieve a single employee tuple, ship it off to the database, which would parse it, optimize it, execute it, and ship the single tuple answer back to the Prolog component. Prolog would then check to see if this employee had a manager, and if so, construct a database query to retrieve a single employee tuple (the manager's), ship it off to the database, etc. The point is that there is a tremendous amount of overhead for what ought to be a simple running of a chain of pointers on disk.

In this paper we consider an integrated approach to providing Prolog with database facilities. The intuition is that we must take ideas developed in the database area, extend them, and incorporate them into the Prolog framework. This involves creating a system that is an extension of standard Prolog systems and which includes disk management and optimization. The Prolog extensions will look very much like standard database system components. The difference from the above approach is that our approach results in a much more integrated system. We emphasize that extensions will have to be made to existing Prolog systems; the primary claim of this paper is that these extensions can be made naturally in the logic programming framework.

The remainder of this paper gives evidence for the desirability of this integrated approach. We give examples of facilities that would be duplicated by connecting two systems and show how extra benefits can be obtained by eliminating the redundancy. We discuss how such issues as buffer management, normally thought to be exclusively a database concern, can be considered profitably in the Prolog framework. We then discuss query optimization and execution in an integrated system. Finally we briefly mention other aspects of a database system, which can, we believe, be elegantly incorporated into the Prolog framework.

Efficiency is an important consideration. For example, we will see that removing redundant functionality can reduce overhead. The question arises as to whether an extended Prolog system can manage the disk as efficiently as a finely-tuned database system. Many of the examples in this paper address this question. In almost every case (the only exception being sort-merge join) there is no problem in extending Prolog to achieve the same disk access pattern as a database system; sort-merge joining is possible, but more difficult to model.

2. Indexing

Standard relational database systems make extensive use of indexes to help search through many facts. Much is known about indexing; many indexing strategies exist, and database research is continuing to develop new ones. Unlike sophisticated database systems, Prolog systems support only a limited and fixed amount of indexing. For example, DEC-10 Prolog [WPP77] indexes on the first field of a relation. Another Prolog system [Bru82] does a primitive kind of indexing on all fields. How might we extend Prolog systems to incorporate the power and flexibility of database techniques?

A brute force approach is to add access methods and index selection algorithms to the internals of the Prolog implementation. In order to specify the available indexes for each predicate, the programmer would have to use some sort of Data Definition Language (DDL). The DDL statements would be interpreted by the Prolog processor and used at run time to determine the appropriate access path for a query. This approach extends the database indexing techniques to the Prolog framework, but results in a grossly complex and unchangable system. For example, in order to add a new indexing technique at a later date, the DDL must be changed and the entire Prolog system must be modfied and recompiled to accommodate it. Thus this approach leads to a combined system, but not an integrated one.

There is a more elegant way to represent and maintain indexes in the Prolog framework: the indexes and their access routines can be specified as Prolog predicates and clauses. Consider a Prolog system that organizes records based on the first field of a relation. The relation *emp* 1(*Empno* ,*Lastname* ,*Sal* ,*Dept*) thus provides fast access to queries given a value for *Empno* . An index on *Dept* corresponds to the predicate *emp_dept_index* (*Dept* ,*Empno*). This index can be used by queries that have Dept bound and Empno unbound, nondeterministically returning each *Empno* for a department. That is, its access routine can be specified as the Prolog clause

```
emp(Empno,Lastname,Sal,Dept) :-
        var(Empno),nonvar(Dept),
        emp_dept_index(Dept,Empno),
        emp1(Empno,Lastname,Sal,Dept).
```

Similarly, each index for *emp* has a corresponding clause, and the collection of these clauses specifies the access strategy of the predicate.

Suppose now that we wanted to organize our employee predicate with two indexes, one on *Dept* and one on *Sal* . The clauses to access the predicate would be as follows:

```
emp(Empno,Lastname,Sal,Dept) :-
        var(Empno),nonvar(Dept),!,
        emp_dept_index(Dept,Empno),
        emp1(Empno,Lastname,Sal,Dept).
emp(Empno,Lastname,Sal,Dept) :-
        var(Empno),nonvar(Sal),!,
        emp_sal_index(Sal,Empno),
        emp1(Empno,Lastname,Sal,Dept).
emp(Empno,Lastname,Sal,Dept) :-
        emp1(Empno,Lastname,Sal,Dept).
```

With this definition of emp, the system will use the index on Dept if possible; otherwise, it tries the index on Sal, and if not possible uses *emp* 1 as the last resort. Note how Prolog's ability to handle multiple clauses allows us to specify the runtime selection of indexes simply and naturally, without the necessity for a separate DDL.

In database terminology, *emp_dept_index* and *emp_sal_index* are called ***inverted indexes***. These indexes take a non-key value and return a key value of *emp* , for use by *emp* 1. *Empno* is called a ***symbolic pointer***. However, access would be more efficient if the index returned a physical pointer instead. To incorporate this capability, we need to extend Prolog to include the notion of disk pointer. One way to treat a disk pointer is as a Prolog structure, consisting of a file name, a tuple location, and a length. A new builtin predicate (called *deref* in [Sci85]) could be used to read a tuple into memory given a disk pointer.

Disk pointers are very useful constructs which give us the control necessary to deal with the disk efficiently. For example, it is straightforward to write file organization routines in Prolog using them. Consequently, we do not need to use Prolog's automatic indexing on the first argument. By writing file organization routines as Prolog predicates, we can use any strategy we choose (say, Btrees or hashing), instead of depending on the default system method. For example, *emp* 1 above may be defined by the program

```
empl(Empno,Lastname,Sal,Dept) :-
        btree(emp(Empno,Lastname,Sal,Dept)).
```

Where *btree* is a general Prolog predicate that implements Btrees. If the first argument, the key, is not bound, *btree* returns all tuples in the relation.

There are several advantages to having the indexing and file organization expressed as Prolog programs. Prolog is a high-level language, so the programs are simpler. Also, there is nondeterminism in the indexing mechanisms that is very naturally expressed and handled by Prolog. Another advantage is that with an optimizing Prolog compiler, we could compile the indexes together with the program and generate a system tuned for that specific query.

One feature that is not available in Prolog is the ability to use range queries while indexing. For example, consider the query

```
p(X),X>5.
```

If predicate *p* is organized as a Btree, then we should be able to use it to get the appropriate records. However, there is no way for Prolog to use the tree; *p* must be accessed sequentially, with each record checked afterwards to see if it is greater than 5. One solution would be to extend the Prolog syntax, allowing goals such as

```
p(X:X>5).
```

It is not clear how powerful an extension to Prolog is required, or even if it is worth the effort.

We have argued that the indexing done in databases can be mirrored in Prolog. There is, however, an additional advantage to be gained from incorporating the indexing in the Prolog system. Prolog will index on rules, not only on facts. Thus Prolog will automatically index what are known in database terms as union views. Consider an example concerning bank accounts from [Ull82] (pp 413-414), which discusses horizontally fragmented relations. The idea is that, depending on the value of an attribute, tuples are put into one of several relations. The total relation is then defined by a view that takes the union of the subrelations. In Prolog terms, the customer relation would be defined as follows:

```
cust(1,Account,Balance,Customer) :- custbr1(Account,Balance,Customer).
cust(2,Account,Balance,Customer) :- custbr2(Account,Balance,Customer).
cust(3,Account,Balance,Customer) :- custbr3(Account,Balance,Customer).
```

The first attribute of cust is the branch office at which the account was opened and resides. Ullman assumes that the subrelations, custbr1, custbr2, and custbr3, are distributed on separate machines. The point of the example is to show that if a query only requires data from one branch, the system can keep from having to access all the subrelations by appropriate optimizations. The optimization described there is given only in general terms, and a footnote points out that the generalized problem is difficult. But note that the standard indexing of clauses done by Prolog achieves the same result in a very natural way. In such cases Prolog can be more efficient than most database systems.

3. Blocking and Buffer Management

One aspect of a database system that is critical to its efficiency is how it handles buffers and the movement of blocks of data from disk to memory. How can we represent the idea of blocking? One way is to define predicate *p* as follows:

p(X,Y,Z) :- p_block(B),p_rec(B,X,Y,Z).

Predicate *p_block* returns each block of *p* nondeterministically, and predicate *p_rec* returns the records in a block. The result is that the records of *p* are retrieved in a two-level fashion, as they should be.

There are various ways in which one could implement this strategy. A simple way is to have *p_block* return B as a list of records, and have *p_rec* be the predicate that tests for membership in a list. A more sophisticated strategy would be to have B correspond to a physical block of memory. Then *p_block* is the routine to read a block, and *p_rec* is the routine to convert each record in the block to a Prolog term. The strategy should be more efficient, but it requires extending Prolog systems with the ability to deal with "memory blocks". For details, see [Sci85].

A database system should also be able to use its memory buffers effectively. Consider the following example: We have two database predicates *p* and *q*. Each has 100 tuples, stored 10 to a block. We wish to compute the cartesian product

p(X),q(Y).

Expanding the predicates by their definitions, we get

p_block(B1), p_rec(B1,X), q_block(B2), q_rec(B2,Y).

Assuming one buffer for each predicate, direct evaluation of this query results in 1010 block accesses; each block of *q* will be accessed for every tuple of *p*.

Now consider the following logically equivalent query:

p_block(B1), q_block(B2), p_rec(B1,X), q_rec(B2,Y).

Prolog's execution of this query requires only 110 block accesses. The query traverses the blocks to return the product of the tuples in the buffers. When the buffers are empty, it backtracks and reads in another block. This strategy is well known to the database community, and is the most efficient way to compute the product. If we look at the two programs, we see that they are logically equivalent, and in fact the second could easily be considered an optimization of the first. (Note however that the order of the tuples is different.) This result suggests that at least part of the buffer management strategy is affected by the query optimizer.

Another feature of a database system is that it manages buffer allocation intelligently. Buffer management is usually done by the operating system, using an all-purpose replacement strategy. Such a strategy is frequently not the one desired by the database system. As a result, it is difficult to integrate database buffer management in a general system. In a Prolog environment, we can use the global stack space to allocate buffers. This space is reclaimed on backtracking, making management of memory space for buffers trivial. Further research into such buffering strategies is required.

4. Caching

It is often useful while computing to be able to save intermediate results in a table; then if the same result is needed later, it can be retrieved from the table and not recomputed. This concept is commonly known as *caching,* and appears in many situations. Consider as an example the following.

A database system keeps a table of open files for use during query processing. This table holds important information about a file (such as format and starting block) that otherwise would require expensive disk processing. So whenever access is required to a file, the system looks in this table to see if that file is already open. If not, it calls the operating system to open the file, determines its format, and does other "initalization" work, storing various collected information in its open file table. Subsequent accesses to the file then use the table to obtain quickly information necessary to carry out the requested operation.

In a Prolog framework, we can think of this table as an optimization performed by the system. For example, the code for accessing a predicate *p* might look like

```
p(X,Y) :- initialize(p,Fd,Fmt,T),  · · ·
initialize(P,Fd,Fmt,T) :- getformat(P,Fmt),getfiledesc(P,Fd),getfirsttup(Fd,T).
```

It is logically correct (and good programming practice) to have each call to *p* invoke *initialize* ; however, if the file is opened several times, this would be inefficient. So we attach a "pragma" to the predicate *initialize* , indicating that the results of *initialize* are to be saved in a table. Then, logically, every open of the file would call the "initialize" predicate but only the first one would actually carry out the code, code that involves disk access and system calls. Later calls would access an in-memory table that was set up by earlier calls.

We call such a table of facts an *extension table,* because it stores the extension (i.e. the tuples) of a rule-defined predicate. A completely general extension table facility would have to handle recursively defined predicates and complex recursive data structures; this is very complex, and would turn Prolog's simple, fast deduction method into the more complicated Earley deduction method [PeW83, She76, War79]. However, there are many uses for extension tables for simple predicates such as the example of the open file table above, and we need to look for special cases which can be implemented simply and efficiently. The database aspects of Prolog seem to contain several of these special cases.

The notion of an intermediate relation is another example of an extension table. If we have the predicate definition

```
t(X,Z) :- p(X,Y),q(Y,Z).
```

then *p* and *q* will be executed each time *t* is called. If, however, we indicate that *t* should be kept in an extension table, the join will be performed only once and saved. In database terms, the extension table is used to store the contents of the intermediate relation *t*

From these two examples, it is evident that an ideal extension table facility will contain many features. For example, the table might start out in memory, but (in the case of intermediate relations) be paged to disk when it gets too big. Or there might be a replacement algorithm that decides the tuples to remove when the table gets too big (in the case of the open file table). The facility would also need a way to know when to invalidate an extension table.

The addition of an extension table facility should make a Prolog system much more flexible than current systems. Currently, caching mechanisms are hard-coded into a system and are very difficult to change. With extension tables, the database system designer could easily change what values are to be cached, simply by adding, deleting or changing a pragma annotation that indicates an extension table should be maintained for a given predicate.

5. Query Optimization

One important component of a relational database system is its optimizer. Indeed, relational database systems, for all their mathematical elegance, would not be efficient enough to be practical were it not for the extensive query optimization they do.

It is also the case that most state-of-the-art compilers include an optimization phase. We assume that an advanced Prolog compiler would have an optimization component; this component will have deterministic optimizations and nondeterministic ones. The deterministic optimizations involve flow analysis, constant propagation, inline expansion of procedures, and also general Lisp-like program transformations. The nondeterministic optimizations try to reduce the search space, and involve re-ordering literals. The nondeterministic optimizations are similar to database optimizations, and will be discussed here. The point of this section is that it is not possible to separate database optimizations from Prolog optimizations, and thus the use of a separate database system must introduce duplication of effort.

Consider a search-intensive Prolog program, such as the eight-queens problem or a map-coloring problem. Several heuristics have been suggested to reduce the search space [Kal83, McC82]. One heuristic is to re-order literals so that literals with the largest number of instantiated variables are executed first [Kal83, War81]. In a database system, re-ordering literals corresponds to determining the proper order in which to join relations. The best ordering also depends on which variables are bound (i.e. the selection conditions). Thus the Prolog problem of re-ordering literals includes the database optimization problem; note that the problem arises from nondeterminism, not from the existence of database predicates. Thus we cannot leave the optimization to a database system. Even if the database system used different algorithms, the analysis of the query necessary to perform the optimizations would be redundant.

In general, it is easier to do database query optimization because we know at compile time when variables become bound. For general Prolog predicates it is necessary to do some analysis. Simple flow analysis can determine that a predicate is not recursively defined, which variables will be bound after the predicate is invoked, and other properties on which the database optimization algorithms depend. Again, it is important to discover simple cases of Prolog programs in which we can use database techniques.

It is also possible that optimization strategies developed for Prolog may turn out to provide insight into why certain database optimization strategies work. Consider the example query:

```
:- p(X,Y),q(X,Z),r(Y,W).
```

Assume that flow analysis can determine that none of these variables will be linked, i.e., the same variable does not occur free in distinct terms. This is trivially true if p, q, and r are database predicates. Now if the Prolog interpreter succeeds through p and q and fails in r, it should not waste time trying to find another solution for q; it would again fail in r for the same reason. Failure in r should cause backtracking into p. Therefore the compiler can generate code so that the choice points laid down in the evaluation of the goal $q(X,Z)$ are spliced out of the backtrack chain while r is being executed, and spliced back in when r succeeds.

This strategy is the idea behind the QUEL decomposition algorithm [WoY76] and Warren's "independent sub-queries" [War81]. The general case is known as ***intelligent backtracking,*** and has been explored by several researchers [BrP84, Cox84, PeP82]. Intelligent backtracking is a runtime execution strategy for reducing the amount of useless search. Its major drawback is that the overhead in maintaining the necessary information at runtime often takes more time than the technique can save. However, flow analysis can be used to detect programs (such as database queries) where the code for intelligent backtracking can be laid down at compile time. In such cases, there is no runtime overhead.

6. Query Execution

Database systems tend to be very inflexible in the way they execute queries. Most are strictly bottom-up processors, processing two relations at a time and creating intermediate temporary relations. Some are top-down (e.g. [Rei82]), but none have the ability to do both. With Prolog, we can combine these strategies.

The natural Prolog execution strategy is top-down; we can use extension tables to get bottom-up behavior. Consider the query

```
a(X,Y,Z,W) :- p(X,Y),q(Y,Z),r(Z,W).
```

We can transform this to

```
a(X,Y,Z,W) :- t(X,Y,Z),r(Z,W).
t(X,Y,Z) :- p(X,Y),q(Y,Z).
```

With standard Prolog execution, this query will execute a top-down join. In order to get some bottom-up behavior, we simply need to specify that p, q, r and t have an extension table. We can get a mixture of the two behaviors by specifying that only some of the predicates have extension tables.

One important feature of bottom-up processing is the ability to perform a sort-merge join. Consider the query

```
p(X,Y),q(Y,Z)
```

Each of these predicates has an extension table; let us assume that both of these tables are sorted on Y. The problem is how a Prolog system can merge these two tables.

The standard top-down strategy is to scan each tuple of q for each tuple of p. Suppose that in the middle of execution we find tuple $p(x,y)$. We now have to scan q. But since q is sorted, we only need to scan a certain part of q. In particular, we know that we can begin scanning q at the tuple where we left off. (That is, assuming Y is a key of q. The case where there are duplicate Y-values is not much harder.) We also know that we can stop scanning q as soon as we find a tuple that does not match. Thus in order to imitate sort-merge joining in Prolog, we need the ability to begin scanning a predicate somewhere other than at the beginning. We have considered a few ways to implement such a feature, but none seem very elegant.

It is important for a system to be able to process several relations at a time. For example, consider the following three-way cartesian product:

```
:- p(X), q(Y), r(Z).
```

Assume that all relations have 100 tuples with a blocking factor of 10, and that 6 buffers are available. If we can only process two relations at a time, the best strategy is to compute the cross product of p and q first, allocating 5 buffers to p and one to q. This would require 10 + 2*10 = 30 block reads. Then cross the resulting temporary relation (of 10,000 tuples) with r, which, using 5 buffers for *r*, would require 10 + 2*1000 = 2010 block reads. The total is 2040 block reads, not including the writing of the intermediate temporary relation.

One way process all three relations at once uses 5 buffers. Allocate 2 buffers to p, 2 to q, and 1 to r. The Prolog approach (with blocking as in Section 3) will require 10 + 5*10 + 5*5*10 = 310 block reads. The cost savings here results because we do not have to scan an intermediate relation.

7. Concurrency

Full database management systems support concurrent access to the database by multiple users. A Prolog interpreter, while interactive, only supports a single user. What we would like to do is allow a single Prolog system to be able to provide, in a natural way, a virtual Prolog interpreter for each of several users. The system should allow some form of communication between the users. The kind of concurrency we need is called "and-parallelism" in Prolog. Consider the following goals

```
process_user(1),process_user(2).

process_user(Termid) :-
        read_query(Termid,Query),
        eval(Query,Answer),
        print(Answer),
        process_user(Termid).
```

The idea is that the main query calls process_user twice to process requests from two terminals. The predicate process_user is essentially a read-eval-print loop to read from a terminal a user's request, carry out the request, print the results, and loop back to read another request. Evaluating the above query with a standard Prolog interpreter would cause all requests from the user on terminal 1 to be processed first, and then (assuming *read_query* fails on end-of-file) all requests from terminal 2.

What we really want is for the processing of requests from terminals 1 and 2 to be done concurrently. This would be achieved by a Prolog control strategy that concurrently executed the two goals of the main query. There are problems that can arise from the presence of concurrency; these problems can arise from goals that reference predicates that have changing clauses, and goals that share variables.

The first case corresponds to the well-known read/write and write/write conflicts. For example, one process may be asserting $p(a)$ while the other one is evaluating $p(X)$. Standard protocols, such as two-phase locking, may be used; see [PCG85] for details. The case where two goals share a variable arises from a main query such as the following:

```
process_user_c(1,X),process_user_c(2,X).
```

The shared variable X can be used as a communications channel to allow the concurrently executing processes to interact; this is the approach of Concurrent Prolog [Sha83]. In message-passing schemes such as this, the problem of serializability is left to the user.

In both of the above cases, standard techniques can be used to improve concurrency. However, an acceptable solution must also take into consideration the fact that a Prolog process can fail and backtrack. This problem of full and-parallelism is known to be difficult. Concurrent Prolog had to eliminate full backtracking from the language in order to achieve a simple concurrent evaluation strategy. However, the work on intelligent backtracking [BrP84, Cox84, PeP82] may lead the way to a solution to the full problem. The general problem in backtracking in a concurrent situation is that the system must be able to determine whether a parallel process used the results of the now-failing process. If so, that process must also be failed; if not, that process should be unaffected. The information saved by the intelligent backtracking schemes allows exactly these kinds of properties to be determined.

8. Conclusion

In this paper we have argued for the desirability of constructing an integrated database-Prolog system. While constructing such an integrated system is significantly more difficult than the more standard approach of combining two already existing systems, there are significant advantages to be gained from the effort. Perhaps the most interesting conclusion we have drawn is how closely related database and Prolog systems are. We have tried to show that each feature of a database system has an undeveloped counterpart in a Prolog system; the best course of action seems to be to develop each part as much as possible.

There are many aspects of database systems that we have not discussed, such as recovery, distribution, authorization, integrity constraints, transactions, etc. To consider recovery, for example, note that since Prolog is a backtracking language, it automatically maintains information necessary to restore the system to an earlier state; it must restore an earlier state every time it backtracks. Its method, the trail stack, is a primitive in-memory log. It is an interesting problem to investigate this connection, and try to integrate the recovery aspects of a database management system with Prolog backtracking. As far as distributed Prolog, Warren [WAD84] describes an algorithm for executing distributed Prolog programs on a broadcast network. That algorithm can be seen as a generalization of a distributed database query processing algorithm that uses semi-joins. Again, this connection deserves further study.

One of the interesting things about a Prolog system is that the language is both a query language and an implementation language. Thus the borders between relations, views, and files are somewhat fuzzy. In particular, if the storage mapper is written in Prolog, then the conceptual level is a view of the storage level, in the same way that the user level is considered a view of the conceptual level. What this means is that a lot of database features can be added simply by defining Prolog predicates.

Thus the issue is what primitive functions we *need* to add to a Prolog system. We have isolated three concepts:

1) Disk pointers. These pointers are used to get a tuple from the disk. A disk pointer conceptually contains a file name, tuple location and length. We are implementing a built-in predicate *deref(P,T)* which takes a disk pointer P and returns the tuple in T.

2) Tuple formats. Prolog systems prefer to keep tuples in a Lisp-like internal pointer-based format for processing efficiency. This format is unsuitable for the disk, which need a more record-oriented format. We are requiring that each disk tuple have an associated *format*, which is a Prolog term. This format is used by a Prolog predicate

convert(Fmt,T,S), which takes the disk tuple *T* and converts it to a Prolog structure *S*.

3) Sophisticated buffer management. Buffers are conceptually long character strings. The most natural way to deal with them in a Prolog system is as long constant names. Database buffers must be reusable, so they are allocated on the heap. Similarly, all database constants should be removed from the name table upon backtracking. Thus we are implementing a more sophisticated name table facility, which provides the necessary flexibility. We also are implementing a dynamic loading facility, so that Prolog predicates are loaded only when they are needed.

The above additions are only a first step; we intend to use them to get a working prototype system. There is a lot more work to be done in order to realize fully the ideals of this paper.

9. References

[Bru82] M. Bruynooghe, "The memory management of PROLOG implementations", in *Logic Programming*, K. L. Clark and S. Taernlund, (eds.), Academic Press, New York, NY, 1982, 83-98.

[BrP84] M. Bruynooghe and L. M. Pereira, "Deduction Revision by Intelligent Backtracking", in *Implementations of Prolog*, J. A. Campbell, (ed.), Ellis Horwood Limited, Chichester, England, 1984, 194-215.

[CKP73] A. Colmerauer, H. Kanoui, R. Pasero and P. Roussel, "Un Systeme de Communication Homme-machine en Francais", Groupe Intelligence Artificielle, Universite Aix-Marseille II, 1973.

[Cox84] P. T. Cox, "Finding Backtrack Points for Intelligent Backtracking", in *Implementations of Prolog*, J. A. Campbell, (ed.), Ellis Horwood Limited, Chichester, England, 1984, 216-233.

[EPP83] Eggert, S. Parker and K. Parsaye, "Prototyping in Prolog: Experiences and Lessons", Unpublished Manuscript, 1983.

[GaM78] H. Gallaire and J. Minker, in *Logic and Data Bases*, Plenum Press, New York, 1978.

[Kal83] L. V. Kale, "Control Strategies for Logic Programming", Technical Report, SUNY Stony Brook, May 1983.

[Kow79] R. Kowalski, in *Logic for Problem Solving*, Elsevier North-Holland, New York, NY, 1979.

[Kow81] R. Kowalski, "Logic as a Database Language", Technical Report, Imperial College, July, 1981.

[McC82] J. McCarthy, "Coloring Maps and the Kowalski Doctrine", STAN-CS-82-903, Computer Science Dept, Stanford University, 1982.

[PCG85] S. Parker, M. Carey, F. Golshani, M. Jarke, E. Sciore and A. Walker, "Logic Programming and Databases", in *Expert Database Systems*, L. Kershberg, (ed.), to appear, 1985.

[Par83] K. Parsaye, "Logic Programming and Relational Databases", *Database Engineering*, **8**, 4 (December 1983), 20-39.

[PeP82] L. M. Pereira and A. Porto, "Selective Backtracking", in *Logic Programming*, K. L. Clark and S. Taernlund, (eds.), Academic Press, New York, NY, 1982, 107-116.

[PeW83] F. C. N. Pereira and D. H. D. Warren, "Parsing as Deduction", *Proceedings of the 21st Annual Meeting of the Association for Computational Linguistics*, Cambridge, MA, June 1983, 137-144.

[Rei82] S. Reiss, "The Efficient Implementation of Database Models", Technical Report, Brown U., 1982.

[Sci85] E. Sciore, "Database Facilities for Prolog", Tech. Rep. 85/012, Dept. of Computer Science, SUNY, Stony Brook, NY, 1985.

[Sha83] E. Y. Shapiro, "A Subset of Concurrent Prolog and its Interpreter", Dept of Applied Mathematics, The Weizmann Institute of Science, Rehovot, Israel, 1983.

[She76] B. A. Sheil, "Observations on Context-free Parsing", *Statistical Methods in Linguistics*, 1976, 71-109.

[Ull82] J. Ullman, *Principles of Database Systems*, Computer Science Press, Rockville, MD, 1982.

[VCJ83] Y. Vassiliou, J. Clifford and M. Jarke, "Access to Specific Declarative Knowledge by Expert Systems: The Impact of Logic Programming", Technical Report, NYU School of Business, 1983.

[WPP77] D. H. D. Warren, L. M. Pereira and F. Pereira, "Prolog - The Language and its Implementation Compared with Lisp", *SIGPLAN Notices/SIGART Newsletter*, 1977.

[War79] D. S. Warren, "Syntax and Semantics in Parsing: An Application to Montague Grammar", Ph.D. Thesis, University of Michigan, Ann Arbor, MI, 1979.

[War81] D. H. D. Warren, "Efficient Processing of Interactive Relational Database Queries Expressed in Logic", *Proceedings of the 7th Conference on Very Large Data Bases*, Cannes, 1981, 272-281.

[WAD84] D. S. Warren, M. Ahamad, S. K. Debray and L. V. Kale, "Executing Distributed Prolog Programs on a Broadcast Network", *Proceedings 1984 International Symposium on Logic Programming*, Feb 1984, 12-21.

[WoY76] E. Wong and K. Youssefi, "Decomposition — A Strategy for Query Processing", *ACM Transaction on Database Systems*, **1**, 3 (September 1976), 223-241.

[YKK84] H. Yokota, S. Kunifuji, T. Kakuta, N. Miyazaki, S. Shibayama and K. Murakami, "An Enhanced Inference Mechanism for Generating Relational Algebra Queries", *Proceedings of the Third Symposium on Principles of Database Systems*, April 1984, 229-238.

PART V:

Expert Database System Architectures, Tools and Techniques

Constraint Management in Expert Database Systems

Allan Shepherd
Hewlett-Packard †

Larry Kerschberg
University of South Carolina ‡

ABSTRACT

This paper argues that *constraint management* will be a key factor in the evolution of Database Management Systems (DBMS) into Expert Database Systems (EDS). This new generation of DBMS will manage not only a database of facts, but also a knowledge base of rules and heuristics regarding various application domains, such as database design and knowledge acquisition, semantic query optimization, user interfaces, and data dictionary/directories.

Constraint management — the specification, distribution, update, mapping, and reasoning on constraints — will be at the heart of the EDS architecture. In this paper constraint formalisms and constraint-based systems in the fields of Programming and Specification Languages, Database Management, and Artificial Intelligence are examined. Their similarities and differences are presented, and knowledge representations for constraint management are discussed. An architecture for a constraint-based EDS is presented, together with important issues that must be addressed for the efficient use of such systems.

1. INTRODUCTION

This paper addresses the need for constraint management in knowledge-based systems. Constraint support is a major component in a system's cost, and a major guarantor of its functional value and stability, and as such should receive careful management. A constraint denotes an abstract relationship between system objects which must be satisfied for the objects to participate consistently in the constrained system. Uncertainty or incompleteness in constraint satisfaction may be allowed if the system is used as a model to approximate the world it represents.

System design and analysis activities can employ constraints as units of explicit specification to represent rules in production systems, plans for problem solving, propositional abstractions of relationships, semantic integrity assertions in logic programming and Database Management Systems (DBMS's), and so forth. Each type of system activity, e.g., design, integrity maintenance, information retrieval, and problem analysis, can not only use and satisfy applicable constraints, but also manipulate the constraints themselves to change the system's intended semantics. For example, in designing a

† Hewlett-Packard, 3L, 1501 Page Mill Road, Palo Alto, CA 94304.

‡ College of Business Administration, University of South Carolina, Columbia, SC 29208.

database schema, new constraints may be specified and old constraints updated, subject to satisfying meta-constraints on these operations. System implementation activities can translate the constraint source specifications into attached procedures, daemons, and structural dependencies.

In this paper it will be useful to think of a complex information (knowledge) system as a multi-level collection of virtual machines with appropriate mappings between successive levels. Within different virtual machines of such a system, constraints are given different representations and roles. To support information modeling, each virtual machine provides a structure for knowledge representation and operations to manipulate the representation.

The goals of constraints are:

- to assure the correct operation of each virtual machine,
- to support effective methodologies for use of the machine,
- to yield efficient run-time modeling, and
- to act as an intuitive unit of specification.

For effective enforcement of constraints, constraints *at all levels* of knowledge systems must be considered in designing constraint representational formalisms and constraint management architectures.

In this work we study the specification and use of constraints in systems found in Artificial Intelligence (AI), Programming Languages (PL), and Database Management (DB). By studying the roles of constraints in these diverse areas, we postulate an architecture and mechanisms for *constraint management* in future knowledge systems. Further, we argue that for Database Management Systems to *evolve* to Expert Database Systems, new architectures incorporating object-oriented data models with explicitly-specified constraints will be needed. These new architectures will require *knowledgeable tools* to manage constraints for semantic integrity enforcement, query optimization, user interfaces, concurrency control, and most importantly, planning and reasoning over diverse application domains.

The paper is organized as follows. In Section 2 we present a multi-disciplinary view of constraints. Our taxonomy framework analyzes constraints as follows: 1) explicit, implicit, and inherent, 2) active versus passive, and 3) object-oriented versus process-oriented constraints. Section 3 presents both an object-oriented and process-oriented view of knowledge representation for constraint specification and processing. This section also provides examples of constraint-based systems. Section 4 discusses the issues in constraint management for Expert Database Systems and presents an architecture for such a system, drawing upon the insights gained from PRISM [Shepherd and Kerschberg 84]. Section 5 presents our conclusions.

2. A MULTI-DISCIPLINARY VIEW OF CONSTRAINTS

Substantial work on constraints has been done in four areas relevant to knowledge systems: Programming and Specification Languages, Database Management, and Artificial Intelligence[1]. The differing goals of these areas are important to a comparison of the roles played by constraints in each area. Their similarities are discussed in Section 4, and incorporated into the proposed architecture.

The Programming Language model generally expects a fully-defined specification instance (program) prior to evaluation (execution). An AI system generally allows extension of its declarative semantics, i.e., the fact base, both before, during (by inferencing and

[1] It is assumed the reader is familiar with the organization of knowledge-based systems such as expert systems [Feigenbaum 83, Hays-Roth 84], and the concept of metadata — data about data [Goldfine 82, Shepherd and Kerschberg, 84].

user interaction), and after an evaluation. Even the knowledge base that specifies the AI system's goals is extensible.

A Database Management System, by comparison, generally expects fully-specified metadata semantics and an unambiguous transaction specification, but will extend the fact base (by insertion, deletion, or modification) during a transaction. Yet, the concept of logical data independence in database management does *theoretically* allow for the extension of metadata while permitting existing applications to continue to function. Moreover, a programming language transaction can be extended to obtain the same overall results as in the other two types of systems, but the scope of rigorous constraint enforcement across multiple transactions through a concurrency control mechanism distinguishes database management systems.

Constraints can be classified as being *inherent, explicit*, or *implicit* [Brodie 78]. Inherent constraints are those which are an integral part of a model, e.g., the parent-child relationship in the hierarchical data model inherently supports a functional map from children to parent segments. Explicit constraints are those that can be expressed independently of model structures in some formalism such as the predicate calculus. Finally, implicit constraints are those derivable from the inherent and explicit constraints. In the database area, database design [Leveson 80] and database schema verification methodologies [Berry 79, Berry 81] provide examples of such specifications.

A constraint specification may be *active* or *passive*, [Mylopoulos 80, 80b, 83]. Active constraints cause transitions or propagation of the effects of updates on the model to maintain the assertive part of any predicate. The roles of active constraints versus passive constraints need to be clearly delineated. Active constraints such as triggers seem appropriate for control of semantics that have indeterminate (perhaps global) scope. Passive constraints seem appropriate for control of local semantics. The activation of these constraints need only be considered when processing touches the context that holds the object constrained.

2.1. Constraints in Programming and Specification Languages

Programming languages are generally designed to ensure that programs and instances of program invocations are internally self-consistent representations. The primary use of constraints in programming languages is to specify and guarantee this internal consistency while a program instance is executing, in particular across transitions between states. A programming language is an example of a virtual machine definition. The semantics of the language express constraints inherent in the machine.

Specification languages, such as SPECIAL [Robinson 77], Ina Jo [Locasso 80], and BETA [Brodie 78], provide formalisms in which a user can express constraints on a model instance in a notation which ideally is uncomplicated by physical enforcement considerations.

In programming and specification languages, *explicit constraints* may be specified using axioms, algebraic notation, denotational semantics, or operational requirements. Sometimes they are packaged into Abstract Data Types (ADT's) and modules. Implicit and inherent constraints are typically represented by object typing mechanisms, and in specification languages by inferencing on propositions.

Explicit Typing of Objects in Programming Languages

Programming languages provide many examples of process-oriented constraints that use explicit typing of objects in the domains and ranges of operators, procedures and functions.

In Pascal, for example, explicit typing of all objects is required [Jensen 75]. Weaker, inherent constraints on cardinality are provided by formal parameter lists. Implicit constraints in Pascal provide that automatic type conversion is not allowed thus restricting operations on instances of types to correctly typed objects. Implied constraints can be specified by declaration of user-defined types as specializations of other types, e.g., subranges of integers. However, data relatability of specialized types is not enforced.

Enforcement of data integrity using such mapping constraints requires a guarantee that only the constrained operations can access the database. ALPHARD, for example, [Wulf 76, London 78] provides such a guarantee for user-defined types by packaging operations into Abstract Data Type capsules. In this respect ALPHARD provides object-oriented security for Abstract Data Type constraints. Types in a programming language imply constraints on instances of the types, i.e., the instances must be correctly manipulable by operations which take them as actual parameters.

To assure that implicit constraints are enforced, access to the instances of ADT's is restricted to operations packaged with the ADT. Invariants specified in an ADT can be used to check whether packaged operations leave instances of the type in an acceptable state. ADT's are thus used to abstract the shared properties of instances. Static properties are abstracted as invariants; behavioral properties are abstracted as packaged operations.

Fully-enforced data relatability can be provided in programming languages through Abstract Data Type packaging. The definition of explicit constraints on procedures that operate on ADT's allows the user to verify that certain properties of the type are invariant throughout the procedure's execution. Additionally, encapsulating the constraints and procedures associated with an abstract data type can guarantee that only specified operations can access the type, thus simplifying verification of the semantic integrity and security of the instances of the type. The restriction of programming languages to particular logic and object spaces has allowed formal mathematical description techniques to be developed for specification and verification of Abstract Data Types.

Explicit constraints for ADT's have been specified in algebraic, axiomatic and denotational notations. Examples of each of these notations have been compared for the 'stack' ADT [Cleveland 80]. Axiomatic constraint specifications have been implemented as assertions in Pascal. Algebraic specifications have also been implemented [Guttag 80b]. Abstract Data Type specifications should be consistent, i.e., no false statement should be derivable from the axioms, and perhaps complete (any well-formed formulae (wff) or not(wff) can be proved by resolution to be true or false, respectively), but at least 'sufficiently complete' [Guttag 80].

Inherent Constraints in Programming Languages

Programming languages provide many inherent global constraints on the semantics of the program instances. For instance, in Pascal, only the current value bound to a simple variable is accessible, i.e., the variable has no past value. Array bounds are not dynamically extensible, and new data types cannot be dynamically created at run time.

2.2. Constraints in Database Management Systems

Database Management Systems must effectively support the management of information as a vital corporate resource. Important components of information value, such as its security, sharability between different applications and users, semantic integrity, consistency, and accessibility, may be protected with a variety of constraint mechanisms. A DBMS supports several virtual machines for modeling at different levels of abstraction. For example, a data model enforces constraints which allow operations on objects such as data types, entities and relationships. Similarly, an end-user uses the definition of an application schema and its operations as a virtual machine to model the application domain.

Under conventional DBMS's, the management of constraints is distributed among diverse subsystems, such as:

- Query processor,
- Database specification tools,
- Physical restructuring and storage management,
- Application programs,
- Integrity subsystem, and
- Security subsystem.

The user's "external view" must model his problem domain faithfully; the various DBMS subsystems must cooperate in managing the constraints that enforce desired system behavior.

Contemporary concerns of data security, data distribution and database integrity seek to maximize the value of information resources to users. Constraint management provides a unified framework for pursuing this goal. Constraint management tools are needed to guarantee, among others, the following:

- Internal consistency of semantic data models — semantic integrity of enterprise models that are constrained to be accurate models (representations) of the real world [Sen 83].
- Logically correct data models and conceptual schemas to ensure unambiguous query processing. For example, the relational model [Codd 70] normal forms are constraints that seek to remove semantic ambiguity from the relational model of data.
- Data security, for instance, access control by query modification. In the following example, the [AND] clause *modifies* the base query, i.e., it attaches additional constraints to be satisfied for the query to be accepted.

```
SELECT EMP WHERE EMP.SALARY LT 10K
    AND CASH_WITHDRAWAL LT $100
    [AND ACCESSOR.STATUS = "MANAGER"]
```

- Correct query decomposition for query processing, particularly for query distribution in systems with heterogeneous logical data representations.
- Correctness of internal schemas, e.g., controlled concurrent access to avoid deadlock and data corruption.
- Access constraints, i.e., correctness of mappings to physical storage.

2.3. Constraints in Artificial Intelligence

The Artificial Intelligence (AI) community uses a wide variety of knowledge representations to capture the semantics of AI problem domains. AI systems can capture inconsistent knowledge at the expense of localized and more costly constraint enforcement. The key to this facility seems to be in a rich typing of both the objects supported and logical relationships between objects. As knowledge is acquired it is typed and added to the base [Davis 76]. AI inferencing schemes provide for non-determinism in reaching transaction goals; Database Management System models are not yet doing so.

In AI systems an initial database, which is an accurate representation of a not-necessarily internally consistent view of reality, is manipulated by transition-creating operations. Constraints are specified for allowable operations and states. Through inferencing on these, the facts in the database, i.e., its extension, are changed such that they satisfy the constraints. The constraint specifications themselves are part of the 'intention' of the model, and are subject to the same inferencing efforts to determine their logical consistency, completeness and value to the system. Constraints may be added or changed and facts maintained by satisfying the constraints or by partitioning the database.

Constraints can constitute the main knowledge base of an AI system, and their consistency [Nicolas 78] and completeness can be a goal of the system. Truth maintenance systems that support models based on incomplete knowledge have been proposed[2]. McDermott and Doyle describe models which in response to new observations revise the assumptions on which the beliefs of active processes are based. Doyle has implemented a truth maintenance system, called TMS, [Doyle 79].

In AI systems, constraints play a variety of roles, including:

1. Methods in object-oriented programming
2. Relationships in modeling and simulation

   Multiple constraints are specified of which all that are applicable must be satisfied.
3. Problem specifications for problem solving

   Multiple constraints may be used to describe the solution space. The problem specification is given as a set of constraints on the allowable solutions.
4. Goals in planning systems

   The goal is added to the system as a true description of the target state.
5. Propositions in inferencing
6. Axioms and theorems in theorem proving, and
7. Facts in knowledge bases.

3. KNOWLEDGE REPRESENTATIONS FOR CONSTRAINT MANAGEMENT

Constraint representational form to a large extent determines the management strategies needed to support the objects constrained. When the computational model being used is object-oriented, constraints specify and modify valid objects, and provide methods for doing this. Whereas, if the computational model is process-oriented, constraints specify invariant conditions that must be satisfied by the system affected by the processes.

In this section we explore various knowledge representations for constraints, and argue for an object-oriented model for constraint specification and management. We summarize various systems that use constraints for their underlying knowledge representation.

3.1. Object-Oriented Versus Process-Oriented Systems

Advantages of Object-Oriented Systems

In object-oriented models, objects can in general be entities or relationships between entities. Constraints specify the creation, deletion, test and modification conditions for allowable objects. The coupling between object definitions and the operations which refer to them is very loose. Thus inherent constraints on operations are minimized.

Context in object-oriented systems provides a semantic scope within which inferencing and selection are encapsulated. Procedural objects, e.g., PROGRAMS [Levesque 79], as well as declarative rules, assertions and frame type directives to interpreters can be activated in a context. The capability to determine dynamically the context of a reference can be exploited to support sophisticated view mechanisms. Context can be provided by 1) selection rules which are activated depending on the problem environment, and 2) a knowledge interpreter's control strategy.

---

[2] Non-monotonic reasoning [McCarthy 80] and non-monotonic logic [McDermott 80, Davis 80].

Object-oriented models share the goal of *logical data independence* with database management systems. Object-oriented models can provide logical data independence between applications and the conceptual knowledge base by encapsulating application-oriented behavior into *abstract operation types* which are themselves objects. Thus, both declarative and procedural aspects of the system can be handled uniformly in object-oriented models.

Specification-Based Object Description

The advantages of *specification-based* descriptions of systems versus operational descriptions have been widely recognized, particularly for system design and prototyping. In an object-oriented definitional environment, *specification-based* object description allows interpreter function to keep pace with theory, and interpreter implementation to suit and improve with technology. This has been given as a rationale for the clear separation of object specifications and interpreter specifications for the Smalltalk programming system [Goldberg 82].

A specifications formalism must have sufficient functional resolution to capture the semantics of the dependencies between objects in information systems. The representation of facts and dependencies as conventional database extensions and intentions, though efficient, places undesirable restrictions on metadata update and interpretation [Brodie 83].

Process-oriented Systems

The efficiency gained from process-oriented solutions to problems is often necessary. In the AI field, production systems exemplify process-oriented models. The operational logic used by the algorithms and heuristics of a production system's control strategy enforces inherent constraints on allowable operations.

A model's metadata is the specification of what constitutes a valid model instance, for example, the conditions to be met by valid mailing address instances, i.e., the (maximum) field length, whether a city can start with a numeric, and how an address can be deleted or changed. To modify a *model's metadata,* process definitions have to be changed; since the metadata is embedded in an inherent or implicit form, i.e., it is hard or costly to change.

Hybrid formalisms, such as frames, which combine declarative and procedural representations, provide a way to trade-off conceptual flexibility for efficiency. Such representations suit specific classes of problems, particularly where hard representational problems are confronted, as in natural language processing.

Semantic Nets as Object-Oriented Systems

Semantic nets provide, for object-oriented systems, a way to structure object indexing in a knowledge representation which is conceptually very flexible. Consequently, semantic nets have been used to model a wide range of problem domains, for example, to model linguistic patterns of association in which the semantic distances in natural language have been represented by path length.

The focus in associative net systems [Findler 79] is on the logical representation of the net and on the knowledge stored at nodes rather than on algorithms to query the knowledge. Semantic nets that support the attachment of rules to nodes exemplify non-deterministic object-oriented models.

Specialized or generic interpreters can traverse a net to retrieve knowledge sources attached to object nodes in order to execute queries on objects. Different interpreters with a variety of purposes and side effects can navigate through a net using the information implicit in the arcs. The behavior of interpreters is dependent upon the constraints and other contextual information stored at nodes as well as upon each interpreter's control strategy.

The knowledge stored in a net can be logically independent of the interpreters that traverse it. Learning in constraint systems, i.e., the acquisition of new constraints, parallels the acquisition of knowledge as general laws or rules in AI systems.

Object Typing

If explicit constraints have their semantics restricted such that constraint instances are wff's in a logic, e.g., first-order logic, logical operations can perform inferencing to extend the fact base of the system in information retrieval [Reiter 78, 80].

Complete typing of objects in an information system can support logical correctness inferencing for *object instantiation*, i.e., testing whether an object, which may be newly created, satisfies the properties of the type of which it is an instance. A formal treatment of object typing in a *deductive database* has been given [Reiter 81b]. And database modeling tools using such inferencing have been described [Lundberg 82, Borgida 80, 82].

Semantic Nets as a Dual of Logic Systems

If the arcs of a semantic net represent logical relationships between nodes, the net can be equivalent to a logical production system or other logic-based schema. Semantic nets in which the arcs and nodes are equivalent to objects in a logic are used in various semantic database models. Deliyanni and Kowalski provide an excellent comparison of various 'extended semantic net' representations as a dual of clausal predicate logic [Deliyanni 79].

Schubert uses semantic nets as 'graphical analogues of data structures representing facts'. Logical *propositions* are described as being able to be represented in semantic nets in many ways [Schubert 76]. For example, a binary predicate can be readily represented by a directed labeled arc between its argument nodes. Where the formalism of rules attached to nodes guarantees that rule instances are wff's in a logical system, interpreters can do inferencing on the rules [Schubert 76]. In a more expressive representation, a subgraph can link a proposition's predicate concept node and argument nodes.

The clustering of associated propositions about concept nodes in semantic nets provides a naturalness of representation that is missing in text representations of propositional logic, and also provides an efficient indexing scheme. Logical quantification, however, is not so readily represented in semantic networks. Schubert describes a notation in which typed, directed arcs are used to represent the direction of decreasing quantifier scope. Schubert gives other notations, and includes an interesting discussion of representations of time in semantic nets and logics.

Propositions in semantic nets have parallels in functional and multivalued dependencies in logical database schemas. The direct equivalence of logical data dependencies in relational data models to some predicate calculus expressions have been shown and used in database design [Sagiv 80, 81, Zaniolo 81]. Using propositions within semantic nets to represent database dependency constraints allows a natural clustering of related concepts and an associated indexing for efficient schema traversal [Shepherd 83].

3.2. Examples of Constraint-Based Systems

Several constraint systems are described below to illustrate the roles played by constraints in a range of systems.

3.2.1. Invariance Assertions in Database Systems

Hammer and McLeod define constraints as invariance assertions on a database [Hammer 75, 76]. A semantic integrity sub-system proposed by Hammer and McLeod for Database Management Systems has five parts; a constraint specification language consistency checker, constraint database system, enforcement processor, and violation action processor.

3.2.2. Abstract Data Types in Programming Languages

As discussed above, ADT's provide a scope within which invariance assertions can be encapsulated.

3.2.3. Deductive Databases

Specific kinds of inferencing are employed to provide derived extensions of databases [Reiter 81b].

3.2.4. Generalized Inferencing

The manipulation of propositional information as data, that is, the update to the intentional part of an information base, using a range of inference tools, has been widely investigated. However, this work has not been integrated with the conventional manipulation of database extensions.

3.2.5. Logical Specification Languages

Tools to assist in the design of information systems have made extensive use of theorem proving techniques to test logical specifications [Berry 81]. However, these specifications have not been integrated into on-line DBMS dictionary/directories. Specification languages which support these design approaches, for example, Ina Jo and SPECIAL, do not encompass heuristic or rule-based problem descriptions.

3.2.6. BETA

Brodie introduces a 'limited generic data model' for static constraints [Brodie 78]. The model has a data type algebra and a schema specification language, named BETA, which supports a methodology for denotational constraint management (2). Constraints that are specified by the generic data model's axioms are termed by Brodie inherent constraints. BETA is used to declare the semantics required of a database. Implicit constraints are given by the syntax and semantics of BETA. Explicit constraints are generated as assertions that have not been shown to be inherent or implicit, and which thus would have to be enforced explicitly for the database schema and instance.

In more recent work, Brodie describes a specification formalism, which can be used to specify behavioral constraints for a database system [Brodie 82].

3.2.7. Constraint-Based Simulation

ThingLab [Borning 79] is a specialized extension of Smalltalk for modeling which provides for abstraction hierarchies. It allows the user to specify constraints declaratively, which are added as objects to a Smalltalk system. Constraints are kept satisfied during manipulation of objects by several predetermined techniques, which are applied through a limited planning process. During execution, dependencies between objects are maintained as logical path names. The object-oriented encapsulation of types provided by Smalltalk is used to model propagation of side effects during constraint satisfaction.

3.2.8. Constraint-Based Programming Languages

A constraint based programming environment has been implemented [Steele 80] which uses dependency-directed backtracking to satisfy constraints. A construct for assumptions about default values that may be used in satisfying constraints, and a mechanism for the automatic retraction of incorrect assumptions are provided.

3.2.9. MOLGEN

In MOLGEN [Stefik 81a 81b], constraints are treated as specifications of goals. To satisfy constraints, Molgen uses hierarchical decomposition of specifications into subgoals. Sub-goals generated during decomposition could interact through updates to the database of objects affected by the constraints. Planning techniques use heuristics to guide the decomposition in order to generate sub-goals which modularize the solution process and avoid inconsistencies in updates to the database. The concept of *constraint posting* is used to post relevant activated constraints so that other subsystems are aware of their use[3].

The MOLGEN program uses a hierarchical planning process to plan genetic experiments. Constraints are used to successively reduce the experiment solution space. This is accomplished by actually *operating* on constraints by means of three operations:

- *Constraint formulation* in which new constraints are formulated and committed as more detailed knowledge is obtained,
- *Constraint propagation* involves the creation of new constraints from old constraints in a plan. This operation allows communication among subproblems, making them aware of their composite information requirements.
- *Constraint satisfaction* is the operation of finding variable values so that a set of constraints on those variables is satisfied.

A novel feature of MOLGEN is its hierarchical planning model consisting of an interpreter and three planning levels: 1) the Strategy Space containing knowledge about planning, 2) the Design Space which knows how to design experiments, and 3) the Laboratory Space with objects and operations of the real laboratory.

Stefik points to some limitations of MOLGEN that are important: 1) constraints can only specify objects and it is desirable to be able to specify *processes*, 2) MOLGEN does not use meta-constraints regarding plans, e.g., a plan should have at most twelve steps, etc., and 3) it cannot reason adequately about *time*; rather, different names are used to represent the same entity in different states at different times.

3.2.10. Constraint-Based Database Modeling

The PRISM architecture [Shepherd and Kerschberg 84] uses constraints and meta-constraints to specify the semantics of information systems. An explicit constraint specifications formalism packages rules to provide object-oriented encapsulation. The rules may express heuristics or expert knowledge to capture heterogeneous semantics, or may express logical propositions, equivalent to Horn clauses. The formalism provides a uniform way of specifying both static and behavioral constraints. Constraint declarations are interpreted directly by modeling tools, and satisfied through updates to data and subordinate constraints. The PRISM architecture employs a semantic net with a small number of logical link types to model hierarchical abstraction, and explicit constraint specifications indexed on object nodes to model other dependencies including aggregation. Data instances reside in a conventional database store, with intentional information in the constraint base.

4. TOWARDS AN EXPERT DATABASE SYSTEM ARCHITECTURE

The previous sections discussed several constraint formalisms and the use of constraints in building constraint-based systems in Programming and Specification Languages, Database Management, and Artificial Intelligence. Differences among constraint formalisms reflect their intended use, i.e., invariance assertions, database consistency and integrity, and planning and reasoning.

In order to *evolve* toward intelligent, or expert database systems (EDS), we should understand the commonalities of these diverse constraint formalisms, so that the key

[3] An example of constraint posting in DBMS can be found in INGRES [Stonebraker, 82], where the integrity subsystem "posts" a conjunction for the query processor to use in query modification (cf. the example in Section 2.2).

features may be incorporated into an EDS. Below is a list of similarities in constraint formalisms:

What All the constraint formalisms give a condition which must be satisfied by the system.

When When to check whether a constraint's condition is satisfied is inherent in most systems, and is usually after every transaction, i.e., before any other user access. Constraints which only need to be checked on demand may be attached to particular queries or transactions, e.g., at audit time, or before a particular report is printed. Within a transaction, states of the information system that do not satisfy applicable constraints are encapsulated to prevent general access to these states.

Systems that use planning to satisfy constraints, test constraints at steps in the plan execution, as for example in ThingLab or MOLGEN.

Where The conditions that determine whether or where a constraint is applicable are captured in many ways. Inherent mechanisms that determine applicability are often associated with contexts and context switching. Scopes provide an implicit way of controlling applicability. 'Where' conditions are specified as, for example, message selectors, or predicates.

How Information on how to satisfy a constraint may take many forms, for example:

- Heuristics or rules used to search for a solution,
- Its weight in a relaxation scheme,
- Its subgoals if it is decomposable, or
- An actual procedure or methods for its satisfaction.

4.1. Integration of Constraint Approaches

Future EDSs will integrate the features mentioned above to maintain security and semantic integrity of databases while providing *knowledge tools* for inferencing and reasoning. Such systems will require new architectures that incorporate *knowledge models* rather than the traditional data models or semantic data models. The knowledge models will be object-oriented in which relationships among objects will be specified in a constraint language.

Reasoning will be supported by *knowledge tools* that will access the knowledge base, that is, the knowledge model and the collection of constraints to infer new knowledge relevant to the user's application. Examples of knowledge tools are the following:

- **Metadata Management** — An important aspect of an EDS will be the transparency between metadata, that is, data about data, and the actual database. Metadata in commercial DBMS is stored in Data Dictionary/Directory systems which are not readily accessible to users. In EDSs this dichotomy will disappear.

  For example, the second author used the INGRES relational database system to manage the papers for the EDS Workshop. Consider the following query involving both data and metadata:

  Which relations is Mike Stonebraker involved in?

  In order to answer this query, the user would have to use the "help" command in QUEL to determine the base relations in the database, and then query those relations using the "retrieve" command. This approach requires the user to be aware of relation schemas, attribute names, etc. Another approach would be to use the UNIX[TM] — INGRES interface to execute the following "shell" commands:

[TM] UNIX is a Trademark of AT & T Bell Laboratories

```
for relation in papers addresses program
do
echo ""
echo $relation
printr eds $relation|grep 'id'
printr eds $relation|grep 'Stonebraker'
done
```

The "for"-loop will range over the relations papers, addresses and program. Note that "printr eds $relation|grep 'Stonebraker'" means "Print the relation "$relation" of database "eds" as a UNIX file and look for the line (or lines) containing the string "Stonebraker." An edited version of the result of executing this shell procedure is given below:

```
papers
id          author                  title
68          Stonebraker et al       Heuristic Search in Data Base Systems

addresses
id          name                    affiliation
68          Michael Stonebraker     Univ. of California-Berkeley

program
id          lastname                name
13          Stonebraker             Michael Stonebraker
```

Thus we see that 'Stonebraker' has submitted a paper, is affiliated with the University of California at Berkeley, and is a member of the EDS Program Committee. In an object-oriented system, the object "Stonebraker" would be a member of relations papers, addresses, and program, and the user interface would allow the user to issue the query given above without having to make a distinction between data and metadata.

- **Expert Query Optimizer** — Much research has been done in query optimization for both centralized and distributed database systems [Selinger 79, Bernstein 81, Kerschberg 82]. Recognizing the large solution space of possible optimization scenarios, these authors have proposed heuristic algorithms which obtain, if not optimal solutions, at least satisfactory solutions, but at reduced optimizer cost.

  More recently, the work in semantic query optimization has shown that user knowledge regarding the inferencing mechanism of PROLOG [Warren 81] can serve as a meta-control strategy for query optimization. Warren notes that the strategy he proposes is similar to that used by System R [Selinger 79].

  In the case where a PROLOG-based expert system is loosely coupled with a relational database system, there is a need to transform tuple-at-a-time PROLOG accesses to associative retrievals against the relational database. Optimization techniques that reason on the set of functional and multivalued dependencies to map PROLOG-to-relational queries should be incorporated into EDS optimizer tools [Jarke 84].

- **Expert User Interface Agent** — With more and more casual users accessing databases, both internal and external to their organizations, it is imperative to develop user interfaces that are knowledgeable about each user, and the various database query formats of external databases accessed by that user. This knowledge would include user preferences for menu versus command-level interfaces, the experience level and the favorite "external" view of the database. The agent would adapt to the user's learning curve and could institute remedial instruction if the user had not used the system for some predetermined time.

- **Database Design — Knowledge Acquisition Expert** — An Expert Database System will have tools to guide the user in designing a knowledge base of facts, rules, and heuristics regarding a particular application. Special interpreters that could reason about data dependencies would advise the user about the implications of adding new facts or constraints to the knowledge base. Thus, this tool must understand how knowledge is represented and organized in order to act as a consultant to the designer.

4.2. PRISM as a Candidate EDS Architecture

The research goal of the PRISM [Shepherd and Kerschberg 84] system was to develop a constraint formalism and language to specify the semantics of information systems. Special features of PRISM are: 1) an information model is a hierarchy of models in which each higher level serves as meta-data for the level below it, 2) the PRISM meta-level concepts can be used to implement a conventional data model in terms of constraints on user-defined objects, 3) the collection of objects in an information model are related by an associative net whose links denote membership in a type, the *isa* or subtype-to-supertype relationship, and a "constraint-on" relationship that maps an object to the collections of constraints on that object, and 4) all constraints are expressed *explicitly* so that they may be examined and reasoned on.

The PRISM architecture organizes the constraints in a knowledge base, and the inference engine accepts user goals, converts them into conjectures, and attempts to prove the conjectures by executing and evaluating applicable constraints.

The PRISM Model Hierarchy

In PRISM, an information system is represented as a hierarchy of object-oriented models. The top level consists of PRISM metadata, that is, the *primitive concepts* available to users to define successively lower model levels. At the top level are such concepts as built-in types (integer, dollar, date, etc.), dictionary types (dictobj, usrobj, dict_name), and modeling primitives (class, map, isa, asa, domainof, rangeof, etc.). The other levels are the Data Model, Schema, and Application levels.

Objects at each level are defined in terms of the metadata of the level above! For example, metadata for a data model is expressed in terms of PRISM modeling primitives, and defines the concepts and rules for that data model, e.g., the Relational Data Model [Codd 70]. Schema metadata consists of the data definition facilities provided by a particular data model. Applications metadata consists of the database types defined in a schema according to a data model, for example, a relational schema for a sales order processing application.

An example of a vertical slice through an information system is shown in Figure 1. Ellipses represent objects. Dotted-lined arcs represent 'asa' links. Only significant 'asa' links are shown. Solid-lined arrows represent 'isa' links. Notice that this information system models, at the two highest levels, PRISM metadata and types associated with the Functional Data Model [Sibley 77, Shipman 81]. The *schema diagram* within the dotted region in Figure 1 shows a database schema defined in the graphical notation of the Functional Data Model, which consists of entity_sets 'order' and 'employee' and functions 'order_taker' and 'ord_#', where order_taker: order —> employee and ord_#: order +-> integer.

The function 'ord_#' serves as a *key* of the 'order' entity_set. This is denoted by the bar on the function arrow. This figure shows the *duality* of representing relationships (functions) as objects. For example, ord_# and order_taker are clearly functions at the Schema Level and also instances of the meta-type 'function' at the Data Model level. Also, the token "order 62 --> 62" represents the mapping under ord_# of order 62 to the integer 62.

The PRISM Constraint Language (CL)

A CL constraint consists of a collection of rules. Each rule consists of a precondition, action and postcondition sequence. Within each precondition and postcondition, predicates are combined with the logical operators AND, OR, NOT and parentheses. Predicates name CL metadata query functions. The optional action statement contains a sequence of simple actions which name CL atomic update procedures.

In PRISM a user request (or goal) is either to ASSERT, DENY or TEST an information system fact. User goals are determined in the precondition clause. Example 1 shows an 'instance' constraint for an object named 'invoice'. The '$' prefix denotes a variable.

Example 1.

```
CONSTRAINT:      instance of: invoice;
PARMS:           $invoice_instance;
PRECONDITION:  roleis(ASSERT);
ACTION:          unitasa: $invoice_instance, invoice;
POSTCONDITION: assert(
  invoice_number($invoice_instance,$integer_instance));
```

An 'instance' constraint specifies the conditions for a user to create or update instances of a type. A CL constraint bundles *functional rules* that specify the semantics of objects. Example 1 has a single rule which says that "To assert the existence of an instance of type 'invoice', the instance must have associated with it an invoice number." The 'invoice_number' object is a mapping between 'invoice' and an integer id-number, that is,

invoice_number: invoice -> integer.

A CL constraint for 'invoice_number' is shown in Example 2. This constraint specifies that two actions will occur: a unitasa and a unitmap only if the system can obtain an integer invoice number from the user, and $inv_num_inst is related to precisely one invoice.

Example 2.

```
CONSTRAINT:      instance of: invoice_number;
PARMS:           $inv_inst, $integer_inst;
PRECONDITION:  roleis(ASSERT) AND
           NOT iscurrinstance( $integer_inst);
ACTION: unitasa: $inv_num_inst, invoice_number;
           unitmap: $inv_num_inst, $inv_inst, $integer_inst;
POSTCONDITION: pmssg  ("Enter invoice number")  AND
           assert (integer($integer_inst) ) AND
           mapcardinality ($inv_num_inst,"1:1")
```

The CL language is also used to express the constraints of PRISM meta-types. The constraint specifications for 'class' and 'map' are provided below:

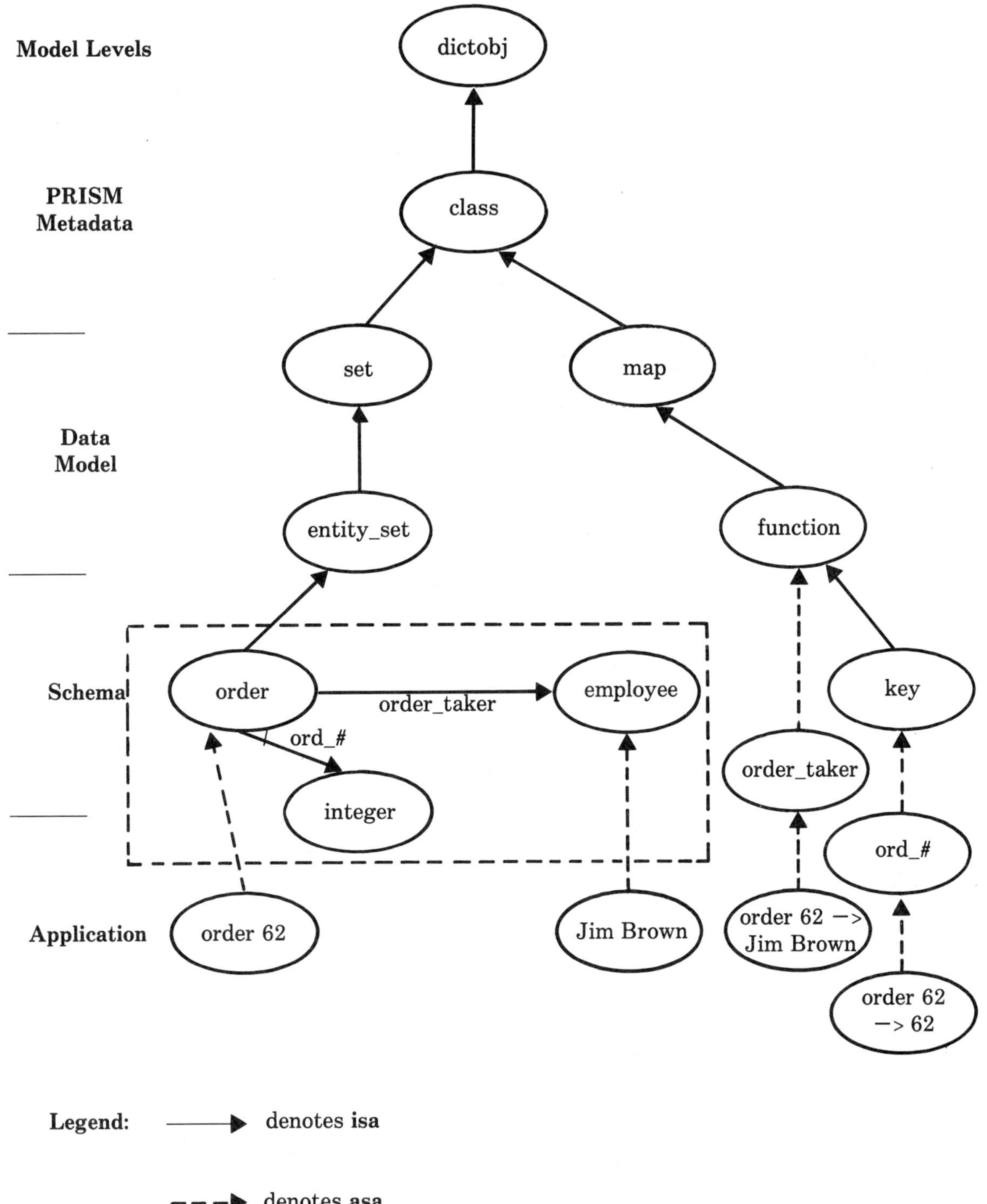

Figure 1: PRISM Model Hierarchy — Metadata and Data

Example 3:

```
CONSTRAINT: instance of: class;
PARMS:$class_i;
PRECONDITION:       NOT roleis(ASSERT);
POSTCONDITION:      mssg("Class role is not avail.") AND
            FALSE;
PRECONDITION:       roleis(ASSERT) AND
            NOT isclass($class_i) AND
            mssg("CLASS IN INSTANTIATION")
    /* build explicit constraint for instantiation */
ACTION:         unitasa:$class_i,class;
POSTCONDITION:      assert(outmapof($class_i,#omap_s)) AND
    /*should assert all outmaps */
            assert(inmapof( $class_i,#inmap_s)) AND
            assert(supertypeof( $class_i));
PRECONDITION:       TRUE;
  /* translate implicit constraints to explicit CON: */
POSTCONDITION:      assert(dictobj($class_i));
```

An instance of the 'class' type, in addition to being a dictionary object, is itself a type. Therefore there may be maps for which an instance is the domain type, including the 'isa' map that specifies any supertypes of it. And there may be maps for which such an instance is the range type, e.g., the 'asa' map.

For example, 'invoice' as an instance of class would be both a dictionary object, the domain type of the 'total_value' map and the range type of the 'invoices_for_client' map. The existence of such maps for a 'class' instance is enforced by propagation of the properties of the 'class' type. The properties are called the 'outmapof' and 'inmapof' types. A further property, the 'supertypeof' type, is propagated on instances of the 'class' type. For example, the supertype of 'invoice' may be 'document'.

Example 4:

```
CONSTRAINT:      instance of: map;
PARMS:         $map_i;
PRECONDITION:   NOT roleis(ASSERT);
POSTCONDITION:  mssg("Map role is not avail.") AND
            FALSE;
PRECONDITION:
            roleis(ASSERT) AND
            NOT ismap($map_i) AND
            mssg("INSTANTIATION OF MAP");
ACTION:        unitasa:$map_i, map;
POSTCONDITION:
      pmssg  ("Defining a map:") AND
      assert (domainof( $map_i, $map_domain_i)) AND
      assert (rangeof($map_i, $map_range_i));
PRECONDITION:   TRUE;
/* translate implicit constraints to explicit CON: */
POSTCONDITION:  assert(dictobj($map_i));
```

Semantics of CL

To determine whether a constraint is satisfied, its logical value is computed to TRUE, FALSE, UNKNOWN, or EXCEPTION as the *conjunction* of the value of each rule in the constraint.

To determine the value of each rule, the logical value of a rule's precondition is first determined. Predicates in preconditions are typically CL query functions on the Fact Base or on environment parameters. If a rule's precondition evaluates to TRUE, the rule fires and its ACTION statement is triggered, then the postcondition is evaluated. The logical value of a fired *rule* is the value to which the postcondition expression evaluates. If a precondition evaluates to FALSE, the rule is not applicable and the value of the rule is *TRUE,* i.e., it does not affect the value of the constraint. Neither the action nor postcondition are evaluated in this case. If any predicate or action evaluates to EXCEPTION, evaluation of the constraint terminates with a value of EXCEPTION. Expressions which evaluate to UNKNOWN combine with logical operators as follows:

```
TRUE    OR  UNKNOWN  ->   TRUE
FALSE   OR  UNKNOWN  ->   UNKNOWN
TRUE    AND UNKNOWN  ->   UNKNOWN
FALSE   AND UNKNOWN  ->   FALSE
```

A user goal is handled as a transaction that is not committed until all subgoals are proved to be correct. Actions, which are derived principally from the update semantics of the Functional Data Model, specify atomic update operations on instances in the Knowledge Base. Atomic updates are only committed, i.e., updated instances moved into the Fact Base, if assert, deny, and test subgoals in postconditions are satisfied. In addition to create, delete and update rules, ordering rules may be added to instantiation constraints such that the creation or deletion of instances of the type propagates the ordering. Security constraints and access constraints are evaluated prior to instance constraints.

The syntax and semantics of CL constraints ensure that an interpreter can complete an evaluation of rules sequentially to derive a logical value for a constraint.

4.3. Issues in Constraint Management for EDS

In the previous sections we have argued for a constraint-based EDS incorporating an object-oriented associative-net knowledge representation in which object behavior, both static and dynamic, is specified by explicit constraints. Several issues related to this representation are given below.

There is a trade-off in the representational form of constraints at each level of abstraction in an information system. Whether constraints are represented inherently, implicitly or explicitly, affects the system's ability to:

1. Enforce a constraint,
2. Translate constraints from one representation to another, for instance, decompile an inherent constraint to an equivalent explicit form,
3. Make inferences based on implicit constraints,
4. Explain to a user or another system the status of a constraint, e.g., its existence, or the history of its enforcement, and
5. Reason about a constraint, e.g., to decide whether to activate it based on its heuristic value which may be determined by reading its specification and computing its expected or actual propagation behavior [Davis 80b].

Embedding a constraint in an inherent representation makes its enforcement predetermined but untraceable (unverifiable at run time). If equivalent implicit or explicit representations of the same constraint are eliminated, the system can not reason about or explain its enforcement behavior. Moreover the embedded constraint could be difficult or impossible to update without recompiling the constraint.

Efficient enforcement requires compilation (translation of constraints into inherent form) of all that it is cost effective to compile since compilation implies a collapse of mappings (query decomposition and modification, and access path mappings) into the lowest expected aggregate cost access paths.

Constraints which are not inherent or implicit have to be enforced interpretively. The resolution of such explicit constraints at all levels to a minimal set should reduce the work of run-time enforcement processors and may point the way to the design of machine architectures optimized for generic constraint enforcement.

A constraint evaluator could be constructed that would maintain a staged virtual execution space, in which constraint specifications would be represented in different levels of readiness for evaluation. For instance, scripts and their associated constraint specifications that are receiving heavy usage could be compiled. A change to a rule in a frame or script would make the compiled version obsolete. If demand for a script is heavy it can be recompiled, otherwise its specification can be maintained in an explicit notation or in an intermediate code ready for direct interpretation.

5. CONCLUSIONS

By comparing the roles played by constraints in various systems, we have shown the importance of the constraint construct to the evolution of information systems. An approach to the management of metadata is emphasized in which the constraint is used as a unit of specification to express the semantics of information models. An architecture is proposed in which a base of constraints can be manipulated by an extensible tool set for knowledge management.

The evolution of information systems may be characterized by progress in the higher-level organization of semantic knowledge and the use of such knowledge in tools, e.g., security verification tools and database design tools. The management of semantic integrity is viewed as the task of optimally organizing semantics as a knowledge resource. This means designing and operating a system for maintaining representations of semantics to which generic and specialized tools can refer. The representational formalisms selected must serve the needs of these tools.

6. REFERENCES

Bernstein 81
Bernstein, P.A., Goodman, N., Wong, E., Reeve, C.L., Rothnie, J.R., Query Processing in a System for Distributed Databases (SDD-1), *ACM Trans. on Database Systems*, 6,4, 1981, pp 602-625.

Berry 79
Berry, O., and King, R., An Abstract Data Type Approach to Database Design, *Proc. 5th Int. Conf. VLDB,* Rio de Janeiro, 1979.

Berry 81
Berry, D. M., Application of the Formal Development Methodology to Database Design and Integrity Verification, *Int. Conf. on Computer Science,* Chile, 1981.

Borning 79
Borning, A., ThingLab: A Constraint-Oriented Simulation Laboratory, *SSL-79-3,* Xerox Palo Alto Research Center, July 1979.

Borgida 80
Borgida, A., Greenspan, S., Data and Activities: Exploiting Hierarchies of Classes, *Proc. Workshop on Data Abstraction, ACM SIGMOD Record,* Feb. 1981, Pingree Park, Colorado, June 1980, pp 98-100.

Borgida 82
Borgida, A. T., Mylopoulos, J., Wong, H. K. T., Methodological & Computer Aids for Interactive Info. Sys. Design, *IFIP Working Conf. on Automated Tools for Information Systems Design & Dev.,* New Orleans, Jan., 1982.

Brodie 78
Brodie, M. L., Specification and Verification of Database Semantic Integrity, Ph. D. Dissertation, *Tech. Report* CSRG-91, Univ. Toronto, April 1978.

Brodie 82
Brodie, M.L., Silva, E., Active and Passive Component Modeling: ACM/PCM, in *Information System Design Methodologies,* ed. T.W. Olle, H.G. Sol, North Holland, 1982.

Brodie 83
Brodie M. L., Research Issues in Database Specifications, *ACM SIGMOD Record,* 13, 3, April 1983, pp 42-45.

Childs 77
Childs, D. L., Extended Set Theory, A General Model for Very Large, Distr., Backend Inf. Syst., *Proc. 3rd Int. Conf. VLDB,* Tokyo, Oct. 1977, pp 28-46.

Cleveland 80
Cleveland, J. C., Mathematical Specifications, *ACM SIGPLAN,* Vol. 15, Dec. 1980.

Codd 70
Codd, E. F., A Relational Model of Data for Large Shared Data Banks, *Comm. ACM,* 13, 6, June 1970, pp 377-387.

Davis 76
Davis, R., Applications of Meta Level Knowledge to the Construction, Maintenance and Use of Large Knowledge Bases, Ph. D. Dissert., Stanford Univ., in *Knowledge Based Systems in Artificial Intelligence,* McGraw Hill, NY, 1980.

Davis 80
Davis, R., Reasoning About Control, *Artificial Intelligence,* 15, 3, pp 179-222.

Davis 80b
Davis, R., Content Reference: Reasoning About Rules, *Artificial Intelligence,* 15, 3, pp 223-239.

Deliyanni 79
Deliyanni, A., Kowalski, R. A., Logic and Semantic Networks, *Comm. ACM,* 22, 3, March 1979, pp 184-192.

Deutsch 80
Deutsch, L. P., Constraints: A Uniform Model for Data and Control, *Proc. Workshop on Data Abstraction, ACM SIGMOD Record,* Feb. 1981, Pingree Park, Colorado, June, 1980.

Doyle 79
Doyle, J., A Truth Maintenance System, *Artificial Intelligence,* Vol. 12, No. 3, 1979.

Feigenbaum 83
Feigenbaum, E.A., and McCorduck, P., *The Fifth Generation: Artificial Intelligence and Japan's Computer Challenge to the World,* Addison Wesley, Reading, MA, 1983.

Findler 79
Associative Networks: Representation and Use of Knowledge by Computer, Academic Press, NY, 1979.

Goldberg 82
Goldberg, A., The Smalltalk-80 System Release Process, *Smalltalk-80,* ed. G. Krasner, Addison Wesley, 1983, pp 3-8.

Goldfine 82
Information Resource Management - Strategies and Tools, NBS Special Publication 500-92, 1982.

Guttag 80
Guttag, J., Notes on Type Abstraction, *IEEE Trans. Soft. Eng.* SE-6, 1, Jan. 1980, pp 13-23.

Guttag 80b
Guttag, J., Horning, J. J., Formal Specification as a Design Tool, *ACM 7th POPL,* Las Vegas, Nevada, Jan. 1980, pp 251-261.

Hammer 75
Hammer, M., McLeod, D., Semantic Integrity in a Relational Database, *Proc. 1st Int. Conf. VLDB,* Framingham, Mass., 1975.

Hammer 76
Hammer, M., McLeod, D., A Framework for Database Semantic Integrity, *Proc. 2nd Int. Conf. on Software Engineering,* San Francisco, 1976.

Hayes-Roth 84
Hayes-Roth, F. et al, *Building Expert Systems,* Addison Wesley, Reading, 1984.

Jarke 84
Jarke, M., Clifford, J., Vassiliou, Y., An Optimizing Prolog Front-End to a Relational Query System, *Proc. ACM-SIGMOD Conf.,* Boston, 1984, pp 296-306.

Jensen 75
Jensen, K., Wirth, N., Pascal User Manual and Report, *Lecture Notes in Computer Science,* 18, 1975.

Katz 80
Katz, R. H., Wong, E., An Access Path Model for Physical Database Design, *ACM SIGMOD Record Conf.,* Santa Monica, Cal., 1980, pp 194-201.

Katz 82
Katz, R. H., Wong, E., Decompiling CODASYL DML into Relational Queries, *ACM TODS,* 7, 1, March 1982, pp 1-23.

Kerschberg 82
Kerschberg, L., Ting, P.D., Yao, S.B., Query Optimization in Star Computer Networks, *ACM Trans. on Database Systems*, December 1982, pp 653-677.

Levesque 79
Levesque, H. J., Mylopoulos, J., A Procedural Semantics for Semantic Networks, in *Associative Networks,* ed. Findler, N., Academic Press, NY, 1979, pp 93-120.

Leveson 80
Leveson, N. G., Applying Behavioral Abstraction to Information System Design and Integrity, *Tech. Report* 47, Lab. of Medical Information Science, Univ. Cal., San Francisco, March 1980.

Locasso 80
Locasso, R., Scheid, J., Schorre, V., Eggert, P., *The Ina Jo Specification Language Reference Manual,* TM-(L)-6021/001/00, System Development Corp., Santa Monica, CA., Jan. 1980.

London 78
London, R. L., et al, Abstraction and Verification in ALPHARD: A Symbol Table Example, *Constructing Quality Software,* ed. P. G. Hibbard, North Holland, 1978, pp 319-349.

Lundberg 82
Lundberg, B., IMT - Information Modeling Tool, *Automated Tools for Information Systems Design,* eds. H-J. Schneider and A. I. Wasserman, North Holland, 1982, pp 21-30.

McCarthy 80
McCarthy. J., Circumscription - A Form of Non-monotonic Reasoning, *Artificial Intelligence,* 13, pp 27-39.

McDermott 80
McDermott, D., Doyle, J., Non-Monotonic Logic I, *Artificial Intelligence,* 13, pp 41-72.

McLeod 80
McLeod, D., Smith, J. M., Abstraction in Databases, *Proc. Workshop on Data Abstraction, ACM SIGMOD Record,* Feb. 1981, Pingree Park, Colorado, June 1980.

Minsky 68a
Minsky, M., Matter, Mind, Models, in *Semantic Information Processing,* MIT Press, 1968, pp 425-435.

Mylopoulos 79
Mylopoulos, J., Bernstein, P. A, Wong, H. K. T., A Language Facility for Designing Interactive Database Applications, *Tech. Rep.* CSRG 105, Univ. Toronto, 1979.

Mylopoulos 80
Mylopoulos, J., Wong, H. T., Some Features of the TAXIS Data Model, *Proc. 6th Int. Conf. VLDB,* Oct. 1980, pp 399-410.

Mylopoulos 80b
Mylopoulos, J., Bernstein, P. A, Wong, H. K. T., A Language Facility for Designing Database-Intensive Applications, *ACM TODS,* 1, pp 185-207.

Mylopoulos 80c
Mylopoulos, J., An Overview of Knowledge Representation, *Proc. Workshop on Data Abstraction, ACM SIGMOD Record,* Feb. 1981, Pingree Park, Colorado, June 1980.

Nicolas 78a

Nicolas, J. M., Yazdanian, K., Integrity Checking in Deductive Databases, in *Logic and Databases,* eds. Gallaire, H. and Minker, J., Plenum Press, NY, 1978.

Paolini 77

Paolini, P., Pelagatti, G., Formal Definition of Mappings in a Data Base, *Tech. Report* 77-2, Istituto di Elettrotechnica ed Electtronica, Politecnico di Milano.

Reiter 78

Reiter, R., On Closed World Databases, in *Logic and Databases,* eds. Gallaire, H. and Minker, J., Plenum Press, NY, 1978, pp 55-76.

Reiter 80

Reiter, R., Database: A Logical Perspective, *Proc. Workshop on Data Abstraction, ACM SIGMOD Record,* Feb. 1981, Pingree Park, Colorado, June 1980, pp 174-176.

Reiter 81b

Reiter, R., On the Integrity of Typed First Order Data Bases, in *Advances in Data Base Theory,* Plenum Press, 1981, pp 137-157.

Robinson 77

Robinson, L., Roubin, O., *SPECIAL - A Specification and Assertion Language,* SRI, Menlo Park, CA., Jan. 1977.

Sagiv 80

Sagiv, Y., An Algorithm for Inferring Multivalued Dependencies with an Application to Propositional Logic, *Journal ACM,* 27, 2, April 1980, pp 250-262.

Sagiv 81

Sagiv, Y., et al, An Equivalence Between Relational Database Dependencies, and a Fragment of Propositional Logic, *Journal ACM,* 28, 3, July 1981, pp 435-453.

Schubert 76

Schubert, L., Extending the Expressive Power of Semantic Nets, *Artificial Intelligence,* 7, pp 163-198.

Selinger 79

Selinger, P., Astrahan, M.M., Chamberlin, D.D., Lorie, R.A., Price, T.G., Access Path Selection in a Relational Database Management System, *ACM-SIGMOD International Conference on Management of Data,* Boston, May 30-June 1, 1979, pp 23-34.

Sen 83

Sen, A., Kerschberg, L., Enterprise Modeling for Information System Design, Working Paper, Univ. South Carolina, Dept. Mgt. Science, 1983.

Shepherd 83

Shepherd, A., PRISM: A Constraint Based Prototyping Information System Manager, *MS Thesis,* Univ. South Carolina, December, 1983.

Shepherd and Kerschberg 84

Shepherd, A., Kerschberg, L., PRISM: A Knowledge-Based System for Semantic Integrity Specification and Enforcement in Database Systems, *ACM SIGMOD Conference, Boston, 1984, pp 307-315.*

Shipman 81

Shipman, D., The Functional Data Model and the Data Language DAPLEX, *ACM Trans. Database Syst.* 6, 1 (March 1981) pp 140-173.

Sibley 77

Sibley, E.H., Kerschberg, L. Data Model and Data Architecture Considerations, *Proc. National Computer Conference,* AFIPS Press (June 1977) pp 85-96.

Steele 80
Steele, G.L., The Definition and Implementation of a Computer Programming Language Based on Constraints, *MIT VLSI Memo. 80-32,* Ph.D. Dissertation, December 1980.

Stefik 81a
Stefik, M., Planning with Constraints (MOLGEN: Part 1), *Artificial Intelligence* **16** (1981) 111-140.

Stefik 81b
Stefik, M., Planning and Meta-Planning (MOLGEN: Part 2), *Artificial Intelligence* **16** (1981) 141-170.

Stonebraker 82
Stonebraker, M., Application of Artificial Intelligence Techniques to Database Systems, *Mem UCB/ERL M82/31,* Berkeley, May 1982.

Warren 81
Warren, D.H.D., Efficient Processing of Interactive Database Queries Expressed in Logic, *Proc. Conf. on Very Large Data Bases*, Cannes, France, 1981, pp 272-281.

Wedekind 80
Wedekind, H. E., Constructive Abstract Data Types (CAD), *Proc. Workshop on Data Abstraction, ACM SIGMOD Record,* Feb. 1981, Pingree Park, Colorado, June 1980, pp 203-206.

Wulf 76
Wulf, W. A., London, R. L., Shaw, M., Abstraction and Verification in ALPHARD: Introduction to Language & Methodology, *TR* Carnegie-Mellon Univ., June 1976.

Zaniolo 81
Zaniolo, C., Melkanoff, M. A., On the Design of Relational Schemata, *ACM TODS,* 6, 1, March 1981, pp 1-47.

Implementation Of A Semantic Integrity Manager With A Knowledge Representation System

Gilles M. E. Lafue
Reid G. Smith

Schlumberger-Doll Research
Old Quarry Road
Ridgefield, CT 06877-4108
USA

Abstract

This paper presents an approach to combining an A.I. Knowledge Representation System and a DBMS which consists of extending the Knowledge Representation System into a DBMS. The Knowledge Representation System provides both the data model for the DBMS and the basic tool for building the DBMS. That is, the DBMS is built by bootstrapping its own data model. This is illustrated with the implementation of the semantic integrity subsystem for the DBMS. One benefit of using a Knowledge Representation System is that the information on which integrity management is based can be encoded declaratively, thus facilitating its generation, modification and interpretation. The paper presents both the salient data modelling features of the Knowledge Representation System and the integrity management system implemented with it.

1 Introduction

A.I. Expert Systems (ESs) typically use relatively complex and variable data, but not in large amounts. The data is assumed to reside in virtual memory. By contrast, a DBMS manages data which reside on files outside virtual memory.[1] There is an increasing need for ESs to process large amounts of data, and for DBMSs to support more complex data. A major problem then, is the reconciliation of data modelling requirements.

This concern arises at a time when data models are being re-visited both for ESs and for DBMSs. ES developers realize that production rules are often insufficient to enable such systems to explain their findings or improve their knowledge, and are proposing general-purpose *Knowledge Representation Systems* (KRSs) to structure ES knowledge (*e.g.,* based on the notion of frames [14]).[2] KRSs determine the types of data structures and operations performed on the data. They can

[1] We ignore for the time being the emergence of main or virtual memory-oriented databases made possible by increased memory size. In any case, even in virtual memory, grouping of data and access mechanisms can significantly impact performance of data operations.

[2] This is not to say that production rules are not valuable. They are indeed the basis for much needed and well understood inference making. They can be used in a complementary fashion with a KRS.

be seen as ES data models. Some of these systems borrow from programming languages and are sometimes referred to as *object-oriented* languages. A KRS is one component of a system, or set of tools, for building ESs; a rule language and an inference engine are examples of other components. To the extent that it provides a good way of organizing software, a KRS can also be a useful tool for building systems other than ESs, for example, DBMSs.

On the database side, after being on its way to becoming a standard, the general-purpose set-oriented relational model has been criticized as insufficient for handling, for instance, meta-data, statistical or scientific data [20], generalizations [21], or complex design data [2,12].

A desirable system would be one combining the KRS modelling richness with the DBMS ability to manage secondary memory. There are four basic ways to realize this combination: *(i)* take an existing DBMS and an existing KRS and interface them; *(ii)* take an existing DBMS and extend its data model into a KRS; *(iii)* take an existing KRS and extend it into a DBMS; and *(iv)* build a system combining the two *de novo.* When faced with these alternatives, one is usually influenced by the utility of what one already has and by the complexity of what is needed.

The first alternative is illustrated with the use of Logic Programming, Prolog in particular, as a way of getting both the inference engine needed by an ES and a connection to a relational DBMS [17,26]. This is reasonable as long as Prolog's inference engine fits the contemplated class of ES, and the relational model is acceptable. As noted in [9], it turns out that neither assumption corresponds to the class of applications considered at Schlumberger: *(i)* ESs for signal interpretation typically make forward-chained inferences (*e.g.*, see [4,24]); and *(ii)* we have a KRS which is richer than the relational model, as we shall see below.

Others, choosing the second alternative, have tried to extend existing DBMSs, relational ones in particular, to embed some of the facilities needed by ESs. Related to this effort are attempts to integrate KRS modelling features such as generalizations into the relational model [21], or into Prolog [25].

The third alternative has been initiated by efforts to extend programming languages into managing permanent data (*e.g.*, Algol [1] or SmallTalk [6]).

This paper presents a case along the third alternative which begins with a KRS called Strobe [22], that is richer than most current data models, and certainly richer than the data models of commercially available DBMSs. Strobe also has a very convenient programming environment: Interlisp-D on Xerox workstations (1100, 1108 and 1132).[3] The combination of Strobe's knowledge representation declarations and its programming environment has been proven to be helpful for building large systems, some aspects of which are described in [23].

[3]The workstations are connected by Ethernet to each other and to other mainframes (*e.g.*, Vaxes). The mainframes provide storage of large files and execution of programs written in other languages, but accessible from Strobe on the workstations. Strobe is implemented in Interlisp-D to run on Xerox workstations and in Mainsail, Common Lisp, and C to run on Vaxes. When we say that Strobe is implemented in some language, we mean *(i)* that Strobe consists of functions or procedures written in that language, and *(ii)* that the operations, or methods, associated with Strobe objects are written in that language. Strobe objects use the same message exchange protocol whether they are on the same workstation, on different workstations, or on both workstations and Vaxes. The rest of this paper concerns the Interlisp-D version of Strobe. Also worth noting is a convenient window and menu-oriented editor for Strobe that makes extensive use of the Interlisp-D graphics primitives [18].

This means that Strobe not only provides a DBMS data model, but also an implementation tool for building the DBMS. The approach taken here is a bootstrapping one in which the DBMS is (progressively) built by using its own data model. It is believed that interfacing Strobe with an existing DBMS would be at least as complicated as, and certainly less integrated than, extending Strobe into a DBMS.

This approach of building systems in Strobe itself has been tested with the implementation of several DBMS components: a semantic integrity manager and a file manager to store and retrieve Strobe objects on secondary memory. Tools that are less database-oriented, but as general and domain-independent, have been implemented in a similar fashion: a production rule interpretation system and a system to execute tasks based on a declarative task representation [11].

The rest of this paper illustrates this approach with the description of the DBMS subsystem for semantic integrity management implemented in Strobe. This subsystem, also referred to as *the integrity manager*, processes information such as integrity constraints to be satisfied by the data, when and how these constraints should be checked, and what do do when they are violated (or satisfied). This information is encoded declaratively, using the knowledge representation features of Strobe, in order to facilitate its generation, modification and interpretation. The integrity manager itself is a simple interpreter for this information which is naturally incorporated into the kernel of Strobe. The novelty is less to be found in the components of integrity management than in their implementation. This system is related to the knowledge-based integrity management system described in [19] in that both systems use knowledge representation features such as generalizations, object datatypes and uniform manipulation of data and meta-data. This integrity manager was implemented during the development of a programming environment for interactive interpretation of logs of geophysical measurements made in oil wells. Other aspects of that environment are described in [23].

The next section shows the salient data modelling features of Strobe both to contrast them with those of commonly available data models and to prepare the reader for the description of the integrity manager. Then, the encoding of the type of information on which integrity management is based is presented, followed by an outline of the interpretation of that information by the integrity manager. The performance of declarative integrity management is discussed next. Finally, the conclusion includes considerations about what remains to be done.

2 Data Modelling in Strobe

Strobe is related to other KRSs (*e.g.,* Loops [3], KEE [8]), and many of the features presented here are general to this type of system. Some Strobe features are also offered by experimental database data models sometimes generically referred to as *semantic data models* (*e.g.,* [13,16]).

2.1 Four Levels of Data Representation

Database data models usually provide three levels of data representation (*e.g.,* databases, relations and attributes) for the relational model. Strobe provides four levels: *knowledge bases*, *objects*, *slots* (*i.e.,* attributes) and *facets*. A knowledge base is a collection of objects, an object has a collection of slots, and a slot has a collection of facets. Facets can be seen as annotations on attributes. Some facets, such as VALUE and DATATYPE, are system-defined and appear in every slot. Others are user-defined.

Facets turn out to be very useful for meta-data encoding. In practice, they have been extensively used in order to convey information about data in a way which is less domain-specific than the data itself. For instance, [23] describes a declarative process representation essentially encoded as facets. In that application, objects and slots correspond to programs, procedures, parameters, and so on. Therefore, their names and values are no more meaningful to people other than their long-time users, than are the names of the programs, procedures or parameters themselves. On the other hand, a relatively small number of facet names and contents has been found useful to describe these objects and slots in more general terms of control and data flow. The documentation that the facets provide is useful to a number of users: the end-user who can use it as concise guideline, the system that controls program execution, and the user-interface system that infers from some of these facets the best way to prompt the user for information such as input parameters. The description of the integrity manager provides other examples of the utility of facets for meta-data encoding.[4]

2.2 Generalizations and Inheritance

Traditional database data models are based on aggregation relationships and are notoriously bad at handling generalizations. Like most KRSs, Strobe tends to favor generalizations while providing for aggregations. It allows multiple generalizations and, like other KRSs, offers inheritance along generalizations. In Strobe, inheritance basically applies to facets. Suppose for example, a message is sent to facet F of slot S in object O. If in O, S has a value for F, this value is returned. Otherwise, the ancestry of O is searched for the first object in which F of S has a value and that value is returned. A common use of inheritance is for default values, which are not supported by DBMSs that impose fixed length-records.

There are two major types of Strobe objects: *class* objects and *individual* objects. The difference is that classes can have specializations, but individuals cannot. Of course, the specializations of a class can include other classes. In general, the set of classes of a knowledge base corresponds to a database schema, and the set of individuals to a database extension.

2.3 User-Defined Datatypes

Traditional database data models usually provide few basic datatypes, typically, integer, real and character. By contrast, Strobe allows user-defined datatypes to become an integral part of

[4]As meta-data encoders, facets may play a role similar to that of slots of high-level objects in a knowledge base organized as a hierarchy of generalizations in the sense that such objects contain general information that applies to their more domain-dependent specializations. The choice between these two alternatives involves fine points of knowledge representation beyond the topic of this paper. We only present here the alternative of encoding integrity information with facets.

```
OBJECT: BITMAP
SYNONYMS:
TYPE: CLASS
GENERALIZATIONS: DATATYPE
   DATUM-EDIT: SYS/EDITBITMAP
   DATUM-PRINT:
      VALUE: SYS/PRINTBITMAP
      DATATYPE: LISP
```

Figure 1: A Datatype Object

knowledge bases. This is particulary useful for scientific applications. It is also central to the implementation of the integrity manager discussed in the next section.

Strobe datatyping works as follows. Every slot has a DATATYPE facet. A datatype is represented by an object, some slots of which are a bit special. They are special because messages sent to facets of slots having that datatype are forwarded to them, unless the slots already have the facets to which the messages are sent. For instance, Figure 1 shows an object called BITMAP which defines the bitmap datatype and has two slots: DATUM-EDIT and DATUM-PRINT.[5] When a message is sent to the PRINT facet of a slot with datatype BITMAP, the message is forwarded to the DATUM-PRINT slot of the BITMAP object (more precisely, to its VALUE facet), which contains the name of the function to print bitmaps. The slots of a datatype object that work as message handlers for the slots having that datatype are recognized by the system on the basis that their name start with "DATUM-". Message forwarding can be seen as another form of inheritance.

Typically, "DATUM-" slots define operations for datatypes. Datatype objects can also have regular slots. Some for example, define datatype constraints, as we shall see in the next section. Also, like all objects, datatype objects can form hierarchies of generalizations. In fact, every Strobe knowledge base starts with a few class objects, one of which is called DATATYPE and is the ancestor of all datatype objects. This is where general datatype operations and constraints can be defined since they can be inherited by all datatypes.

2.4 Actual and Virtual Data

Being an object-oriented language, Strobe provides a message passing mechanism which makes data access uniform, whether data is actual or virtual (*i.e.*, re-computed as needed). Messages are

[5]The figures showing objects are to be read as follows. General information about the object (such as its name, its synonyms, whether it is a class or an individual, its immediate generalizations) is shown first. Slots are then shown indented with respect to the object general information, and when shown, the facets of a slot are indented with respect to the slot name. When a slot has a value and the facets of the slot are not shown, then the value is printed following the slot name.

sent to facets of slots, typically, but not exclusively, VALUE facets. The effect of sending a message to a facet is to evaluate the content of the facet. If the content is data, atomic or structured, that data is returned. If it is a function name or a function definition, the function is applied to the contents of the message and its value returned.

2.5 Active Values

Strobe provides a demon mechanism by which the activation of functions can be associated with data operations (*e.g.*, the access or update of slot values, or the creation or deletion of slots or objects. Several functions can be associated with a given data operation, and it is possible to specify whether invocation should take place before or after the associated operation.

2.6 Set Representation

Database data models do not always support a one-to-one correspondence between real world entities and database entities. While aggregation abstractions in models like the relational model support the grouping of properties as a single type, they do not necessarily support the reference to a set of instances as a single entity. Often, one needs to define a view (or query) in order to refer to such sets. With an object-oriented KRS such as Strobe, which does not impose *flat* objects (in the relational sense), one can reference such a set with an object slot. More generally, slot values can be sets or elements. A related feature of Strobe is the notion of *group*. A group is simply a named collection of objects.

2.7 Query Language

Strobe query language is a combination of Interlisp-D and Strobe functions. Strobe functions are functions written in Interlisp-D that access or update slots or facets of single objects or retrieve special sets of objects (typically defined by generalization or specialization relationships). Control is essentially provided by Interlisp-D. Interlisp-D offers at least the expressive power of set-oriented query languages like the relational calculus (with logical connectives and arithmetic comparators provided by Interlisp functions and quantifiers by macros). However, it supports no query optimization beyond the optimization provided by Strobe functions.

3 Semantic Integrity Management

Integrity management has three major components:

Constraints (or *conditions*) are relationships defined by the user between variables. In our case, variables are facets of Strobe slots (particularly, the VALUE facet). Currently, our constraint language is a combination of Interlisp-D, Strobe and a way to reference Strobe slot facets as free variables rather than via Strobe messages. It supports only limited analysis for the automatic generation of checking information (described next).

Checking is a mechanism to evaluate constraints. This mechanism is based on the following information. First, the mechanism needs to identify the variables of a constraint so that operations on those variables activate evaluation of the constraint and the variables can be bound to facet contents in the current database. Second, it is useful for the mechanism to know which operations on the variables may violate the constraint (assumed to be currently satisfied), so as to perform checking discriminately. Third, it would also be useful to have, for each such operation, a transform of the constraint which is more efficient to check than the original constraint.

Ideally, the information for checking should be automatically generated by the system based on the constraint definitions. In our current implementation, this generation is only semi-automatic because our current constraint language doesn't support all the necessary formal analysis. Variables are automatically identified. The operations on variables that may violate constraints are automatically generated because they correspond to the most probable case rather than as the result of formal analysis—and therefore, they can be overridden by the user. Transforms of constraints are not derived by the system.[6]

Maintenance is a set of actions to take in case of constraint violation and/or satisfaction.[7] Maintenance may be specified by the user but the system provides a default for the cases left unspecified, which typically, consists of rejecting the database updates that violate a constraint.[8]

Integrity management can be hard to specify, complicated to implement, and costly to execute. We want to make the information for the three components of integrity management easy to specify and efficient to check and maintain, and to make the checking and maintenance mechanism simple and uniform. The requirement for ease of specification and interpretation is partly answered by the declarative nature of integrity information encoding. As for performance, it is sometimes involved in a trade-off with simplicity, as we shall see below.

[6]Although the automatic generation of checking information is not the focus of this paper, it is worth noting that first order logic is an example of a language that offers techniques to determine which operations can violate a constraint, and which operations cannot [5,7]. It also offers ways of symplifying constraints for these operations. It is also worth noting that the checking considered here is performed after atomic database operations, not transactions of updates.

[7]An example of an action prompted by the satisfactory checking of a constraint consists of keeping a log of the possible side-effects caused by the checking of the constraint, so as to be able to undo these side-effects in case the current operation is aborted due to violations of other constraints.

[8]This is a major difference between DBMS integrity rules and ES production rules. The conditions of production rules are like integrity constraints, and their actions are like maintenance actions, except that they are usually not defaulted by the system.

4 Integrity Information

4.1 Types and Location of Integrity Constraints

Integrity constraints are first distinguished according to the number of slots they involve. *Single-slot constraints* involve a single-slot and *multi-slot constraints* several slots. There are two kinds of single-slot constraints: *datatype constraints*, which apply to all the slots having a particular datatype, and *regular single-slot constraints*, or *single-slot constraints* for short, which apply to one particular slot. Since slots can be set-valued, constraints are further divided into *element constraints* (that apply to every element of a slot value) and *set constraints* (that apply to a slot value as a set). The distinction between element and set constraints is a convenience for the user rather than a necessity.

Both for clarity and for performance, it seems natural to associate integrity information with the slots and objects involved in the checking. The integrity information which is specific to a particular slot is stored in the slot itself. As for the information concerning a constraint involving more than one slot, there is a trade-off between performance and simplicity. This trade-off is between duplicating integrity information for fast access versus not duplicating it for the sake of uniqueness and simplicity. In general, we have opted for the latter.

Integrity information concerning a datatype constraint is in the datatype object (rather than duplicated in every slot). Similarly, information about a multi-slot constraint is in a separate slot (*i.e.*, a slot whose sole purpose is to encode the constraint). If all the constrained slots are in the same object, the slot implementing the constraint is in that object; if they are in different objects, the slot implementing the constraint is one of those objects. There is nc other fundamental difference between multi-slot constraints among slots of the same object and among slots of different objects. Therefore, for clarity, the rest of this discussion will consider that the slots involved in a multi-slot constraint are in the same object.

In this implementation, information specifying constraints, their checking and their maintenance, is stored in facets. For single-slot constraints, these facets belong to the constrained slots; for datatype constraints, they belong to slots of datatype objects; and for multi-slot constraints, they belong to the slots used to encode the constraints.

We now turn our attention to the facets containing integrity information. These facets are first presented without any consideration of how they are generated.

4.2 Information For Single-Slot Constraints

A single-slot constraint applies only to the slot to which it is associated, independently of the slot's datatype. An example is shown in Figure 2. That figure shows the class object that represents the location of a well in terms of a town, county, state, country, and continent.[9] The value of the continent slot is constrained to belong to a set of legal continent names.

[9] Names that appear in curly brackets after a slot name are synonyms of that name.

```
OBJECT: WELL-LOCATION
TYPE: CLASS
GENERALIZATIONS: OBJECT
  WELL
  TOWN {TOWNSHIP}:
  COUN {COUNTY PARISH}:
  STAT {STATE PROVINCE}:
  NATI {NATION COUNTRY}:
  CONT {CONTINENT}:
    VALUE:
    DATATYPE: EXPR
    CONDITION: (MEMBER *VALUE* CANDIDATES)
    FACETS: CANDIDATES
    CANDIDATES: (EUROPE NORTH-AMERICA SOUTH-AMERICA ASIA AFRICA AUSTRALIA)
    OPERATIONS: (PUT ADD)
    CORRECTION: (ERROR *VALUE* "is not one of:" CANDIDATES)
```

Figure 2: A Single-Slot Constraint

All the information pertaining to a single-slot constraint is declared as facets of the constrained slot as follows.

An element constraint is indicated by a CONDITION facet. This facet contains an s-expression or a function. In the example, CONDITION contains an expression stating that a CONTINENT value must be one of the names contained in the CANDIDATES facet. The interpretation and binding of constraint variables is explained below. In addition, it can have a set constraint declared in a SET-CONDITION facet.

The facets that contain checking information are the following.

FACETS identifies the facets of the current slot involved in the constraint, *i.e.*, the variables of the constraint. The facets appearing in FACETS are referenced in the constraint freely by their name, rather than by using Strobe access operations. At checking time, the integrity manager binds the constraint's variables to the contents of the designated facets. These facets are also bound to corresponding variables in maintenance actions. In the example, FACETS points to the CANDIDATES facet which is used freely in both the constraint and the correction. *VALUE* represents the VALUE facet, that is, the facet affected by the constraint by definition. In an element constraint, *VALUE* is repeatedly bound to each element of the slot value and the constraint checked each time. In a set constraint, it is bound to the whole value.

OPERATIONS specifies the operations for which the element constraint in the CONDITION facet should be checked. It can specify one or several of the atomic update operations: PUT, ADD and REMOVE. SET-OPERATIONS specifies the operations for which the set constraint in SET-

CONDITION should be checked.

The facets containing maintenance information are the following.

The CORRECTION facet contains an expression or a function to execute in case the element constraint is violated. In the example, the CORRECTION facet contains an expression that issues an error message. CANDIDATES is bound at checking time to the corresponding facet of the current slot, and *VALUE* to each value element, as for constraints. CORRECTION is optional. If specified, the value it returns is taken as the corrected value element. If not specified, the system rejects the current value element. Similarly, SET-CORRECTION specifies what to do in case of set constraint violation.

The ACTION facet contains an expression or a function to execute in case the element constraint is satisfied. Its variables are bound to facets, as in constraints and corrections. ACTION is optional. If specified, its returned value becomes the current value element for the update. SET-ACTION plays an analogous role for set constraints.

4.3 Information For Datatype Constraints

As mentioned earlier, some of the slots of a datatype object define facets common to all the slots having that datatype (the "DATUM-" slots). Typically, these slots implement operations for the datatype. Other slots of a datatype object may be used to define integrity constraints for the datatype. A datatype constraint is represented by one and only one slot. Several such slots in a datatype object are interpreted as a conjunction of datatype constraints. Figure 3 shows the MEASUREMENT (or DIMENSIONED-QUANTITY) datatype object and some of the constraints that apply to slots of datatype measurement.

The slots of a datatype object that represent integrity constraints are denoted by a ROLE facet whose content is either DATATYPE-CONDITION (for element constraints) or DATATYPE-SET-CONDITION (for set constraints).

A datatype constraint is implemented as an expression or a function whose name appears in the VALUE facet of the slot representing the constraint.[10] In figure 3, the constraint represented by the LIMIT-VALUES-CONDITION slot is implemented by an expression and the INTERNAL-UNITS-CONDITION by the function InternalUnitsCondition.

The facets containing checking informations are the following.

A datatype constraint can have two sorts of variables: *(i)* properties of the datatype, and *(ii)* properties of the slots having that datatype. The former correspond to slots of the current datatype object and are identified in the SLOTS facet of the datatype constraint. The latter correspond

[10]The apparent lack of uniformity between single-slot constraints and datatype constraints regarding the facet that contains the constraints is explained as follows. Integrity information for a single-slot constraint is added to other facets of that slot; in particular, the VALUE facet of that slot is already used. By contrast, a datatype constraint is encoded in a slot entirely devoted to that constraint. In particular, the VALUE facet is free to contain the constraint itself. As seen later, this is also the case for multi-slot constraints.

```
OBJECT: MEASUREMENT
SYNONYMS: DIMENSIONED-QUANTITY
TYPE: CLASS
GENERALIZATIONS: DATATYPE
  LOWER-LIMIT:
  UPPER-LIMIT:
  LIMIT-VALUES-CONDITION:
    VALUE: (AND (≥ *VALUE* LOWER-LIMIT)(≥ *VALUE* UPPER-LIMIT))
    DATATYPE: LISP
    SLOTS: (LOWER-LIMIT UPPER-LIMIT)
    ROLE: DATATYPE-CONDITION
    OPERATIONS: (PUT ADD)
  INTERNAL-UNITS-CONDITION:
    VALUE: InternalUnitsCondition
    DATATYPE: LISP
    FACETS: (INTERNAL-UNITS)
    ROLE: DATATYPE-CONDITION
    OPERATIONS: (PUT ADD)
    CORRECTION: InternalUnitsConversion
```

Figure 3: Datatype Constraints

to facets of the slots having the current datatype, and are identified in the FACETS facet of the datatype constraint. The purpose of the SLOTS and FACETS facets is similar to that of the FACETS facet of single-slot constraints.

For instance, in Figure 3, the `LIMIT-VALUES-CONDITION` slot implements the constraint that slots representing measurements must be within the limit values defined for their measurement. The limit values for a given measurement are the same for all the slots whose datatype is that measurement, and therefore, belong in that datatype object. They are represented in the `LOWER-LIMIT` and `UPPER-LIMIT` slots, which both appear in the SLOTS facet of the `LIMIT-VALUES-CONDITION` slot.

Slots of datatype `MEASUREMENT` can require their values to be expressed in some specific units, called here *internal units.* While all such slots can make this requirement, their internal unit varies from one slot to the next, and therefore, must be associated with each slot individually. This is done in a facet called `INTERNAL-UNITS`. The `INTERNAL-UNITS-CONDITION` slot in figure 3 implements the constraint that a value assigned to a measurement slot must be expressed in the required internal units and `INTERNAL-UNITS` appears in the FACETS facet. In case of violation, the function declared in the CORRECTION facet makes the necessary conversion.

The OPERATIONS facet indicates the operations for which a datatype element constraint must be checked and SET-OPERATIONS the operations for which a datatype set constraint must be

```
OBJECT: CHANNEL-FILE
TYPE: CLASS
GENERALIZATIONS: DSK-FILE
  MEASUREMENT:
    VALUE:
    DATATYPE: MEASUREMENT
    PUT-MULTI-SLOT-CONDITIONS: MEASUREMENT-AND-UNIT-CONSTRAINT
    CARDINALITY: (1 . 1)
  UNITS:
    VALUE:
    DATATYPE: UNITS
    PUT-MULTI-SLOT-CONDITIONS: MEASUREMENT-AND-UNIT-CONSTRAINT
    CARDINALITY: (1 . 1)
  MEASUREMENT-AND-UNITS-CONSTRAINT:
    VALUE: (MEMBER UNITS (MESSAGE MEASUREMENT 'UNITS))
    DATATYPE: LISP
    ROLE: MULTI-SLOT-CONDITION
    SLOTS: (MEASUREMENT UNITS)
    CORRECTION: (ERROR UNITS "are not units of" MEASUREMENT)
```

Figure 4: A Multi-Slot Constraint

checked.

Maintenance information is indicated in CORRECTION (and/or SET-CORRECTION) and ACTION (and/or SET-ACTION) facets.

4.4 Information For Multi-Slot Constraints

An example multi-slot-constraint is shown in Figure 4. That figure shows some slots of an object called CHANNEL-FILE that defines files of measurements (or dimensioned quantities). The slot MEASUREMENT indicates the kind of measurement a file of this class is to contain, and the slot UNITS indicates the units in which the quantities in the file are expressed. There is a constraint between MEASUREMENT and UNITS such that units must belong to the set of known units for the measurement.

The slots of an object which represent multi-slot constraints are denoted by a ROLE facet whose content is MULTI-SLOT-CONDITION (or MULTI-SLOT-SET-CONDITION). Like a datatype constraint, a multi-slot constraint is represented in a slot devoted to it and is contained in the VALUE facet of that slot (as an s-expression or a function). Like a datatype constraint, it may also have a SLOTS facet, an OPERATIONS (or SET-OPERATIONS) facet, a CORRECTION (or SET-CORRECTION) facet and an ACTION or (SET-ACTION) facet.

The constraint of the example is in the MEASUREMENT-AND-UNITS-CONSTRAINT slot. The slot names MEASUREMENT and UNITS appear both in the SLOTS facet of MEASUREMENT-AND-UNITS-CONSTRAINT, and as variables in the constraint and in the correction. A Strobe message is used to retrieve the set of units from the object that defines the measurement.

In addition, the slots involved in multi-slot constraints have facets that point to these constraints when some operation is performed on them. For example, MEASUREMENT and UNITS have a PUT-MULTI-SLOT-CONDITIONS facet which indicates that the constraint in the MEASUREMENT-AND-UNITS-CONSTRAINT slot must be checked when a value is PUT into them. Several constraints appearing in a such a facet are interpreted as a conjunction and checked in the order in which they appear. Similar facets exist for ADD and REMOVE.

5 Interpretation of Integrity Information

The facets containing integrity information provide documentation both for the end-user that inspects a knowledge base and for the integrity manager. This documentation allows the integrity manager to be implemented as a single simple mechanism.

The integrity manager uses the Strobe datatype mechanism. There are currently three operations that require integrity checking: *putting* a value into a slot, *adding* one or several elements to the current value of a slot, and *removing* one or several elements from the current value of a slot. Each of these operations is implemented by a simple function whose name is inserted into the DATUM-PUT, DATUM-ADD and DATUM-REMOVE slot of the DATATYPE object, respectively. The DATATYPE object is shown in Figure 5. Since DATATYPE is the ancestor of all datatype objects in a Strobe knowledge base, these slots, and therefore the handling of PUT, ADD and REMOVE messages, is inherited by all datatypes.

The way the functions for these operations work is outlined as follows. A value put into, added to, or removed from a slot is checked for every constraint that applies to the slot. Element constraints are checked first and set constraints second, because the composition of a set may be altered as a result of maintenance actions taken on its elements. For each type, datatype constraints are checked first, single-slot constraints second and multi-slot constraints last. A constraint is only checked when all its variables have a value. After each check, the value may be modified by a correction or an action.

The handling of a PUT message is now described in more detail as an example; ADD and REMOVE cases are similar.

The datatype element constraints to check are represented in the slots of the datatype object whose ROLE is DATATYPE-CONDITION and whose OPERATIONS includes PUT. Prior to every constraint check, the constraint's variables are bound to the facets of the slot being checked that are referenced in the FACETS facet (if any), and to the values of the slots of the datatype object that are referenced in the SLOTS facet (if any). Then, the constraint is repeatedly checked for every value element (bound to *VALUE*) by sending a message to the VALUE facet of the slot representing the constraint. If a check succeeds and the constraint slot has an ACTION facet,

```
OBJECT: DATATYPE
TYPE: Class
GENERALIZATIONS: ROOT
  DATUM-EDIT:
  DATUM-PRINT:
  DATUM-GET: SYS/MGETVALUE
  DATUM-PUT: DATATYPE-PUT
  DATUM-ADD: DATATYPE-ADD
  DATUM-REMOVE: DATATYPE-REMOVE
  DATUM-ANALYZE-CONSTRAINT: DATATYPE-ANALYZE-CONSTRAINT
  CARDINALITY-CONSTRAINT:
    VALUE: CARDINALITY-CONSTRAINT
    DATATYPE: LISP
    ROLE: DATATYPE-SET-CONDITION
    FACETS: CARDINALITY
    OPERATIONS: (PUT ADD REMOVE)
    CORRECTION: (ERROR *VALUE* "is not within" CARDINALITY)
```

Figure 5: DATATYPE Object For Integrity Management

a message is sent to that facet. If a violation occurs and the slot has a CORRECTION facet, a message is sent to that facet. Actions and corrections have their variables bound to the same values as the constraints. If there is no correction or the correction returns NIL, the current value element is deleted from the assigned value; otherwise, checking proceeds to the next constraint.

Then, the integrity manager checks whether the slot has a CONDITION facet, representing a single-slot element constraint. If such a facet is found and the OPERATIONS facet includes PUT, the constraint in the CONDITION facet is evaluated with its variables bound to the facets of the slot that are referenced in the FACETS facets and for each value elements. Actions and corrections may be invoked as a result.

If after all the element constraints have been applied, there are some elements left in the assigned value, set constraints are applied. Datatype set constraints are represented by the slots whose ROLE facet is set to DATATYPE-SET-CONDITION and OPERATIONS facet includes PUT. The whole assigned value is bound to *VALUE* and may be passed to, and altered by, actions and corrections. The process is repeated if there is a set single-slot constraint represented in the SET-CONDITION facet and if PUT appears in the SET-OPERATIONS facet.

Finally, if all the previous constraints are satisfied, then constraints referenced in the PUT-MULTI-SLOT-CONDITIONS facet of the slot (if it exists), are evaluated until all succeed or one fails. The evaluation of each constraint starts with binding the constraint's variables to the values of the slots of the current object that are listed in the SLOTS facet.

The DATUM-ANALYZE-CONSTRAINT slot contains a function for analyzing constraints. The user can send an ANALYZE-CONSTRAINT message to any slot representing a constraint. The result is the automatic creation and filling of the facets containing integrity checking information (*e.g.*, SLOTS, FACETS, OPERATIONS, PUT-MULTI-SLOT-CONDITIONS).[11]

DATATYPE also defines a general datatype set constraint, called CardinalityConstraint, which allows the user to set minimum and maximum cardinalities for slot values. CardinalityConstraint is checked for all update operations. The facet it uses is CARDINALITY, a dotted pair of the minimum and maximum cardinality (see, for example, MEASUREMENT and UNITS in CHANNEL-FILE).

6 Performance of Declarative Integrity Management

Any form of integrity management slows down the execution of data updates. Declarations may help to the extent that they provide information that can be used to improve efficiency. One the other hand, they may also cost to the extent that they require interpretation. We consider first some ways of reducing the cost of integrity management by providing better declarations, and then the cost of interpreting declarations.

There are at least two ways of making integrity checking cheaper: avoid it, and make it more discriminating. In some cases our integrity manager avoids checking just because of the expected cost. For example, when the VALUE facet of a slot is updated, the constraints in which it is involved are checked, these constraints being readily identified in facets of the slot. However, when a facet other than VALUE is updated, the constraints in which it may be involved, *i.e.*, datatype or single-slot constraints, are not checked. This is because identification of these constraints would require searching the appropriate datatype object and the current slot and because it would necessitate the development of a special mechanism to trap the updates of all facets, which may be expensive.

Integrity checking can be made more discriminating by using better information. An example would be to consider the sources of slot updates. Some sources may be trusted enough that the updates they perform need no checking. Another example could consist of taking advantage of *dependencies* among variables of constraints ([10,15]). A variable in a constraint is *independent* if is not affected by the constraint (*i.e.*, if it may not be updated for the purpose of maintaining the constraint). On the other hand, a *dependent* variable may be updated for maintenance purposes. If the number of such dependencies is significant, performance may be improved by re-scheduling constraint evaluations based on them ([10]). Dependency specifications could be naturally encoded with facets.

As for declarative encoding, one way of reducing its interpretation cost consists of *compiling* high-level declarations into lower-level, more efficient declarations (or even into executable code). For example, quite of bit of integrity management is based on searching objects for slots with particular facet names and/or contents (*e.g.*, slots with a ROLE facet set to DATATYPE-CONDITION and an OPERATIONS facet including PUT). This kind of search has its cost. One way to reduce this cost

[11] The filling of OPERATIONS facets is based on the most probable case, rather than on formal analysis, and therefore, it can be overridden by the user.

is to maintain slot indices that point to the slots having particular facet names and/or contents. Such slot indices are slots themselves. For instance, datatype objects have (or inherit) a PUT-ELEMENT-CONDITIONS slot that points to the slots of the current datatype object which have a ROLE facet filled with DATATYPE-CONDITION and an OPERATIONS facet that includes PUT (similar slots exist to index datatype set conditions as well as ADD and REMOVE operations).

7 Conclusion

We have described a representation system which is useful both as a data model for DBMSs due to its modelling richness, and as a convenient tool for implementing software systems like DBMSs. The latter was illustrated with the implementation of an integrity manager. This approach has also been used for building a system to manage objects on disk files. The intention is to continue building other DBMS features for Strobe, in a similar bootstrapping manner. Of all the DBMSs issues still to face, the most pressing ones at the moment, are improvement of the object-oriented file system and design of a transaction-oriented query language.

Regarding object-oriented file management, current DBMSs are not always of great help. Relational DBMSs for example, tend to group tuples on disk according to their structures (*e.g.,* the tuples of the same relation in the same file), rather than according to their expected or observed patterns of access, and they tend to prefer fixed length-records. (These observations are less true for some CODASYL DBMSs.) More generally, there is a need to handle arbitrary groupings of objects, variable length-records, indexing on slots and facets, efficient implementation of generalizations and of inheritance (along generalizations, datatypes or user-defined relationships), a mixture of data and code, and query optimization that takes into account the fact that objects can be found both in files and in the virtual memory managed by a KRS like Strobe.

One advantage of having the same language, Interlisp-D, as the query and constraint language on one hand, and the language for applications on the other hand, is that data manipulation and applications are unified instead of being separated and under the control of completely different systems, as in current DBMSs. However, there is a need to augment the current query language. This is not for reasons of user friendliness but rather in order to support *(i)* complete automatic derivation of integrity checking information, and *(ii)* transactions for query optimization, integrity management, crash recovery and concurrency control.

Acknowledgements

The participants in the Crystal project are acknowledged for contributing to the framework for this system, especially Eric Schoen who contributed more than his share. Bob Young, Eric Schoen and the referees made valuable comments about an earlier draft of this paper.

References

[1] M. Atkinson, K. Chisholm, and P. Cockshott. PS-Algol: Algol with a persistent heap. *SIG-*

PLAN Notices, 17(7), July 1982.

[2] D. S. Batory and A. P. Buchmann. Molecular objects, abstract data types and data models: a framework. In *Tenth International Conference on Very Large Data Bases*, VLDB, Singapore, 1984.

[3] D. G. Bobrow and M. J. Stefik. *The LOOPS Manual.* Technical Report, Xerox Palo Alto Research Center, December 1983.

[4] R. Davis, H. Austin, I. Carlbom, B. Frawley, P. Pruchnik, R. Sneiderman, and J. A. Gilreath. The Dipmeter Advisor: interpretation of geologic signals. In *Proceedings of the Seventh International Joint Conference on Artificial Intelligence*, pages 846–849, August 1981.

[5] H. Gallaire and J. Minker, editors. *Logic and Data Bases.* Plenum Press, New York, 1978.

[6] Adele Goldberg and David Robson. *Smalltalk-80: The Language and its Implementation.* Addison-Wesley, Reading, MA., 1983.

[7] M. Hammer and S. Sarin. Efficient monitoring of database assertions. In *International Conference On Management of Data*, ACM/SIGMOD, 1978.

[8] *KEE User's Manual.* IntelliGenetics, 3rd edition, 1984.

[9] G. M. E. Lafue. Basic decisions about linking an Expert System with a DBMS: A case study. *IEEE Database Engineering*, 6(4), Dec. 1983.

[10] G. M. E. Lafue. Semantic integrity dependencies and delayed integrity checking. In *Eighth International Conference on Very Large Data Bases*, VLDB, Mexico City, 1982.

[11] G. M. E. Lafue and R. G. Smith. A modular tool kit for knowledge management. In *Proceedings of the Ninth International Joint Conference on Artificial Intelligence*, pages 46–52, August 1985.

[12] R. Lorie. Issues in databases for design applications. In J. Encarnacao and F. Krause, editors, *File Structures and Data Bases for CAD*, North-Holland, 1982.

[13] D. McLeod and R. King. Semantic database model. In S.B. Yao, editor, *Principles of Database Design*, Prentice Hall, 1982.

[14] M. Minsky. A framework for representing knowledge. In P. H. Winston, editor, *The Psychology Of Computer Vision*, McGraw-Hill, 1975.

[15] M. Morgenstern. The role of constraints in databases, expert systems and knowledge representation. In L. Kerschberg, editor, *Expert Database Systems.*

[16] J. Mylopoulos, P. Bernstein, and H. K. T. Wong. A language facility for designing interactive database-intensive applications. *ACM Transactions on Database Systems*, 5(2), 1980.

[17] K. Parsaye. Logic programming and relational databases. *IEEE Database Engineering*, 6(4), Dec. 1983.

[18] E. Schoen and R. G. Smith. Impulse, a display-oriented editor for Strobe. In *Proceedings of the National Conference on Artificial Intelligence*, pages 356–358, August 1983.

[19] A. Shepherd and L. Kerschberg. Constraint management in expert database systems. In L. Kerschberg, editor, *Expert Database Systems.*

[20] A. Shoshani, F. Olken, and H. K. T. Wong. Characteristics of scientific databases. In *Tenth International Conference on Very Large Data Bases*, VLDB, Singapore, 1984.

[21] J. Smith and D. Smith. Database abstractions: aggregation and generalization. *ACM Transactions on Database Systems*, 2(2), June 1977.

[22] R. G. Smith. Strobe: support for structured object knowledge representation. In *Proceedings of the Eighth International Joint Conference on Artificial Intelligence*, pages 855–858, August 1983.

[23] R. G. Smith, G. M. E. Lafue, E. Schoen, and S. C. Vestal. Declarative task description as a user interface structuring mechanism. *Computer*, 17(9):29–38, September 1984.

[24] R. G. Smith and R. L. Young. The design of the Dipmeter Advisor System. In *Proceedings of the ACM Annual Conference*, pages 15–23, ACM, New York, October 1984.

[25] S. Tsur and C. Zaniolo. An implementation of GEM - supporting a semantic data model on a relational back-end. In *International Conference On Management of Data*, ACM/SIGMOD, 1984.

[26] Y. Vassiliou, J. Clifford, and M. Jarke. How does an expert system get its data? In *Ninth International Conference on Very Large Data Bases*, 1983.

The Role of Constraints in Databases, Expert Systems, and Knowledge Representation

Matthew Morgenstern

SRI International
333 Ravenswood Ave.
Menlo Park, Calif. 94025

Abstract

There are similarities between the representation of inter-relational constraints in databases and the representation of knowledge in some expert systems. Several avenues of interaction among databases, knowledge representation frameworks, and expert systems are explored in this paper. Attention is then focused on the representation and use of constraints as as a unifying paradigm applicable to these superficially different systems. The recent development of Constraint Equations provides a concise declarative language for expressing inter-relational constraints in database schemata, and helps to extend the KL-ONE knowledge representation system. These Constraint Equations have a more natural and perspicuous structure than the predicate calculus formulas into which they may be translated, and they conveniently express both universal and existential quantifiers. For a subclass of these constraint expressions, a prototype compiler automatically generates programs which incorporate a structured set of condition-action rules to enforce these constraints and perform the actions needed to reestablish consistency.

1. Introduction

There are similarities between the representation of inter-relational constraints in databases and the representation of knowledge in some expert systems. In this paper we explore the concept of constraints as as a unifying paradigm for a variety of superficially different systems which demonstrate expertise.

In addition, we consider other means of interaction between expert systems and databases that offer potential benefits. For example, database technology will become more important to Expert systems as the latter utilize increasingly large databases of rules and facts. In the other direction, Expert systems can aid database design and query optimization. And the similarities between database schema and knowledge representation frameworks may help to extend the semantics expressible in schemata.

Knowledge and expertise can be perceived as consisting of representation and performance. Paralleling the distinction made in [Steele80], the *representation* component contains the factual information and statements of relationships that ultimately define the desired result. The *performance* component then deals with the strategy and tactics for manipulating and combining this information so as to actually achieve this result efficiently. Constraint expressions help provide the *representation* of what the system is to achieve. The constraint propagation and maintenance strategies provide the *performance* component of how the system is realized.

Some of the differences among systems which demonstrate expertise arise from the different needs of these systems and, in turn, the different way in which the logical constraints (often implicit) of an application are transformed into programs. In comparing knowledge based systems, we find that alternative uses of the same information can give rise to different implementations as a result of the differing efficiency concerns of these systems.

A potential benefit of looking at several forms of knowledge representation as deriving from a common concept of constraints is that the same representation of knowledge may be utilized in different ways for different problems, rather than using different systems for parts of the same expertise. Furthermore, a common foundation provides a handle on the issue of multiple representations for alternative problem solving strategies.

Previous work on constraint-based systems include [Borning79], [Fikes81], [Steele80], [Stefik80], and [Sussman80]. Lafue has studied delayed enforcement of integrity constraints [Lafue82], and his paper in this volume [Lafue84] touches on this issue. The Shepherd and Kerschberg paper in this volume illustrates the prevalence of constraints in different kinds of systems, and also describes the way in which they chose to represent constraints in their PRISM system [Shepherd84].

Here we describe the recent development of Constraint Equations, which provides a declarative representation for inter-relational constraints, as well as constraints involving several database objects. The specifics of this representation are presented together with their application in extending the KL-ONE knowledge representation system. A subset of these Constraint Equations can be automatically enforced in a database which supports triggers, as described below.

2. Constraints and Rule-based Systems

Real world expertise must be structured in a useful form, stored, and efficiently accessed. Rule based expert systems require at least a Rule Database (RDB) of production (condition-action) rules, as well as a database of currently true assertions -- typically referred to as the Working Memory (WM). In addition, some expert systems utilize a large Fact Database describing the problem domain at hand -- this database may be separate or may be combined with either the Rule Database or Working Memory, depending upon system architecture. For example, in the ACE system for analysis of telephone cables [Vesonder83], a large separate database already existed, and the expert system utilized it both for its record of recent problems and for its information as to the layout of the telephone network.

The production rules found in expert systems describe consequences of certain information, and typically can be expressed in the form that *if* certain conditions are true *then* take certain actions. Often these actions will assert additional information (the deletion of information is ignored for the moment). Forward chaining operation of a production rule system creates a succession of production rule activations and consequent assertions of additional information. It is a data driven inference process in which all derivable data is explicitly computed subject to the rules and then stored. These rules thus can be viewed as constraints between the facts which enabled the rule and the resultant derived data.

We could view a rule-based system as a means of maintaining a complex database which is governed by the rules, or constraints, of the system. This similarity is more evident if we consider the memory of the rule system to be cumulative and to contain all facts which have been asserted. The production rules then correspond to derivation rules (or integrity constraints) for the database in which all derivable data is explicitly stored.

The initial action which begins the sequence of rule invocations manifests itself as an assertion. This could be an observation of a malfunction of some system, and the resultant rule activations can derive and store the set of suspect defective components which are to be analyzed further. In the same manner, the initiating action may be the addition of a new employee to a database, and the resultant derivation process executes all consequential changes which are to be made to personnel, benefits, salary files, etc.

Constraints express relationships which must hold between different pieces of information. Inter-relational constraints and logic formulae are non-procedural representations of knowledge which can be used in alternative performance engines -- eg. for forward inference or backward chaining. Similarly, production rules can be interpreted as constraints/theorems which also can be used in both directions depending upon the need. Though on the surface there may appear to be directionality of use, from the condition part to the action part, production rules often can be used in the reverse direction too. For example, given a set of such rules and the fact that a certain action has occurred, we can determine which rules could have had that effect and what conditions could have enabled those rules.

An example of such operation for a rule-based system is found in EMYCIN [Hayes-Roth83], which uses goal-driven backward chaining to determine the set of facts needed to support an hypothesis. This strategy helps to determine, for example, the set of laboratory tests needed to diagnose a suspected illness. The rules of such a system are a form of constraint between initial findings and diagnoses. The goal-driven exploration of the constraint network is a way of dynamically determining the dependency structure and logical support for an hypothesized outcome.

3. Database Schema and Semantic Networks

Database schema present a limited but useful set of declarative semantics for an application. The particular semantics expressed depend on the data model, and may include the keys for unique identification of data, functional and multi-valued dependencies, existence and update dependences, etc. The similarity to semantic network style knowledge representation systems such as KL-ONE [KL1] is best seen with respect to the entity-relation data model [Chen76], the entity-based Daplex model [Shipman81], and to some extent with respect to the binary relational model [Abrial].

In these data models, attributes are organized around entities -- also referred to as objects[1] -- and are associated with them by binary relations. The value of an attribute may be either a literal value or an object instance. Entities may be of different types, and in Daplex the types may be organized into a type hierarchy or a lattice. The fact that a jet plane and a propeller plane are types of aircraft may be directly represented in the type structure of the schema. Thus a 747 type of plane would inherit the schematic attributes or characteristics of aircraft as well as the special attributes appropriate to a jet plane.

The parallel to the KL-ONE knowledge representation system is considerable. KL-ONE is a semantic network of typed concepts having roles which are restricted as to the number and the type of fillers for each role. The type structure is a lattice which allows inheritance from multiple superconcepts. A concept corresponds to the object or entity of a database model. Roles correspond to the binary relations which define the attributes of an entity, and which may limit the number of attribute values which are allowed.

An important aspect of the KL-ONE system is the automatic classification of a newly defined concept with respect to the existing semantic network, based upon the type of the concept and the types of the concepts which fill its roles, etc. In effect, this classification process determines at concept creation time certain implications or inferences deducible from the semantic network/schema. Such automatic classification is useful for large KL-ONE semantic nets which arise in applications such as natural language understanding and in modelling of user interfaces to computer systems. The classification process does not have a direct parallel in common database applications, though a similar process could be important when issues such as incremental changes to database schema and evolution of databases are given careful attention.

4. Constraints in Database Systems

A database application is, in some sense, a model of a portion of the real world. The integrity and consistency of a database require that a variety of implicit and explicit constraints be maintained among the data. An accurate model of the world would require many constraints which are not captured by typical database schemata. Such semantic constraints too often are either ignored or are implicit in the protocol of use rather than being explicitly stated and enforced by the system.

There are several ways in which constraints can arise in databases. They may express application dependent rules for consistency among several data objects and relationships -- thereby enabling the database system itself to know what dependent changes must be made when updates occur to

---

[1]not to be confused with the *objects* discussed in hypergraph-based models; see [Maier83] and [Morgenstern85]

certain data objects or relationships. Constraints thus help to define and delimit the behavior of the system as the database changes. Rules for derived data also are a form of constraint between the resultant data and the components on which it depends. Whether or not there is a distinction between consistency rules and derived data is largely a matter of which data is stored and one's perspective.

Views also involve constraints, since the selection and possible transformation of the underlying data establishes constraints between the base data and the information presented in the view. Capabilities for incremental browsing and for interaction directly with the data presented in views [Morgenstern83] will require that the constraints defining the view be enforceable in both directions wherever possible. Three forms of dynamic change need to be supported: (1) updates to the view directly [Dayal78], (2) dynamic maintenance of the view as the underlying data changes, (3) and dynamic maintenance of the visible information as the view definition is modified by the user.

Schema declarations currently provide a very limited set of constraints which supplement the actual data. For example, one may determine from different schemata the relations which connect attributes or entities, the keys of a relation, or the allowed multiplicity for attributes. The various data models differ with respect to their coverage of these constraints and the defaults they assume. By expressing these constraints and dependencies explicitly, the perceived differences between these data models would be reduced. We then would be better able to see how the constraints inherent in one data model are represented or not by another data model. In a similar manner, transformations among different data models can be expressed as constraints which define and enforce the translation among these multiple representations [Morgenstern81].

5. Constraint Equations

Constraint Equations (CEs) provide a concise declarative language for expressing invariant relationships which must hold among specified data objects involving several relations. This is preferable to writing procedural code to express and enforce the constraints. Furthermore, the declarative Constraint Equations have an executable interpretation, and can be compiled directly into routines for automatic maintenance of the Constraints. This case of automated generation of programs from constraint specifications has been demonstrated in the prototype implementation.

The declarative nature of Constraint Equations together with their executable interpretation have an analogy with algebraic equations. For example, the equation `X = Y + Z` is a declarative statement of an equivalence between the expressions on either side. If this is to be treated as a constraint which is to be maintained by the system, then there is an executable interpretation which may be thought of as two condition-action rules: (1) if Y and/or Z change, then revise the value of X accordingly, and (2) if X changes, select between the alternatives of disallowing the change, revising Y, or Z, or both.

The following example of a Constraint Equation (CE) in an entity-relationship database specifies that the Projects of a Manager are to be the same as the set of Projects which his/her Employees work on.

```
MANAGER.PROJECT  ==  MANAGER.EMPLOYEE.PROJECT
```

Here the dot "." may be thought of as standing in for the relationship between the entities (objects) appearing on either side of it. In general, the dot allows a form of ellipsis in which the attribute or entity name may be omitted.

The CE may be read from left to right as "the Manager's Projects are the same as the Manager's Employee's Projects." Since MANAGER begins the path of associations on both sides of the CE, it serves as the *Anchor* or common binding for both paths. The CE is to hold for each instance of Manager in the database.

Each side of the CE describes a sequence of relations from the Anchor on the left to the *Target* object on the right of the path. There will be a set of one or more Target instances associated with one Anchor instance by these relationships. This CE says that the sets of Projects that arise from both sides must be equal, and that this must be true for each Manager.

The *Path Expression* on each side of a Constraint Equation is an abbreviated representation for a sequence of data objects and relationships from the schema for the application. The elided components are determined by comparing the abbreviated path with the database schema. Consider the following partial Entity schema, where the indicated attributes of Manager are the only ones directly relating it to an Employee and to a Project. (The -->> symbol denotes a multi-valued attribute.)

```
MANAGER  Entity
         OVERSEES -->> PROJECT
         MANAGES  -->> EMPLOYEE

EMPLOYEE Entity
         WORKSON -->> PROJECT
```

The translation of the above Constraint Equation from abbreviated Path Expressions into the fully expanded *Connection Paths* is shown here:

```
[ (MANAGER) OVERSEES (PROJECT) ]  =

[(MANAGER) MANAGES (EMPLOYEE) WORKSON (PROJECT)]
```

In general, a simple *Connection Path* is a sequence of the form:

```
[ (E0) R1 (E1) R2 ... RN (EN) ] ,
```

where Ei denotes an entity (object) type, and Ri denotes a (binary) relationship/attribute from E_{i-1} to Ei. (Entities are shown in parentheses when there may be ambiguity between the names of entities and relationships.)

A Connection Path defines a derived relation Rcp in terms of a sequence of Joins over relations Ri. For each pair of relations Ri and R_{i+1} shown above, the natural join is taken with respect to their common domain (Ei). The tuples resulting from the whole path are then projected onto the domains E0 and En, which are the *Source* and *Target* domains, respectively, of the Connection Path.

When a set of instances is provided for domain E0 (or En) of the derived relation Rcp, the Connection Path defines the selection of tuples from Rcp based on these instances, and their projection onto the other domain -- thus providing a mapping from one set of instances to a related set of instances. In particular, for one instance of the Anchor E0, the Connection Path provides a mapping to a set of Target instances, En. Also, a *composition* of Paths is itself a new Connection Path which defines a derived relation. Thus a Connection Path, or composition of subpaths, can be used wherever a relation is used in a Constraint Equation.

5.1. CEs in Logic

Constraint Equations can be viewed as a compact shorthand for a class of predicate calculus constraints. Consider the following generic CE expressed in abbreviated form and then expanded into the full Connection Paths:

```
E0.E1   = E0.E2.E3

[ (E0) R1 (E1) ] = [ (E0) R2 (E2) R3 (E3) ]
```

Each relation may be viewed as a binary predicate, such as R1(E0, E1). Since each side of the CE is a derived (binary) relation, the equality of the two sides may be expressed in predicate calculus with set notation as follows:

$$\{ (E0\ E1) \mid R1(E0\ E1) \} =$$

$$\{ (E0\ E3) \mid \exists E2\ (R2(E0\ E2) \wedge R3(E2\ E3)) \}$$

An alternative formulation emphasizes the fact that a CE may be thought of as being implicitly iterated over the instances of the Anchor E0.

$$\forall E0\ \{ E1 \mid R1(E0\ E1) \}$$

$$= \{ E3 \mid \exists E2\ (R2(E0\ E2) \wedge R3(E2\ E3)) \}$$

Here, each E0 instance serves as an Anchor by providing a common binding for both sides. And each side defines a mapping to a set of Target instances -- the Target sets for the left and right sides being {E1} and {E3}. The CE constrains these two sets to be equal for any such Anchor instance.

5.2. Path Quantifiers

The set-oriented semantics of Constraint Equations can naturally express a spectrum of quantifiers, including existential and universal quantifiers. Existential quantifiers are implicit in CEs. For the CEs we have discussed above, the two Connection Paths comprising a CE have had existential quantification on all intermediate objects along the Connection Path (other than the Anchor and Target objects). This means that each such Path produces the *union* of the Target instances for an Anchor.

The *Universal quantifier* is needed for a constraint such as: the Projects of a Department are those Projects on which all the Employees of that Department work. In other words, *the Projects of a Department are those which are common to every Employee of that Department.* This notion of commonness to all sets of instances arising from a (possibly derived) association is represented as a *Path Intersection Quantifier* " ∩/ " -- which replaces the implicit union for a path with an explicit *intersection over* the Target sets. This example is represented as:

```
DEPARTMENT.PROJECT  =  [DEPARTMENT.EMPLOYEE ∩/ PROJECT]
```

We may expand this CE into a full Connection Path using the previous entity definitions together with the following Department entity:

```
DEPARTMENT entity
           DIRECTS -->> PROJECT
           EMPLOYS -->> EMPLOYEE

[ (DEPARTMENT) DIRECTS (PROJECT) ]  =

[ (DEPARTMENT) EMPLOYS (EMPLOYEE) ∩/ (EMPLOYEE) WORKSON (PROJECT) ]
```

The Path Quantifier on the right side of this expanded CE is expressed as an intersection over the subsets of Projects, one such subset for each and every Employee of that Department (ie. each Employee works on a subset of Projects). The resulting intersection contains just those Projects which are common to these Employees. The CE requires that this set of common Projects is to be equal to the set of Projects which the Department directs. We can express this constraint in terms of predicate calculus with set notation as follows:

```
∀DEPARTMENT

{ PROJECT | DIRECTS(DEPARTMENT PROJECT) }
=
{ PROJECT | ∃EMPLOYEE ( EMPLOYS(DEPARTMENT EMPLOYEE) ) ∧
            ∀EMPLOYEE ( EMPLOYS(DEPARTMENT EMPLOYEE) ⇒
                        WORKSON(EMPLOYEE PROJECT) ) }
```

In the second set expression above, a Project is included in the resulting set if *all* Employees of the Department work on that Project. Note that the first clause of this set expression requires the existence of least one Employee in the Department. This clause is needed here to ensure that the predicate calculus Universal Quantifier does not become satisfied for each and every Project in the case that there are no Employees in a Department! Such a clause might be too easily overlooked when writing the predicate calculus expression, but it is taken care of automatically by the semantics of the *Path Intersection* quantifier.

Consider the general Path Intersection expression and its expansion into a full Connection Path:

[E1 . E2 ∩/ E3 . E4]

[(E1) R2 (E2) ∩/ (E2) R3 (E3) R4 (E4)] .

For an E1 instance, this path yields *those* E4 *instances which are common to every* E2 -- ie. an E4 instance is related to an E1 by this path if this E4 is related to every E2 associated with this E1. The universal quantifier applies to the entity E2 which immediately precedes the Path Intersection symbol (∩/) in the expressions above. The scope of the universal quantifier is the immediately containing bracketed path expression. The other intermediate objects along the path (here E3) are existentially quantified as usual:

$$\{ (E1\ E4) \mid \exists E2\ (\ R2(E1\ E2)\ ) \wedge \forall E2\ (\ R2(E1\ E2) \Rightarrow \exists E3\ (\ R3(E2\ E3) \wedge R4(E3\ E4)\ ))\ \} .$$

Since this represents a derived relation Rcp(E1, E4), the above Path Intersection expression (from E1 to E4) can be used as part of a larger Path. Thus quantified expressions can be nested within each other.

5.3. Spectrum of Quantifiers

The Path Quantifier concept may be extended to provide a spectrum of quantification capabilities ranging from existential to universal quantifiers. In particular, universal quantification required above that E4 be related to *every* E2, whereas existential quantification requires that E4 be related to *at least one* E2 for an Anchor instance.

We define ${}_{m}\cap/_{n}$ to be a *Limited Path Quantifier*. If it is used in place of the unconditional intersection quantifier ∩/ above, it means that an E4 instance is included if it is related (for a given E1) to at least m E2 instances and not more than n E2 instances. We let |E2| denote the size of the set of E2's which are related to the given E1. The upper bound n defaults to this set size |E2|, and may be different for each Anchor instance. The lower bound m defaults to the smaller of the upper bound and |E2| -- so these defaults are consistent with the unsubscripted path intersection symbol ∩/ .

For example, the constraint that a Department is responsible for helping to direct a Project if at least three employees of that Department are working on the Project, may be written as:

DEPARTMENT.PROJECT = [DEPARTMENT ${}_{3}\cap/$ EMPLOYEE.PROJECT]

It can be seen that for the previous path from E1, ${}_{|E2|}\cap/$ is equivalent to the unconditional *Path Intersection* (universal) quantifier $\cap/$, since this explicit lower bound requires that for an E4 to be included in the result, it must be related to *all* E2s of an E1. Furthermore ${}_{1}\cap/$ is equivalent to the *existential quantifier*, since for an E4 to qualify, it must be related to just *one* or more E2s. Thus we have a spectrum of quantifiers.

6. Constraint Equations and KL-ONE Representation of Knowledge

The KL-ONE [Schmolze83] semantic network discussed above is a taxonomy of *concepts* (intentional objects) which are related by specialization -- indicated by a superconcept (is-a) link. The attributes of a concept are referred to as roles, and may include restrictions such as the number and type of values that may fill the role. Role Constraints (role value maps) are intended as a way of mutually restricting the values that may fill two or more roles. As an example, a Role Constraint for a locally employed person (LE-PERSON) is that his/her home is in the same city as the company which employs the person. The following KL-ONE diagram from [Moser83] shows this requirement.

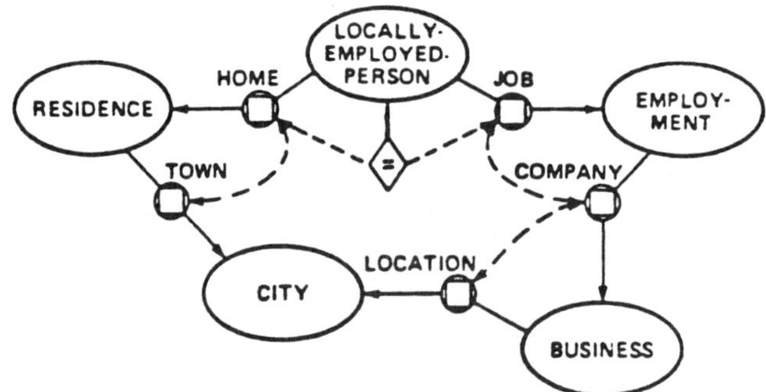

A Constraint Equation which represents this constraint is shown in both its abbreviated and complete path forms:

```
LE-PERSON.HOME.TOWN  =
LE-PERSON.JOB.COMPANY.LOCATION
```

```
[ (LE-PERSON) HOME (RESIDENCE) TOWN (CITY) ] =
 [(LE-PERSON) JOB (EMPLOYMENT) COMPANY (BUSINESS) LOCATION (CITY)]
```

Thus far, universal quantifiers have not been expressible in KL-ONE.[2] However, the universal quantifier is captured by Path Intersection in a Constraint Equation. If the person in this example worked for more than one business, then the requirement might be that the LE-Person

---

[2]Some consideration had been given by KL-ONE designers to the use of a separate predicate to filter the cross product of values from the several roles, and thereby select those combinations which mutually satisfy the Role Constraint [Bobrow83].

must live in a city in which all these Businesses have locations. This constraint may be expressed by the following CE -- where the intersection is over the sets of cities arising from the businesses of that LE-Person:

LE-PERSON.HOME.TOWN $\subseteq$

LE-PERSON.JOB.COMPANY $\cap$/ LOCATION

As another example of a constraint that has not been expressible in KL-ONE, consider the requirement that a person's friends are those people who are friends of *all* his/her brothers. This is represented by the following CE:

PERSON.FRIEND = [PERSON.BROTHER $\cap$/ FRIEND]

If the CE did not include the Path Intersection ($\cap$/), then any friend of any brother would be one of the person's friends, rather than requiring friendship with all the brothers in order to qualify.

Thus Constraint Equations overlap with other knowledge representation schemes, and they provide a natural extension to the already rich KL-ONE semantic network.

7. Condition-Action Rules for Constraint Equation Enforcement

When changes occur to the database, one or more Constraint Equations may be affected. The interpretation of a Constraint Equation as a structured set of condition-action rules provides the basis for automatic enforcement of the constraints. If there is no way of reestablishing the constraint, then the initial change will not be accepted. Usually however, the rules can determine and execute the consequential actions which are needed.

A condition-action rule which helps to enforce a consistency constraint would state the change or combination of changes to the data which serve as the condition for activating the rule. And it would indicate the action to be taken -- typically an expression of how to reinstate consistency. Other forms of action might be to disallow the change, provide information to the user, or invoke a more general procedure to execute an arbitrary action.

When a change occurs to a relationship on one side of a CE, a compensating change may be made to a relationship on the other side in order to reestablish satisfaction of the constraint. Since there may be more than one relation on a side, the one to change is indicated by the "!" symbol to the left of or in place of a relation name (the "!" is used in lieu of the dot "."). The designated relation can be thought of as a *weak bond*, since it is more readily modified in response to an initial change to the other side of the CE.

As an example, consider the constraint that an Employee's Phone's Backup (the extension which takes messages when the phone is busy or does not answer) is the same as the Employee's Project's Secretary's Phone. This is expressed by the following CE:

```
EMPLOYEE.PHONE!BACKUP  =  EMPLOYEE.PROJECT.SECRETARY.PHONE
```

The designation of a weak bond on the left indicates that if any of the associations on the right change (eg. a Project's Secretary) then the Backup extension for the Employee's Phone will be changed. The absence of a weak bond on the right indicates that a change directly to the relations on the left is *not* allowed *if* it would cause a violation of the constraint. For example, the Employee's Phone could be changed to any other Phone having the same Backup without violating the constraint. Alternative update semantics are specifiable as discussed below.

The update semantics are rather obvious when relationships are single valued, and are well defined when relationships are multi-valued. For example, if an Employee changes to a different Project, and all the relationships, except the changed relation and the weak bond relation, are single valued, then the Secretary's Phone is clearly defined, and there is a simple change of Backup extension for that Employee's Phone. On the other hand, if a Secretary for a Project changes, then multiple Employees will be affected by the consequential change to the Backup extension.

As another example, consider the CE presented earlier where a Manager oversees those Projects his/her Employees work on:

```
MANAGER!PROJECT = MANAGER!EMPLOYEE.PROJECT
```

The weak bond on each side here indicates that Projects stay with the Employee if there are any other changes. Thus if a Manager adds a Project, then he adds those Employee(s) who work on that Project.

The Constraint Equation specifications are used by the CE Compiler to automatically generate a set of such condition-action rules -- one for each relation that may change in the Equation.[3] The condition part of such a rule indicates the relation change which would activate this rule. The action or response indicates a relation of the CE to which the compensating change should be made. Thus for the above CE, the following condition-action rules are generated by the CE compiler (shown here in abbreviated form):

```
IF MANAGER.EMPLOYEE is-changed  THEN  revise MANAGER.PROJECT
IF EMPLOYEE.PROJECT is-changed  THEN  revise MANAGER.PROJECT
IF MANAGER.PROJECT  is-changed  THEN  revise MANAGER.EMPLOYEE
```

The specific revisions that occur in response to an update follow from the invariant condition represented by the CE. When the revision is completed by the appropriate rule, the CE will be satisfied, so that the consequential changes do not result in a cycle of rule activations within a

[3]The CE Compiler currently accepts existentially quantified CEs, with universal and cardinality quantifiers planned for the next version.

CE. For example, the last rule above indicates that if a Manager takes charge of an existing Project, then the rule may add Employees to the Manages relation for that Manager. Based on the original CE, the complete rule will find and add all those Employees who Workon that Project. The result will now satisfy the CE.

7.1. Specialized Update Semantics

The algorithms stated above assume that a change to one side of a CE may be responded to by a change to the designated weak bond relation on the other side. There are cases when a change warrants different responses. We provide this by annotations which express exception rule(s). The normal update rule that would be generated by the CE compiler is then replaced by the exception rule which has the same condition part.

In the exception rule, the condition part may also indicate the type(s) of change (insertion, deletion, update) which are to trigger this rule. The action or response may be of arbitrary complexity, but typically indicates a relation of the CE to which the compensating change should be made -- thus allowing the weak bond relation to be conditional on which change occurred. In addition, if a predicate is provided on the action side, it is taken as a filter which limits the creation of new instances for the selected weak bond relation in the insertion algorithm. The filter can monitor the initial changes and thus can conditionally reject invalid changes by disallowing compensating actions.

The following CE is similar to the one presented earlier, except that here the semantics indicate that a change of Manager for an Employee changes the Projects the Employee works on. The additional rule overrides the base semantics of the weak bond on the left side of the CE. The rule is invoked when the relationship indicated by MANAGER.EMPLOYEE is changed, and the response is to treat the relation EMPLOYEE.PROJECT as the weak bond for this case.

```
MANAGER ! PROJECT = MANAGER ! EMPLOYEE.PROJECT
    except
    IF MANAGER.EMPLOYEE is-changed  THEN  revise EMPLOYEE.PROJECT
```

Another example is repeated below with a new response. Here a change of the Project's Secretary would cause the compensating change to be made to the Phone of the new Secretary -- in order that the Backup number (and the phone associated with the Project) stay the same:

```
EMPLOYEE.PHONE ! BACKUP  =  EMPLOYEE.PROJECT.SECRETARY.PHONE
    except
    IF PROJECT.SECRETARY is-changed  THEN  revise  SECRETARY.PHONE
```

8. Constraint Maintenance - Implementation Strategies

8.1. Indices for Rule Triggering

The efficiency of the recognize-act cycle of rule-based Expert systems can benefit from specialized application of database indexing strategies. Each cycle recognizes which rules are enabled and selects the rule whose action part is then executed -- thus the efficiency of this cycle is of central importance. Condition-Action rules are considered enabled when their condition part is satisfied by the assertions in Working Memory (WM). The action part of such rules may add or delete elements in WM, potentially changing the enabled status of other rules. A straightforward approach to determining which rules are activated would retest each condition of each rule on each cycle. For large expert systems having many rules, such an approach would become prohibitively expensive.

Analysis of the Rule Database (RDB) can produce a discrimination net of the rules -- this is essentially a hierarchically structured index of the rules based upon the token types and/or relations referenced in the condition part of each rule. Furthermore, since the enabled status of a rule can change only due to changes in WM, the status of these rules can be treated differentially. That is, the subconditions of each rule which have already been satisfied can be remembered so that the discrimination index can be used to determine just the changed effects on subcondition satisfaction due to a change in WM [McDermott78, Hayes-Roth75]. When the complete condition for a rule becomes satisfied, the rule is enabled. If multiple rules are simultaneously enabled, then the Conflict Resolution Strategy of the system determines the next rule to execute.

In a straightforward implementation of the recognize-act cycle, the cost of recognizing the enabled rules could grow as the product of the sizes of the RDB and WM. The use of a discrimination index and a table of partially satisfied subconditions of rules can allow the cost of each recognition phase to be relatively insensitive to the size of RDB and the WM. The approach described in [McDermott78] has a cost which is linear in the number of rules which have not been disqualified -- ie. could be enabled on subsequent cycles.

8.2. Constraint Propagation Strategies

In its broadest sense, one might say that the implementation of programs corresponds to the choice of strategies for constraint propagation and maintenance. More immediately, it might be interesting to determine how many problem solving algorithms can be described as specialized methods of solving a system of constraints. This section discusses strategies for propagation and maintenance of constraints, and does so in the context of Constraint Equations, though the techniques are generally applicable.

Straightforward maintenance of the CEs utilizes a triggering mechanism. Condition-action update rules are generated from a CE as described above. The executable representation of such a rule is referred to as a demon. It is invoked when database changes occur to satisfy the condition part of the rule. As the number of constraints increases, the efficiency of this maintenance becomes important, and a range of alternative strategies needs to be explored. One spectrum for constraint maintenance may be characterized by *when* the constraint is enforced.

Another dimension for optimization of constraint maintenance is *aggregation of constraints.* Since the activation of a CE can result in additional changes to relationships, a chain of activations of several CEs may arise. Each such activation serves to propagate the consequences of the initial change. Aggregation of individual constraints into compound constraints can optimize constraint maintenance by reducing the overhead for triggering and by eliminating redundant access and update operations. Similar issues regarding constraint propagation arise in truth maintenance systems [Doyle78].

Along the dimension of *when* propagation is done, the most obvious approach is that maintenance of the constraint be done immediately when the original change occurs -- this is naturally referred to as *immediate propagation.* Alternatively, maintenance can be delayed until the dependent attribute is retrieved -- *propagation when used.* Maintenance can be delayed even further when timeliness of the data is not critical to the user, such as for aggregate data based upon slowly changing values -- *scheduled propagation.*

Between immediate propagation and propagation when used is an intermediate strategy of *delayed constraint propagation* and maintenance -- in which the time of propagation is based upon other criteria. This option has been referred to as *opportunistic propagation* -- both in the sense of doing the work of constraint propagation when the computer is idle, and in the sense of using priority ranking of the constraints to select the order in which they should be considered for propagation.

When maintenance of the constraint is delayed until use, there is the additional option of whether to store the dependent value or association which has been derived. If not stored, then we have the common approach for *derived data,* in which the derivation is done anew for each reference -- a useful choice if updates are expected more frequently than retrievals. On the other hand, the newly derived value may be stored for reuse later -- this is a form of *caching* the values, and also is referred to as a *memo function*[4] in some artificial intelligence applications.

When maintenance of the constraint is done opportunistically (delayed propagation), the derived value must be cached or memoized. Whatever the reason for caching, when a change occurs to the database, all constraints and derived data that depend on that changed data must be alerted that any previously cached data may be dirty, that is, may be invalid. This can be a difficult problem if the chain of dependencies is long.

[4]That is, a *memo* is made of this derived value. When subsequent access is attempted, if this memo value is still valid, then it is used, otherwise recalculation occurs. In either case the results are the same, but the efficiency may differ. The set of indexed memo values may be thought of as a *memo function.*

Furthermore, both the semantics of the application and operational statistics -- including frequency of use, selectivity, and sparseness -- can be used to improve the efficiency of constraint propagation and maintenance. For example, the constraints may be given priorities relative to the application, and these priorities used to determine the order of propagation. Also, if old data can be tolerated by the application, then additional flexibility is possible for delaying the propagation of constraints until some scheduled point in time.

These alternatives as to when propagation is done are related to the notions of *forward chaining* and *backward chaining* -- which characterize the *direction* along which a chain of associations or logical inferences is followed. Forward chaining starts from the updated stored data, following the chain of associations or inferences forward to the consequences. Backward chaining characterizes the process of following the chain of associations from the dependent consequent object (or goal) which is being accessed, back to the source data to determine if changes might affect this dependent object (and rederiving information as needed). Thus *immediate propagation* of constraints dictates *forward chaining*, while (re)calculation of *derived data* upon use gives rise to a form of *backward chaining.*

The efficiency of constraint maintenance also is affected by the efficiency of access to objects, attributes, and relationships. Software caching of relevant indexes, and of object instances which are retrieved from secondary storage, can be helpful. Several forms of compile time aggregation can be used to avoid duplicated access to the same data. For example, several separately specified Constraint Equations can be aggregated into one demon or procedure based upon either (a) a common triggering pattern -- *parallel aggregation*, or (b) based upon a chain of constraints such that one constraint takes an action which serves as a trigger for another constraint -- *chained aggregation*. More elaborate compile time analysis could determine which user programs have the potential of triggering specific constraints, and then *open coding* these constraints into those programs.

The alternatives for constraint propagation and maintenance which have been highlighted here include: the relative time at which constraint propagation is executed, the direction of such propagation, remembering newly derived results, caching of information obtained from slower storage media when cost of re-access and likelihood of re-use are high, aggregation of constraints to reduce net overhead, and open-coding the constraints into those programs which could trigger these constraints.

In the long term, the database or rule-based expert system should be taking an active role in monitoring its own performance and incrementally reorganizing itself to adapt to a changing environment. Such dynamic optimization might well utilize an internal rule-based expert system to determine which improvements are cost effective and how they are best accomplished.

9. Conclusion

The different types of constraints which arise in databases, semantic network representations, and rule-based systems may well warrant different implementations due to the different ways in which these constraints are utilized. However, when efficiency is put aside, part of the conceptual representation which underlies these systems shows greater similarity of the concepts and constructs than is commonly acknowledged. The efficiency issues then may be seen as strategies for constraint propagation and maintenance relative to the different uses of constraints -- these efficiency issues being the primary reasons for the different structures of these problem solving systems.

Constraint Equations (CEs) have been described as an example of what such a constraint paradigm might include. CEs provide a concise declarative representation for modularly expressing a variety of inter-relational constraints in application-based terms. CEs have a more natural and perspicuous structure than the predicate calculus formulas into which they may be translated. Yet a form of both universal and existential quantifiers are expressible conveniently in CEs.

Automatic constraint enforcement is provided in the prototype implementation by compilation of a basic CE specification into the equivalent of condition-action rules. The code which is generated will perform the actions needed to reestablish consistency. Since the activation of a Constraint Equation can result in additional database changes, a chain of activations of several Constraint Equations may arise. The set of such activations defines the consequences of the initial change. Strategies for such constraint propagation include *when* the propagation is done as well as potential aggregations of constraints.

References

[Abrial] J.R. Abrial, *Data Semantics*, in Data Base Management, eds. Klimbie and Koffeman, 1974, pp.1-60.

[Bobrow83] Rusty Bobrow, *NIKL - A New Implementation of KL-ONE*, Bolt Beranek and Newman, Cambridge, Mass., January 1983, draft.

[Borning79] Alan Borning, *Thinglab - A Constraint-Oriented Simulation Laboratory*, Stanford Univ. report STAN-CS-79-746, July 1979, Ph.D. thesis.

[Chen76] P.P.S. Chen, *The Entity-Relationship Model: Toward a Unified View of Data*, ACM Trans. on Database Sys., vol.1, no.1, March 1976, pp.9-36.

[Doyle78] Jon Doyle, *Truth Maintenance Systems for Problem Solving*, Masters Thesis, M.I.T., January 1978, A.I. TR-419, 97pp.

[Dayal78] U. Dayal & P.A. Bernstein, On The Updatability Of Relational Views, Proc. 4th Very Large Data Base Conf. West Berlin, Sept. 1978.

[Fikes81] Richard E. Fikes, *Odyssey: A Knowledge-Based Assistant*, Artificial Intelligence Jour., v.16, 1981, pp.331-361.

[Hayes-Roth75] Fredrick Hayes-Roth and David J. Mostow, *An Automatically Compilable Recognition Network for Structured Patterns*, 4th Int'l Conf on A.I. (IJCAI), Sept 1975, pp.246-252.

[Hayes-Roth83] Fredrick Hayes-Roth, Donald Waterman, & Douglas Lenat, eds., *Building Expert Systems*, Addison-Wesley Pubs., 1983.

[KL1] Proc of the 1981 KL-ONE Workshop, eds James G. Schmolze and Ronald J. Brachman, May 1982.

[Lafue82] G.M.E. Lafue, *Semantic Integrity Dependencies and Delayed Integrity Checking*, Eighth Int'l Conf. on Very Large Data Bases, Mexico City, Sept. 1982, p.292.

[Lafue84] Gilles M.E. Lafue and Reid G. Smith, *Implementation of a Semantic Integrity Manager with a Knowledge Representation System*, Expert Database Systems, 1985 (this volume).

[Maier83] David Maier, *The Theory of Relational Databases*, Computer Science Press, 1983, 637pp.

[McDermott78] J. McDermott and C. Forgy, *Production System Conflict Resolution Strategies*, pp.177-202 in [Waterman78].

[Morgenstern81] Matthew Morgenstern, *A Unifying Approach For Conceptual Schema To Support Multiple Data Models*, Second Int'l Conf. on Entity-Relationship Approach, Washington, D.C., October 1981, pp.281-299.

[Morgenstern83] Matthew Morgenstern, *Active Databases As A Paradigm For Enhanced Computing Environments*, Ninth Int'l Conf on Very Large Data Bases, Florence, Italy, Oct 1983, pp.34-42.

[Morgenstern84] Matthew Morgenstern, *Constraint Equations: Declarative Expression of Constraints With Automatic Enforcement*, Tenth Int'l Conf. on Very Large Data Bases, Singapore, August 1984.

[Morgenstern85] Matthew Morgenstern, *Connections Among Application Based Objects in Directed Edge-Labelled Hypergraphs*, IFIP Conference on Theoretical and Formal Aspects of Information Systems (TFAIS-85), Barcelona, Spain, April 1985, North Holland publishers.

[Moser83] M.G. Moser, *An Overview of NIKL, the New Implementation of KL-ONE*, pp.7-26, in Research in Knowledge Representation for Natural Language Representation, October 1983, Bolt Beranek & Newman, Report No.5421.

[Schmolze83] James G. Schmolze and Thomas A. Lipkis, *Classification in the KL-ONE Knowledge Representation System*, Proc 8th Int'l Joint Conf. on A.I., August 1983, Germany, pp.330-2.

[Shepherd84] Allan Shepherd and Larry Kerschberg, *Constraint Management in Expert Database Systems*, Expert Database Systems, 1985 (this volume).

[Shipman81] David W. Shipman, *The Functional Data Model and The Data Language DAPLEX*, Trans on Database Sys, v.6, no.1, March 1981, pp.140-173.

[Steele80] Guy Lewis Steele, Jr., *The Definition and Implementation of a Computer Programming Language Based on Constraints*, M.I.T. A.I. Lab Tech Report AI-TR-595, Aug 1980, PhD thesis, 371pp.

[Stefik80] Mark Stefik, *Planning with Constraints (Molgen: Part 1)*, Artificial Intelligence Journal, vol.16, 1980, pp.111-140.

[Sussman80] Gerald Jay Sussman and Guy Lewis Steele, Jr, *CONSTRAINTS -- A Language for Expressing Almost-Hierarchical Descriptions*, Artificial Intelligence Journal, v.14, 1980, pp.1-39.

[Waterman78] D.A. Waterman and Fredrick Hayes-Roth, *Pattern-Directed Inference Systems*, Academic Press, 1978, 658pp.

[Vesonder83] Gregg T. Vesonder, S.J. Stolfo, J.E. Zielinski, J.F.D. Miller, D.H. Copp, *ACE: An Expert System for Telephone Cable Maintenance*, Proc. 8th Int'l Joint Conf on A.I. (IJCAI), Aug 1983, 116-121.

SPECIFICATION AND DESIGN OF EXPERT DATABASE SYSTEMS

Forouzan Golshani

Department of Computer Science
Arizona State University
Tempe, Arizona 85287

ABSTRACT

We propose the combination of semantic evaluation and proof theoretic techniques as a suitable machinery for the design of expert database systems. We regard expert databases as dynamic objects and use a system of modal logic for the specification of their dynamic properties. The possible worlds of the modal system are the instances of the expert system which are defined as many-sorted algebras. Thus our framework is a modal logic system of algebras where the signature of algebra is the basis for the schema of the expert database. We indicate how, in addition to ordinary database operations, sophisticated expert facilities can be naturally provided. We cater for hypothetical queries, queries involving transitive closure, queries involving making inferences and some other types.

1. Introduction

Often expert systems are idealized as systems which imitate human beings that, given a situation, can make decisions. There is however a significant difference between man and machine - Humans can learn without being programmed. Obviously, "learning" is distinguished from "being programmed". The search for discovering a suitable class of concepts which can be learnt in a reasonable, perhaps polynomial, number of computation steps is a major challenge of artificial intelligence [Va-84]. This is precisely the central problem in the field of expert systems. Given a pool of information (i.e. a database), what would the system need (e.g. satisfactory algorithms, rules, etc.) in order to "learn" enough so that it can answer queries of various complexity. We will find that the process of learning (or deduction) severely limits the types of questions than can be answered by the expert system.

In addition to giving precise and complete answers to some questions, expert database systems (EDBS) should be able to act as consultants to the users. The following are a few types of queries for which, one would hope, an expert system can be useful:

- what would be the consequence if X happens? The system should make predictions based on certain assumptions. We will refer to this type as "hypothetical queries".
- why would X happen? With this type of question we investigate the reasons for the occurrence of a situation.
- what could prevent the occurrence of X?
- which object <u>can</u> be candidates for solutions (in addition to the definite answers obtained from the database).

The task of expert database system (EDBS) becomes considerably more complex when some other factors such as time-varying (dynamic) data, incomplete data, tentative reasoning and probabilistic (fuzzy) reasoning are allowed. Obviously, the complexity increases in direct relationship with the size of the underlying database [St-82].

Our aim in this paper is to provide a framework for the specification of expert database systems that is rich enough to cater for all the usual database activities such as querying and updating, as well as the ability to make inferences based on the facts available in the database and a given set of inference rules. In this work we make use of the specification methods presented in [Go-83] and [GMS-83]. Previously, we were concerned only with the issues in databases and the design of the query language **Varqa.** Below is a summary of our approach.

We consider expert database systems as dynamic objects, but we note that we are also interested in every instance of this dynamic object. The reason for this treatment is an obvious one; updates change the state of the database while the instances are used for answering queries. The distinction between query level and update level enable us to distinguish between static integrity constraints and dynamic integrity constraints (or transition constraints). For the dynamic part we develop a logic system that is based on a special kind of modal logic. Modal logic, which began as an extension to first order predicate logic, is the logic to deal with necessity and possibility. A proposition is "necessary" if it holds in all admissible worlds, and it is "possible" if it holds in some [Ch 80]. Modal logic has been used for several different purposes in the field of computer science and is particularly suited for the study of dynamic systems such a databases.

We will see that our modal system has similarities with Hoare-style program logic [Gold 82] and is in agreement with temporal logic [Ma-81], [MP-79]. The domain of interpretation (or the universe) of our modal system is the set of database instances. Following the developments in [Go-83] we regard a database instance as a collection of sets together with a collection of functions on these sets. The database instance is therefore seen as a many-sorted algebra. There are names associated with every function and every sort. These symbols are collected together in a "signature" (see, for example, [ADJ-78]). The signature also has the typing rules for the database mappings. Thus, the signature is the basis for the database schema and is the specification for the "syntax checker" and the "type checker" of the language. With this approach type errors can be detected statically; that is, only those expressions that satisfy the typing rules will proceed to evaluation. In our approach, the ordinary notion of functions is extended in two ways. Firstly, we permit functions which return sets of objects. Secondly, by introducing an error object, we extend all partial functions (i.e. those functions which are not everywhere defined) into total [Go-85]. Computation power is provided by including a sufficiently rich collection of operations (such as arithmetic, set theoretic, etc.) which are fixed across all applications. Ordinary database queries are simply expressions which are built up out of the symbols in the signature together with the operation symbols and which comply with the precise formation rules given by the query language. The semantics of a query is defined to be the value which is assigned to it by the algebra representing a database instance.

Two other notions must also be presented here: integrity constraints and inference rules. Although at the formal level, these two groups have similar characteristics, a distinction between the two is required. The reason for this distinction is the fact that, although both groups are used for making correct inferences, it is only the integrity constraints that must be considered in updates. Both the integrity constraints and the inference rules are expressions of type boolean constructed by using the symbols of the signature and the modal operators.

We must emphasize that the admissible worlds of our modal system are the database instances of a common database schema (i.e. many-sorted algebras with a common signature). We note that a similar formalism may be developed based on many-sorted logic rather than universal algebra.

To end the introductory section, we present the following as the aims of this paper.

i) to provide a formal framework for the specification of the schema for the expert database systems.

ii) to construct a system of deduction (inference system) based on i) above.

iii) to indicate how a query language based on i) and ii) can be constructed.

iv) to specify the dynamic aspects of the expert database system, i.e. those dealing with updates.

The mathematical model for the above goals will be presented in section 3.

2. Related Work

There are several phrases used in the literature by different researchers whose meanings overlap considerably. Amongst these phrases are: expert systems, knowledge based systems, inferential databases, intelligent question-answering systems and decision support systems. Added to these are the particular terminologies adopted by researchers in artificial intelligence and by those interested in specific applications such as medical diagnosis, management planning support, geological exploration and others. Therefore the name "expert system" may mean different things to different people, and for this reason, it is difficult to identify and single out an area as expert systems.

A survey and tutorial on expert systems is presented in [St-82]. In this paper, the authors embark from the field of artificial intelligence and describe many concepts which are important in expert systems. A study of knowledge and database management can be found in [Wi-84]. In this paper, distinction is made between a database and a knowledge base, and between intensional knowledge and its extension. Recent attention to Prolog has created some interest for logic-based expert systems. APES [HS-84] is a system based on the Horn clause subset of first order logic augmented by negation as failure. APES inherits the properties of Prolog systems and the underlying inference mechanism. The work presented in [VCJ-83] notes the limitations of using Prolog directly as a database system and considers a wider framework which is Prolog plus the relational theory of databases (see [GMN-81] and [GMN-82]). This paper suggests four stages for enhancing expert systems with database management facilities thus enabling the expert system to handle large amounts of data. The paper outline strategies for the establishment of communication between the two types of systems. Also in [Ko-81] a metalanguage representation of relational database systems is considered for deductive question-answering systems. The FOL system described in [We-80] has been developed with attention to ideas in first order logic. Although FOL is not a formal system, it makes use of notions such as partial models (in their terminology, simulation structures) and metatheory level. More on various expert systems and their applications can be found in [Sh-76], [Sp-82], [Se-80] and [BF-78].

On the framework for specification, several papers should be mentioned. Different variations of modal logic (temporal) have been used for the specification of various aspects of databases in [CB-80], [CF-82], [GMS-83] and [Ku-84]. In [CB-80], a language based on variant of dynamic logic has been defined. Using this language, a number of concepts such as database schema and database states are defined. In [CF-82] a family of languages have been defined which are based on an extension of temporal logic [MP-79]. The extension to temporal logic is that of Wolper's and is presented in [Wo-82]. Temporal logic has been used in [Ku-84] for database specification and verification. The author considers three parts (namely, static, temporal (dynamic) and operations for transitions) and then verifies the specifications of these parts.

3. Expert Database Specification and Design of Suitable Languages

Most computer languages need a fairly small collection of logical and mathematical tools for their construction. In fact, we can distinguish two principal components. The first component is the elementary mathematical entities (such as sets, functions, relations, etc.) and the corresponding operators which operate on these entities. The other component is the objects that are used by the first group, such as natural numbers, sequences, strings and the like [Ab-84]. This general statement is certainly true of our area of work.

We assume an alphabet Λ given. Based on this alphabet, we define the vocabulary of our formal system to be the collection of several groups of symbols. For the static part we distinguish four groups: "sort symbols", "function symbols", "operation symbols" and "local variable symbols" (a local variable of a particular sort ranges over the elements of the set which is associated with that sort at a given database instance. It is different from "global variables" which can stand for the potential objects of a particular sort as well as the "concrete" objects of that sort in a database instance. This approach is different from that of [GMS-83]. See [HC-68] for a detailed treatment of the problem associated with each approach, and also see [Ma-81]). It is assumed that the form of each symbol determines to which group it belongs.

We first develop the framework for the static part and then construct the dynamic part on top of it. The overall view of the formalism is as follows:

A1 We use the signature of the many-sorted algebra to define a schema for the EDBS. We also specify the collections of well- formed expressions (on the signature) which will be used for the specification of a query language as well as the static integrity constraints and deduction rules.

B1 We associate a set with every sort symbol and a function with every function symbol of the signature, thus constructing an EDBS instance (i.e. a many-sorted algebra that satisfies the schema).

A2 We extend our signature by including update symbols. For every update symbol u we define a corresponding modal operator [u]. Using these extensions we specify transition constraints and other dynamic characteristics of the EDBS.

B2 We define a collection of update functions, one for each update symbol introduced in A2, where every update function maps an instance to another and satisfies the transition constraints.

Note that A1 and A2 are the syntactic components of our definitions and B1 and B2 give the semantic aspects.

Many-sorted algebras have been important in both practise and theory of the specification of a number of concepts in computer science, in particular, abstract data types. The primary aim in abstract data type specification is to precisely describe a data type independently of any representation of its data objects and independently of any implementation of the operations. Using algebra as the framework allows us to abstract ourselves from details of data structuring and the physical organization and representations.

3.1. EDBS Schema and Instance

It is assumed that two sorts boolean and integer are present in all specifications. We first discuss syntactic matters.

We define inductively simple-type-expressions to be sort symbols or of one of the forms: $\alpha_1 \bigcup \alpha_2$, $(\alpha_1 * \alpha_2 * \cdots \alpha_n)$ and $\mathbf{P}(\alpha_1)$ where for some n for $1 \leq i \leq n$, α_i is a simple-type-expression. For any natural number n, a function-type-expression of arity n has the form $\alpha_1, \alpha_2, \cdots, \alpha_n \rightarrow \alpha_{n+1}$ where for $1 \leq i \leq n+1$, α_i is a simple-type expression. Operation-type-expressions are defined in a similar manner. For example, the operation type expression for the operation symbol "+" is

$$\text{int, int} \rightarrow \text{int.}$$

<u>Definition:</u> A <u>signature</u> is a function which assigns a function-type-expression to every function symbol and a sort symbol to every variable symbol. (Note that the variables, both local and global, are typed by the signature and not by the user. There is an unlimited supply of variables of each type). Thus the signature is the specification for the types-checker and the syntax-checker of the language.

<u>Example:</u> Part of an EDBS for medical purposes can be specified as follows: sort symbols 'patients', 'diseases', 'drugs', etc.; function symbols 'illness_of', 'cures_of', 'results_of_having', 'is_taking', etc. Below, the unique type-expressions for some of these functions are presented:

consumers_of	drugs → **P**(patients)
illnesses_of	patients → **P**(diseases)
results_of_having	diseases → **P**(diseases)
cures_of	diseases → **P**(drugs)
is_taking	patients, drugs → boolean
age_of	employees $\bigcup$ patients → integers

Thus, we know precisely which types are allowed as the arguments of the functions and what type of object the function should return. We will see that this will enable us to carry out static type checking prior to the evaluation of expressions.

Given a signature, we define the set of well-formed expression on that signature in the usual way (and in accordance with [Go-83]).

Amongst the operations provided, there are a number of variable binding operators [KMM-80] such as the logical quantifiers and the set construction operator. Bound and free occurrences of variables in expressions can be detected syntactically in the usual way. For instance, given a variable X and two expressions Ω_1 and Ω_2, any occurrence of X in $\{\Omega_1 \mid \Omega_2\}_X$ is a bound occurrence. (Obviously the type of the expression Ω_2 must be boolean).

Static Integrity Constraints on a given signature Σ are defined to be a collection of well-formed expressions of type boolean on Σ. We use Γ_Σ for a set of integrity constraints on a signature Σ.

Example: Below are examples of static integrity constraints on our medical EDBS (variables are written in capital letters).

- Ages of all employees are greater than 18

```
forall EMP ( age_of(EMP) GT 18 )
```

- The fact that the function consumers_of and the relation is_taking represent exactly the same information can be expressed by the following constraint:

```
forall P forall D
    (P is_taking D implies P isin consumers_of(D)) and
    (P isin consumers_of(D) implies P is_taking D)
```

Given a signature Σ, inference rules on Σ (denoted by Ψ_Σ) are defined as closed expression of type boolean on Σ. Note that the formal definitions of integrity constraints and inference rules are the same and the only distinction is in their designation. Recall that integrity constraints are those which must be checked when an update is being carried out, whereas inference rules are statements which are used, in conjunction with the constraints, for the deduction of new facts.

Example: Here are the formulations of some inference rules on the medical EDBS.

- If a person has an ulcer, he cannot take Aspirin.

```
forall P (ulcer isin illnesses_of(P) implies
    Aspirin is_unsuitable_for P)
```

- If a patient who is over 65 suffers from high blood pressure, then he must be put under special care.

```
forall P ((P has high_blood_pressure and
    age_of(P) GT 65) implies special_care(P))
```

Definition: An EDBS schema is the triple (Σ, Γ_Σ, Ψ_Σ) where Σ is a signature, Γ_Σ is a (possibly empty) set of constraints on Σ, and Ψ_Σ is a (possibly empty) set of inference rules on Σ, such that $\Gamma_\Sigma \bigcup \Psi_\Sigma$ is consistent. Note that if Ψ_Σ is empty, then we have an ordinary database system. In fact, this definition can be regarded as the definition of a database schema (Σ, Γ_Σ) and its conservative enrichment to (Σ, Γ_Σ, Ψ_Σ). Also note that so far as we have only discussed syntactic matters.

3.2. Queries

Although we cannot yet define hypothetical queries (because they are expressions of the modal system) it is appropriate to look at the way in which other types of queries can be constructed. Hypothetical queries will be introduced after discussing our modal logic system.

Given a signature Σ, a query is a closed expression on Σ in which any variable is bound only once (this assumption of each variable being bound only once is made solely to simplify communication with naive users; that is, the user does not need to be aware of concepts such as "hole in the scope").

As examples, we construct a few queries of different types on our medical EDBS. The first query is an ordinary database query.

1. What are the illnesses of all those patients who are currently taking Aspirin?

    { illnesses_of(P) | P is_taking Aspirin }P

"illnesses_of" is a function which returns a set of diseases, simply because it has the function-type-expression patients → **P**(diseases). P is a variable of type patients. The appearance of P on the very right indicates the variable which is being bound by the set construction operator.

2. If a patient complains of headache and diarrhoea, what are the possible diseases he may have?

    { D | headache isin symptoms_of(D) and
        diarrhoea isin symptoms_of(D) }D

The set-construction operator builds up a set of diseases.

3. What are the cures of all those diseases that can be caught as a result of having an ulcer?

This query will require the computation of transitive closure of the set-valued function "results_of_having", i.e. we must find out the diseases that can come as a result of having the ulcer, then find out the diseases that can be caught due to having the newly computed diseases and so on for all computed diseases. By using a "where clause" the query is expressed by induction as follows: (Proofs on least fixed point and termination are presented in [Go-83]).

    { (D1, cures_of(D1)) | D1 isin S } D1

    where

    S = results_of_having (ulcer) union
        Union { results_of_having(D2) | D2 isin S } D2

"union" is the ordinary set theoretical operator $\bigcup$. "Union" is the operator which, when given a set of sets, computes the union of all included sets. Note that in the inductively defined part we have results_of_having(ulcer) as the base for induction.

4. Which drugs cure headache?

This very simple (database) query is formulated as:

cures_of(headache)

Now recall the inference rule that was presented in the previous section: "if a person has an ulcer, he cannot take Aspirin". Suppose the query is to find cures for headache of Jack who has an ulcer. The formulation uses a special construct which refers to the inference rules:

cures_of(headache) for P

where

(P has headache) and (P has ulcer)

The "for" construct invokes the use of the inference rules in answering this query. There are several other constructs similar to this.

3.3. Semantics

So far, in sections 3.1 and 3.2, we have discussed only syntactic matters. The notions of algebra will be used for giving semantics. A many sorted algebra is a function which assigns a set (called a carrier in [ADJ- 78]) to every sort symbol and a function to every function symbol.

Recall that we allowed several forms to be simple-type-expressions. For a simple-type-expression α, the set of all objects of type α in an algebra **A**, denoted by $|\mathbf{A}|_\alpha$ is defined as follows:

- if α is a sort symbol then $|\mathbf{A}|_\alpha = \mathbf{A}(\alpha)$, i.e. the set that is assigned to it by the algebra.
- if α is $\alpha_1 \bigcup \alpha_2$ then $|\mathbf{A}|_{\alpha_2}$
- if α is $(\alpha_1 * \alpha_2 * \cdots * \alpha_n)$ then $|\mathbf{A}|_\alpha = |\mathbf{A}|_{\alpha_1} * \cdots * |\mathbf{A}|_{\alpha_n}$
- if α is $\mathbf{P}(\alpha_1)$ then $|\mathbf{A}|_\alpha = \mathbf{P}(|\mathbf{A}|_{\alpha_1})$, i.e. the powerset.

The evaluation in **A** of expressions is carried out in the usual way. Given an EDBS schema $S = (\Sigma, \Gamma_\Sigma, \Psi_\Sigma)$ where Σ is a signature, and Γ_Σ and Ψ_Σ are as before, an algebra **A** is an S-algebra iff:

1. For every function symbol Φ in the domain of **A**, if $\Sigma(\Phi)$ is $\alpha_1, \alpha_2, \ldots, \alpha_n \rightarrow \alpha_{n+1}$ then $\mathbf{A}(\Phi)$ returns an element of $|\mathbf{A}|_{\alpha_{n+1}}$ when given an element of $|\mathbf{A}|_{\alpha_1}$, an element of $|\mathbf{A}|_{\alpha_2}$, $\cdots$, and an element of $|\mathbf{A}|_{\alpha_n}$.
2. The evaluation in **A** of all of the expressions in Γ_Σ results in true.

For an EDBS schema $S = (\Sigma, \Gamma_\Sigma, \Psi_\Sigma)$, an EDBS instance is the ordered pair (S,**A**) where **A** is an S-algebra. Given an expression Ω of type boolean, for an EDBS instance, we write $i \models \Omega$ iff i evaluates Ω as true. We will use I to indicate the collection of EDBS instances on a given schema.

3.4. The Modal Logic System

We will use a system of modal logic, comparable with temporal logic, for reasoning about dynamic characteristics of the EDBS. The system was first introduced in [GMS-83] and therefore we avoid repeating irrelevant details.

Syntactically, we need to make a number of extensions. Σ will be extended to Σ' by including:

- update symbols $u_0, u_1, \cdots$, and the corresponding modal operators $[u_0], [u_1], \cdots$.
- global variable symbols $X_0^\alpha, X_1^\alpha, \cdots$ of each sort α of Σ.

The set of well-formed expressions over Σ is extended to well-formed expressions over Σ' by allowing the construct $[\mu]\Omega$ as an expression of type boolean, where Ω is of type boolean and μ is an update symbol. The expression $[\mu]\Omega$ is read as: "after the update is performed μ will be true". Note that the $[\mu]$ act as operators in a similar way to the more familiar modal operators always $\blacksquare$, sometimes $\bigtriangledown$ and next $\bigcirc$ In fact, one can think of the $[\mu]$ as the $\bigcirc$ operator of temporal logic which is parameterized with respect to the specific update being made.

Given Ω, Ω_1 and Ω_2 as expressions of type boolean on Σ' and X as a global variable, we can extend our logic for deriving consequences by adding the following axioms and rule:

Axiom schemas:

1. $\vdash [\mu](\Omega_1 \rightarrow \Omega_2) \equiv ([\mu]\Omega_1 \rightarrow [\mu]\Omega_2)$
2. $\vdash \neg[\mu]\Omega \equiv [\mu]\neg\Omega$
3. $\vdash$ for all X $[\mu]\Omega(X) \equiv [\mu]$ for all X $\Omega(X)$

   (X must be a global variable.)

Inference rules:

1. If $\vdash \Omega_1 \rightarrow \Omega_2$ and $\vdash \Omega_1$, then $\vdash \Omega_2$.
2. If $\vdash \Omega$, then $\vdash [\mu]\Omega$.

Note that we do not want the quantification axiom to hold for local variables. By using global variables we can state assertions about all those data values which may at some point be in a database instance.

There are similarities in notation between our logic, program logic [Gold-82] and the interval logic presented in [SMV-83]. The semantics, however, differ significantly, as we will see shortly. Each modal operator [u] is specific to the update that is being performed, for example, [insert-patient(Jack)] which will add Jack to "patients".

Now we define semantics for the modal extensions. For every update symbol μ in Σ' we consider a function $\bar{\mu}$ which when given an EDBS instance returns an EDBS instance. Thus,

$$\bar{\mu}: I \rightarrow I$$

where I is the set EDBS instances.

Recall that we used i $\models \Omega$ to indicate that instance i evaluates Ω as true. We extend this notion of satisfaction to cope with modal expressions. For any update symbol μ and the corresponding update function $\bar{\mu}$ we have:

$$i \models [\mu]\Omega \text{ iff } \bar{\mu}(i) \models \Omega.$$

Checking the soundness of the axioms and the rule is straightforward and thus omitted.

Other modal operators are not essential for our purposes but we can easily capture them by the following definitions: ($\blacksquare$ is the necessity operator and $\bigtriangledown$ is the possibility operator. They concern "all admissible EDBS instances" and "some admissible EDBS instances" respectively.)

$$i \models \blacksquare\,\Omega \text{ iff } \bar{\mu}_0(\bar{\mu}_1 \cdots \bar{\mu}_n(i) \cdots) \models \Omega$$

for all sequences $\bar{\mu}_0, \bar{\mu}_1, \cdots, \bar{\mu}_n$ of updates,

and

$$i \models \bigtriangledown\,\Omega \text{ iff } \bar{\mu}_0(\bar{\mu}_1 \cdots ,\bar{\mu}_n(i)...) \models \Omega$$

for some sequence $\bar{\mu}_0, \bar{\mu}_1, \cdots, \bar{\mu}_n$ of updates.

Should we allow these operators into our logic, obviously, we would need to include the usual axioms that are specified for them, such as $(\blacksquare\,\Omega_1 \rightarrow \Omega_2)$ iff $(\blacksquare\,\Omega_1 \rightarrow \blacksquare\,\Omega_2)$, etc. See e.g. [MP-79].

Transition constraints are boolean type expressions over Σ' . For example, the constraints "ages cannot be reduced" is expressed as follows:

forall X forall Y ((age_of(X) is Y) implies ([u] (age_of(X) GE Y)))

This expression reads as follows: for any person X and any age Y, if the age of X is Y then after performing any update u the age of X will be at least Y.

3.5. Hypothetical Queries

By this type of query the user asks the expert system to make predictions based on some assumptions. For example, in a company, the manager may wish to ask this simple question: "if I increase Jack's salary by 1,000 dollars, would he then be earning more than George?"

Such a query is expressed as follows:

[increase_salary(Jack, 1,000)] sal_of(Jack) GT sal_of(George)

In this query the system will not make the update effective but will assume that the update is performed and then answers the question. This type of question-answering is particularly needed for decision support systems.

Similarly, suppose the management decides to ensure that no employee shall earn less than 20,000 dollars and they want to know whether a uniform 10% pay raise would achieve this. Such a query is formulated as:

forall EMP ([increase_salary(EMP, sal_of(EMP)/10)] sal_of(EMP) GT 20000)

This expression reads as follows: "For every employee, after increasing the salary of that employee by 10%, is it true that her salary will be more than 20,000 dollars?".

And finally, here is an example from our medical EDBS: All patients who will be in critical condition if a certain drug, say isophane, is not available. (Suppose there is a rule in our EDBS stating that: "for some diseases, if a patient has the disease and the drug which is the sole cure for that disease is not available, then the patient is in critical condition.")

{ P | [unavailable(isophane)] critical_condition(P) }P

4. Conclusions

In the past, most efforts for the design of expert systems were implementation oriented. Recent contributions to computer science, such as functional/logic programming and the theory of abstract data types, allow the users to use the system without much attention to the representation or implementation detail. In the case of databases, this trend is very obvious as witnessed by the recent publications such as [BNF-81], [GM-78], [Ma-77] and [CCF-82]. One of the advantages of having a powerful mathematical foundation for the database is that, in many cases, we can do more than just the elementary database operations. This is certainly true about the functional based databases [BNF-81] and the logic based ones [GMN-81]. However, there is one drawback about the Prolog-based expert systems: they treat the data and the rules uniformly, and any fact finding is carried out by theorem proving. Unfortunately, at least with the present technology, theorem proving is not a sufficient machinery for large databases [VCJ-83].

In our approach, we have combined proof-theoretic techniques for deriving consequences from rules with semantic interpretation, thus providing a framework which can accommodate, in addition to the ordinary database operations, the tools for making queries which are not usual to the database systems. The basis of the work presented here is the language **Varqa** which is a functional query language based on the notation of conventional mathematics. (Work on the implementation of this language is currently in progress.) Our methodology has allowed us to handle the problem of incomplete data quite easily at the semantic level. In [Go-82] we have presented how the interpretation of queries can be carried out despite the existence of null values in the database. We have used the formal framework used here but have extended it to allow each algebra (representing a data base instance) to be an approximation for another algebra which has more information (i.e. we construct a partial ordering on algebras).

One issue that we have not addressed here is that of updating the inference rules. Ideally, we want the ability to change or extend our inference system, thus working with a more general and more powerful system. Separation of integrity constraints and inference rules allows for this facility, though we should bear in mind that in some cases the distinction between constraints and rules is very vague. For example, if we wish to include in the EDBS the statement "certain diseases once caught cannot be cured", it is not clear whether this should be a constraint or a rule.

Finally, we should add that our method of specification has the same advantages as the specification methods for abstract data types in that the implementor can decide on the best method of implementation and can prove the correctness of his activity.

Acknowledgement

The author wishes to than Tom Maibaum for many stimulating discussion. The was work carried out by the support of a grant from SERC of the U.K.

References

[Ab-84] Abrial J R
"Program Construction as a Mathematical Exercise"
Talk given at the Royal Society Meeting on Mathematical Logic and Programming Languages - London 15-16 February 1984

[ADJ-78] Goguen J A, Thatcher J W, Wagner E G
"An Initial Algebra Approach to the Specification, Correctness, and Implementation of Abstract Data Types"
In "Current trends in programming methodology", Vol. IV, pp 81-149, Prentice Hall 1978

[BF-78] Buchanan B G, Feigenbaum E A
"DENDRAL and Meta-DENDRAL: Their Applications"
Artificial Intelligence 11, pp 5-24, 1978

[BNF-81] Buneman P, Nikhil R, Frankel R
"A Practical Functional Programming System for Databases"
Proceedings ACM Conference on Functional Programming and Machine Architecture, 1981

[CB-80] Casanova M A, Bernstein P
"A Formal System for Reasoning about Programs Accessing a Relational Databases"
ACM TOPLAS, Vol 2, No. 3 July 1980, pp 386-414

[CCF-82] Castilho J, Casanova M A, Furtado A L
"A Temporal Framework for Database Specifications"
Proceedings 8th VLDB Conference, Mexico City, September 1982, pp 28-291

[CF-82] Casanova M A, Furtado A L
"A Family of Temporal Languages for the Description of Transition Constraints"
Workshop on Logical bases for databases, Toulouse, 1982

[Ch-80] Challas B F
"Modal Logic; an introduction"
Cambridge University Press, 1980

[GM-78] Gallaire H, Minker J
"Logic and Databases"
Plenum Press, New York, 1978

[GMN-81] Gallaire H, Minker J, Nicholas J-M
"Advances in Database Theory"
Vol. 1, Plenum Press, New York 1981

[GMN-82] Gallaire H, Minker J, Nicholas J-M
Proc. Workshop of Logical Bases for Databases
Toulouse, France, December 1982

[GMS-83] Golshani F, Maibaum T, Sadler M
"A Modal System of Algebras for Databases Specification and Query/Update Language Support"
Proceedings 9th International Conference on VLDB, Florence, November 1983, pp 331-339

[Go-82] Golshani F
"Growing Certainty with Null Values"
Research Report DoC 82-22, Imperial College, London UK
(To appear in Information Systems, Vol. 10, no. 2)

[Go-83] Golshani F
"A Mathematically Designed Query Language"
Research Report DoC 83-1, Imperial College, London UK

[Gold-82] Goldblatt R
"Axiomatising the Logic of Computer Programming"
Lecture Notes in Computer Science 130, Springer-Verlag, 1982

[HC-68] Hughes G E, Cresswell M J,
"An Introduction to Modal Logic"
Methuen and Co. Ltd, London, 1968

[HS-84] Hammond P, Sergot M
"APES: Reference Manual"
Logic Based Systems, Ltd., 40 Beaumont Ave., Richmond, Surrey, UK

[KMM-80] Kalish D, Montague R, Mar G
"Logic, Techniques of Formal Reasoning"
Second Ed. 1980
Harcourt Brace Jovanovich inc.

[Ko-81] Konolige K
"A Metalanguage Representation of Relational Databases for Deductive Question-Answering Systems"
Proceedings of IJCAI-81, pp 496-503

[Ku-84] Kung C H
"A Temporal Framework for Database Specification and Verification"
Research Report, Department of Computer Science, The Norwegian Institute of Technology
Trondheim, Norway, 1984

[Ma-77] Maibaum T S
"Mathematical Semantics and a Model for Databases"
Proceedings IFIP 1977, (Gilchrist Ed.) pp 133-138

[Ma-81] Manna Z
"Verification of Sequential Programs: Temporal Axiomatization"
Report No. STAN-CS-81-877, Stanford University, 1981

[MP-78] Manna Z, Pnueli A
"The Modal Logic of Programs"
Report No. STAN-CS-79-751, Stanford University, 1979

[Ni-82] Nicolas J M
"Logic for Improving Integrity Checking in Relational Databases"
Acta Informatica Vol. 18, 1982, pp 227-253

[Se-80] Sergot M
"Programming Law: LEGOL as a Logic Programming Language"
Research Report, Department of Computing, Imperial College, 1980

[Sh-76] Shortliffe E H,
"Computer-Based Medical Consultation: MYCIN"
New York, Elsevier/North Holland, 1976

[SMV-83] Schwartz R L, Miller-Smith P M, Vogt F H,
"An Interval Logic for Higher-Level Temporal Reasoning"
Computer Science Laboratory, SRI International, Manlo Park, California, 1983

[Sp-82] Speedie S M, et al
"Evaluating Physician Decision Making: A Rule-Based System for Drug Prescribing Review"
Proceedings First IEEE Conference on
Medical Computer/Science/ Computational Medicine,
Pennsylvania, September 1982

[St-82] Stefik M, et al
"The Organization of Expert Systems: A Prescriptive Tutorial"
Palo Alto Research Center, Xerox, Palo Alto, California, January 1982

[Va-84] Valiant L G,
"Deductive Learning"
Talk given at The Royal Society Meeting on Mathematical Logic and Programming Languages, London, 15-16th February, 1984

[VCJ-83] Vassiliou Y, Clifford J, Jarke M
"How does an expert system get its data?"
Extended Abstract, Proceedings 9th International Conference on VLDB, Florence, November 1983, pp 70-72

[We-80] Weyhraunch R W
"Prolegomena to a Theory of Mechanized Formal Reasoning"
Artificial Intelligence, Vol. 13, 1980, pp 133-170

[Wi-84] Wiederhold G
"Knowledge and Database Management"
IEEE Software, January 1984, pp 63-73

[Wo-81] Wolper P
"Temporal Logic Can Be More Expressive"
Proceedings of 22nd Symposium on Foundations of Computer Science, Nashville, Tennessee, October 1981

TOWARDS A UNIFIED APPROACH FOR EXPERT AND DATABASE SYSTEMS

M. Missikoff, G. Wiederhold*

Computer Science Department
Stanford University

ABSTRACT

This paper addresses the organization of tools for applications that require both the deduction and problem solving capabilities of an expert system, and the management of a large base of facts, typically kept in a DBMS. In the first part of the paper the principal approaches considered today are summarized: most of these approaches embody database functions in an expert system frame.

In the second part we state the criteria required for an *Expert Database System* (EDS) and propose an approach based on database concepts. Such a system must be able accept knowledge as a new type of object, to be stored and managed within an expanded database framework.

The proposed approach requires that the knowledge be organized with more structure than is usually adopted in existing systems. To achieve this the concept of a knowledge cluster is introduced and a way of structuring the knowledge similar to the structure of a relational database is suggested.

1. INTRODUCTION

Expert Systems (ES) are a significant application of Artificial Intelligence. An expert system consists of a body of knowledge pertaining a specific domain and the mechanisms to process the knowledge in order to find solutions to complex problems. The behavior of an expert system is intended to be comparable to that of a *human* expert in the specific field. Given a problem instance, an ES is capable of using its expertise to *reason* and to derive possible solutions implied by what it knows about the general situation.

The first expert systems were developed more than a decade ago [Haye:83]; since then ES have been used in a variety of application domains, with encouraging results. The successes of many ES in the last few years has had the effect of increasing the demand for ES on more vast and complex application fields.

Presently the knowledge embodied in an ES is typically represented by frames and rules that model the relationships within a specific subset of reality. The rules govern the interactions among the entities and their evolution over time. Many of the entities dealt with are defined at a high level of abstraction, i.e., as entity types. The rules describe general relationships among entity types.

An ES also contains built-in knowledge, namely some inference mechanism to invoke the application of the rules. The built-in inference engine may be aided by meta-rules, which encode reasoning about the application-domain rules.

* Visiting from IASI-CNR, Rome (Italy).

On the other hand a database management system (DBMS) models a given subset of reality by recording its extension. The actual state of the given reality, as consistent as possible at any given moment, is represented. The transitions from one state to the next are performed by the application procedures. These procedures have to satisfy constraints, equivalent to the rules in a knowledge-base. The procedures may be aided by explicit constraint statements or by dependency definitions supplied with the database [Ston:75], [Wied:83], [Ullm:82].

The general and abstract descriptions of an ES and the set of extensional facts kept in a DBMS represent, in a very different but strictly related way, the same reality. However, the former tracks general issues and the latter records detail. Both general and detailed knowledge are needed when information is needed for difficult decisions about specific tasks. Therefore a unified approach that can merge these representation techniques for the same reality is highly desirable.

ES and DBS technologies have evolved along different lines. Research is addressing the problem of enhancing the power of both types of systems [Kono:81]. Database systems are evolving in the direction of capturing more semantics in their schemas; expert systems are trying to deal with applications that require an increasing amount of existential facts to be stored to complement the general rules.

On the database side the proposals mainly concern the semantic data models, as in [Hamm:78], [Smit:77], [Wied:78]. These models allow the representation of some semantics in the schema of the database. The objectives are mainly to enforce the consistency of data (e.g., integrity constraints [Fagi:78]), to simplify access [Wied:84], optimize query processing [King:81a], [King:81b], [Hamm:80]; other proposals use the inheritance of properties, in hierarchical semantic models (as in the Enriched E-R model [Sche:80] [Bati:82]), to enhance the modeling capabilities of the schema of the database.

On the ES side many different applications require the use of large amounts of data in conjunction with specific expertise. In particular in (i) CAD systems [Brown:83], (ii) systems to assist the maintenance of complex machinery [Gene:82], (iii) weather forecasting, (iv) geological prospection [Duda:77], and (v), in a closed loop system, the extraction of knowledge from medical databases [Blum:82].

In such applications the database stores the operands of the applications. In examples (i) and (ii) the data are the specifications of parts and components. In (iii) it is a base of examples, i.e., typical patterns that imply the evolution of the reality towards a probable successor situation. For examples (iv) and (v) it is a base of observed facts. In (iv) data about the chemical composition of families of rocks used to infer additional facts; in (v) the medical records of many patients are analyzed to increase the knowledge base which drives the inference mechanism itself.

The incorporation of concepts the database side and the expert systems side into systems based in the other area can occur at different levels, as seen within this proceedings [Brac:85]. We find integration at the symbolic level of structures which represent types of knowledge [Deer:85] and at the knowledge level, when the unified frame refers to the content of the knowledge base and the functionality provided by the knowledge-based system [Brod:85]. This trend will continue until a general tool, capable of managing in a unified fashion different types of knowledge, and related facts, is available and has been accepted.

However, the advantage of combining knowledge about the facts and the facts themselves into one environment also has disadvantages. The inference engine will not distinguish the two, but the two may have different weight. In larger systems we find specialists interacting with distinct aspects of information: changes to data are made by clerical staff, changes to the organization of the data are made by a database administrator, and knowledge is supplied by experts. Retrieval is made by programs for routine reporting and these reports are scanned to note and correct discrepancies. Planners work by applying knowledge to the data, often ignoring minor data inconsistencies and aberrations. In all these instances the operational semantics of knowledge and data are distinct.

Our objectives are hence not fulfilled by simply building a large and fast system. It must also be a well-structured and smart system in which the components work synergistically. Maintenance of system and contents will be a concern. The need to have common functionalities, knowledge representation, and architecture was a major concern in the Working Group on Knowledge Base Management Systems.

In the next section we present a brief overview of the proposed approaches for joining of ES and DBS; in Section 3 we propose a different approach oriented to define a new class of systems, called Expert Database System (EDS), characterized by a unified approach to the representation, the manipulation and the inquiry into the various types of knowledge (namely facts, rules, and meta-rules; and their descriptions, i.e., schemas). The final section will address the primary difficulties that are encountered in facing such a challenging objective, indicating the research lines that need to be followed when proceeding towards the design of an EDS.

2. EXPERT SYSTEMS WITH LARGE BASES OF FACTS

In this section we first introduce a simple example of a knowledge base that encompasses both facts and rules, and allows to manage them in a unified way. The intent is to clarify some definitions. The reader familiar with the issues can skip the next paragraph.

Subsequently we present the principal techniques that have been adopted in combining expert system and database technology. The presentation follows the classification introduced by [Jark:83] (see also [Vass:83]). On top of that we superimpose a more general distinction between two broader classes: homogeneous and heterogeneous approaches.

2.1. The "family" database

This simple example presents a database having two relations: father and mother having factual instances, and a base of rules representing a body of elementary knowledge about parenthood. This knowledge allows derivation of four more relations (deduced relations). The example is presented in a formalism taken from the PROLOG language [Cloc:81].

```
    * Rules *

grandfather(X,Y) :- parent(X,Z), father(Z,Y).

grandmother(X,Y) :- parent(X,Z), mother(Z,Y).

parent(X,Y) :- mother(X,Y).
parent(X,Y) :- father(X,Y).

child(Y,X) :- parent(X,Y).

    * Facts *

father(John,Ted).
father(Alfred,Ted).
father(Mary,Peter).
father(Peter,Arthur).

mother(John,Amy).
mother(Ted,Nancy).
mother(Alfred,Amy).
```

For sake of conciseness we are not going to further develop the example, the reader can see that in addition to simple queries as: "who is the father of Peter?", the system has enough knowledge about the family to answer to queries like:

- Who is the grandfather of Mary?

- Who is the child of Nancy?

- How many children does Ted have?

After adding to the example a relation of facts, having a schema:

person(name,address,age)

we can ask questions like: "what is the age of the grandmother of Alfred?". This example shows the capability of dealing with deduced relations in the same fashion as actual relations.

We see above that the important feature of managing in the same context both the rules and the facts is supplied in a natural way within a PROLOG system. The PROLOG system supplies the formalism (the language itself) to represent the two forms of knowledge (facts and rules) and the mechanisms to process that knowledge. The mechanism includes an inference engine and a pattern matching mechanism. This combination forms the basis for the approaches described in the remainder of this section.

2.2. The Homogeneous Approach: Deductive Databases

The homogeneous approach integrates data manipulation functions and deductive functions into a single system. This type of systems has been called a Deductive Database System [Lloy:83]. The approach uses the same programming system to represent both aspects of a given reality: the deductive aspects and those related to facts. We note already that this approach does not provide an intrinsic capability to distinguish data and knowledge.

A typical framework is represented by logic programming [Kowa:79], in particular the programming language PROLOG [Cloc:81]. Using PROLOG it is easy to write a program that contains both rules and facts, and the approach allows us to treat both conceptually in the same way. It has been shown that first order logic can be used to express both facts and rules. The relational model [Date:81] represent a natural way to organize facts (i.e., data) in a PROLOG programming environment [Pars:83b]. The example presented above shows how a deductive database can be built in PROLOG.

The two cases which follow present different types of deductive databases, classified by the extent to which they embody database technology in the PROLOG logic programming environment.

a) Elementary Deductive Database

A PROLOG program may embody in a unified way complex knowledge (facts and rules) of a given domain and allows the user to easily manage (query, modify, etc.) the facts as well as the knowledge. Moreover the language is particularly well suited to implement additional features as a friendly interface, integrity constraints enforcement, and query optimization [Warr:81], [Pars:83a].

This approach appears to be very suitable for simple applications or for prototype implementation of complex applications [SIGS:82]), since it allows to program at a higher level of abstraction than is possible when using traditional algorithmic languages; furthermore the programs appear to be easy to modify. These features are particularly useful in a stage of a project when on the one hand the specifications are still being developed, while preliminary tests of certain functions, say a user interface, are needed to guide the development.

In elementary deductive databases the mechanisms to manage the knowledge, essentially the pattern matching and the inference engine, are used as implemented within the PROLOG system. This represents one of the major arguments for using PROLOG, since it reduces the time required to develop a system; conversely this facility represents a limitation for two reasons. The first is due to the access method and the second is due to the homogeneity of the storage structure.

The data structures and the algorithms which manage the rules and the facts are strictly those supplied by the PROLOG system itself; this does not allow any flexibility to adjust these for specific applications. The necessity for the program and the related bases of rules and facts to reside in main memory in order to be executed either limits the size, if real memory is used, or leads to unpredictable paging patterns, when the memory is virtual.

The first drawback has been addressed by many researchers. Richer access methods for the object code of PROLOG programs have been implemented by [Samm:83]. The second problem is partially overcome by the advance of technology, mainly the availability of large main memories. Nevertheless the elementary approach to deductive database appears to be still quite limited.

b) Advanced Deductive Database

In advanced deductive databases the principal enhancement is the capability to manage data residing on an external device; this capability includes access methods typical of database technology and are integrated in the PROLOG framework. Now we have a PROLOG system with the principal functions of a DBMS.

The implementation can be very general. If the PROLOG system itself is extended, also any program developed using it obtains data handling capabilities, as for instance in MU-PROLOG [Nais:82]. If the extension is oriented to a particular expert system (or a family of ES), as seen in Maxwell [Egge:84] the efficiency may be great, but the benefit is limited.

Other experiences show analogous approaches for ESs developed using other programming environment than PROLOG, as the object oriented language STROBE: a similar approach of enhancing the original data handling capability of the system has been presented in [Lafu:85]. Subsequent experience, using concurrent PROLOG, is found here [Dahl:85].

Generally in those experiences the original programming environment has been preserved, but the data handling functions have been implemented using an algorithmic language, as in Maxwell, where the lower parts of the system have been implemented in the C language.

This approach avoids the two major difficulties of the previous one, i.e., space limitation and poor data structures; however the proposed systems end up with a large amount of code, since they tend to implement all the functions of a standard DBMS besides the inference capabilities of a deductive programming environment.

To reduce the implementation effort while keeping the advanced data handling capabilities, a suitable approach is that of connecting an expert system to an existing database system. This approach is referred as the heterogeneous approach.

2.3. The Heterogeneous Approach: ES plus DBMS

This approach refers to the cooperation of two distinct systems, one for knowledge management, the expert system, and one for massive data management, the database management system. In this approach the key issue is the interface that allows the two systems to communicate. In designing this kind of interface there are essentially two possibilities, that lead to a loose or a tight coupling.

c) ES-DBMS Loosely Coupled

This approach tends to maintain for each component its identity: the ES essentially devoted to deductive functions, the DBMS manages the database. The DBMS acts as a server to the ES, supplying on demand the data that the latter requires. This is the approach indicated in the Japanese 5th generation documents, although we expect considerable refinement to occur as their research progresses, e.g., [Ohsu:82].

In a simplified way the interactions among the two can be described as follows. The ES has a window on the facts and can access directly only those facts currently loaded on the window. When the data actually held in the window have been processed the ES asks the DBMS for new data.

This approach has been also referred to as the *compiled* approach [Chak:82], since it is based on two distinct phases (eventually repeatedly performed): first a computation on the side of the ES, which, using its knowledge, generates the queries for the DBMS; then the execution of the queries on the side of the DBMS and the delivery of the result to the former.

One of the major advantages of that approach is represented by the possibility of using existing databases, to which the ES can be connected as one of the application programs. In this way the database will continue to serve all its users without the necessity of any data replication.

If the expert system is implemented in a logic programming language, as PROLOG, the implementation of an interface with a relational database appears particularly natural due to the common theoretical foundation of the two environments [Kuni:82].

The principal drawback of this approach is represented by the necessity of separating in a precise way the deductive phase and the data retrieval phase; furthermore, if the selected data can not fully reside in main memory (due to window size limitations), an additional mechanism must be implemented in order to allow the window to shift back and forth on the full set of relevant data. Finally a problem of consistency may arise if the data collection extracted from the database (which essentially represents a *snapshot*) is used while the original version is updated.

d) ES-DBMS Tightly Coupled

In a tightly coupled approach the interactions between ES and DB can take place at any moment, the data of the database represents indeed a natural extension of the knowledge encompassed by the ES. Now the limitations due to the presence of the window are overcome and access to data can be performed during the deductive processes. The other problem seen in the loosely coupled approach: the consistency of data accessed by ES, is also avoided since the accesses are performed in real-time relative to the status of the database. However, this kind of free interaction can cause a severe slowdown for the ES operations. Using a database machine [Hsia:83], [Leil:83] may help [Koga:84].

In regard to the interface between the two systems, the user sees the database just as an extension of his program. The decisions when and how access the database relies on the ES frontend. The interface still represents a very critical point, both in terms of efficiency and reliability.

2.4. A First Assessment

The brief survey presented shows that a convergence of the two technologies, namely expert system and database system, is on the way, but also that a general solution is still far away. The main problem is that these two technologies are presently too different, even though in their evolution they tend to overlap. Database technology deals with simple objects, namely facts, organized in well-formulated structures. Structuring occurs both at a low level, to achieve an effective physical organization, and at a high level, to allow the conceptual modeling of data [Wied:83].

The technology of expert systems is presently characterized by the management of complex objects (the knowledge) organized into relatively simple structures [Barr:81]. ES research has concentrated on knowledge representation at an intermediate level, with less attention to the problems located at the two ends of the scale of abstraction: at a lower level, the storage structures, and at a higher level, the intensional aspects related to the description of the knowledge. The problem of representation of knowledge about knowledge is particularly hard. These problems become critical when an application requires large knowledge bases, e.g., for today's technology: over a thousand rules.

Merging of DB and ES technologies should lead to systems capable of managing a large base of complex knowledge in an integrated way. To this end it is necessary to conceive, for the different types of knowledge, highly effective storage structures on the one hand and a hierarchy of abstractions in knowledge representation on the other hand [Smit:85].

Since databases have addressed issues of storage structures and use of intension to control the extension, this technology appears likely to offer the right framework for an effective management of the knowledge.

To be able to deal with knowledge, the database technology must be substantially extended over today's capabilities. In order to manage the knowledge with the flexibility and the reliability available today for data, several problems must be solved:

(i) at a lower level: storage structures must deal with complex objects

(ii) at a higher level: multiple levels of abstraction must be supported to manage expert knowledge.

In modern applications of databases, for instance design support, the database system must already cope with complex objects [Lori:82]. Objects which have repeating groups and entries of variable lengths are dealt with in bibliographic database systems.

New methods for knowledge structuring and knowledge description are being investigated as databases recognize functional relationships within extended schemas as seen in DAPLEX [Ship:81] and the Universal relation [Ullm:82]. Success in those issues will allow to define schemas and views for knowledge, as we currently do for data.

3. THE FIFTH WAY

We now consider a system, which we call Expert Database System (EDS), conceived to manage knowledge consisting of both facts and rules in a uniform, database-like frame.

3.1. Criteria for an Expert Database System (EDS)

An EDS is seen here as an evolution of DBMSs, both in terms of type of objects managed and functions performed. Additional functions and new object types aim to endow the EDS with the ability to manage knowledge and obtain the deductive power of expert systems. The principal criteria for an EDS are:

- Application independence

  The EDS ought to be a general purpose system with a spectrum of applicability covering a large set of different application domains.

- Application capability

  The domain knowledge required by an application must be managed within the EDS, and not delegated to outside procedures.

- Expandability

Knowledge acquisition and update is a critical issue. For an EDS the management of the knowledge, in its different forms as facts, rules, heuristics, must be managed as updatable data and schemas are managed in a modern DBMS today.

- Deductive power

  This is a key contribution coming from ES technology. The EDS implements a large set of the functions related to deduction available in the more advanced ES.

- Alternative strategies

  Unlike most ES, the EDS will have a choice of different search strategies. To help decide which strategy is good for what problem accessible sets of rules must be able to control search strategy invocation. We will refer to this capability as the *skill* of the system.

- Manipulation of Degrees of Confidence

  The EDS must support imprecise reasoning. There should be a mechanism dealing with certainty factors for each rule that is applied during inferencing. In solving a given problem the composite confidence assessment refers to a specific path in the search graph. This capability can be extended to data, allowing the update of the factual knowledge with values having a certain degree of uncertainty.

- Transparent reasoning

  The system must have the capability to explain, during its processing and once it has found a solution, the reasoning by which it reaches any state.

- Multiuser environment

  Similarly to many DBMS the system can be used for different purposes by different users. To achieve this the concept of *views* must be imported from database field, but with the warning that *knowledge views* are much more complex that *data views*. Multiuser support permits specialists to work cooperatively, through the knowledge and database, but independently.

A unified frame in which different forms of knowledge can be treated in the same fashion is the key feature of EDS. This objective can be attained only if there exists an underlying information model that can represent homogeneously the different forms of knowledge.

For the storage of facts we adopt the relational model. Many advanced applications find the relational model too sparse, so that models as the Entity-Relationship (E-R) model [Chen:77], the Structural Model [Wied:83], and the Functional Models [Bune:80] have been developed to capture the semantics of relationships. In the approach we propose here such semantics will be captured by the knowledge base. Since the relational model captures all factual information within its relations, it provides an adequate basis for this work. Knowledge about relationships between relations now can capture static and dynamic constraint information, as found in the structural model, but not instance information about relationships, as found in the E-R model.

We now introduce the main components of a structured representation of knowledge; this representation is based on the notion of a Knowledge-Cluster, or *kluster* for short, that will permit the building of parallel organizations for factual and deductive aspects of knowledge.

3.2. The Structuring of Knowledge

We define structuring to be the process of classifying and organizing knowledge by type or function. The objective is to modularize the knowledge to improve its accessibility and management. The structuring of the knowledge appears to be an important step towards advanced expert systems [Clan:83]. Some proposals for structuring knowledge have been presented in Section 2. Among these, the frame organization [Mins:75] appears to be very suitable for a structured representation of knowledge. Another proposal is derived from concepts of semantic networks and it suggest a partitioning of a given semantic network in order to represent knowledge structure [Hend:77].

Both techniques support concepts as hierarchical inheritance, explicit references to related knowledge concepts, and the capability to bind knowledge to database facts. Structurally the approaches can be viewed as duals of each other. We tend to favor a frame-based representation since keeping knowledge in frames, rather than in links, is easier modeled using well-understood relational database concepts. The capability required from frames: dealing with multiple entries in a slot, does mean that a knowledge concept cannot be managed as a single relational tuple.

In the next sections we introduce the main lines of a proposed model for structured knowledge representation. The model is largely independent of the basic representation technique chosen for the knowledge: frames, production rules, logic, etc. We will use the general term rules to identify the knowledge units in the subsequent descriptions. We deal first with the overall organization that allows us to structure the database and rulebase of a EDS.

As shown in Figure 1, this organization structures the knowledge along two dimensions:

1) horizontally with the partitioning of the sets of rules and data and introducing clusters and views,
2) vertically with the introduction of different levels of abstraction.

The data and knowledge concepts at the various levels of abstraction are cross-linked. For instance, the knowledge schema refers to attribute descriptions for the database.

3.3. The Kluster

The knowledge organization is parallel to the one used by a relational database to manage the facts. In the database the facts are organized at different levels of aggregation. Single facts are connected to form a tuple, similar tuples are gathered to form relations with descriptive relation schemas, several relations will participate in a view, and finally the database encompasses all the source relations and their relation schemas.

In a rule-based system we have the atoms that compose a rule, then we have a set of rules that compose the knowledge base. To build an organization for rules which is similar to that used for facts, we need an intermediate level of aggregation, represented by the kluster.

The kluster represents essentially the locality that can be found in different sections of a large knowledge base. In a rule-based system we find groups of rules that tend to be activated within the search for a given class of problem. For those rules we can say that they form *problem related* clusters. Alternatively we can see that for other rules whenever one rule is activated there is a high probability that the remaining others are activated as well; in this case we can say that those rules form a *context related* cluster.

We do not proceed with an analysis of different types of localities and clusters that can be found in the knowledge, since we intend mainly to introduce the guidelines of the structured representation of knowledge based on a parallel structure to the relational data model.

Expert — Database — System

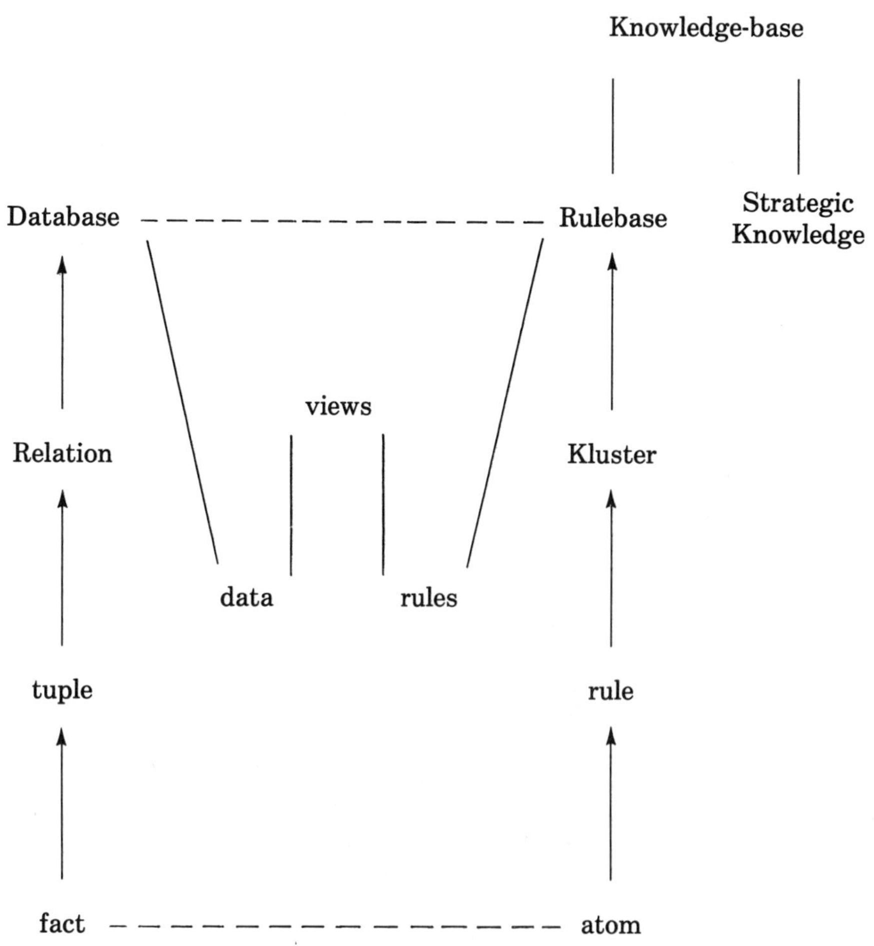

Figure 1: Structure of an EDS

The second aspect we introduce is the representation of different levels of generality or abstractions within a knowledge base. The problem is harder than for databases, where two main levels are clearly separated: the extensional level containing the ground information, i.e., the facts, and the intensional level containing the schema, namely the descriptions of the facts.

For the rules such a neat distinction does not exist. Nevertheless there are rules that apply to facts and meta-rules that apply to other rules. Figure 1 represents the hierarchy of aggregations in the proposed model and shows the parallel organization for facts and rules. Above the dotted line we represent the reality, decomposed in entities, whose states are modeled in the database, and relationships that determine the interactions between entities, that are modeled in the rulebase.

The figure represents the extensional aspects of the data and the knowledge base; besides it the system needs the schemas and the heuristics to accomplish effective problem solving strategies.

In Figure 1 the kluster is to be a set of rules that show common properties. The kluster defines rule sets which have similar predicates, so that they will be triggered by similar conditions.

For applications views are defined. Views are subsets of the content of the EDS, and may overlap each other to an arbitrary extent. The rule portion of a view represents a collection of klusters used by the applications. We have not yet tried to define operations which select or project rules from a kluster. Otherwise the views are similar to user views in database technology.

Views may also be helpful to define a specific source of expertise. Such a view can collect rules, which, before updating the overall rulebase will be subjected to validity constraints similar to the constraints which have to imposed to database updates through views [Keller:80]. This concept can simplify the knowledge update problem, especially when a new rule must be validated. Checking first if a new rule conflicts with preexisting knowledge in the view is less costly than scanning the entire rulebase. The cost can be further be reduced by an effective clustering of the rule base.

The rulebase represents the complete set of deductive knowledge on the specific domain. The figure represents the skill of the system, that is the knowledge related to search strategies, as strategic knowledge.

3.4. The Intensional Level of the Knowledge Base

As in the factual database a schema is introduced to describe properties of the entities represented in the knowledge base. In a database the schema specifies the realization of the model and also defines guidance about access structures to be maintained with the database. During execution the schema provides the names used by the user to address the database.

The k-schema serves the same purposes. Description of the rules and frames will increase the representational power of the system and will be particularly useful in the interactions with users. The k-schema must also provide guidance to tasks that access different sections of the knowledge base when searching for solutions. The k-schema can refer to the data schema (d-schema).

The problem solving activities rely greatly on the k-schema to realize effective strategies and reduce the search space [Rich:84]. The EDS should be able to use different search techniques and chose the most suitable depending on the kind of problem or the section of knowledge: the kluster or view, it is using.

The design of an actual knowledge base will present difficulties comparable with those encountered with the databases. The main point is the design of the klusters. The rules for designing a database by collecting attributes which functionally depend on the same key attributes cannot be literally transplanted.

Klusters may be more or less comprehensive and more or less bound to one another. As in relational database design, an initial k-schema can be defined and, later, refined based on the experiences of the users.

3.5. Consistency of the Knowledge Base Changes of Facts and Changes of Rules

Changes in the knowledge base can affect the validity of facts in the database. Today, some database schema changes have equivalent effects. We see the separation of knowledge and data within one system as an essential aspect of knowledge base design.

If all facts would be known to be correct, then no knowledge which contradicts any fact would be acceptable. In practice large databases contain errors. The inferential power of a data item which does not meet expectations will be insufficient to affect the knowledge base automatically. Depending on the strategy in force a warning may be produced, the database fact will be eliminated or flagged, or the certainty factor associated with the rule can be reduced.

4. THE EDS: ENTITIES AND FUNCTIONALITIES

The EDS manages three basic classes of objects: facts that represent the real-world state of the entities of a given domain; rules that represent the relationships under which the entities relate each other and evolve over time, and the heuristics or skill that allows effective processing of the knowledge when the solution of a problem is required.

To manage these objects there is the k-schema and d-schema.

We now provide a summary of the operations that an EDS is required to perform on those objects, essentially inquiry and update operations. Note that the problem of initial knowledge design and schema definition is beyond the scope of this paper.

4.1. Knowledge Inquiry

This function has a very different effect depending on the type of knowledge one addresses.

* Fact retrieval *

For factual inquiry the system acts like a traditional relational database system. It accepts queries in a relational language, uses the k-schema to enforce views, security and semantic constraint, and supplies the factual answer to the user.

* Rule retrieval *

The system can be queried about the knowledge it possesses on the given domain. Here notion of kluster and k-view is particularly effective. It is possible to formulate complex queries about single rules, about set of rules sharing a given property or satisfying a conditional expression on properties.

The query language is a critical feature. It must allow easy interaction with the system, both in the formulation of queries and in the presentation of the responses in a readable form to the user. It is recommended that the formalism for communicate with the user be independent from but mappable to the internal representation used to store the knowledge in the system.

* Inference *

This is the typical function expected by an ES. It refers to the deductive process performed in order to solve a given problem. The system will combine rules and facts to search for solutions. The way in which it actually proceeds in the search depends on the skill it has and on the specific strategy adopted. The system may use different search strategies for different problems or knowledge sections.

* Reasoning *

To inquire from the system about its reasoning means to ask for an explanation about the way it reaches the final or current state. The system must be able to recite the logic steps taken, the reasons for the choices made and why candidate alternative solutions were discarded. This is the trace of the inference process, it makes the user aware of the functioning of the system and leads to improvement of its performances.

* Heuristics *

The system can be asked to reveal the different strategies it has available and uses when solving problems. There may be alternate heuristic techniques and a history of their effectiveness. Rules can decide which is best to use on the basis of the previous experiences, allowing a flexible policy, similar to a dynamic strategy using a cache organization for its access structure.

The heuristics to be held by the system are essentially of two kinds. One kind is related to the domain and best embodied in the rules that describe the behavior of the reality, that we called skill. The second refers to the way the system works internally, when its search space is the knowledge itself. The search strategies are the well known, and include techniques as backward or forward chaining, depth first or breadth first search, and so on [Pear:84].

* Knowledge structure *

This type of inquiry refers to the schemas of the system. It requires descriptive information about the meta-knowledge and meta-data kept within the system, and its organization. This function is similar to database schema retrieval functions. It provides the user with the information to make decision about the applicability of a given EDS to a task.

4.2. Update Functions

The knowledge base must evolve according to the reality it is modeling. The evolution concerns the three type of knowledge, that can be accessed by the user and updated: facts, rules and search strategies, that we refer to as skill.

Updating facts is necessary in order to guarantee the consistency of the data kept by the system with the corresponding real-world entities. The evolution of these data is subject to the known constraints that rule the specific domain. Therefore any update of facts must be checked against the pertinent rules; generally it is sufficient to refer to one kluster. We discussed in Section 3.5 the alternatives when conflicts occur.

Any change of the real-world rules, or any discovery of new rules, or refinement of existing rules with more precise ones must be reflected by the rulebase of the system. The rules can be changed explicitly by the users or the system itself can reach, through a process of learning, a state in which a change appears timely to be introduced with or without human intervention.

Skill represents the way experts, using their knowledge about facts and rules of a given domain, proceed in finding a solution to a given problem. Skills include knowledge about different types of strategies, rules of thumb, and general heuristics. Skills may improve, therefore updates are necessary; they improve mainly due to experience and study. In systems that requires an activity of successfully solving problems and obtaining feedback about the quality, speed and accuracy of the solutions found are essential.

The update functions may also affect the way the knowledge has been modeled, structured and implemented on the computer. This type of organizational update is a management function. It is very similar to the function of a databases administrator. This person can also intervene with the operation of the system. This function may, of course, be distributed, and in turn be subjected to rules.

Such organizational update functions may realign the relational conceptual schema which models the facts, and change the clustering of the knowledge and the data structures that implement the knowledge base in order to speed up certain functions. Included in this level of update is also the establishment and modification of views, and the definition of rules and authorization for updates from views.

5. CONCLUSIONS

In this paper we defined criteria and a structure for an Expert Database System, a system capable to manage complex knowledge, namely facts and rules, and its *skill*. Skill refers to the ability that an expert shows in finding solution to problems.

The proposal is intended to move expert system technology on a new track. By trying to move within database technology we hope to deal with advanced and quantitatively large structures. The structures may contain complex objects which can support machine-processable knowledge.

To make progress within this framework it is necessary to carry out specific research in order to define more precisely the characteristics of EDS. In particular the following points should be investigated.

(i) The definition of a structured model for knowledge representation that allows description and representation of knowledge having several levels of abstraction. The notion of *kluster* defines a high organization level of extensional knowledge, and a knowledge schema provides its intension.

(ii) A better understanding of different types of knowledge is required. In particular a clear separation between domain knowledge, i.e., facts and rules, and skill, i.e., the heuristics that the expert uses to solve problems, ought to be investigated.

(iii) At a lower level, research on storage organization for the different type of knowledge and search techniques is required. Frames may provide the basis for the representation. That will lead to the introduction of a structure seen within databases as the internal schema.

ACKNOWLEDGMENTS

Research leading to this paper has been partially supported by DARPA contract N39-82-C-250 for research into Knowledge Based Management Systems (KBMS). Revisions were guided by discussions during the 1984 Kiawah Island workshop, and we thank all the participants who helped us clarify our thinking.

6. REFERENCES

[Barr:81]
A.Barr, E.A.Feigenbaum, and P.Cohen: *The Handbook of Artificial Intelligence*; William Kaufmann Pub., 1981.

[Bati:82]
C.Batini and M.Lenzerini: *A Methodology for Data Schema Integration in the Entity Relationship Model*; Universita' di Roma, Istituto di Automatica, R.82-09, Jun.1982.

[Blum:82]
R.L.Blum: *Discovery and Representation of Causal Relationships from a Large Time-Oriented Clinical Database: The RX Project*; Springer Verlag, 1982.

[Brac:85]
R.J.Brachman and H.S.Levesque: "What Makes a Knowledge Base Knowledgeable -- a View of Databases from the Knowledge Level"; in this volume.

[Brod:85]
M.Brodie and M.Jarke: "On Integrating Logic Programming and Databases"; in this volume.

[Chak:82]
U.S.Chakravarthy, J.Minker, and C.Tran: "Interfacing Predicate Logic Languages and Relational Databases"; *Proc.of First Int'l Logic Programming Conference*, Marseille, 1982.

[Clan:83]
W.J.Clancey: "The Epistemology of a Rule-Based Expert System: a Framework for Explanation"; *Artificial Intelligence*, no.20, 1983.

[Cloc:81]
W.F.Clocksin and C.S.Mellish: *Programming in PROLOG*; Springer-Verlag, 1981.

[Dahl:85]
V.Dahl: "Logic Programming for Constructive Expert Systems"; in this volume.

[Date:81]
C.J.Date: *Introduction to Database Systems (III ed.)*; Addison Wesley, 1981.

[Deer:85]
M.Deering and J.Falletti: "Database Support for Storage of AI Reasoning Knowledge"; in this volume.

[Duda:77]
R.O.Duda, P.E.Hart, N.J.Nilsson, and G.L.Sutherland: "Semantic Network Representations in Rule-based Inference Systems"; *Workshop on Pattern-Directed Inference systems*, Honolulu, Hawaii. May.1977.

[Egge:84]
P.R.Eggert, D.S.Parker, and K.Parsaye: "Prototyping in PROLOG: Experiences and Lessons"; *IEEE Conf.on Logic Programming*, Atlantic City, Feb.1984.

[Fagi:78]
R.Fagin: "On an Authorization Mechanism"; *ACM Trans.on Database Systems*, vol.3 no.3, 1978.

[Gene:82]
M.R.Genesereth: "Diagnosis Using Hierarchical Design Models"; *Proc. of AAAI-82*, Pittsburgh PA, pp.278-283, Aug.1982.

[Hamm:78]
M.Hammer and D.McLeod: "The Semantic Data Model: A Modelling Mechanism for Database Applications"; *Proc.of SIGMOD Conf.*, 1978.

[Hamm:80]
M.Hammer and S.Zdonik: "Knowledge-based Query Processing"; *Proc.of VLDB 6 Conf.*, 1980.

[Haye:83]
F.Hayes-Roth, D.A.Waterman, and D.B.Lenat (Eds.): *Building Expert Systems*; Addison-Wesley, 1983.

[Hend:77]
G.G.Hendrix: "Expanding the Utility of Semantic Networks through Partitioning"; *Proc.of IJCAI 4*, 1977.

[Hsia:83]
D.K.Hsiao (Ed.): *Advanced Database Machine Architectures*; Prentice Hall, 1983.

[Jark:83]
M.Jarke and Y.Vassiliou: "Coupling Expert Systems with Database Management Systems"; *Artificial Intelligence Application for Business*, Proc.of the NYU Symp., May 1983.

[Lafu:85]
G.M.E.Lafue and R.G.Smith: "Implementation of a Semantic Integrity Manager with a Knowledge Representation System"; in this volume.

[King:81a]
J.J.King: "Query Optimization by Semantic Reasoning"; Tech.Rep.STAN-CS-81-857, CS Dept.Stanford Un., May 1981.

[King:81b]
J.J.King: "QUIST: A System for Semantic Query Optimization in Relational Databases"; *Proc.of VLDB 7 Conf.*, Sep.1981.

[Koga:84]
D.Kogan.: "The Manager's Assistant, An Application of Knowledge Management"; *IEEE Data Engineering Conference* 1, Los Angeles, Apr.1984.

[Kono:81]
K.Konolige: "The Database as Model: A Metatheoretic Approach; Technical Note 255, Artificial Intelligence Center, SRI International, Menlo Park CA, Sep.1981.

[Kowa:79]
R.Kowalski: *Logic for Problem Solving*; North Holland, 1979.

[Kuni:82]
S.Kunifuji and H.Yokota: "PROLOG and Relational Databases for Fifth Generation Computer Systems"; *Proc.of Workshop on Logical Bases for Databases*, Toulouse, Dec.1982.

[Leil:83]
H.O.Leilich and M.Missikoff (Eds.): *Database Machines*; Springer Verlag, 1983.

[Lloy:83]
J.W.Lloyd: "An Introduction to Deductive Database Systems"; *The Australian Comp.Jour.*, May 1983.

[Lori:82]
R.Lorie and Wilfred Plouffe: "Complex Objects and their Use in Design Transactions; IBM Research report RJ 3706, Aug.1982.

[Mins:75]
M.Minsky: "A Framework for Representing Knowledge"; in *The Psychology of Computer Vision*, P.Winston (Ed.), McGraw-Hill, 1975.

[Ohsu:82]
S.Ohsuga: "Knowledge Based Systems as a New Interactive Computer System of the Next Generation; Computer Science and Technologies, 1982, North-Holland, pp.227--249.

[Pars:83a]
K.Parsaye: "Database Management, Knowledge Base Management and Expert System Development in PROLOG"; *Proc.of ACM-SIGMOD Conf*, San Jose, June 83.

[Pars:83b]
K.Parsaye: "Logic Programming and Relational Databases"; *IEEE Database Engineering*, Dec.1983.

[Pear:84]
J.Pearl: *Heuristics: Intelligent Search Strategies for Computer Problem Solving*; Addison-Wesley, 1984.

[Rich:84]
E.Rich: "The Gradual Expansion of Artificial Intelligence"; *IEEE Computer*, May 1984.

[Samm:83]
C.A.Sammut and R.A.Sammut: "The Implementation of UNSW-PROLOG"; *The Australian Comp.Journal*, May 1983.

[Sche:80]
P.Scheuermann and G.Schiffner: "Abstraction Capabilities and Invariant Properties Modeling within the Entity-Relationship Approach"; *Entity-Relationship Approach*, Chen(ed), North-Holland 1980.

[SIGS:82]
Special Issue on Rapid Prototyping; in ACM SIGSOFT, Software Engineering Notes, Dec.1982.

[Ship:81]
D.W.Shipman: "The Functional Data Model and the Data Language DAPLEX"; *ACM TODS*, Vol.6 No.1, Mar.1981, pp.140--173.

[Smith:77]
J.M.Smith and D.C.P.Smith: "Data Base Abstractions: Aggregation and Generalization"; *ACM Trans.on Database Systems*, vol.2 no.2, June 1977.

[Smit:85]
J.M.Smith: "Expert Database Systems: A Database Perspective"; in this volume.

[Sowa:80]
J.F.Sowa: "A Conceptual Framework for Knowledge Based Systems"; *ACM-SIGMOD 1980*, pp.193--195.

[Sowa:81]
J.F.Sowa: *Conceptual Structures: Information Processing in Mind and Machine*; Addison-Wesley, 1981.

[Ston:75]
M.Stonebraker: "Implementation of Integrity Constraints and Views by Query Modification"; *ACM-SIGMOD 75*, King(ed.), San Jose, Jun.1975, pp.65--78.

[Ullm:82]
J.D.Ullman: "The U.R. strikes back"; *ACM-PODS 1*, Aho(ed), Mar.1982.

[Vass:83]
Y.Vassiliou, J.Clifford, and M.Jarke: "How Does an Expert System Gets Its Data?" (extended abstract); *Proc.of VLDB 9 Conf.*, Florence, Oct.1983.

[Warr:81]
D.H.Warren: "Efficient Processing of Interactive Relational Database Queries Expressed in Logic"; *Proc.of VLDB 7 Conf.*, Cannes, June 1981.

[Wied:78]
G.Wiederhold: "Introducing Semantic Information into a Database Schema"; *Proceedings of the CIPS Session '78*, Canadian Information Processing Society, Sep.1978, pp.338-391.

[Wied:83]
G.Wiederhold: *Database Design (2nd ed.)*; McGraw-Hill, 1983.

[Wied:84]
G.Wiederhold: "Knowledge and Database Management"; *IEEE Software*, vol.1 no.1, Jan.1984, pp.63--73.

An Expert Database System Architecture Based on an Active and Extensible Dictionary System

by

Edgar H. Sibley

George Mason University
and
AOG Systems Corporation
Fairfax, VA

ABSTRACT

The commercial products known as Information Resource Dictionaries (IRDS) today are usually extensible and many have active interfaces to Database Management Systems (DBMS). This suggests a combined IRDS/DBMS architecture that implements the extensibility feature through a meta-meta-meta-data interface. If this is provided, then a set of "triggered" operations at and between the four levels (data, meta-data, meta-meta-data, and meta-meta-meta-data) provides an effective architecture for the modern IRDS. The implementation of one commercial relational DBMS (SQL/DS) is used as an example of how this control/dictionary interface is presently provided and how it could be "improved."

Because this structure allows both definition and control facilities to be consistently applied in the combined architecture, and because the triggers (currently "database procedures" like SQL statements) may work at and across several levels to provide constraints, the architecture may be used for implementation of an Expert Database System. Additional modules to produce such a system would need to include a program generator that takes the set of rules to produce the triggered action and a mechanism for rule proving and ordering of the application.

Work discussed in this paper was partially supported by the Ada Joint Program Office and the Office of Naval Research under Contract Number N00014-83-C-0335.

1.Ø Introduction

The term "Information Resource Dictionary System" (IRDS) is relatively new, though early implementations of "Catalog" or "Data Dictionary Systems" -- DDS -- could be deemed prototypes. Because there is a general lack of understanding of the concepts of such systems and their value in the information system life cycle, a short introduction seems in order; more detail will be found in the literature; e.g., references 1 and 2.

The history of the IRDS can be traced to early Database Management System (DBMS) schema concepts. In fact, the literature of the modern commercially available Relational DBMS (R-DBMS) often states that the product has an integrated Data Dictionary; this is generally only a slightly augmented schema for use by the R-DBMS, though the privileged user may add textual definitions and query the dictionary/catalog/tables as though the schema was a normal database (set of relations).

However, the early DDS's of the late 6Ø's or early 7Ø's did much more than store the database schema. Indeed, some (e.g., U.C.C.'s UCC-1Ø) provided good facilities for maintaining and reporting on

* data (from textual definition to data typing and structure),
* the user community (security level, manager of group, etc.),
* the user/system programs (data parameters, programmer, permission list, language, etc.), and
* communication facilities (designated terminals, lines, configuration, etc.).

The relationships among these four "meta-entities" could also be given and reported.

The systems could respond to queries like:

1. Who is allowed to execute a given program?
   Is there any restriction on the location of the terminal from which it may be initiated (e.g., only those physically assigned to the Personnel Department)?
2. Who may modify the data elements in a certain record?
   Is there any time restriction (e.g., only between Ø9ØØ and 13ØØ ZULU)?
3. Which programs were last modified by a certain person?
   Was this within 3 days of his leaving the organization?

Three IRDS features (implementation architecture, passive or active or dynamic interfaces to a DBMS, and dictionary schema extensibility) are interrelated. These are now discussed; however, first a remark is necessary on notation. Here, the term "entity," without any adjective as qualification, is normally used here to convey the meaning of an "abstract data type" that represents a kind of user object. This must be distinguished from an instance (or occurrence) of the entity (type), which will be described using the adjective "instance" (i.e., entity instance). The same will be used to distinguish relationship and attribute types and instances; relationship and relationship instance or attribute and attribute instance. Thus the "entity type" is redundent, since "type" is not strictly needed to be added; however, in a few cases, it will be used to clarify the meaning.

1.1 Passive and Active Dictionary Interfaces

Even the earliest implementations of IRDS could be observed to have one of two different architectures, possibly driven by different "storage philosophies." These, in turn, gave rise to two different "control interfaces" -- though they do not map specifically to the architectures:

1. An external interface, where the IRDS is free standing.
2. An internal interface, where the IRDS is implemented on a DBMS.

In the first, the IRDS has its own mechanism for storing and retrieving the meta-database (the data about the customer's database). Vendors of such IRDS point out, as an advantage of their product, that it is not dependent on any particular DBMS. In the second, the advantages of the DBMS for storage and manipulation of the meta-database are obvious.

In order to make IRDS more attractive to customers, interfaces to other parts of the user system are added. These typically include --

(a) Means of reading any program data definitions (such as COBOL Data Divisions or an IMS DBDGEN and PCBGEN) as a method of preloading the dictionary with some important facts about the data names and program usage.

(b) Ways of generating the Data Definition or schema (for a COBOL program or a DBMS) from the dictionary entries.

(c) Collection and recording of run time information (e.g., IMS access times, automatically collected) to be stored in the dictionary database for future administrative use; e.g., database tuning.

These features are, however, cosmetic in nature and do not really tie the IRDS and DBMS with close control links; they are thus termed "passive," because they are only recording and managing meta-data (storing, retrieving and reporting it).

This passive interface could, however, be modified to allow the IRDS to control the operations of any DBMS to which it is tied. In the extreme, the IRDS may completely control the DBMS. As an example, in several early information systems implementations using UCC-1Ø, the programmer was restrained from compiling a COBOL program that reacted with an IMS database unless the COBOL field names (other than those for temporary/working storage) had been defined in the dictionary -- i.e., a precompiler aborted the compilation or the library manager refused to store the code unless the meta-database contained all externally referenced names. Such controls are imposed through active interfaces (though the active interfaces that are applied at run time have alternatively been called dynamic interfaces).

The question of whether an IRDS uses a DBMS or not is moot. Cullinet will provide its DDS product without the user previously buying IDMS (some of whose modules and interfaces are used in implementing its DDS). Such a buyer is not, however, able to use the full DBMS without additions (involving a new contract).

1.2 Dictionary Schema Extensibility

As the IRDS concept developed, users found that the vendor-provided entities, relationships, and attributes (instances of meta-entities) did not always suit their needs: the dictionary systems only provided a prespecified (fixed) schema. What was needed was a mechanism for adding instances of meta-entities, then of augmenting the instances of meta-relationships between the given and added instances of meta-entities, and finally defining new instances of meta-attributes to be added to the instances of either the meta-entities or meta-relationships. This is "dictionary schema extensibility."

Naturally, the added meta-entities, etc., should all be treated in the same way as the original set when making queries about them or generating reports; in other words, the user should not have to know whether a meta-entity such as "requirements documentation" is original or added when requesting a report on it.

2.0 Information Resource Dictionary Systems

2.1 Passive IRDS

The passive IRDS has a meta-database and a set of routines to manage it. Because the system needs so many of the functions of a DBMS, there are some advantages in using one as a "passive" meta-database management device. Data may be entered either by hand or collected from previously defined "formats" and schema. Typical entries can be broken into three categories (with communication data as a possible fourth):

1. Meta-data referring to application system data:

   Schema information:
   Internal-, Conceptual-, and External-Schema (subschema or view) names or traditional file names.

   Schema component information:
   Entity, attribute, and relationship names (or the equivalent for specific DBMS, such as record, field name, and set for network/CODASYL), group or record names in traditional.

   For entities, attributes, and relationships:
   Textual description, Password, Protection-Type.

For entities:
Index name, physical attributes.

For attributes:
Data type -- integer, character with maximum length, data class.

For relationships:
Names for special structures, such as Contains (as in "Table Contains Column") and also Is-validated-by (as in "attribute Is-validated-by validation-procedure"), physical aspects, such as forward and backward pointers or pointer arrays.

2. Meta-data on the application programs and procedures:

   For procedures, modules, etc.:
   Program-class, program or module name, language, query name, Validation procedure name, and

   For program structure:
   Relationships, like Calls ("program name Calls module name").

3. Meta-data on people:

   Creator-, programmer-, and user-type, creator, programmer, and user name, manager-type and name.

   For management structure:
   Relationships like Manages ("manager name manages programmer name") and Owns ("creator name owns table name").

There are, of course, also interrelationships between the meta-data objects; these include:

Relationships, like Uses ("user name Uses program name") and Has-authority-for ("creator name has-authority-for schema").

2.2 Active IRDS and their Interface Properties

A DBMS schema may be considered a prototype dictionary. Indeed, many relational DBMS consider the schema tables to be an example of one -- , and this is true, in a strict sense, though its value is less than that of most stand alone commercial products.

The earliest of the DBMS required a schema, but possibly the first implementation to have consistency of operations between its database and its schema was the Philips' PHOLOS system, a CODASYL network model introduced in the early 70's. SPIRES had a similar capability. In PHOLOS, the schema was stored as records and sets, where the meta-database/schema contained meta-records that were populated as records and sets, as shown in figure 1. The illustration shows that at the next highest level of schema (the schema of schemas or meta-meta-database), the <u>entities and</u>

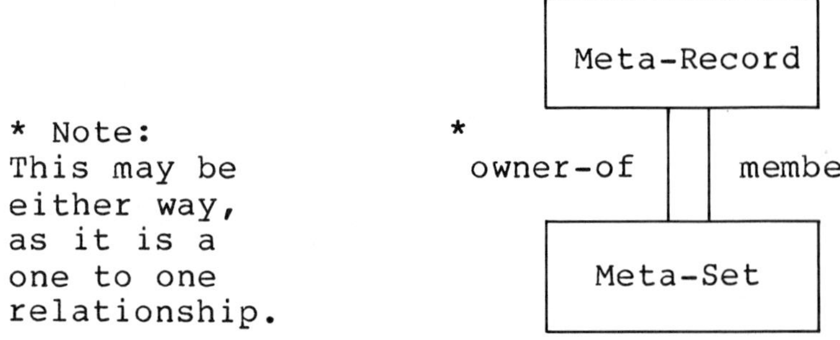

(a) The Schema of Schemas (meta-meta-database)

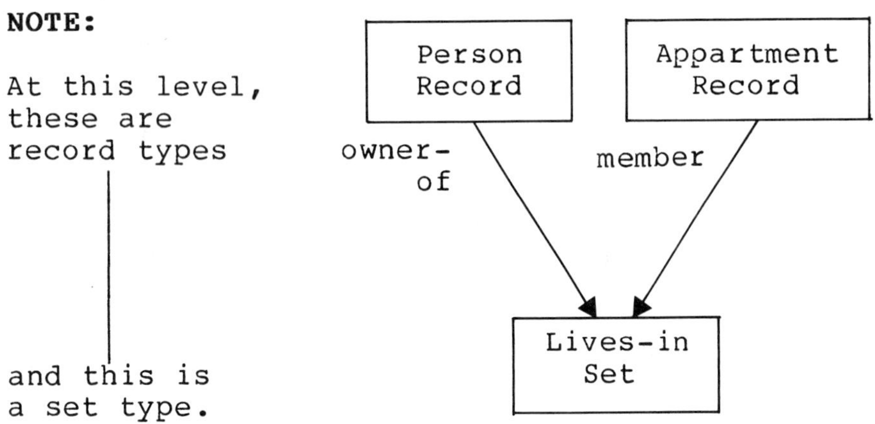

(b) The Schema or Subschema (meta-database)

An Instance of the Schema of Schemas

Figure 1. The PHOLOS Schema "Bootstrap"

relationships of the next lower level (records and sets) are meta-entities at the higher level. The beauty and simplicity of such an approach is that the operations on data are equally applicable to all levels -- schema or subschema and data! Thus PHOLOS would check that a new subschema was valid by traversing it and at the same time traversing the schema, thus ensuring that the subschema did not have any constructs that were inconsistent with those of the schema.

Some recent implementations of R-DBMS have a similar approach, as illustrated by IBM's SQL/DS, where the schema and some parts of "the schema of schemas" are stored in the SQL/DS System Catalogs. These are described (see reference 3) as a set of tables which "are created automatically during database generation."

There are many tables that make up the System Catalogs. Specific details are not of importance here, but the following introduces the major tables and shows how they present the equivalent of a dictionary. Components are:

(a) The main entities (tables and views). The main attributes (column names) and validation methods (duplicates allowed for indexed fields, data type, nulls allowed or not, etc.). The relationships or auxiliary tables with common columns; i.e., the inherited or "foreign keys," which should be controlled along with the columns of the original tables for update and deletion consistency.

SYSCATALOG has a row for each table or view (including itself and the other catalog tables); it names the table creator. SYSCOLUMNS has a row for each column of each table or view; this provides data type and length, and whether nulls are allowed. SYSINDEXES has a row for each index, with creator, columns covered, and whether field values must be unique. SYSSYNONYMS has an entry for all synonyms and their creator. SYSVIEWS receives the definitions of views at the time of processing the SQL statement that created it.

(b) The assignment of right-to-access the system, initially through passwords; the creator of the table or author of the program (the table "owner," though the DBA has authority to assign space and assign authority) -- the owner may then grant access rights to others.

SYSUSERAUTH contains passwords of users and of holders of special privileges (these are: the DBA, who has the only right to access this table, and the RESOURCE, SCHEDULE, and CONSTRUCT authorities); SYSUSERLIST is a view of this, owned by the SQLDBA, but without password information. SYSTABAUTH is the main access granting table; it contains user names privileged to access entire tables and views plus the source of the right (such as another user). Program priviledges are granted to the programmer (from the owner) and from the programmer to the user; the table is also used in revokation of rights. The entry is time-stamped. SYSCOLAUTH contains

UPDATE rights on tables and views, if they are on a column by column basis; it is linked to SYSTABAUTH by the same time-stamp. SYSPROGAUTH contains privileges of users to run the programs and to grant rights to others.

(c) Space allocated and used; storage structure control.

SYSCATALOG has a list of all space (DBSPACE) for the tables, with statistics about its use by the data. SYSDBSPACES contains a row for each DBSPACE (including those allocated but not yet acquired) with user name, owner, and present percentage free space. SYSUSAGE records dependencies between objects of the dictionary, such as programs and their dependency on access modules and other system objects (e.g., indexes).

As pointed out in reference 4:

> "Since the SQL/DS catalogs are defined as normal tables with public read authorization, you can use SQL query statements to retrieve information."

The actions of CREATE, ALTER, and DROP TABLE or GRANT and REVOKE access rights (among others) have the effect of changing the catalogs. It is interesting therefore to see what interactions there are between the schema (catalog) and the database. There are, in fact, two distinctly different ones:

(a) Commands like CREATE TABLE and SELECT act on only one level. Thus although, in both cases, the command may access tables at different levels (data and meta-data), it never ever crosses levels during the same application. The first will update the SYSCATALOG, SYSCOLUMNS, and DBSPACES (where the table is to be stored), assuming user RESOURCE authority in SYSUSERAUTH. SELECT retrieves data from the tables or from the catalogs (if the user is so authorized).

(b) Commands like DROP TABLE must both change the meta-data and the data. This is because the catalog no longer needs to retain data on the table and its columns, nor any of its previous privileges and finally it is necessary to delete the table itself.

Obviously, the side effects of the DROP TABLE command are more complicated than those of CREATE TABLE. And if SQL were to have an "add column" command (it is not provided), there would have to be simultaneous update of two tables (data and meta-data). This could require substantial change; as an example, if the column entries were constrained to be "non-null and non-repeating" the system would have to ask the user what to add to each row.

The SQL/DS implementation could be said to embody the "active" dictionary concept in some ways, since some automatic updating and integrity controls may be defined in the schema/dictionary and imposed at the database level, but interaction is limited.

The properties of an active interface tie the operations of the IRDS and DBMS closer, particularly when the IRDS is extensible.

2.3 IRDS Extensibility

The need for extensibility of the IRDS arises when the user groups decide that the "IRDS schema" is too restrictive in the classes of meta-entities it allows. But in order to consider some of its ramifications, a more formal discussion of the terms is needed. In the following, the applications database exists at level Ø.

To illustrate the terms, a running example will be given. However, a special point must be made about the names of tables and other entities, such as columns, in the R-DBMS. The database at level Ø is the set of rows in all the tables. The level 1 schema consists first of the entity names that are used to define the tables and rows; of course, more is required, but these are not of concern to this explanation. The entity names are, however, "internal" and are often not the same as the words used in displaying the table with its column headers. Thus for a very small level Ø database with one table consisting of two rows:

<Jones, 92, 17/Ø3/55, Mechanic>,
<Shade, 28, 24/11/48, Writer>

Output of the table may result in the headers:

Personnel Table

Name	Number	date/birth	skill

But the relevant entries for the table and columns in the DBMS-schema or dictionary-database may be:

Dictionary Table

Meta-entity	Meta-entity_Name (instance)
Table	Personnel Table
Column	Emp-name
Column	Emp-num
Column	DoB
Column	Emp-skill
Column_Header	Name
Column_Header	Number
Column_Header	date/birth
Column_Header	skill

2.3.1 Level 1 -- Meta-data

The level 1 components consist of entities, relationships, and attributes. In IRDS terms, these form the "dictionary database" while the instances are in the "applications database." Each entity, relationship, and attribute is defined as having a type, which classifies it by providing a direct or indirect definition of its allowed component(s) or value set(s). An attribute can be associated either with an entity or a relationship. Note that in some dictionary systems, the "name" of an entity, or relationship, or attribute is not considered one of its attributes, but a special property. To repeat the example from level Ø, the level 1 entities are: "Emp-table", "Emp-name", "Emp-num", "DoB", and "Emp-skill".

Relationships between data entities are not specifically defined in the relational system; they are represented by a special table with the same columns as those in the entities to be related. Constraints (in the form of triggered procedures) may be stored at level 1. As discussed below, they are, however, enforced at level 2.

To demonstrate this, let us suppose that another table called "Job-assignment" is to be related to the Personnel table at this level. A new table named "Assigned" is then added, as follows:

Personnel Table

	Name	Number	date/birth	skill
	...	....	....	..
------>		X		
	...	....	....	..

Job-assignment Table

	Job-name	Job-num	Total-price
	......	.....	....
------>		Y	
	......	.....	....

Assigned Table

	Emp-num	Job-number	Hours
	.....	....	...
------>	X	Y	
	.....	....	...

A validation procedure "Assgn-rel-val" must be defined to check that any new row in this table is consistent with entries in the other two tables; it may be defined at level 1 as:

"Assgn-rel-val: When adding a row in the table Assigned, the value to be added for the Emp-num column must exist as a

Number entry in the table Emp-table and the corresponding value for Job-number must exist as a Job-num in table Job-assignment."

As discussed later, another way of achieving this validation is by parameterizing a generic procedure; this is illustrated in figure 2. However, such a description assumes that the generic procedure is one level higher than the instantiated procedure; the generic procedure is therefore at level 2 (and enforced one level higher).

2.3.2 Level 2 -- Meta-meta-data

The level 2 components are meta-entities, -relationships, and -attributes. Thus every type of component (entity, relationship, and attribute) at Level 1 is represented by a meta-entity at level 2, as illustrated in the Meta-Entity Table of figure 3. Other level 2 components may be used to describe the structure of the dictionary (see the Meta-Attribute and Meta-Relationship Tables), and also to specify rules to be applied/enforced on level 1 components; e.g., constraint on the length of entity names (Column-Name, Maximum-Length in the Meta-Attribute Table).

Any allowable dictionary structure is therefore defined through meta-relationships; in a system other than an R-DBMS, one might allow a meta-attribute to be associated with a meta-entity that represents a relationship; however, in an R-DBMS the constraint between tables is really an equivalent of this.

It should be noted that one meta-entity has already been cited: the generic procedure. With this, the specific constraint at level 1 (Assgn-rel-val) can be replaced by:

"Rel-val" with its seven parameters --
[Rel-name, c1, c2, e-1-name, c3, e-2-name, c4] is:
"When adding a row in Rel-val-name, c1 must be the same as an entry in c3 of the table e-1-name and c2 must be the same as an entry in c4 in table e-2-name."

The meta-meta-database definition of figure 3 shows, in effect, one structure of an R-DBMS, in a way somewhat analogous to that in Hardgrave's Set Processor implementation (reference 5), but it is at this level that new meta-entities are added to extend the system. However, level 3 is needed to make validation of the structure easy.

2.3.3 Level 3 -- Meta-meta-meta-data

This, which has been termed the meta-schema level, is not implemented in current commercial IRDS. However, if it were available (explicitly), Level 3 components would be the types of the existing Level 2 components. Moreover, the application of some of the concepts suggested here is the basis for one apparently valuable architecture of an extensible IRDS with active interfaces to a

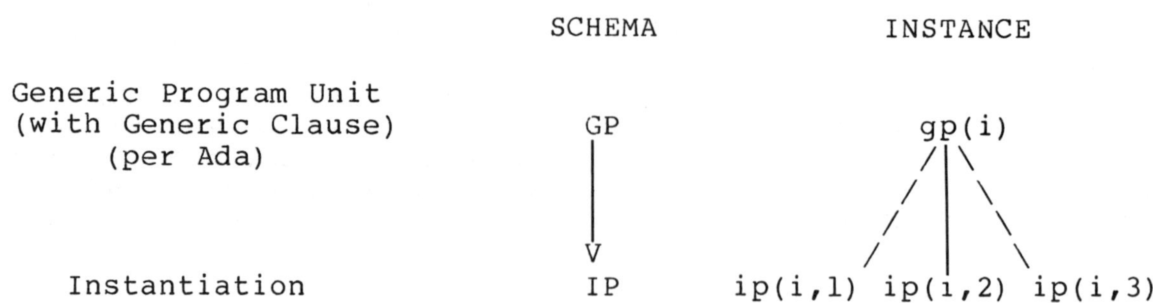

(a) Generic/Instantiation Procedures as a "Program Schema"

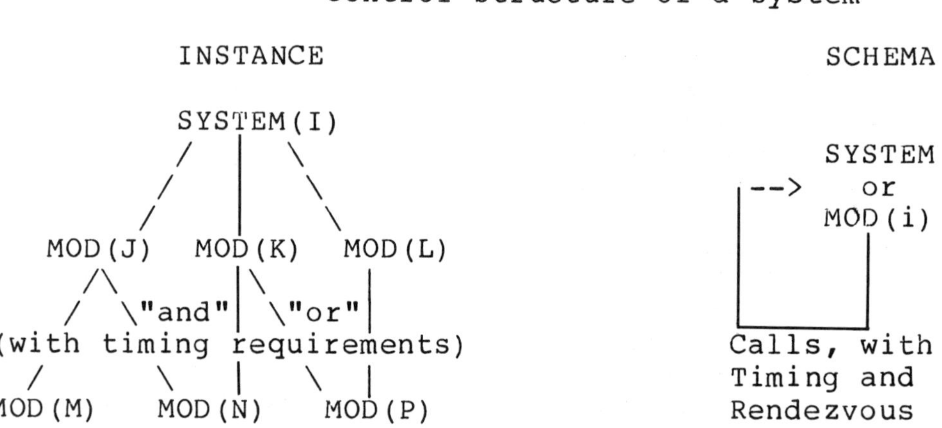

(b) Instantiation of the "Control Schema"

Figure 2: The Program Schema and Control Schema Concept

Meta-Entity Table

Meta-Entity	Meta-Entity-Name	Example at Level 1
Entity	Table	"Personnel Table"
Entity	Row	--
Entity	Item	"date of birth"
Entity	Column	skill
Relationship	Contains	--
Relationship	Domain	--
Attribute	Cardinality	2 rows
Attribute	Owner	Steerforth
Attribute	Description	"Textual informn."
Attribute	Validation-Name	Assgn-rel-val
Attribute	Degree	4 columns

Meta-Attribute Table

Meta-Entity-Name	Meta-Attribute-Name
Maximum-Length	Table-Name
Maximum-Length	Column-Name

Meta-Relationship Table

M-Relationship-Name	From	To	M-Attribute-instance
Containment	Contains	Table	First
Containment	Contains	Row	Second
Rows of table	Having	Table	First
Rows of table	Having	Cardinality	Second

Figure 3: A Relational IRDS Schema
(meta-meta-database)

DBMS and hence to an Expert DBS.

The meta-meta-entities at level 3 are made up of the meta-entities, -relationships, and -attributes at level 2. Some other possible meta-meta-entities for information resource management and control are:
attribute-validation-procedure and attribute-validation-data, and life-cycle-stage-name and life-cycle-status-name.

A meta-attribute may also be associated with a meta-relationship through a meta-meta-relationship; one reason for this would be to describe the components of more-than-binary relationships in system descriptions where only binary relationships are allowed (this is the case in the definition of a FIPS IRDS for the Federal Government, see also reference 6). There, every relationship (type) is defined with instances of two meta-meta-entities such as:

MRT (relationship[-type], entity[-type]-1)
with the meta-attribute FIRST (or SOURCE) and
MRT (relationship[-type], entity[-type]-2)
with the meta-attribute SECOND (or TARGET).

It should be noted that MRT is an example/instance of a mete-meta-entity and that consequently any additional information about it is really at level 4. Indeed, there, two meta-meta-entities are needed to define a meta-relationship. Tertiary or higher order relationships are then possible by having a THIRD and FOURTH meta-attribute, etc. This then allows the definition of such complex relationships as are needed in some life cycle control systems.

Other meta-meta-relationships are those where components are: meta-entity and meta-attribute, meta-relationship and meta-entity, and meta-relationship and meta-attribute. The four Levels are illustrated in figure 4. Level 3 may be a useful way of allowing parameterization of a procedure for its execution at a lower level. This is easiest seen in the way that the so-called "semantic constraint" has had to be added to relational systems (because they heretofore lacked the generic procedures available in CODASYL/network DBMS; e.g., "automatic" insertion of a record into a "set" is generic, as it constrains the action of addition for any "record" into a "set" that is so defined). Now in order to achieve this same property in the older or "traditional" relational system (assuming the availability of triggered procedures), the procedure must be rewritten, with each parameter inserted in the definition, for each relationship that needs an automatic insertion property.

The requirement for a generic procedure may better be met at a "higher level" by using a Lambda-calculus definition with parameterization by data, meta-data, or meta-meta-data (depending on the level of abstraction), and then executed at the lower level.

Level	Type of Data	Name in DBMS	Name in IRDS
Ø	Data		--
1	Meta-Data	Database	IRDS Database
2	Meta-Meta-Data	Schema	IRDS Schema
3	Meta-Meta-Meta-Data	Schema Schema	"IRDS Meta-Schema"
		--	

Some Controls:

1. Validation of Application Data --
   Statement (e.g., like SQL query) at Level 1
   Action on Level Ø

   [Note that this is a specific constraint]

2. On Structure of IRDS entities --
   Statement (e.g., a meta-relationship) at Level 2
   Action at Level 1, with side effect (if active interfaced) at Level Ø

   [Note that this is also a specific constraint]

3. Generalized Structural Constraint --
   Statement (e.g., a meta-meta-relationship) at Level 3
   Instantiation at Level 2
   Action at Level 1, with side effect (if active interfaced) at Level Ø

   [Note that this is a generic constraint]

4. On the IRDS Schema --
   Statement at Level 3
   Action at Level 2

   [Note that this is also a specific constraint]

5. Generalized IRDS Schema Constraint --
   Statement at Level 4
   Instantiation at Level 3
   Action at Level 2

   [Note that this is also a generic constraint]

Figure 4. The IRDS Levels

3.0 Control Using an Active Extensible IRDS/DBMS Interface

Figures 5 and 6 illustrate changes to the meta-database of an extensible IRDS built on an R-DBMS.[++] It should, however, be obvious that the use of an R-DBMS is irrelevant -- a similar system could be designed using Cullinet's IDD, which primarily uses the IDMS network data model as its basis, though it also has an integrated relational interface for the same database. In the diagrams, the original set of tables is in figure 3; additions of figure 5 will allow use of an entity called "requirements" and another called "stored program" and make a relationship between them (by defining a table). However, as stated previously any constraint is imposed at a higher level. Then, the additions in figure 6 allow the definition of a generic/instantiated program concept (as in the Ada (R) language [**]) and also some interesting representations of control structures.

If the system interfaces are active/dynamic then the entities, etc. that are added can control the operation of the DBMS through constraints and triggers, which may be either specific or generic and initiated on the occurrence of an event, such as a change in any data item. The procedures, as previously, can be one of several types:

1. Operative at one level.
This occurs in the computation of age given the date of birth and "today's date".

2. Operative from a higher level to its next lower level.
As an example, a child table entry (a row) in the database must be deleted if neither parent is an employee (this means that when an employee leaves, the child entry is deleted unless the other parent is still an employee).

3. Operative from one level, but cascading over several.
This happens when an action must be recorded at the level affected, but it causes an action at other lower levels; typically, the constraint structure is changed or the meta-meta-entities are altered (such as the changes to the table definition cited in section 2.2).

The triggers which cause the operation are therefore embedded at each level, and the actions (which may be passive, in the sense of a conditional returning a logical variable, or active, initiating an action) may cascade other actions by setting triggers in other places -- sometimes at other levels, and hence the need for a control structure, as shown in figure 2.

Footnote:
[++] Obviously, this IRDS definition bears a familial resemblance to the Catalogs of section 2.2, but the added features attempt to correct some deficiencies and provide consistency through the use of a meta-meta-meta-database architecture.
[**] Ada is a registered trademark of the U S Government, Ada Joint Program Office.

Meta-Entity Table (Additions only)

Meta-Entity	Meta-Entity-Name
Entity	Requirements
Entity	Program
Relationship	Implements
Attribute	Program-Name
Attribute	Program-Body
Attribute	Requts-Author

Meta-Attribute Table (Additions only)

Meta-Entity-Name	Meta-Attribute-Name
Program	Program-Name
Program	Program-Body
Requirement	Reqt-Name
Reqt-Auth	Date-Accepted

Meta-Relationship Table (Additions only)

M-Relationship-Name	From	To	M-Attribute-instance
Implementation	Implement	Program	First
Implementation	Implement	Requirement	Second
Writes	Reqt-Auth	Author-Name	First
Writes	Reqt-Auth	Reqt-Name	Second

Figure 5: An Extended Relational Representation

Meta-Entity Table (additions only)

Meta-Entity	Meta-Entity-Name
Entity	Generic-Prog
Entity	Validation-Program
Attribute	Function/Subroutine
Relationship	Instant
Attribute	Program-Size
Relationship	Contains/Calls
Relationship	Triggers

Meta-Attribute Table

Meta-Entity-Name	Meta-Attribute-Name
Program	Program-Size
Generic-Prog	Owner
Cont/Call	Function/Subroutine

Meta-Relationship Table

M-Relationship-Name	From	To	M-Attribute-instance
Instantiation	Instant	Generic-Prog	First
Instantiation	Instant	Program	Second
Calling Sequence	Cont/Call	Program	First and Second
Calling Method	Triggers	Item	First
Calling Method	Triggers	Validation-Program	Second

Figure 6: Relational Representation of Program and Control Schemas

4.0 An Architecture for Expert DBS Using IRDS

The architecture presented here consists of four levels of data (as shown in figure 4); at each of the levels, there are three major "objects" (data, procedure, and control) with levels and interfaces, as shown in figure 7. The four levels are used to define the entity and its abstraction. Thus the instance level is the place where the data, program, and control mechanisms exist and operate, while the schema level is where they are defined, the meta-schema level is where the concepts at the schema level may be extended, and the fourth where the extensions may be enforced. It is interesting to note that the levels can also be considered to consist of: object, meta-object, meta-meta-object, and enforcing meta-meta-meta-object.

The definition of the prime data objects involves the three parts: Entities, Relationships, and Attributes. The Objects must be Referenceable, Persistent, and Typed and they may need to be organized (possibly using faceted classification, though a simple typing mechanism may be sufficient). There are some special Relationships that are only constraining at Run-time; these are the Control Relationships, with their Control Structures, working in conjunction with other procedural Objects (Modules and/or tasks).

The obvious result of this is:

1. Types are objects that control values of other objects;
2. Active objects perform operations on other (passive) objects;
3. Operations are controlled through Rules;
4. Rules are themselves objects;
5. A Relationship may be an ordered set of other objects;
6. An attribute is a function of an object.
   It returns another object.
   Normally this is a Representation;
   possibly atomic, but maybe also a structure.

Thus, the structure of figure 7 will be sufficiently general to allow the implementation of Expert DBS.

5.0 Conclusions

Semantics of Levels higher than 2 must be investigated further, since it is difficult to decide if they are theoretically based or merely arbitrary or contrived. Though this might destroy the layered approach presented here, relationships between entities and meta-entities appears to be useful.

Some questions to be answered about the interactions are:

1. From Data to Control:
   Is the "trigger" the only necessary mechanism?
   How much generalization is enough?
   Is there a natural structure of the control schema?
   Does it differ from that needed for "Control to Program"?

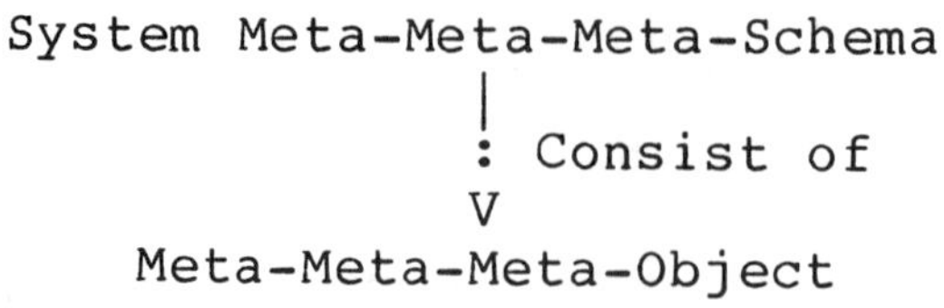

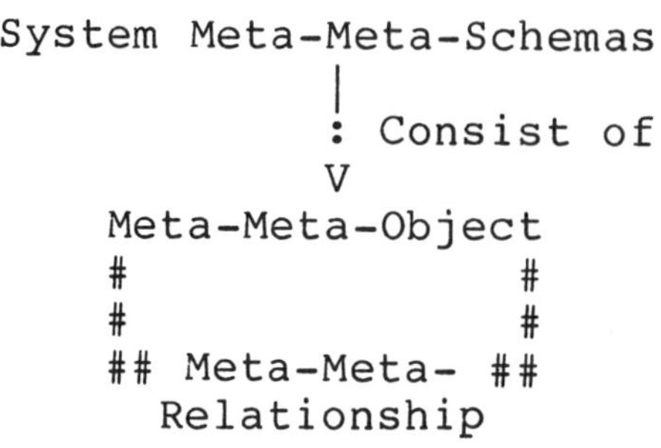

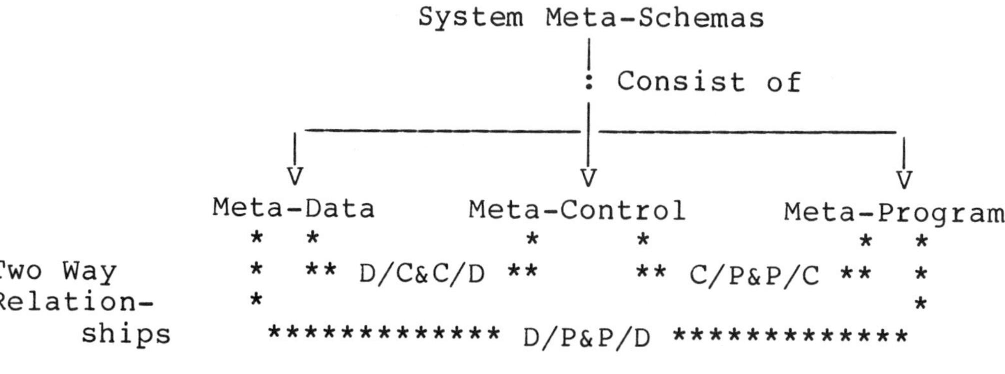

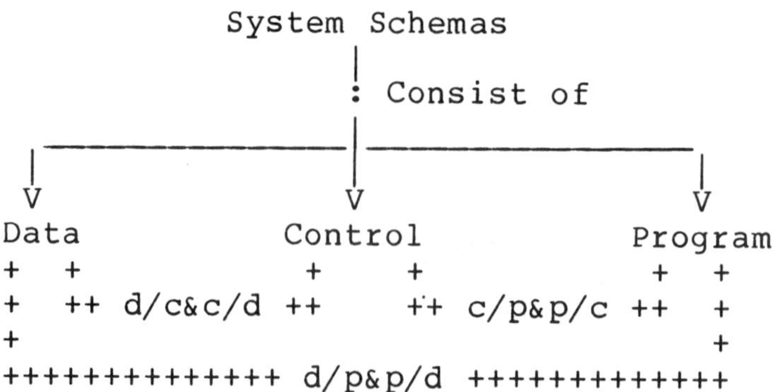

Figure 7: The Meta-System and Components

2. From Control to Program:
   Is this only a control structure?
   What might be the use of a meta control structure?

3. Control Structure and the "Meta-Control"
   Does the control of a meta system reflect that of a system? (For the meta-data system, it does)

4. Data Structure and the Meta-Data Interactions
   Some concepts of extensibility can only be provided by the use of trigger initiated procedures; is this the only interaction needed between data and control, or is there more?

5. Rules for Data-to-Control/Control-to-Program
   It appears that a Rule-based method could be used for generation of the controls in a trigger and task oriented system; Is this so? Is there a better way?

6.Ø Acknowledgements

The author would like to thank the following:

Dr. H. C. Lefkovits of AOG Systems Corporation for proposing the problem partially addressed here, early discussions, and careful reading and correcting of the manuscript. Drs. Raymond T. Yeh and N. J. Roussopoulos of the Department of Computer Science, University of Maryland, for discussions that led to concepts and overall architectures in the final sections of this paper. And to Dr. Ann E. Reedy for aid in clarification of many rough spots.

7.Ø References

1. Lefkovits, H. C., Sibley, E. H., and S. L. Lefkovits: "Information Resource/Data Dictionary Systems." Q.E.D Information Sciences, Inc. 1983 (6Ø4 pages).

2. Leong-Hong, B.W. and B.K. Plagman: "Data Dictionary/Directory Systems: Administration, Implementation, and Usage." John Wiley and Sons, 1982 (328 pages).

3. IBM Corp.: "SQL/Data System Terminal User's Guide." SH24-5Ø16-Ø, Programming Publications, Endicott, NY, 1981

4. IBM Corp.: "SQL/Data System Application Programming." SH24-5Ø18-Ø, Programming Publications, Endicott, NY, 1981

5. Koll, M.B., Hardgrave, W.T. and S.B. Salazar: "Data Model Processing." NCC Proceedings 1982, pp 571-578.

6. ANSC X3H4, Proposed American National Standard, IRDS, December 1984.

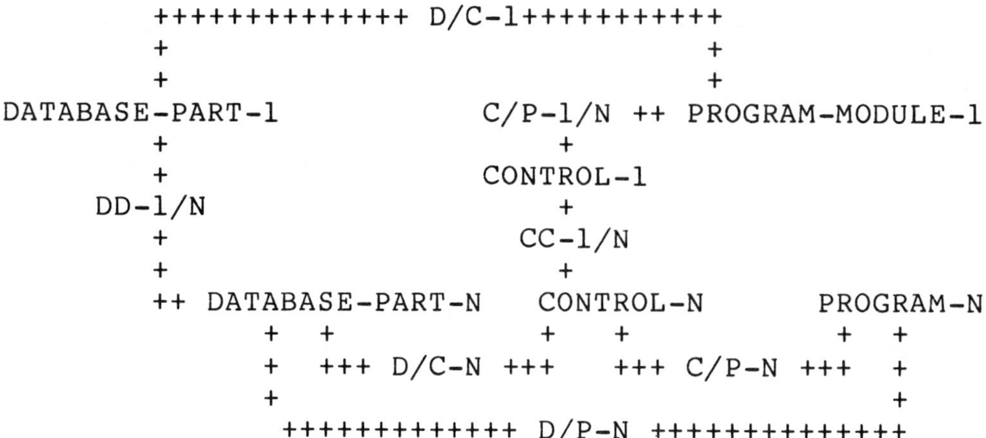

Figure 8: The Meta-System and its Component Interactions

An Interactive Data Dictionary Facility for CAD/CAM Data Bases

Stephanie J. Cammarata
Michel A. Melkanoff

Computer Science Department
and
Manufacturing Engineering Program
University of California
Los Angeles, CA 90024

1. Introduction

Over the past ten years, major advances have been made in the area of Computer Aided Design/Computer Aided Manufacturing (CAD/CAM). These advances are evident in many application areas such as computer aided drafting systems, engineering analyses, and numerical control (NC) machine operations. When CAD/CAM application systems were first introduced, they each operated independently and data was prepared manually as input to the individual programs. As a result, enormous overhead costs were incurred in the management of design and manufacturing data. Gradually, engineers and computer scientists recognized production inefficiencies due to gaps in the data flow, and sought to bridge these gaps in a variety of ways. Today, it is generally accepted that a solution can only be reached through a Computer Integrated Data Base Management System (CIDBMS) which will serve as a repository for the data needed by each of three major systems: Design, Manufacturing, and Business/Administration.

Numerous attempts are being made to use existing DBMS (Data Base Management Systems) for storing and manipulating CAD/CAM data; however, many features of CAD/CAM data are troublesome for current DBMS. Also, designers and engineers need additional capabilities which conventional data management systems do not offer.

Our preliminary studies have reviewed existing CAD/CAM DBMS and analyzed the capabilities required to represent and maintain CAD/CAM data. The main goal of this paper is to present the design of a *network-structured* data base dictionary facility with an *interactive graphical user interface* for CAD/CAM data management. We show how these two features provide high-level user facilities for *dynamic schema generation* and *interactive constraint specification*, not possible in existing data base systems. This research is the first phase in a major effort at UCLA toward developing a sophisticated Computer Integrated Manufacturing System [MEL84]. In the following sections we first motivate this work by outlining some of the problems of CAD/CAM data management, and discuss the desired functionality of CAD/CAM data base systems. We then present our design of an interactive dictionary facility in terms of its functionality. We conclude with a discussion of the contributions of this research in the areas of data modeling, CAD/CAM DBMS technology, and artificial intelligence methodology.

2. Problem Discussion and Motivation

In this section we first talk about problematic features of CAD/CAM data and then show why existing DBMS facilities cannot effectively manage such data.

2.1. Characteristics of CAD/CAM Data

First, CAD/CAM data is *heterogeneous.* Graphical, textual, procedural, and mathematical data are stored in their specialized formats and models [EBE82]. Graphical data, generated during the engineering design and drafting phase, include geometrical (metric) entities such as lines, points, arcs, splines, and curves; and topological entities such as faces, edges, and surfaces. A CAD drafting system usually manages graphical data and therefore, it is stored in system dependent formats [MEI83]. Textual data is found in all phases of CAD/CAM, from design through marketing. File systems and generalized DBMS frequently maintain the textual data. Procedural data consists of sequences of actions; which, for manufacturing planning may include a process plan; for numerical control (NC) operations may be an APT program; and during inspection, may refer to an inspection sequence. Finally, mathematical data is needed for many engineering computations and analyses such as load stress and other physical calculations.

Second, CAD/CAM data is characterized by its *dynamic schema.* A schema defines the allowable structures for data instances and is generally viewed as a static collection of data types. The data types represent attributes, entities, and relationships of the application being modeled. CAD/CAM data differs from business-oriented data because the structure of CAD/CAM data actually grows with the design of the artifact and therefore cannot be completely defined in a static schema. At each manufacturing phase, schema specification is interleaved very closely with the construction of an object [EAS82, EBE82].

A third characteristic of CAD/CAM data is its *entity-oriented* or *object-oriented* nature. A recursive organization where objects have other objects as their parts is typified by a Bill of Materials (BOM) data base. However, in addition to BOM hierarchies, CAD/CAM entities also have structural descriptions in terms of other entities. Many of these descriptions preclude the use of a strict hierarchy, necessitating a network organization. For example, geometrical entities, such as points, lines, and arcs compose topological entities, like faces and edges, which in turn compose solid objects. Relationships such as *inside, connected to, bounded by, on top of, next to* convey structural descriptions of objects, and imply additional facts about the object. For instance, if the relationship *connected to* exists between two beams, it would imply that the length of the two *connected* beams is the sum of their separate lengths. Although such relationships are used for modeling an assembly or part, data base users admit that the most frequent way of accessing the data is by entity, not relationship. Based on these observations, CAD/CAM data is most naturally represented by an object-oriented network.

Finally, CAD/CAM data objects exhibit *object-specific relationships.* To model each assembly or part, designers express many unique relationships that can differ from part to part. No fixed set of relationships describes all entities. For example, all airplanes do not contain the same parts; moreover, each L-1011 was customized and therefore contained different specifications. In large diverse manufacturing environments there is little uniformity in the structure or content of data across different products.

2.2 DBMS Limitations

Current DBMS cannot effectively manage data with all the characteristics described above. First, they do not have adequate facilities to maintain heterogeneous data. Current commercial systems have evolved from record and file based systems to hierarchical and network set/owner models and most recently to flat relational models. Given this heritage, the predominant data structure is still a strictly typed, textual record. As such, current systems are best suited for applications with homogeneous, well-structured data such as numeric business data.

Specialized CAD systems and drafting systems represent graphical data using entities most suitable for displaying graphical images. These entities are usually simple geometric primitives such as point, line segment, circle, curve segment. In this representational approach, any semantic content implied by the graphical data is lost. For instance, by viewing a display, it may be obvious that one surface is orthogonal to another; however, it is impossible to derive this fact by querying the graphical data file. Some general graphics systems, especially 3-D representation systems, incorporate a good deal more semantic information in a structured way. However, the structure is fixed depending on the representation used, (i.e. boundary representation, cell decomposition, constructive solid geometry) and it is difficult to integrate other kinds of data such as textual or mathematical data. Also, an engineering drawing contains an even higher level of application-dependent semantic information. For example, manufacturing planners study drawings to produce a sequence of manufacturing processes, called a process plan, for fabricating a part. Queries like those below are posed by the planners while they are generating a process plan for a rotational part to be manufactured on a lathe:

Is the largest diameter in the middle or end of the part?
Are there any slots or keys?
Is there any internal turning required?

The number of similar queries is virtually unbounded. Therefore, a data base which can respond to these queries must be very rich in semantic knowledge and inference capabilities.

Second, most DBMS adhere to a static schema definition. Schema definition and generation are expensive off-line tasks. The enormous overhead for data base reconfiguration due to schema modifications prohibits the practical use of an interactive dynamic schema in most existing systems. Thus, the desired structure of the entities to be represented is completely defined at the time they are entered into the data base, and cannot be subsequently modified. An increasing number of DBMS are allowing schema revision to the extent that revisions are upwardly compatible with the old schema, and previously loaded data. However, this limitation still requires a user to make a strict distinction between schema definition and data specification, and the operations for performing each.

Describing object-oriented CAD/CAM data in the relational model exposes a third limitation of existing DBMS systems. In the relational model, a 2-dimensional table represents all data items participating in a given relationship, and data is accessed primarily through relations. This organization is unnatural and inefficient for CAD/CAM applications where primary access is by part. Forcing data to conform to a relational model can create two situations generally regarded as undesirable: ragged relations with repeating groups and null values [GUT82]; or expensive join operations across many relations [ULL80].

A final deficiency is the lack of expressive power in existing implementations of various data models. Current DBMS are used for applications requiring relatively few relationships to be represented compared to the large amount of data to be stored. Furthermore, these relationships are constant and uniform across all data instances. In contrast, CAD/CAM data requires many complex and part-specific relationships linking heterogeneous data items. Merely expressing M:N relationships is particularly cumbersome and restrictive in a CODASYL network and IMS hierarchy [CAR79, DAT81, ENC83]. Although network and hierarchical models, in general, can accommodate complex entities and relationships; particular implementations of these models limit the expressive power of the representation, resulting in an unnatural modeling environment.

3. Desired Functionality of CAD/CAM DBMS

The above characterization of CAD/CAM data, and critique of existing

DBMS systems, suggest the need for user capabilities unavailable from current data base models. Because a CAD/CAM data base is generated and used within many facets in a manufacturing organization, it is necessary to be able to *merge or integrate different sources of data* which reside in various files or data bases distributed both logically and physically. For example, the wing of an aircraft would have associated design, engineering, and manufacturing data. Although each category of data describes the same entity, the divisions represent a functional decomposition of the data. Moreover, within a category, different data types (graphical, textual, procedural, mathematical) should be accommodated.

The dynamic quality of the schema and data necessitates some highly *flexible and interactive user facilities.* Users need to interactively view or navigate the data base dictionary, and dynamically modify the schema for three purposes. First, they need to retrieve schema information such as the attributes which are defined for a given entity or the kinds of relationships that have been described. Second, a user may want to query specific data values such as the radius of drilled hole or the material of a particular part. Third, a user should be able to retrieve information such as file identifiers, auxiliary data bases, and program identifiers to aid future queries or data searching within or outside the data base system. Corresponding operations for modifying the schema and data should also be available. These facilities include initial generation of a new schema when designing a new part, and interleaving the schema definition with the storing of specific data values.

Maintaining integrity and consistency of CAD/CAM data has even greater importance in a highly robust modeling environment. Users need the capability to specify *integrity constraints* over a single data item or among many different data items. Constraints could take the form of restrictions on data values, like a range of temperatures for heat treatment of a given material; or, they could express relationships between data values which must hold, such as a mathematical equality between spindle speed, cutting speed and tool diameter for an NC operation. The user may also need to specify how constraints should be enforced, or what action to take if they are violated. For example, if the dimensions of a part are changed, the modifications should effect other changes in the data base such as graphical and cutter path data. Often it is desirable to have the changes automatically reflected in the data base, or in other cases, users might want to be notified of changes in order to make the appropriate modifications themselves. For instance, if the dimensions changed drastically, the part may need re-engineering in order to adhere to structural requirements. Furthermore, users may want to disable constraint maintenance temporarily during part design. A CAD/CAM DBMS should allow a designer to generate data base instances without immediate concern for integrity constraints, however, permit the user to query for constraints which are violated.

CAD/CAM data base users have also expressed a need for *application knowledge* to automate many CAD/CAM processes. Two areas which have shown potential are automatic generation of group technology codes and automatic process planning. Most of the data necessary to perform these processes is available in some form in the data bases. However it is necessary, first, to represent the data in a form amenable to the various application processes, and, second, to incorporate knowledge for manipulating the data and inferring absent data. The second task, namely, developing inference mechanisms, is beyond the scope of this research, although, work in that area is also being carried out in the Manufacturing Engineering Program at UCLA.

We have discussed four desirable capabilities of CAD/CAM DBMS. These features, and the functionality implied by them, are the subject of the following section.

4. A User-Oriented Dictionary Facility

A data base dictionary is a specification of the data base schema for a particular application. In traditional DBMS, the dictionary is constructed by the data base administrator (DBA) during the ***data base design*** phase [CAR79, TSI82]. The system discussed below will shift the design away from the DBA, to the users, by providing them with interactive facilities to define a schema and combine schema definition with generation and access of data.

A ***user-oriented*** dictionary represents a high-level organization of data from the user's point of view. This dictionary facility will allow a user to model the data in a fashion as close to reality as possible, so that data and relationships do not need to be contrived to fit a given structure. The dictionary also provides a common model for interfacing to many other sources of data. It is a starting point for navigating through a variety of different representations where information may be physically local or distributed. The construction of a user-oriented dictionary facility entails the definition of three major components, discussed below: the structure of the schema and data (from a user's viewpoint), facilities for maintaining the integrity of the data by constraint satisfaction, and user operations for viewing and manipulating the schema and data.

4.1 Data Dictionary Network

From a user's point of view, the main purpose of a data dictionary is to locate, define, and control the data to which a schema pertains [MCC82]. These three functions are particularly important in CAD/CAM applications because of the variety and magnitude of data, and because of the variety of ways in which the data is stored. Despite the seemingly lack of uniformity of the data, we have observed through our studies that one of the underlying structures of CAD/CAM data organizations is the Bill of Materials (BOM) hierarchy or some variation of it. In its simplest form, a BOM tree represents the ***uses*** or ***contains*** relation between assemblies and parts. A partial BOM hierarchy for a car is shown below purposes, mathematical data for simulation and analysis, manufacturing data for product fabrication and assembly. Not all of the data will necessarily be stored in the object data structure but symbolic and textual pointers will help a user determine where certain information can be found and possibly how to access the data. In this fashion, a node represents an abstraction of the underlying data associated with the object.

For example, *CAR*, the root node in the above BOM tree, could have some specification data in the form of attribute/value pairs such as:

CAR
<*size specification data*>
height: *53 in.*
wheelbase: *178 in.*
length: *98.8 in.*

Associated with the *BEARING* node may be some data about where to find the engineering drawings for this part and characteristics about the drawings:

BEARING
<*graphics data*>
drawing-file: */a/bearing-351/drawing/meet-data*
drawing-size: *11 in. x 17 in.*
drawing-medium: *b/w scope*
graphics-system: *CADAM*

Fabrication data and information about stress analysis programs need to be stored for a machined part like *PISTON*:

PISTON
<*fabrication data*>
drilling-processes: *(twist-drill, rough-ream, finish-bore)*
stress-analysis-program: *finite-ele-analy-1*

Notice the variety of data types represented here: text strings, units identifiers, filenames, lists, and program names. Other potential data types include arrays, data base identifiers, mathematical equations and specifications.

A user can navigate through a BOM-like network until the object in question is located. (A directed network structure is favored over a hierarchy because a part is likely to be used in more than one assembly.) Alternatively, a user could access a portion of the network by entering an object name or key identifier to focus directly on a part. At this level of abstraction the user bypasses much of the detailed data about objects which are of no interest. Once a user focuses on the object of interest, the corresponding node of the network is expanded allowing the user to "look inside" the object node to view the next

with explicit named links:

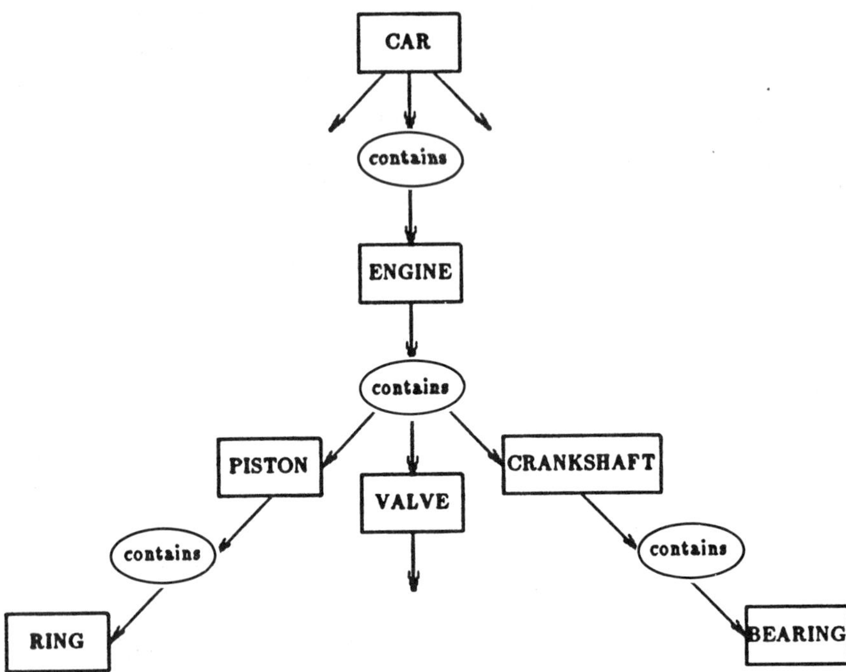

Each node in the tree represents a particular manufacturing entity or object, such as an assembly, sub-assembly, part, or sub-part. Links in the downward direction indicate the ***uses*** or ***contains*** relation; upward links represent the ***used by*** or ***is-contained-in*** relation. Any manufactured or purchased object will be found as a node somewhere in some BOM hierarchy and the majority of queries and updates are keyed on these objects. In existing engineering and manufacturing DBMS, the main navigational mechanism is the BOM data base which in itself may be very extensive. (In aerospace industries, generating a complete BOM listing for a commercial aircraft is a batch job taking several hours of CPU time.) Also, BOM data bases are output from many CAD systems and drafting packages as an interface to commercial product data bases.

We are extending the notion of a BOM hierarchy by viewing each node, not simply as an object declaration, but as its own data base directory encompassing the data about that particular object. The BOM organization provides a decomposition of an object based on its physical components. A non-leaf node can be viewed as a ***physical*** aggregation of its descendent nodes in the same way as a *CLASS* object is an ***conceptual*** aggregation of the individual components *COURSE*, *SEMESTER*, *INSTRUCTOR*, *ROOM* [SMI77]. Different decompositions including those discussed in [EAS78] will be introduced below for different descriptions of an object.

For each node in the tree, additional data about the object may include descriptions in the form of attribute/value pairs, graphical data for display level of detail and data values associated with the object.

A *geometrical* decomposition is the representation of an object based on its geometrical properties. For example, a triangular bracket in which two sides form a right angle is described by the network below:

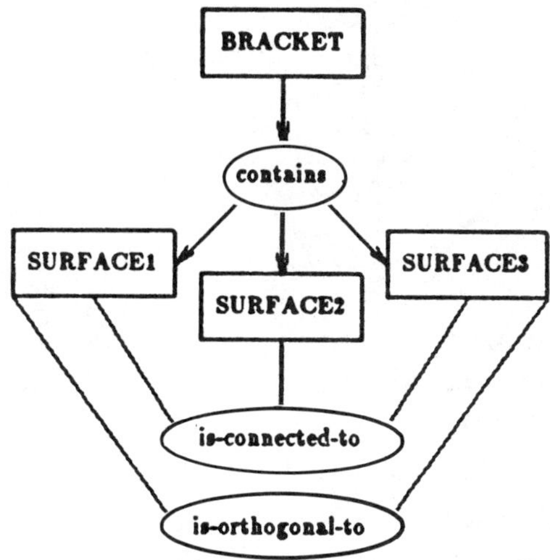

In addition to the ***contains*** links, we have introduced additional links to represent geometrical relationships describing the connectivity of surfaces. Similar geometric networks are presented by [LIL78] and [ULF82] for describing wire frame representations. They use relationships such as ***is-bounded-by***, ***is-a-chain-of***, ***delimits***, ***is-start-of***, and ***comes-after*** to describe geometry elements.

Spatial decompositions can also be represented as a network structure. A spatial description of a prototypical ARCH is shown below using spatial relationship links.

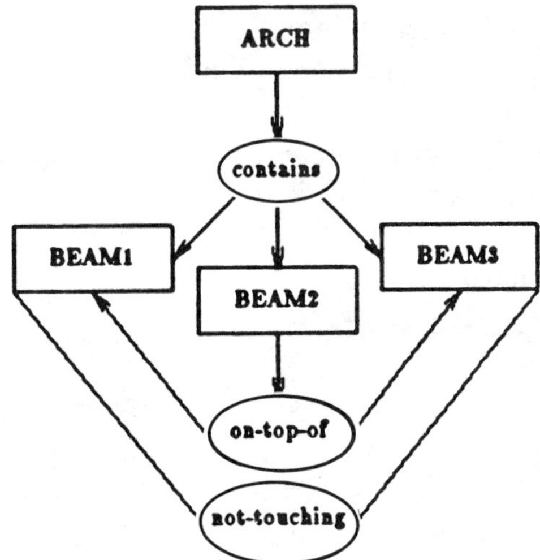

Different decomposition networks for the same object can be viewed individually or combined depending on the needs and requests of the user. The relationships presented above describe only the spatial qualities of the *ARCH* object; whereas, the network below describes the *functional* characteristics of its components:

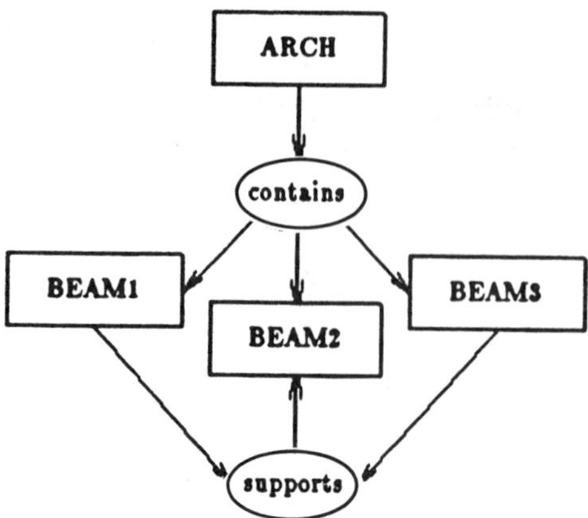

These network organizations promote interleaving of data with schema thus allowing a dynamic schema. As discussed earlier, for design data, a dynamic schema is an important characteristic because design engineers do not know a priori the exact structure of the object to be modeled. The semantics of a part or assembly can be viewed from many different perspectives: physically, structurally, geometrically, spatially, or functionally. Allowing users to define their own perspectives, generate new relationships, and build their own networks in an easy fashion encourages the development of a richer, more robust modeling environment.

4.2 Expressing and Satisfying Integrity Constraints

Links in the dictionary model can play different roles. The most general role is simply to express a relationship or mapping across two or more domains. Functions are represented in the network as directed links from the domain to the range. Named links can also express *integrity constraints*. The dictionary model enables a user to specify restrictions on data values or provide a procedure for the enforcement of constraints. Mathematical relationships such as *is-equal-to* or *is-greater-than* can be expressed as a relation link joining two object nodes. Because object nodes may also represent constants, users can express absolute or relative value restrictions such as:

tolerance < .00050
feed-rate = 2(spindle-speed)(feed)

The equation for feed-rate not only specifies a constraint but also implies a *procedure* for maintaining the constraint: if the values of spindle-speed or feed are changed, then recompute feed-rate according to the equation. Thus, mathematical relationships can help maintain the integrity of the data as well as express constraints. Other constraint relationships do not inherently prescribe an enforcement procedure; however, relation links have an additional feature which allow arbitrary procedures to be attached to the relation. The procedure will be triggered if data values linked to the relation change in a way which violates the constraint. For instance, in the relationship "*part-material is-element-of (cast-iron steel graphite)*", if the value of *part-material* violates the restriction, the following procedure may be triggered:

If cutting-tolerance < .00010 then set part-material to cast-iron
else if cutting-tolerance < .00050 then set part-material to steel
else if cutting-tolerance < .00100 then set part-material to graphite.

These constraint relationships are very similar to constraint equations [MOR84] which provide a declarative language for expressing constraints among relations. As an alternative to triggering attached procedures, a user may choose to be warned of potential inconsistencies resulting from data modifications. For example, if the dimensions of a part change more than some given threshold, the designer and engineer will be notified of the change by an on-line message. Below is one of the previous example networks where the *not-touching* relationship has been replaced by the relationship, "*distance > 0*", which can be viewed as a procedural specification of *not-touching*.

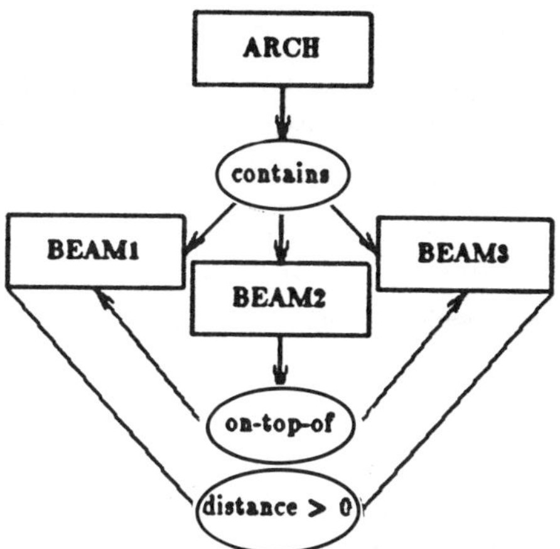

A spatial decomposition network with inequality constraint

The user will also have the capability to *enable* and *disable* constraint validation. During product design phase, data is incomplete and constantly being modified. Merely specifying a constraint, or updating a data value, should not necessarily trigger constraint validation. When a constraint is entered into the dictionary, it is initially in a disabled state. By setting a flag or switch, the user will enable constraint checking and maintenance. While a constraint is in the enabled state, any modification of associated data will trigger integrity checking and enforcement prescribed by the respective attached procedures.

By building a network of object nodes and constraint relationships, a user can express methods for sophisticated *constraint satisfaction*. Constraint specification can be viewed as a means of incorporating knowledge into the dictionary model by expressing design, engineering, and manufacturing *standards* as constraints. During early stages of part design at Lockheed Corporation, engineers must iteratively submit their drawings, parts list, and bill of materials to be validated against extensive industry standards. As one engineer stated "...it's the rule, not the exception, that there will be errors during the first passes of constructing the geometry and parts list data..." Incorporating such data in this fashion is a step toward *integrating application knowledge* into a data management system. Providing the designer and engineer with the facility to build their models by adding part-specific constraints themselves, and utilizing predefined corporation restrictions, further enhances the modeling environment.

4.3 User Interface

Throughout this research, a main goal has been to target the dictionary facilities to the data base user, not the DBA, application programmer, or computer specialist. For CAD/CAM applications, users include designers, engineers, or manufacturing planners. This goal will be achieved through the use of an *interactive graphical interface*. Data structures have been intentionally formulated as a network organization because networks are inherently graphical. Although a conventional terminal monitor cannot display as much information as a large computer-generated or manually prepared chart, it can present information more dynamically, and therefore, more effectively. Also, there is evidence that information overload occurs when humans are presented with more than a dozen artifacts to process visually. The interface facilities discussed below allow a user to direct attention to a portion of a network, thereby focusing on and displaying a manageable subset of the available data.

Viewing data in the network dictionary differs from conventional data base query operations. Viewing in this environment includes viewing the schema, its associated data, and constraint specifications. Display and manipulation routines will allow a user to easily *pan* and *zoom*. Panning, or changing the user's view of the network, will use commands to shift the display window onto different portions of the network. Zooming, or expanding a particular node, will permit users to vary the level of detail displayed. One technique is to use a mouse or light pen to navigate through the network. A high-level display of the network will show only schema information consisting of object nodes and relation links. *Indicating* or *pointing at* an object node will expand it to show the data type, any associated data values, and any auxiliary data. Similarly, relation links will expand to show constraints and attached procedures.

User facilities will be provided to build and modify the dictionary network, as well as view it. By pointing at an object node, the user will instruct the system to draw a relation link emanating from the indicated object node. To draw an object node, a user will point to an existing relation link. Commands or menus may be used for adding or modifying the contents of a selected node depending on the node type. Finally, commands of the type *store* and *retrieve* will be used to save and reload the network structures.

5. Research Contributions

In this final section we outline the contributions of this research in the areas of data modeling and CAD/CAM DBMS technology. We include a presentation of other research which relates to these contributions, and discuss the relevance and application of work in artificial intelligence.

- *Integration of Heterogeneous Data*

Data integration is a major design goal of most industrial CAD/CAM data base projects. The network dictionary will enable dramatic improvement of data integration in design and manufacturing applications. In fact, the dictionary permits *varying* degrees of integration. For example, a quick and limited integration could be achieved by designing object nodes to contain strictly symbolic pointers to other data bases, file systems, programs, or even other computer installations. In this fashion it would be used as a directory to help users determine *where* their data is located, without actually retrieving it. Engineers and manufacturers at Rockwell International expressed a strong desire for a facility as simple as this to keep track of their highly distributed data files.

The IPAD (Integrated Programs for Aerospace-Vehicle Design) program has concentrated on developing tools for the efficient integration of design and analysis data [FIS83, DUB83]. Other government sponsored programs such as ICAM (Integrated Computer Aided Manufacturing) and organizations such as CAM-I (Computer Aided Manufacturing - International, Inc.) are dedicated to the goal of increased productivity and efficiency through integration. An integrated data base design presented by Karna and Chu [KAR83] has been implemented as a CODASYL-like network system. The system exhibits some data integration, and improved facilities for part definition and multiple data descriptions; however, the issues of data independence, interactive user capabilities, and simple subschema definition are ignored. Most industrial efforts have focused on adapting the existing data models and data base systems to accommodate the needs of a CAD/CAM DBMS. The underlying limitations of the current models are, therefore, still present.

- *Object-Oriented Network of Item and Relation Nodes*

Our network organization allows richer data semantics to be modeled and expressed in an easy fashion. Many existing CAD/CAM DBMS refer to their data storage capabilities as a *data base system*, however, in reality they are sophisticated record filing systems. File organizations such as Lockheed's CADAM system [FLY76] have extremely limited and inflexible representation facilities and are very closely coupled to a drafting system. As discussed earlier, expressing M:N relationships in CODASYL network models and hierarchical models such as IMS is an awkward task. The schema description requires intermediate link records or pointer segments. These extra structures do not add semantics to the representation; they are only necessary because of the lack of data independence in these models. The relational model is an improvement with respect to data independence, but is relation-oriented not object-oriented.

Researchers in the area of data modeling are also concerned about expressibility. The Entity/Relationship Model [CHE76] and the Semantic Data Models [BOR80, TSI82] suggest a network organization of entity and relationship nodes, but do not address issues of integrity maintenance or provide user facilities. These models are used mainly as data base design tools. Other efforts at representing CAD/CAM data have produced variations of the relational model such as allowing null values and repeating groups within a relation [LOR82, GUT82]. Most of these projects, however, have been conceived and developed strictly to enhance the expressive power of a representation. They may be useful for data base design (defining the schema and data dictionary information) but the final schema is intended to be translated into a conventional data base model [TSI82, ROU75].

Network organizations for representing knowledge have also been the subject of work in Artificial Intelligence (AI), specifically Expert Systems research [BAR81]. Formalisms like semantic networks [BRA79] and conceptual graphs [SOW76, SOW84] were developed for representing human knowledge. These representations are composed of *nodes*, interconnected by various kinds of *associative links*. The nodes are considered to be *word concepts*, and links from one concept node to another make up a definition, just as dictionary definitions are constructed from sequences of words defined elsewhere in the same volume. One feature of these models is that they serve as a general inference mechanism for implicit knowledge, as well as a representational scheme for explicit information. This research applies these AI techniques for the explicit representation of CAD/CAM data. Having developed a rich, expressive representation, such as the network organization described, attacking the inference issue is an area for future investigation.

- *Graphical User Interface*

This research merges the notions of a rich semantic model with graphical, interactive user facilities. Languages built for many commercial DBMS are strictly procedural and are designed to be incorporated in an algorithmic programming language [MYL80, ROW79]. For example, generating a parts explosion listing in a Bill of Materials data base requires a recursive procedure [DAT81], or information about how many levels to descend for an iterative solution [CHA80]. Interactive query languages have been advertised more recently with the advent of commercial relational systems. QBE, a graphical user interface [DAT81], incorporates desirable interactive features, but is specifically designed for use with a relational model and therefore cannot easily express the part-oriented networks exhibited by manufacturing data. The data base language GEM [ZAN83] provides a graphical representation for schemas but again, it is an extension of a relational language, QUEL [STO76]. An image data base facility is being developed at the University of Toronto [ECO83] which focuses on user interaction to generate and query graphical images. Their system uses a menu of graphical icons to *draw* images on the display screen.

- *Interactive and Dynamic Schemata*

The need for dynamic schemata has been motivated by CAD/CAM technology. Although *sub-schema* definition by a user is frequently allowed in commercial DBMS, the structure of the resulting sub-schema is dictated by the underlying schema definition. Relational systems, like System-R [DAT81], allow less restrictive sub-schema definition across relations, however, they are still limited by a pre-defined schema. The data base language, Floreal [FOI82], provides two ways of describing entities: a *type* entity to model static objects, and an *object* entity to represent dynamic objects which may be altered by the designers during the design process. Their approach is to segregate information which is known to be static from data structures which are expected to change over time.

- *Constraint Specification and Satisfaction*

In a dynamic modeling environment, constraint satisfaction is even more critical than in a static domain. The constraint mechanism we have presented, will enable users to add constraints in parallel with schema and data generation. This facility encourages *application-specific* constraints to be entered by design engineers. Constraints can be augmented with procedures to specify how the constraints are to be enforced. The Floreal system [FOI82] also allows application knowledge in its Knowledge Data Base. This information, however, is fixed and cannot be altered by a user. In most systems, the DBA specifies constraints during the data base design phase. Typically, constraint specification, like static schema definition, is performed as an off-line task. Once the data base system is initialized, the constraints are *compiled* into the system.

Constraint satisfaction and procedural attachment originated in Artificial Intelligence research [BOR79, STE80, STE81]. Using these mechanisms to encode knowledge in a data base applies ideas from AI knowledge representation for enhancing the functionality of a DBMS.

Bibliography

[BAR81] Barr, A. & Feigenbaum, E.A. *The Handbook of Artificial Intelligence: Volume I.* Los Altos, CA: William Kauffman, Inc., 1981.

[BOR79] Borning, A. THINGLAB: A constraint simulation laboratory. Report No. CS-79-746, Computer Science Department, Stanford University, 1979.

[BOR80] Borkin, S.A. *Data Models.* Cambridge, MA: The MIT Press, 1980.

[BRA79] Brachman, R.J. On the epistemological status of semantic networks. Findler, N. (ed.), *Associative Networks.* New York: Academic Press, 1979.

[CAR79] Cardenas, A.F. *Data Base Management Systems.* Boston, MA: Allyn and Bacon, Inc., 1979.

[CHA80] Chamberlin, D.D. A summary of user experience with the SQL data sublanguage. Deen, S.M. & Hammersley P. (eds.), *Proc. International Conference on Data Bases.* University of Aberdeen, Scotland: Heyden & Son, Ltd., 1980.

[CHE76] Chen, P.P The entity-relationship model: Toward a unified view of data. *ACM Trans. Database Syst.*, 1976, 1, pp. 9-36.

[DAT81] Date, C.J. *An Introduction to Database Systems.* Menlo Park, CA: Addison-Wesley, 1981.

[DUB83] Dube, R.P. & Smith, M.R. Managing geometric information with a data base management system. *IEEE Computer Graphics and Applications,* 1983, Vol. 3, no. 7, pp. 57-62.

[EAS78] Eastman, C.M. The representation of design problems and maintenance of their structure. Latombe, J. (ed.), *Artificial Intelligence and Pattern Recognition in Computer Aided Design.* Amsterdam: North Holland Publishing Co., 1978.

[EAS82] Eastman, C.M. & LaFue, G.M.E. Semantic integrity transactions in design databases. Encarnacao, J. & Frause, F. (eds.), *File Structures and Data Bases for CAD.* Amsterdam: North Holland Publishing Co., 1982.

[EBE82] Eberlin, W. & Wedekind, H. A methodology for embedding design databases into integrated engineering systems. Encarnacao, J. & Frause, F. (eds.), *File Structures and Data Bases for CAD.* Amsterdam: North Holland Publishing Co., 1982.

[ECO83] Economopoulos, P. & Lochovsky, F.H. A system for managing image data. Computer Systems Research Group, University of Toronto, Toronto, Canada, 1983.

[ENC83] Encarnacao, J. & Schlechtendahr, E.G. *Computer Aided Design.* Heidelberg, FRG: Springer-Verlag, 1983.

[FIS83] Fishwick, P.A. & Blackburn, C.L. Managing engineering data bases: The relational approach. *Computers in Mechanical Engineering,* 1983, No. 1, pp. 8-16.

[FLY76] Flygare, R.M. Distributed CAD/CAM with database management common to both engineering and manufacturing. Report No. MS76-738, Society of Manufacturing Engineering, Dearborn, MI, 1976.

[FOI82] Foisseau, J. & Valette, F.R. A computer aided design data model: Floreal. Encarnacao, J. & Frause, F. (eds.), *File Structures and Data Bases for CAD.* Amsterdam: North Holland Publishing Co., 1982.

[GUT82] Guttman, A. & Stonebraker, M. Using a relational database management system for computer aided design data. *Database Engineering,* 1982, No. 6, pp. 21-28.

[KAR83] Karna, K.N. & Chu, D.F Computer-aided engineering in communications satellite design. *Computer,* 1983, No. 4, pp. 69-82.

[LIL78] Lillehagen, F.M. Modelling in CAD systems. CAD Tutorial, SIGGRAPH Conference, Atlanta, GA, 1978.

[LOR82] Lorie, R.A. Issues in database for design applications. Report No. R53176 (38982), IBM Research Laboratory, San Jose, CA, 1982.

[MCC82] McCarthy, J.L. Megadata management for large statistical databases. *Proc. Very Large Data Base Conference,* 1982, Mexico City, pp. 234-243.

[MEL84] Melkanoff, M.A. The CIMS database: goals, problems, case studies and proposed approaches are outlined. *Industrial Engineering:* 1984, (forthcoming).

[MEI83] Meister, A.E. The problems of using CAD-generated data for CAM. *Proc. Autofact 5 Conference,* 1983, Computer and Automated Systems Association of SME, pp. 38-48.

[MOR84] Morgenstern, M. Constraint equations: Declarative expression of constraints with automatic enforcement. *Proc. Very Large Data Base Conference,* 1984, Singapore, (forthcoming).

[MYL80] Mylopoulos, J., Bernstein, P.A. & Wong, H.K.T. A language facility for designing database-intensive applications. *ACM Trans. Database Systems,* 1983, Vol. 5, No. 2, pp. 185-207.

[ROU75] Roussopoulos, N. & Mylopoulos, J. Using semantic networks for data base management. *Proc. Very Large Data Base Conference,* 1975, Framingham, MA, pp. 144-172.

[ROW79] Rowe, L.A. & Shoens, K.A. Data abstraction, views, and updates in rigel. Memorandum No. UCB/ERL M79/5, Electronics Research Lab - College of Engineering, University of California, Berkeley, 1979.

[SMI77] Smith, J.M. & Smith, D.C.P. Database abstractions: Aggregation. *Communications of the ACM,* 1977, Vol. 20, No. 6, pp. 405-413.

[SOW76] Sowa, J.F. Conceptual graphs for a database interface. *IBM Journal of Research & Development,* 1976, Vol. 20, No. 4, pp. 336-357.

[SOW84] Sowa, J.F. *Conceptual Structures.* New York: Addison-Wesley, 1984.

[STE80] Stefik, M.J. Planning with constraints. Report No. 80-784, Computer Science Dept., Stanford University, 1980.

[STE81] Stefik, M.J. An examination of a frame structured representation system. *Proc. International Joint Conference on Artificial Intelligence,* 1981, Vancouver, British Columbia, pp. 845-852.

[STO76] Stonebraker, M., Wong E., Kreps, P. & Held, G. The Design and Implementation of INGRES. *ACM Trans. Database Systems,* 1976, Vol. 1, No. 3, pp. 198-222.

[TSI82] Tsichritzis, D.C. & Lochovsky, F.H. *Data Models.* Edgewood Cliffs, NJ: Prentice-Hall, Inc., 1982.

[ULF82] Ulfsby, S., Meen, S. & Oian, J. Tornado: A data-base management system for graphics applications. Encarnacao, J. & Frause, F. (eds.), *File Structures and Data Bases for CAD.* Amsterdam: North Holland Publishing Co., 1982.

[ULL80] Ullman, J.D. *Principles of Database Systems.* Potomac, MD: Computer Science Press, 1980.

[ZAN83] Zaniolo, C. The Database Language GEM. *ACM SIGMOD Record, Proc. of Database Week,* 1983, Vol. 13, No. 4, pp. 207-218.

A Database Management System Based on an Object-Oriented Model

Roger King

University of Colorado
Department of Computer Science
Boulder, Colorado, 80309

Abstract

Sembase is a database management system based on an object-oriented, or semantic, model. Its goal is to determine whether object-oriented modeling can be transformed from an abstract design tool into an effective data management tool. Sembase attempts to capitalize on the expressiveness of object-oriented models by providing special data structures and access methods which allow complex information to be maintained efficiently. Also, Sembase supports a data language and a graphics interface which are specially designed to support object-oriented data applications. The system is currently under development at the University of Colorado, with the physical implementation and the data language complete. The graphics-based user interface is under construction. Sembase is written in C and runs on a Sun workstation under Unix. The physical implementation and data language require approximately 350k of memory.

1. Motivation

Object-oriented, or semantic modeling grew out of semantic network research. It was developed in an attempt to more naturally model the relationships inherent in computerized data. See [KKT77] for an early discussion of the issues involved in data modeling and [KM84c] for a general discussion of semantic modeling. Zaniolo, in the paper "Prolog: a Database Query Language Interface for All Seasons" in this book, argues that object-oriented models are well suited to the integration of knowledge base and database management systems. This paper presents an object-oriented database system called Sembase.

Essentially, object-oriented models have three advantages over traditional hierarchical, network, and relational models. First, a database can be viewed as a collection of abstract objects, rather than a (possibly interrelated) set of flat tables. Second, at least two sorts of relationships may be differentiated. Typically, an object-oriented model supports explicit constructs for representing abstraction (or

This work was supported by IBM under a Faculty Development Award (1984).

attribute interconnections) and generalization (or subtyping). Third, an object-oriented schema more easily captures integrity constraints. In particular, the attributes of abstract objects can be viewed as functions; this allows much more precise notation in specifying constraints.

It is this extra expressiveness which gives object-oriented modeling the name "semantic" modeling, and makes it worth studying in the realm of expert databases. The goal of object-oriented data modeling is to provide constructs for capturing more of the semantics of an application environment than is possible with a traditional model. Clearly two significant tradeoffs are the added implementation complexity and the resulting rigidity of an object-oriented schema. While an object-oriented schema may be extended easily (this is discussed is section 4), it is more difficult to restructure relationships which are already defined. This is in contradistinction to a relational model, which places very few initial constraints on legitimate relationships (at the expense of meaningless joins). The Sembase project has attempted to resolve the issue of the first tradeoff by building an effective implementation. Sembase also illustrates the utility of providing extra expressiveness in a data model, thus making the resulting rigidity an acceptable tradeoff.

Besides structures to represent abstract objects, abstraction, and generalization, two other capabilities are needed to make an object-oriented model useful. A mechanism for specifying subtype membership is necessary. This generally consists of a predicate language for isolating objects according to the values of its attributes. The other required capability is a set of object-oriented data manipulation primitives.

Although object-oriented modeling has been pursued actively, and a large number of research papers have been generated on the topic, object-oriented modeling is still viewed as solely a database design tool and as a documentation aid. A few researchers have addressed implementation issues; in particular [Ch82] describes an object-oriented database physical implementation. [Za83] describes an object-oriented data language built on top of a relational system. Smalltalk is an example of a general-purpose, object-oriented language; see [GR83]. There has also been some important work in the theoretical analysis of object-oriented modeling, including [AH84] and [HK81].

Sembase is designed as a DBMS which capitalizes on the richness of an object-oriented model, rather than merely implementing one in a naive fashion. An object-oriented model naturally supports complex derived information. Sembase provides unique data structures and algorithms designed to ensure the efficient maintenance of derived data, so that the added complexities of object-oriented queries and updates do not seem unjustifiably expensive.

Also, Sembase's data language and interface provide a convenient means of manipulating object-oriented databases, so that the user may benefit from the power of the underlying model. In particular, the data language provides data operators and control structures specifically designed for object-oriented database manipulations. And, the interface allows the user to interactively organize the information in an object-oriented schema, by using special graphics operators to peruse and manipulate the schema. The user may also extend the schema with either the language or interface.

The next section describes the model underlying Sembase. The third section describes the physical implementation of Sembase, and the fourth section discusses the data language. The fifth section describes the proposed graphics interface, which is currently under construction. Finally, the sixth section gives directions for the future.

2. Sembase's Object-Oriented Model

The model underlying Sembase was developed as a "generic" object-oriented model in that it attempts to encompass (in a simplified form) the constructs found in most object-oriented models. This model is defined in detail in [KM82], [KM84a] and [KM85]. Briefly, the model represents an application environment as a collection of *objects.* All objects are instances of *types* and *subtypes,* which are arranged into hierarchies according to type/subtype relationships. There are two kinds of objects: *Descriptor* objects are atomic values of character strings, integers, booleans, and reals, and generally serve as symbolic identifiers in a database. *Abstract* objects are non-atomic entities, defined in terms of their relationships with other objects through *attributes.* An attribute is a relation between two types. A subtype is formed according to a predicate based on the values of the attributes of the parent type. A subtype may also be defined as being *arbitrary,* meaning that a data operation (see the description of data operators below), not a static predicate, is used to define its membership.

At any time, and for each attribute of a type, each object of the given type (attribute domain) is related to a specific set of objects which is a subset of the modifying type (attribute range). Several constraints may be specified with each attribute definition. For example, an attribute may optionally be defined as being unique, single- or multi-valued, or non-null. An attribute of a given object type may also be required to "exhaust" its value type, meaning that every instance of the value type is a value of the given attribute for some instance of the given object type. Also, two attributes may be defined as being inverses of each other. A subtype inherits all the attributes of the parent type (or subtype), and may have additional attributes.

Descriptor subtypes are formed by placing bounds on the values of numbers or by placing bounds on the lengths and values of strings. Abstract objects are formed into subtypes using standard boolean operators (and, or, not), set comparators (equals, intersects, contains), and string comparators (=, <>, <, >, >=, <=). Predicates are formed by composing attributes and using them as right and left hand sides of comparator operators within simple predicates, and then grouping simple predicates into disjunctive or conjunctive normal form. Arithmetic operations and several special functions (e.g., Count) are also allowed in predicates.

Throughout this paper, the familiar parts/suppliers database is used as a source of examples. As an example of an object-oriented schema, Suppliers, Parts, Shippers, Sales Orders, Purchase Orders, and Customers may be considered abstract object types. Suppliers has the attribute Supplier Open Orders (range of Purchase Orders); Parts has the attributes Cost (range of Reals) and Part Number (range of integers);

Customers has the attribute Customer Open Orders (range of Sales Orders); Sales Orders has the attribute Parts (range of Parts); Purchase orders has the attribute Parts (range of Parts). Shippers have the attributes Days (range of Integers) and Mode (range of strings). A subtype of Sales Orders might be Big Sales defined as all Sales Orders such that the Parts on the order have as a sum of the values of their costs a number greater than 10,000.

The predicate mechanism of Sembase provides a form of intelligence. It allows the database to specify one sort of data in terms of other sorts of data. In this way, a subtype such as Big Sales may be statically defined within the database and need not be recomputed by the application program every time it is needed. This is the sort of capability which would be very useful in an "expert" database.

Database manipulations are performed via *data operations.* These operations include:

Retrieve Database, which loads a given database and prepares it for processing.

Save Database, which stores a database at the end of a processing session.

Apply Attribute, which evaluates an attribute of some object.

Create Object, which creates an object of a type (without any attribute values).

Delete Object.

Insert Attribute, which assigns a value or values to an attribute of some object.

Remove Attribute, which removes an attribute value.

Insert Object, which places an existing object in an arbitrary subtype.

Remove Object, which takes an object out of an arbitrary subtype (but does not delete the object).

First, which locates the first instance of a type, subtype, or multi-valued attribute.

Last, which locates the last instance of a type, subtype, or multi-valued attribute.

Next, which is used to locate successive instances of a type, subtype, or multi-valued attribute.

Previous, which is used to locate the preceding instance of a type, subtype, or multi-valued attribute.

It should be noted that abstract objects may be ordered according to any atomic valued attribute of the given type. As an example, Parts may be ordered according to the Cost attribute. Then, the First, Next, and Previous operators will follow this ordering. Also, Create Object may not be applied to a subtype, and Delete Object may not be applied to an arbitrary subtype. Further, if a Delete Object is applied to a subtype, the object referenced is deleted from all types in the relevant type hierarchy.

3. The Semantic Database Constructor

The Semantic DBMS implementation has been constructed with a tool called Sedaco (the SEmantic DAtabase COnstructor). Sedaco is described in [FKM84] and [FKM85]; it provides primitives for implementing databases designed with the generic object-oriented model. Sedaco constructs memory-resident structures which are used to maintain schema information. These structures form the Schema Dictionary. Sedaco also constructs secondary memory-resident structures which are used to maintain data. All database objects are stored according to unique internal identifiers. Sedaco consists of approximately 200k of optimized C object code and runs under Unix.

In addition to supporting the data manipulation primitives described in the previous section, Sedaco supports a number of operations for constructing object-oriented database schemas, including:

Create Type, which takes as an argument the name of the new type.

Create Attribute, which takes as arguments, the name for the new attribute, a domain name, a range name, and a set of constraints.

Create Predicate, which takes as arguments the name of the predicate and the specification of the predicate.

Create Subtype, which takes as arguments the name of the subtype, the name of the parent type, and a name of a predicate to define the subtype.

Sedaco also supports Delete Type, Delete Attribute, Delete Predicate, and Delete Subtype. These operators return a success/failure result.

Sedaco supplies operators for perusing a schema. List Types, List Subtypes (given a parent type as an argument), List Attributes (given a type as an argument), and List Predicates (given a parent type as an argument) all return the names of the desired schema components.

It is necessary to refer to schema components as arguments in various data operators. The following operators are used to translate a schema component name into an internal reference: Locate Type (given a type name), Locate Subtype (given a parent type name and a subtype name), Locate Attribute (given a type name and a domain name), and Locate Predicate (given a type name and domain name).

Sedaco maintains the inverse value of every attribute in order to simplify the execution of a Delete Object operation. When an object is deleted, that object will have associated with it all objects that "point" to it via attributes. These attribute values must of course be deleted. Sedaco also uses a process similar to data flow analysis (see [AU78]) to simplify the execution of other operators. The schema is preprocessed and extra information is stored in the Schema Dictionary. For example, all predicates that refer to a given attribute are associated with that attribute. Then, when an Assign Attribute or Remove Attribute operation is performed, the subtypes whose membership may be affected by the update are found without having to examine any other subtypes.

When performing an update to a subtype, Sedaco checks only the specific objects whose subtype membership may be affected. Each database object is associated with all other objects it is dependent on. For example, a sales order may be in the subtype Big Sales because the cost of the one part associated with it is greater than 10,000. Sedaco would note the dependency between the sales order and the cost of the part. If the cost of only the one part were changed, only the one sales order (assuming no other order involved that part) would be checked for new subtype memberships.

Sedaco is also being augmented to allow batching of updates to attributes and subtypes. This will extend the concept of differential files to include object-oriented structures.

4. The Semantic Data Language

The SEMantic DAta Language (Semdal) is a data definition and manipulation language written in C, using the Unix tools YACC and LEX (see [KS84]). It is callable through C. Semdal supplies the Sedaco data and schema operators and also provides control structures and a convenient syntax.

Sembase's object-oriented model represents derived information in the form of predicate-defined subtypes. Semdal extends this notion and allows attribute values to be specified with predicates, in the same manner as subtype memberships. Attributes may also be composed to form new, derived attributes. In this fashion, one could define an attribute of Purchase Orders called Total Cost, which consists of the sum of the costs of the parts on each purchase order.

Thus, with Semdal, a user can extend his or her schema with derived information, by specifying predicate-defined subtypes, predicate-defined attributes and composed attributes at data manipulation time. This tailoring is viewed as a powerful advantage of object-oriented modeling. The central goal of Semdal is to make data definition and data manipulation as indistinguishable as possible.

Below, is a very simple Semdal transaction. It creates the parts/suppliers database. Note that the inverse attributes of Parts of Purchase orders and Parts of Sales Orders are given explicit names. Then, a subtype of Parts is created. This subtype consists of all parts such that they are on both a sales order and a purchase order. This indicates which parts are being ordered from suppliers to meet specific needs of customers, not just to fill out the company's stock. Then, Total Cost of Purchase Orders is created. Finally, the transaction creates a part, and assigns if a part number and a cost.

```
Transaction parts/suppliers db:

Create Type parts
```

```
Create Attributes of parts
     cost from reals > 0, single-valued, non-null
     number from strings, single-valued, unique, non-null

Create Type suppliers

Create Attribute of suppliers
     supplier open orders from purchase orders, multi-valued

Create Type customers

Create Attribute of customers
     customer open orders from sales orders, multi-valued

Create Type shippers

Create Attributes of shippers
     mode from strings, single-valued, non-null
     days from integers, single-valued, non-null

Create Type purchase orders

Create Attribute of purchase orders
     parts from parts, multi-valued
          with inverse on purchase orders

Create Type sales orders

Create Attribute of sales orders
     parts from parts, multi-valued
          with inverse on sales orders

Create Subtype committed parts
     all parts where parts.on sales order and
          parts.on purchase order <> null

Create Attribute of purchase orders
     total cost:
          sum of purchase orders.parts.cost

Create Object in parts
     part.cost = 6.00
     part.number = aj6000
```

5. The Semantics-Knowledgeable Interface

Semdal is intended as a programmer's interface to Sembase. Currently a graphics-based interface is under construction. It is called the Semantics-Knowledgeable Interface, or Ski. A preliminary design of Ski is described in [KM84b]. Ski combines the expressiveness of object-oriented modeling and the visual power of graphics, and provides an interface which allows a user to peruse a database in a truly semantic manner.

The key to providing a graphics interface to a semantic DBMS lies in finding an effective visual representation of object-oriented constructs. There are three important criteria for measuring the usability of an object-oriented model representation. First, as an object-oriented database consists of non-atomic objects, the possibly intricate interconnections of a schema must be made understandable. Simply using a graph notation is insufficient, as this leads to a possibly complex maze of arcs. This approach is also not conducive to visually isolating a schema subset from the remainder of the schema.

Second, as for any type of interface, an object-oriented model representation should be able to exhibit information related to the data a user has isolated. Naively, there are only two ways to relate information in an object-oriented database: attribute interconnections and subtyping. However, due to the complexity of subtyping mechanisms, the user must be able to follow more distant relationships. As an example, a smart student may be defined as one who gets an A in a course such that the professor who teaches that course is known to give tough grades. The information about a professor's grading history may not be "near" the student's information schematically, but the two are very closely related. In other words, a fixed view of a schema will not necessarily provide a convenient interface for all users.

The third requirement is that an object-oriented representation should assist the user in displaying the effects of a data update. Again, because of the capability to define derived data via predicates, the effects may be far-reaching and therefore difficult for the user to predict. The challenge is to provide an interface which gives the user a semantic, and not a purely structural view of the database, so that he may determine the true consequences of a data manipulation.

The philosophical thrust of Ski is to provide an interface which capitalizes on the underlying object-oriented model. Thus, Ski not only supports standard object-oriented data definitions and manipulations, it also provides an extra level of intelligence by supporting operations which locate far-reaching data relationships and update effects. Ski, therefore, might be useful in an expert database system, in that it has a certain amount of deductive capability built into it.

With Ski, the processes of viewing object-oriented data, isolating related data, and determining the effects of an update are centered around the concept of a *session view.* During a session with the interface, the user selects schema components of interest and peruses the schema for related information. This perusing is not performed navigationally, but semantically. The user may locate schema components related through attributes. He may also locate the subtypes of a more general type. He may also, given a schema component and a specific data operator, locate any other components which may be affected by updating the first. Gradually, the user constructs his session view and uses graphics commands to visually isolate the elements of his view. The user is then ready to update the schema or perform a data manipulation. The interface will also provide methodological and graphics support during query and transaction formulation.

Very little work has been done in the area of object-oriented database user interfaces. Some very insightful work has been done in the area of multi-dimensional knowledge representation ([Wi80a], [Wi80b], and [He80]). In [SK82] a graphics based relational browser is described; while it does not use an object-oriented model, it does support powerful window and icon manipulations. MPS ([Wi83]) uses relational tables to represent non-atomic objects. Guide ([WK82]) uses a fixed network of boxes (representing types) and rhombuses (representing attributes) to support an entity/relationship-like model. Also, a (non graphics) interface based on an object-oriented model is described in [Mo83].

In Ski, there is no notion of a statically defined graphical layout. Instead, Ski uses the semantic relationships inherent in the schema definition to dynamically drive the graphical representation. The portions of the database to be displayed and the types of relationships depicted vary with each user's area of interest, as indicated through their use of the Ski operators.

5.1. Overview

Ski uses a formated screen, a three button mouse, and a number of semantically-motivated operators. These operators allow a user to examine and access a database while taking full advantage of the semantic relationships inherent in the schema. The user never peruses the schema randomly or by navigating a graph of relationships. Rather, he constructs a session view based on the meaning of the data, and directly controls both the selection of schema components and the arrangement of items on the screen.

When interfacing with Ski, a user constructs a session view. This view consists of some subset of the schema, and possibly new types, attributes, constraints, and subtypes. A user may permanently record any or all new schema components. And, at any time during the construction of a session view, the user may drop into the language Semdal.

Figure 1 shows the high-level interactions of the Ski windows during the construction of a session view. First, the user enters the Hello subsystem, which provides a brief summary of the functions of Ski, points out the existence of the Help subsystem, and recalls any previously saved schema and session view. The Schema View subsystem is then entered; it is used to construct and/or peruse a session view. The Data View subsystem is used to examine the attribute values and subtype memberships of the session view. The user may of course only view string, boolean, real, or integer valued data. The Data View also provides access to the language Semdal. The Report Generation subsystem is used to format data for output. The Help subsystem documents the structure of Ski and provides tutorials on the use of the various operators. Finally, the Exit subsystem is used to store a session view.

The next two subsections describe some possible Ski operators and the screen layout. The following subsection describes a user scenario.

5.2. The Formated Screen

While constructing a session view using the Schema View subsystem of Ski, the user is presented with a formated screen. See figure 2. The screen provides a medium for representing the complicated structure of object-oriented schemas. The screen is broken into a variable number of horizontal stripes. The top stripe represents one or more parent types, which may be any of the types or subtypes in the schema. The next stripe represents attributes of the parent types.

Attribute ranges are shown in the third stripe. Predicates based on any of the parent types are shown in the next stripe and subtypes of the parent types are shown in the fifth stripe. Then, the sixth stripe (not shown in the figure) represents attributes of the range types from the third stripe. The seventh through ninth stripes show the ranges, predicates, and subtypes of the range types from stripe three. The stripes continue in this fashion. Any predicate stripe may reference a type or subtype from the parent stripe or any range stripe.

A three button mouse (figure 3) is used to control Ski operations. The Drag button is used to scroll, expand, collapse, or move icons on the screen; it will be described in the scenario. The Select button is used to bind a schema component on the screen as a parameter to an operation. The Menu button is described immediately below, and is used to place schema components on the screen. Any component placed on the main screen becomes part of the session view. Certain operations (as described below) use a separate screen; in order for objects appearing on a separate screen to be placed in the session view, a special operator must be used.

The user may scroll up or down to view all stripes; for added screen space, any stripe may be removed from the screen (but not from the session view) by selecting the Collapse operator from the top menu stripe (in the black border on figure 2) with the Menu button. Expand is used to make a stripe reappear. Also, square icons may appear at either end of each stripe (see figure 5h). If there is a token which has "fallen off" a stripe, a square will appear; more than one square means that a number of tokens have fallen off. The user may scroll to see the end of the stripe to find these tokens. Scrolling is performed by picking the appropriate arrow (above the squares) with the Drag button of the mouse.

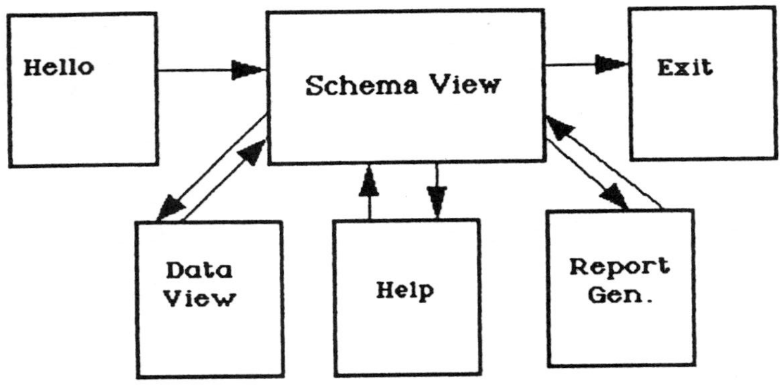

Figure 1. The interaction of the SKI screens.

Figure 2.

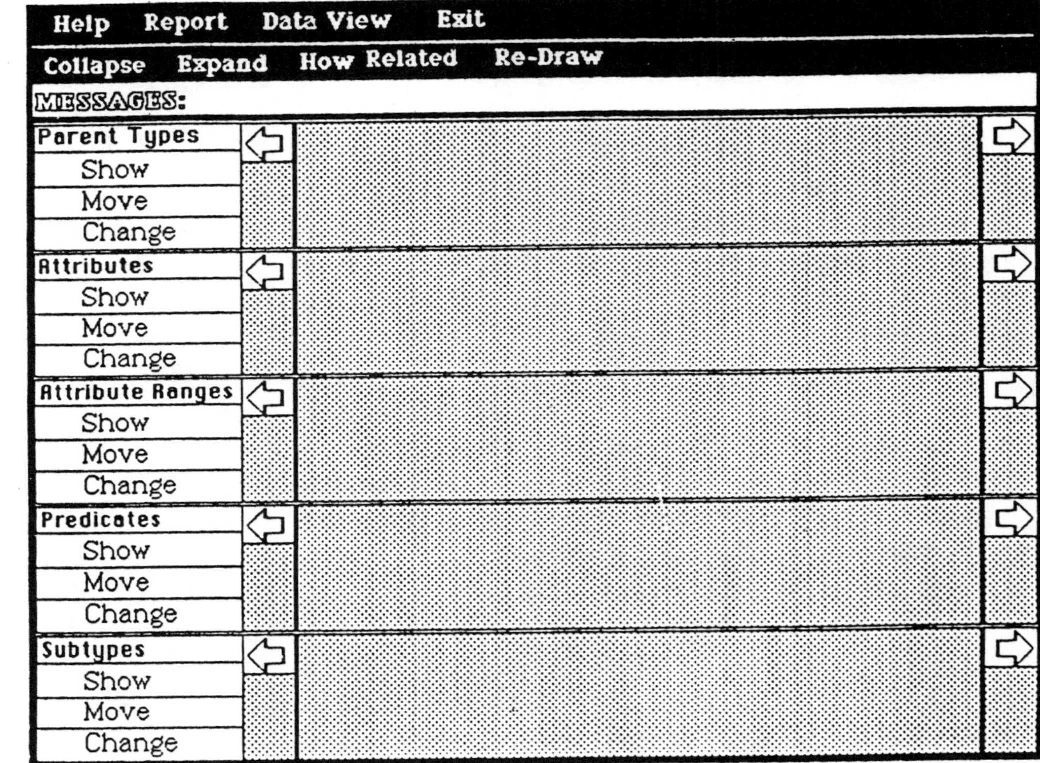

The initial screen.

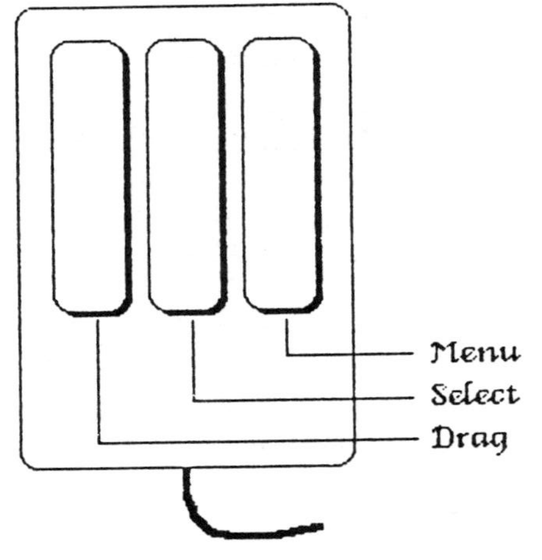

Figure 3. The Mouse.

5.3. Ski Operators

Figure 4a illustrates the submenu interactions of Ski. Next to each stripe is a menu; the user chooses an operation by picking it with the Menu button. This will either invoke an operation or cause another menu to appear. As an example, if the user selects the Change menu, he will have the choice of then selecting either a Modify, Delete, Create, Accept, or Reject operation. Modify is used to change a token; when this operation is chosen and an icon is picked with the Select button, that icon is blown up on the screen so the text in it may be edited. Delete is used to delete a component from the schema (and the session view); Create makes a new component for the schema (and the session view); and Accept and Reject are used to either permanently keep or remove a change. The Reject operation may also be used directly to remove any component from the view.

The Show menu varies according to the stripe involved and is used to add schema components to a session view or delete components from a session view. Figure 4b illustrates the Show menus for the five types of stripes. Under the Parent Types stripe, Show All will select any schema component not currently in the view and display them on the Parent Types stripe. A Show All on the subtype stripe will show all subtypes of all parent types in the view. Under the Attribute stripe, Show All will show all attributes of all types or subtypes on the above Parent Types or Subtypes stripe. If this operation is performed, the ranges are not shown unless explicitly asked for with a Show Excluded on the Attribute Range stripe; this is done to simplify the display. A Show All on the Range stripe will reveal the ranges of all attributes of the Parent Types stripe, even if these ranges are not yet in the session view. A Show Excluded on the Predicates stripe will show all predicates involving any types, subtypes, or attributes in the view.

The user may also request to add certain predicates to his or her view because they involve certain components. In this case, the user chooses a set of schema components with the Select button and then chooses Show Predicates Involving on the Predicate stripe with the Menu button.

On the Parent Types, Attribute Ranges, and Subtypes stripes, Show Duplicates will make any duplicate images of a component selected with the Select button flash. If a duplicate is off-screen, the appropriate square or squares will change shading. As an example, a type may appear as both a parent type and as the range of some attribute.

Under the Parent Type or Subtype stripes, the user may choose to show the attributes of a type or subtype; the attributes will appear on the stripe below. Under the Subtype stripe, the user may ask for inherited attributes, noninherited attributes, or all attributes. On the attribute stripe, the user may choose to show the inverse attribute of a given attribute; this inverse need not necessarily have a name in the schema. Under the attribute stripe, the user may also request to add the ranges of any attributes to the session view.

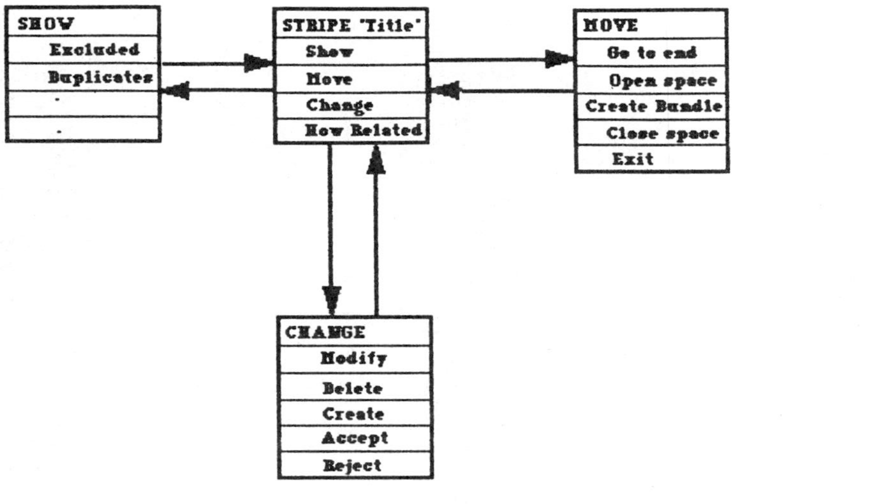

Figure 4a. The interaction of the SKI submenus.

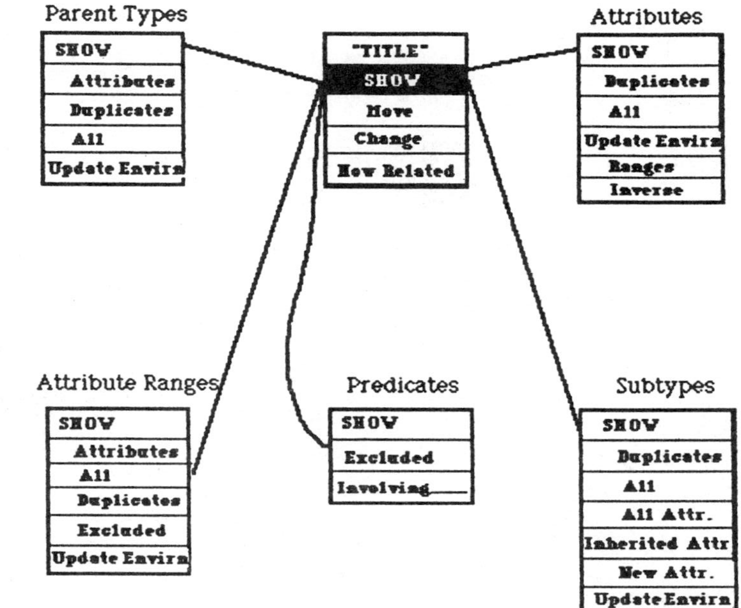

Figure 4b. The various SHOW submenus.

Under the attribute stripe, constraints are represented in two ways: graphically or by menu. Whether an attribute is single or multi valued is modeled by either a single or a double arrowhead leading to the attribute range. The remainder of the constraints may be displayed by a separate menu. Constraints are not shown in any of the figures.

In the database interface Guide ([WK82]), a user may specify a general radius of concern in viewing a schema. The size of the radius is expressed syntactically, in terms of graph arcs. This sort of a function is clearly very important. Ski provides a semantically-motivated way of requesting information which is related to a given schema component. The How Related menu (chosen by picking How Related from the top border with the Menu button) is used to show how two schema components are related, and is described in the scenario. Two components may be related via type/subtype relationships, attributes, or predicate definitions. The schema components discovered in this fashion may be included or excluded from the view. If two components are related in more than one way, all possible relations may be viewed by using the How Related Next or Previous operations.

Another way of isolating semantically-motivated relationships is with the Show Update Effects operator. If the user chooses Show Update Effects on any stripe and then selects a component, another menu will appear (see figure 6h). This menu consists of a number of data operations. The user chooses the operation and the system informs the user which components might be affected by performing the given operation on the given component.

The last menu is the Move menu. It is used to go to the end of a stripe, open or close a space, or move a component. Components are moved in bundles; a description of a bundle move appears in the scenario.

5.4. A Sample Session

The ABC Widget Company is a distributor of widgets. Customers submit sales orders for desired parts. If there are not enough parts in inventory to fill a sales order, a purchase order is placed with a supplier. Unfortunately, ABC is suffering from a cash flow problem. They have no money to pay suppliers. Mr. Fred Jones, the president of ABC, is about to use the Ski user interface to assess the consequences of this problem.

Mr. Jones begins his quest by in figure 5a by using the menu button to choose the operator Show All under the Parent Types stripe. This adds the four parent or 'root' types to his session view.

Figure 5b illustrates Mr. Jones' next operation, a How Related, with the types Suppliers and Customers chosen (with the Select button) as parameters. Mr. Jones is trying to find out what will happen to his customers if he does not pay his suppliers.

The How Related operator gives Mr. Jones a separate screen, shown in figure 5c. In 5d, he chooses Next from the How Related submenu, which gives the next (i.e., the

Figure 5a.

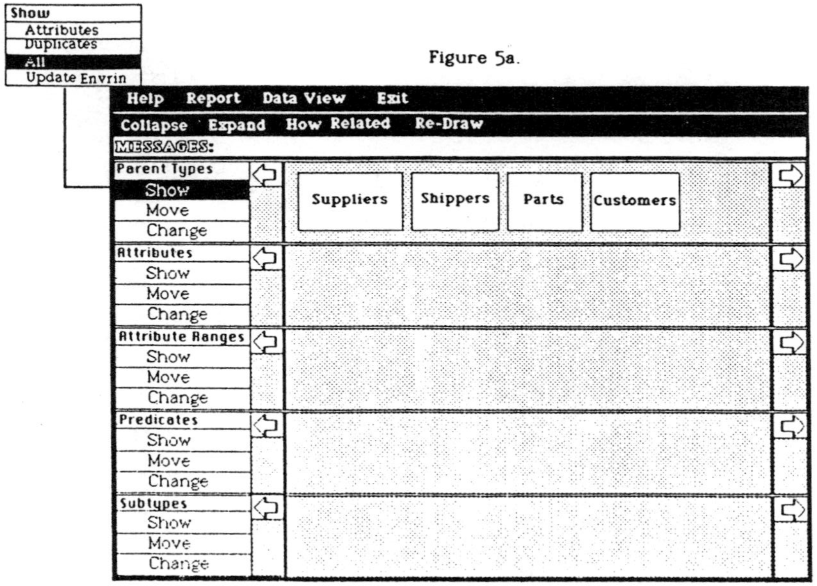

The user performs a Show and chooses All Types from the submenu.

Figure 5b.

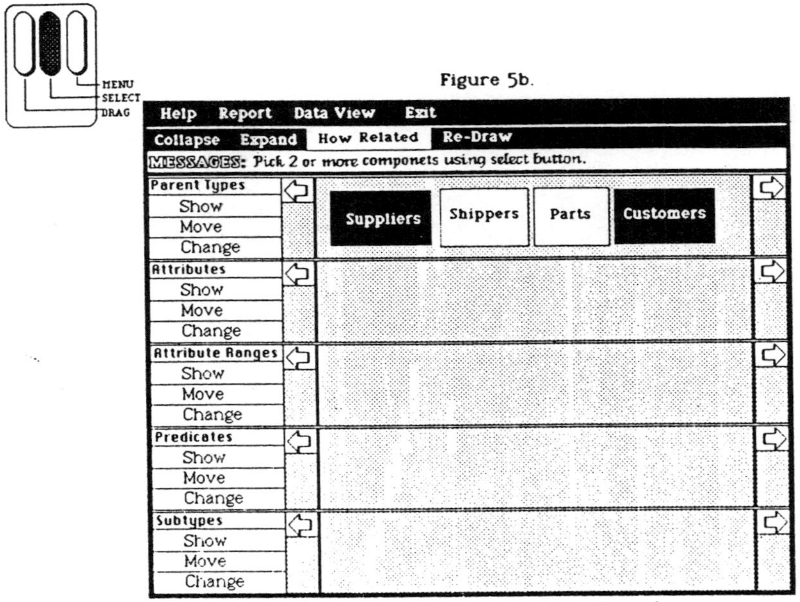

The user selects Suppliers and Customers and performs a How Related.

Figure 5c.

The How Related screen.

Figure 5d.

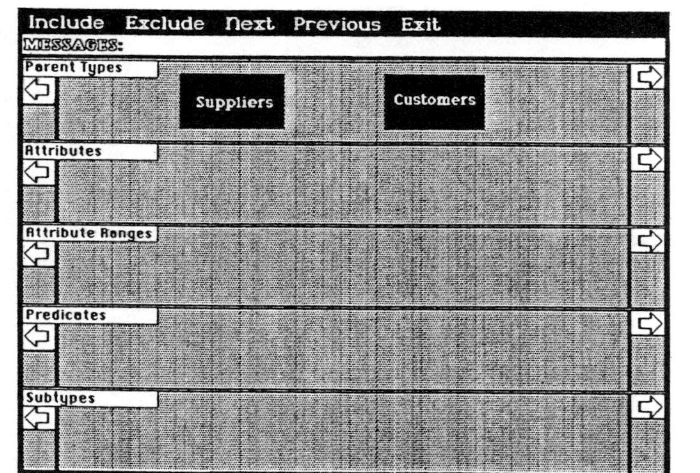

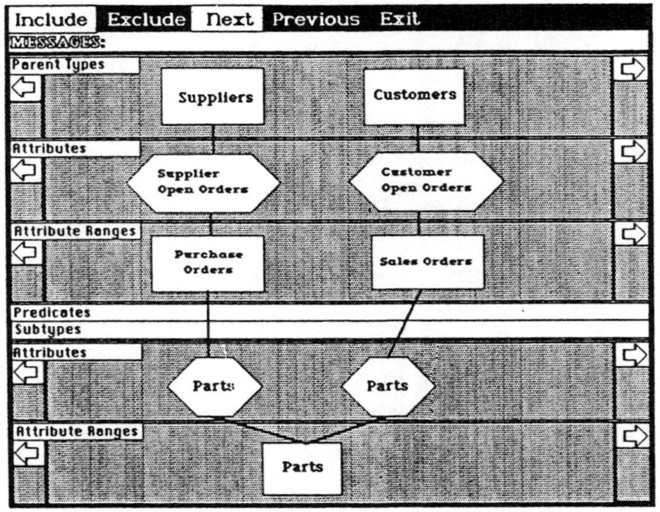

The user requests the Next shortest How Related path. The results are to be Included in the session view.

first) relationship between the two components. Mr. Jones sees that Suppliers and Customers are related through Parts via the two Open Orders attributes. Mr. Jones uses the Menu button to include this information in his session view, and exits the How Related screen. Figure 5e shows the result of this Include operation.

Note that on the How Related screen, only those schema components lying on the connecting path are displayed. If Ski relied upon a pre-defined (i.e. static) graphical representation of the schema, any attempt to show how two schema components were related would be likely to include considerable "noise"; that is, additional schema components not relevant to the current query. Using a dynamic representation allows rapid isolation of pertinent schema components.

Mr. Jones would like some more information about Parts. He is searching for some reference to money. He chooses a Show Attributes operation on the Parent Types stripe. He uses the Select button to choose Parts. The result is shown in figure 5f. (Note that Mr. Jones has also collapses the Predicate and Subtype stripe in order to simplify his screen image. This was performed with the Menu button to choose the operator from the top and with the Select button to choose the stripes to collapse.)

Mr. Jones notices that Parts have a cost. He then selects the Move Bundle operation on the Parent Types stripe. He selects Suppliers and Customers (figure 5g), and using the Drag button, moves the bundle to the right of the screen. The result is shown in figure 5h. The continuation icons have appeared, informing Mr. Jones that there is information off screen. It should be noted that a Drag operation may result in a number of crossed lines; the user may use the Re-Draw operation from the top border to simplify line positions.

It is time for Mr. Jones to isolate the data he needs. He expands the Predicate stripe (figure 5i), and chooses a Change Create operation on the Predicate stripe (figure 5j). Mr. Jones uses the skeleton to create his predicate, as shown in figure 5k. What he wants is all parts that are on both sales and purchase orders. He may bind the attributes in the predicate with either the Select button or by using text. In the example, Mr. Jones writes in Parts of Sales Orders and Parts of Purchase Orders (using dot notation), two set inclusion operators (which may also be chosen from a menu), the free variable X, and the logical and operator (which may also be chosen from a menu. He names the new subtype Committed Parts, and views the resulting data; see figure 5l.

5.5. An Alternate Scenario

By way of comparison, an alternate formulation of the above session is given here. The essential difference is that, in the second session, Mr. Fred Jones elects to use the Update Environment operation rather than the How Related operation. This illustrates the two ways of determining far-reaching semantic relationships with Ski. The first is structurally motivated, the second is based on the dynamics of the Sedaco operators.

Figure 5e.

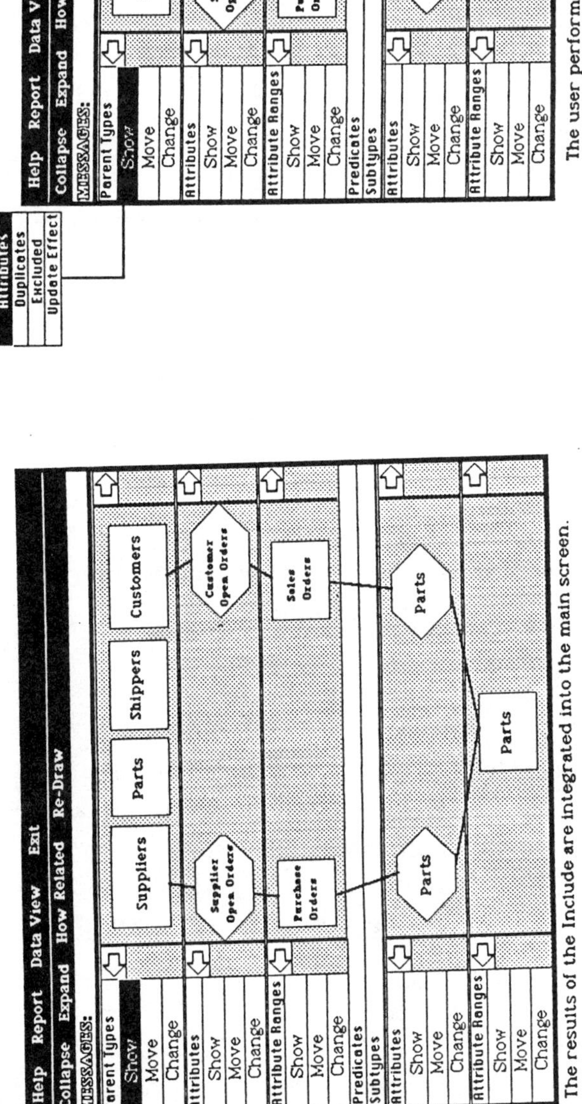

The results of the Include are integrated into the main screen.

Figure 5f.

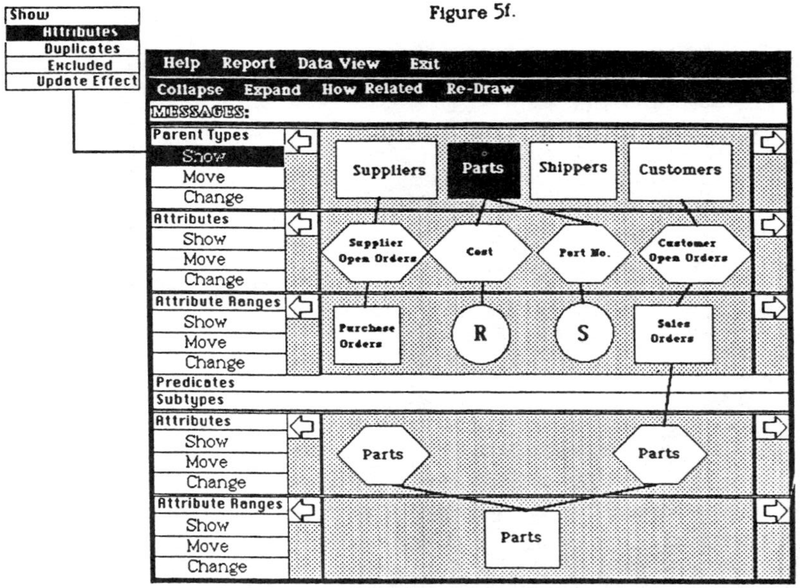

The user performs a Show Attributes operation on the selected Parent Types.

Figure 5g.

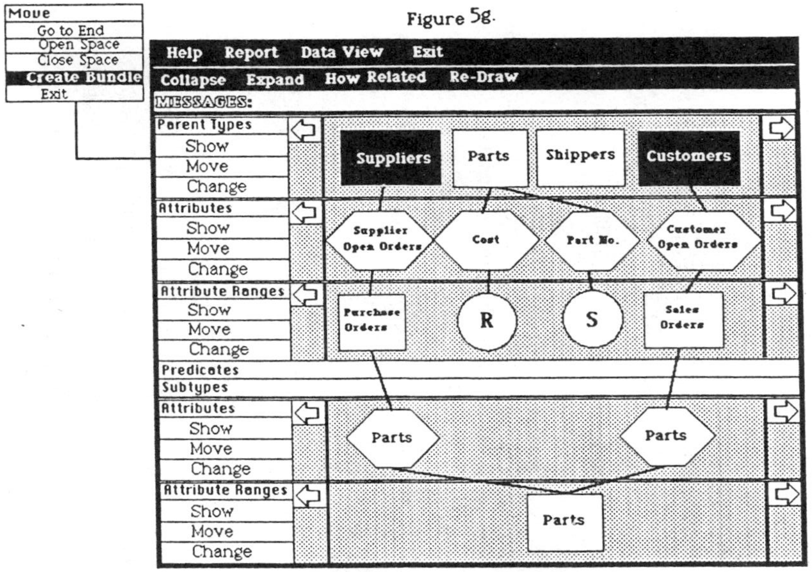

The user performes a Move on the top stripe and requests a Bundle operation.

Figure 5h.

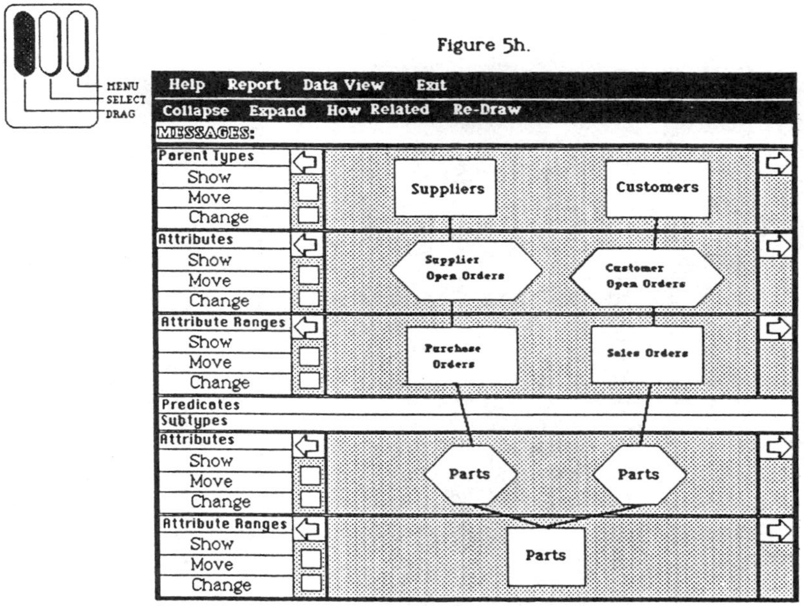

Using the mouse, the Bundle is dragged to the right of the screen.

Mr. Jones begins this alternate session in figure 6a by performing a Show All on the Parent Types stripe. Then, in 6b, he adds all attributes of these types to his session view. In 6c, Mr. Jones views the ranges of these attributes.

Mr. Jones digs deeper into the schema by choosing Show All Attributes on the Range stripe. He discovers that Sales Orders and Purchase Orders have attributes with a common range: Parts. See figure 6d.

In order to visually isolate the schema components he is concerned with, Mr. Jones uses the Move Create Bundle operation and the Drag button to move Suppliers, Customers, and their attributes to the right of the screen. The selection of the operation and the selection of components is shown in 6e. The result is illustrated in 6f.

In order to get a better perspective on the relationship between Purchase Orders and Sales Orders, Mr. Jones requests to see the Inverse Attributes of the attributes Parts of Purchase Orders and Parts of Sales Orders. Figure 6g shows this operation. Note that the database designer has given these inverse attributes explicit names; if they had not been named, the system would have generated names for them.

Figure 6h shows Mr. Jones performing an Update Environment operation on the Attribute Ranges stripe. He wants to know what will happen if he performs a Delete operation on the type Purchase Orders. This will tell him what schema components will be affected if he cancels all his purchase orders. The result, as show in figure 6i, is that two sorts of information will be affected. First, any suppliers who had any open orders, and secondly, any parts which were on purchase orders. Clearly, Mr. Jones is interested in the second subtype.

In 6j, the subtype of Parts is further refined by Mr. Jones. He locates the parts which are also on sales orders. Figure 6k illustrates this subtype being added to the session view. See 6l for the result. Mr. Jones now knows what parts he must buy in order to fill active orders. The rest of his purchase orders may be ignored.

6. Directions

Sembase in an object-oriented, or semantic, DBMS which supports intelligent databases. Such databases may embody complex data types, such as predicate-defined derived information. Sembase also supports a data language which allows a user to dynamically extend a schema. The user interface to Sembase, Ski, supports object-oriented manipulations and navigations, and provides capabilities for examining complex relationships within an object-oriented database.

One drawback of Sembase is that the simple deductive capabilities it supports are spread throughout the model, language, and interface. Predicates are defined at the model level, schema extensions at the language level, and complex relationships at the interface level. Therefore, before Sembase could be used as a firm foundation for an expert database system, these aspects would have to be integrated cleanly so that they could be smoothly extended into a true expert system, complete with very powerful deductive capabilities.

Figure 5i.

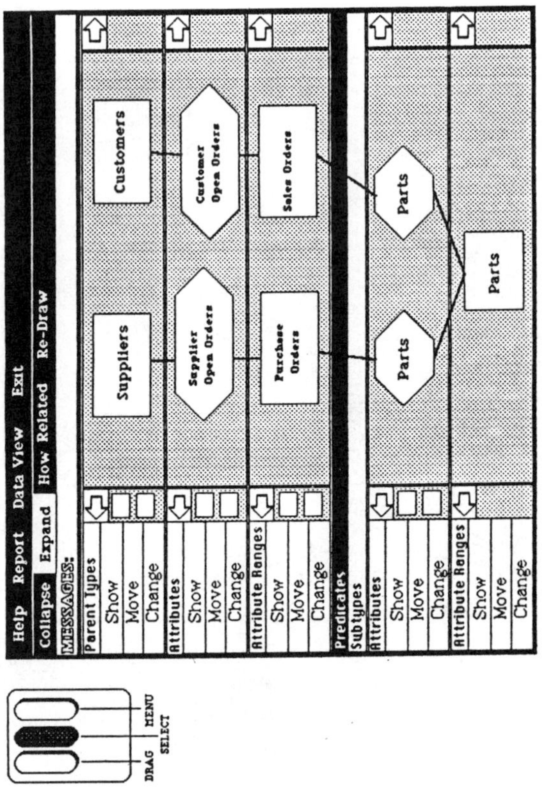

The user wishes to create a Subtype.

Figure 5j.

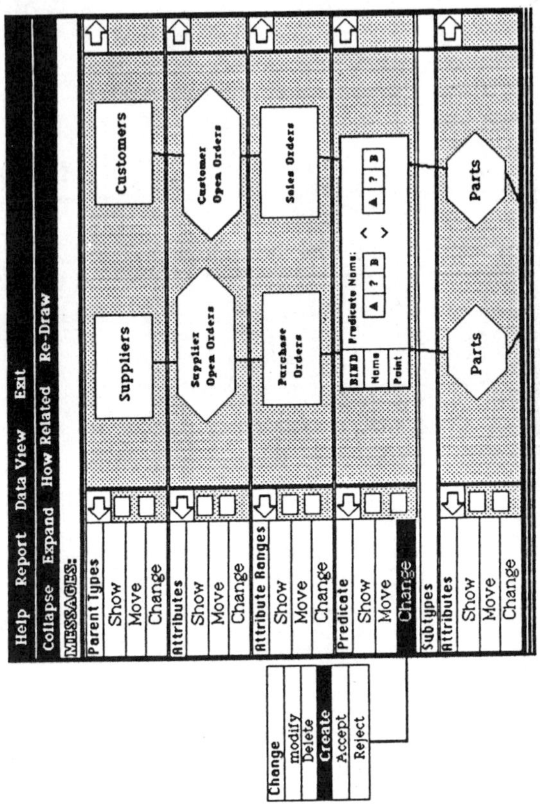

The predicate skeleton appears.

Figure 5k.

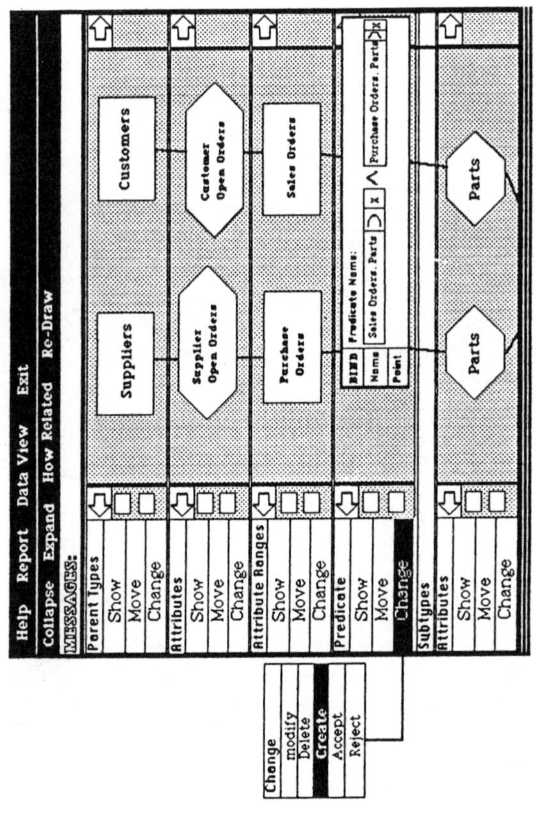

The predicate of the Subtype is Specified

Figure 5.L

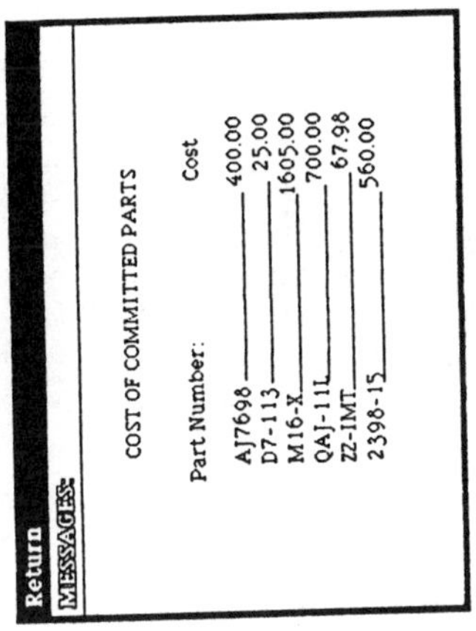

COST OF COMMITTED PARTS

Part Number:	Cost
AJ7698	400.00
D7-113	25.00
M16-X	1605.00
QAJ-11L	700.00
ZZ-IMT	67.98
2398-15	560.00

The Corresponding data is viewed.

Figure 6a.

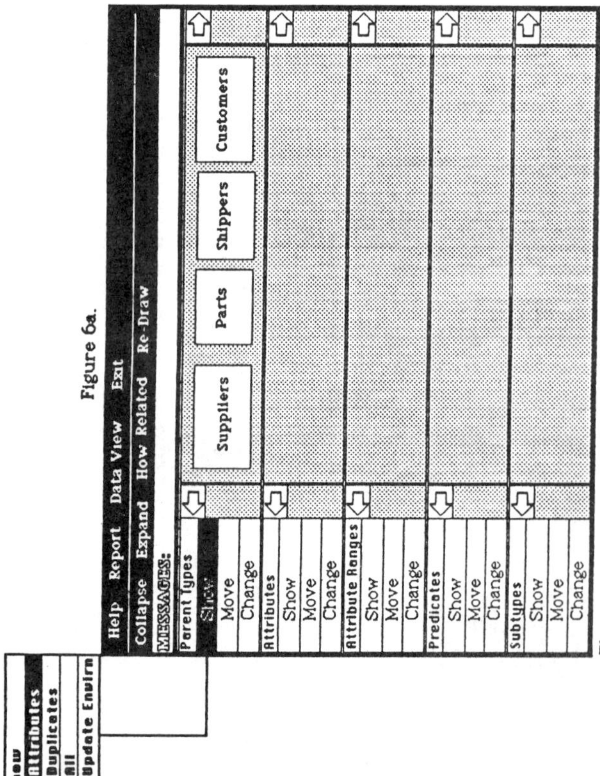

The user performs a Show All on the Parent Type stripe.

Figure 6b.

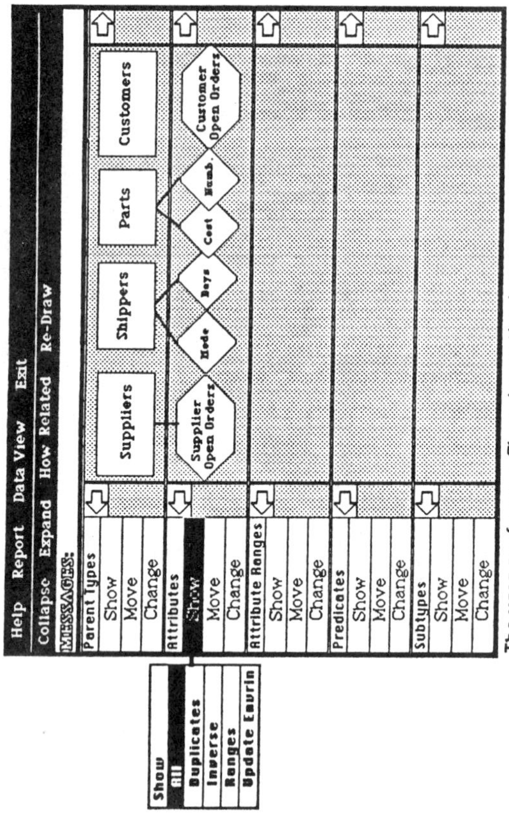

The user performs a Show All on the Attribute stripe.

Figure 6 c.

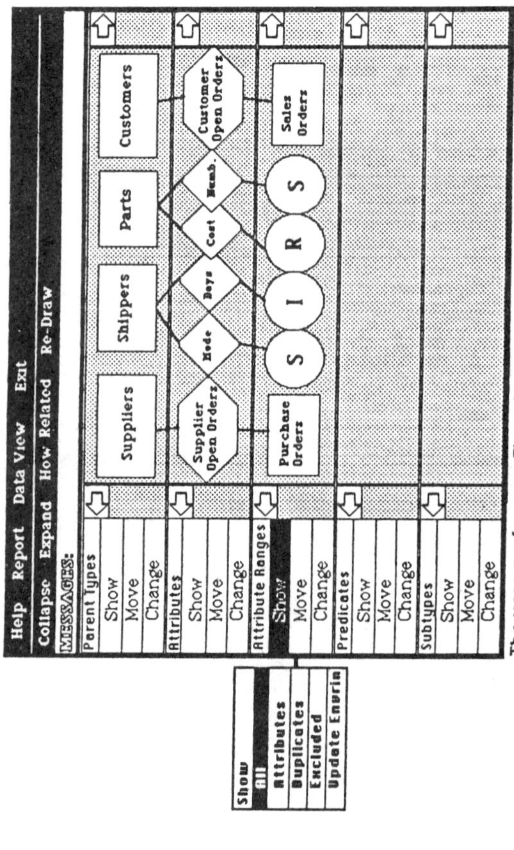

The user performs a Show All on the Attribute Range stripe.

Figure 6d.

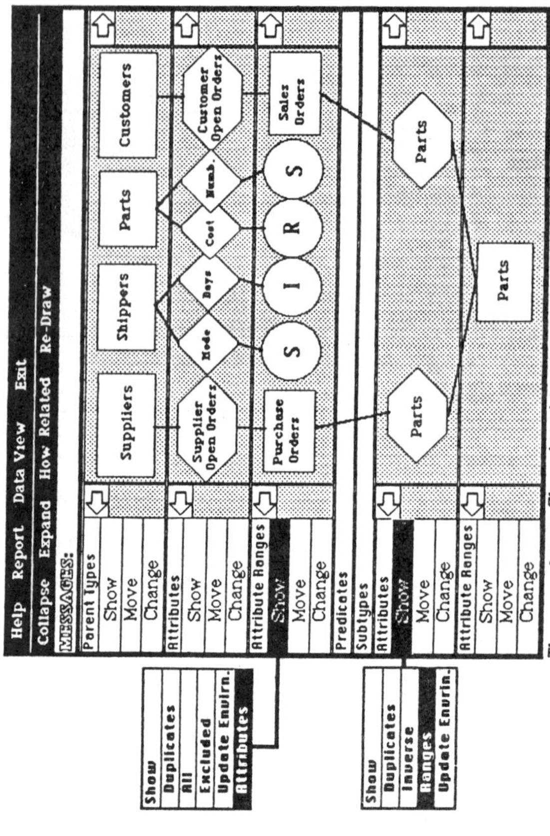

The user does a Show Attributes on the Range, and a Show Ranges on the Attribute stripe. He then sees the relationship.

Figure 6 e.

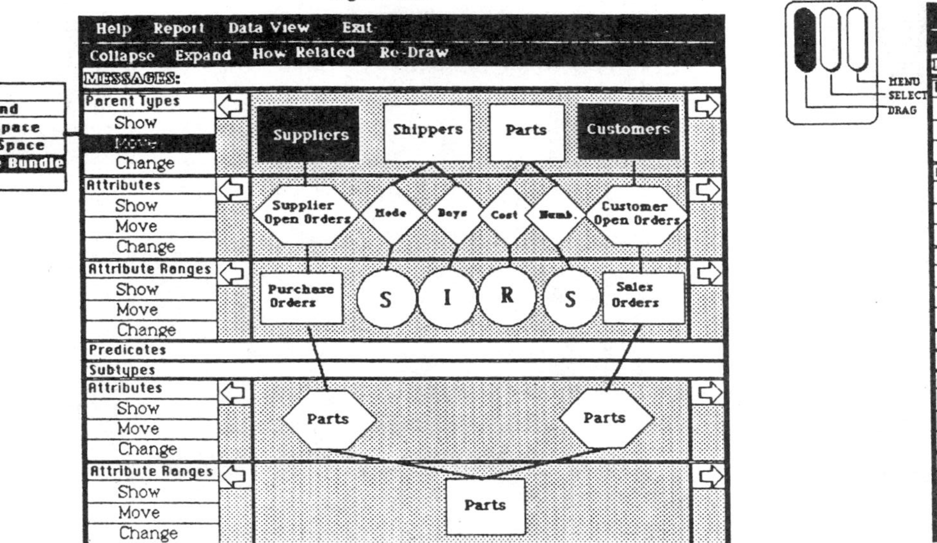

The user performs a Move on the top stripe and requests a Bundle operation.

Figure 6f.

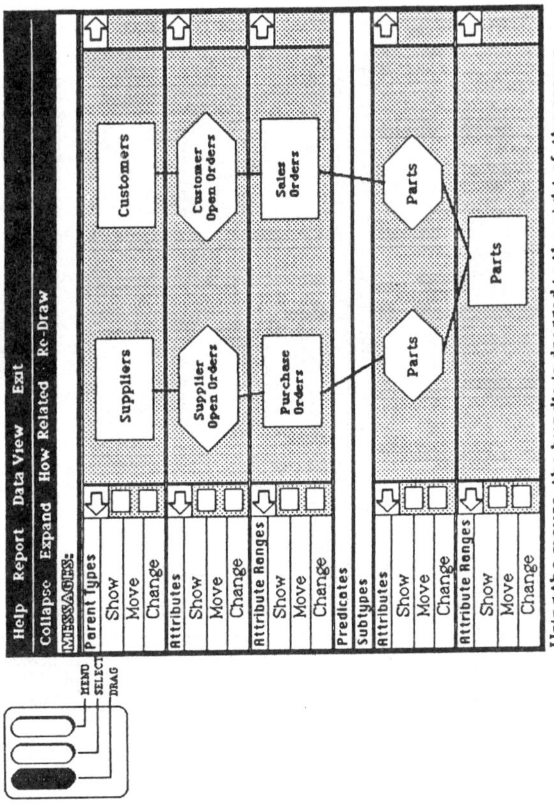

Using the mouse, the bundle is dragged to the right of the screen.

Figure 6g.

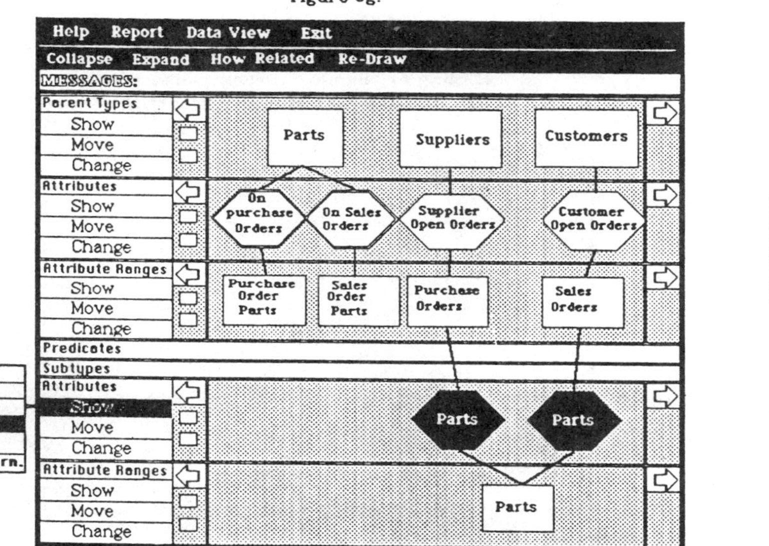

The user performs a Show Inverse Attributes on the selected Attributes.

Figure 6h.

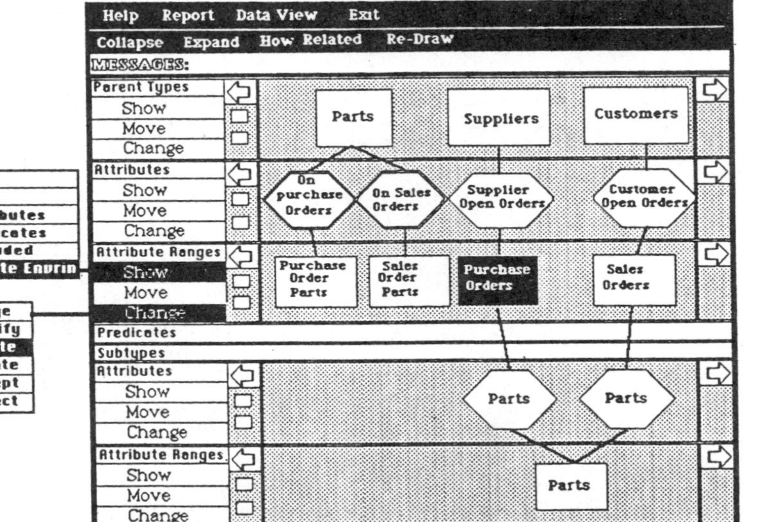

The user wishes to see the effect of deleting all Purchase Orders.

Figure 6i

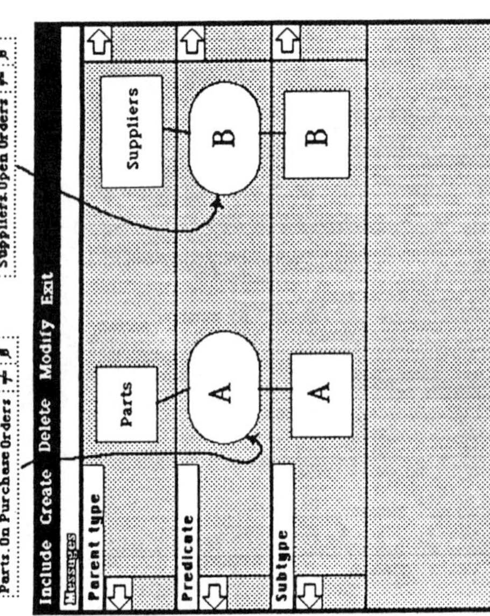

The update Environment is shown. The Subtype contains the effected data.

Figure 6j.

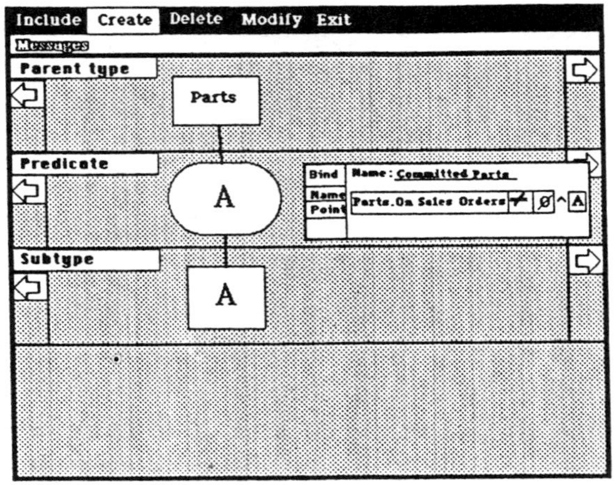

The User Creates another Subtype from the previous predicate.

Figure 6k.

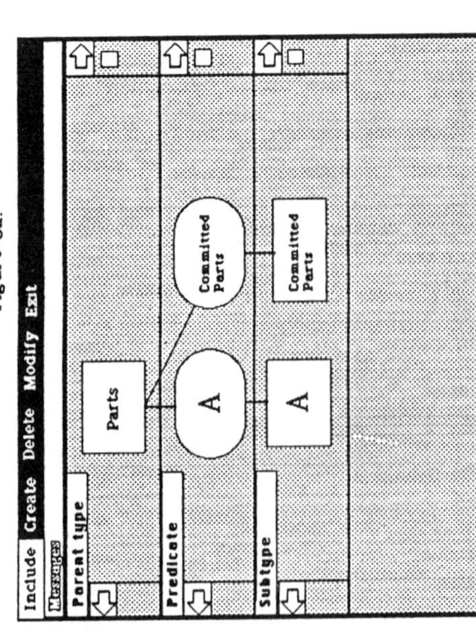

The resulting subtype is integrated in the session view.

Figure 6L.

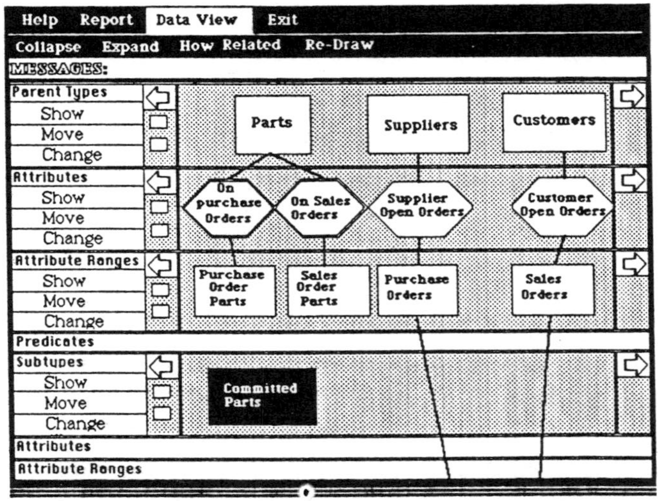

The Subtype is then chosen for viewing.

Currently, Sembase is being expanded into a multi-user, distributed system. Sembase does not support rollback and recovery. A long-range goal is to tailor the DBMS to support textual data (see [SK82] for an example of a relational database interface which includes a text editor).

References

* [AH84]

Abiteboul, S. and R. Hull, "IFO: A Formal Semantic Database Model" University of Southern California Technical Report, and the *Proceedings of the 3rd Symposium on Principles of Databases Systems,* 1984, pages 119-132.

* [AU78]

Aho, A.V., and J.D. Ullman, *Principles of Compiler Design,* Addison-Wesley, 1977.

* [Ch82]

Chan, A., S. Danberg, S. Fox, W.-T.K. Lin, A Nori, and D. Ries, "Storage and Access Structures to Support a Semantic Data Model", *Proceedings of the Eight International Conference on Very Large Data Bases,* September 8-10, 1982.

* [FKM84]

Farmer, D., R. King, and D. Myers, "A Tool for the Implementation of Databases", *Proceedings of COMPDEC '84, Computer Data Engineering Conference,* Los Angeles, CA, April 1984.

* [FKM85]

Farmer, D., R. King, and D. Myers, "The Semantic Database Constructor", *The IEEE Transactions on Software Engineering,* July, 1985.

* [GR83]

Goldberg, A. and D. Ronson, *Smalltalk-80: The Language and its Implementation,* Addison-Wesley, 1983.

* [He80]

Herot, Christopher F., "Spatial Management of Data", *ACM Transactions on Database Systems,* December 1980, Volume 5, Number 4, pages 493-513.

* [HK81]

Hecht, M.S., and L. Kerschberg, "Update Semantics for the Functional Data Model", Bell Laboratories Technical Report, Holmdel, New Jersey, January, 1981.

* [KKT77]

Kerschberg, L., A. Klug, D. Tsichritzis, "A Taxonomy of Data Models", *Systems for Large Databases,* edited by Lockemann and Neuhold, North Holland, 1977

* [KM82]

King, R. and D. McLeod, "The Event Database Specification Model", *Proceedings of the Second International Conference on Databases: Improving Usability and Responsiveness,* Jerusalem, Israel, June 1982.

* [KM84a]

King, R. and D. McLeod, "An Approach to Database Design and Evolution", *Data Modeling,* eds. M. Brodie, J. Mylopoulos, and J. Schmidt, Springer-Verlag, 1984.

* [KM84b]

King, R. and S. Melville, "A Semantics-Knowledgeable Interface" *proceedings of the Tenth International Conference on Very Large Databases,* Singapore, August, 1984.

* [KM84c]

King, R., and D. McLeod, "Semantic Database Models", in *Database Design,* editor S. B. Yao, Prentice Hall, 1985.

* [KM85]

King, R. and D. McLeod, "A Database Design Methodology and Tool for Office Information Systems" *The ACM Transactions on Office Information Systems,* January, 1985.

* [KS84]

King, R. and S. Sonke, "A Semantic Data Language", proceedings of the *1984 Trends and Applications Conference,* May 23-24, 1984.

* [Mo83]

Morgenstern, Matthew, "Active Databases as a Paradigm for Enhanced Computing Environments", *proceedings of the Ninth International Conference on Very Large Databases,* October 31 - November 2, 1983 pages 34-42.

* [SK82]

Stonebraker, M. and J. Kalash, "TIMBER: A Sophisticated Relation Browser", in *Proceedings of the Seventh International Conference on Very Large Data Bases,* 1982, pp. 1-10.

* [Wi80a]

Wilson, G. A., "Three-Dimensional Knowledge Presentation", Technical Report, Computer Corporation of America, Cambridge MA, December 1980.

* [Wi80b]

Wilson, G. A., "Semantics vs. Graphics - To Show or Not to Show", *Proceedings of the International Conference on Very Large Databases,* Montreal, Canada, October 1980.

* [Wi83]

Wilson, G., E. Domeshek, E. Drascher, and J. Dean, "The Multipurpose Presentation System", *proceedings of the Ninth International Conference on Very Large Databases,* October 31 - November 2, 1983 pages 56-69.

* [WK82]

Wong, W.K.T., and I. Kuo, "Guide: Graphical User Interface for Database Exploration" Proceedings of the International Conference on Very Large Databases, Mexico City, 1982, pages 22-32.

* [Za83]

Zaniolo, C., "The Database Language Gem", in *Proceedings of the ACM-SIGMOD International Conference on Management of Data,* May 1983, pages 207-218.

MILK : MULTI LEVEL INTERACTIVE LOGIC SIMULATOR AT KEIO UNIVERSITY

Experience in using the CONSTRAINTS language

Masahiro Nakazawa++, Michio Isoda, Jun Miyazaki, and Hideo Aiso

FACULTY OF SCIENCE AND TECHNOLOGY
Department of Electrical Engineering
Keio University

14-1, HIYOSHI, 3 CHOME, KOHOKUKU, YOKOHAMA
Yokohama 223, JAPAN

ABSTRACT

This paper presents an interactive logic simulator, MILK (Multi level Interactive Logic simulator at Keio university). MILK provides multi level descriptions, back tracing, graphic user interfaces, and the other useful facilities for interactive logic simulations. By using MILK, a user can verify and correct digital logic circuits effectively in the initial processes of the design. The first version of MILK was implemented on a VAX-11/750 UNIX+ (4.1BSD) using FRANZ LISP. MILK has been constructed using the hierarchical description language CONSTRAINTS. This paper gives a description of this language and the functions necessary to make logic simulations possible. We also present some simple execution examples.

KEYWORDS

FRANZ LISP
CONSTRAINTS
hierarchical description
object oriented language
interactive logic simulation
EVENT-DRIVEN

+UNIX is a Trademark of Bell Laboratories.
++The author is on the staff of the Nihon Digital Equipment Corporation.

1. Introduction

Due to the recent development of highly integrated and low priced of LSIs, the designing of large scale logic circuits has become necessary. As a result, the importance of the logic simulator as a designing and testing tool has greatly increased. In the early stages of the design work, many errors are to be expected. It is necessary to fina these errors and correct them as quickly as possible. Because of this, much work has been done on logic simulators. The main fields of concern have been the speed and user interface of the logic simulator [Abra 82], [McWi 80], [Szyg 72], [Toko 78], [Ulri 80], [Ulri 82]. Interactive execution between the user and the logic simulator allows the design of logic circuits in a trail and error manner. Most existing logic simulators are based on batch processing, and thus, no form of interactive simulation is allowed. In this paper we will describe an interactive logic simulator referred to as MILK (Multi level Interactive Logic simulator at Keio university). We will also present implementation methods and the CONSTRAINTS language, which is employed in this project.

2. What is CONSTRAINTS ?

The concept of the CONSTRAINTS language is introduced in this simulator. This concept, originally appeared in [Stee 80],[Deut 80]. However, only the basic part of this idea has been implemented as the kernel of MILK. The basic concepts of CONSTRAINTS language are as follows:

(1) program = constraints + constraint networks

CONSTRAINTS is a new programming paradigm and is a uniform model for data and control. Constraints, a uniform model, is a single kind of object. A program consists of the connections formed between constraints. These connections are called constraint networks. Each constraint has been created by its constraint-type. A constraint can be called an instance or an object. This is analogous to the wire-wrapping done between the IC pins of a circuit board, if we imagine the constraint to be an IC and constraint networks to be the wires.

(2) CONSTRAINTS language is similar to object-oriented languages.

The SMALLTALK language [Xero 81] is object-oriented; conceptually all computation occurs through one object passing messages to another. This message passing method is, therefore, already very similar to the CONSTRAINTS language, the primary difference being that in CONSTRAINTS the computation is bidirectional in nature.

(3) Local propagation

The sending and receiving of data is limited to those instances which are directly connected to each other by constraint networks.

(4) Almost-hierarchical descriptions

CONSTRAINTS can be expressed in a hierarchical fashion. digital circuits are also expressed in a hierarchical fashion, for instance, a Flip-Flop is made of several gates. Therefore CONSTRAINTS can express digital circuits in natural fashion.

We have used the CONSTRAINTS language as the basis for the MILK logic simulator because of points (1) and (4) listed above. CONSTRAINTS enables us to perform interactive simulations by terminating one connection and creating a new connection with another instance. Hierarchical descriptions allow the user to construct a new program from programs that already exist in the library. This using of existing programs lightens the burden of the programmer to a great extent.

When CONSTRAINTS language is used as a description language for the MILK logic simulator, the following problems occur:

(1) The evaluation sequence of an instance is determined by the availability of needed data.

(2) The input evaluation sequence is not determined by simulation time.

In logic simulators, time management is necessary when checking propagation delays.

(3) Connections are singular.

In logic circuits many multiple connections such as address buses and data buses exist. However, CONSTRAINTS does not support such group connections.

3. Extension of the CONSTRAINTS language in MILK

In MILK, the problems described above are solved as follows. For problems 1 and 2 in Section 2, a time scheduler and an event history have been incorporated, while for problem 3, a parallel value simulation has been incorporated.

(1) Time scheduler.

The EVENT-DRIVEN method is incorporated in MILK. Time in the simulator is advanced only by a fixed increment. All of the input data (EVENTs) which are put into each instance are recorded in the EVENT list according to the order of their input time. The EVENTs also have references which point to the input terminals.

In MILK, a simulation proceeds in the following manner. The EVENT is executed by following the output line to all elements that its fanouts are connected to (local propagation). Each element that is fanned out is re-evaluated with the new value taken on by the output line. New outputs for these instances are scheduled as EVENTs which will occur at some future point in the simulated time.

(2) EVENT history.

All of the EVENTs which were executed during the simulation are registered at each connection of the output line (repository). In MILK, back tracing is made possible using this history.

(3) Parallel value simulation.

Values in digital circuits are either "0"'s or "1"'s. But in simulations, three values ("0", "1" and "x"(unknown)) or five values (adding "upward transition" and "downward transition") are used. In MILK, the method using three values is incorporated to simplify the time flow mechanism and improve the simulation speed. Having EVENT history, the two additional values are represented by using three. Using this method, it is possible to represent the values with 2 bits.

On the other hand, each line of the address bus or data bus has a common simulation time and common references because the EVENTs are propagated on these lines simultaneously. So we can treat these lines as a group. Each line contains a value different from the other lines. Because the mechanism is implemented by "bignum" in FRANZ LISP, any number of lines can be treated as a group.

4. System diagram of MILK

In the section, we describe the system diagram of MILK using the extented CONSTRAINTS language in the previous section. MILK is implemented in FRANZ LISP on UNIX, and the normal user interface is a keyboard. However, a graphical interface is also supported by using a CP/M machine (OKI IF800 model 30 color graphic terminal) to facilitate a simpler user interface. Through interactions with the user, the graphic interface program generates for MILK the information which is necessary for the simulation. To simulate logic circuits, first, instances are created from desired constraint-types. Second, the created instances are connected to construct the desired circuit. When the simulation begins, the time scheduler synchronizes all the instances. However, the actual data propagation is only limited to the instances which are directly connected (local propagation). Simulation ends when all the events are exhausted or when it stops at a break point which is preset by the user.(Figure 4.1)

5. Data structures in MILK

Now, we will describe details of the data structures in MILK. The data structures in MILK are implemented using a specific array, "HUNK", which was prepared using FRANZ LISP. The following is a detailed description of the MILK data structure.

(1) Data structure constraint-type.

In CONSTRAINTS, a constraint-type contains the "program text" (rules for computation), its own name, and the names of the parameters (Figure 5.1-(1)). In MILK, an internal constraints list is added to the original constraint-type. Information concerning the internal hierarchical relation is stored in this list only if the constraint-type has a hierarchical structure (Figure 5.2-(1) CTYPE-INTERNAL).

(2) Data structure instance (constraint).

The data structure instance in CONSTRAINTS language consists of the following three parts:

a) The entry point (Figure 5.1-(2)),

b) cells (Figure 5.1-(3)),

c) and a repository(ies) (Figure 5.1-(4)).

The data structure instance in MILK is based on the one found in Steele's paper on CONSTRAINTS language[Stee 80]. To this we have added the following:

1) The entry point (Figure 5.2-(2)).

2) If the instance has a hierarchical structure, it contains numerous sub-instances (CON-INTERNAL).

3) A repository(ies) (Figure 5.3).

The following data has been added to the existing repository:

a) The simulation time at which the EVENT occurred (REP-PASSTIME),

b) a past EVENT list (REP-OUTCELLS),

c) and a future EVENT list (REP-FUTURES).

6. Extended constraint-type

In MILK, by using hierarchical descriptions in the CONSTRAINTS language, a functional level module (e.g. F.F.,COUNTER) can be constructed with gate level modules (e.g. AND, OR) as the basic elements. On the other hand, in order to describe a functional level module without basic elements, an extension of the constraint-type function is necessary. In general, after an operation a gate level module with a single output has a propagation delay. But, this method cannot be incorporated into a functional level module. This is because it usually has multiple inputs and multiple outputs, and propagation delays differ between input terminals. Therefore, instead of setting the propagation delay after an operation, we must set it before an operation. Because of these consideration, we will introduce the following three kinds of constraint-types:

1) a functional description constraint-type,

2) a propagation delay setting constraint-type,

3) and a timing check constraint-type.

A functional level module is a connection of instances created from these constraint-types. Some of these functional level modules must have a storage function (e.g. F.F., register, memory). Therefore, we have added the storage mechanism to the constraint-type. It is implemented with an array in FRANZ LISP instead of using data structure cells and repositories. In order to protect memory elements from illegal references, actual array names cannot be directly referenced by the user. In addition, the debugging monitor is also of a constraint-type. Thus, the simulation control mechanism is simplified. Due to this fact, the debugging monitor can be set by connecting it to the instance in the same manner.

7. Examples of using MILK

In this section a description of the constraint-type representation in MILK and the execution of simulations is presented. First, we will show an example of a gate level module (EXAMPLE 1). The list following "parts" shows that this gate has three terminals (A B Y). The list following "rules" consists of three parts: input((A B)), output((Y)) and rules to be applied (the list following "case"). For example, the underlined part of the rule is represented in the following manner. If the output Y is an L-level value and both inputs A and B are set as H-level values, output Y will become an H-level value after 18 nsec.

EXAMPLE 2 shows a functional level module (SN7474 D-F.F). The definition of a functional level module consists of four constraint-types: a Timing Check constraint-type, a Delay Setting constraint-type, a Functional Description constraint-type, and a Connection constraint-type. Like a gate level module each constraint-type has three parts (input, output, and rules). Each constraint-type in this example can be defined as follows:

1) The Timing Check constraint-type (e.g. constraint-type SN7474tck) contains information that checks the timing conditions. In this case, the data set up time (Tsu), the data hold time (Th), and the minimum pulse width (Tw) are checked.

2) The Delay Setting constraint-type (e.g. constraint-type SN7474ptm) contains propagation delay time information. The user can set the delay time of each terminal.

3) The Function Description constraint-type (e.g. constraint-type SN7474func) characterizes the logical function of this module. In this case, the function of the D-F.F. is described. In other words, the level of the D-terminal is registered at the rising edge of the clock and is then output at the Q-terminal.

4) The Connection constraint-type has information for connecting the three types described above. In this case, the three constraint-types are connected as shown in Figure 7.1.

Now, we will show a simple result of an execution of MILK (EXAMPLE 3). Figure 7.2 shows a simulation circuit (SN7474 D-F.F.) and its input and output timing chart. First, the user creates instances used in the simulation. Using the function "crystal" (1), a 2 kHz clock instance "hclock" is created from constraint-type CLOCK and is recorded in time scheduler. An instance "dff" is created from the constraint-type SN7474 using the function "create" (2). Next, the user appropriately connects the instances. In this case, the user attaches the clock instance "hclock" to the terminal "CK" of the instance "dff" (3) and sets the "PR", "CLR" ,and "D" terminals to the H-level (4, 5, 6). That ends the preparation which will allow the user to start the simulation. The function "start" is used for this purpose (7).

During a simulation process, MILK puts out a record of the simulation state and the rules corresponding to the change of the input data. The user can recognize both the details of the transition state and its cause.

A user can use MILK in the above manner, but because this

method of execution is rather complicated, MILK provides another method of communication using the graphic editor. Figure 7.3 shows an example of a circuit diagram drawn by the graphic editor in MILK. When a user draws a circuit diagram like Figure 7.3, input commands are generated automatically.

While drawing circuit diagrams, the user may select graphic instances (D-F.F., and-gate, or-gate, etc.) from the constraint-type library. Then, MILK creates instances of corresponding constraint-types (EXAMPLE 3 (1),(2)). Next, the user may connect graphic instances, and at the same time MILK will generate connection information (EXAMPLE 3 (3)-(6)). The user can register the circuit diagram in the constraint-type library, which can be used later.

8. Conclusion

The interactive logic simulator, MILK, was implemented on a VAX-11/750 UNIX (4.1 BSD) using FRANZ LISP. MILK is based on the hierarchical description language CONSTRAINTS. To the original CONSTRAINTS language, we added a time scheduler, the EVENT history mechanism, which allows the user to execute back tracing, and group connection capability. With these additions give MILK the facilities for dynamic tracing in the simulation process. Thus, MILK can be used as a powerful tool in the interactive debugging of logic designs.

The execution speed of MILK is slower than existing logic simulators. However, MILK is supposed to be used for small size circuits in the early stage of the logic design process and we believe that the powerful facilities available in MILK more than make up for its lack of speed.

9. Acknowledgement

The authors would like to acknowledge the generous advice of Professor Mario Tokoro of Keio University. We also wish to thank Mr. Hideharu Amano for his valuable discussions and suggestions. We would also like to express our appreciation to Mr. Allen Shepherd for informing us of the existence of the workshop and suggesting that we present this paper.

REFERENCES

[Abra 82] M. Abramovici et al, "A logic simulation machine", Design Automation Conference 1982.

[Deut 80] L. Peter Deutsch, "CONSTRAINTS:A UNIFORM MODEL FOR DATA CONTROL", PROCEEDING OF THE WORKSHOP ON DATA ABSTRACTION, DATABASES AND CONCEPTUAL MODELLING Pingree Park, Colorado June 23-26, 1980.

[McWi 80] Thomas M. McWilliams, "The SCALD Timing Verifier: A New Approach to Timing Constraints in large Digital Systems", Design Automation Conference 1982.

[Saka 81] Takashi SAKAI et al, "Design verification with on interactive Logic Simulation SIM/D-IS", EC81-54 1981.

[Stee 80] Guy Lewis Steele Jr., "The Definition and Implementation of a Computer Programming Language Based on CONSTRAINTS", Technical report No.595, Artificial Intelligence Laboratory, MIT, Cambridge, Massachusetts, August 1980.

[Szyg 72] S.A.Szygenda, "TEGAS2--anatomy of a general purpose test generation and simulation", Design Automation Conference 1972.

[Toko 78] Mario Tokoro, Masayuki Sato, Masayuki Ishigami, Eiji Tamura, Terunobu Ishimitsu, and Hisashi Ohara, "A module level simulation technique for systems composed of LSI's and MSI's", Design Automation Conference 1978.

[Ulri 80] Ernst Ulrich, "Table look up technique for fast and flexible digital logic", Design Automation Conference 1980.

[Ulri 82] Ernst Ulrich, "Speed and accuracy in digital network simulation based on structural modeling", Design Automation Conference 1982.

[Xero 81] Xerox Learning Research Group, "The Smalltalk-80 System," Special Issue on Smalltalk-80 System, BYTE, Vol.6, No.8, Aug., 1981.

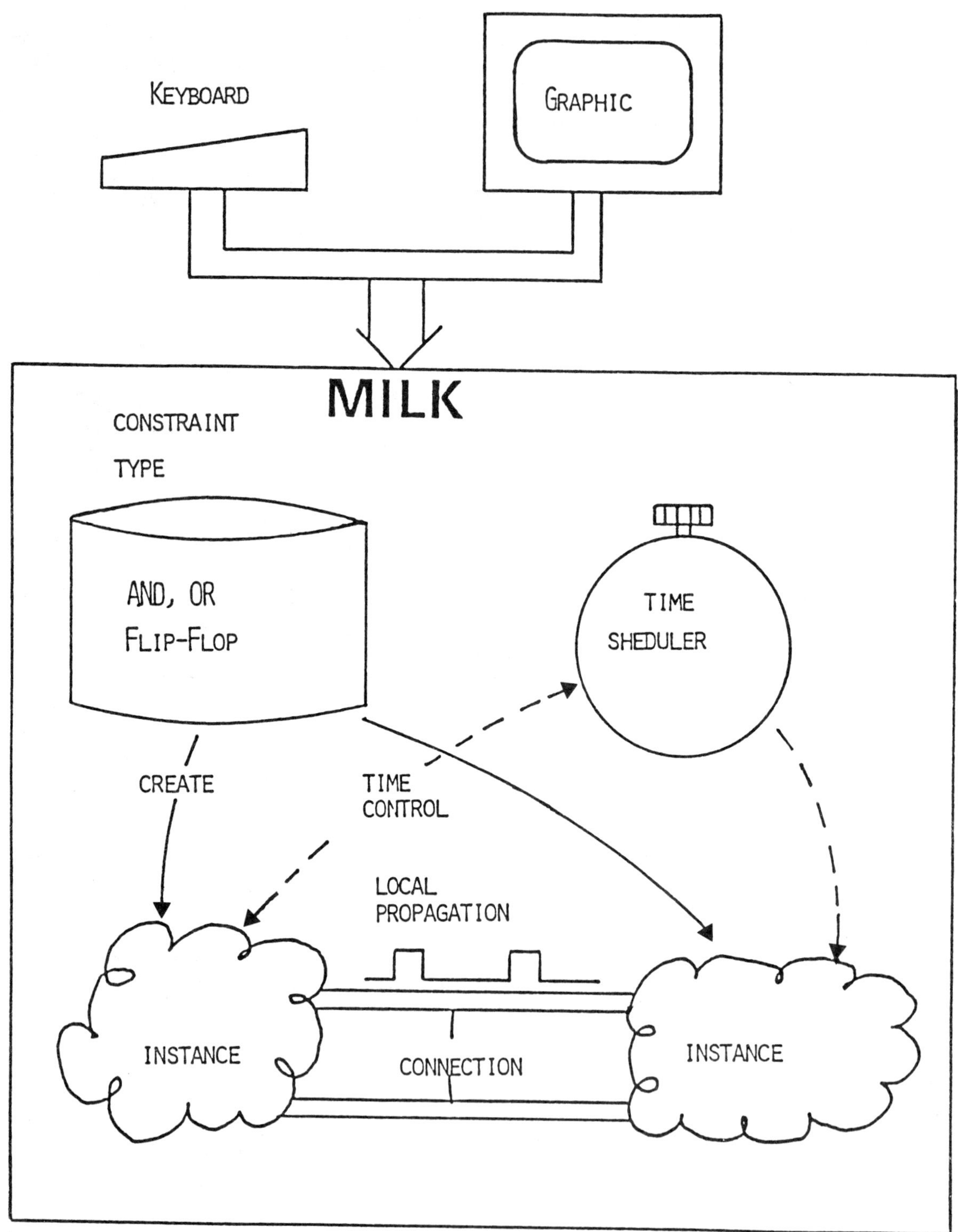

Figure 4.1 System diagram of MILK

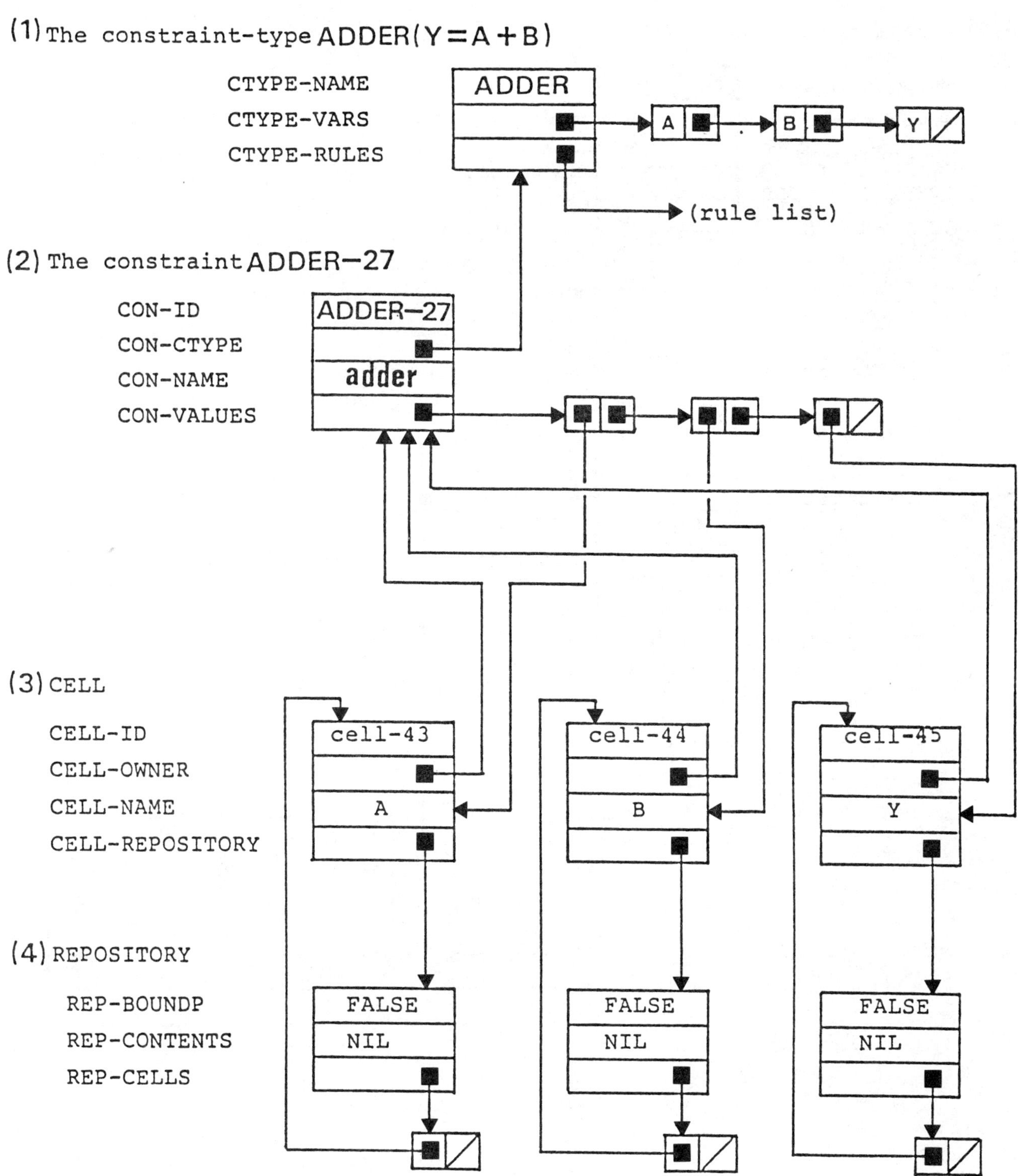

Figure 5.1 The ADDER constraint-type and an instance.

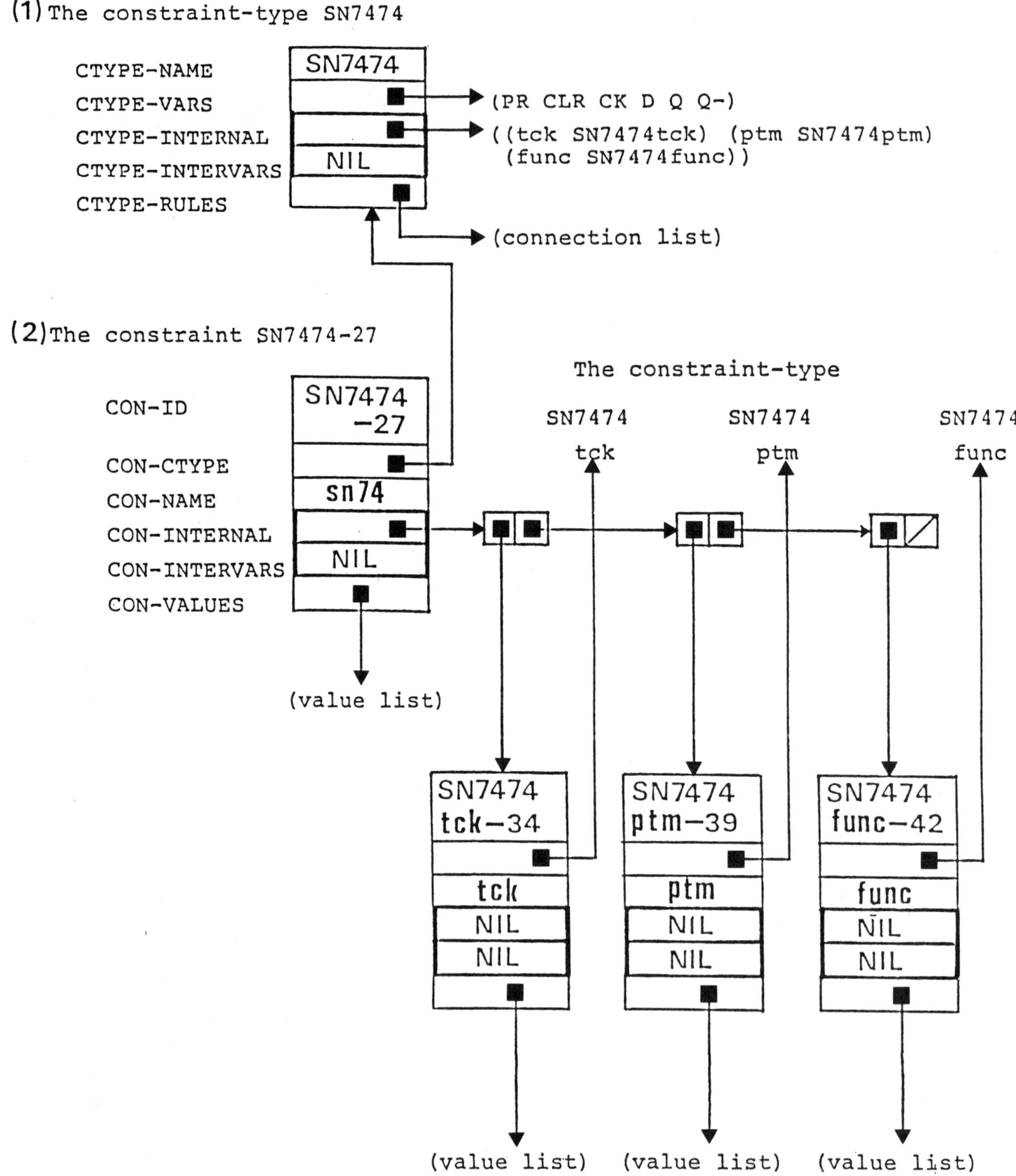

Figure 5 .2 The SN7474 constraint-type and an instance.

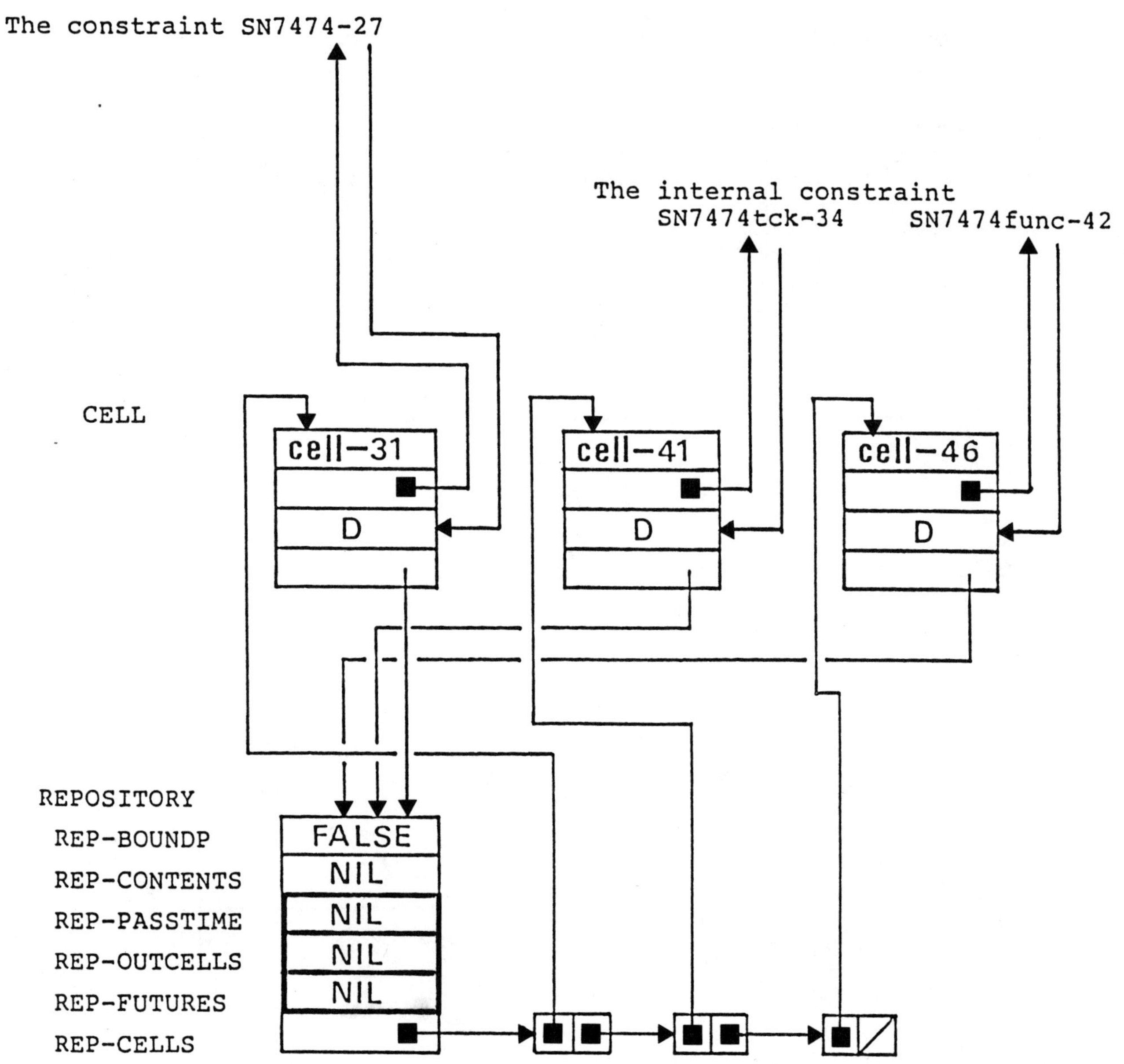

Figure 5.3 The Result of the Creating a terminal(D) for SN7474.

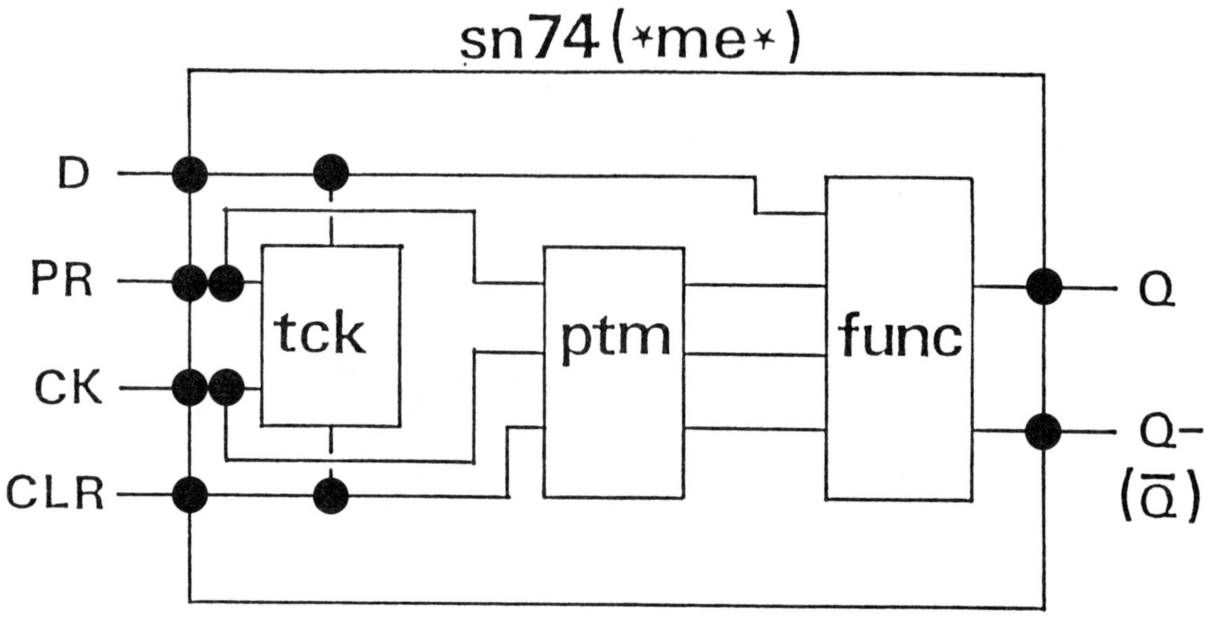

Figure 7 .1 internal connection

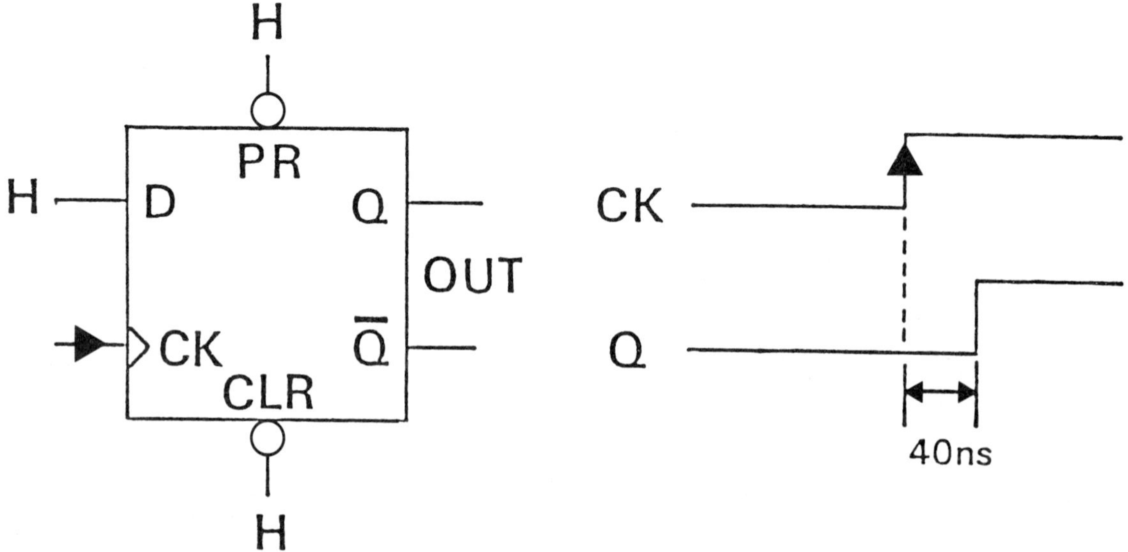

Figure 7.2 SN7474(D-F.F.)and input and output timing chart.

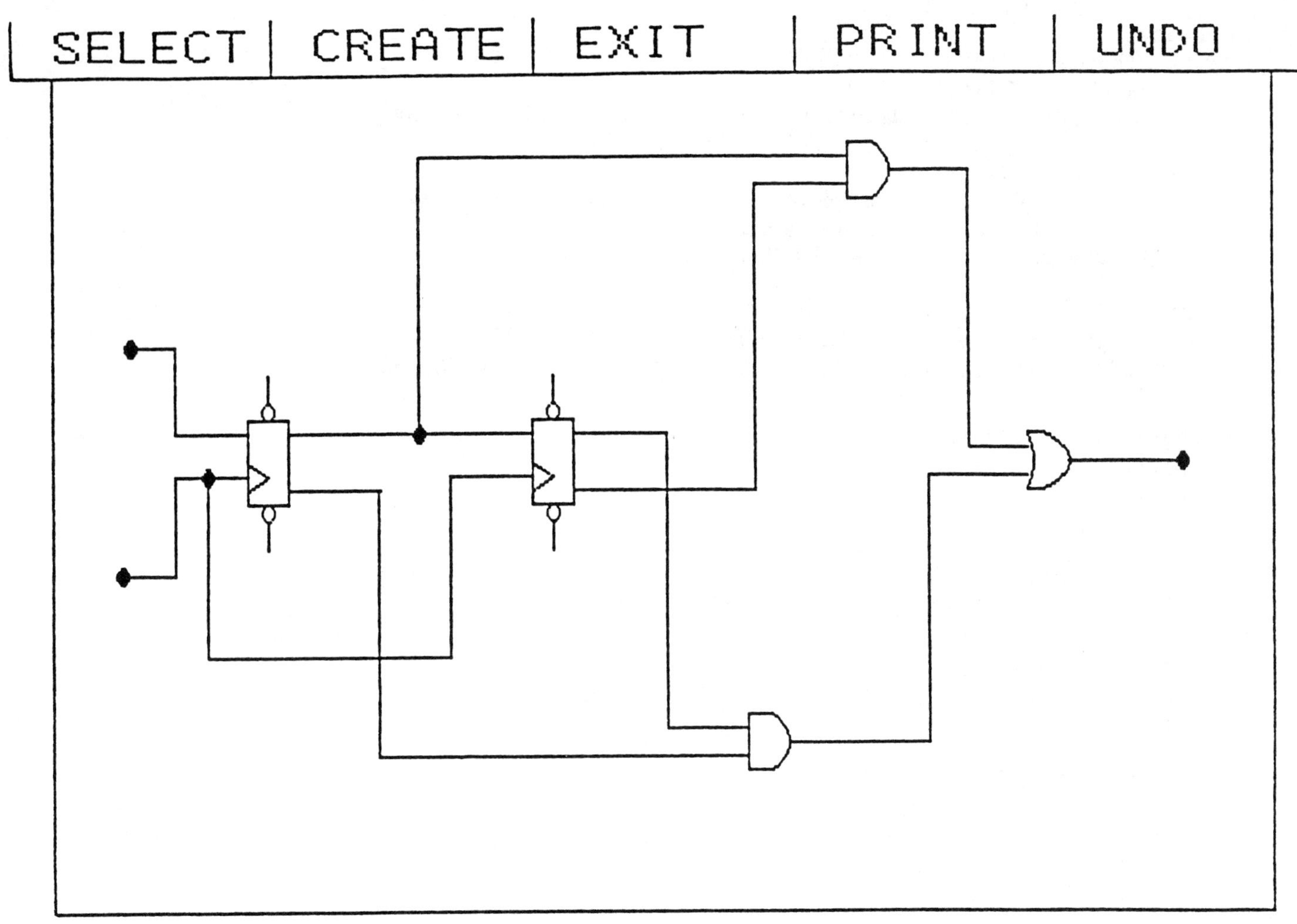

Figure 7.3 a circuit diagram with graphic editor

EXAMPLE 1

```
(constraint AND2 (parts (A B Y))
(body
       (rules
              ((A B) (Y) (case (Y A B)
                           ((L H H) (setcl Y H 18) )))
              ((A B) (Y) (case (Y A B)
                           ((H L H) (setcl Y L 12))))
              ((A B) (Y) (case (Y A B)
                           ((H H L) (setcl Y L 12))))
              ((A B) (Y) (case (Y A B)
                           ((H L L) (setcl Y L 12))))
))     )
```

EXAMPLE 2

```
(constraint SN7474tck
  (parts (CK D PR CLR))
  (body
   (timingcheck
    ((PR CLR CK D) nil
     (case (PR CLR (risingedge CK) (=< (Tsu D 20) global-time))
           ((H H t t) (Tw CK 30) (Th D 5))))
    ((PR CLR CK D) nil
     (case (PR CLR (risingedge CK) (> (Tsu D 20) global-time))
           ((H H t t) (lose "error"))))
    ((PR CLR CK D) nil (case (PR CLR (fallingedge CK))
                             ((H H t) (Tw CK 37))))
    ((PR CLR) nil (case (PR CLR) ((L H) (Tw PR 30))))
    ((PR CLR) nil (case (PR CLR) ((H L) (Tw CLR 30))))
    ((PR CLR) nil (case (PR CLR) ((L L) (Tw CLR 30) (Th CLR 30))))
)))
(constraint SN7474ptm
  (parts (CK CK1 PR PR1 CLR CLR1))
  (body
   (passingtime
    ((CK) (CK1) (setcl CK1 CK 40))
    ((PR) (PR1) (setcl PR1 PR 40))
    ((CLR) (CLR1) (setcl CLR1 CLR 40))
    )))
(constraint SN7474func
  (parts (PR CLR CK D Q Q-))
  (body
   (rules
    ((PR CLR CK D) (Q Q-)
     (case (PR CLR CK D)
          ((H H (risingegde CK) H) (setc Q H) (setc Q- L))))
    ((PR CLR CK D) (Q Q-)
     (case (PR CLR CK D)
          ((H H (risingegde CK) L) (setc Q L) (setc Q- H))))
    )))
(constraint SN7474
  (parts (PR CLR CK D Q Q-)
   internal
    ((tck SN7474tck) (ptm SN7474ptm) (func SN7474func)))
  (body
   (connections nil
;
        (== (<< CK *me*) (<< CK tck))
        (== (<< PR *me*) (<< PR tck))
        (== (<< CLR *me*) (<< CLR tck))
        (== (<< D *me*) (<< D tck))
;
        (== (<< CK *me*) (<< CK ptm))
        (== (<< PR *me*) (<< PR ptm))
        (== (<< CLR *me*) (<< CLR ptm))
;
        (== (<< CK1 ptm) (<< CK func))
        (== (<< PR1 ptm) (<< PR func))
        (== (<< CLR1 ptm) (<< CLR func))
;
        (== (<< D *me*) (<< D func))
        (== (<< Q *me*) (<< Q func))
        (== (<< Q- *me*) (<< Q- func))
        )))
```

EXAMPLE 3

```
(1) (MILK):(crystal hclock 2000.0)
    <cell-20> (CK of CLOCK-19(hclock)) : LOW 2000.0 Herz passtime is 0ns>
(2) (MILK):(create dff SN7474)
    <dff:SN7474-21>
(3) (MILK):(== (<< CK hclock) (<< CK dff))
    ;|Awakening <dff:SN7474-21> because its CK got the value LOW.
    done
(4) (MILK):(== (<< PR dff) H)
    ;|Connected cell-28 (value = HIGH) trigger time = 0 ns
    ;| and <cell-25 (PR of SN7474-21(dff)) : >.
    done
(5) (MILK):(== (<< CLR dff) H)
    ;|Connected cell-29 (value = HIGH) trigger time = 0 ns
    ;| and <cell-26 (CLR of SN7474-21(dff)) : >.
    done
(6) (MILK):(== (<< D dff) H)
    ;|Connected cell-30 (value = HIGH) trigger time = 0 ns
    ;| and <cell-22 (D of SN7474-21(dff)) : >.
    done
(7) (MILK):(start)
    ;|Awakening <dff:SN7474-21>
     because its (D - - PR CLR CK) got the value (H - - H H L)
    ;|      0 ns.
    ;|Awakening <dff:SN7474-21> because its CK got the clock 250000.0
    ;|      clock level HIGH.
    ;|<dff:SN7474-21> computed the value HIGH for its Q
    ;|<dff:SN7474-21> computed the value LOW for its Q-
    ;|<dff:SN7474-21> hold time 5 ns : D
    ;| need-hold-time is 250005.0 ns.
    ;|<dff:SN7474-21> propagation delay time 40 ns : Q
    ;| passtime is 250040.0 ns.
    ;|<dff:SN7474-21> propagation delay time 40 ns : Q-
    ;| passtime is 250040.0 ns.
    ;|owner is <dff:SN7474-21> :parts (- Q Q- - - -) is (- H L - - -)
     passtime: 250040.0 ns.
    ;|Awakening <dff:SN7474-21> because its CK got the clock 500000.0
    ;|      clock level is LOW.
    done
    (MILK):
```

HANDLING CONSTRAINTS AND META-DATA ON A GENERALIZED DATA MANAGEMENT SYSTEM

ADIBA, M.
NGUYEN, G.T.

IMAG
Laboratoire de Génie Informatique
Université de Grenoble
BP 68
38402 ST-MARTIN-D'HERES Cedex (France)

Abstract:
Sophisticated applications such as office automation and computer aided design require improved semantics and data management facilities. Large and complex objects are stored and modified (e.g documents, graphics), and complex and multiple representations are often used (e.g VLSI circuits definition). Semantic relationships between objects and representations must be defined and maintained with respect to numerous and intricate consistency constraints.

We propose to enhance a generalized data management system called TIGRE with a validation sub-system in order to :

- define, control and manipulate the semantics of a generalized model of data,
- define, control and manipulate the consistency constraints associated with sophisticated applications implemented on TIGRE.

This leads to the specification of a meta-model that includes the fundamental concepts captured in the model and the ability to modify dynamically the application schemas and their associated consistency rules.

Our approach is being experimented on a prototype that is implemented in PROLOG and cooperates with TIGRE in an integrated fashion. TIGRE provides the large and complex objects storage and manipulation facilities, whilst the semantics definition, control and manipulation is off-loaded to PROLOG, in a cooperative approach.

Experiments are made on office automation and CAD for VLSI circuits.

This work is supported in part by Agence de l'Informatique (contract 84061).

I. INTRODUCTION.

The scientific and industrial community is faced nowadays to the problems of task automation and electronic data processing. In the past, they have been solved with algorithmic programming languages and file management systems. Database management systems (DBMS) offer today easier ways to deal with this. This is especially true for relational DBMS, which have popularized non-procedural languages, in which the user tells the system what he wants, not the way he wants it to be done. They lack however of powerful semantics definition facilities, as well as the associated control mechanisms.

In parallel, one can observe the growing impact of logic programming, and particularly of languages such as PROLOG /COL83/. In such languages, one declares ground facts, general properties of data, and with the same formalism, programs defined in their own particular logic. It was therefore clear that expert systems for instance, would take advantage of both DBMS and logic programming technologies /PAR83, VAS83, WAL83, ZAU83/. Other recent research efforts tend also to use such facilities for specific application requirements, such as graphics database management in PROLOG /PER83/.

Our work deals with the representation and control of the SEMANTICS of applications developed on a generalized database system called TIGRE. By semantics of applications, we mean :

- the objects involved,
- their static properties,
- their processing,
- the dynamic constraints they must obey.

We want to enlight the possibilities of implementing applications which require, as in AI or CAD, sophisticated data models and powerful processing tools to handle usual, but also large and/or complex objects. We propose for this to enhance TIGRE with logic programming, and thus provide a validation sub-system that will control both schema definition and user operations on the data.

We use here logic programming to define (Fig. 1) :

- the semantics associated to the conceptual schema of an application,
- the access and manipulation of data stored in a relational-like DBMS or in a database of PROLOG clauses, at the internal schema level,
- the definition of the execution procedures at the external schema level.

Indeed, some applications need powerful tools for the definition of data (e.g VLSI or aerodynamic profiles representation), for the definition of the processing (e.g aerodynamic structures vibrations), and sophisticated semantics control capabilities (e.g VLSI layout).

	PROLOG		TIGRE
data access and manipulation	facts and knowledge	internal level	relational DBMS
data types and constraints	rules and semantics	conceptual level	generalized data model
data processing	clauses and inference	external level	application programs

Fig. 1. Using logic programming with TIGRE.

We assume here that the DBMS TIGRE exists, and that it allows for the modelling of such applications, using a generalized data model /LOP83/. This one provides the user with a strong data typing capability, with such notions as entity, relationship, classes, aggregation and generalization.

As it stands today, TIGRE provides the user with a high level data definition and manipulation language, called LAMBDA /VEL82/. In particular, complex objects and large objects (e.g documents) are handled as standard data. In the future, graphics and voice processing capabilities will be incorporated in the system. Another aspect of the project concerns the development of intelligent workstations. Sophisticated applications such as office automation and CAD for VLSI circuits are being experimented using TIGRE /ADI84/.

A prototype of TIGRE in currently being implemented at IMAG on a Honeywell DPS 8/70 machine, running the MULTICS operating system. The delivery is planned for the end of 1984. It does not however include powerful constraint checking mechanisms on the schema definition and manipulation (e.g attribute inheritance, schema modifications), neither on the control of the dynamic behavior of objects (e.g update propagation through relationships).

We integrate TIGRE and PROLOG to solve these problems, and provide TIGRE with a deductive component (Fig. 2). We shall thus have a generalized and logic DBMS, in the sense of /GAL83/, and be able to handle generalized data stored in TIGRE, and off-load the semantics definition and control capabilities to PROLOG. We are therefore able to implement with this approach a meta- knowledge management facility. It will include semantics information concerning the definition, control and modification of application schemes and consistency control strategies (e.g rule modification laws).

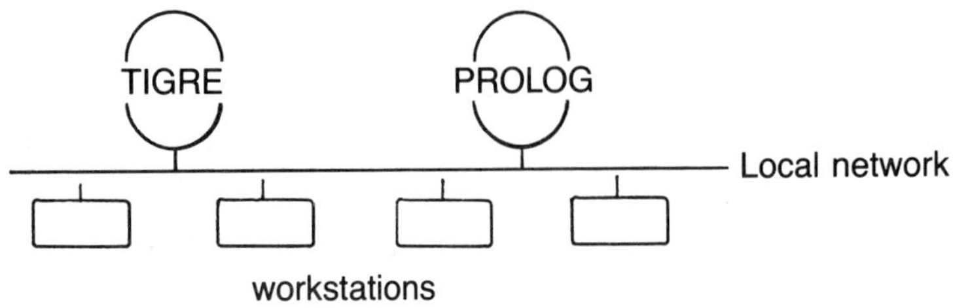

Fig. 2. Environment of the research.

On one hand, TIGRE will provide the data management facilities to store, retreive and modify large and/or complex objects. On the other hand, PROLOG will provide the semantics representation, control and manipulation capabilities for applications using these objects.

We are not trying here to provide general tools, but rather to show the feasability of our approach. An implementation of all the following proposals is described in /NGU84, OLI83/. As do some other recent research efforts /COL83, GAL83, PAR83, VAS83, WAL83, ZAU83/, we aim at proving how easily the fundamental concepts of databases and knowledge bases can be defined and cooperate through PROLOG.

All our examples, some of which have been drawn from /LOP83/, are written in the Edimburgh version of PROLOG, which is available at IMAG on DEC LSI-11 machines, running the RT-11 operating system.

We suppose the reader familiar with PROLOG /CLO81/. Recall that a clause :

```
p(X,Y) :- q(X), r(X,Y), s(Y,_).
```

is evaluated as an logical implication :

"for all X and Y such that q(X) and r(X,Y) and s(Y,_) are true, then p(X,Y) is true".

An assertion s(a,b) is an predicate which is always true. Variables start with an uppercase letter. Constants and predicate names with a lower case letter. An anonymous variable, noted "_", is not significant for the evaluation of a predicate. Finally, an alternative is noted :

```
     p(X,Y) :- t(X,Y).
     p(X,Y) :- s(X,Y).
or : p(X,Y) :- t(X,Y) ; s(X,Y).
```

A list is enclosed in square brackets, noted : °X!Y§. X is the head of the list. Y is the tail of the list.

First, we give the principles for modelling in Prolog the generalized data of TIGRE (Section II). This provides a meta-model definition capability to control the definition of consistent schemas, with respect to the fundamental concepts of the data model.

We emphasize on the representation in PROLOG of the SEMANTICS associated to applications involving generalized data described with the model of TIGRE. We show with the help of examples, drawn from office automation and from CAD for VLSI circuits, the consistency of this representation with that of TIGRE.

We then outline some implementation considerations, for the operations of the inference mechanisms on TIGRE (Section III). In particular, we show how semantics management and knowledge processing in PROLOG can be used in cooperation with TIGRE. We thus stress the complementarity of logic programming and of generalized DBMSs like TIGRE. Section IV is made of conclusions.

II. META-DATA AND MODELLING PRINCIPLES.

2.1 Basic principles.

TIGRE and PROLOG both operate on very different concepts. The generalized model of data of TIGRE is an extension of the entity-relationship model /CHE76/. It includes the notion of data type, class, generalization and aggregation. The associated data definition and manipulation language, called LAMBDA, is non procedural. Besides, PROLOG allows for the manipulation of complex data, structured in lists and trees. It also provides a powerful tool for the definition and manipulation of semantics data /ADI84, PAR83, VAS83, WAL83, ZAU83/.

Integrating both TIGRE and PROLOG implies finding a level of consistency.

In fact, there are three main possibilities :

- the data model level,
- the language level,
- the physical data structure level.

The latter has been eliminated, since the data structures in TIGRE and PROLOG are specific to each system. In particular, the database server of TIGRE uses the relational model of data. It is now being implemented with an extended version of a DBMS developed at IMAG, called MICROBE /NGU82/. Further, PROLOG uses a proper implementation of data values and variables, which excludes on available interpreters the communication with external programs. Binding the two systems at this level would have required heavy data formatting facilities.

The integration of the manipulation languages seems more appropriate but requires the compatibility of all the data concepts they operate on. It is thus necessary to show the compatibility of the data model of TIGRE with PROLOG /OLI83/.

Indeed, if we can represent in PROLOG any data type defined with the model of TIGRE, we can guarantee that any constraint concerning the data types, the belonging of elements to classes, the inheritance of properties and the semantic constraints will be in our cooperative approach implemented and controlled in PROLOG. Moreover, we shall be able in such a case to write programs with the same formalism. An implementation of this proposal is described in /ADI84, NGU84/. It concerns a CAD application for VLSI circuits.

This approach guarantees also that all information handled by PROLOG can be syntactically and semantically consistent with any application developped on TIGRE.

So, we shall be able in the future to handle in LAMBDA any data managed by a PROLOG expert system, and vice-versa (Fig. 3).

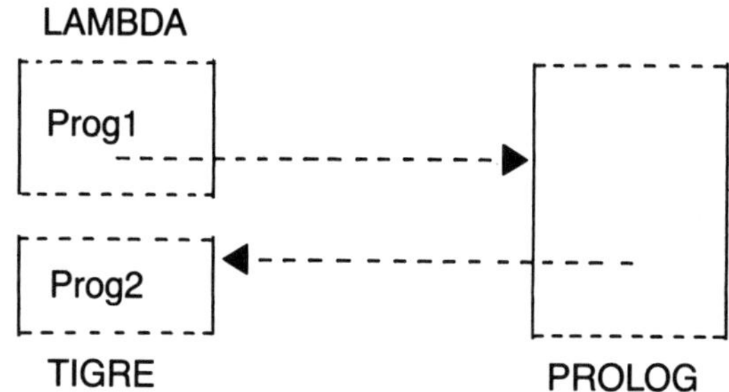

Fig. 3. Integrating TIGRE and PROLOG.

Schematically, the different steps for the modelling and the manipulation of TIGRE data in PROLOG are in our approach (Fig. 4) :

1 - generation of a kernel of basic operators on data types, in the form of PROLOG clauses,
2 - translation of the user data types in PROLOG,
3 - interpretation in PROLOG of the user defined operations, in accordance with the above data types and basic operators.

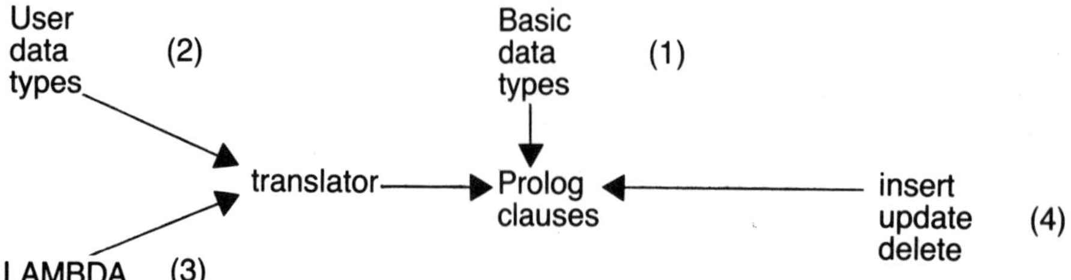

Fig. 4. Cooperation schema.

First, we GENERATE a set of PROLOG clauses (steps 1, 2 and 3) that define the constraints that apply on the data and consistency rule definitions (§ 2.2 to 2.6).

Next, we define how to use these constraints in programs which correspond to user programs at step 4 (Section III).

If we only want to use PROLOG for the implementation of type checking constraints or schema and consistency rule modification, in some kind of a procedural way, we can stop this modelling approach prior to step 4. The clauses defined so far will deliver boolean values, i.e constraint checking predicates true or false, usable in LAMBDA programs. This is explained in Section III.

2.2 Basic type definitions.

The first step corresponds to the definition in PROLOG of the basic data type operations. These include /VEL82/ :

- basic type derivation, e.g scalar type,
- constructed types, e.g record, array,
- specialization of entities and associations,
- aggregation of entities.

These operators will guarantee the consistency of the data definitions and data manipulation operations already defined in TIGRE.

We automate this translation of data definition statements from LAMBDA in PROLOG clauses. The specifications of a program implementing this translation is out of the scope of this paper. One knows that PROLOG fits well to the requirements of syntactic transformation rules of this kind. Providing that the source language is defined with a BNF grammar, which is the case for LAMBDA, one can write easily a rewriting system.

Ex1 The definition of the basic types, derived types and constructed types of LAMBDA becomes in PROLOG :

```
type(X)               :- basic-type(X) ; derived-type(X) ;
                         constructed-type(X).
basic-type(X)         :- integer(X) ; char(X) ; bool(X) ;
                         interval(X) ; string(X) ; scalar(X).
constructed-type(X)   :- array(X) ; record(X) ; document(X).
class-type(X)         :- entity-type(X) ; relationship-type(X) ;
                         generalization(X) ; aggregation(X).
generalization(X)     :- specialization(X) ; union(X) ;
                         intersection(X).
```

2.3 Derived and constructed types.

In the second step, i.e the translation of user defined data types, the basic data types above are used. As for the abstract data type mechanism, we can define new data types from elementary ones. We use for this PROLOG clauses calling predicates that have already been defined (Fig. 5).

```
LAMBDA                          PROLOG

basic-type (A)                  basic-type (A).
derived-type (B)                derived-type (B).
constructed-type (C)            constructed-type (C).
type D = x1 : A,                D-type :- A(x1),
         x2 : B,                          B(x2),
         x3 : C.                          C(x3).
.........................       ...........................
```

Fig. 5. Type derivation in LAMBDA and PROLOG.

Ex2 The qualification of a secretary is defined by a scalar type :
qualification : (steno, dactylo).
this is interpreted in PROLOG by the two following clauses :

```
scalar(qualification).
qualification(X) :- type(qualification),
                    (X=steno ; X=dactylo).
```

This mechanism is recursive. It follows that complex object structures can be defined, e.g documents (Fig. 6). For instance, a document in which we can include sub-sections into sections has the following definition :

```
document(manual).
manual(M,P) :- type(manual), structure(manual,M),
               parameters(manual,P).
structure(manual,°Preface,Introduction,List-sect,Appendix§):-
               text(Preface),
               Introduction is °Title!Content§,
               string(Title,20),
               text(Content),
               list-sections(List-sect),
               text(Appendix).
list-sections(é§).
list-sections(°Title!Content§):-
               string(Title,20),
               °C!Cont§ is Content,
               text(C), liste-sections(Cont).
parameters(manual,°Version§):- integer(Version).
```

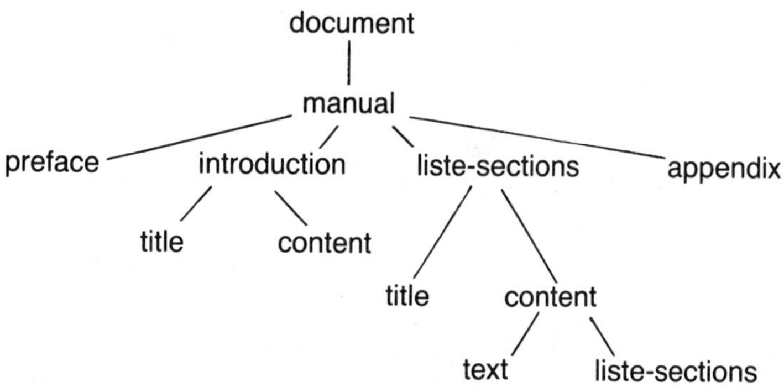

Fig. 6. Example of document structure.

2.4 Entity type.

The definition of entity types and association types involve a more complex procedure. Not only must the elementary data types be verified, but so must be the entity or association attributes. This control provides at the same time the access mechanism to the data. We use here the CONSTRUCTOR concept. It provides for the definition of the logical structure of entities, independently of the operations on the data.

The entity EMPLOYEE, which is defined in LAMBDA by :

```
Ex3 Define entity EMPLOYEE
        key number : integer end
            name   : string(1..30)
            salary : amount
            categ  : (engineer, secretary, programmer)
            address: type-address
            contrac: type-contractr.
```

is in PROLOG :

```
entity-type(EMPLOYEE).
constructor(EMPLOYEE,°NUM,NAME,SAL,CAT,ADR,CONT§):-
        type(EMPLOYEE),
        key(EMPLOYEE,NUM),
        integer(NUM),
        string(NAME),
        amount(SAL),
        categ(CAT),
        type-address(ADR),
        type-contract(CONT).
```

where amount, categ, type-address and type-contract are user defined types.

2.5 Entity abstraction.

LAMBDA provides for two abstraction mechanisms on entity classes, namely : generalization and aggregation. The first one is implemented by three type operators which are : the union, intersection and specialization of classes.

Semantic controls as those defined in the examples given so far are not powerful enough. Each entity involved in a specialization will have to be checked for its logical structure as well as its attribute types. We use for this an explicit CONSTRUCTOR clause.

Ex4 The entity SECRETARY defined on the entity EMPLOYEE as a specialization in the LAMBDA statement :

```
Define EMPLOYEE SECRETARY where category = "secretary"
       bilingual : (yes,no)
       qualific  : (steno,dactylo).
```

has a PROLOG constructor defined by :

```
specialization(secretary,employee).

constructor(secretary(NUM,NAME,SAL,CAT,ADR,CONT,BILINGUAL,QUAL)):-
       specialization(secretary,_),
       arg(2,specialization(secretary,_,_),E),
       constructor(E(NUM,NAME,SAL,CAT,ADR,CONT)),
       bool(BILINGUAL), qualific(QUAL),
       CAT="secretary".
```

where arg(n,f(x1,x2,...,xk),E) assigns the value xn to the variable E, where k>=n.

Similarly, the union and intersection of entity classes are defined by specific constructor clauses.

2.6 Relationships.

Just as we can generate constructors for entity types in LAMBDA, we can generate them for the relationships between entities.

Ex6 The OFFICE-LOCATION relationship between the EMPLOYEE entity and the LOCATION entity, which is defined by :

```
Define OFFICE-LOCATION between
       EMPLOYEE : staff (1,*)
       LOCATION : site  (1,*)
       since    : date
```

is controlled in PROLOG by the following clauses :

```
relationship-type(office-location).
relationship(office-location,employee,location)
role(office-location,staff,employee).
role(office-location,site,location).

constructor(office-location(EMPLOYEE,LOCATION,DATE):-
      'relationship-type(office-location).
       entity-type(employee),
       key(employee,EMPLOYEE),
       entity-type(location),
       key(location,LOCATION),
       date(DATE).
```

III. META-DATA AND CONSTRAINT MANAGEMENT.

In Section II, we have shown how object models and relationship models can be defined in PROLOG. This is used to define a META-MODEL that includes the basic concepts in the data model and the rules for defining, enforcing and modifying schemas and consistency rules for particular applications.

In this section, we deal with the practical aspects of this proposal, that is : objects and relationships instantiation and management. In the following (§ 3.1 to 3.3), we use the term "object" for "object instance".

We consider two specific points, which concern :

- the user interface for data and semantics manipulation (§ 3.1 and 3.2),
- the management of knowledge bases developed in PROLOG, for application programs that process generalized data stored in TIGRE (§ 3.3). This is illustrated by a CAD application for VLSI circuits /ADI84, NGU84/.

One knows that PROLOG provides for the DEFINITION of general properties of data which are at the same time executable programs that can CONTROL these properties.

This capability permits us to implement a set of clauses that can altogether :

- specify the type and semantics of the data,
- implement procedures that will check whether these semantics are

fulfilled by application programs.

3.1 Data manipulation.

In order to simplify the user interface, and alleviate the systematic scan of the entire search-space by the inference mechanisms of PROLOG, a few primitives are provided to allow for the data and the semantics manipulation, i.e :

- object instantiation,
- static properties control,
- processing procedures description,
- dynamic behavior control.

The primitives concerning the objects are :

- create an object in the database (primitive object),
- derive an object from an existing one (dependent object),
- copy an object (making a dependent object independent),
- replace an object (making a (in-)dependent object dependent),
- modify an object (update the value of one or more attributes),
- delete an object.

Recall that in PROLOG, L=..°X§ takes the head H of the list X and gives the variable L the value H(tail-of-X).

The creation in the user database of a data object X is controlled and made effective by calling the predicate create(X) defined by :

```
Ex7 create(X) :- L=..°X§ , constructor(L), asserta(L).

                           type checking   creation
```

The static properties are controlled by the constructor clauses. The processing procedures must be written by the designers when the system is being implemented. They are application dependent. So far, the dynamic behavior definitions are not generated automatically. They must therefore be explicitly put down by the designers. This is explained in the following paragraph (§ 3.2).

3.2 Semantics management.

We have defined some basic mechanisms to implement in PROLOG a META-MODEL which includes :

- basic operators on data types,
- constructors, which are clauses specifying semantic constraints

on the logical structure of the data.

It is clear that we can also specify with this approach specific application constraints, e.g privacy of data, object version management for CAD, etc. (Fig. 7).

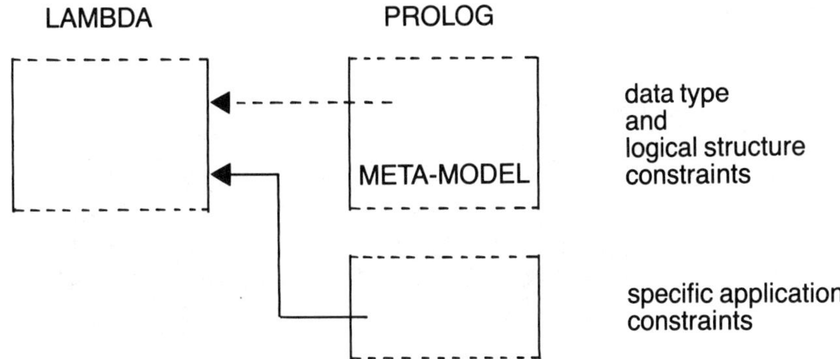

Fig. 7. Data type and specific application constraints.

Once data constructors have been generated, it is possible to define very easily a semantic control capability which is application tunable. We can therefore control each particular semantics of specific data management applications.

In our approach, we assume that dynamic behavior constraints can be ENTIRELY modelled and maintained through relationships among the database objects. We provide for this purpose some primitives for the instantiation and manipulation of two specific types of relationships, namely : weak and strong relationships.

A WEAK relationship between two objects can be created explicitly by the user. It can also be created by the system, when an object is instantiated by invocation of the COPY primitive (§ 3.1). This enforces the sibling relationship between the original object and its copy. It permits the control of the logical structure and of the static properties of both objects when the constructor clauses are invoked by application programs. Further modifications of one of these objects do not imply modification of the other.

A STRONG relationship can be created by the user. It can also be created by the system when :

- deriving an object from an existing one,
- replacing an object by another.

This implies modification of the descendants of the parent objects. Further, modifications on strongly related objects are visible to the each other. We plan to explore in the near future protocols to control the usage of relationships by concurrent users of TIGRE.

In this approach , which we shall call horizontal, the application programs developed on TIGRE use the inference mechanisms of PROLOG to check logical data structures and semantics constraints. It is possible to extend it to access from TIGRE knowledge bases developed in PROLOG.

In such a case, which we shall call a vertical approach, deductions and other sophisticated processing, needed for instance for AI or CAD applications, are off-loaded by the system to PROLOG. This is explained in the following section (§ 3.3).

3.3 Application to CAD/VLSI.

Since CAD is basically a trial and error process, the non determinism and backtracking features of PROLOG are well suited to implement it. Further, in most CAD applications, designers must manipulate several representations of the same objects. Consistency among these representations must be enforced. Again, the formalism of PROLOG, which allows the definition of the data, of the semantics and the processing procedures of user applications, with the same concepts and syntax, provides a very convenient way for the consistency control.

We are involved in the development of a CAD application for VLSI circuits, in which the knowledge associated to the logic, electric and physical representations of a circuit is stored as PROLOG clauses (Fig. 10) /ADI84, NGU84/. Simplification rules of the electric layout are also stored as a set of clauses. As stated earlier, they include STATIC properties of electric components, e.g the connections of transistors must obey precise rules. They also include DYNAMIC behavior constraints, such as the consistency rules between the different circuit representations during the generation of a component. For instance, connecting a transistor in parallel to others imply some simplifications under particular connection configurations.

Circuit specifications
↓
logic representation
↓
electric representation
↓
Physical representation
↓
Layout specifications

Fig. 10 Circuit design steps.

Most of all, besides these knowledge management facilities, the inference mechanisms guarantee that in such an application, all possible versions of a circuit corresponding to the designers requirements, can be generated.

As contrasted to relational DBMS, which must be extended with new features to handle this kind of problem, inference machines should be for our purpose LIMITED in some way, so as to leave to the designer the decision power for the circuit caracteristics. Indeed, he probably does not care about ALL solutions to his problem, but only about a few ones. For this, interacting query-answer clauses are introduced wherever needed, so that he can specify partial solutions or requirements.

Apart from performance considerations /BER83/, he is guaranteed to obtain ALL potential versions of an object INSIDE a particular representation, if he wishes. All versions of the objects at the other levels (e.g electric and physical), corresponding to a particular instance of an object at a given level (e.g logic), can also be designed.

IV. CONCLUSION.

We have presented the enhancement of a generalized data management system, with the inference mechanisms of logic programming. This is used to define a meta-model that includes the semantics of schema and consistency rule definition, control and modification.

A first implementation of our proposal has been written on DEC LSI-11 machines, using the Edinburgh version of PROLOG.

A prototype of the system TIGRE, is being implemented at IMAG in cooperation with the BULL Corporate Research Center in Grenoble. For this purpose, we are now using an extended version of PROLOG, running on the MULTICS operating system /DON83/. It allows communication, via procedural calls, with external Pascal programs. It also provides for the management of an effective database of PROLOG clauses.

We emphasize in this paper on the representation of the SEMANTICS of sophisticated applications, such as office automation and CAD for VLSI circuits, to provide the users with :

- a generalized data model,
- powerful data manipulation and semantics representation and control facilities.

We have shown that extended entity-relationship-like concepts can be easily modelled and manipulated in PROLOG. This offers to the users of TIGRE all the inference mechanisms of logic programming. It is thus possible to off-load the semantics definition and control to a PROLOG system, in a cooperative approach, whilst large and /or complex objects are handled by TIGRE.

It leads to :

- the extension of the functionnalities of TIGRE,

- the cooperation of generalized database systems with knowledge bases developed in PROLOG,
- the integration of DBMS management facilities, specially those concerning the manipulation of large and/or complex objects, with artificial intelligence techniques, such as those using knowledge and semantics representation through logic programming.

Acknowledgments.

The authors are greatly indebted to Ms. Ofelia CERVANTES, Judith OLIVARES and Pascale WINNINGER, for experimenting many of the ideas presented above during the last few months, in partial fulfillment of their respective Doctorate Degrees.

They also thank MM. Jacques LECOURVOISIER and Christian JULLIEN from CAD Research Dept at CNET (French National Research Center for Telecommunications), for numerous discussions that lead to refine many ideas presented here.

REFERENCES.

/ADI83/ ADIBA M. et al.
Présentation générale du projet TIGRE.
Research Report TIGRE n° 1. Lab. IMAG. January 1983.

/ADI84/ ADIBA M., NGUYEN G.T
Information Processing for CAD/VLSI on a generalized data management system.
Proc. 10th International Conference on Very Large Databases. Singapore. August 1984.

/ADI84b/ ADIBA M., NGUYEN G.T
Logic programming for a generalized data management system.
Research Report TIGRE n° 12. Lab. IMAG. January 1984.

/BER83/ BERGER-SABBATEL, J.C IANESELLI, NGUYEN G.T
A Prolog database machine.
Third international workshop on database machines.
Munich (FRG). September 1983.

/CHE76/ CHEN P.P
The entity Relationship Model. Toward a unified view of data.

ACM TODS. Vol. 1, n° 1. 1976.

/CLO81/ CLOCKSIN, W.S, MELLISH C.S
Programming in Prolog.
Springer-Verlag. 1981.

/CNE83/ CNET-Grenoble.
Présentation générale de CASSIOPEE.
French National Research Center for Telecommunications.
CNET Grenoble. October 1983.

/COL83/ COLMERAUER A.
Prolog en dix figures.
CNET working conf. on logic programming.
Lannion (France). March 1983.

/DON83/ DONZ P.
FOLL : une extension au langage Prolog.
CRISS. Université des Sciences Sociales.
Grenoble. November 1983.

/GAL83/ GALLAIRE H.
Prolog et bases de données.
Ibid. /COL83/.

/LOP83/ LOPEZ M., PALAZZO J., VELEZ F.
The TIGRE data model.
Research Report TIGRE n° 2. Lab. IMAG. November 1983.

/NGU82/ NGUYEN G.T, L. FERRAT, H. GALY
A high level interface for a local network database system.
Proc. INFOCOM conf. Las Vegas (USA). March 1982.

/NGU84/ NGUYEN G.T, ADIBA M.
Knowledge engineering for CAD/VLSI on a generalized data management system.
Proc. IFIP Working Conference on Knowledge Engineering in Computer Aided Design.
Budapest (Hungary). September 1984.

/OLI83/ OLIVARES J.
Coopération entre une machine Prolog et une base de données généralisées.
DEA Report. Lab. IMAG. September 1983.

/PAR83/ PARSAYE K.
Database management, knowledge base management and expert system development in Prolog.
ACM-IEEE database week. San-Jose (USA). May 1983.

/PER83/ PEREIRA C.N
Can drawing be liberated from the Von Neumann style ?
Ibid. /PAR83/.

/VAS83/ VASSILIOU Y. et al.
How does an expert system get its data ?
Proc. 9th Very Large Data Base Conf.
Florence (Italy). October 1983.

/VEL82/ VELEZ F.
LAMBDA : un langage de définition et de manipulation de données généralisées.
ADI working conf. on databases. Toulouse (France).
November 1982.

/WAL83/ WALKER A.
Databases, expert systems and Prolog.
IBM Research Lab. RJ 3870. San-Jose (USA). April 1983.

/ZAU83/ ZAUMEN W.T
Computer assisted circuit evaluation in Prolog for VLSI.
Ibid. /PAR83/.

DISTRIBUTED DATABASE CONSIDERATIONS IN AN EXPERT SYSTEM FOR RADAR ANALYSIS

Andrew S. Cromarty, Thomas L. Adams, Gerald A. Wilson, James F. Cunningham, Carl J. Tollander, and Milton R. Grinberg*

Advanced Decision Systems, 201 San Antonio Circle, Suite 286, Mountain View, California 94040, USA

* Heuristic Programming Project, Department of Computer Science, Stanford University, Stanford, California 94305

ABSTRACT

A knowledge-based research prototype has been created for analyzing existing radar systems. The expert system, called ASTA, interactively accepts values for system attributes, subsystem attributes, or signal parameters, and then incrementally infers the value of as many other attributes as it can. The ASTA knowledge base represents the first known effort to structure information about radar design as a function of observable operating characteristics.

We present the architecture of ASTA as a working example of an expert system that faces and solves several practical problems in the marriage of an expert system to distributed databases. ASTA ensures database concurrency across differently structured databases, and yet meets the pragmatic constraints of integrity and timeliness of the data required by the expert system. This is achieved in part by the use of a distributed message-passing architecture with explicit time-stamping of messages. We also discuss ASTA's current interface to external DBMS's and propose a new technique which would enable the inference engine and the DBMS to cooperate more closely in the selection of data when the query is imprecise.

INTRODUCTION

The challenge of developing consultation systems which provide knowledge-based support for people performing complex tasks is both formidable and important. Real problems require an integrated use of problem-specific knowledge, current and background data, and effective tools for handling the cooperation between the human user and the computer system. In this paper we describe the knowledge representation and data base issues, and their solutions, which have been addressed in an ongoing project. The objective of this project is to develop a knowledge-based consultation system, called the Assistant for Science and Technology Analysis (ASTA), which assists individuals attempting to predict the architecture and performance characteristics of modern electronic systems given only a description of the observed operating behavior of the system.

Three aspects of this project are discussed in this paper. First, we describe the approach employed in representing the knowledge and data required for the inference engine. The data, as well as some of the knowledge, must be maintained in a form appropriate for interaction with the human user through our MPS [1] interface. At the same time, these data must be available in a form appropriate for the inference engine to employ for hypothesis generation. Second, because the same data must be maintained in each of the two major processes (the interface and the inference engine) of the system, there must be a means to maintain the consistency of the two representations. Third, the inference process also requires access to supporting data maintained by one or more DBMS's external to ASTA. Each of these aspects is discussed below.

KNOWLEDGE-BASED RADAR SYSTEM ANALYSIS: A BRIEF OVERVIEW

ASTA is tailored to radar systems by virtue of its database of symbolic facts and heuristics that define how new information should be inferred from existing evidence and previously reached conclusions. Because of the heuristic nature of much of the information that such a database contains, it is properly called a *knowledge base.* The ASTA knowledge base represents the first known effort to structure information about radar design as a function of observable operating characteristics, rather than from the point of view of the design process. The knowledge comes from expert radar designers and analysts and from radar design handbooks. This includes general knowledge about radar systems, such as the physics of radar signals and the relationship between different components of radar systems. ASTA also has knowledge about itself: it contains explicit rules identifying (a) the ways it can use logic to solve problems, (b) the problems that are worth solving, and (c) the order in which interesting problems can most effectively be solved.

ASTA's knowledge may express either numeric or logical relationships. By separating declarative knowledge about radar physics and radar analysis problem-solving techniques from the generic inference-related control aspects of the computer program (its *inference engine*) that operates on that knowledge, ASTA facilitates inspection of its knowledge base and its line of reasoning in order to explain why new values were inferred. Further, its body of radar facts and analysis techniques can be modified by non-programmers, and it can operate robustly in the face of the partial or errorful data that typify analysis tasks.

Radar is an echo-location system wherein pulses sent out at a given frequency (the Pulse Repetition Frequency) are listened for as they return after reflection off environmental objects. The presence of an object is indicated by a strong return, and its velocity and range can be determined by the length of time from transmission until the echo is heard and by the way the object alters characteristics of the transmitted radar signal. A pictorial representation of a typical radar waveform and scanning sequence, which constitutes the raw data described in the formatted reports that ASTA accepts as

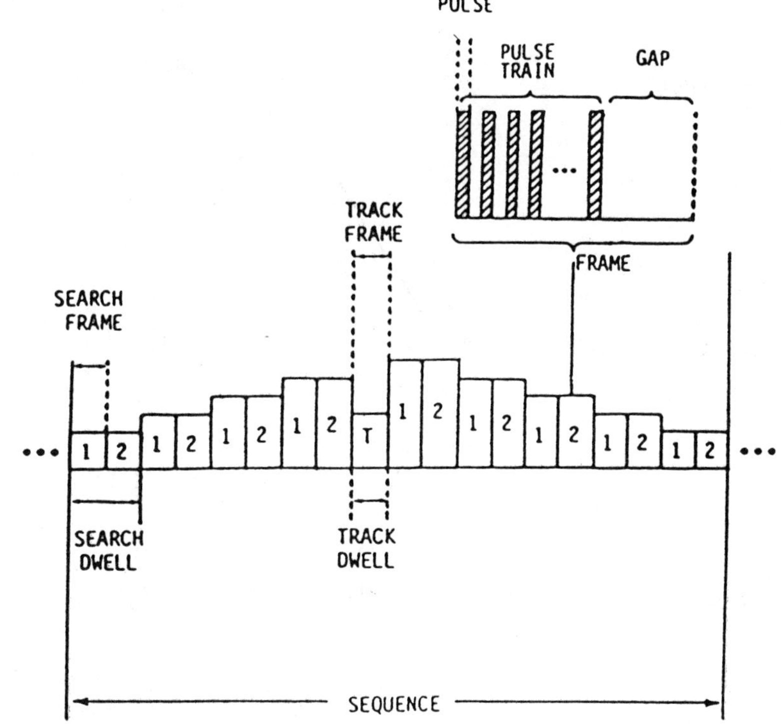

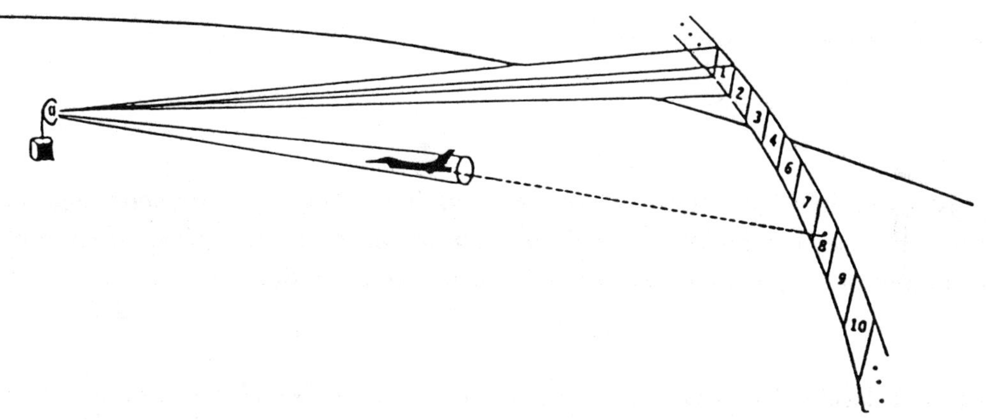

Figure 1: A Pictorial Representation of Waveform and Scan Pattern

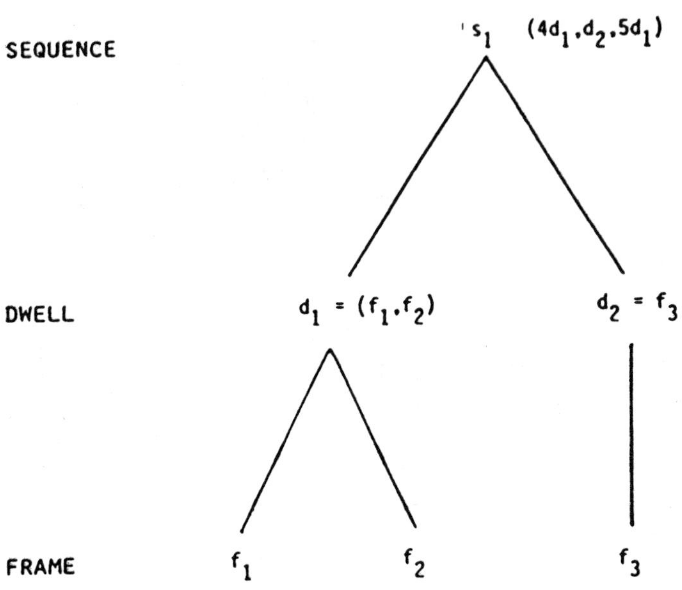

Figure 2: ASTA's Internal Representation of Waveform and Scan Pattern

input, is given in Figure 1. (A tree diagram indicating the corresponding internal structures we use to represent such data is shown in Figure 2.) ASTA represents the waveform and operational characteristics according to the following taxonomy:

- *Frame level information*: A description of the basic waveform parameters of each of the pulse trains used in the system.

- *Dwell level information*: A description of how the individual pulse trains are used together to achieve the intended radar function. In the example, two frames are used sequentially to search for as yet unseen objects and a single frame is used to track an object already observed. During a dwell, the radar antenna is focused on (dwells on) one location in the sky and is attempting either to search that location for undetected objects or to track an already-observed object believed to be at that approximate location.

- *Sequence level information*: A description of the method by which the operational modes of the radar are multiplexed, i.e. the way that search and track dwells are interleaved to allow the radar system to both keep track of objects it does know about and find new ones it has not yet detected. In the example, only one object is being tracked, and the radar search mode is interrupted periodically every tenth spatial dwell to accomplish tracking. (This is an important problem for airports where a single air traffic control radar must become aware of new planes that are coming in for landing while known planes are being observed, for example, when multiple planes may be attempting to land at once.)

An example of the rule knowledge contained in ASTA's knowledge base is given in Figure 3, which portrays a fragment of the rule graph structure that ASTA employs to infer the kind of radio tube used in the amplifier of the radar transmitter under study, given only a description of the characteristics of a signal observed to have been emitted by the radar. Figure 4 provides the corresponding modified predicate calculus form that MRS uses to represent the knowledge depicted in Figure 3, with their English equivalents. The lower-level frame parameter processing rules used to establish the maximum instantaneous bandwidth and the nominal frequency are not shown for the sake of brevity. Rule 1, which defines the fractional instantaneous bandwidth, is enabled whenever the instantaneous bandwidth and the nominal frequency have been previously calculated and stored in the collection of facts describing the current state of knowledge of the system. Thus the rule contains not only the expression used for calculating the result, but also the more general information that the expression can only be solved for the independent variable, if the two dependent variables are known. Rule 2 states that, if the number of elements in the set of signal frames satisfying the high duty cycle and high PRF condition is equal to the total number of signal frames (thereby establishing that every signal frame satisfies the condition), then the radar system employs pulsed Doppler modulation. This example shows that (1) the conditions for triggering a symbolic conclusion can depend on an arithmetically calculated precondition and (2) the set of objects over which the constraint is satisfied can be specified in the rule. Rule 3 is of the purely symbolic type commonly employed in expert systems. Rule 4 illustrates how the satisfaction of a symbolic constraint and an arithmetic constraint can be used as preconditions for a symbolic conclusion.

This example illustrates how ASTA can employ a wide variety of mixtures of symbolic and arithmetic expressions to obtain its conclusions, and also how two parallel reasoning paths (pulse characteristics to infer bandwidth and PRF to infer pulsed Doppler) can be combined to produce the desired conclusion (klystron tube type). Readers interested in the radar analysis problem will find more detailed explanations and examples in [2].

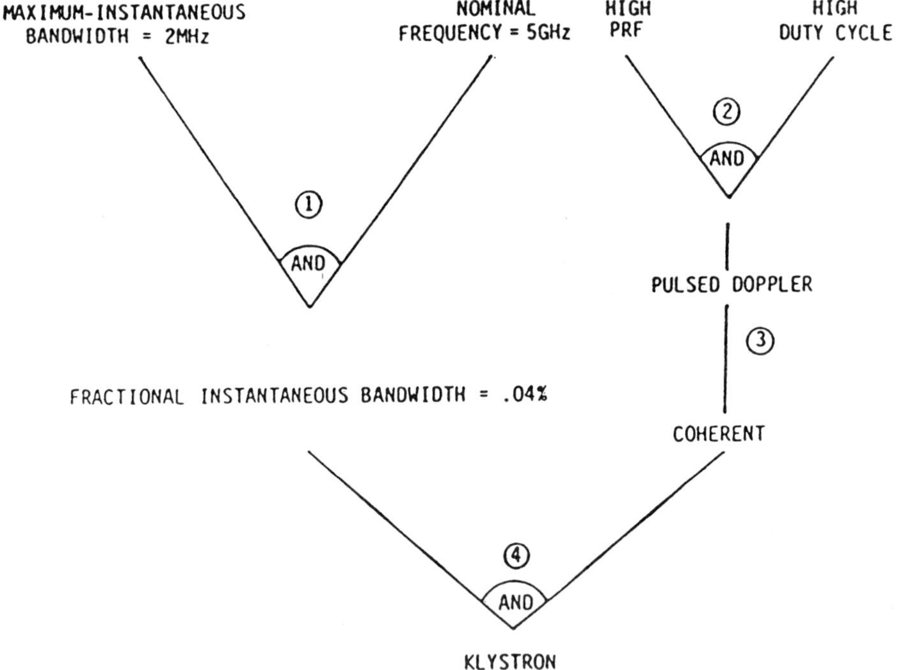

Figure 3: Rule Graph Fragment for Transmitter Output Tube Type Determination

(1)
```
(if (and (inst-bandwidth radar-xmtr $x)
         (nominal-frequency radar-xmtr $y)
         (is (// (// $x $y) 1000.0) $z))
   (frac-inst-bandwidth radar-xmtr $z))
```

"The fractional instantaneous bandwidth is the instantaneous bandwidth divided by the nominal frequency of the transmitter."

(2)
```
(if (and (setof $n (and   (radar-signal-frame $n)
                          (PRF $n $a)
                          (> $a 8)
                          (duty-cycle $n $b)
                          (> $b 3))
                $q)
         (setof $m (radar-signal-frame $m) $p)
         (length $p $c)
         (length $q $d)
         (= $c $d))
   (modulation-type radar-system p-dop))
```

"If every frame observed has a PRF greater than 8 KHz and a duty cycle greater than 3%, then the radar system employs pulsed-Doppler modulation."

(3)
```
(if (modulation-type radar-system p-dop)
   (coherent radar-xmtr))
```

"Pulsed-Doppler systems normally employ coherent modulation."

(4)
```
(if (and (frac-inst-bandwidth radar-xmtr $x)
         (< $x .05)
         (coherent radar-xmtr))
   (tube-type radar-xmtr klystr ))
```

"The klystron is the preferred transmitter tube type for a narrowband, coherent system."

Figure 4: Inference Rules for Transmitter Output Tube Type Determination

AN OVERVIEW OF THE ASTA IMPLEMENTATION

The ASTA implementation comprises three parts: the interactive, menu-driven, forms-oriented user interface based upon the Multipurpose Presentation System (MPS) [1]; the Metalevel Representation System (MRS) [3] for constructing rule-based systems; and the COP control and communications system [4] to perform message routing and system task planning functions. The underlying architecture for ASTA is thus a functionally partitioned, multiple-process message passing design, depicted in Figure 5. The separation of the expert system *per se* from its user interface was motivated by several goals:

- The desire for a *clean modular design* with effective information hiding. The conviction that a module should "do only one thing and do it well" argues for making accessible to a given module exactly and only those data it needs to perform its job, without providing access to ancillary data and hence introducing a risk of inadvertent data collisions or unintended data dependencies.

- The need for a *reliable incremental development environment* with minimal subpart interaction. An important aspect of the ASTA specification was the requirement that the knowledge base be amenable to continued development well after the user interface had stabilized; this can be achieved by divorcing the rule set from the data base that supports user interface activity and defining a narrow bandwidth communication mechanism between the two.

- The desire to employ *locally optimal representations for each subtask* of the problem that ASTA is trying to solve. That is, separation of the component modules allows different data representation techniques to be employed rather than forcing reliance upon a single representation that optimally supports only one (or neither) of the two tasks, reasoning and user interaction, that ASTA must perform.

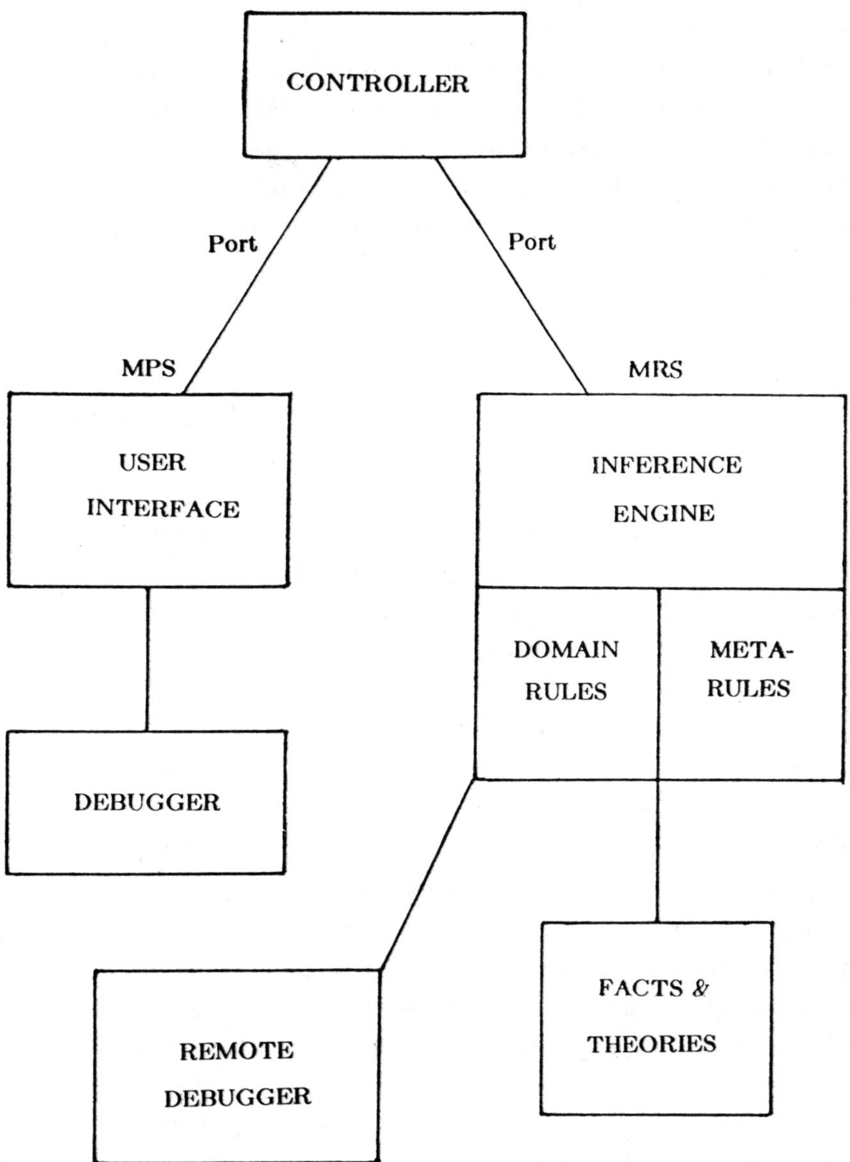

Figure 5: The ASTA Multiple-process Message Passing Architecture

THE EXPERT KNOWLEDGE DATABASE

The knowledge base of facts, rules, and metarules is contained entirely within a process that is assigned the responsibility of pursuing the inferences required to support the analysis. MRS provides the general purpose inference engine and data base capability used within ASTA to store and derive radar system parameters. It supports a rule-based approach that employs a knowledge base of facts and rules along with a flexible control structure used to guide the inference strategy. MRS is a domain-independent reasoning and representation system in which knowledge about any field may be represented. In the ASTA system, MRS stores and maintains all of the domain specific knowledge of radar systems including the initial default values for physical constants, the current known radar parameters that have been entered by the analyst, the radar parameters that have been derived from one or more known parameters, the rules used to relate the radar parameters to each other, and the meta-level knowledge used to control the use of the rules and data. The information that the system uses may be numeric or symbolic in nature. MRS has the ability to make mathematical calculations or to draw inferences based on symbolic information to derive new symbolic information. Furthermore, symbolic information can be used to select the appropriate form of a calculation or to provide constraints on the range of values in the terms of an equation. Because the analysis domain is characterized by information that is informal, imprecise and incomplete, we stores all of this knowledge declaratively, rather than procedurally. By storing the inferencing procedures declaratively, the system has the ability to reason with them, manipulate them, and use them only when enough information exists to derive new data from the existing data. The inference process is therefore very flexible and can use the information it has available to make all the conclusions it can, but will not be hindered or rendered useless when certain radar parameters are unknown.

The **stash** operation is used to store *assertions* (facts and rules describing the current problem domain) in the database. These assertions are stored as n-tuples in MRS. Intermediate inferences need not always be stored in the database, so the meta-level control is used to define when and where assertions are stashed. For the ASTA application, we have chosen to represent the radar system parameters in 3-tuples consisting of a property, object, and value, where the object can be thought of as an index into a table of values for all objects with the specificied property. For example, the 3-tuple (prf f1 15) states that the property "prf" has the value "15" for the radar frame indexed by "f1". Assertions are retrieved from the database by the "truep" ("truth" predicate) operation. It queries the database for evidence concerning the validity of a statement given the current context. The system will determine if this statement is true by searching the database for it; if the fact is not present, MRS will then try to infer the validity of the statement from the database using the known facts along with the rules of inference.

The rules in MRS are of the common *if-then* production rule form, with the *if* clause consisting of one or more antecedents (preconditions) that, when true, imply that the consequent statement associated with the *then* clause is true. Any logical proposition can be encoded as a set of rules in this form by first putting it into conjunctive normal form and converting each disjunct into an appropriate rule. MRS then allows these rules to be used in two ways: either in a data-driven, forward chaining direction, from antecedents to consequents, or in a goal-directed, backward chaining direction, from consequents to antecedents. In the data-driven direction, the system will try to match the information it has against the antecedents of the rules, and when successful, will add the consequent of the matched rules to the database. Conversely, when performing goal-directed reasoning, the system will hypothesize that a particular goal is true and try to find rules that contain the desired goal in its consequent. If such rules are found, the system will attempt to match the antecedents of these rules against the database, and if at least one rule is successful, will then add the desired consequent to the database. If no such rule succeeds, the system may try to find further rules with the unsuccessfully matched antecedents in the consequent of another rule and attempt to determine the truth of these using the same procedure. For example, ASTA has the following rule in its database:

```
(if (and (pulse-modulation $f psk)
         (chip-duration $f $p))
    (compressed-pulse-duration $f $p))
```

The antecedent assertions are the clauses with the properties "pulse-modulation" and "chip-duration", while the consequent clause has the property "compressed-pulse-duration". (Variables are distiguished by a "$" preceeding the name, and can match against any instantiated term in another clause.) In this example, the first antecedent has the variable "$f" which will match the first index it finds with the property "pulse-modulation" that has the value of "psk". When using this rule in the forward chaining direction, the system will try to match these antecedents, which must both be true since they are joined by the "and" operator, against the database. If successful, it will assert the consequent with the property "compressed-pulse-duration" using the same instantiations for the variables that it used for the antecedents. As an example of applying the previous rule in the backward chaining direction, suppose it is desired to determine the compressed-pulse-duration of a particular frame "f1" as the instantiation for "$f". The compressed-pulse-duration can be thought of as a goal that the system will try to prove using the database of current assertions along with the applicable rules. MRS does this by instantiating the antecedents of this rule; if these can be matched against the database, MRS will use the same instantiation in the consequent clause to assert the fact. If one or more of the antecedents does not occur in the database, the system may post them as new goals and try to prove them true using the same backward chaining mechanism.

The method of search and chaining direction is selected by the ASTA design team on a case-by-case basis and implemented through the use of the meta-level rules (with default search techniques employed where appropriate). Meta-level control operations provide control over the use of the rules as well as a means of manipulation of the environment of assertions that are currently valid. The meta-level consists of both assertions and rules of the same form as the base level rules and assertions, stored in the same database. The meta-level assertions dictate how the system uses rules. For example, they can proscribe the use of backward chaining or forward chaining mechanisms, control the stashing of results in the database, or specify whether it is appropriate to seek out more than one instantiation of a particular goal.

Meta-level assertions can be used to affect the current context of applicable databases that are valid. MRS allows multiple databases, called "theories", to be used for stashing both rules and assertions. The meta-level defines which theories are currently "active" (searchable) and how to change the state of a theory between active and inactive. The meta-level rules may contain context dependent conditions that determine when the meta-level assertions are applied. These rules have the same form as the base level rules; however, the base level rules embody knowledge about the particular domain, whereas the meta-rules adapt the use of those rules to the current situation. This mechanism allows the system to understand its effect in the current context and then adapt to the constantly changing situations that it encounters.

These database mechanisms allows ASTA to work with multiple, mutually exclusive hypothesis simultaneously. Competing hypothesis data are manipulated in different databases, and storage and retrieval are managed using meta-level rules. Specifically, the ASTA system will activate a theory to store the hypothesized values and values derived from inferences made using these hypothesis. The theory may also contain specific rules that are only activated with the theory and, therefore, only with the one set of data associated with the particular hypothesis. If the hypothesis is found to be valid, the assertions made in its local theory may be moved to a more global theory, or this theory may simply be moved into a new context within the global framework. If the hypothesis is found to be invalid, the assertions may be discarded or moved to an inactive state which will not affect the other theories.

The ASTA knowledge base also contains a network of *justifications*, used to generate explanations. Every assertion in the system has an associated explanation of how it was derived, either from the user as an input parameter, from a system constant, or a value derived from a rule. For each assertion that is derived from a rule, the explanation database must save the rule that was used to derive the fact, the current meta-level control that was in effect when the rule was fired, and a binding list of the instantiations of the variables in the rule. From this information, the system can trace the derivation of a value, and the rules that were applied to the input parameters to infer the value that is in question.

THE USER INTERFACE DATABASE

The MPS user interface system maintains a database, physically but not logically independent of the MRS knowledge base, that is focused on the specific problem of providing efficient access to the data that specify the state of the interaction with the user.

The MPS user interface is object oriented. Text input boxes, captions, and menu selections are stored in the MPS data base as dynamic record structures. These objects are the components of a special kind of object called a ***presentation surface***, which handles their display and manipulation by the inference engine and the user. MPS is composed of a number of presentation surfaces along with a toolkit of primitives for their creation, modification, and manipulation.

At the present time, the allowable object types are:

- **caption**: simple text strings placed the screen at a specified location.
- **selection**: like captions, but the user may position the cursor on the text string and select it as a menu option.
- **input**: a reverse video box placed on the screen at a specified location, into which the user may type text strings.

A presentation surface, and the form or menu that it displays, are created by the function **NewForm**, which sequentially evaluates the object specifications for captions, selections and inputs found in a template file. These specifications take the form of the relations:

(**caption** *coordinates unique-id initialization-string-value*)

(**selection** *coordinates unique-id initialization-string-value*)

(**input** *coordinates unique-id field-size field-type*)

The *field-type* argument permits some simple type checking for integer, floating point and string values. The **caption**, **selection**, and **input** abstract relations are grouped together to form presentation surfaces using the relation

presentation-surface-id = (*bptr clist slist ilist*)

where *bptr* is a pointer to the bitmap of the display form, *clist* is a list of unique caption identifiers, *slist* is a list of unique selection identifiers, and *ilist* is a list of unique input identifiers. Each such identifier is in turn a relation:

identifier = (*row column value* [*field-size*] [*field-type*])

We thus achieve ***object orientation*** in part through the mechanism of unique naming, making each data object a uniquely identifiable object with an existence of its own, i.e. not dependent on its relationship to other data objects for its identity. Some of the advantages of this approach over the use of primary keys as a data object unique identifier are discussed by Codd [5], where he refers to them as ***surrogates*** corresponding to an implicit ***E-attribute*** (entity-designation attribute) of the data object (tuple) of interest.

Each radar signal component structure (e.g. frames, dwells, sequences) and each radar system component structure (e.g. antenna, transmitter, receiver) is mapped by **NewForm** onto a presentation surface at initialization time. There is thus a one-to-one correspondence between the "f1" radar signal frame data object of the inference process and the form displayed by the presentation surface called "f1". The properties of the components are mapped onto an MPS "input" record.

The inference process may manipulate MPS structures through a variety of primitives, although most operations of interest can be achieved using the primitive relations **Show**, **SSet** and **SGet**, which we have added as a common extension to both the MRS and MPS systems.

- (**Show** *presentation-surface*): Transfer control to a given presentation surface, refresh the form involved, handle cursor movement and user input.
- (**SSet** *presentation-surface object-type object-unique-id Slot-name value*): Set a slot in a record by tracing the path given by the argument list.
- (**SGet** *presentation-surface object-type object-unique-id Slot-name*): Get a slot value, again by tracing the given path.

If the user enters several values on a form, these values are stored directly in the MPS database and the values are sent to the inference process as a list of ordered triples of the form "(input-slot form value)". Each such triple can be stashed without modification into the knowledge base, since the MPS representation (form slot value) directly corresponds to the MRS representation of (property component value). For example, if the inference engine stashes a value as a result of some inference, such as

(**stash** '(prf f1 12.5))

then a procedural attachment is activated, which stashes the value into the knowledge base and initiates the following events:

- Determines whether "(prf f1 12.5)" is isomorphic to one of several legal patterns (in this case "(slot form value)") and, if so, sets slot to prf, form to f1, and value to 12.5.

- Invokes the remote MPS call "(SSet 'f1 'input '(prf f1) 'value 12.5)", which tells the presentation surface "f1" to set its "prf" slot to "12.5". MPS alters the display accordingly.

The MPS primitives always perform a last evaluation on their arguments before sending themselves as a message to the inference process. This allows the MRS assertions to be of arbitrary complexity so long as their structure is isomorphic at the top level to one of the accepted patterns.

MAINTAINING CONSISTENCY: THE COP COMMUNICATION AND CONTROL SYSTEM

The inference and user interface processes contain data that are largely distinct semantically: rules are under the purview of the inference process, while the details of the presentation surface are the domain of the user interface alone. The two processes do, however, experience overlap in several semantic domains, most notably for (a) data entered by the user and (b) inference results that are to be presented to the user. Because multiple copies of these data exist in the two name spaces and because of their time-varying nature, the potential exists for inconsistency between the two databases. For example, the inference process could erroneously work on obsolete data if newly entered data held in the user interface database are not yet installed in the inference process's knowledge base; similarly, incorrect results (or none at all) could be displayed to the user even after the inference process had determined the proper values, if the corresponding entries in the user interface database have not been updated.

We need not solve all the problems addressed by a distributed DBMS such as SDD-1 [6], since only one data source (the user or expert system) can be updating the database at any moment in time. ASTA is, however, faced with the problems of maintaining multiple copies of a single logical database that a distributed DBMS must solve. In order to ensure consistency and integrity of the common data across the two processes, ASTA employs a *time-stamping* data communication architecture with message routing between the two processes explicitly managed by a semi-intelligent controller. The time-stamping, message-passing architecture from which ASTA has been constructed is the COP system [4].

In its full generality, the COP communications and control system provides for resource management and planning functions as well as communications; within the ASTA implementation, however, we use it primarily to ensure timely and reliable interprocess communications. COP provides to each of the two client processes (user interface and inference) a message-passing view of the external computational environment. All communication between modules is effected by means of a single **send-message** primitive having the following structure:

(**send-message** *from to timestamp class* [*text*])

where *from* and *to* identify the sender and receiver, *class* is a member of the set of permissible remote operations which the sender may invoke (in the case of ASTA, the set {**SSet, SGet, Show**}), and *timestamp* is a structured message identifier that includes a timestamp timed according to the sender's clock and guaranteed to be unique across all clients in the system. Where messages take argments, *text* specifies those arguments, in keyword (attribute-value) form. (The *from* value is provided by the communications slave, described below, to minimize the potential for implementation errors on the part of the client module's designer and to prevent message forgery.)

Each client is transparently provided with a communications slave that performs two functions:

- It dispatches messages sent by the client using **send-message**.
- It responds to incoming messages, either directly or by dispatching them to the appropriate client function.

If an incoming message is a member of the client's set of permissible messages, message receipt is transformed into a call to the client's corresponding function. If the message is not a member of the client's operator set, the slave determines whether it is an otherwise known message class (such as a bookkeeping request from the controller which the slave itself can execute); if not, an error message is transmitted back to the controller by the slave.

As described above, our approach to ensuring consistency for inferred facts and hypotheses relies upon *procedural attachments* within the inference process. These procedural attachments are essentially explicit per-rule and per-relation specifications of the corresponding relation(s) in the companion database that depend upon the value of the attached rule or relation. For example, the inference engine is instructed to check for and execute procedural attachments whenever a new fact is inferred in order to ensure immediate update of the user interface database.

Depending upon the specifics of the rule or relation so attached, the procedural attachment may specify either a *remote procedure call* form of update, wherein the inference engine waits until the companion database has been updated before proceeding, or a pure ***message delivery update***, in which messages are queued for delivery to the companion process but the sender does not wait for delivery. (In the latter case a remote procedure call is guaranteed to wait until all pending update messages have been delivered and acknowledged.)

Emulation of remote procedure call is supported by allowing the sender to "block" itself until a return message is received; this blocking action is a primitive of the communications slave, which continues to listen to the input port and process incoming messages, either queueing them on an agenda of tasks to feed the client once it is resumed or executing them directly if they are communications-specific (such as a request for a message indicating the client's status). This restricted use of message passing permits two clients to synchronize their state: for example, the sender client may ask for a datum from the target client's database and then wait, blocking all other analysis- and display-related operations within its name space until a (time-stamped) return value is received.

CONVERSING WITH AN EXTERNAL DATABASE

A wide variety of data bases are already in use by radar system designers and analysts, and clearly ASTA will benefit if it can capitalize on the prior existence of massive collections of relevant domain data. Unfortunately, these data bases are mutually incompatible, are frequently poorly organized, and are supported on a variety of DBMS's. An important task in the design of ASTA has therefore been the development of a uniform method of providing the inference process with access to external database systems.

Our solution to this practical problem has been to isolate the knowledge about specific external database query languages and schemas in a single additional ***database access expert*** process that maps data requests from the inference engine to the appropriate database query. This prevents the inference process's knowledge base from becoming cluttered with arcane knowledge of the external DBMS, provides a potential degree of parallelism (in that inference can proceed while the database access expert formulates a database query), and modularizes the DBMS-specific knowledge so that no changes to the inference process's knowledge base are necessary (at least in principle) in order to support access to additional external databases or to change the query protocol as external databases evolve.

While this meets our immediate pragmatic goal of providing access to external DBMS's, several problems still present themselves during the construction of the database access expert. For example, a separate access capability (whether in a monolithic access expert or multiple indpendent such experts) must be provided for each external DBMS. Furthermore, the schema of the external DBMS must be duplicated in the database access expert, and thus changes in the external database schema still require a corresponding alteration of the database access expert. Finally, the database access expert must contain knowledge not only of the query language syntax, but of the computational semantics of query language constructs as well, in order to effectively map inference process requests into database queries. Whereas this semantic mapping is normally performed either by a human user of a conventional database or by a transaction designer, the database access expert cannot appeal to either source of interpretive expertise and thus must carry the additional burden of maintaining and applying that knowledge of query semantics itself.

On the basis of our experience with the expert system–external database interface, we observe that a more effective solution is at hand if data base systems provide an additional query capability not currently supported: that of ***query predicate*** satisfaction. That is, an ideal external database from the standpoint of the expert system would be one that accepts not merely a static query but a predicate that can be executed within the name space of the database.

Such a query predicate could contain, for example, a weighted vector of values or ranges which would be applied to candidate tuples in the database by the DBMS to produce a ***degree-of-match*** measure, where a database tuple is considered to itself be a vector in n-space. In the simplest case, attributes of a relation would be objects with considerable mathematical structure on them (such as values in $\mathbf{R}^n$ with the elements of the basis set being semantically compatible -- for example, a database that contained only latitude and longitude information), and the metric for degree of match is little more than a variance calculation. In more difficult cases where, for instance, the range of data values for an attribute is nominal-level (i.e. no ordering relation applies), the query predicate must contain more information in order to convey the ***goal*** of the "user" (in this case, the inference engine) in posing the query. For instance, if the attribute in question is a spectral color, the degree to which "yellow" is a satisfactory match for a query that requested tuples that are "like orange" is a function of the intent of the inference engine in using that color information, which intent must be reflected in the query predicate's handling of the color attribute. This predicate would then allow the database to perform a better-informed search (i.e. provide better recall performance) by virtue of semantically-derived information provided as a part of the query by the agent (the inference engine) formulating that query.

An obvious extension of this approach, and one especially useful in expert system applications, would be a DBMS that provides not only the tuples that match above some threshold or according to semantic constraints embodied in the query predicate, but also the degree-of-match measure as defined by the query function for each tuple satisfying the query predicate.

A database system that supported query predicates would offer a potential performance improvement in several respects: raw query-satisfaction speed, decreased inter-process traffic, and decreased requirements for post-processing of query results by the inference engine, all by virtue of the knowledge contained in the query that focuses the database search process. Such cooperation between the expert system and the external database would greatly facilitate the development of knowledge-based problem solvers in practical problem domains. We know of no database systems that currently provide such a facility.

SUMMARY AND CONCLUSIONS

We have described a knowledge-based consultation system which uses a combination of AI inference techniques and distributed data base management. In developing this system we have been able to provide workable solutions to the merging of a Predicate Logic based inference engine and a relational data base. This required both the maintenance of copies of the same data in two quite different representations, as well as the development of efficient mechanisms by which the two data bases remain consistent. This would not be new or interesting if these were simply two data bases. What is significant is that we were able to utilize techniques quite similar to the time-stamping approach of SDD-1 with one copy of the data in a DBMS and the other in a predicate logic based system.

An approach has also been incorporated into ASTA which allows the knowledge-based system to access and query external DBMS's. The approach allows the inference engine to generate queries to the data bases in a predicate logic form, and to have these queries transformed into appropriate DBMS queries to the external data base. The results of the query are then used to instantiate the predicate logic assertions which are delivered back to the inference engine as if they were obtained directly by the inference engine. We have proposed an extension to this technique which would enable the inference engine and the DBMS to more closely cooperate in the selection of data with an imprecise query. This is an important problem which needs to be solved for many DBMS/Inference-Engine interactions in support of knowledge-based systems.

ACKNOWLEDGMENTS

The authors wish to acknowledge the efforts of the many people who have contributed to the ASTA project, especially: Victor Askman, John L. Allen, Eric Domeshek, Ellen Drascher, Nancy English, Milissa Feeney, Brian P. McCune, Sonia Schwartzberg, David S. Spain, Richard P. Wishner, and James L. Whitaker.

REFERENCES

[1] Wilson, G., Domeshek, E., Drascher, E., and Dean, J. (1983). The Multipurpose Presentation System. *Proc. Ninth International Conference on Very Large Data Bases.* Florence, Italy, October 1983.

[2] Adams, T., Cromarty, A., McCune, B., Wilson, G., Grinberg, M., Cunningham, J., and C. Tollander (1984). A Knowledge-Based System for Analyzing Radar Systems, invited paper, Proceedings of Military Microwaves '84, London, England.

[3] Genesereth, M. (1982). An introduction to MRS for AI experts. Technical Report HPP-80-24, Stanford University Heuristic Programming Project, November 1982.

[4] Cromarty, A. (1984). COP: A framework for the intelligent Control of Processes using Communication over Ports. (In preparation.)

[5] Codd, E. (1979). Extending the database relational model to capture more meaning. *ACM Transactions on Database Systems* 4(4):379-434.

[6] Rothnie, J., Bernstein, P., Fox, S., Goodman, N., Hammer, M., Landers, T., Reeve, C., Shipman, D., and Wong, E. (1980). Introduction to a system for distributed databases (SDD-1). *ACM Transactions on Database Systems* 5(1):1-17.

PART VI:

Reasoning in Expert Database Systems

Database Support for Storage of AI Reasoning Knowledge

Michael Deering

Fairchild Laboratory for Artificial Intelligence Research
4001 Miranda Avenue
Palo Alto, CA 94304

Joseph Faletti *

Division of Computer Science
University of California, Davis
Davis, CA 95616

ABSTRACT

Databases for artificial intelligence have differed greatly from conventional databases in the past. More recently they have been moving toward a common ground, but each still has far to go. This paper discusses the nature of that common ground, what each type of database lacks, and how traditional concepts could be applied to the implementation of AI databases to provide the features necessary for AI applications.

1. Introduction

Until recently, databases designed for research in artificial intelligence have differed significantly from conventional databases. There have been several types of interactions between the database and AI fields including the following:

1. Use of an AI natural language front-end translating queries in English to a conventional database query language.
2. An intelligent system for database query optimization.
3. Applications of AI to expert tasks involving the use of a (conventional) database.
4. The use of a database system to store a large number of interrelated facts and rules for a rule-based AI system.

This paper is mostly concerned with this last intersection. The principal notion that we wish to explore is the use of conventional databases to support AI systems in the way that AI database languages have supported them in the past. The primary difference involves the rules that are being fired during the course of AI processing. Rather than being in a memory-resident Lisp program as is currently common, they would be dynamically fetched from a much larger disk-based database of rules. While this is a less commonly explored intersection, a few AI programs have been moved to a conventional database from a memory-resident Lisp program. For example, Wilensky, Arens & Chin (1984) mentions that (in work done with Stonebraker and Mueller) the use of Ingres to support the AI language analyzer PHRAN resulted in slower performance on a small database of linguistic knowledge but significantly better performance on much larger databases.

*Joseph Faletti's research was done at the University of California at Berkeley and the University of California at Davis, and was sponsored in part by the Office of Naval Research under contract N00014-80-C-0732 and the National Science Foundation under grant IST-8007045.

However, as AI applications go, the demands placed upon a database by PHRAN were slight.

This paper is concerned with what properties a database system must have to provide in an efficient manner the features that AI programs are likely to want. While utilizing disk-resident rules would allow for the larger expert systems that will be needed in the future, it will be shown that a conventional database system will not be sufficient. Techniques from memory-resident AI language database systems will be described briefly and then extended to disk-basing. We will also discuss how such a disk-based AI database system might be constructed. We are currently exploring the design and construction of a prototype system.

2. What AI Needs in a Database

Our point of view in this paper is influenced by having implemented and extensively used PEARL (Package for Efficient Access to Representations in Lisp), an AI database language which was built at Berkeley on top of Lisp (Deering, Faletti, and Wilensky (1981, 1982))*. PEARL's early design was influenced both by conventional database concepts and by frame-based AI languages such as FRL (Roberts and Goldstein (1977)) and KRL (Bobrow and Winograd (1977)). More recently it has been influenced by KLONE (Brachman (1978)). We are currently exploring the modification of PEARL to use disk-resident databases as described below. For a good summary of the current features provided by frame-based AI languages in this volume, see Fox, Wright and Adam (1985).

An AI program requires a certain set of functions from a database system, some of which are not currently provided by conventional databases. In (Wiederhold (1984)) many possible close interactions of AI and database systems are discussed, but it is always assumed that the AI portion uses its own separate "knowledge base". Since the "knowledge base" is becoming a significant portion of the data that an AI program must manipulate, it becomes important remove this distinction. This section discusses the set of functions that such knowledge bases need, focusing on those functions which are not provided by conventional databases.

2.1. The Contents of AI Databases

The knowledge stored in an AI database is usually a large collection of typed slot-filler objects similar to records in Pascal or structures in C. Each type of object must be predefined to have a finite set of slots which usually have their types specified. In particular, the values of slots will commonly be other slot-filler objects and are not restricted to simple integer or string values.

AI databases tend to contain two kinds of objects:

A. facts about objects and events, and

B. knowledge rules used for inference from facts.

In many languages this distinction is artificial but it is useful in this context for describing the features that a rule-based inference process requires.

Facts about objects and events will behave much like objects in a conventional database in that they will usually have their slots completely filled out. For example, if the salary of an employee record is missing, it will contain some default value such as 0 or a guess like $16,000. Many AI systems allow an additional value meaning *unknown* or *unbound.* For a system consisting solely of such objects, a conventional database would be close to sufficient.

---

* PEARL is distributed as part of Franz Lisp with the 4.2 Berkeley Software Distribution(BSD) of Unix. However, several of the features described below are not yet in the distributed version. A post-4.2-distribution version of PEARL also runs under Franz on Suns under 4.2 and under Zetalisp on the Symbolics 3600 Lisp Machine.

2.2. Rules in an AI Inference Loop

However, most AI systems also include a second knowledge base of *rules* which are used to make *inferences* from facts about objects and events. This process can be characterized in the following way. (This is much simplified for illustrative purposes.)

The processing in an AI system can be considered as a cycle in which each newly-learned fact or event is used in combination with other currently-known facts to fire (i.e., select and apply) inference rules which can enhance the system's knowledge by providing a new fact to be added to the fact database. The cycle then repeats with this new fact. For example, upon being told that someone moved to a new home, a rule which states that if someone moves to a new place they no longer live in their old place may be applied. This new fact might cause further inferences, for example, that they will cancel their old utilities.

An inference rule differs from a fact in that it is a general statement about objects or events and as such, must be much less specific about its slot values than the facts from which it makes inferences. Rules for such situations must be allowed to have almost any component filled with a *pattern-matching variable* which is allowed to match any corresponding element in a query. Since the collection of rules must also be stored in a database, it is mandatory that objects in an AI database contain such variables.

AI programs often take this one step further by encoding some of their processing knowledge into rules in a database. This involves the concept of *metarules* which are used to suggest other inference rules to be applied. For example, upon noting that someone just left in a vehicle, a story understanding program might have a metarule which suggests that the system look for rules explaining the goals which that particular vehicle satisfies. This rule will be retrieved from a database via the fact and provide a new query to be used to find other rules that might be applicable. Note that a metarule will not only contain variables, but it will share variables with an object which will be used as a further query.

AI databases must allow queries to be stored in slots of objects in the database and to be treated first as data, and later as queries. The usual AI solution to this is to make queries and data identical. In most conventional database systems queries are essentially pieces of code to be executed. Query-By-Example is an exception in that queries at least at the user interface level appear very much like database objects. In this volume, Kung et al (1985) propose an extension to QUEL for Ingres to allow queries to be stored as data and then executed as queries. But queries remain fundamentally different from data.

AI queries more than resemble database objects — usually they *are* database objects. That is, queries to AI databases are made via *patterns* which are objects in the same form as objects in the database, but which describe the type of knowledge being requested by specifying for each slot the kind of value desired. Each slot in a query pattern may contain either (A) a constant value which constrains the acceptable values for that slot or (B) a variable which will *match* any value. Such a variable is called a *pattern-matching variable*, a named variable that may or may not have a value. If the variable is free then, in addition to matching any value, the variable becomes *bound* to the value it matched as a side-effect of matching. In this case, later occurrences of the variable are no longer free and are used to restrict later slots to contain the same value as was found previously. Slots with variables may also have *predicates* which constrain the values which a variable will match. Even if the value in a slot at one level is a constant, that "constant" may be another slot-filler object containing variables at lower levels, possibly shared with slots at higher levels, as they are in metarules.

Since there may be more than one metarule, each suggesting more than one set of inference rules to be considered, this process is recursive and will often require that the current context be stacked for later backtracking. This context will contain the values of pattern-matching variables for each currently active query and result.

2.3. More on Matching

In conventional database systems there also exists the concept of a database entry "matching" a query (or more specifically, a portion of a query.) There is no standard definition of this match function, as in extreme cases it may be an arbitrary function written by the user. A typical semantics of matching is for the query to specify constraints upon slots of an object. The usual constraints include equality, inequality, numeric range restrictions, and recursive constraints upon other objects "pointed to" by the slot of an object. More complex constraints may involve the computation of a value based upon the contents of several slots. Constraints can usually be strung together by logical connectives; the default is *and* supported by a selection from *or*, *not*, and *exclusive or*. In many ways, most query languages consist in large part of constructs for specifying matching, the other parts being aggregate functions, update, printing, etc. (The relational algebra provides a structured basis for query operations in relational database systems, but all real implementations augment the algebra with additional capabilities in an ad hoc manner.)

The semantics of match functions is in much the same state in most AI languages. However recently several languages have settled upon the formal operation of *unification* as a standard match function. The power of unification over simpler forms of matching is the aforementioned ability to allow the inclusion of pattern-matching variables in both the query *and the data.*

AI systems support a wide range of matching services. The simplest ones resemble simple template matches with no variables. The next stage allows variables to occur in queries but not in the data. Predicates can be (optionally) attached to slots in the query. Full unification adds the ability to have variables in the data as well as the query. Even more complex matching functions allow predicates and demons in both the query and the data. (Demons restrict operations upon the object that they are attached to. In database terminology they are very similar to integrity constraints and the like. From another perspective demons are a way of obtaining object-oriented programming techniques.)

2.4. Summary of What's Hard

Thus, the key features of AI database methods that present problems for conventional databases are:

- variables in queries,
- variables in data,
- the equivalence of queries and data,
- queries stored in the database,
- context stacking for backtracking.

3. Implications for Efficiency

These features of AI databases present advantages for efficient implementation but they also introduce problems.

3.1. Hashing

Slot-filler structures aid efficiency because it is possible to hash entries in the database. That is, the database can be organized in such a way that a search can be narrowed to a portion of the database containing all objects of that type. All objects of a particular type may be further subdivided based on the values filling certain *key slots* so that restrictions by the query on a particular value in a key slot may restrict the search to a subset of the objects of that type. This limited form of hashing might be generalized with the addition of several key slots which all participate in the subdivisions of objects as in PEARL. However, this seems to be uncommon in conventional databases.

The fact that both queries and data may contain pattern-matching variables in key slots has several important consequences for object storage representations, indexing of objects, and the management of the state of query processing.

Given the presence of variables in a key slot of a query, the system is unable to choose the most specific place in the database. It must instead search all values of this type. Thus there is some loss of efficiency with variables in a query, although the use of multiple key slots may lessen the impact. There must also be several entries in the database for each item, once for each place that a query might look for it. (In a totally memory-resident database this simply requires multiple pointers.)

Another problem for hashing is the allowance of variables in the database. Given a query containing a constant value in a key slot, possible matches in the database may or may not have a variable in that slot. Therefore, for such a query to succeed in finding all relevant pieces of knowledge, it must look in both places. Again, this is only a minor problem in a memory-resident program. The implications of these are more serious for a disk-based system and are discussed below.

Thus, there needs to be a certain amount of heuristic knowledge in the hash mechanism of an AI database to allow it to look in the best place for answers to a query. Ideally, the user wishes to create some data and present queries and let the system deal with making this process efficient. Unfortunately, the variety of ways that users represent data make such an analysis difficult. In PEARL and most hashing schemes, the user is required to suggest slots which should be used as *keys* for hashing and fetching and these are used in deterministic ways to determine the fetch strategy. If the queries are at the fairly-high object level as in PEARL, the system can use this information to guide the search. In this volume, Kung et al (1985) demonstrate the potential negative consequences resulting from users being allowed to specify in code the method of fetching. They then contrast this with the benefits that accrue from having the database system compile queries at a higher level based on information about the organization of the database. This suggests the need for exploration of the use of such query interpretation methods in the hashed object-query methods of AI. Furthermore, partial results from one query will often be of use in a subsequent query. Rowe (1984) describes some steps toward noticing connections between adjacent queries and combining them.

3.2. Internal Representation of Objects

The two principal problems in having conventional database systems handle AI query processing are that the objects in the AI database are not easily represented in conventional database systems *and* that the queries in AI systems are usually expressed as *objects*. As an example, unification is defined upon classes of objects that are not efficiently expressed as simple relations in the relational database model. Unifiable objects are recursive slot-filler objects in which slots may be filled with pattern-matching variables or with other slot-filler objects of arbitrary type. While such objects can be expressed as relations with slots having values of unique ID's of other relation entries, this would require potentially several disk accesses to pull together what unification thinks of as one object. To illustrate this, in Schank's Conceptual Dependency notation (Schank, 1975) the rule *A plan for going somewhere is to walk there yourself* would be represented as:

```
(PlanFor
    (Goal (Goal (State (Position (Planner ?planner)
                                 (Location ?loc)))))
    (Plan (PhysicalTransfer (Actor ?planner)
                            (Object ?planner)
                            (To ?loc))))
```

(Here pattern-matching variables are indicated by the conventional question-mark prefix.) But in a relational database system one would have to represent this as:

PlanForDatabase = { ..., <ID: #120, Goal: #344, Plan: #654>, ... }
GoalDatabase = { ..., <ID: #344, State: #846>, ... }
PositionDatabase = { ..., <ID: #846, Planner: ?planner, Location ?loc>, ... }
PhysicalTransferDatabase =
    { ..., <ID: #654, Actor: ?planner, Object: ?planner, To: ?loc>, ... }
IsADatabase = { ... , <Object: #120, IsA: PlanFor>,
    <Object: #344, IsA: Goal>,
    <Object: #846, IsA: Position>,
    <Object: #654, IsA: PhysicalTransfer>, ... }

(Even this is not quite right, as some method must be chosen to represent pattern-matching variables. One possibility would be that negative unique ID's could indicate that the object is a variable.) Note the number of relational table accesses that would be required to access all parts of this rule. So while the space efficiency of the relational system is fine, fixed tuples of strongly-typed data tends to spread simple AI objects all over the disk.

One could criticize the AI representations as being made up of random pointers, but this is not usually the case. Some AI systems do use networks and one might think that perhaps the older network-oriented DBTG systems would be more appropriate for representation of AI data. While some Lisp-based AI programs in the past have had a superficial resemblance to DBTG-style representations, they are significantly less constrained. In particular, slots in DBTG records are strongly typed, and usually can only contain references to objects of one specified type. In AI systems a piece of knowledge can refer to other pieces of knowledge without type restrictions.

An implication of having data and queries contain variables is that for access efficiency, AI objects must be stored contiguously in one physical location, and each object may be of a different length. Because of all this, the fundamental AI database objects must be thought of as variable length, mostly non-relational objects, and database systems for AI must be constructed accordingly.

AI objects do have a relational component. When one object must refer to another, rather than use a random pointer, some modern systems will refer to a unique symbol that also occurs in the second object (but the symbol must be unique to this second object in this context), exactly as in relational database data representations. At least conceptually, some AI systems cast all data into this form. For example, Krypton (Brachman, Fikes and Levesque (1983)) and KODIAK (Wilensky (1984)) view all objects as triples, that is, representations of the form:

<object, role, role-filler>

Unfortunately this seeming resemblance to relational database format is only conceptual; the actual implementation representations are rarely of this simplistic relational form.

4. Disk Implementation Considerations

Most of the above efficiency considerations are important for implementations aimed at either virtual memory or disk. We will now address some additional considerations raised by the prospect of a disk-based AI system.

4.1. Why on a Disk?

The knowledge bases of AI programs are changing in two ways that push them toward database technology:

A. They are approaching the physical memory limits of non-virtual-memory machines and the performance limits of virtual memory machines.

B. They have become both large enough and static enough to benefit from long-term storage on disk.

With these two needs alone, the move toward conventional databases with their large storage capacity and longevity of data would be quick, were it not for several problems that they cannot handle.

4.2. Non-Fixed Size Data

Most database systems usually assume that simple database objects have a fixed size, or at least a known maximum size. For example, relational systems assume that all entries into a particular relation are of the same fixed size. Unfortunately, as discussed in the section on representations above, AI objects are extremely variable in size. This requires more complex secondary storage management techniques than are typically found in existing database systems. This is a further reason why existing database systems cannot be efficiently used to support AI databases.

4.3. Binding Environment Problems

Due to the dynamic backtracking nature of most AI inference processing loops, unknown and unlimited amounts of variable binding data must be kept around for potential future re-use. A complete disk-based solution of even a simple inference loop must also address the problem of how to manage this data (and move it to secondary storage when applicable). Because of the wide range of environment requirements of various inference loop styles, and due to space limitations, further details of this important subproblem cannot be discussed here.

5. How To Do It

We will now examine one possible technique of supporting AI database operations directly on disk. We will start with simple known implementation techniques, and modify them as additional requirements are added.

Data on disk may be hashed in a fashion similar to that described above. Consider the indexing of tuples in database systems for a simple matching query. In a simple case there is only the linear list of tuples, and an exhaustive search must be made to identify those tuples that "match" the query. If a field of the relation has been noted as "key", then the tuples could be stored in order ranked by this numeric key value, utilizing any of several suitable secondary storage data structures, such as B+ trees. Thus to check the database for all matches of the query, only a subset of the database as indicated by the key value need be accessed and checked. However this will only work if the value of the key field is given in the query. If it is a free variable, then the key feature is not usable, and the whole database must be searched. If such an unfortunate occurrence seems likely, then the database can be organized such that *two* fields are declared "key". In this way rapid access can be made as long as at least one key field value is present in the query, though at the expense of duplicating the entire database, once for each sort order (plus all the update overhead that goes with such a system). Alternately, the second database can contain pointers into the first database, at the cost of increasing disk accesses. This can of course be generalized to any number of key fields.

In some cases a single key field, even when present, may not provide enough information to narrow down the subportion of the database to be searched as much as one would wish (for example "Smith" in a telephone book). In such a case, it is advantageous to hash on two or more fields at once. The most general feature would be to always run all queries through an intelligent hash function to generate an index into a hash table. The hash function would choose which combination of slots to hash upon, based upon user-specified data and features of the particular query at hand. (These query-dependent features include such things as which slots contain known values.) The hash function computed for simple queries would be the usual key indexing, but complex queries with many variables would hash upon some combination of many slots.

There are a number of techniques available for implementing the hash table. One good one is to set up the hash table as an array of pointers to disk pages of collision chains. To save space, the collision chains could be lists of pointers to unique instances of the objects in the database, but to reduce disk seeks it is often better to let each list contain duplicates of the database entries that belong on that chain.

If the collision chain entries are much smaller than the disk page size, it may be possible to allow multiple chains to share a single page. During update, if a chain grows beyond the space available on its current disk page, then it can be moved to a new disk page (if it had been sharing a page before), or the chain can point to another disk page where it will continue. Of course whenever possible this next logical disk page should be as near as possible to the physical disk page. If a database of rules is constant enough over time (which is many times the case) then a good global analysis and careful layout could almost always make this the case. If the database grows so large that most collision chains occupy more than one page, the hash array should be expanded. This can be performed via rehashing of the entire database if rule growth is slow. The technique described in (Fagin, Nievergelt, Pippenger and Strong (1979)) can be used if one wishes to avoid this rehashing overhead.

Assuming such a system of indexing inference rules, inference processing of the normal inference loop would now proceed in the following fashion:

> Given the initial fact, construct a pattern describing rules about that fact, hash this rule and index into the rule database in order to gather up all rules that might be applicable to this fact. The result of this operation should be one or more collision chains of potentially usable rules. Then each rule would be matched against the query, and each rule successfully matching would suggest new inferences. The order of trying these new inferences would depend upon the particulars of the inference system. Breadth-first processing would try to follow all in parallel; depth-first would recursively check out each one in order, backtracking upon failure. Assuming depth-first search, the first successfully matched rule would suggest a list of new inferences. The first of these would become the new current fact, and the whole process would repeat. During this processing, whenever no further inferences can be found for a particular fact, the system must back up to the most recent choice point where other facts remain to be processed.

Other types of more complex inference, such as the meta-level reasoning in (Genesereth (1983)), would only use the query accessing as primitives employed by a more complex inference loop. But the disk access property would be the same.

What sort of disk access pattern would such processing generate? If the hash array is small enough to always be in core then no disk seeks are required to access it. Otherwise one seek is needed. Most collision chains will be small enough to be obtained with just one seek, and hopefully the multiple disk pages of long chains will be close by on disk. Thus in the best case the list of matches to most queries will generate only one seek with a worst case of a few seeks. Of course the results of disk access should be cached against probable near-term re-use. In fact when the total database size that a system desires to support (including duplicates) can fit into the virtual memory of a machine, it may be expedient to leave direct control of the disk to a virtual memory system. However to keep disk accesses down it is still necessary even in this case to arrange the data in the efficient access structures described above.

6. Processing Time Analysis

Current-technology disk drives have an average random access time of approximately 30 milliseconds, though many inexpensive disks have much worse access times. For processing the inference loop presented above, most systems will perform several query match functions per hash chain accessed. (Each hash chain accessed will typically generate one disk seek.) For general AI languages written in Lisp, the match time can range from 10 to 100 or more milliseconds, and in such cases the disk seek time is not a bottleneck. However, in highly efficient compiled inferencing languages with stripped down match functions (such as Prolog), the match function can run in well under 0.1 milliseconds. Fortunately these systems tend to have a high degree of locality in their access pattern as they tend to recursively use rules during processing. Even so the techniques described in this paper may not always be applicable to these systems. In the more typical case one finds AI code performing a number of non-database operations between each query step.

7. Custom Machines

The techniques described in this paper have application beyond the context of conventional computers. Custom database machines and AI machines face the same problems, but have the freedom to cast a portion of the solutions into hardware. The Fairchild FAIM-1 machine provides a good example. This massively parallel multiprocessor machine contains large amounts of custom CAM for rapid, associative indexing of AI rules. Each processor has an attached pipelined unification engine to speed the matching process. (This unifier hardware is augmented with built-in predicates such as numeric range restriction to support the processing of more complex matching functions.) The complex hashing functions advocated above as being necessary for the indexing of rule data containing variables are available via a custom hashing chip. This chip will be able to directly track down data cached in banks of DRAM, but can also be used to provide addresses for use in a disk-based search.

8. Other Database Features

Included among the things that conventional databases do but that AI databases currently seldom worry about are: multiple users, using the disk to good advantage, security, reliability and query optimization. These should be (and are likely to be) considered in the future. For these issues, the standard database techniques are more than sufficient.

9. Other AI Needs

The needs of AI databases discussed above are those that are currently the best understood and that are already provided. However, as AI systems grow and become more sophisticated in the kinds and complexity of knowledge they wish to store, it is becoming necessary to join groups of slot-filler objects into larger objects whose structure cannot be reduced to a simple hierarchy of slot-filler objects filling the slots of other objects. In many cases it is desirable for variables to be shared among many slot-filler objects in such a conglomeration. These collections of objects are often treated as separate databases (or as partitions of the database). Although it is possible to attain a certain degree of such partitioning with multi-key hashing, this quickly becomes unwieldy. These large structures currently present problems for AI database systems but as they are resolved, these problems (and with luck, their solutions) will devolve on future expert database systems.

We have concentrated in this paper on the things that are best understood and can easily be transferred to expert database systems. As a result, the focus was fairly low-level. At the same time we are striving to build systems on top of this aimed more directly at the level of knowledge that our programs want to deal with. For a discussion of these important issues, see Brachman and Levesque (1985) in this volume.

10. Conclusions

Traditional database techniques are useful for the support of large databases of AI rules. But problems associated with providing indexing for rapid retrieval require extensions of the normal database indexing methods. The AI view of queries as data requires more complexity to be added to the underlying data objects supported by database systems. Therefore existing database systems are not currently well-suited for efficiently supporting large AI reasoning systems. Techniques for constructing database systems which are better-suited to AI applications were suggested. Some custom machines under design are already employing similar techniques to address this important issue. There are still many problems to be solved in the future.

11. References

Bobrow, D., and Winograd, T. 1977. An Overview of KRL, a Knowledge Representation Language. *Cognitive Science.* Vol. 1, No. 1, Jan.-Mar. 1977.

Brachman, R. 1978. *A Structural Paradigm for Representing Knowledge,* Technical Report 3605, Bolt Beranek and Newman, Inc., May, 1978.

Brachman, R., Fikes, R., and Levesque, H. 1983. KRYPTON: A Functional Approach to Knowledge Representation, *IEEE Computer*, October, 1983.

Brachman, R., and Levesque, H. 1985. What Makes a Knowledge Base Knowledgeable -- A View of Databases from the Knowledge Level. In this volume, 1985.

Deering, M., Faletti, J., and Wilensky, R. 1981. PEARL: An Efficient Language for Artificial Intelligence Programming. In the *Proceedings of the Seventh International Joint Conference on Artificial Intelligence.* Vancouver, British Columbia. August, 1981.

Deering, M., Faletti, J., and Wilensky, R. 1982. The PEARL Users Manual. Berkeley Electronic Research Laboratory Memorandum No. UCB/ERL/M82/19. March, 1982.

Fagin, R., Nievergelt, J., Pippenger, N., and Strong, H. 1979. Extendible Hashing — A Fast Access Method for Dynamic Files. *ACM Transactions of Database Systems.* Vol. 4, No. 3, Sept. 1979.

Fox, M., Wright, J., Adam, D. 1985. Experiences with SRL: An Analysis of Frame-Based Knowledge Representation. In this volume, 1985.

Genesereth, M. 1983. An overview of Meta-Level Architecture, in *Proceedings AAAI-83*, Washington, D.C., August, 1983.

Kung, R., Hanson, E., Ioannidis, Y., Sellis, T., Shapiro, L. and Stonebraker, M. 1985. Heuristic Search in Data Base Systems. In this volume, 1985.

Roberts, I., and Goldstein, R. 1977. NUDGE, A Knowledge-Based Scheduling Program. In *Proceeding of the 5th International Joint Conference on Artificial Intelligence.* Cambridge, MA. August, 1977, 257-263.

Rowe, N. 1984. Steps Toward Parsing of Query Sequences to a Database. *Proc. First International Workshop on Expert Database Systems*, L. Kerschberg (editor), Kiawah Island, SC 1984.

Schank, R. 1975. *Conceptual Information Processing.* Amsterdam: North Holland.

Wiederhold, G., Knowledge and Database Management, *IEEE Software,* January 1984.

Wilensky, R., Arens, Y., and Chin, D. 1984. Talking to UNIX in English: An Overview of UC. *Commun. ACM.* Vol. 27, No. 6, June 1984.

Wilensky, R. 1984. KODIAK: A Language for Meaning Representations. *Proceedings of the Cognitive Science Conference.* Boulder, CO. June 1984.

HEURISTIC SEARCH IN DATA BASE SYSTEMS

by

Ru-Mei Kung
ESL, Inc.
495 Java Dr.
Sunnyvale, Ca.

and

Eric Hanson, Yannis Ioannidis, Timos Sellis, Leonard Shapiro, and Michael Stonebraker
Department of Electrical Engineering and Computer Science
University of California
Berkeley, Ca.

ABSTRACT

This paper proposes extensions to a relational database system to support the selection and execution of algorithms for shortest path search problems. An expert system can employ this extended DBMS to provide unified management of data and part of the knowledge base. Several search algorithms have been prototyped using the database extensions. Their performance characteristics are described and comparisons with main memory algorithms are made.

1. INTRODUCTION

A wide variety of so-called expert systems have a significant component which performs heuristic search over a sizable data space. Examples include R1 [MCDO80] which searches the space of possible ways of allocating VAX printed circuit boards to a cabinet. The algorithm used is a greedy algorithm with no backtracking. Other examples include GA1 [STEF78] which attempts to identify a chemical molecule from component pieces by generating options in a orderly way and then pruning ones that are infeasible.

There are several identifiable classes of algorithms (e.g. hill climbing, branch and bound, dynamic programming) which can be applied to search problems. An extensive discussion of options is presented in [PEAR84, STEF82]. Moreover, there are many ways to implement a given type of algorithm, and expert system performance may be quite sensitive to the specific implementation chosen and the actual data on which the algorithm is run. Hence, one of the tasks of an expert system implementor is to discover which class of algorithms appears practical for his problem and then to code a variation of the algorithm which performs effectively on his data. In addition, if the expert system in question must deal with dissimilar data sets, then the implementor must either code a collection of algorithms and have a meta expert system to perform algorithm selection or accept poor performance on some data sets.

The basic objective of our research is to move the search portion of an expert system into a data base management system. On large data sets, a DBMS is a practical necessity; hence, expert systems for such data sets must act as application programs to a data

This research was sponsored by the U.S. Air Force Office of Scientific Research Grant 83-0021 and by the Naval Electronics Systems Command Contract N00039-78-G-0013.

base manager. Consequently, one has the opportunity of selectively moving function from such application programs into the DBMS. Common function can thereby be written once within the DBMS and not once per application as is common today. Moreover, performance improvements are often realizable from such function migration.

There are two components to heuristic search in an expert system, namely the selection of which of several possible algorithms to use, and the execution of the chosen algorithm. In this paper we will show that with relatively minor extensions to a classical query language such as QUEL [STON76] it is possible to integrate the execution of many algorithms into a DBMS. In addition, we show how selection of an efficient algorithm can be effectively performed within the DBMS.

We have focused on a particular shortest path problem as the context for our study. We have coded several of the popular heuristic algorithms for this problem and measured their performance in a DBMS context. Our results are quite different from those predicted for main memory data [PEAR84].

The remainder of this paper is organized as follows. In Section 2 we explain our example shortest path problem in detail. Then in Section 3, we present an extended version of the query language QUEL [STON76] which will allow us in Section 4 to express a variety of common algorithms for this problem. Section 5 then indicates experimental results on a real data base. We turn in Section 6 to automatic selection of an efficient algorithm by the DBMS and suggest several appealing strategies. Lastly, Section 7 contains our conclusions from this study.

2. THE OVERLAND SEARCH PROBLEM

The task we will focus on is to move a vehicle from a given point (say San Francisco airport) to a second point (say the Computer Science building at the University of California in Berkeley) in minimum expected cost. The applicable cost function might be the minimum expected time of travel or the minimum expected gasoline consumption.

There can be many constraints on the feasible path. For example, certain vehicles (e.g. Hertz rental cars) are restricted to travel on roads while other (e.g. tanks, off road vehicles) can choose an overland route. Even overland vehicles are constrained in route selection because they cannot pass through rivers greater than a certain depth or traverse terrain which exceeds a specific pitch. Additionally, the cost of certain paths can vary with time of day or day of week; for example the cost of traveling on a highway changes during rush hour.

The specific search problem is to find a minimum cost route from a point START to a point FINISH that satisfies a collection of constraints of the above form. Moreover, it is a simple bookkeeping problem to keep track of the total route; hence we will content ourselves with simply finding the cost of the best route.

We assume that a topographical map of the area in question is available. It is a separate problem to process the raw map data into a form usable by a heuristic search program. For the moment, we assume that the map has been processed into a relation of the form

FEASIBLE (source, dest, cost)

where the cost attribute indicates how difficult it is to travel from point "source" to point "dest". We also assume the availability of point as a fundamental DBMS data type in this discussion. It can be realized as a built-in data type or added through the mechanism proposed in [STON83].

Notice that if a map is discretized at 100 foot intervals, this will result in about 2500 points per square mile. If each point is accessible from its eight nearest neighbors, we require 20,000 tuples in FEASIBLE per square mile. A 50 mile by 50 mile map would then consume about 600 Mbytes if each tuple requires 12 bytes. Clever coding of the data might reduce this amount; however, it should be clearly noted that FEASIBLE is a very large relation. Hence, it is not reasonable to assume that it is a main memory data structure as is commonly done by algorithm designers [PEAR84].

We now turn to describing an extended version of QUEL which will allow us to express a collection of solutions to this problem.

3. DATA BASE SOLUTIONS

It is clear that for all paths between pairs of nodes in

FEASIBLE (source, dest, cost)

the transitive closure of FEASIBLE contains and edge. In fact, assuming that FEASIBLE is acyclic, the following algorithm will generate the cost of all possible paths from any START to any FINISH:

```
retrieve into TEMP (FEASIBLE.all)

repeat
   append to TEMP ( TEMP.source, FEASIBLE.dest,
                cost = FEASIBLE.cost + TEMP.cost)
   where TEMP.dest = FEASIBLE.source
until TEMP does not grow
```

The cost of the best path between two points START and FINISH is the minimum "cost" value in TEMP with source equal to START and dest equal to FINISH. The goal of any heuristic search algorithm is to do better than the above computation.

It should be noted that the computation of transitive closure cannot be expressed in QUEL (or in most of the relational query languages that we are aware of). Only QBE [ZLOO75] and ORACLE [ORAC84] have limited capabilities to express such recursive calculations. Hence, our first task must be to enlarge QUEL with the appropriate function. We follow the extensions of [GUTT84] in including a * operator in QUEL.

Using the * operator, the above calculation becomes:

```
retrieve into TEMP (FEASIBLE.all)
append* to TEMP ( TEMP.source, FEASIBLE.dest,
             cost = FEASIBLE.cost + TEMP.cost)
where TEMP.dest = FEASIBLE.source
```

Basically, the semantics of APPEND* are to repeat the command forever. In practice, the execution of the command can cease when an iteration produces no additional tuples in TEMP. Similar semantics hold for REPLACE*, DELETE* and RETRIEVE* into a result relation. For example, consider the following alternate algorithm that computes the cost of the best path between all pairs of points (even for cyclic graphs):

```
range of F1 is FEASIBLE
range of F2 is FEASIBLE
retrieve into TEMP (F1.source, F2.dest, cost = INFINITE) where
      F1.source != F2.dest
replace TEMP (cost = FEASIBLE.cost) where
      TEMP.source = FEASIBLE.source and
      TEMP.dest = FEASIBLE.dest
range of T is TEMP
replace* TEMP( cost = T.cost + FEASIBLE.cost) where
      T.cost + FEASIBLE.cost < TEMP.cost and
      T.dest = FEASIBLE.source and
      FEASIBLE.dest = TEMP.dest
```

The semantics of REPLACE* are to execute the command indefinitely. In practice execution can cease when one of two things happens:

1) the qualification becomes false. In this case one need not continue to execute the command because it will not have any effect at any time in the future.

2) the command fails to update a tuple. Again, continuing to run the command will have no effect.

Two comments should be made at this time. First, in the case that there is more than one adjacent point that can be used to lower the cost of a given tuple in TEMP, the REPLACE* command will attempt to replace a single data item by two or more calculations. This is an example of a non-functional update [STON76] which is allowed by some versions of INGRES and disallowed by others. Non-functional updates will be discussed further in section 4. Second, notice that it is possible to define REPLACE* as non-terminating. For example, one could simply make the command inactive until some other update caused the data base to change so that the command could be rerun and have an effect. For example the following command will run forever and update the salary of Mike to be equal to that of Leonard whenever Leonard's salary is changed:

```
range of E is EMPLOYEE
replace* EMPLOYEE (salary = E.salary) where
        EMPLOYEE.name = "Mike" and
        E.name = "Leonard"
```

In this paper we assume that * commands terminate. The efficient implementation of the non-terminating version of these commands (which are in effect triggers [ESWA76]) is described separately [STON84].

Our second necessary construct is the notion of storing collections of QUEL commands in the data base and then being able to execute them. For example, suppose both routines for constructing TEMP are stored in the relation, COMMANDS:

```
COMMANDS (id, QUEL-desc)
```

If one has id "mostly-replace" and the other "mostly-append", then we could execute the "mostly-replace" routine as follows:

```
range of C is COMMANDS
execute (C.QUEL-desc) where C.id = "mostly-replace"
```

Suppose we change the "mostly-replace" routine so that the first retrieve and replace commands are stored separately in COMMANDS as a routine called "warm-up". Then, the REPLACE* is changed into a simple REPLACE and stored in "inner-loop". The following commands are an equivalent specification of the "mostly-replace" routine:

```
execute (C.QUEL-desc) where C.id = "warm-up"
execute* (C.QUEL-desc) where C.id = "inner-loop"
```

In the next section we turn to expressing a collection of popular search algorithms in this extended language, QUEL*.

4. SHORTEST PATH PROBLEMS IN QUEL*

We have coded and simulated two kinds of algorithms, Breadth-First and Best-First. By Best-First we mean that only the node(s) with the least accumulated cost are expanded in each iteration. This section contains QUEL* code for these algorithms and an extension of the algorithms which uses a hierarchical decomposition of the map space.

In addition to the FEASIBLE relation, each algorithm will also use a relation describing the state of the system as the algorithm progresses:

```
STATES ( dest, cost)
```

where cost is the cost of the cheapest path, found by the algorithm so far, from START to the node labeled dest. We use the following range variables in the QUEL* code:

```
range of s,t is STATES
range of f is FEASIBLE
```

Our first coding of the algorithms follows the classic approach, in which only visited nodes are kept in the state space.

BREADTH FIRST - VISITED NODES

```
/* Initially STATES consists only of the starting point */
append to STATES(cost = 0, dest = START)

execute*
{       /* Append the newly expanded nodes */
        append to STATES(dest = f.dest, cost = f.cost + s.cost) where
        s.dest = f.source

        /* Delete states that are dominated */
        delete s where
        s.dest = t.dest and s.cost > t.cost      /* t is a cheaper path */
                or
        s.cost > t.cost and t.dest = FINISH /* the cost of getting to s is already more
                                    than the cost of getting to FINISH */
}
```

BEST FIRST - VISITED NODES

```
/* In the best first algorithms, a status field is added to the STATES
relation, with values "open", "current" and "closed". The value "open"
means the node has not been expanded, "current" means it is being
expanded in the current step, and "closed" means it has been expanded. */

retrieve into STATES (dest = START, cost = 0, status = current)

execute*
{       /* expand best node */
        append to STATES (dest = f.dest, cost = s.cost + f.cost, status = open)
        where f.source = s.dest and s.status = current

        /* Close the state that was expanded */
        replace s(status = closed) where s.status = current

        /* Delete states that are dominated */
        delete s where
        s.status = open and
        s.dest = t.dest and s.cost > t.cost

        /* Mark best nodes as current */
        replace s(status = current) where
        s.status = open and s.cost = min(t.cost where t.status = open)
        and s.dest != FINISH        /* If we are done, nothing is marked current */
}
```

We also coded these two algorithms with a state space equal to all nodes, i.e. one state for each node in the graph. This allows us to use fewer calls to the database inside the loop, which may improve performance for reasons we discuss below. While the routines which keep only visited nodes in STATES use an append followed by a delete, our next approach needs only a replace* command to accomplish most of the processing.

BREADTH FIRST - ALL NODES

```
/* Initially all nodes in STATES have infinite cost, except that START has zero cost */

retrieve into NODES (s.dest)
range of n is NODES
append to STATES(n.dest, cost = INFINITE)
replace s(cost = 0) where s.dest = START

/* In this algorithm, all the processing is done by one replace* */

replace* t (cost = s.cost + f.cost) where
        f.source = s.dest and  f.dest = t.dest  /* f is path from s to t */
                and
        t.cost > f.cost + s.cost          /* this path is cheaper */
```

The code above includes a non-functional update [STON76]. In the case that the cost of a given tuple in STATES can be improved in more that one way, the system will attempt to update it multiple times. Many database systems refuse non-functional updates, including the version of INGRES used for the performance tests that follow. The stated reason is that such an update replaces a value by two or more different values and the last value processed is the one that persists. Hence, a random answer is recorded as a result of such an update. However this will not lead to incorrect results in the above code, since a better improvement will be chosen in the next iteration of the loop to replace the random improvement selected. If the system does not allow non-functional updates, additional queries must be added to the above code.

Finally, in the routine for the "best first - all nodes" algorithm that follows, we have added tuples (z,z,0) to the FEASIBLE relation for all nodes z. This results in fewer queries in the loop.

BEST FIRST - ALL NODES

```
/* In this routine a field "open" is added to the STATES
relation, with values true or false. A state is open (i.e.
its open attribute is "true") if it has not been expanded */

retrieve to nodes (s.dest)
range of n is nodes
append to STATES(n.dest,cost = INFINITE, open = true)
replace s(cost = 0) where s.dest = START
append to FEASIBLE(n.dest,n.dest,0)

execute*
{ /* find the minimum cost node */
        retrieve(mincost = min(s.cost where s.open = true) )
        retrieve(mindest = min(s.dest where s.open = true and s.cost = mincost) )

        /* expand that node */
        replace t(open = (t.cost != mincost), cost = s.cost + f.cost) where
        s.dest = mindest /* s is being expanded */
                and
        f.source = mindest and f.dest = t.dest /* t is neighbor of s, or s = t */
                and
        (
                t.cost > f.cost + s.cost/* This route is cheaper */
                        or
                t.dest = s.dest          /* or s = t */
        )
}
```

It is possible to improve the performance of all the algorithms by using a variety of estimators to decide which nodes should be expanded, but we do not address that subject in this paper. It is also possible to improve the algorithms if every point in FEASIBLE is required to have exactly four adjacent points. Lastly, some algorithms can be improved by maintaining a temporary relation which contains the points which were updated during the last iteration and then investigating only points adjacent to this set in the current iteration. These optimizations would be performed in a production setting. However, they would lead to much more complex examples and have not been pursued in this paper.

If START and FINISH are widely separated, and the maps are of fine granularity, then the algorithms may take prohibitively long to find a shortest path, even with a judicious use of estimators. To deal with such problems, we can embed the above algorithms in a hierarchical algorithm which uses main road maps. The main road algorithm can be expressed in QUEL, so it together with any of the above algorithms will provide a mechanism for finding shortest paths over a wide range of START and FINISH points.

In the hierarchical algorithm we assume that the database is presented with a tree of maps, each in the form of the FEASIBLE relation. The leaves of the tree are detailed maps and the higher levels include only nodes from the lowest levels which are on main roads. For example, the leaves might be plat maps, the second level might have main road maps through a city, and the highest level could have main roads through a state. There are at least two ways to use the main road maps in the search process, a top down or a bottom up approach. In the top down approach, one first finds a main road from the plat containing START to the plat containing FINISH and then searches the individual plats for a path from the chosen main road to the START and FINISH points. The bottom up approach first finds shortest paths from START and FINISH to any main road, then searches the main road network for the shortest path between the two chosen points on the main roads. Each model has its own advantages and the choice of bottom up vs top down again depends on the data. An improvement to either algorithm would go straight to the bottom level if the points in question are close enough together. Any of these choices can be easily coded in QUEL*,

5. PERFORMANCE RESULTS

We coded the algorithms from the previous section in EQUEL [ALLM76] on the Relational Technology version of INGRES by simulating the effect of the * operator by rerunning a command until the tuple count of modified tuples was zero. We also coded the Best-First algorithm in FORTRAN using virtual memory data structures in the program address space for STATES and FEASIBLE. This program kept only visited states in its data structure for STATES. Our data set was a 36 square mile area of Santa Cruz county, California. This area is extremely mountainous with deep valleys and an extensive river system. It was digitized into three FEASIBLE relations of different granularity, representing grids which are 10, 20 and 30 nodes on each side. The START and FINISH points were at opposite corners of the map.

The CPU time of the various algorithms is indicated in Table 1. All times are in seconds.

	10 by 10	20 by 20	30 by 30
FORTRAN	24	1,010	6654
Breadth first - Visited Nodes	949	62,071	...
Best first - Visited nodes	108	964	2962
Breadth first - All nodes	84	718	1361
Best first - All nodes	126	1449	4455

Figure 1: CPU time of algorithms

The times for the FORTRAN program are growing much more rapidly than those for the best QUEL* algorithm. This supports our thesis that a database manager is a practical necessity for large maps. The reason that the FORTRAN code is not as fast as INGRES is because it does joins by scanning one relation repeatedly for every tuple of the other relation (the nested loops approach to join processing). On the other hand, the INGRES query optimizer considers a nested loops approach as well as a sort-merge tactic. On this data sort-merge is far superior. Of course, the FORTRAN program could have coded a sort-merge join and obtained considerably better performance. However, that would have made the program a great deal longer. In addition, it is not clear that sort-merge is the algorithm of choice on all maps. Hence, a dynamic query optimizer is a valuable tool for this problem.

The FORTRAN program was two pages of code, while the QUEL* program was one half page long. This supports our thesis that shortest path algorithms will be easier to write in QUEL* than in a programming language.

Within the different QUEL* algorithms, we note that the Breadth-First algorithm with all nodes in STATES outperforms all other choices. The Best-First approach (known as the A* algorithm when augmented with estimators) is known [PEAR84] to be more efficient than the Breadth-First approach when the database can fit in main memory. We speculate that Breadth-First is generally better in a database environment because it makes few calls to the set-oriented database system. Hence, it may expand a larger number of nodes than Best-First, but each node is expanded more efficiently. Hence, algorithms with good performance in main memory environments do not necessarily exhibit the same behavior in a data base context.

The performance of Breadth-First when only visited nodes appear in STATES is especially poor. This is because in our formulation of the algorithm all nodes in the STATES relation are expanded in every execution of the append statement. Towards the end of processing, the STATES relation contains many tuples, most of which no longer need to be expanded. Hence, care must be taken in efficiently coding an algorithm of a given type, because large performance differences can be observed.

6. SELECTION OF AN ALGORITHM

In previous sections a query language was described in which a variety of shortest path algorithms can be implemented and performance results are presented for several of them. Since each algorithm is relatively straight-forward to specify in QUEL*, it is apparent that a library of alternate algorithms and of various implementations of the same algorithm could be easily constructed. This section suggests ways in which algorithm selection from such a library could be performed using the DBMS.

We will suggest two levels of facilities that can be implemented in this context. In the discussion which follows, we assume the presence of an algorithms relation

COMMANDS (id, alg-name, type, QUEL-desc, ...)

where "id" is a unique identifier for the routine in "QUEL-desc," "alg-name" is the name of the algorithm implemented by that routine and "type" specifies the function of the algorithm, e.g. "shortest-path." We assume that QUEL-desc contains QUEL* with a variety of parameters. For example, one could specify the following routine (using '$' to denote parameters):

```
retrieve into $result ($name.$source, $name.$dest, cost = $name.$cost)
append* to $result ($result.$source, $name.$dest,
            cost = $name.$cost + $result.cost)
      where $result.$dest = $name.$source
```

Assuming that the above routine has id "mostly-append" one requires a syntax such as:

```
range of C is COMMANDS
execute (C.QUEL-desc with (name = FEASIBLE, source = source,
                 dest = dest, cost = cost, result = TEMP))
where C.id = "mostly-append"
```

In the sequel we assume that a parameterized mechanism such as the above would be used in practice, but for simplicity we code specific examples on the FEASIBLE relation.

The first level of routine selection is the EXECUTE-1 command. Suppose one has several routines in the COMMANDS relation implementing an algorithm with the name "dy-prog". One could specify that one be executed by:

```
execute-1 (C.QUEL-desc) where C.alg-name = "dy-prog"
```

After the collection of appropriate routines has been found, the query optimizer must choose exactly one to execute. Our suggestion is to run the optimizer on all the routine descriptions to find the expected cost of each collection of commands. In the case that only normal QUEL appears, the optimizer can generate a complete estimate for the cost using the techniques of [SELI79] and then choose the one with expected minimum cost. In the case that statements in QUEL* appear, the choice is much more difficult because the number of iterations is not known for the various routines. In this case we suggest the following heuristics:

1) Assume that any QUEL* expression will be executed a constant number of times. Choose the expected cheapest routine on this basis.

2) Assume that any QUEL* expression will be executed a number of times equal to the cardinality of the largest relation which it acts on. Choose the expected cheapest routine on this basis.

3) Run each QUEL* expression once and record how many tuples were changed. Assume that the number of iterations is equal to this number. Choose the expected cheapest routine on this basis.

Other heuristics appear possible. It is a problem for future research to generalize a query optimizer to choose a good candidate in this extended environment.

Notice that the query optimizer can make its selection decision based only on expected execution time of the candidate routines. This formulation has several shortcomings. First, a user may have additional constraints. For example, he may insist on obtaining the optimal answer rather than an approximate one. Second, the running time of a routine and the quality of its answer depend crucially on the characteristics of the data. For example, any implementation of a greedy algorithm will perform well on a flat uniform landscape (such as Illinois) but will perform poorly in mountainous terrain. Such data specific information is not captured by the above formulation. Moreover, a knowledgeable user may know that a dynamic programming algorithm is always preferable to a greedy algorithm unless the terrain is perfectly flat. Such comparative information is not captured by a mechanism minimizing expected algorithm running time.

In order to solve the above problems, we suggest the inclusion of an algorithm selection level, which uses one or more relations containing auxiliary information. Moreover, we will need another extension to QUEL to properly utilize the added information. The QUEL extension is to allow a QUEL qualification to be a data type in a relation. This would allow statements of the form:

```
execute (relation.QUEL) where relation.qualification
```

For a given relation with fields of type QUEL and qualification, the QUEL commands would be executed in each tuple for which the qualification field evaluated to true. This construct is used in the auxiliary relations, an example of which is the BEATS relation:

```
BEATS (winning-alg, losing-alg, condition)
```

The two algorithm name fields identify algorithms appearing in the COMMANDS relation while the condition field contains a qualification in the QUEL language. A tuple in this relation indicates the conditions under which a given winning algorithm should be chosen in preference to a given losing algorithm. Assuming that there is a relation

```
path(START,FINISH)
```

containing one tuple specifying the start and finish points of the desired path, the following insert specifies that the Best-First algorithm is preferable to the Breadth-First algorithm if the distance between START and FINISH is less than 10.

```
append to BEATS (
        winning-alg = "Best-First",
        losing-alg = "Breadth-First",
```

condition = "distance(path.START, path.FINISH) < 10)"

We expect that a skilled algorithm designer will insert such conditions. To utilize the knowledge contained in this relation, we would expect the designer of an expert system to obtain a command from an end user of the form:

```
range of CO is COMMANDS
execute-1 (CO.QUEL-desc) where CO.type = "shortest-path"
```

The expert system could alter this command to the following:

```
retrieve into CANDIDATES (CO.id, CO.alg-name, CO.QUEL-desc)
      where CO.type = "shortest-path"
range of CA1 is CANDIDATES
range of CA2 is CANDIDATES
range of B is BEATS
delete CA2 where CA2.alg-name = B.losing-alg and
                 CA1.alg-name = B.winning-alg and
                 B.condition
execute-1 (CA2.QUEL-desc)
```

In this way the condition is checked in BEATS whenever both a winning and losing algorithm appear in CANDIDATES and the loser is removed if the condition is true. Hence, the knowledge in BEATS has been used to eliminate choices and the EXECUTE-1 command has fewer options to evaluate. Some other relations which might be useful are:

```
IS-REASONABLE (alg-name, condition)
WONT-WORK (alg-name, condition)
HAS-SMALL-RUNNING-TIME (alg-name, condition)
```

The job of the expert system implementor is to accept a specification from an end user of the command to be run and then to utilize the information in the relations such as the one above to restrict the options to be evaluated. This restriction process can be programmed completely in QUEL. The last QUEL command in such a program should be an EXECUTE-1 command to turn over final routine selection to the data base system.

7. CONCLUSIONS

We have shown that our proposed extensions to QUEL make it possible both to express search algorithms as collections of DBMS commands and to support the selection of a candidate algorithm based on performance considerations. This is a first step to capturing general knowledge bases inside a data base management system.

We have shown that an expert system can employ this extended DBMS to provide unified management of data and part of the knowledge base. For the moment, an expert system designer is required to intervene between the end user and the data base system to specify how algorithm knowledge should be used to restrict the search for a candidate algorithm. In the future we will investigate how to factor more of the algorithm selection process into the data base system.

We implemented several common search algorithms in a data base context. We found that Breadth-First parallel algorithms consistently outperformed serial Best-First ones. This contradicts the behavior that would be expected on main memory resident data sets. Additionally, data base algorithms were found to be competitive against a hand coded Fortran program.

The requirement that updates be functional was found to cause substantial increase in running time of the dynamic programming algorithm. It is thus desirable to allow non-functional updates as a user-selectable option in a relational data base system.

REFERENCES

[ALLM76] Allman, E. et. al., "EQUEL Reference Manual," ERL Report, University of California, Berkeley, 1976.

[ESWA76] Eswaren, K., "Specification, Implementation and Interactions of a Trigger Subsystem in an Integrated Database System," IBM Research, San Jose, Ca., Research Report RJ1820, August 1976.

[GUTT84] Guttman, A., "Extending a Relational Data Base System to Effectively Manage CAD Data," PhD Thesis, University of California, Berkeley, June 1984.

[MCDO80] McDermott, J., "R1: A Rule Based Configurer of Computer Systems," Carnegie Mellon Univ., Pittsburgh, Pa., Computer Science Report CMU-CS-80-119, April 1980.

[ORAC84] "ORACLE REFERENCE MANUAL," ORACLE, Inc., Menlo Park, Ca., 1984.

[PEAR84] Pearl, J., "Heuristics: Intelligent Search Strategies for Computer Problem Solving," Addison Wesley, Reading, Mass., 1984.

[SELI79] Selinger, P. et. al., "Access Path Selection in a Relational Data Base System," Proc. 1979 ACM-SIGMOD Conference on Management of Data, Boston, Mass., June 1979.

[STEF78] Stefik, M., "Inferring DNA Structure from Segmentation Data," Artificial Intelligence 11, pp. 85-114, 1978.

[STEF82] Stefik, M. et. al., "The Organization of Expert Systems: A Prescriptive Tutorial," Xerox Palo Alto Research Center, Palo Alto, Ca., Memo VLSI-82-1, January, 1982.

[STON76] Stonebraker, M., Wong E., Kreps P. and Held G., "The design and implementation of INGRES," ACM Transactions on Database Systems, Vol. 1, No 3, pp. 189-222, (Sep. 1976).

[STON83] Stonebraker, M., et. al., "Application of Abstract Data Types and Abstract Indices to CAD Data," Proc. Engineering Applications Stream of the ACM-SIGMOD International Conference on Management of Data, San Jose, Ca., May 1983.

[STON84] Stonebraker, M., "A Novel Specification and Implementation of Data Base Triggers," (in preparation).

[STON84a] Stonebraker, M. et. al., "QUEL as a Data Type," Proc. 1984 ACM-SIGMOD Conference on Management of Data, Boston, Mass., June 1984.

[ZANI83] Zaniolo, C., "The Database Language GEM," Proc. 1983 ACM-SIGMOD Conference on Management of Data, San Jose, Ca., May 1983.

[ZLOO75] Zloof, M., "Query-by-Example: Operations on the Transitive Closure," IBM Research, Yorktown Heights, N.Y., Research Report 5526, July 1975.

RELATIONSHIPS BETWEEN DEDUCTIVE AND ABDUCTIVE INFERENCE IN KNOWLEDGE-BASED DIAGNOSTIC PROBLEM SOLVING[1]

Dana S. Nau and James A. Reggia

Computer Science Dept.
University of Maryland
College Park, MD 20742

Abstract

Most knowledge-based computer systems are based on a production rule format which proves to be very difficult to apply to many diagnostic problems. In this paper, we argue that this is because diagnostic problem solving is a problem in abductive inference rather than deductive inference. The usual rule format does not provide sufficiently rich knowledge representation capabilities to allow abductive problems to be translated into deductive ones. We also show how abductive problems can be translated into deductive problems by using a rather different rule format than is usually used in knowledge-based computer systems, and discuss an algorithm for diagnostic problem solving based on this rule format. This algorithm has been successfully used to create expert computer systems in several different problem domains.

1. Introduction

The vast majority of expert systems for diagnostic problem solving which have been developed by artificial intelligence researchers are based on the use of production rules to do deductive inference [3]. Even systems such as Prospector [1] which use semantic networks or similar knowledge representation structures still use production rules to do their reasoning.

Production rule systems for diagnostic problem solving are based on techniques for deductive inference. Such systems typically use rules of the form

IF *conjunct of manifestations* THEN *disorder*

to construct chains of deductive reasoning showing that the existence of some set of manifestations provides evidence for the presence of various causes or disorders. Such reasoning proceeds from the rule of modus ponens: if "A implies B" is true and if "A" is true, then "B" is true. However, diagnostic problem solving is basically an abductive process rather than a deductive one. Abductive inference proceeds from a rule which goes in the reverse direction from modus ponens: if "A implies B" is true and "B" is true, then *possibly* "A" is true.

In this paper, we argue that in diagnostic problems where more than one disorder occurs simultaneously, the usual deductive approach used in production rule systems can lead to severe problems. We briefly describe an abductive approach to diagnostic problem solving which overcomes some of these problems, and discuss some knowledge-representation and control issues which arise in the abductive approach.

---

[1] This work was supported in part by Contract NB83SBCA2124 from the National Bureau of Standards, and in part by Contract N60921-83-C-0107 from the Naval Surface Weapons Center.

2. Diagnostic Problem Solving

In order to compare various approaches to diagnostic problem solving, we first need to formalize what is meant by a diagnostic problem. In our formation every diagnostic problem domain has the following characteristics:

1. There are various disorders which can occur in that domain which may or may not be present in specific diagnostic problems. The set of all possible such disorders we call D. For the purposes of this paper, we assume that all members of D are independent of each other.

2. If a disorder d are present, then it may cause one or more symptoms, signs, or *manifestations* of its presence. The set of all possible manifestations in a given problem domain we call M. We let $C \in D \times M$ be the relation between disorders and the manifestations they cause; i.e., $(d,m) \in C$ if and only if d is capable of causing m. In this paper, we assume that a disorder does not necessarily always cause all of the manifestations it is capable of causing, as is often the case in real-world diagnostic problems.

Thus, a problem domain may be specified as a three-tuple $<D,M,C>$.

Within a problem domain, a diagnostic problem occurs when one or more manifestations are present. Thus a diagnostic problem P may be specified as a four-tuple $P = <D,M,C,M^+>$, where $M^+ \subseteq M$ is the set of all manifestations which are actually present. Given P, the task is to find the set of disorders $D^+ \subseteq D$ which is responsible for the presence of the manifestations in M^+.

It may not be possible unambiguously to determine D^+, as there may be more than one set of disorders capable of causing M^+. Several possible criteria have been proposed for how to determine D^+, and some of them are listed below.

Criterion 1. D^+ is the set of all disorders capable of causing any of the manifestations in M^+.

Criterion 2. Every set of disorders capable of causing M^+ is an alternate hypothesis for the identity of D^+.

Criterion 3. Not all of the alternate hypotheses produced by Criterion 2 need be considered. If (as we are assuming) all disorders are independent of each other, then it follows that the simplest possible explanation for a set of manifestations M^+ is a minimum[2] set of disorders capable of causing M^+. From Ockham's razor, it follows that such a set of disorders is likely to be the correct diagnosis. In general, there may be several smallest sets of disorders capable of causing M^+, and according to Criterion 3 these sets are alternate hypotheses for the identity of D^+.

Criterion 4. Although not all of the alternate hypotheses produced by Criterion 2 need be considered, more than just the minimum sets should be considered. For example, suppose that M^+ can be caused either by one very rare disorder d_1, or by two very common disorders d_2 and d_3. Then even though $\{d_1\}$ is a simpler explanation, $\{d_2,d_3\}$ may be more likely and should also be considered as a hypothesis. However, a set such as $\{d_1,d_2\}$ need not be considered as a hypothesis, because if d_1 is present, then it alone is capable of causing all occurring manifestations and so there is no evidence for the additional presence of d_2. As a generalization of this example, the set of possible

---

[2] i.e., having the smallest possible cardinality

alternatives for D^+ according to Criterion 4 is the set of all minimal[3] sets of disorders capable of causing M^+.

3. An Example

As an example, consider the following problem domain:

disorder d_1 can cause manifestation m_1;
disorder d_2 can cause manifestations m_1 and m_2;
disorder d_3 can cause manifestations m_2, m_3, and m_4;
disorder d_4 can cause manifestation m_4;
there are no other disorders;
all of the disorders are independent of each other;
a disorder does not always cause all of the disorders it is capable of causing.

Three diagnostic problems in this problem domain are discussed below.

Problem P1: suppose that m_1 is present. Then the correct answers according to each of the criteria are

Criterion 1: d_1 & d_2;
Criterion 2: $d_1 \mid d_2 \mid (d_1$ & $d_2)$;
Criterion 3: $d_1 \mid d_2$;
Criterion 4: $d_1 \mid d_2$.

Problem P2: suppose that both m_1 and m_2 are present. Then the correct answers according to each of the criteria are

Criterion 1: d_1 & d_2 & d_3;
Criterion 2: $(d_1$ & $d_3) \mid d_2 \mid (d_1$ & $d_2) \mid (d_2$ & $d_3) \mid (d_1$ & d_2 & $d_3)$;
Criterion 3: d_2;
Criterion 4: $(d_1$ & $d_3) \mid d_2$.

Problem P3: suppose m_1, m_2, m_3, and m_4 are present. Then the correct answers according to each of the criteria are

Criterion 1: d_1 & d_2 & d_3 & d_4;
Criterion 2: $(d_1$ & $d_3) \mid (d_2$ & $d_3) \mid (d_1$ & d_2 & $d_3) \mid (d_1$ & d_3 & $d_4)$
$\mid (d_2$ & d_3 & $d_4) \mid (d_1$ & d_2 & d_3 & $d_4)$;
Criterion 3: $(d_1$ & $d_3) \mid (d_2$ & $d_3)$;
Criterion 4: $(d_1$ & $d_3) \mid (d_2$ & $d_3)$.

Note that in this example, if the answers are considered as Boolean expressions, then in each case the answer produced by Criterion 3 implies the answers produced by Criteria 2 and 4, and the answers produced by Criteria 2 and 4 are equivalent. Although the proof is beyond the scope of this paper, this property can be proved to be true in general.

4. Problems with Production Rule Systems

Let us consider how a production rule system might perform in the above example. If we were to write the problem domain knowledge naively in the form of production

[3] i.e., a set D^+ such that no proper subset of D^+ has the same property.

rules, we might write

R1. IF m_1 THEN d_1 (c_1)
R2. IF m_1 & m_2 THEN d_2 (c_2)
R3. IF m_2 & m_3 & m_4 THEN d_3 (c_3)
R4. IF m_4 THEN d_4 (c_4)

where c_1, c_2, c_3, and c_4 are the relative certainties with which we believe that the disorders d_1, d_2, d_3, and d_4 are present. The results produced by these rules are

d_1 in Problem P1;
d_1 & d_2 in Problem P2;
d_1 & d_2 & d_3 & d_4 in Problem P3.

Only in Problem P3 does the answer exactly fit any of the four criteria. Part of the problem is that not enough rules fire, since each rule requires the presence of all of its preconditions in order to fire. This problem can be handled by adding additional rules referring to all combinations of manifestations which can be caused by each disorder:

R5. IF m_1 THEN d_2 (c_5)
R6. If m_2 THEN d_2 (c_6)
R7. IF m_2 THEN d_3 (c_7)
R8. IF m_3 THEN d_3 (c_8)
R9. IF m_4 THEN d_3 (c_9)
R10. IF m_2 & m_3 THEN d_3 (c_{10})
R11. IF m_2 & m_4 THEN d_3 (c_{11})
R12. IF m_3 & m_4 THEN d_3 (c_{12})

If these rules are added, then the system will produce (with varying certainties)

d_1 & d_2 in Problem P1;
d_1 & d_2 & d_3 in Problem P2;
d_1 & d_2 & d_3 & d_4 in Problem P3.

These results all fit Criterion 1.

It seems fairly clear that the Criterion 1 is not really an adequate characterization of the solution to a diagnostic problem. However, if we are restricted to using rules of the form

IF *manifestations* THEN *disorder*

then the production rule approach cannot be made to satisfy Criteria 2, 3, or 4 because the only conclusions it will be able to produce are conjuncts of disorders.

5. Another Approach

Part of the reason why the usual rule-based approach cannot produce diagnoses satisfying Criteria 2, 3, or 4 is that the information contained in the production rules is simply incorrect. The underlying causal knowledge is not of the form

IF *manifestations* THEN *disorder*

typically found in rule-based expert systems but is instead of the form

IF *disorder* THEN *manifestations.*

Suppose, for example, that a manifestation m_1 can be caused by any of the disorders d_1, d_2, and d_3. If m_1 is present, then we cannot deduce the presence of d_1, nor of d_2, nor of d_3. The correct action would instead be to postulate d_1, d_2, and d_3 as alternate possible hypotheses for what is causing m_1. However, if we further knew that d_1, d_2, and d_3 were the *only* disorders capable of causing m_1, then we could correctly deduce that at least one of d_1, d_2, and d_3 must be present. This is a special case of a diagnostic principle which we will call the *principle of abduction*:

Theorem 1. Suppose that M^+ is a set of manifestations which can be caused by any of the sets of disorders $D_1, D_2, ..., D_k$, and that there are no other sets of disorders capable of causing M^+. Suppose also that the manifestations in M^+ can never occur without being caused. Then if these manifestations are present, then one of the sets of disorders $D_1, D_2, ..., D_k$ must be present.

Proof. Immediate from modus ponens.

The principle of abduction allows us to translate causal knowledge of the form

IF *disorder* THEN *disjunct of manifestations*

into equivalent diagnostic knowledge of the form

IF *manifestation* THEN *disjunct of causes.*

For example, the information about the problem domain used for Problems P1, P2, and P3 can be directly written as a problem in abductive inference with the following set of rules. Note that these rules go in the reverse direction from rules R1 through R4, and that (in terms familiar to the logician) these rules are not Horn clauses.

A1. IF d_1 THEN m_1
A2. IF d_2 THEN $m_1 \mid m_2$
A3. IF d_3 THEN $m_2 \mid m_3 \mid m_4$
A4. IF d_4 THEN m_4

The principle of abduction allows us to translate this abductive problem into a deductive problem having the following set of rules.

D1. IF m_1 THEN $d_1 \mid d_2$
D2. IF m_2 THEN $d_2 \mid d_3$
D3. IF m_3 THEN d_3
D4. IF m_4 THEN $d_3 \mid d_4$

These rules will produce the diagnoses

$d_1 \mid d_2$ for Problem P1;
$(d_1 \mid d_2)$ & $(d_2 \mid d_3)$ for Problem P2;
$(d_1 \mid d_2)$ & $(d_2 \mid d_3)$ & d_3 & $(d_3 \mid d_4)$ for Problem P3.

If considered as Boolean expressions, the answers produced by the rules {D1, D2, D3, and D4} are logically equivalent to the answers produced by Criterion 2 and the answers produced by Criterion 4. Furthermore, they contain all of the disorders appearing in the answers produced by Criterion 1. From this it follows that each answer produced by the rules {D1, D2, D3, D4} can be transformed exactly into the answers produced by Criteria 1, 2, 3, and 4 by means of the following operations:

1. To transform the answer into the one produced by Criterion 1, take the conjunct of all the disorders appearing in the answer.

2. To transform the answer into the one produced by Criterion 2, treat it as a Boolean expression and find all implicants.

3. To transform the answer into the one produced by Criterion 3, treat it as a set covering problem and find all minimum set covers.

4. To transform the answer into the one produced by Criterion 4, treat it as a Boolean expression and find all prime implicants.

6. Control Strategies

The previous section described a general approach to diagnostic problem solving. The main steps in the approach are as follows:

Step 1. Formulate the diagnostic problem as an abductive problem using the direct causal knowledge about the problem. This results in a set of rules similar to rules A1 through A5.

Step 2. Use the Principle of Abduction to translate the abductive problem into an equivalent deductive problem. This results in a set of rules similar to rules D1 through D5.

Step 3. Apply the deductive rules to the problem.

Step 4. Use one of the transformational techniques listed above to find an answer satisfying Criteria 1, 2, 3, or 4 as desired.

In implementing this approach, a number of problems must be solved. Five major ones are described below.

1. Diagnostic problem solving normally requires sequential hypothesize-and-test approach. Typically, only a few of the members of M^+ will be known to be present at the outset. The diagnostician will have a tentative hypothesis sufficient to explain the members of M^+ that are known to be present, and based on this hypothesis he or she will perform tests or ask questions to discover additional members of M^+. As these new manifestations are discovered, the hypothesis is revised to account for them. In order to be broadly useful, knowledge-based diagnostic problem solving systems must perform in a similar way.

2. Although our approach has been described in terms of four separate steps, it is often more efficient--particularly in the case of Criteria 3 and 4--to write a procedure which solves the problem directly as a problem in abductive inference.

3. While solving large diagnostic problems, the alternate hypotheses for sets of disorders capable of causing M^+ can become quite large and unwieldy. A representation is needed which is compact, efficient, and easily understandable.

4. Although this paper has so far ignored the issues raised by the use of certainty factors in diagnostic problem solving, a way is needed to handle them.

5. The rule format

   IF *conjunct of manifestations* THEN *disorder*,

   is the standard form for production rules in knowledge-based computer systems. If (as this paper proposes) we instead use rule formats such

   IF *disorder* THEN *disjunct of manifestations*.

   or

   IF *manifestation* THEN *disjunct of disorders*,

   then it is no longer clear how to do rule chaining.

We have developed an algorithm for diagnostic problem solving using Criterion 3 which handles the first four problems described above [7] [8], and which has been successfully used as the control strategy for knowledge-based diagnostic problem solvers in several different domains [9]. This algorithm is summarized below; for a more detailed treatment, the reader is referred to [7] [8]. We are currently extending the algorithm to handle the fifth problem (how to do inferential chaining) [6], and to work for Criterion 4 as well as Criterion 3 [11].

Three main data structures are used in the algorithm:

1. MANIFS $\subseteq M^+$ is the set of manifestations known to be present so far, i.e., our current hypothesis for the identity of M^+.
2. SCOPE $\subseteq D$ contains every disorder capable of causing at least one of the manifestations in MANIFS (note that this is the answer Criterion 1 would produce).
3. FOCUS is the family of all minimum sets of disorders capable of causing MANIFS. This is the set of alternate hypotheses for D^+ according to Criterion 3. FOCUS is also our solution to the problem of how to represent the alternate hypotheses compactly: it is expressed as a disjunct of conjuncts of disjuncts, and is manipulated directly in that form.

At the top level, the algorithm is a hypothesize-and-test loop which looks roughly as follows:

```
procedure HT
    MANIFS := SCOPE := FOCUS := ∅
    while not all of M+ is known do
        perform a test to discover a new manifestation m ∈M+
        MANIFS := MANIFS ∪ {m }
        SCOPE := SCOPE ∪ {d ∈D | (d ,m )∈C }
        adjust FOCUS to accomodate m
    endwhile
    return FOCUS
end HT
```

The knowledge base for this procedure is a set of frames, one for each disorder $d \in D$. These frames are generalizations of abductive rules such as the rules {A1, A2, A3, A4} discussed earlier. The frame for a particular disorder d contains all the information we may have about d--what manifestations it is capable of causing, what conditions govern whether it may occur, etc. These frames thus define the causal relation C. In addition, the frames contain information about how likely it is to cause each of its manifestations, and this information is used to determine the relative likelihoods of the various alternate hypotheses. This provides a straightforward solution to the problem of how to handle certainty factors.

In adjusting FOCUS to accomodate a new manifestation m, there are two possible cases which may occur:

1. Some of the sets of disorders in FOCUS may be capable of causing MANIFS $\cup \{m\}$. In this case, it can be proved that the family of minimum covers capable of causing MANIFS $\cup \{m\}$ is a subfamily of FOCUS. Thus FOCUS must be adjusted to remove the sets of disorders that no longer work.
2. MANIFS $\cup \{m\}$ cannot be caused by any set of disorders in FOCUS. In this case, it can be proved that each minimum set of disorders capable of causing

MANIFS ∪ $\{m\}$ has cardinality exactly one more than the cardinality of each minimum set of disorders capable of causing MANIFS. In this case, FOCUS must be completely recomputed, but the problem is not as difficult as it might be in general since we know exactly how many disorders will appear in each set.

7. Another Example

We now illustrate the operation of the algorithm on Problem P3. Just how tests are generated in line 3 is described in [9]. The final result produced is independent of the order in which these manifestations are discovered, so for now, let us assume the members of M^+ are discovered in the order m_1, m_2, m_3, m_4. Then the following events occur.

1. Initially, MANIFS = SCOPE = FOCUS = $\emptyset$.
2. m_1 is found to be present. Then MANIFS is set to $\{m_1\}$. SCOPE is set to $\{d_1,d_2\}$, the set of all disorders which can cause m_1. MANIFS can be caused by d_1 alone or d_2 alone, so FOCUS is the expression $d_1|d_2$.

   If we were solving Problem P1, then at this point no more manifestations would be found and the program would terminate, returning FOCUS. This would be the correct answer to P1 according to Criterion 3.
3. m_2 is found to be present. The disorders capable of causing m_2 are d_2 and d_3. These are added into SCOPE, yielding SCOPE = $\{d_1,d_2,d_3\}$. MANIFS can still be caused by d_2, but not by d_1. Thus FOCUS is the expression d_1.
4. m_3 is found to be present. The only disorder capable of causing m_3 is d_3; thus SCOPE does not change. No single disorder can now explain MANIFS. Thus FOCUS is recomputed, looking for sets of two disorders each. Both $\{d_1,d_3\}$ and $\{d_2,d_3\}$ work, and thus FOCUS is represented as the expression $(d_1 \mid d_2)$ & d_3.

   If we were solving Problem P2, then at this point no more manifestations would be found and the program would terminate, returning FOCUS. This would be the correct answer to P2 according to Criterion 3.
5. m_4 is found to be present. m_4 can be caused by either d_3 or d_4, and thus SCOPE becomes $\{d_1,d_2,d_3,d_4\}$. m_4 can be caused by both of the sets of disorders represented in the previous FOCUS, so FOCUS does not change.
6. No more manifestations are found. Thus the program terminates and returns FOCUS, which is the correct answer to Problem 3 according to Criterion 3.

8. Conclusions

We have discussed four different criteria for what constitutes the solution to a diagnostic problem. The ordinary deductive production rule approach to diagnostic problem solving uses rules of the form

IF *conjunct of manifestations* THEN *disorder*,

and this approach is sufficient to meet only the least sophisticated of these criteria.

Part of the reason for this problem is that diagnostic problem solving is more properly an abductive problem rather than a deductive one: the causal knowledge we have about diagnostic problems is not of the form given above, but rather is of the form

IF *disorder* THEN *disjunct of manifestations.*

The principle of abduction stated in this paper shows how to translate this kind of knowledge into knowledge that can be used in deductive problem solving. This results in rules of the form

IF *manifestation* THEN *disjunct of disorders.*

Implementing a rule-based problem solver using this kind of knowledge requires a much different kind of control strategy than is normally used in production systems. We have discussed the basics of a control strategy for this approach.

Production rules have been criticized in the past as a representation of diagnostic knowledge [10], and our approach appears in at least some cases to be a more intuitively plausible descriptive representational formalism and model of diagnostic reasoning. A knowledge-based reasoning system based on this approach has been implemented and successfully used for several diagnostic medical problems. [9].

The inference method used in INTERNIST [2] differs but is rather close to our approach [8] and some similar techniques have also been used on an immunological problem [4] [12]. However, this approach has not to our knowledge been previously examined in detail as a model of general diagnostic reasoning.

Our approach also appears to have application (perhaps in modified form) to other types of problems as well. It has been used for several non-medical "toy" diagnostic problems, and an effort is underway to use it for a non-diagnostic problem in automated manufacturing [5].

9. References

[1] Duda, R. O., Hart, P. E., Barrett, P., Gaschnig, J. G., Konolige, K., Reboh, R., and Slocum, J., Development of the Prospector Consultation System for Mineral Exploration, Tech. Report, SRI International, Menlo Park, CA, Oct. 1978.

[2] Miller, R., Pople, H., and Myers, J., Internist-1: An Experimental Computer-Based Diagnostic Consultant for General Internal Medicine, *NEJM* **307**, pp. 468-476, 1982.

[3] Nau, D. S., Expert Computer Systems, *Computer* **16**, 2, pp. 63-85, Feb. 1983.

[4] Nau, D. S., Markowsky, G., Woodbury, M. A., and Amos, D. B., A Mathematical Analysis of HLA Serology, *Mathematical Biosciences* **40**, pp. 243-270, 1978. (An early version is available as Tech. Report RC 6803, IBM T.J. Watson Research Center, Yorktown Heights, NY, Oct. 1977.)

[5] Nau, D. S., Reggia, J. A., Blanks, M. W., Peng, Y., and Sutton, D., Artificial Intelligence Approaches for Automated Process Planning and Control, Tech. Report, Computer Science Dept., University of Maryland, College Park, Md., Feb. 1984. Submitted for publication.

[6] Peng, Y., Ph.D Dissertation, in progress. 1984.

[7] Reggia, J. A., Nau, D. S., and Wang, P. Y., A Formal Model of Diagnostic Inference, Part One: Problem Formulation and Decomposition, submitted for publication, 1983.

[8] Reggia, J. A., Nau, D. S., and Wang, P. Y., A Formal Model of Diagnostic Inference, Part Two: Algorithmic Solution and Applications, submitted for publication, 1983.

[9] Reggia, J. A., Nau, D. S., and Wang, P. Y., Diagnostic Expert Systems Based on a Set Covering Model, *International Journal of Man-Machine Studies*, pp. 437-460, Nov. 1983.

[10] Reggia, J. A., Nau, D. S., and Wang, P. Y., Diagnostic Expert Systems Based on a Set Covering Model, To appear. Nov. 1983.

[11] Reggia, J. A., Peng, Y., and Nau, D. S., A Formal Model of Diagnostic Inference, Part Three: Exploring the Nature of Parsimony, In preparation, 1984.

[12] Woodbury, M., Ciftan, E., and Amos, D., HLA Serum Screening Based on an Heuristic Solution to the Set Cover Problem, *Comp. Pgm. Biomed.* **9**, pp. 263-273, 1979.

A Temporal Logic for Reasoning About Changing Data Bases in the Context of Natural Language Question-Answering

Eric Mays

IBM T.J. Watson Research Center
P.O. Box 218
Yorktown Heights, NY 10598

1.1 INTRODUCTION

In this paper we present a modal temporal logic for reasoning about change in data bases with the primary consideration being the effect of such a capability on the sorts of behaviors produced by a natural language question answering system. The logic has the ability to represent necessity and possibility as well as temporal relations such as before and after. That is, we can reason about events within alternative futures.

1.1.1 Problem Description

It is generally accepted that a natural language query system often needs to provide more than just the literal answer to a question. By incorporating a model of the data base in which a dynamic view is allowed, answers to questions can include an offer to monitor for some condition which might possibly occur in the future. The following is an example:

U: "Is the Kitty Hawk in Norfolk?"
S: "No, shall I let you know when she is?"

But just *having* a dynamic view is not adequate, it is necessary that the dynamic view correspond to the possible evolution of the world that is modelled. Otherwise, behaviors such as the following might arise:

U: "Is New York less than 50 miles from Philadelphia?"
S: "No, shall I let you know when it is?"

An offer of a monitor is said to be *competent* only if the condition to be monitored can possibly occur. Thus, in the latter example the offer is not competent, while in the former it is.

Reasoning about prior possibility admits a class of queries dealing with the future possibility of some event or state of affairs at some time in the past. These queries have the general form: "Could it have been the case that p?". That is, was there some time in the past from which there might be a future time at which p is true. This class of queries will be termed counterhistoricals in an attempt to draw some parallel with counterfactuals.

The future correlate of counterhistoricals, which one might call futurities, are of the form: "Can it be the case that p?", i.e., in the sense of: "Might it ever be the case that p?". That is, might there be a future time at which p is true. The most interesting aspect of this form of question is that it admits the ability for a query system to offer a monitor as a response to a question for relevant information the system may become aware of at some future time. A query system can only competently offer such monitors when it has this ability, since otherwise it cannot determine if the monitor may ever be satisfied.

1.1.2 Extended Responses in Natural Language Question-Answering Systems

Research in the area of natural language based question-answering systems has recently been moving away from the initial interest of providing a correct answer to the literal interpretation of a query (e.g., LUNAR, LADDER, PLANES) towards more cooperative responses attempting to address the questioner's intent ([AP80], [HR78], [Kaplan82]).[1] Human factors studies have shown that a questioner's expectations of the computer system are increased when the mode of interaction is natural language [Schneiderman78]. Indeed, Joshi [Joshi80] has pointed out that a questioner's expectations of a computer based question-answering system may even exceed those of similar human exchanges.

[1] These extended responses need not be confined to just natural language interactions. (See [Motro84].)

It is from this perspective that the work reported here is intended to be placed, namely, attempting to provide responses that fulfill increased user expectations and address the intent rather than the literal meaning of a question.

The initial work in natural language question-answering systems viewed an utterance whose surface structure was that of a question as either a proposition whose truth value was to be determined or an open formula for which the extension of the free variables was to be determined. It has been noticed, however, that an utterance carries more than its truth value. Thus, for example, the surface question, "Can you pass the salt?", while in some contrived situations might actually be just asking of some individual whether or not they possess the capability to actually "pass the salt," is generally a request to actually "pass the salt." In the context of natural language question-answering systems we will provide several examples of such responses. We will assume in each case that these responses would not necessarily be expected of a system based on formal query languages.

An answer to a question often requires more information than actually requested. For example (from [Kaplan82]), the question "What are the phone numbers of CIS faculty?" is not appropriately answered by just providing a list of the phone numbers -- the corresponding names must be provided as well. Similarly, Allen and Perrault [AP80], in their analysis of information seeking dialogues at train reservation counters, observed that requests for train departure times were most appropriately responded to by including the track number as well, since presumably the goal of the questioner was to board the train.

A response to a question may also preempt additional questions that the user might reasonably pose. Justifications and explanations fall into this category. For example, in the following exchange the response justifies the answer.

U: "Is John a sophomore?"
S: "No, he's passed less than 8 courses."

This response will preempt an additional question from the user if say, John had been in school for two years and the user believed that class status was determined by years in attendance rather than courses passed. In the case of direct yes-no questions, if the proposition under question is false, an appropriate response might be to include information that does hold. For example,

U: "Is John a freshman?"
S: "No, he's a sophomore."

In addition to preempting additional questions an extended response could be used to correct any misconceptions which the lack of a qualification might implicitly confirm. Kaplan [Kaplan82] investigated responses of this type which corrected presumptions of a query which failed to have an extension in the data base. For example, the following response implicitly confirms that CIS523 was offered in spring 83.

U: "Which students failed CIS523 in spring 83?"
S: "None."

If it was the case that CIS523 was not offered in spring 83, it would be better to to include that information in the response. In [Mays80] presumptions which fail intensionally, that is, because the posited relation could never hold, were investigated. A response of this sort is the following.

U: "Which students teach courses?"
S: "Students don't teach courses. Faculty teach courses. Students take courses."

By allowing the user to pose questions in natural language the range of questions that the system is expected to cover increases. McKeown [McKeown82] has investigated generating responses to questions that are about the *structure* rather than the *contents* of the data base. The ability to answer questions such as these becomes increasingly important as the potential set of questioners becomes less familiar with the structure of the domain.

Notice that to produce these sorts of responses the system must attempt to address the intentions of the user, determine what kind of response is appropriate, and determine which information is relevant to include. (We do not claim that the above mentioned work has solved these problems.) With regard to the problem under consideration here, there are two points to be made. First, reasoning about change is an important aspect of each of the extended responses given. That is, the temporal dimension is as fundamental as any other dimension of knowledge when providing additional information, justifying responses, correcting misconceptions, and explaining the data base structure. For example, the additional information provided in a response could include information about some previous state of the data base. Similarly, a justification may involve stating how the present data base state evolved from some previous state or why some hypothetical data base state could not evolve from the present one. It is also apparent that the user may have some misconceptions about how the data base evolves over time and thus may need an explanation of that process. The second point is that the determination of the relevance of a response which depends on reasoning about change should be no more difficult a problem than relevance in any other context.

While the traditional view of natural language data base question-answering systems has been that of a static data base modeling a snapshot of the world, we believe that it is important to consider a dynamic data base that models a changing world. In the traditional (static) view of the data base query process, as viewed by the query system, there is one state of the data base modeling one state of the world. Any provision made for capturing information about previous or future data base states is encoded in the present data base state. Furthermore, the data base cannot reason about how it might change over time. The user interacting with the data base through the natural language interface is forced into this view, even though the user might have a crucial interest in viewing the world as modelled by the data base changing over time. In a dynamic view of the data base query process there are previous and future data base states in addition to the present state. These data base states model the present, previous, and future states of the world. The world states and thus the data base states are temporally related to each other. We intend to relate multiple states of a data base by a relation of temporal change as a model of a sequence of snapshots of a world responding to change over time. We claim that this places the user in proper view of the data base query system.

1.1.3 Distinguishing Kinds of DB Change

There are three distinct ways in which the contents of a DB might change.

1. The actual world modelled by the DB has changed (i.e., some event has taken place) and the DB is updated to reflect that change.

2. The knowledge of some prior event or state of affairs is refined. (e.g., The fact that "John owns a car" may be refined to "John owns a Ford.") The easiest and perhaps most appealing way to deal with this is to simply allow for any refinement of knowledge. Under this optimistic view, we will not allow that we will never know the answer to a question. If we adopt a more pessimistic view, the description of future states of knowledge needs to be distinct from the description of future states of the world. That is, we cannot distinguish these cases by holding that actual change corresponds to stating "at some point in the future p is true," and refinement of knowledge is "at some point in the future p is true now." The following example illustrates the sort of responses that might be given.

   U: "Has John passed CSE110?"

   S: "I don't know. The semester has ended, but Prof. Tardy hasn't turned in his grades. Shall I let you know when I find out?"

3. A previous update was in error, thus causing the present DB state to be inaccurate. The DB must be modified to correct the error. (The distinction between types 2 and 3 is that 3 gives rise to an inconsistency, whereas 2 will not necessarily.) Natural language interaction should not be based on this description of change, since any valid static data base state then becomes a valid dynamic one. In this case an extended form of truth maintenance is required to effectively maintain consistency in the discourse context as well as in the data base.

Each of these types of DB change is important to consider in the development of natural language question-answering systems, and each type of change requires a different technique to be invoked when updating the DB. Here, however, we are only concerned with the first.

1.1.4 Representation Considerations

The major division of methods for knowledge representation is between those based on network methods and those based on formal logic. One could very well imagine incorporating some network based method for process description (e.g., Petri nets) into an existing semantic network based knowledge representation language or semantic data model, most likely yielding an object ripe for relatively efficient implementation. We have instead opted to use formal logic as the representation. Although this track does not lend itself quickly to efficient implementation, it excels in expressive power. To realize an efficient implementation it is then necessary to (perhaps) restrict the logical theory in some reasonable way. That is, we want to investigate the *theory* of change in data bases, and then when that is (hopefully) right, turn our attention to *implementation grounded in that theory.*

There are two basic requirements which lead us toward logic and away from methods such as Petri nets. First, it may be desirable to assert that some proposition was or will be the case without necessarily specifying exactly *when.* ("It was the case that p." vs. "It was the case that p at t.") Secondly, our knowledge may be disjunctive. That is, our knowledge of temporal situations may be incomplete and indefinite, and as others have argued [Moore82] (as a recent example), methods based on formal logic (though typically argued for first-order) are the only ones that have so far been capable of dealing with problems of this nature.

In contrast to first-order representations, modal temporal logic makes a fundamental distinction between variability over time (as expressed by modal temporal operators) and variability in a state (as expressed using propositional or first-order languages). Modal temporal logic also reflects the temporally indefinite structure of language in a way that is more natural than the common method of using state variables and constants in a first-order logic. The syntactic forms of the modal temporal formulas are considerably simpler than their first order counterparts. That is, the modal operators directly capture exactly those relations which are of most interest.

1.1.4.1 Temporal Reasoning

Bruce [Bruce72] develops a formal model for temporal reference in natural language. The application of this model is demonstrated in a question answering system. Ordering relations are defined on sequences contained in linearly ordered subsets of a partially ordered set. An example is *before(A,B)*, which means that all elements in *A* are earlier than any element in *B*. Using relations such as *before*, *after* , *during*, and *same-time* an analysis of the representation of the concepts of order, aspect, duration, frequency of occurrence, and modality is given. The approach of Allen [Allen81] is similar to that of Bruce in the set of primitives that are provided. In Allen's work constraint propagation techniques are used along with hierarchical organization of intervals to maintain temporal relationships. Kahn and Gorry [KG77] propose a time specialist for problem solving situations. Their idea is to construct a program to which problems pertaining to temporal knowledge may be posed by a more general problem solver. This program organizes temporal knowledge by date, reference events, and before/after chains, providing the facilities to update, query, and maintain consistency of the knowledge organization.

McDermott [McDermott82] proposes a temporal logic for reasoning about processes and plans. The basic features of this logic are the branching of the future and the continuity of time. While the applicability of modal logic to temporal logic is acknowledged, the setting chosen is first order logic. The idea is that the first order logic expresses the interpretation of the modal logic.

In [CW83] an intensional logic based on the work of Montague is presented as a semantics for time in historical data bases. The basic idea is that the time varying attributes of a data base are represented as functions from a set of times into values. A more computationally oriented approach is taken in [Anderson81]. There a conceptual level data base model is extended with a set of time modeling primitives and access functions. Also, a Petri net like process representation is given.

In [LCC84] a logical data base model is presented which treats various temporal aspects of administrative data bases including the support of temporal inferencing. It is part of a larger effort for the logical modelling of administrative data bases [Lee80].

1.1.4.2 Modal Temporal Logic

The work on temporal logic has been primarily in philosophy [Prior57], [Prior67], [Prior68], [RU71], but recently there has been interest in computer science for program verification [MP81], [BMP81], [GPSS80]. The idea in modal logic is to consider various possible worlds or states of affairs. Each possible world may differ on the truth value of particular predicates. For example, the statement "It is raining" may be true or false depending on the time and location at which it is made. Additionally, there is an accessibility relation between possible worlds. The properties of this relation depend on the intended structure of the area of application. We might reasonably consider the future tense relation to be transitive, for example.

In modal temporal logic the idea is to consider the possible worlds as states in time which are temporally related via the relations earlier-than and later-than. In the application to program verification, the temporal states are taken to be states in the execution of a program which are related by the next-instruction relation.

There are several possible structures that one could reasonably imagine over states in time. The one we have in mind is discrete, backwards linear, and infinite in both directions. Due to the nature of the intended application, we have assumed that time is discrete. It should be stressed that this decision is not motivated by the belief that time itself is discrete, but rather by the data base application. Furthermore, in cases where it is necessary for the temporal structure to be dense or continuous, there is no immediate argument against modal temporal logic in general. (That is, one could develop a modal temporal logic that models a continuous structure of time [RU71].) That we admit branching in the future, but require a linear past, reflects the asymmetry of our knowledge of the past and the future. We allow branching into the future to capture the idea that it is open, but the past is determined. The future does not influence the past, whereas the past does influence the future. (But knowledge acquired in the future may influence knowledge about the past.) Although we could imagine several possible futures from the past, each possible future traces a path backwards into now.

1.2 UNIFIED BRANCHING TEMPORAL STRUCTURES

A modal temporal structure is composed of a set of states. Each state is a set of propositions which are true of that state. States are related by an immediate predecessor-successor relation. A branch of time is defined by taking some possible sequence of states accessible over this relation from a given state. The future fragment of the logic is based on the unified branching temporal logic of [BMP81], which introduces branches and quantifies over them to make it possible to describe properties on some or all futures. This is extended with an "until" operator (as in [Kamp68], [GPSS80]) and a past fragment. Since the structures are backwards linear the existential and universal operators are merged to form a linear past fragment.

1.2.1 Syntax

Formulas are composed from the symbols,

- A set $\mathcal{P}$ of atomic propositions.
- Boolean connectives: $\vee$, $\neg$.
- Temporal operators: $\forall X$ (every next), $\exists X$ (some next), $\forall G$ (every always), $\exists G$ (some always), $\forall F$ (every eventually), $\exists F$ (some eventually), $\forall U$ (every until), $\exists U$ (some until), L (immediately past), P (sometime past), H (always past), S (since).

$\forall U$, $\exists U$, and S are binary; the others are unary. For the operators composed of two symbols, the first symbol ($\forall$ or $\exists$) can be thought of as quantifying universally or existentially over branches in time; the second symbol as quantifying over states within the branch. Since branching is not allowed into the past, past operators have only one symbol.

using the rules,

- If $p \in \mathcal{P}$, then p is a formula.
- If p and q are formulas, then $(\neg p)$, $(p \vee q)$, $(p \wedge q)$, $(p \Rightarrow q)$, $(p \Leftrightarrow q)$ are formulas.
- If m is a unary temporal operator and p is a formula, then $(m\ p)$ is a formula.
- If m is a binary temporal operator and p and q are formulas, then $(p\ m\ q)$ is a formula.

1.2.2 Semantics

A temporal structure T is a triple (S, Π, R) where,

- S is a set of states.
- $\Pi:(S \rightarrow 2^{\mathcal{P}})$ is an assignment of atomic propositions to states.
- $R \subseteq (S \times S)$ is an accessibility relation on S.

Each state is required to have at least one successor and exactly one predecessor -- i.e., $\forall s(\exists t(sRt) \wedge \exists! t(tRs))$.

Define b to be an s-branch: $b = (\ \ldots, s_{-1}, s = s_0, s_1, \ldots\ )$ such that $s_i R s_{i+1}$. The relation $<$ is the transitive closure of R.

The satisfaction of a formula p at a state s in a structure T, $<T, s> \models p$, is defined as follows: (Following the definition of each of the temporal operators is a brief description.)

$<T, s> \models p$ iff $p \in \Pi(s)$, for $p \in \mathcal{P}$

$<T, s> \models \neg p$ iff not $<T, s> \models p$

$<T, s> \models p \vee q$ iff $<T, s> \models p$ or $<T, s> \models q$

$<T, s> \models \forall Gp$ iff $\forall b \forall t((t \in b \wedge t \geq s) \Rightarrow <T, t> \models p)$

(p is true at every time of every future)

$<T, s> \models \forall Fp$ iff $\forall b \exists t(t \in b \wedge t \geq s \wedge <T, t> \models p)$

(p is true at some time of every future)

$<T, s> \models p \forall Uq$ iff $\forall b \exists t(t \in b \wedge t \geq s \wedge <T, t> \models q \wedge \forall t'((t' \in b \wedge s \leq t' < t) \Rightarrow <T, t'> \models p))$

(q is true at some time of every future and until q is true p is true)

$<T, s> \models \forall Xp$ iff $\forall t(sRt \Rightarrow <T, t> \models p)$

(p is true at every immediate future)

$<T, s> \models \exists Gp$ iff $\exists b \forall t((t \in b \wedge t \geq s) \Rightarrow <T, t> \models p)$

(p is true at every time of some future)

$<T, s> \models \exists Fp$ iff $\exists b \exists t(t \in b \wedge t \geq s \wedge <T, t> \models p)$

(p is true at some time of some future)

$<T, s> \models \exists Xp$ iff $\exists t(sRt \wedge <T, t> \models p)$

(p is true at some immediate future)

$<T, s> \models p \exists Uq$ iff $\exists b \exists t(t \in b \wedge t \geq s \wedge <T, t> \models q \wedge \forall t'((t' \in b \wedge s \leq t' < t) \Rightarrow <T, t'> \models p))$

(q is true at some time of some future and in that future until q is true p is true)

$<T, s> \models Hp$ iff $\forall b \forall t((t \in b \wedge t \leq s) \Rightarrow <T, t> \models p)$

(p is true at every time of the past)

$<T, s> \models Pp$ iff $\exists b \exists t(t \in b \wedge t \leq s \wedge <T, t> \models p)$

(p is true at some time of the past)

$<T, s> \models Lp$ iff $\forall t(tRs \Rightarrow <T, t> \models p)$

(p is true at the immediate past)

$<T, s> \models pSq$ iff $\exists b \exists t(t \in b \wedge t \leq s \wedge <T, t> \models q \wedge \forall t'((t' \in b \wedge s \geq t' < t) \Rightarrow <T, t'> \models p))$

(q is true at some time of the past and since q is true p is true)

1.2.3 Axioms

The following form a sound deductive system [Mays84].

Axioms

1.	$[Df(\exists G)]$	$\exists Gp \Leftrightarrow \neg \forall F \neg p$
2.	$[Df(\exists F)]$	$\exists Fp \Leftrightarrow \neg \forall G \neg p$
3.	$[Df(\exists X)]$	$\exists Xp \Leftrightarrow \neg \forall X \neg p$
4.	$[Df(P)]$	$Pp \Leftrightarrow \neg H \neg p$
5.	$[K(\forall G)]$	$\forall G(p \Rightarrow q) \Rightarrow (\forall Gp \Rightarrow \forall Gq)$
6.	$[K(\forall X)]$	$\forall X(p \Rightarrow q) \Rightarrow (\forall Xp \Rightarrow \forall Xq)$
7.	$[K'(\exists G)]$	$\forall G(p \Rightarrow q) \Rightarrow (\exists Gp \Rightarrow \exists Gq)$
8.	$[K(H)]$	$H(p \Rightarrow q) \Rightarrow (Hp \Rightarrow Hq)$
9.	$[K(L)]$	$L(p \Rightarrow q) \Rightarrow (Lp \Rightarrow Lq)$
10.	$[T(\forall G)]$	$\forall Gp \Rightarrow p$
11.	$[T(\exists G)]$	$\exists Gp \Rightarrow p$
12.	$[T(H)]$	$Hp \Rightarrow p$
13.	$[D(\forall G, \forall X)]$	$\forall Gp \Rightarrow \forall Xp$
14.	$[D(\exists G, \exists X)]$	$\exists Gp \Rightarrow \exists Xp$
15.	$[D(H, L)]$	$Hp \Rightarrow Lp$
16.	$[D(\forall X)]$	$\forall Xp \Rightarrow \exists Xp$
17.	$[D!(L)]$	$Lp \Leftrightarrow \neg L \neg p$
18.	$[5_c(\forall G, \forall X)]$	$\forall Gp \Rightarrow \forall X(\forall Gp)$
19.	$[5_c(\exists G, \exists X)]$	$\exists Gp \Rightarrow \exists X(\exists Gp)$
20.	$[5_c(H, L)]$	$Hp \Rightarrow L(Hp)$
21.	$[I(\forall X)]$	$\forall G(p \Rightarrow \forall Xp) \Rightarrow (p \Rightarrow \forall Gp)$
22.	$[I(\exists X)]$	$\forall G(p \Rightarrow \exists Xp) \Rightarrow (p \Rightarrow \exists Gp)$
23.	$[I(L)]$	$H(p \Rightarrow Lp) \Rightarrow (p \Rightarrow Hp)$
24.	$[T^+(L)]$	$L(\forall Xp) \Rightarrow p$
25.	$[T^+(\exists X)]$	$\exists X(Lp) \Rightarrow p$
26.	$[T5!(\forall U)]$	$p \forall Uq \Leftrightarrow q \vee (p \wedge \forall X(p \forall Uq))$
27.	$[T5!(\exists U)]$	$p \exists Uq \Leftrightarrow q \vee (p \wedge \exists X(p \exists Uq))$
28.	$[T5!(S)]$	$pSq \Leftrightarrow q \vee (p \wedge L(pSq))$
29.	$[D(\forall U, \forall F)]$	$p \forall Uq \Rightarrow \forall Fq$
30.	$[D(\exists U, \exists F)]$	$p \exists Uq \Rightarrow \exists Fq$
31.	$[D(S, P)]$	$pSq \Rightarrow Pq$

Rules

1.	[TAUT]	If p is a tautology, then $\vdash p$.
2.	[MP]	If $\vdash p$ and $\vdash (p \Rightarrow q)$, then $\vdash q$.
3.	$[N(\forall G)]$	If $\vdash p$, then $\vdash \forall Gp$.
4.	$[N(H)]$	If $\vdash p$, then $\vdash Hp$.

1.3 MODELLING CHANGE IN DATA BASES

In this section we investigate the ways in which the temporal logic outlined earlier may be employed to represent and reason about change in a data base. We intend to present a method for modelling a data base with this logic and then turn to the posed problems of historicals, counterhistoricals, and futurities (including monitor competence).

Note that the logic we will be using is a propositional one, while a data base is generally considered to require first-order logic. In the discussion we will consider a first-order logic, but now we consider just the propositional logic for the following reasons. Primarily it is a simplifying first step. That is, it is easier to analyze and develop proof procedures. Second is that much of a data base is actually propositional rather than first-order in nature. This is especially evident if we adopt Reiter's closed domain assumption [Reiter80] which states that the only individuals in the data base are the constants which appear (i.e., $\forall x(x = c_1 \vee \ldots \vee x = c_n)$). This reduces the data base to a (possibly very large) propositional theory.

1.3.1 Basic Modelling Strategy

The set of propositional variables for modelling change in data bases is divided into three classes. A state proposition asserts the truth of some atomic condition. An event proposition associates the occurrence of an event with the state in which it occurs. A time proposition names the state at which it is true. The idea is to impose constraints on the occurrence of events and then derive the appropriate state description. To be specific, let $Q1_s \ldots Qn_s$ be state propositions, $Q1_e \ldots Qn_e$ be event propositions, and $Q1_t \ldots Qn_t$ be time propositions. If φ is a Boolean formula of state propositions, then formulas of the form:

$$(\varphi \Rightarrow \exists X Qi_e)$$

are event axioms. To derive state descriptions from events frame axioms are required:

$$(Qi_e \Rightarrow ((L\varphi) \Rightarrow \psi)),$$

where φ and ψ are Boolean formulas of state propositions. In the blocks world, an event axiom would be that if block A was clear and block B was clear then move A onto B is a next possible event:

$$((cleartop(A) \wedge cleartop(B)) \Rightarrow \exists X move(A,B)).$$

Two frame axioms are:

$$(move(A,B) \Rightarrow on(A,B))$$

and

$$(move(A,B) \Rightarrow ((L on(C,D)) \Rightarrow on(C,D))).$$

While this strategy does not exercise much of the power of the logic, it appears to be about as expressive as most planning languages. That is, the event axioms specify sufficient conditions for an event to occur (corresponding to the pre-conditions in planning) and the frame axioms specify how events change the world (corresponding to the add-lists and delete-lists in planning languages). It would thus appear possible to suitably restrict the syntactic form of the non-logical axioms in such a way that the heuristics devised for solving planning problems may be used to prove formulas of the form $\exists F\varphi$. More powerful search techniques, such as those described by Rosenschein [Rosenschein81], might yield solutions for less restricted non-logical axioms.

An obvious defect of this strategy is that the number of frame axioms becomes extremely large as the number of propositions grows. To a certain extent this may be aided with quantification. Ignoring any problems with quantification for now, the frame axioms for *move* with respect to *on* are just:

$$x \neq y \wedge cleartop(x) \wedge cleartop(y) \Rightarrow \exists X move(x,y)$$

$$move(x,y) \Rightarrow on(x,y)$$

$x \neq x' \wedge y \neq y' \wedge move(x,y) \Rightarrow (Lon(x',y') \Leftrightarrow on(x',y'))$

$y \neq y' \wedge move(x,y) \Rightarrow (Lon(x,y') \Rightarrow \neg on(x,y'))$

$x \neq x' \wedge move(x,y) \Rightarrow (L\neg on(x',y) \Rightarrow \neg on(x',y))$

However, there is a different sort of problem which occurs when specifying that an event type leaves a predicate unchanged. The standard example in the blocks world is that moving a block does not alter the color of the block.

$move(x,y) \Rightarrow (Lcolor(x,x') \Leftrightarrow color(x,x')) \wedge (Lcolor(y,y') \Leftrightarrow color(y,y'))$

If there are a lot of event-predicate pairs like *move* and *color* there will be a lot of frame axioms which have the effect of complicating a simple situation. But if the world is simple enough, we may employ the "every until" ($\forall U$) operator to cut down the complexity of the description in cases where a predicate is affected by a small number of events. In the blocks world we can use the following axiom.

$color(x,c) \forall Upaint(x,z) \vee \forall Gcolor(x,c)$

This states that the color of any block x is c until x is painted some color z or, because $\forall U$ implies $\forall F$, the color of x is always c. This eliminates the need to state that *move* leaves *color* unaffected, since we would have:

$move(a,b) \wedge \neg paint(a,x)$

and

$color(a,c) \forall Upaint(a,x) \vee \forall Gcolor(a,c)$

implies

$paint(a,x) \vee (color(a,c) \wedge \forall X(color(a,c) \forall Upaint(a,x))) \vee (color(a,c) \wedge \forall X \forall Gcolor(a,c))$

which implies

$color(a,c)$.

Of course, if the world is a complicated one, there will be quite a lot of complicated frame axioms.

1.3.1.1 Extending the Basic Strategy

This basic strategy needs to be extended in order to determine that some condition can never arise or to reconstruct previous states from the current one, for example. An obvious way to do this is to place necessary conditions on the occurrence of an event. From the previous blocks world example, we might have:

$cleartop(A) \wedge cleartop(B) \Leftrightarrow \exists Xmove(A,B)$.

Thus if we know that:

$move(A,B)$.

We can derive:

$L(cleartop(A) \wedge cleartop(B))$,

partially reconstructing the previous state. Also if we add the axiom:

$H(\forall G \neg cleartop(B))$.

(Perhaps another block is glued on top of it.) Then we can derive:

$\neg \exists Fmove(A,B)$.

This is an example of showing that some event can never occur.

Another way of extending the modelling strategy is to allow for the possibility that a certain condition requires some event to happen next. These axioms have the form:

$\varphi \Rightarrow \forall X \psi$.

An example of this type occurs in the context of course registration. When the semester has advanced to a particular point such that courses may no longer be dropped a student must then complete the course, i.e., receive a grade.

We might also wish to allow for some condition to hold at any previous time, rather than just now, in order for some event to occur:

$P\varphi \Rightarrow \exists X \psi$.

Similarly, we could allow some event to occur at some point in the future but not necessarily next:

$\varphi \Rightarrow \exists F \psi$.

1.3.1.2 Modelling Simultaneous Events

Genuine simultaneity of events is somewhat problematic to model, but fortunately it is also fairly rare. By genuine simultaneity we mean the sort of situation that is required when the window cleaners on a tall building wish to raise the platform on which they are standing. They must simultaneously pull the two ropes at each end of the platform in order to ensure that the platform remains level as it rises.

In the logic this problem takes the following form. We might have

$\varphi \Rightarrow \exists X p_e \wedge \exists X q_{e.}$

If we assume that only one event takes place in each state, we would have

$\varphi \Rightarrow \exists X(p_e \wedge \neg q_e) \wedge \exists X(q_e \wedge \neg p_e)$.

Without this assumption, we do not have

$\varphi \Rightarrow \exists X(p_e \wedge q_e)$

which is, of course, good since $p_e \wedge q_e$ may be inconsistent. In order to obtain this we need to add the axiom

$\exists X p_e \wedge \exists X q_e \Rightarrow \exists X(p_e \wedge q_e)$.

In this way we can effectively model simultaneous events. Furthermore, it would be mistaken to suppose that we could have it any other way, since simultaneity properly belongs in our non-logical theory of the domain.

1.3.2 Completion of History

As previously mentioned, we assume that the past is determined (i.e., backwards linear). However this does not imply that our knowledge of the past is complete. Since in some cases we may wish to claim complete knowledge with respect to one or more predicates in the past, a completion axiom is developed for an intuitively natural conception of history. Examples of predicates for which our knowledge might be complete are presidential inaugurations, employees of a company, and courses taken by someone in college.

Consider a first order theory T where the only occurrence of the predicate Q is:

$(C1) \quad (Q\ c_1) \wedge \ldots \wedge (Q\ c_n)$.

We may form a completed theory T_c with respect to Q by replacing C1 with the following completion axiom:

$(C2) \quad \forall x((Q\ x) \Leftrightarrow x = c_1 \vee \ldots \vee x = c_n)$.

From right to left on the biconditional this just says what the original theory T did, that Q is true of $c_1 \ldots c_n$. The completion occurs from left to right, asserting that $c_1 \ldots c_n$ are the only constants for which Q holds. Thus for some c' which is not equal to any of $c_1 \ldots c_n$, it is provable in the completed theory T_c that $\neg(Q\ c')$, which was not provable in the original theory T. This axiom captures our intuitive notions about Q.

The completion axiom for temporal logic is developed by introducing time propositions. The idea is that the conjunct of a time proposition, T, and some other proposition, Q, within the scope of the temporal operator P (previously), $P(Q \wedge T)$, denotes that Q was true at time T. There would also be axioms specifying an ordering on the time propositions. Consider a temporal theory M where the only occurrence of Q is of the form:

$$(C3) \qquad P(Q \wedge T_1) \wedge \ldots \wedge P(Q \wedge T_n).$$

We may form a completed theory M_c with respect to Q by adding the following completion axiom:

$$(C4) \qquad H(Q \Longleftrightarrow T_1 \vee \ldots \vee T_n).$$

Note that the temporal completion is of slightly different character than first-order completion, since replacing all occurrences of Q in M with the completion axiom would work only if in M with C3 removed it was the case that the following is provable:

$$(C5) \qquad P(T_1) \wedge \ldots \wedge P(T_n).$$

That is, C4 without the presence of C5 does not imply C3. Therefore C3 must be replaced by the conjunction of C4 and C5. Analogous to the first-order completion axiom, the direction from left to right is the completion of Q.

An equivalent first-order theory to M in which each temporal proposition T_i is a first-order constant t_i and Q is a monadic predicate,

$$(Q\ t_1) \wedge \ldots \wedge (Q\ t_n),$$

has the first-order completion axiom (with Q restricted to time constants of the past, where t_0 is now):

$$\forall x \le t_0((Q\ x) \Longleftrightarrow x = t_1 \vee \ldots \vee x = t_n).$$

One might wish to ask a more general question regarding the possibility of completing an arbitrary temporal theory. We can only point out some simple examples. In the following we use $[\varphi] \rightarrow \psi$ to mean the completion of φ is ψ.

$$[Lq] \rightarrow \forall G \neg q \wedge Lq \wedge LLH \neg q$$

$$[Hq] \rightarrow \forall X \forall G \neg q \wedge Hq$$

$$[Pq] \rightarrow \forall X \forall G \neg q \wedge q \wedge LH \neg q$$

$$[Lq \wedge LLLq] \rightarrow \forall G \neg q \wedge Lq \wedge LL \neg q \wedge LLLq \wedge LLLLH \neg q$$

The universal future operators may be completed similarly, but there is no satisfactory completion available for the existential future operators.

1.3.3 Futurities

A query regarding future possibility has the general logical form: $\exists Fp$. That is, is there some future time in which p is true. The basic variations are: $\forall Fp$, must p eventually be true; $\exists Gp$, can p remain true; $\forall Gp$, must p remain true. These can be nested to produce great variation. However, answering direct questions about future possibility is not the only use to be made of futurities. In addition, futurities permit the query system to competently offer monitors as responses to questions. (A monitor watches for some specified condition to arise and then performs some action, usually notification that the condition has occurred.) A monitor can only be offered competently if it can be shown that the condition might possibly arise, given the present state of the data base. Note that if any of the stronger forms of future possibility can be derived it would be desirable to provide information to that effect.

For example, if a student is not registered for a course and has not passed the course and the time was prior to enrollment, a monitor for the student registering would be competently made given some question about registration, since

$((\neg register_s \wedge \neg (Ppass_e) \wedge \forall X(\forall Fenroll_t)) \Rightarrow (\exists Fregister_e))$.

However, if the student had previously passed the course, the monitor offer would not be competent, since

$((\neg register_s \wedge (Ppass_e) \wedge \forall X(\forall Fenroll_t)) \Rightarrow \neg (\exists Fregister_e))$.

Note that if a monitor was explicitly requested, "Let me know when p happens," a futurity may be used to determine whether p might ever happen. In addition to the processing efficiency gained by discarding monitors that can never be satisfied, one is also in a position to correct a user's mistaken belief that p might ever happen, since in order to make such a request s/he must believe p could happen. Corrections related to the divergence of the user's beliefs with those of the system regarding the temporal aspects of the data base are of two types:

1. The present instance of the data base is such that the proposition will never be true in the future.
2. While the present state of the data base is such that the proposition may be true in the future, the intervening course of events creates a data base state such that the proposition will never be true in the future from that state.

The first case corresponds to showing $\neg\exists Fp$. In the second case we can show $\exists Fp$, but the actual course of events causes a data base state in which $\neg\exists Fp$ is provable. The implication of this is that when a monitor is set, it should be periodically checked to see if it is still satisfiable. That is unless it is provable that $\forall G \exists Fp$.

The application of the constraints when attempting to determine the validity of an update to the data base is important to the determination of monitor competence. The approach we have adopted is to require that when some formula p is considered as a potential addition to the data base that it be provable that $\exists Xp$. Alternatively one could just require that the update not be inconsistent, that is not provable that $\forall X \neg p$. The former approach is preferred since it does not make any requirement on decidability. Thus, in order to say that a monitor for some condition p is competent, it must be provable that $\exists Fp$.

1.3.4 Counterhistoricals

A counterhistorical may be thought of as a special case of a counterfactual, where rather than asking the counterfactual, "If kangaroos did not have tails would they topple over?", one asks instead "Could I have taken CSE110 last semester?". That is, counterfactuals suppose that the present state of affairs is slightly different and then question the consequences. Counterhistoricals, on the other hand, question how a course of events might have proceeded otherwise. If we picture the underlying temporal structure, we see that although there are no branches into the past, there are branches from the past into the future. These are alternative histories to the one we are actually in. Counterhistoricals explore these alternate histories.

Intuitively, a counterhistorical may be evaluated by "rolling back" to some previous state and then reasoning forward, disregarding any events that actually took place after that state, to determine whether the specified condition might arise. For the question, "Could I have registered for CSE110 last semester?", we access the state specified by last semester, and from that state description, reason forward regarding the possibility of registering for CSE110. However, a counterhistorical is really only interesting if there is some way in which the course of events is constrained.

In the logic, the general counterhistorical has the form: $P(\exists Fp)$. That is, is there some time in the past at which there is a future time when p might possibly be true. Constraints may be placed on the prior time: $P(q \wedge \exists Fp)$, e.g., "When I was a sophomore, could I have taken Phil 6?". One might wish to require that some other condition still be accessible: $P(\exists F(p \wedge \exists Fq))$, e.g., "Could I have taken

CSE220 and then CSE110?"; or that the counterhistorical be immediate from the most recent state: $L(\exists Xp)$. (The latter is interesting in what it has to say about possible alternatives to -- or the inevitability of -- what is the case now. [WM83] shows its use in recognizing and correcting event-related misconceptions.) For example, in the registration domain if we know that someone has passed a course then we can derive the counterhistorical that they could have not passed: $((Ppass_e) \Rightarrow P(\exists F \neg pass_e))$.

1.3.5 Example

The propositional variables reg_t, add_t, $drop_t$, $enroll_t$, and $break_t$ are time points intended to denote periods in the academic semester on which certain activities regarding enrollment for courses is dependent. (Note that these form a cycle.) The event propositions are reg_e, $pass_e$, $fail_e$, and $drop_e$; for registering for a course, passing a course, failing a course, and dropping a course, respectively. The only state is reg_s, which means that a student is registered for a course. Note that the following are true at all points in time. That is, if φ is one of the following non-logical axioms then $H(\forall G\varphi)$ is true.

1. $reg_t \Leftrightarrow (\forall X add_t)$ -- add follows reg
2. $add_t \Leftrightarrow (\forall X drop_t)$ -- drop follows add
3. $drop_t \Leftrightarrow (\forall X enroll_t)$ -- enroll follows drop
4. $enroll_t \Leftrightarrow (\forall X break_t)$ -- break follows enroll
5. $break_t \Leftrightarrow (\forall X reg_t)$ -- reg follows break
6. $\neg(i_t \wedge j_t)$, for $i \neq j$ (e.g., $\neg(enroll_t \wedge break_t)$)
7. $((reg_t \vee add_t) \wedge \neg reg_s \wedge \neg(Ppass_e)) \Leftrightarrow (\exists X reg_e)$ -- if the period is reg or add and a student is not registered and has not passed the course then the student may next register for the course
8. $((add_t \vee drop_t) \wedge reg_s) \Leftrightarrow (\exists X drop_e)$ -- if the period is add or drop and a student is registered for a course then the student may next drop the course
9. $(enroll_t \wedge reg_s) \Leftrightarrow (\exists X pass_e)$ -- if the period is enroll and a student is registered for a course then the student may next pass the course
10. $(enroll_t \wedge reg_s) \Leftrightarrow (\exists X fail_e)$ -- if the period is enroll and a student is registered for a course then the student may next fail the course
11. $(enroll_t \wedge reg_s) \Rightarrow (\forall X(pass_e \vee fail_e))$ -- if the period is enroll and a student is registered for a course then the student must next pass or fail the course
12. $reg_e \Rightarrow (reg_s \forall U(pass_e \vee fail_e \vee drop_e))$ -- if a student registers for a course then eventually the student will pass or fail or drop the course and until then the student will be registered for the course
13. $pass_e \vee fail_e \vee drop_e \Rightarrow \neg reg_s$
14. $((L \neg reg_s) \wedge \neg reg_e) \Rightarrow \neg reg_s$ -- not registering maintains not being registered
15. $\neg(i_e \wedge j_e)$, for $i \neq j$ (e.g., $\neg(reg_e \wedge pass_e)$) -- only one event at a time

Given the above non-logical axioms, we can derive the following kinds of data base contents, response conditionals. The antecedent corresponds to the data base contents and the consequent to the response. In the first proof, for example, given the data base contains $Ppass_e$, we can respond $Preg_s$ to a request regarding registration status. The proofs make use of the logical axioms in section 1.2.3 and the theorems at the end of this section.

- Reconstructing a previous database state

Proof $(Ppass_e) \Rightarrow (Preg_s)$

[1] $H((\exists X pass_e) \Rightarrow reg_s)$ [$Axiom9$]

[2] $H((L\exists X pass_e) \Rightarrow Lreg_s)$ [$1, D(H, L), G!(H, L), K(L)$]

[3] $H(pass_e \Rightarrow Lreg_s)$ [$2, T_c^-(L)$]

[4] $(Ppass_e)\Rightarrow(PLreg_s)$ — [3, $K'(P)$]

[5] $(Ppass_e)\Rightarrow(Preg_s)$ — [4, $5_c(H, L)$, $G!(H, L)$]

- Counterhistorical

Proof $(Ppass_e)\Rightarrow(P\exists Ffail_e)$

[1] $(Ppass_e)\Rightarrow P(reg_s \wedge enroll_t)$ — [Similar to previous proof]

[2] $(Ppass_e)\Rightarrow P(\exists Xfail_e)$ — [1, $Axiom10$]

[3] $(Ppass_e)\Rightarrow P(\exists Ffail_e)$ — [2, $D_c(\exists X, \exists F)$]

- Incompetent monitor

Proof $Ppass_e \Rightarrow \neg\exists Freg_e$

[1] $\forall G(H(\exists Xreg_e \Rightarrow \neg Ppass_e))$ — [$Axiom7$, $G(\forall G, H)$]

[2] $\forall G(reg_e \Rightarrow L\neg Ppass_e)$ — [1, $D(H, L)$, $K(L)$, $T_c^-(L)$]

[3] $\forall G(reg_e \Rightarrow \neg pass_e \wedge LH\neg pass_e)$ — [2, $Axiom15$, $Df(P)$]

[4] $\forall G(reg_e \Rightarrow H\neg pass_e)$ — [3, $T5!(H, L)$]

[5] $\forall G(reg_e \Rightarrow \neg Ppass_e)$ — [4, $Df(P)$]

[6] $\forall G(Ppass_e \Rightarrow \neg reg_e)$ — [5]

[7] $\forall GPpass_e \Rightarrow \forall G\neg reg_e$ — [6, $K(\forall G)$]

[8] $Ppass_e \Rightarrow \neg\exists Freg_e$ — [7, $T^+(\exists F)$, $Df(\exists F)$]

- Answering a query

Proof $Ppass_e \Rightarrow \neg reg_s$

[1] $\forall G(\neg reg_s \wedge \forall G\neg reg_e \Rightarrow \forall X(L\neg reg_s)\wedge\forall G\neg reg_e)$ — [$T_c^+(\forall X)$]

[2] $\forall G(\neg reg_s \wedge \forall G\neg reg_e \Rightarrow \forall X(L\neg reg_s \wedge \forall G\neg reg_e))$ — [1, $5_c(\forall G, \forall X)$, $R(\forall X)$]

[3] $\forall G(\neg reg_s \wedge \forall G\neg reg_e \Rightarrow \forall X(\neg reg_s \wedge \forall G\neg reg_e))$ — [3, $Axiom14$]

[4] $\neg reg_s \wedge \forall G\neg reg_e \Rightarrow \forall G(\neg reg_s \wedge \forall G\neg reg_e)$ — [3, $I(\forall X)$]

[5] $H(pass_e \Rightarrow \forall G\neg reg_e)$ — [Previous proof, $T(H)$, $Df(\exists F)$]

[6] $H(pass_e \Rightarrow \neg reg_s \wedge \forall G\neg reg_e)$ — [$Axiom13$, 5]

[7] $H(pass_e \Rightarrow \forall G(\neg reg_s \wedge \forall G\neg reg_e))$ — [4, 6]

[8] $H(pass_e \Rightarrow \forall G\neg reg_s)$ — [7]

[9] $Ppass_e \Rightarrow P\forall G\neg reg_s$ — [8, $K'(P)$]

[10] $Ppass_e \Rightarrow \forall G\neg reg_s$ — [9, $T^+(P)$]

- Competent monitor

Proof $reg_t \wedge \neg reg_s \wedge \neg Ppass_e \Rightarrow \exists Freg_e$

[1] $reg_t \wedge \neg reg_s \wedge \neg Ppass_e \Rightarrow \exists Freg_e$ — [$Axiom7$, $D_c(\exists X, \exists F)$]

- Competent monitor

Proof $enroll_t \wedge reg_s \Rightarrow \exists F \neg reg_e$

[1] $enroll_t \wedge reg_s \Rightarrow \exists F \neg reg_e$ [*Axioms*9 and 15, $D_c(\exists X, \exists F)$]

- Competent monitor

Proof $enroll_t \wedge reg_s \Rightarrow \exists F pass_e$

[1] $enroll_t \wedge reg_s \Rightarrow \exists F pass_e$ [*Axiom*9, $D_c(\exists X, \exists F)$]

Theorems Used in the Example

1.	$[K'(P)]$	$H(p \Rightarrow q) \Rightarrow (Pp \Rightarrow Pq)$
2.	$[G!(H, L)]$	$L(Hp) \Leftrightarrow H(Lp)$
3.	$[G(\forall G, H)]$	$H(\forall Gp) \Rightarrow \forall G(Hp)$
4.	$[R(\forall X)]$	$\forall X(p \wedge q) \Leftrightarrow \forall Xp \wedge \forall Xq$
5.	$[D_c(\exists X, \exists F)]$	$\exists Xp \Rightarrow \exists Fp$
6.	$[T5!(H, L)]$	$Hp \Leftrightarrow p \wedge L(Hp)$
7.	$[T_c^-(L)]$	$p \Rightarrow L(\exists Xp)$
8.	$[T_c^+(\forall X)]$	$p \Rightarrow \forall X(Lp)$
9.	$[T^+(P)]$	$P(\forall Gp) \Rightarrow \forall Gp$
10.	$[T^+(\exists F)]$	$\exists F(Hp) \Rightarrow Hp$

1.4 DISCUSSION

1.4.1 First-order Temporal Logic

It was noted earlier that a data base is generally considered to be a first-order logical theory. The most straightforward approach to extending this propositional temporal logic to a first-order temporal logic would be to have the universe remain constant across every state. It is questionable whether this assumption is consistent with our notions of data bases, since it seems unreasonable to suppose that the present data base state contains all individuals present in future data base states. This assumption may also be analyzed by examining the validity of the temporal status of the Barcan formula (BF) and its converse (BFC), as the universe varies across states.

- BF: $\forall x \forall G \varphi(x) \Rightarrow \forall G \forall x \varphi(x)$
- BFC: $\forall G \forall x \varphi(x) \Rightarrow \forall x \forall G \varphi(x)$

Note that if the universe is constant both BF and BFC are valid. However, the following argument, which is due to Kripke [Kripke63], demonstrates that neither are valid with varying universe.

For BF suppose that new individuals are added as time passes for which φ is false.
$U(s_0) = \{c_1\}$ $s_0 \models \varphi(c_1)$
$U(s_1) = \{c_1, c_2\}$ $s_1 \models \varphi(c_1)$ $s_1 \not\models \varphi(c_2)$
Assume that every $s_i, i > 1$ is like s_1.
Then $s_0 \models \forall x \forall G \varphi(x)$, since for each $s_i, i \geq 0$, $s_i \models \varphi(c_1)$.
But $s_1 \not\models \forall x \varphi(x)$ and thus $s_0 \not\models \forall G \forall x \varphi(x)$.

For BFC suppose that the universe contracts as time passes. We will use the assumption that $\varphi(c)$ is false in any state in which c does not exist.
$U(s_0) = \{c_1, c_2\}$ $s_0 \models \varphi(c_1)$ $s_0 \models \varphi(c_2)$
$U(s_1) = \{c_1\}$ $s_1 \models \varphi(c_1)$ $s_1 \not\models \varphi(c_2)$
Assume that every s_i, $i > 1$ is like s_1.
Then $s_0 \models \forall G \forall x \varphi(x)$, since $s_0 \models \varphi(c_1)$, and $s_0 \models \varphi(c_2)$, and for each s_i, $i \geq 1$, $s_i \models \varphi(c_1)$.
But $s_1 \not\models \varphi(c_2)$ and thus $s_0 \not\models \forall x \forall G \varphi(x)$.

It may be reasonable in the case of data bases to suppose that the universe does not contract, in which case BFC is valid. The following allow us to express varying universes.

- Universe expands: some individual existing next does not exist now. $\exists X \exists x L \neg \exists y(x = y)$
- Universe contracts: some individual existing now does not exist next. $\exists x \exists X \neg \exists y(x = y)$

There is however the additional question of how to resolve the standard problems of substitutivity in modal contexts. In the temporal context, the problem is the following. It is true that Reagan is the President and the President always lives in the White House. It follows that Reagan always lives in the White House, but of course this is not true. There is a proposal that has been made about data bases in the static setting that eliminates this sort of problem. Reiter's proposal [Reiter80] is that a data base is function free and that distinct constants denote distinct individuals (i.e., $c_i \neq c_j$, for $i \neq j$).

Additionally, we would see as reasonable the following two observations regarding data bases. The first is Reiter's domain closure assumption (i.e., $\forall x(x = c_1 \vee \ldots \vee x = c_n)$). We would adopt this with slight modification, in that the present and past would obey domain closure while the future would not. The second observation is part of Codd's Tasmanian proposal [Codd79]. Specifically, that with each entity an internal constant is uniquely associated. This fits nicely with the reference account advanced by Kripke[Kripke72] that reference is made via a chain of communication to the initial "baptism." The internal constant provides a referent which allows us to identify individuals across states.

1.4.2 Conclusion

We have addressed the problem of reasoning about a changing data base from the perspective of a natural language based question answering system. The sorts of response behaviors that arise when the data base is viewed as a dynamic rather than a static object include historicals, counterhistoricals, and futurities with the resulting ability to competently offer monitors. In addition to directly providing this response capability, this type of reasoning plays a role in other types of response behaviors as well. We argued that for the purposes of natural language interaction with a data base, the aspect of data base change which should be considered is that which corresponds to a change in the real world rather than change due to error correction or refinement of knowledge.

The logic developed here depends heavily on previous work in program verification logics. The sort of structures we proposed were forward branching and backwards linear. The chief feature of this logic is the ability to quantify over branches as well as over states within the branches. It is this ability, which to our knowledge is not available in any proposed representation in AI, that provides the power to represent and reason about changing data bases.

We demonstrated how this logic may be employed to represent and reason about data base change. It was claimed that this logic, which is based on discrete change, models a wide range of data base situations. One line of investigation would be to look at the continuous case and attempt to evaluate this claim.

Perhaps the most interesting area to pursue is the first-order, in contrast to propositional, modal temporal logic. This must be investigated in order to make the connection to real world data bases. Our stated goal was to investigate the theory of change in data bases and then (when that is hopefully right) turn our attention to implementation grounded in that theory. It is hoped that the logic presented here does so, since it expresses exactly those relations which are of interest in a wide range of cases. Now it is necessary to look at the first-order problems and attempt in some way to realize an appropriate implementation. That is, how to make a connection between this logic and a standard data base management system. In [Mays84] an implemented theorem prover is described, but any theorem proving strategy based on present techniques is not feasible for anything close to a real world problem.

One alternate strategy would be to see if there was some way to restrict the logical theory that would yield more efficient search strategies. The idea would be to try to find something that did for this logic what Prolog does for first-order logic.

Another interesting direction, in the spirit of[Chang78], would be to look at some strategies for finding proofs which might transform a temporal query into a standard query on the data base. That is, we want to construct partial proofs, such that the premises on which the partial proofs depend are interpretable in some way outside of the proof procedure.

1.5 BIBLIOGRAPHY

[AP80]
J.F. Allen, C.R. Perrault.
Analyzing Intention in Utterances.
Artificial Intelligence, 15, 1980.

[Allen81]
J.F. Allen.
Maintaining Knowledge About Temporal Intervals.
In *Proceedings of IJCAI 81*, Vancouver, August, 1981.

[Anderson81]
T.L. Anderson.
The Database Semantics of Time.
PhD Thesis, University of Washington, 1981.

[BMP81]
M. Ben-Ari, Z. Manna, A. Pneuli.
The Temporal Logic of Branching Time.
In *Eighth ACM Symposium on Principles of Programming Languages*, Williamsburg, Va., January, 1981.

[Bruce72]
B.C. Bruce.
A Model for Temporal References and Its Application in a Question Answering Program.
Artificial Intelligence, 3, 1972.

[Chang78]
C.L. Chang.
Deduce 2: Further Investigations of Deduction in Relational Data Bases.
In H. Gallaire, J. Minker (editors), *Logic and Data Bases*, Plenum, New York, 1979.

[CW83]
J. Clifford, D.S. Warren.
Formal Semantics for Time in Databases.
ACM Transactions on Database Systems, 8, 1983.

[Codd79]
E.F. Codd.
Extending the Database Relational Model to Capture More Meaning.
ACM Transactions on Data Base Systems, 4, 1979.

[GPSS80]
D. Gabbay, A. Pneuli, S. Shelah, J. Stavi.
On the Temporal Analysis of Fairness.
In *Seventh ACM Symposium on Principles of Programming Languages*, 1980.

[HR78]
J.R. Hobbs, J. Robinson.
Why Ask?.
Manuscript, SRI International, Menlo Park, Ca., October, 1978.

[Joshi80]
A.K. Joshi.
Mutual Beliefs in Question-Answer Systems.
In *Proceedings of the Social Science Research Council "Colloquium on Mutual Knowledge"*, Guilford, England, September, 1980.

[KG77]
K. Kahn, G.A. Gorry.
Mechanizing Temporal Knowledge.
Artificial Intelligence, 9, 1977.

[Kamp68]
J.A.W. Kamp.
Tense Logic and the Theory of Linear Order.
PhD Thesis, UCLA, 1968.

[Kaplan82]
S.J. Kaplan.
Cooperative Responses from a Portable Natural Language Query System.
Artificial Intelligence, 19, 1982.

[Kripke63]
S.A. Kripke.
Semantical Considerations on Modal Logic.
Acta Philosophica Fennica, 16, 1963.

[Kripke72]
S.A. Kripke.
Naming and Necessity.
Harvard University Press, Cambridge, 1972.

[LCC84]
R.M. Lee, H. Coelha, J.C. Cotta.
Temporal Inferencing on Adminstrative Databases.
Manuscript, Dept. of Decision Sciences, University of Pennsylvania, Philadelphia, Pa., 1984.

[Lee80]
R.M. Lee.
CANDID: A Logical Calculus for Describing Financial Contracts.
PhD Thesis, University of Pennsylvania, 1980.

[MP81]
Z. Manna, A. Pnueli.
Verification of Concurrent Programs, Part 1: The Temporal Framework.
Manuscript, Stanford University, Stanford, Ca., 1981.

[Mays80]
E. Mays.
Failures in Natural Language Systems: Applications to Data Base Query Systems.
In *Proceedings of AAAI 80*, Stanford, Ca., August, 1980.

[Mays84]
E. Mays.
A Modal Temporal Logic for Reasoning About Changing Data Bases With Applications to Natural Language Question Answering.
PhD Thesis, University of Pennsylvania, 1984.

[McDermott82]
D. McDermott.
A Temporal Logic for Reasoning About Processes and Plans.
Cognitive Science, 6, 1982.

[McKeown82]
K.R. McKeown.
Generating Natural Language Text in Response to Questions about Database Structure.
PhD Thesis, University of Pennsylvania, 1982.

[Moore82]
R.C. Moore.
The Role of Logic in Knowledge Representation and Commonsense Reasoning.
In *Proceedings of AAAI 82*, Pittsburgh, Pa., August, 1982.

[Motro84]
A. Motro.
Query Generalization: A Technique for Handling Query Failure.
In this volume.

[Prior57]
A. Prior.
Time and Modality.
Oxford University Press, London, 1957.

[Prior67]
A. Prior.
Past, Present, and Future.
Oxford University Press, London, 1967.

[Prior68]
A. Prior.
Papers on Time and Tense.
Oxford University Press, London, 1968.

[RU71]
N. Rescher, A. Urquhart.
Temporal Logic.
Springer-Verlag, New York, 1971.

[Reiter80]
R. Reiter.
Equality and Domain Closure in First-Order Databases.
Journal of the ACM, 27, 1980.

[Rosenschein81]
S.J. Rosecschein.
Plan Synthesis: A Logical Perspective.
In *Proceedings of IJCAI 81*, Vancouver, Canada, August, 1981.

[Schneiderman78]
B. Schneiderman.
Improving the Human Factors Aspect of Database Interactions.
ACM Transactions on Data Base Systems, 3, 1978.

[WM83]
B. Webber, E. Mays.
Varieties of User Misconception: Detection and Correction.
In *Proceedings of IJCAI 83*, Karlsruhe, Germany, August, 1983.

PART VII:

Intelligent Database Access and Interaction

EXPERT HELPERS TO DATA-BASED INFORMATION SYSTEMS

*A.L. Furtado * and C.M.O. Moura ***

* Departamento de Informatica
Pontificia Universidade Catolica do Rio de Janeiro

** Latin American Systems Research Institute, Rio de Janeiro
IBM do Brasil

ABSTRACT

This paper discusses some features of software tools — expert helpers — to provide expert assistance in the specification, usage and maintenance of data-based information systems. A simple PROLOG prototype and an example information system are used to illustrate the discussion.

1. INTRODUCTION

Expert systems have achieved considerable success in coping with specialized application areas [St]. They usually include a knowledge base, i.e., a repertoire of general rules, besides a conventional data base consisting of given facts. Through an inference capability, new facts are derived as combined consequences of the general rules and the given facts.

The present research considers some desirable features of software tools, to be called *Expert Helpers* (EHs), to aid in the specification, usage and maintenance of information systems. EHs combine the purpose of other software tools. Like data dictionaries they document the information system. Like running specifications, they allow experimenting with the information system. Their additional distinguishing feature, which justifies calling them "expert," is the inferential capability which can use general rules to synthesize sequences of function applications leading from the current state to a state where certain desired facts hold or cease to hold (see [SMF] and, for plan-generation in general, [Ni]).

To make the discussion more concrete, we shall refer to a simple prototype EH that is being developed modularly in micro-PROLOG [CM]. The prototype contains two kinds of modules: specific and general. The *specific modules* refer to an application, i.e., a particular data-based information system. In the application module the conceptual schema of the application is specified, while view modules cover external schemas. The *general modules* permit one, given an application, to selectively interrogate its conceptual schema (the dictionary module) or run experiments on example data, both at the conceptual and at the external schema level (the processing module); another general module (the interface module) connects the EH with the operational data base proper, via shared sample files.

2. THE SPECIFIC MODULES

2.1. Application

Application modules contain the specification of some application at the conceptual schema level. Taking the abstract data type approach, we regard an application as an abstract data type, which can therefore be specified in terms of the functions defined on it

[BZ].

The query functions correspond to the (conceptual) facts. The update functions are defined by:

- the domains from which come the values of their parameters;
- each fact added by each function;
- each fact deleted by each function;
- the (pre-) conditions to apply each function.

So, the effects of functions are the facts they add and/or delete. Besides the additions and deletions originally intended, others may be required to preserve the static and transition integrity constraints [NY]. The enforcement of constraints may also require (pre-) conditions to the application of a function. Such conditions consist of sets of positive and/or negative facts that must hold at the state immediately before its application.

Clearly this function-oriented style of specification defines the (update) functions explicitly, whereas facts are only implicitly mentioned as participating in the effects and conditions of functions.

As an overly simplified example, we consider an academic data base where the facts are that courses are offered and that students take courses. The integrity constraints require that students can only take offered courses (static constraint) and that the number of courses taken by a student cannot drop to zero during the academic term (transition constraint). The functions are:

- offer(x), with x ε course
  facts added: {offered(x)}
  facts deleted:{ }
  conditions: { }

- cancel (x), with x ε course
  facts added: { }
  facts deleted: {offered(x)}
  conditions: {NOT takes(z,x), for any z ε student}

- enroll(x,y), with x ε student, y ε course
  facts added: {takes(x,y)}
  facts deleted: { }
  conditions: {offered(y)}

- transfer(x,y,z), with x ε student, y ε course, z εcourse
  facts added: {takes(x,z)}
  facts deleted: {takes(x,y)}
  conditions: {offered(z)}

We claim that this kind of specification is relatively simple and does not require that designers have a profound theoretical background. The only somewhat more involved problem is that of deriving the conditions (and additional effects, a case that does not occur in our example) necessary to enforce the constraints. Such problems, of course, must be attacked in a systematic way, as argued in [VF].

And yet, although the specification seems to say all that we need to know about the application, it is still incomplete. We should say what happens

(a) if a condition fails;

(b) if a fact that should be added is already present or a fact that should be deleted is absent;

as also

(c) what happens with facts not explicitly mentioned as added or deleted by a function (this corresponds to the well-known *frame problem*).

Most specification methodologies either answer questions like these by introducing assumptions informally or by supplying additional rules. The former solution lacks rigor. The latter tends to clutter the specification, leading to the combinatorial growth of its size. We prefer to provide a formal general solution to questions (a), (b), (c) that seems acceptable for a broad class of applications and is specified once and for all (see section 3.2).

2.2. Views

The view modules contain the specification of external schemas. They consist, first of all, of a number of *external facts*, implicitly defined by their *mappings* into conceptual facts.

The module may also include the predicate, is-a, as developed in connection with semantic hierarchies in the area of artificial intelligence. With this predicate we can introduce new domains through a view and declare that they are specializations of given conceptual domains. Objects of the specialized domains inherit the properties of the corresponding more general ones, besides having new properties of their own.

We have included one view for our example application (the view of a user *i*, or the ith-view). The ith-view introduces the domain:

- lab, where lab is-a course

and the external facts:

- beginning(x), with x ε student
  mapping: {takes(x,y), with y ε (course - lab)}
  condition: { }

- practicing(x), with x ε student
  mapping: {takes(x ,c2) ^ takes (x,y), with y ε lab}
  condition: {takes(x,c2) at the current state}

The specification defines as beginning students those who are taking any course that is not a lab (laboratory) course. To do laboratory work, which raises him to the practicing status, a student must already be taking *at the current state* (and should continue to take) the co-requisite course c2.

View modules might also contain the definition of external update functions. For simplicity we preferred not to have that, assuming that views would be updated through sequences of conceptual update functions; as seen, the mappings of external facts may impose special conditions to the application of such sequences.

3. THE GENERAL MODULES

3.1. Dictionary

The dictionary module allows one to ask questions about the specification. Dictionaries are often defined as "meta data bases", in that they contain facts about what kinds of facts (and other elements) are maintained in the data base. At the present stage of our prototype, the dictionary module informs only about application modules. Using it we may ask:

- with respect to facts:

  - what kinds of facts are maintained;
  - from what domains come the values of their parameters;
  - what functions can add their occurrences;
  - what functions can delete their occurrences;
- with respect to functions:
  - what functions are defined;
  - from what domains come the values of their parameters;
  - what are the conditions for their application;
  - what kinds of facts they can add;
  - what kinds of facts they can delete.

Since only functions are explicitly defined, the questions on facts are answered by looking at how facts are referred to in the function specifications. This gives us the possibility to check if such references have been done consistently. For example, we can adapt the question

- From what domains come the values of the parameters of a fact?

so that we can verify whether all functions involving the fact have parameters in the same corresponding domains. Suppose we had in our example application a function f(x,y) with the effect of deleting takes(x,y), and suppose further that the parameters of f were declared x ε course, y ε course. Clearly this would be inconsistent with the other functions, which expect x to be a student in takes(x,y).

3.2. Processing

The processing module allows one to run the specification, as expressed declaratively in specific application and view modules. It also fulfills the fundamental role of completing such specifications by providing solutions to questions (a), (b), (c) of section 2.1.

First, we introduce the concepts of:

- *valid* application of a function — the application of a function is valid if the function has been invoked with the correct number of parameters of the prescribed domains (syntactical validity), and all conditions for its application are preliminarily satisfied (semantic validity);
- *productive* application of a function — the application of a function is productive if all facts that the function should delete are present and all facts that it should add are absent before its application.

Productive applications exclude trivial situations, as for example trying to transfer a student to a course that he is already taking, or from a course that he is not taking. A consequence of excluding these two situations is that an attempt to transfer from a course to the same course is also excluded.

Now we can say that an assertion holds in a data base state only if one of the cases below applies:

- case 1 — the assertion corresponds to a stored fact, which means that it holds at the current state;
- case 2 — the assertion corresponds to a fact to be added by a function, and therefore holds at the state reached by a valid and productive application of the function;
- case 3 — the assertion corresponds to a fact that is not deleted by a function; so, if it held at the state to which the function is applied, it also holds at the state reached by its application.

Another predicate, not-holds, is defined dually to handle negative assertions. The definition of holds and not-holds is complemented by the criterion known as *negation as failure*

[Cl], according to which an assertion is false unless provable from the, possibly recursive, stated rules.

We conclude that either a function meets all its syntactical and semantic requirements and achieves all its effects and only these, or it does nothing at all and hence no state change is operated. This principle is precisely stated through the axioms of the processing module (plus negation as failure).

To write the axioms we have followed the idea, introduced in [Ko], to treat facts and functions as terms. Other axioms adapt an algorithm [Wa1] to derive alternative *sequences of function* applications leading to a state (partially) characterized by an indicated set of positive and/or negative facts. Such a set is treated as a conjunction of possibly interacting goals; interaction induces a partial order on function application. Conditions to function application are established as sub-goals. If there is an inconsistency involving goals or sub-goals, no sequence is generated.

The sequences of function applications are represented internally in a nested notation but are displayed in a more readable "linear" format. To compare alternative sequences, we can examine what facts each sequence adds, deletes or preserves. We can actually execute a chosen sequence to obtain a new current state.

Finally, the module also allows views to be queried or updated, by working on the underlying conceptual facts and states. To determine the generation of external states, however, the present version only permits the indication of sets of *positive* external facts.

3.3. Interface

The interface module permits a simple communication between the EH and the associated data base via shared sample files, i.e. subsets of the operational files whose contents are considered, with respect to some criterion not to be investigated here, representative of the situations that can arise.

Two features are available, allowing to

- read a sample file and add its contents as new facts of a given kind;
- use the facts of a given kind, holding at the current state, to write a sample file.

Since we are running micro-PPOLOG under MS-DOS, on an IBM Personal Computer, sample files are standard format MS-DOS files. The relational DBMS dBASE II [AT] is being used in our experiments. We had to make provision for little problems, such as expecting or not end-of-record or end-of-file marks.

The sample MS-DOS files can be written or read by dBASE II, using the commands "copy to <file> for <expression> sdf" and "append from <file> sdf", respectively. All modules are fully listed in the APPENDIX. We must warn the reader that different releases of any system tend to require minor adjustments (our release of micro-PROLOG is 3.1). The syntax follows the general format of PROLOG versions, especially notable deviations being that unary predicates are displayed in postfix notation and binary predicates in infix notation, and "if" is substituted for the more usual left-directed arrow. Unary predicates can be used as commands, as we have done with the predicates "state", "external-state", "in-predicate" and "out-predicate". A set-former capability [Wa2] is provided, which we have used extensively. Our immediate plans include a thorough revision to improve efficiency; in particular, considerable time is being taken for the processing module to convince itself that it cannot generate any further sequences of function applications.

4. USING THE PROTOTYPE

We begin by showing how to learn about the conceptual schema of an application.

— *Dictionary look-up*:
(load the application and the dictionary modules)

- "what kinds of facts are kept ?"
  which(x : facts(x))
  answer: ((takes X Y) (offered Z))

- "what are the domains of 'takes' ?"
  which(x : fact-domains(takes x))
  answer: (student course)

- "which functions add 'takes' ?"
  which(x : fact-adders(takes x))
  answer: ((transfer X Y Z) (enroll x y))

To conduct experiments with example elements, we introduce:

instance(student John)
instance(student Peter)
instance(course c1)
instance(course c2)

and a current state, s0, with the following facts (noting however that we have always the option to start with the "empty" state, consisting only of the dummy fact()):

fact((offered c1))
fact((offered c2))
fact((takes John c1))
fact((takes Peter c2))

— *Querying the current state*:
(load the application module)

- "does John take c1 ?" (a yes/no-question)
  is(fact((takes John c1)))
  answer: YES

- "what courses are offered ?" (a wh-question)
  which(x : fact((offered x)))
  answer: c1
  c2

— *Deriving sequences of function applications*:
(load the application and the processing modules)

- "how can we reach a state where c1 is not offered and John takes c2 ?" (a how-to-do-question)

```
one(x : plans(((not offered c1) (takes John c2)) y) and
   linear(y x))
answer: (s0 ; transfer John c1 c2 ; cancel c1)
```

- "what are the consequences of executing the sequence above ?" (a what-if-question)

```
one((to be added x to be deleted y and remains z) :
    plans(((not offered c1) (takes John c2)) X) and
    seq-added(x X) and
    seq-deleted(y X) and
    seq-preserved(z X))
answer: (to be added ((takes John c2)) to be deleted ((takes
        John c1) (offered c1)) and remains ((takes Peter c2)
        (offered c2)))
```

— *Obtaining a new current state*:
(load the application and the processing modules)

- "obtain a state where John takes c2."

```
state((takes John c2))
answer: (s0 ; enroll John c2)
       (s0 ; transfer John c1 c2)
choose one option
.2
```

inspecting the new current state

```
list(fact)
(offered c1) fact
(offered c2) fact
(takes Peter c2) fact
(takes John c2) fact
```

— *Querying and updating the ith-view*:
(load the application, the view and the processing modules)

First we add a new element:

instance(lab c3)

- "what external facts hold corresponding to the conceptual state above ?"
which(x : external-fact(i x))
answer: (beginning John)
(beginning Peter)

- "from the previous state, obtain a state where both John and Peter are practicing."
external-state(i ((practicing John) (practicing Peter)))
answer: (s0 ; offer c3 ; enroll John c3 ; enroll Peter c3)
(s0 ; offer c3 ; enroll Peter c3 ; enroll John c3)
choose one option
.0 /* if 0 is typed, no state-change is performed */

— *Communicating via sample files with a DBMS*:
(load the interface module)

- "read 'takes' facts from file alpha."
in-predicate(takes "alpha.txt" ((CON 5)(CON 2)) (x y))
/* from this point on the added facts can be treated like any others */

- "write all 'takes' facts on file beta."
out-predicate(takes "beta.txt" ((CON 5)(CON 2)))
/* if the file does not exist it is created, otherwise it is overwritten */

5. CONCLUSIONS

It is a widespread conjecture that we shall see large intelligent data-based information systems in the near future. Our point in this paper is that, even if size and intelligence are incompatible with efficiency given the present state of the art, intelligence may be present in smaller software tools, such as our proposed expert helpers, "connected" somehow with the larqe systems.

The processing module of our EH can be regarded as an interpreter when it generates and executes a sequence of function applications. As seen, function applications may be conditional. Also, we have iteration, as may be induced by the conditions of the cancel(x) function: if there are students taking course x, the set {NOT takes(z,x)}, for all such students z, will be established as sub-goal, causing the repeated invocation of transfer(z,x,y). So, the three main program control structures (sequence, selection and iteration) are present. Although we synthesize executions rather than programs [BF], a similar result is achieved, with the usual loss in terms of efficiency inherent in the choice of interpretive instead of compilation-oriented solutions.

The highly non-procedural ability of the prototype to perform conceptual and external state transitions, by indicating target sets of facts, is at present its most interesting feature. Other features, related to expert assistance at the specification phase and during the life-time of an application, should be identified by future research and gradually incorporated.

6. REFERENCES

[AT] Ashton-Tate - "dBASE II assembly-language relational database management system" - reference manual - Ashton- Tate (1982).

[BF] A. Barr and E.A. Feigenbaum (eds.) - "Automatic Programming"- in *The handbook of artificial intelligence* - vol. 2, chapter 10 - HeurisTech Press and William Kaufman (1982) 295-379.

[BZ] M.L. Brodie and S.N. Zilles (eds.) - Proc. of the Workshop on Data Abstraction, Databases and Conceptual Modelling - SIGMOD Record, vol. 11, n. 2 (1981).

[Cl] K.L. Clark - "Negation as failure" - in *Logic and data bases* - H. Gallaire and J. Minker (eds.) - Plenum Press (1978) 293-322.

[CM] K.L. Clark and F.G. McCabe - *Micro-PROLOG: programming in logic* - Prentice-Hall (1984).

[Ko] R. Kowalski - *Logic for problem solving* - North-Holland (1979).

[Ni] N.J. Nilsson - *Principles of artificial intelligence* - Springer-Verlag (1982).

[NY] J.M. Nicolas and K. Yazdanian - "Integrity checking in deductive data bases" - in *Logic and data bases* - H. Gallaire and J. Minker (eds.) - Plenum Press (1978) 325-344.

[SMF] C.S. dos Santos, T.S.E. Maibaum and A.L. Furtado - "Conceptual modelling of data base operations" - *International Journal of Computer and Information Sciences* - vol. 10, no. 5 (1981) 299 - 314.

[St] M. Stefik et al - "The organization of expert systems - a tutorial" - Artificial Intelligence - vol. 19, n. 2 (1982) 135-173.

[VF] P.A.S. Veloso and A.L. Furtado - "Towards simpler and yet complete formal specifications" - *Proc. of the IFIP Working Conference on Theoretical and Formal Aspects of Information Systems* (1985).

[Wa1] D.H.D. Warren - "WARPLAN: a system for generating plans" - memo 76 - University of Edinburgh (1974).

[Wa2] D.H.D. Warren - "Higher-order extensions to PROLOG: are they needed?" -in *Machine intelligence* -vol. 10 - J. E. Hayes, D. Michie and Y.H. Pao (eds.) - Halsted Press (1982) 441-454.

7. APPENDIX

A. Application module

```
(offer X) operation (course)
(cancel X) operation (course)
(enroll X Y) operation (student course)
(transfer X Y Z) operation (student course course)

(offered X) added (offer X)
(takes X Y) added (enroll X Y)
(takes X Y) added (transfer X Z Y)

(offered X) deleted (cancel X)
(takes X Y) deleted (transfer X Y Z)

conditions ((offer X) () Y)
conditions ((cancel X) Y Z) if
        Y isall (not takes x X : (takes x X) holds Z)
conditions ((enroll X Y) ((offered Y)) Z)
conditions ((transfer X Y Z) ((offered Z)) x)
```

B. View module

```
map (i (beginning X) ((takes X Y)|Z)) if
        student domain X and
        () isall (x  : lab domain x and
        (takes X x) fact) and
        course domain Y and
        not lab domain Y and
        Z isall (not takes X x : lab domain x)
map (i (practicing X) ((takes X c2) (takes X Y))) if
        student domain X and
        (takes X c2) fact and
        lab domain Y

lab is-a course
```

C. Dictionary module

```
X facts if
        Y isall (Z : CL (((added Z x)|y) 1 z)) and
        Y no-duplicate X

X fact-domains Y if
        X fact-adders Z and
        (x|y) ON Z and
        x function-domains z and
        APPEND ((x)  z X1) and
        CL (((added (X|Y) X1)|Y1) 1 Z1) and
        /

X fact-adders Y if
        Y isall (Z : CL (((added (X|x) Z)|y) 1 z))

X fact-deleters Y if
        Y isall (Z : CL (((deleted (X|x) Z)|y) 1 z))

X functions if
        X isall (Y : CL (((operation Y Z)|x) 1 y))

X function-domains Y if
        CL (((operation (X|Z) Y)|x) 1 y)

X function-conditions Y if
        CL (((conditions (X|Z) x y)|z) 1 X1) and
        (x|z) simplify Y

X function-adds Y if
        Y isall (Z : CL (((added Z (X|x)) y) 1 z))

X function-deletes Y if
        Y isall (Z : CL (((deleted Z (X|x))|y) 1 z))

() no-duplicate ()
(X|Y) no-duplicate Z if
        X ON Y and
        / and
        Y no-duplicate Z
(X|Y) no-duplicate (X|Z) if
        Y no-duplicate Z

(X) simplify X if
        /
X simplify X
```

D. Processing module

```
X state if
        Y isall (Z : X plans Z and
                Z linear x and
                x PP) and
        y isall (z : z ON Y) and
        PP (choose one option) and
        X1 R and
        choose (y X1 Y1) and
        Y1 exec

X plans Y if
        plan (X () s0 Y)

plan ((X|Y) Z x y) if
        / and
        solve (X Z x z X1) and
        plan (Y z X1 y)
plan (() X Y Y) if
        /

solve ((not|X) Y Z ((not|X)|Y) Z) if
        X not-holds Z
solve ((not|X) Y Z ((not|X)|Y) x) if
        X deleted (y|z) and
        (y|z) syntax-OK and
        achieve ((not|X) (y|z) Y Z x)
solve ((not|X) Y Z x y) if
        / and
        FAIL
solve (X Y Z (X|Y) Z) if
        X holds Z
solve (X Y Z (X|Y) x) if
        X added (y|z) and
        (y|z) syntax-0K and
        achieve (X (y|z) Y Z x)

achieve (X (Y|Z) x y (result (Y|Z) z)) if
        conditions ((Y|Z) X1 y) and
        plan (X1 x y z) and
        (result (Y|Z) z) productive and
        x preserved (result (Y|Z) z)
achieve (X Y Z (result (x|y) z) (result (x|y) X1)) if
        retrace (Z (x|y) Y1) and
        achieve (X Y Y1 z X1) and
        (result (x|y) X1) productive and
        conditions ((x|y) Z1 X1) and
        (X) preserved (result (x|y) X1) and
        Z1 preserved X1
```

```
retrace (((not|X)|Y) Z x) if
        X deleted Z and
        / and
        retrace (Y Z x)
retrace ((X|Y) Z x) if
        X added Z and
        / and
        retrace (Y Z x)
retrace ((X|Y) Z (X|x)) if
        retrace (Y Z x)
retrace (() X ())

X preserved Y if
        (forall Z ON X
        then    Z preservedl Y)

(not|X) preserved1 Y if
        / and
        X not-holds Y
X preserved1 Y if
        X holds Y

(X|Y) syntax-OK if
        (X|Z) operation x and
        Y syntax-OK1 x

(X|Y) syntax-OK1 (Z|x) if
        Z domain X and
        Y syntax-OK1 x
() syntax-OK1 ()

X domain Y if
        X instance Y
X domain Y if
        CL (((is-a Z X)) 1 x) and
        Z domain Y

(result (X|Y) Z) productive if
        (forall x deleted (X|Y)
        then    x holds Z) and
        (forall x added (X|Y)
        then    not x holds Z)

X holds s0 if
        X fact
X holds (result (Y|Z) x) if
        X added (Y|Z) and
        (Y|Z) syntax-OK
X holds (result (Y|Z) x) if
        / and
        X holds x and
        not X deleted (Y|Z)
```

```
X not-holds s0 if
        not X fact
X not-holds (result (Y|Z) x) if
        X deleted (Y|Z) and
        (Y|Z) syntax-OK
X not-holds (result (Y|Z) x) if
        / and
        X not-holds x and
        not X added (Y|Z)

s0 linear (s0)
(result (X|Y) Z) linear x if
        Z linear y and
        APPEND (y (; X|Y) x)

choose (X O Y) if
        / and
        FAIL
choose (((X|Y)|Z) 1 (X|Y)) if
        /
choose (((X|Y)|Z) x y) if
        SUM (1 z x) and
        choose (Z z y)

s0 exec
X exec if
        Y seq-added X and
        Z seq-deleted X and
        (forall x ON Y
        then   (x fact) add) and
        (forall y ON Z
        then   (y fact) delete)

X seq-added Y if
        X isall (Z : Z holds Y and
                not Z holds s0)

X seq-deleted Y if
        X isall (Z : Z holds s0 and
                not Z holds Y)

X seq-preserved Y if
        X isall (Z : Z holds s0 and
                Z holds Y)

X external-fact Y if
        map (X Y Z) and
        Z external-fact1
```

```
() external-fact1
(X|Y) external-fact1 if
        X fact and
        Y external-fact1
((not|X)|Y) external-fact1 if
        Y external-fact1 and
        not X fact

maps (X () ())
maps (X (Y|Z) x) if
        map (X Y y) and
        maps (X Z z) and
        APPEND (y z x)

(X Y) external-state if
        Z isall (x : maps (X Y x)) and
        Z states y and
        y states1

() states ()
(X|Y) states Z if
        x isall (y : X plans y and
                y linear z and
                z PP) and
        X1 isall (Y1 : Y1 ON x) and
        Y states Z1 and
        APPEND (X1 Z1 Z)

X states1 if
        PP (choose one option) and
        Y R and
        choose (X Y Z) and
        Z exec
```

E. Interface module

```
(X Y Z x) in-predicate if
        Y OPEN and
        Y SEEK (0|0) and
        APPEND (Z ((CON 2)) y) and
        in-predicate1 (X Y y x)
(X Y Z x) in-predicate if
        Y CLOSE

in-predicate1 (X Y Z x) if
        x copy y and
        APPEND (y (z) X1) and
        FREAD (Y Z X1) and
        not X1 eof and
        ((X|y) fact) add and
        in-predicate1 (X Y Z x)

() copy ()
(X|Y) copy (Z|x) if
        X VAR and
        Y copy x
(X|Y) copy (X|Z) if
        not X VAR and
        Y copy Z

(X|Y) eof if
        Z STRINGOF X and
        x CHAROF 26 and
        x ON Z

(X Y Z) out-predicate if
        Y CREATE and
        Y SEEK (0|0) and
        APPEND (Z ((CON 2)) x) and
        y eor and
        (forall (X|z) fact
        then   APPEND (z (y) X1) and
        FWRITE (Y x X1)) and
        Y CLOSE

X eor if
        Y CHAROF 13 and
        Z CHAROF 10 and
        (Y Z) STRINGOF X
```

Query Generalization: A Method for Interpreting Null Answers

Amihai Motro

Department of Computer Science
University of Southern California
Los Angeles, CA 90089

Abstract

A frustrating event in the course of interaction with a database management system is query failure: a query is submitted to the database, but instead of the anticipated printout, the system responds with an empty set of data items. While such null answers are always correct from a technical point of view, quite often they are unsatisfactory. Most efforts to deal with this problem have been in the context of natural language interfaces. In this paper we outline a simple mechanism for handling query failures in a typical database management system, which has only formal language interfaces, and only limited knowledge on the data it stores (such as types and relationships). The mechanism is demonstrated with the Loose Structure data model, which adopts an object-oriented, logic-based approach. Its principles, however, may be implemented with other data models and user interfaces.

1. Introduction

A frustrating event in the course of interaction with a database management system is *query failure*: a query is submitted to the database, but instead of the anticipated printout, the system responds with an empty set of data items (a *null answer*).

Query failure occurs when no data items satisfy the condition expressed in the query. While such null answers are always correct from a technical point of view, quite often they are unsatisfactory. Many null answers reflect undetected errors in the queries. Obviously, if such errors are recognized, interaction with the database will be improved. But even when null answers reflect genuine failures, more informative answers can be provided.

In this paper we outline a mechanism for providing *interpretations* for null answers. Each null answer is accompanied with an interpretation, which classifies the failure as either a user error or as a genuine null. In the former case it attempts to point out the error; in the latter case it attempts to delimit the scope of the failure and provide partial answers.

In interpreting failures the database management system demonstrates cooperative behavior and thus improves the interaction between the user and the database system. Improving man-machine interaction through cooperative systems is an active research area, where much of the effort focuses on the interface between natural language users and database management systems. An example of cooperative behavior is monitoring of changing data[1]. When a query generates a negative answer that may possibly change to a positive answer in the future, a cooperative system will offer to monitor the situation and inform the user when the change occurs. For example, the query "Has flight 909 landed yet?" will be answered with "No. Shall I let you know when it does?" Additional examples of cooperative behavior may be found in [3, 4, 5, 2, 7]. Of particular relevance to this paper is the system CO-OP, designed by Kaplan [3], which implements some of the conventions of cooperation in human conversation. These include *corrective*

---

[1] See the paper by Eric Mays elsewhere in this book.

responses, that detect erroneous presuppositions, and *suggestive* responses, that anticipate follow up queries. CO-OP was designed for natural language interaction, and relied on domain specific knowledge. In contradistinction, our approach here is to obtain similar effects in a typical database management system, which has only formal language interfaces, and only standard knowledge on the data it stores (e.g. types, attributes, relationships). Thus, the mechanism outlined here is less ambitious, but also less expensive. It is envisioned as a *help* key that users may press after a query fails. Our approach is similar to that adopted by Corella et al [1]. But while we share many basic principles, the research reported here takes a more general approach. For example, a limitation of Correla's technique is that it handles only a limited class of queries: conjunctive queries with a single variable, where each conjunct specifies a simple matching requirement. Also, since their data model is extremely simple, only limited analysis is possible. This analysis cannot detect, for example, user misconceptions about the *structure* of the data.

The next section discusses the sources of null answers and classifies them into two types. This classification is the basis for the failure interpretation mechanism, described in Section 3. While the principles of this mechanism hold for all data models and user interfaces, this mechanism is implemented most naturally within a logic-based, object-oriented data model, such as the Loose Structure data model [6]. This model is summarized in Section 4, and the details of the failure interpretation mechanism for this particular model are described in Section 5. Section 6 concludes with a short summary and some remaining problems.

2. Sources of Null Answers

A query submitted to a database can either be *rejected* or *evaluated*. However, a query that is evaluated is not necessarily "correct": a query may be acceptable to the system but somehow not model correctly the intentions of the user. Such queries are said to have *mistakes*; queries that are rejected by the system are said to have *errors*. The distinction between errors and mistakes is based, therefore, on the ability of the system to detect a problem in the query. Queries that contain errors or mistakes will be referred to collectively as *incorrect*.

2.1. Null Answers that Are Results of Mistakes

Experience shows that quite often null answers are interpreted by users as indication of mistakes. This happens when the user believes that the query should have matched some data, and therefore concludes that something went wrong. The user's reaction then is to examine the query for a possible cause: perhaps a misspelled name, or an operation used incorrectly, or simply insufficient understanding of the database. Clearly, the user interprets such answers as "mistake messages". Needless to say, null answers are very unsatisfactory mistake messages. Consequently, the user may end up trying different versions of this query in an attempt to understand the reason for its failure.

In contradistinction, when the database management system actually detects an incorrect query, it rejects it with an informative message. After considering such a message the user can correct the query promptly. It follows that a database management system that rejects a query is superior, in terms of cooperation, to systems that evaluate this query.

A principal source of mistakes in queries is *misconception*: as users form queries on the basis of their conceptions of the data stored in the database[2], inaccurate conceptions may lead to queries that do not implement the intentions of the users correctly. Other sources of mistakes are insufficient command of the query language, misspellings, etc.

While mistakes may result in non-null answers as well, because null answers tend to occur more frequently, and since they carry the least information on the error that caused them, analysis of null answers is a promising technique.

Mistakes occur more frequently when the organization of the data is not known to the user (or when the data model does not enforce organization). In addition, naive database users usually make more mistakes. In general, user interfaces based on *procedural* queries, in which the user specifies action-by-action how to obtain the target data, are less susceptible to such situations, as the user can monitor the progress of the evaluation

---

[2]These conceptions usually reflect they way these users perceive the real life environment which is modelled with this database.

of the query. On the other hand, user interfaces based on *specification* queries, in which the user qualifies the target data by a condition, tend to detect less mistakes, returning more null answers instead.

2.2. Genuine Null Answers

Even *genuine* null answers, i.e. null answers that are not the result of mistakes, are sometimes disturbing, as often, the information they provide amounts to a "shrug".

This is in contrast with human behavior, where a negative answer is usually accompanied with some kind of additional information. For example, when presented with the question "Do you know of a nearby supermarket with a good selection of wines at low prices?", a person without a satisfactory answer may still respond with something like "No, but I know several that are not around here".

In general, such answers are helpful, as they inform the person asking that the question was indeed meaningful, and that its failure was genuine, not the result of some misconception. More importantly, such answers tend to delimit the scope of the failure; in the previous example a negative answer could have been caused by a more fundamental inability to satisfy the question (it may be that the person asked does not even know of any nearby supermarket) and the person asking could be left wondering what is the real cause for the negative answer. Finally, sometimes such answers anticipate subsequent questions, as often negative answers trigger follow up questions.

Similarly, a database management system can be programmed so that genuine null answers are always accompanied with interpretations that achieve the very same benefits: assure the user that the query was meaningful, delimit the scope of its failure, and anticipate possible future queries.

3. The Failure Interpretation Mechanism

The failure interpretation mechanism attempts to detect mistakes in failed queries (they become errors...). Failed queries are thus classified into mistakes and genuine failures. This classification is then used to produce an interpretation of the failure (and provide further assistance). The method used to detect mistakes can be regarded as an extension of methods already in use. Following is an examination of the source of query rejection in typical database management systems.

One obvious cause of query rejection is *syntactic*: the query does not obey the syntax rules of the query language. Other rejections may be described as *schematic*. For example, assume a relational database and the query "select all tuples from relation **R** where attribute **A** has value **v**". If there is no relation **R** in the database, or relation **R** does not include attribute **A**, the query is rejected at the "schema" level. For an example of a rejection which is neither syntactic nor schematic, assume a functional database with the function **WORKS-FOR** from **EMPLOYEE** into **PROJECT**, and the query "list all values of **PROJECT** for **EMPLOYEE=Smith** by the function **WORKS-FOR**". If **Smith** is not in the domain **EMPLOYEE**, the query is rejected after the "content" of the database had been examined.

Except perhaps for syntax-based rejections, these examples of rejections can all be classified as misconceptions. To qualify their target data, all queries provide certain information, such as navigation paths, names of relationships, names of data items, and so on. This information reflects the user's conception of the database. During query processing the validity of this conception is checked against the actual database, and, if found incorrect, the system is able to reject the query with an appropriate message. The previous queries, for example, were rejected because, contrary to the user's conceptions, there is no relation **R**, relation **R** does not have attribute **A**, **Smith** is not an **EMPLOYEE**, etc.

Assume now a database on currently available recordings of music, with information on the composer, the title and the artist. Consider the query "List all different recordings of Chopin's Piano Concerto No. 3 by Rubinstein". As Chopin did not compose a third piano concerto, there will be no such recordings. Still, most database management systems will simply return a null answer without rejecting the query, although this query too reflects a misconception.[3] By detecting such misconceptions many queries, that would otherwise fail, can be rejected with appropriate messages.

3.1. Definitions

A *database* is a set of values. A *(retrieval) query* Q against a database D is a function that evaluates to a subset of D, called the *answer* to Q and denoted $Q(D)$. A query Q *fails* if $Q(D)$ is the empty set; Q is also said to have a *null answer*. The mechanism that evaluates queries is part of the *database management system*.

Consider the queries "List all different recordings of Chopin's Piano Concerto No. 2" and "List all different recordings of Chopin's Piano Concerto No. 2 by Rubinstein". Clearly, the former query is more general than the latter. This query relationship is defined as follows: given two queries Q and Q', Q is *more general* than Q' if $Q(D)$ contains $Q'(D)$. As it is based on containment, *generalization* is a partial order among the different queries.

As another example, consider the query "**1** List all female employees who earn more than \$30000". Some more general queries are "**2** List all female employees who earn more than \$20000" or "**3** List all employees who earn more than \$30000". The latter can be generalized further by the query "**4** List all employees". "**5** List all persons" is still more general. The most general, of course, is "**6** List everything". This example demonstrates some different methods to generalize queries: weaken a condition (from **1** to **2**), remove a condition altogether (from **1** to **3**, or from **3** to **4**), and substitute a more general concept (from **4** to **5**, or from **5** to **6**).

The database management system incorporates a *query generalizor*. Given a query Q this component generates a set of queries $\mathcal{Q}$, all more general than Q, and none related through generalization relationships. Queries in $\mathcal{Q}$ are all *minimally* more general than

---

[3] Admittedly, to identify this misconception positively, it must be assumed that the database includes complete information on composers and their compositions. But even when this so-called "closed world assumption" cannot be made, it should always be possible to reject this query with a message "there are no recordings of Chopin's Piano Concerto No. 3 by *any* artist".

Q; that is, all other queries more general than Q that can be generated by this mechanism, are also more general than some query in $\mathbf{Q}$.

To perform this task the query generalizor incorporates various strategies, all based on information stored in the database. Possible strategies are discussed in more detail in a Section 5. The query generalizor is the main component of the *failure interpretation mechanism*.

3.2. Principles

Consider again the query "List all female employees who earn more than $30000". We can assume the user who formulated it believes there may be female employees who earn more than $30000 (otherwise why bother ask). It is reasonable to assume that this user is even more confident that some employees (either males or females) indeed earn more than $30000. Furthermore, this user is quite certain that employees earn salaries. In other words, while a query that is presented to a database conveys the conceptions of the user about the database with some uncertainty, its more general queries convey user conceptions with a greater degree of confidence. This suggests a simple heuristic to estimate the conceptions of a user from the query.

This heuristic, which assumes most queries risk only minimal uncertainty, states that *while users expect their queries may possibly have null answers, they tend to be confident that every more general query would not fail.*

Under this heuristic, the generalizations of a query become indicators of the conceptions of the user. When a query fails, these conceptions can be tested by evaluating the generalizations. Each generalization that fails suggests a misconception. If all succeed, the original failure is interpreted as a genuine failure, and the answers obtained are offered as "partial answers" (i.e. "the best the system could do to satisfy the query").

Assume Q' and Q'' are both generalizations of Q, but Q'' is more general than Q'. If both succeed, then the partial answer returned by Q' is better. If both fail, then the misconception indicated by Q'' is stronger. This suggests that after a failure we should look for *minimal generalizations that succeed*, or *maximal generalizations that fail*.

The failure interpretation mechanism applies these principles in the following way. When a query Q fails the query generalizor is called to generate its set $\mathcal{Q}$ of minimally more general queries, and this set is evaluated. Then

- If all queries in $\mathcal{Q}$ succeed (Q is a maximal failure), then the failure of Q is genuine, and the answers to the generalizations are offered as partial answers. The interpretive message **partial answers available (yes/no)** accompanies the null answer. Responding **yes** the user gets a list of possible partial answers.

- If some queries in $\mathcal{Q}$ fail, then the failure of Q is due to misconceptions. In a recursive process, each of the failed queries in $\mathcal{Q}$ is generalized, until a set of maximal failures is obtained (every query in this set fails, but all its generalizations succeed). The interpretive message **possible misconceptions (yes/no)** accompanies the null answer. Responding **yes** the user gets a list of the possible misconceptions.

This procedure can be summarized as follows: when a query fails, its associated set of maximal failures is derived. If this set contains only the query itself, then it is a genuine null; otherwise, each maximal failure describes a misconception. Therefore, the interpretation of query failure is always provided by its associated maximal failures. This leads to the conclusion that *only maximal failures are significant*.

4. The Loose Structure Data Model

The Failure Interpretation mechanism can be implemented with different data models and user interfaces. Its main component, the query generalizor, should employ strategies that take advantage of the features of the particular data model. An object-oriented, logic-based data model is a convenient environment to demonstrate a very general strategy. The Loose Structure data model provides such an environment, and will be used here.

While most data models emphasize structure, thereby requiring substantial investment in their design and maintenance (update and reorganization), the Loose Structure model permits databases that are unstructured heaps of facts. These facts can generate further facts through inference rules, and are monitored by integrity constraints.

The appropriate mechanism for retrieval from a Loosely Structured database is *browsing*: exploratory searching that does not assume any knowledge about the database and its organization (or even the very existence of such organization). While the Loose Structure model supports a standard retrieval language based on predicate logic, this language is intended primarily to help formalize different browsing techniques.

This model is particularly suitable for modelling environments which are subject to constant evolution (or of which our conception is continuously evolving). It is a natural tool for modelling those environments that do not lend themselves to "massive" classifications. In general, this alternative model can be employed whenever we prefer to trade retrieval efficiency, for minimal investment in organization.

The Loose Structure model may be classified as a binary, object-oriented, logic-based data model. However, as it formalizes the notion of a unit of information (a fact) and allows one to describe such units "one by one", it does not require "modelling", as this activity is usually understood. A brief description follows. For more details see [6].

The most basic units of data are *entities*. Let $\mathcal{E}$ be a universe of distinctly named entities. This universe is partitioned into three sets, which are not necessarily disjoint: a set of *types* $\mathcal{T}$, a set of *tokens* $\mathcal{V}$ and a set of *relationships* $\mathcal{R}$. Relationships between entities are represented with *facts*, which are pairs of types or tokens named with a relationship. Thus, facts are elements of $(\mathcal{T} \cup \mathcal{V}) \times \mathcal{R} \times (\mathcal{T} \cup \mathcal{V})$. Some examples of facts are *(JACK,BROTHER-OF,JILL)*, *(JACK,∈,BOY)* and *(BOY,LIKES,DOG)*[4].

In particular, $\mathcal{V}$ includes all the numbers, and $\mathcal{R}$ includes the relationships $=$, $\neq$, $<$, and $>$. We assume that for every two different number entities *N1* and *N2* exactly one of the following facts is included: either *(N1,<,N2)* or *(N1,>,N2)*, depending on whether *N1* is smaller than *N2* or not. In addition, we assume that for every two

---

[4]The relationship ∈ describes membership; it is discussed in the next section.

entities $E1$ and $E2$ (not necessarily numbers) exactly one of these two facts is included: either $(E1,=,E2)$ or $(E1,\neq,E2)$, depending on whether $E1$ and $E2$ are identical or not.

When an entity of a fact is substituted with a *variable* the result is a *template fact*. A template fact is a restriction on its variables to entities that form existing database facts. Template facts are then used to construct formulas. A *formula* is constructed from template facts using negation, conjunction and disjunction operations, and universal and existential quantifiers.[5]

Closed formulas (i.e. all variables are bound) are used to express *integrity constraints*. For example, the following constraint guarantees the transitivity of the $<$ relationship:

$$(\forall x)\ (\forall y)\ (\forall z)\ (((x,<,y) \wedge (y,<,z)) \Rightarrow (x,<,z)).$$

As another example, the constraint that a child cannot be older than his father is expressed with the formula:

$$(\forall p_1)\ (\forall p_2)\ (\forall a_1)\ (\forall a_2)\ (((p_1,\in,PERSON) \wedge (p_1,AGE,a_1) \wedge (p_2,\in,PERSON) \wedge (p_2,AGE,a_2) \wedge (p_1,FATHER\text{-}OF,p_2)) \Rightarrow (a_1,>,a_2)).$$

Formulas can also be used to express inference. *Inference rules* require closed formulas of the form: $(u)\ (v \Rightarrow w)$, where v is a subformula, w is a template and u is universal quantification. For example, the following rule inserts every student with GPA greater than 3.5 into the honor category:

$$(\forall x)\ (\forall y)\ (((x,\in,STUDENT) \wedge (x,GPA,y) \wedge (y,>,3.5)) \Rightarrow (x,\in,HONORS))$$

If the database includes the facts $(JOHN,\in,STUDENT)$ and $(JOHN,GPA,3.7)$, then, using this rule the fact $(JOHN,\in,HONORS)$ may be inferred. An inference rule may therefore be regarded as a collective representation of facts.

Finally, a Loosely Structured database is a set of facts $\mathcal{P}$, a set of inference rules $\mathcal{I}$, and a set of integrity constraints $\mathcal{C}$, such that the closure of $\mathcal{P}$ under $\mathcal{I}$ does not falsify any of the constraints of $\mathcal{C}$.

Formulas are also instrumental in retrieval. A formula with free variables is a *query*.

---

[5]Although not necessary, implication is often used for clarity.

Let Q be such a query, and let $x_1,...,x_n$ be its free variables. The *value* of Q, denoted $\{Q\}$, is the set of tuples $(c_1,...,c_n)$ that satisfy it.

For example, the query

$$Q(x) = (x,\in,BOY) \wedge ((\exists y)\ (y,\in,GIRL) \wedge (x,BROTHER\text{-}OF,y))$$

lists all boys who have a sister. Assuming a database that includes all previously mentioned facts, the value of Q includes the entity *JACK*.

5. Query Generalization in the Loose Structure DBMS

Through the use of inference rules and integrity constraints the Loose Structure model permits the database designer to introduce as much structure as desired. In this section we discuss several rules that are necessary for proper query generalization.

The fundamental relationship between tokens and types is *membership*: a token is an instance of a type. To express this relationship with facts a special entity $\in$ is used. Example are *(JACK,*$\in$*,GIRL)* and *(2.5,*$\in$*,REAL-NUMBER)*.

A frequent relationship between types is *generalization*: the concept described by one type is more general than the concept described by the other type. To express this relationship with facts a special entity $\prec$ is used. Examples are *(GIRL,*$\prec$*,FEMALE)* and *(REAL-NUMBER,*$\prec$*,NUMBER)*.

A third basic relationship is between relationships and it is called *consequence*: one relationship always implies another relationship between the same two entities. To express this relationship with facts a special entity $\Rightarrow$ is used. Examples are, *(LOVE,*$\Rightarrow$*,LIKE)* and $(<,\Rightarrow,\neq)$.

The relations $\in$, $\prec$ and $\Rightarrow$ must be *disjoint* and their union must be *cycle-free*: two entities should not be related via more than one of these relationships, and an entity should not be related to itself through a chain of memberships, generalizations and consequences.

The following rules express part of the semantics of membership, generalization and consequence (existential quantifiers, as well as some parenthesis, are omitted):

$(x,\in,a)\ (a,\prec,b) \Rightarrow (x,\in,b)$,
$(x,r,y)\ (r,\Rightarrow,r') \Rightarrow (x,r',y)$,
$(a,\prec,b)\ (b,\prec,c) \Rightarrow (a,\prec,c)$, and
$(a,\Rightarrow,b)\ (b,\Rightarrow,c) \Rightarrow (a,\Rightarrow,c)$.

The first rule ensures that if a token is a member of a type, then it is also a member of every more general type. The second ensure that when two entities maintain a relationship, they also maintain every consequential relationship. The last two rules state the transitivity of generalizations and consequences.

A fact such as *(BOY,LOVES,DOG)* could have different meanings. For example, it could mean that *every* boy loves *every* dog, or that *every* boy loves *some* dogs, or that *some* boys love *some* dogs, etc. The desirable semantics can be enforced with appropriate inference rules. We adopt the weakest interpretation ("*some-some*") as the "standard" semantics. According to this interpretation, if *(JACK,LOVES,FIDO)* and *(FIDO,*$\in$*,DOG)* are facts, then *(JACK,LOVES,DOG)* should also be a fact. If *(JACK,*$\in$*,BOY)* is a fact then also *(BOY,LOVES,DOG)*. If *(BOY,*$\prec$*,PERSON)* then also *(PERSON,LOVES,DOG)*. If *(DOG,*$\prec$*,ANIMAL)* then also *(PERSON,LOVES, ANIMAL)*. Similarly, if *(LOVES,*$\Rightarrow$*,LIKES)* then also *(PERSON,LIKES,ANIMAL)*. These inferences are described by the following set of rules:

$(x,r,y) \wedge (x,\in,x') \Rightarrow (x',r,y)$,
$(x,r,y) \wedge (y,\in,y') \Rightarrow (x,r,y')$,
$(x,r,y) \wedge (x,\prec,x') \Rightarrow (x',r,y)$,
$(x,r,y) \wedge (y,\prec,y') \Rightarrow (x,r,y')$ and
$(x,r,y) \wedge (r,\Rightarrow,r') \Rightarrow (x,r',y)$.

The query generalizor in the Loose Stucture database management system receives a query Q that failed, and returns a set $\mathcal{Q}$ of queries that are minimal generalizations of Q. If Q specifies a total of n entities, then $\mathcal{Q}$ contains n queries: each is obtained by applying the generalization procedure to a different entity of Q. The mechanics of this procedure are different for types (or relationships) and for tokens.

5.1. Generalizing Types and Relationships

The previous rules guarantee that if a type specified in a query is substituted with a more general type, or if a relationship is substituted with a consequence relationship, a more general query is obtained. The generalization procedure substitutes a type or a relationship by the immediate generalization or consequence (or a conjunction of substitutions, if several immediates exist). Thus, among all more general queries that may be formed by substitutions this procedure selects the minimal one.

Consider this query to list all beer lovers:

$Q(x) = (x,\in,PERSON) \wedge (x,LOVES,BEER)$,

and assume the following facts represent the closest generalizations of the *PERSON*, *BEER* and *LOVES*:

(PERSON,≺,LIVING-THING),
(BEER,≺,ALCOHOLIC-BEVERAGE) and
(BEER,≺,FERMENTED-BEVERAGE).
(LOVES,⇒,LIKES),

The query generalizor produces three different queries:

$Q_1(x) = (x,\in,LIVING\text{-}THING) \wedge (x,LOVES,BEER)$,
$Q_2(x) = (x,\in,PERSON) \wedge (x,LIKES,BEER)$ and
$Q_3(x) = (x,\in,PERSON) \wedge (x,LOVES,ALCOHOLIC\text{-}BEVERAGE) \wedge$
$(x,LOVES,FERMENTED\text{-}BEVERAGE)$.

These queries return, respectively, all living things that love beer, all persons who merely like beer, and all persons who love beverages which are alcoholic and fermented.

When queries produced by the query generalizor fail, the generalization procedure is applied again. In the case of type or relationship generalization, the very same process is repeated.

5.2. Generalizing Tokens

Each token specified in Q required ***strict*** matching by a database token. The controlled relaxation of this requirement is the principle that governs the generalization procedure for tokens. For each token of Q a *neighborhood* is defined, and in the more general query matching is satisfied by ***any*** entity in this neighborhood. Defining a neighborhood of a token is like defining an ad-hoc type to which the token belongs.

Assume Q specifies a token E. Let N_E designate the neighborhood of E and let y be an existential variable not used in Q. The generalization of Q on E is obtained by substituting E with y and requiring that $y \in N_E$. Thus, if a query that requests a listing of all programmers who know PASCAL fails, and ALGOL, PL/1 and ADA are in PASCAL's neighborhood, then a more general query would be to list all programmers who know at least one of these languages. The more general query is then satisfiable by any other instance of this type. Obtaining a satisfactory neighborhood N_E is the major point to consider in this process.

Every database fact can be regarded as a characterization of each of its participating entities. Thus, two database entities that appear in similar facts (i.e. facts that are identical except for these two entities) share a common characterization. The more such common characterizations exist, the more similar the two entities are perceived. This leads to the following definitions of *neighborhood*, *immediate neighborhood* and *relevant neighborhood*.

Let X be an entity, and let *(X,Y,Z)* be a fact. The set of all database entities that match the query $Q(x) = (x,Y,Z)$ is called a *neighborhood* of X. An intersection of neighborhoods is also a neighborhood.

By intersecting all the neighborhoods to which X belongs we obtain a neighborhood of entities that share all the characterizations of X. As an example, if *(JOHN,∈,CITIZEN)*, *(JOHN,DRINKS,BEER)* and *(JOHN,LIKES,MARY)* are database facts, then *JOHN* belongs to three neighborhoods: the citizens, the beer drinkers, and those who like Mary. The intersection of these neighborhoods is the set entities that are most like John: the beer-loving citizens who like Mary.

Depending on the facts which describe an entity, the size of intersection neighborhoods may vary widely. If an entity is described by a unique fact, such as *(JOHN,TELEPHONE,743-6710)*, then the intersection neighborhood will include itself only. For the purpose of generalization, neighborhoods that do not encompass any additional entities are useless.[6] Consequently, when intersecting neighborhoods to obtain the set of entities most similar to the given entity, single element neighborhoods should not participate. While this, of course, does not guarantee an intersection with more than a single element, single element neighborhoods formed this way are more plausible: an entity is "truly unique" when no other entities share all its *non-identifying* characteristics. The *immediate neighborhood* of X is the intersection of all the multiple element neighborhoods to which X belongs.

Assume now a database on apartments available for rent in Los Angeles County is presented with the following query to list all apartments in Santa Monica.

$$Q(x) = (x,\in,APARTMENT) \wedge (x,LOCATED\text{-}IN,SANTA\text{-}MONICA).$$

When Q fails, it may be desirable to generalize it on the entity *SANTA-MONICA*. However, this entity may have many characterizations in the database, only some of which are relevant to its role in this query as apartment location (for example, the fact *(SANTA-MONICA,MAYOR,CLARK)* is a characterization of Santa Monica which is irrelevant to its present role). The role of *SANTA-MONICA* in Q is defined as *LOCATED-IN*, which is the relationship in the template in which it appears. Assume that the following characterizations of *SANTA-MONICA* are relevant to the role *LOCATED-IN*:

(SANTA-MONICA,RENT-CONTROL,STRICT),
(SANTA-MONICA,POLLUTION-LEVEL,LOW) and
(SANTA-MONICA,BEACH-ACCESS,YES).

Using a relationship called *relevant*, denoted @, this information is stored in three facts:

(LOCATED-IN,@,RENT-CONTROL),
(LOCATED-IN,@,POLLUTION-LEVEL) and
(LOCATED-IN,@,BEACH-ACCESS).

When the neighborhood of *SANTA-MONICA* is formed, *LOCATED-IN* is taken as its role, and the relationship *relevant* is used to identify *RENT-CONTROL*, *POLLUTION-LEVEL* and *BEACH-ACCESS* as relevant characterizations. The relevant neighborhood of *SANTA-MONICA* then includes all locations with the same

[6] And neighborhoods that are extremely wide are ineffective.

kind of rent control, pollution level and beach access. Consequently, the query generalizor outputs the following query:

$$Q'(x) = (x,\in,APARTMENT) \wedge ((\exists y)\ (x,LOCATED\text{-}IN\ y) \wedge (y,RENT\text{-}CONTROL,STRICT) \wedge (y,POLLUTION\text{-}LEVEL,LOW) \wedge (y,BEACH\text{-}ACCESS,YES)).$$

It is easy to verify that queries generated by immediate or relevant neighborhoods are indeed generalizations of the input queries (i.e. their answers contain the answers to the input queries). Of course, relevant neighborhoods can be formed only when the role of this entity is specified (i.e. not a variable), and the relationship @ provides some relevant characterizations. Otherwise, immediate neighborhoods are formed. Further generalization of a query that underwent immediate or relevant neighborhood substitution is done best by expanding the neighborhood, through removal of one of the characterizations used to form the neighborhood (this corresponds to the deletion of one of the conjuncts introduced in the substitution). Thus, if the neighborhood was single element, it immediately goes into further generalization.

5.3. Generalizing Numbers

Consider the following query to list all employees with four children:

$$Q(x) = (x,\in,EMPLOYEE) \wedge (x,NO\text{-}OF\text{-}CHILDREN,4)$$

and assume generalization on the entity 4 is attempted. In the case of number tokens, neighborhoods are readily available in the form of symmetric intervals around the number. A possible generalization of Q is:

$$Q'(x) = (x,\in,EMPLOYEE) \wedge (\exists y) \wedge (x,NO\text{-}OF\text{-}CHILDREN,y) \wedge (y,\geq,3) \wedge (y,\leq,5))).$$

Q' relaxes the requirement that the number of children must be 4; instead, this number should be in the interval $[3,5]$.

In this example, the lower and upper bounds chosen to replace 4 were the closest integers that create an interval with more than 4 itself. This seems suitable when substituting a value that represents number of children; when substituting, say, yearly salary, broader intervals should be used. For a meaningful substitution, the query generalizor looks for a fact that describes the appropriate *step*. This step relationship is denoted with the symbol Δ. Thus, facts such as *(NO-OF-CHILDREN,Δ,1)*, *(SALARY,Δ,1000)*, or *(BUDGET,Δ,10%)* describe the steps that should be used in enlarging the scope of a query involving this attribute. If a step fact is not available, then a system constant (such as 10%) may be used.

If the relationship involving the number is an arithmetic comparator, such as $\leq$ or $=$, then a simple reduction may be performed. Consider this input query to list all employees with salaries over **$30,000**:

$$Q(x) = (x,\in,EMPLOYEE) \wedge (\exists y)\ ((x,SALARY,y) \wedge (y,\geq,30000))$$

and assume *(SALARY,Δ,1000)*. The previous procedure generates the output query

$$Q'(x) = (x,\in,EMPLOYEE) \wedge ((\exists y)\ (x,SALARY,y) \wedge (\exists z)\ ((y,\geq,z) \wedge (z,\leq,31000) \wedge (z,\geq,29000))).$$

Q' may be reduced to

$$Q''(x) = (x,\in,EMPLOYEE) \wedge (\exists y)\ ((x,SALARY,y) \wedge (y,\geq,29000).$$

Since we assume that all valid mathematical facts are present, all queries generated by substituting numbers with intervals around these numbers are generalizations of the original queries. When further generalization is necessary, queries that were generalized by number substitution go into the very same process again.

6. Conclusion

Whether they reflect mistakes or are genuine failures, null answers are rarely satisfactory. By a simple analysis of null answers, we showed how every null answer can be provided with an interpretation.

We defined the concepts of query generalization and maximal failure, and adopted the assumption that a user who formulates a query expects all its generalizations to succeed. Consequently, these generalizations become indications of the user's conceptions. When a query fails these conceptions are tested in the computation of the maximal failures. If the query is already a maximal failure, the failure is classified as genuine, and the answers to the immediate generalizations are offered as partial answers. Otherwise each maximal failure is reported to the user as a possible misconception. In either case, an appropriate interpretation is provided.

The principles of the failure interpretation mechanism are independent of the data model used. Each implementation exploits the features of the particular data model. For example, in a relational database system, query generalization may be done by weakening mathematical conditions, or by deleting conjuncts from queries. In data models that incorporate a type hierarchy (these are often referred to as "semantic" data models) type substitution can be performed. In object-oriented data models ad-hoc neighborhoods may be created to replace tokens that cannot be matched.

Thus, our mechanism uses information already included in the database, without requiring additional meta-information to help the system understand queries (the @ and Δ facts are possible exceptions). In this respect it can be incorporated inexpensively into available systems. For more profound reasoning about queries, additional meta-information must be stored (and appropriate mechanisms to manipulate this information must be defined).

One possible drawback of our mechanism is that the number of possible generalizations is proportional to the number of entities specified in the query. For complex queries this could limit the utility of the mechanism. A pruning strategy, perhaps based on the cardinalities of the answers, may be desirable. Another important consideration is the cost of failure interpretation. As this is mainly the cost of evaluating the follow up queries, a retrieval strategy that avoids the need to evaluate each follow up query from scratch is very desirable.

References

[1] Corella et al.
Cooperative Responses to Boolean Queries.
In *Proceedings of the First International Conference on Data Engineering*, pages 77-85. Los Angeles, California, 1984.

[2] A. K. Joshi.
Mutual Beliefs in Question Answering Systems.
In N. Smith (editor), *Mutual Belief*. Academic Press, 1982.

[3] J. Kaplan.
Cooperative Responses from a Portable Natural Language Data Base Query System.
PhD thesis, Department of Computer and Information Science, University of Pennsylvania, 1979.

[4] E. Mays.
Failures in Natural Language Systems: Application to Data Base Query Systems.
In *Proceedings of the First Meeting of the American Association for Artificial Intelligence*. Stanford, CA, 1980.

[5] E. Mays et al.
Natural Language Interaction with Dynamic Knowledge Bases: Monitoring as Response.
In *Proceedings of 8-IJCAI*. Vancouver, BC, 1981.

[6] A. Motro.
Browsing in a Loosely Structured Database.
In *Proceedings of ACM-SIGMOD International Conference on Management of Data*, pages 197-207. Boston, Massaccusetts, 1984.

[7] B. L. Webber and E. Mays.
Varieties of user Misconceptions: Detection and Correction.
In *Proceedings of IJCAI-8*. Karlsruhe, Germany, 1983.

THE IRUS TRANSPORTABLE NATURAL LANGUAGE DATABASE INTERFACE

Madeleine Bates
M.G. Moser
David Stallard

BBN Laboratories
Cambridge, MA

1. INTRODUCTION

In a previous publication [Bates83] and in a public demonstration [ACL83] , we have presented a natural language query system called IRUS[1] which is transportable among domains and also among database systems. This paper describes the characteristics of that interface and several of its components, and gives examples of its current capabilities.

Many systems boast of having a "user-friendly" or "English-like" or even "English" interface, but may use shallow, relatively ad hoc techniques that are not robust or linguistically sound. This can result in exchanges which appear to be correct but which are actually misleading, as the following example illustrates (it was obtained using the demonstration version of a commercially available natural language system):

User: Are all the vice presidents male?
System: Yes.
User: Are any of the vice presidents female?
System: Yes.
User: Are any of the male vice presidents female?
System: Yes.

Given the fact that there was nothing unusual about the database being accessed (or the people represented in it), this "conversation" does not inspire confidence that the system understands the user's questions. Just what are the limits of computer "understanding" of natural language? In a review paper [Bates84] we describe the state-of-the-art in natural language understanding and list a number of criteria for judging natural language interfaces. Many other researchers have also investigated similar issues and have designed and/or developed systems and written about the problems in the field [Boguraev83, Codd78, Davidson83, Ginsparg83, Grosz83, Guida83, Hendrix82, Moore82, Salveter84, Schwartz82, Sondheimer81, Templeton83, Thompson83, Walker81, Waltz77, Waltz78].

IRUS attempts to understand the user's queries before figuring out how to retrieve the answer. IRUS is a knowledge-based system, with procedural components that are independent of any particular domain and data base structure. These components use knowledge bases that are domain- and database-dependent. IRUS also contains a knowledge base creation module that allows users to conveniently create and maintain these knowledge structures.

---

[1] IRUS stands for **I**nformation **R**etrieval **U**sing the **RUS** parser. The primary members of the development team are Lyn Bates, Rusty Bobrow, Peggy Moser, and Dave Stallard.

2. EXAMPLES OF IRUS'S CAPABILITIES

To use IRUS (once it has been set up for a particular domain), a user needs only to call the IRUS program and begin typing English questions or commands. Here are some examples of interactions (slightly edited for compactness) using IRUS to access information about people in a company and material that they may have written. The comments point out some of the complex features of English that the system can handle, and some of the particularly nice characteristics of the interface.

>> **How many people in dept. 45 don't live in Cambridge or boston**

```
------RESPONSE----
  19
-----------------
```

IRUS understands simple negation, conjunction, and disjunction. Its dictionary contains many abbreviations, such as "dept." for "department". Note that IRUS does not demand that capitalization and punctuation be correct.

>> **List their names.**

```
------RESPONSE------

LASTNAME    FIRSTNAME
Bates       Madeleine
Bobrow      Robert
 . . .
Tobiason    Beverly
-----------------
```

IRUS allows the use of many referring expressions such as "its title", "that man", etc. In this case, it interprets the referent of "their" to be the people in dept. 45 who don't live in Cambridge or Boston.

>> **Have any of them written papers about "syntax"**

```
------RESPONSE----
Yes,  1 out of 19
-----------------
```

A special case of referring expressions is the use of simple pronouns , such as "they", "them", and "he". IRUS does not take yes/no questions literally, but attempts, where possible, to provide additional information that the user might find helpful. In this case, if the answer had been a simple "yes", the user might have had to ask "How many of them?".

>> **Who is it?**

```
------RESPONSE------

LASTNAME    FIRSTNAME
Bates       Madeleine
-----------------
```

In this case, the pronoun "it" is used to refer not to an entity in the previous query but to an entity in the system's response.

>> **Who in dett 42 lives in Arlington?**

DETT=DEPT ? yes

------RESPONSE------

LASTNAME	FIRSTNAME
Gentner	Dedre
Larkin	Kathy
Steinberg	Cynthia
Stevens	Albert

IRUS is written in Interlisp and uses the Interlisp spelling corrector to attempt to correct spelling errors. If the spelling corrector fails, the user is given an opportunity to correct the word or to define it.

>> **dept 41?**

------RESPONSE------

LASTNAME	FIRSTNAME
Caglayan	Alper

IRUS recognizes this stand-alone noun phrase as an elliptical utterance, and interprets it by finding an entity in the previous utterance which is semantically similar enough to the current utterance to allow a substitution.

>> **Journals sponsored by the IEEE.**

------RESPONSE------
IEEE Trans Med. Imaging
Computer
IEEE Trans. Syst. Man Cyber.
. . .
IEEE Spectrum
IEEE J. Ocean Eng.

Because there is no way to interpret this stand-alone noun phrase as an instance of ellipsis, IRUS implies the existence of the imperative verb "show".

>> **list the 10 most recent articles about "syntax"**

Sorry, there are only 4 of what you asked for. I'll go ahead and answer your question for them.

------RESPONSE------
Text-Critiquing with the EPISTLE System
Planning Units and Syntax in Sentence Production
Syntax in Automatic Speech Understanding
The Use of Syntax in a Speech Understanding System

IRUS understands a wide range of comparisons and superlatives , such as "List THE TEN LARGEST departments" and "Do any journals cost MORE than the AVERAGE cost of THE THREE MOST EXPENSIVE medical journals?" In this case, there were only four articles of the type specified; rather than failing, IRUS informs the user of the situation and provides what information it can.

>> **Did Smith write all the papers on "koala bears"?**

------RESPONSE------
Sorry, but there aren't any such
bibliographical items in the database

IRUS recognizes the presupposition that there are papers on koala bears in the database, and informs the user that this presupposition has failed. This is a far more helpful response than the literal answer "no".

>> **has every woman in dept 45 written a paper since 1979?**

------RESPONSE------
No, just 4 out of 10

Again, IRUS attempts to be helpful, and provides additional information rather than responding literally to the yes/no question.

These examples show IRUS to be a flexible, helpful database retrieval interface with the capability of understanding a wide variety of natural English sentences.

3. COMPONENTS OF IRUS

In order to have an appropriately modular system, it is necessary to separate the user's conceptual view of the domain from the details of both the database structure and the particular database system being used. The result of parsing and semantic interpretation are expressed in terms of the user's conceptual structure so that the database structure can be changed without having to modify the language understanding part of the system. This representation (interpretation) has a clear formal semantics, so that it is possible to determine whether the system has adequately represented ("understood") the user's input before accessing the database.

Figure 1 shows a schematic diagram of the two major modules of the IRUS system. The natural language module contains a parser (the RUS parser, which is based on techniques described in [Bobrow78, Bates78] and a semantic interpreter. Together, their task is to process an English query or command and to "understand" it as far as is possible *without* using any knowledge of any particular database system. This level of understanding is represented as an expression in a formal Meaning Representation Language (MRL).

MRL is the primary semantic representation used by IRUS, and has a formal declarative semantics that can be expressed in the predicate calculus as well as a formal procedural semantics [Woods81]. The procedural semantics for MRL makes it possible to define the operation of the system in any database which can provide generators for the entities that are referred to by noun phrases, and procedures to filter such generators to represent predicates. Any database system for which such a procedural semantics can be defined can be interfaced to the MRL output.

The next step in processing is to fill out the interpretation using additional linguistic (but domain independent) information. This includes resolving pronouns and other anaphoric references, completing ellipsed elements, and disambiguating references by using discourse information.

Figure 1. Overview of the IRUS System.

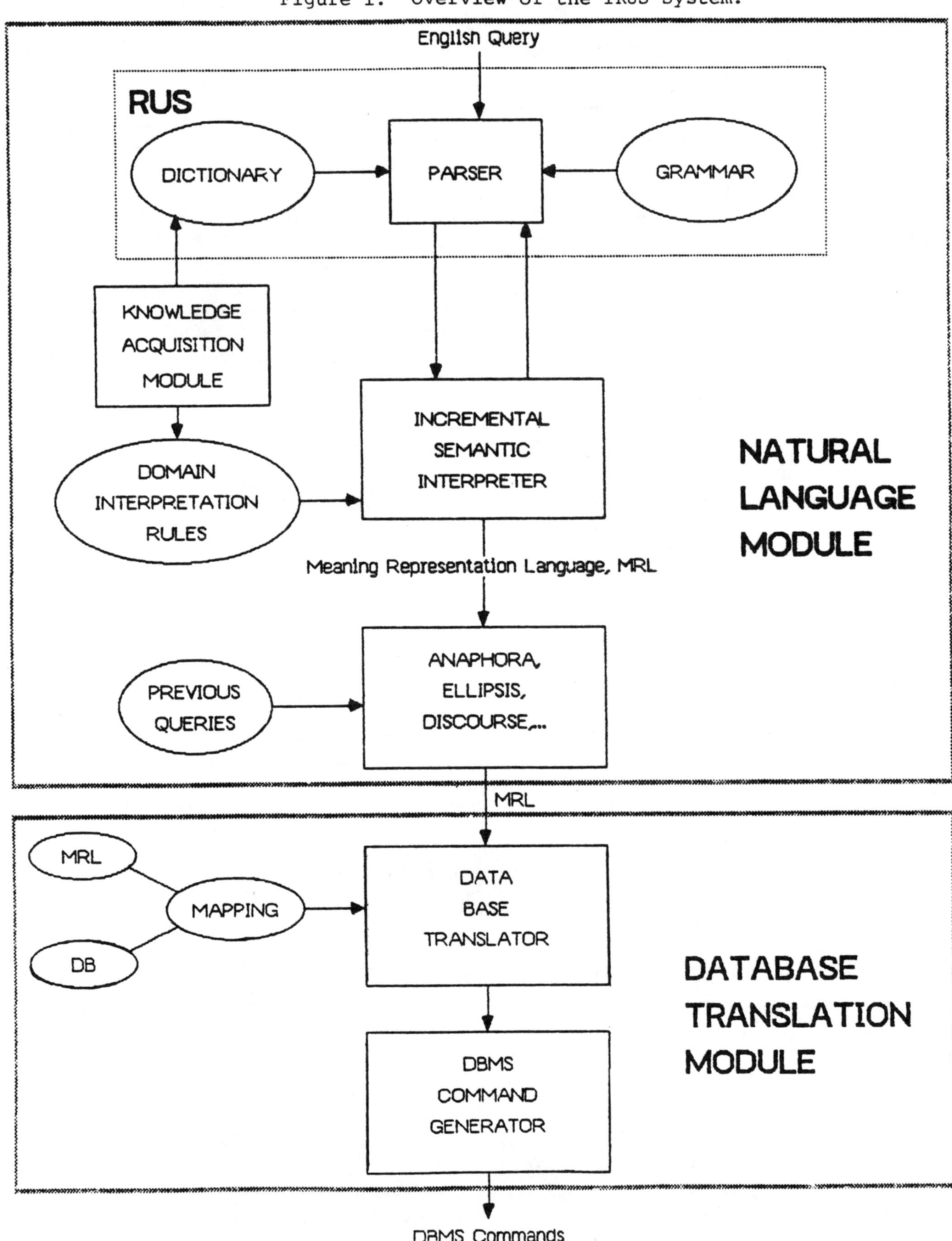

Several knowledge bases contribute to the syntactic, semantic, and discourse processing. They are:

1. a dictionary of English words (which is largely domain-dependent),
2. a large grammar of English (which does not change from one domain to another),
3. a set of semantic rules (also very domain-dependent),
4. the MRL representations of previous inputs by the user.

The dictionary contains information about word and phrase substitutes (such as "Unitedtes" for "USA"), parts of speech, and syntactic features (such as whether a particular verb takes a direct object or not). The grammar is used to syntactically analyze the sequence of words in the input, and the semantic rules determine whether the incremental syntactic assignments (such as the subject of a particular verb) produce interpretable structures.

The last knowledge base, the dialogue context, is used to determine the referents of pronouns (such as "Where does HE live?") and other referring expressions (as in "Who wrote THAT PAPER?"), to resolve some ambiguities, and to fill in elliptical utterances.

3.1. Domain Dependent Semantic Rule Acquisition

A very important module pictured in Figure 1 is the Knowledge Base Acquisition Module, which allows users to create dictionary entries and semantic rules to extend the domain. The lexical acquisition process (which allows a user to define the parts of speech and syntactic features of words) has been described elsewhere [Bates]; this section will focus on the semantic rule acquisition process. The method relies on user-generated English examples of domain sentences, relieving the user of the need to know the underlying representation. The component performing this process is called IRACQ (for Interpretation Rule ACQuisition).

Semantic knowledge is used by the processor to (1) decide which phrases are meaningful, and (2) compute the meaning of those phrases. This is a recursive process. Typically, a phrase, the matrix phrase, is composed of constituent phrases. The matrix is meaningful if all its constituents are meaningful and are combined in an acceptable way. The meaning of the matrix is computed from the constituent meanings.

This section presents an example of how IRACQ acquires the knowledge needed to compute these interpretations. In this example, IRACQ is going to acquire the semantic knowledge needed to interpret the verb "write", in the sense of writing papers and books. More precisely, IRACQ will acquire the information needed to interpret phrases which refer to things in the WRITE-ACTION semantic class. (A semantic class is some set of things in the domain.) In the IRUS test domain, "write", "author" (when used as a verb), and "publish" are all used to talk about the same semantic class. The first step in the acquisition dialogue is for the user to enter an example sentence which we will call an exemplar.

The following dialogue was obtained using the IRACQ system. Input from the user is shown in boldface, output from the system is in regular face, and comments are in italics.

Enter an exemplar SENTENCE using WRITE: **JONES WROTE SOME ARTICLES**

IRACQ uses the full language processor of IRUS to parse the exemplar and interpret all its constituents. In this case, the last name "Jones" is interpreted as a reference to a member of the semantic class PERSONNEL.

JONES is in the semantic class PERSONNEL.
Choose one of these generalizations: PERSON, AGENT, <CR>(to keep PERSONNEL),
or Exemplar (to give a new constituent): **PERSON**

IRACQ needs to know whether the subject constituent must refer to a member of the class PERSONNEL or to a member of one of the more general classes PERSON and AGENT.

In case there was an error in the exemplar, e.g., the user thought "Jones" was the name of an organization, the user may enter another exemplar constituent. Now that IRACQ has elicited a selectional restriction on the subject of "write", it goes on to ask about the object.

ARTICLE is in the semantic class BIBLIOGRAPHY.

Choose one of the generalizations: WRITTEN-MATERIAL,
HOLDING,
<CR> (to keep BIBLIOGRAPHY),

or Exemplar (to give new constituent): **BIBLIOGRAPHY**

Now IRACQ asks whether there are any prepositional phrases likely to modify "write".

Any Prepositional Phrases (PPs)? **Yes**

When additional constituents are possible, IRACQ will continue to prompt for more exemplars. This obviates the need for the user to include all possible interpretable constituents in the first exemplar.

Enter an exemplar PP: **IN NEWSWEEK**

IRACQ now asks for synonyms for the preposition.

What PREPs besides IN can be used this way: **FOR**

NEWSWEEK is in the semantic class JOURNAL.

Choose one of the generalizations: WRITTEN-MATERIAL,
HOLDING,
<CR> (to keep JOURNAL),

or Exemplar (to give a new constituent): **JOURNAL**

Enter an exemplar PP: **OK**

The "ok" signals the end of the user's specification of PPs, and IRACQ summarizes the information it has elicited.

To interpret: JONES writes ARTICLE in NEWSWEEK.
requires: (JONES to be PERSON class)
(ARTICLE to be BIBLIOGRAPHY class)
(NEWSWEEK to be JOURNAL class)

For each constituent slot the user has specified, IRACQ uses its exemplar to create a "tag" name for it. This statement is generated to inform the user of the tags IRACQ has created and the selectional restrictions the user specified for the constituent represented by each tag. Here, the tag ARTICLE has been created for the object slot of the phrase, and IRACQ knows it must be something in the BIBLIOGRAPHY class.

Now IRACQ knows all the constituent slots and the selectional restrictions for them, it needs to know the semantic relations among the constituents. How should the system construct the meaning of a WRITE-ACTION phrase, given the meanings of a PERSON subject and BIBLIOGRAPHY object? The user is asked to use the tags to specify how to combine the constituents to compute this meaning.

Enter predicates, just 'OK' when done.
  Enter a predicate: **(AUTHOR JONES ARTICLE)**
  Enter a predicate: **(IN-JOURNAL ARTICLE NEWSWEEK)**
  Enter a predicate: **OK**

Predicates represent relations between the semantic classes in the domain. For now, we assume the user knows something about what predicates are understood by the system. IRACQ tags are used to specify how to instantiate the predicates when the semantic knowledge is used.

This concludes the annotated example of an interaction with IRACQ.

Much of the knowledge needed by an English processor is language specific, rather than domain specific. This includes both syntactic and semantic information. The grammar of a language and the syntactic features of words are (almost) domain independent. The semantics of quantifiers, determiners, and other "closed class" words tend to be domain independent, and are built into the basic IRUS system rather than acquired by the mechanism illustrated above.

What has to be acquired for each new domain? There are three kinds of domain dependent semantic knowledge:

- Domain Model. What kinds of things will be talked about in the domain? What generalizations of the classification will be useful? What are the relations between the classes? For instance, in the example above, things were classified into PERSONNEL, BIBLIOGRAPHY, and JOURNAL. PERSONNEL is generalized by the classes PERSON and AGENT, and the AUTHOR relation holds between the PERSON and BIBLIOGRAPHY classes.
- Interpretability. Which of the possible syntactic constructions make sense? What are the selectional restrictions, the kind of thing which should fill each syntactic slot in a phrase? The processor must be able to recognize that, in a particular domain, a phrase of the form "PERSON-in-DEPARTMENT" is meaningful, but not "PERSON-in-BOOK". The example above established the NP-V-NP-PP syntax as meaningful when the verb is "write", "author", or "publish" and the first NP refers to members of the PERSON class.
- Predication. How should the constituents be combined to form the interpretation of the phrase?

Each class in the domain model is a semantic class. For each class, the processor must be able to recognize (and produce meaning representations of) the phrases that refer to entities in that class and relate them to other classes. To do this, the processor will use a "phrase description", generated by the domain dependent semantic acquisition. One way to think of a phrase description is as an abstraction of all the ways of talking about a semantic class. Each time a phrase refers to something in the class, then, it will be a specific instance of our abstraction. A phrase description associates relations between the semantic classes with constituent syntax and selectional restriction configurations.

The phrase description produced for the WRITE-ACTION class in the example above includes:

- **the head words.** "write", "author", and "publish".
- **the PEOPLE to BIBLIOGRAPHY relation.** Expressed by a PEOPLE subject and BIBLIOGRAPHY object in a WRITE-ACTION phrase. This relation is (AUTHOR subject object).
- **the BIBLIOGRAPHY to JOURNAL relation.** (IN-JOURNAL object object-of-prep).

A phrase description only needs to identify the most basic syntactic form which expresses the restrictions and relations being defined. Complex constructions such as relative clauses and questions are derived from the simpler ones by the language processor using rules of the grammar.

The IRACQ approach is example driven rather than model driven. An important feature of the system is that it isolates just the part of the IRule that constitutes the domain dependent semantic knowledge. All of the detail of the IRule representation, much of which is system specific or language specific, is handled by IRACQ. Furthermore, the exemplar will constrain the possibilities when acquiring the selectional restrictions, so the user does not need to know semantic class names.

Example directed acquisition is a natural, user-friendly approach to semantic acquisition. However, it does put the burden of completeness on the user. During the acquisition dialogue, the user may give many exemplars when a phrase description has many constituents. There is no guarantee, though, that all the relevant ways of talking about the semantic class and relating it to other semantic classes will occur to the user during this process.

3.2. Data Modeling in the Database Translator

One aspect of natural language understanding systems that is often overlooked is the process by which these systems compute the answers to queries once they have interpreted them. This is more difficult than it first appears. First, and in most general terms, how does one associate the elements of the domain of discourse with the relations in the database? Second, how does one use the retrieval operations of the database in such a way as to handle the most general possible class of queries? In what follows we assume a relational organization of data; however, what we have to say generalizes readily to other models.

To apply a natural language system to an existing database system, one must take the query language that DBMS provides as the target of the translation process. Unfortunately, the basic operations of such query languages are often very limited in expressive power, and they must accordingly have recourse to loops and conditional branching to handle many queries. This notion of expressive power should be distinguished from "relational completeness" — the ability to select any set of tuples in the database [Codd72]. Suppose the database contains the following relations:

PERSONNEL(EMPNUM, EMPNAME,SALARY,DEPTNO)
MEETINGS(MEETNUM,TOPIC,LOCATION,DATE)
ATTENDANCE(EMPNUM,MEETNUM)

Many query languages equivalent to Codd's relational algebra [Codd70] could not handle the following queries without explicit loops and branches:

"Who attended every meeting?"

"What is the average salary in each department?"

Both sentences are readily parsed by the linguistic component of IRUS. The first query, of course, is an example of universal quantification; it requires the relatively uncommon DIVIDE operator [Date77]. The second query is a request for values of what is effectively an attribute of an entire set of tuples; it could not be expressed with the standard relational operators. A natural language system that uses only the standard operations of the target query language would be unable to provide answers for these queries.

The point to be made here is that the difficulty has nothing to do with linguistic considerations. Indeed, its occurrence in a query could not be predicted from them. One could express the sentences above in any alternative syntax (such as "Who wrote all the articles on syntax?") and the problem would still be the same. A system with such an incapacity limits the user on the level of a "deep structure" that has nothing to do with linguistics, nor fundamentally, with computation cost, but rather with the *interior* expressive power of the system. This has important implications for the success of the whole enterprise. We have gained rather little if we free users from limitations of syntax only to hobble them in what they can to do with it.

Another class of difficulties for the system has nothing to do with the query language per se; it arises instead from anomalies in the logical organization of the database. Some of these are discussed in [Konolidge79]. Suppose that in the relation PERSONNEL a city is represented by name and in the relation SALES by some code. How do we refer to the set of all cities, as in the query "How many cities do you know about?". One must also deal with queries like "Who lives in the city with the highest sales rating?", which would require a join on SALES and PERSONNEL. This is an example of a general alternative naming problem, in which entities of a given kind in the real world can have more than one unique identifier in the database. We can expect it to arise frequently in real applications, particularly those which are distributed across several independent databases.

A similar problem has to do with "derived attributes" — those which are not explicitly present in any relation but which can be derived from other attributes. For example, suppose we have a relation

PERSONNEL(EMPNUM,EMPNAME,SALARY,TAX)

and want to ask questions like "What is the average net pay?", where "net pay" is defined as the expression (SALARY - TAX). IRUS approaches both these problems by providing the linguistic component with a database-independent "conceptual model" of the domain in which it may express its interpretation of the query. Further details of query computation are then not the concern of the linguistic component.

Finally there are the issues of transportability and maintenance. We would like our system to be transportable to a variety of DBMS systems with different target query languages (and data models other than the relational) as well as to handle reorganizations in the logical structure of the data base, such the as addition of a new relation that relates employees and the projects they work on. It is important, if only from the vantage point of good software engineering, that neither modifications nor movement to new database systems require extensive re-programming.

Suppose we have a sample database which is organized into two relations:

PERSONNEL(EMPNUM,LASTNAME,FIRSTNAME,SAL,EMPDEPT)
DEPT(DEPTNO,DEPTNAME,MGR)

However, it could just as easily be organized with the same PERSONNEL relation but a different DEPT relation and a third relation called MANAGER:

DEPT(DEPTNO,DEPTNAME)
MANAGER(MGR,MDEPT)

Notice that nothing about the company has changed; the database still represents the same information. To get the department manager of an employee, however, now requires two joins instead of one. A natural language processor that converted its inputs from English directly into queries against the relations of the database would have to be modified each time the relations were modified and in every place where it used those relations. This would certainly not be economical, nor could it be made very easy for a database administrator to do.

The root of the reorganization problem is the confusion between WHAT a user asked for how and HOW to get it for him. IRUS rigorously separates these two questions by having its linguistic processor output its interpretations of English queries in terms of a "conceptual model" of the application domain.

The problem of keeping up with database reorganization must be distinguished from the problem of portability between different database management systems. IRUS solves the latter by interposing a standard query language between itself and the DBMS.

The reader may wonder why the relational data model, which is supposed to be a "high-level" view of data, is not adequate as a conceptual model. There are three reasons why it is not. First of all, the relational model does not deal on the logical level with "things in the world", but with lexical tokens — employee numbers and so on — that are supposed to name them. This accounts for what we have called the "alternative naming problem" — the way in which a given city can be represented in one relation by its name, and in another by some code. The conceptual model would have just one class, CITIES, whose members could have as attributes both a name and a city code.

A second point to be made is that the relational model does not include a facility for defining semantic classes like those of our conceptual model as members of a set. If a particular element of the domain, such as cities, does not have a relation all to itself, it becomes difficult to ask anything about the set of all cities.

Finally, the relational data model tends to lump different relationships together into one compound statement about something. This is at the root of the reorganization problem. For example, each tuple of the PERSONNEL relation presented earlier makes several statements about a given employee: name, salary, and department. Each of these three relationships is separate from the others, yet to to refer to any one of them it is necessary to remember that they are all grouped together in the same database relation. There is nothing to prevent them from being encoded in three separate database relations instead of one. Furthermore, two attributes, LASTNAME and FIRSTNAME, are part of the same relationship — that which is between a person and his or her name. They are thus part of a group, yet there is nothing in the relation which informs us of this fact.

In summary, while the relational model is most useful for representing efficiently facts about individuals, it is not so useful for describing particular classes of things or the application domains of which they are a part. To do this, IRUS introduces a conceptual modeling layer between the English input and the dbms command output.

Our approach to these problems is to make "question-answering" a separate subproblem of the natural language understanding system, with its own issues and methods. The linguistic processor outputs a formal representation of the user's query; it is then up to the question-answering component to come up with the answer. This has the advantage that both parts of the system can then be separately developed and improved — something which has proved very helpful in the development of the IRUS system.

4. CONCLUSIONS AND FUTURE DIRECTIONS

The initial version of IRUS (interfacing to the dbms System 1022) was operational at the end of January 1983. The existence of a mature, well-engineered parser, the power of the Interlisp program development environment, and our past experience with natural language understanding systems made it possible to implement this first version of IRUS with only a few person-months of effort, but it has been under nearly continuous development since that time.

The modularity of the parser's design, together with the potential for effective guidance from the cascaded interaction with semantic knowledge, will permit us to continue the development of linguistically well-founded extensions to the parser. In particular, we plan to extend the techniques now being used (similar to those proposed by Weischedel and Sondheimer [Weischedel79, Weischedel80, Sondheimer80, Weischedel81]) to process input that is syntactically ill-formed.

In the long term, a number of important research problems still exist in such areas of anaphora resolution, ellipsis processing and the discourse model, but the current IRUS system demonstrates that partial solutions to these problems can provide a habitable, useful natural language interface.

References

ACL83.
Association for Computational Linguistics and the Naval Laboratory, ACL,, *Conference on Applied Natural Language Processing*, Santa Monica, CA, February, 1983.

Bates83.
Bates, Madeleine and Robert J. Bobrow, "A Transportable Natural Language Interface for Information Retrieval," *Proceedings of the 6th Annual International ACM SIGIR Conference*, ACM Special Interest Group on Information Retrieval and American Society for Information Science, Washington, D.C., June, 1983.

Bates84.
Bates, Madeleine and Robert Bobrow, "Natural Language Interfaces: What's Here, What's Coming, and Who Needs It," in *Artificial Intelligence Applications for Business*, Ablex Publishing Company, 1984.

Bates.Bates, M. and R.J. Bobrow, The RUS Parser, User's Guide, unpublished BBN manuscript.

Bates78.
Bates, M., "The Theory and Practice of Augmented Transition Network Grammars," in *Natural Language Communication with Computers*, ed. L. Bolc, Springer-Verlag, 1978.

Bobrow78.
Bobrow, R.J., The RUS System, Section of BBN Report No. 3878,, Bolt Beranek and Newman Inc., 1978.

Boguraev83.
Boguraev, B.K. and K. Sparck Jones, "How to Drive a Database Front End Using General Semantic Information," *Proceedings of the Conference on Applied Natural Language Processing, ACL and NRL,*, Santa Monica , CA, February, 1983.

Codd70.
Codd, E.F., "A Relational Model of Data for Large Shared Data Banks," *CACM*, vol. 13, no. 6, June 1970.

Codd72.
Codd, E.F., "Data Base Systems," in *Courant Computer Science Symposia Series*, Englewood Cliffs, NJ, 1972.

Codd78.
Codd, E.F., R.S. Arnold, J-M. Cadiou, C.L. Chang, and N. Roussopoulos, RENDEZVOUS Version 1: An Experimental English-Language Query Formulation System for Casual Users of Relational Data Bases, IBM Research Report RJ2144, San Jose, CA, January, 1978.

Date77.
Date, C.J., *An Introduction to Database Systems,* Addison-Wesley Publishing Company, 1977.

Davidson83.
Davidson, James and J.S. Kaplan, "Natural Language to Access Data bases: Interpreting Update Requests," *AJCL*, vol. 9, no. 2, pp. 57-68, April-June 1983.

Ginsparg83.
Ginsparg, J.M., "A Robust Portable Natural Language Data Base Interface," *Proceedings of the Conference on Applied Natural Language Processing*, ACL and NRL, Santa Monica, CA, February, 1983.

Grosz83.
Grosz, B.J., "TEAM, a Transportable Natural Language Interface System," *Proceedings of the Conference on Applied Natural Language Processing*, ACL and NRL, Santa Monica, CA, February, 1983.

Guida83.
Guida, G. and C. Tasso, "IR-NLI: An Expert Natural Language Interface to Online Data Bases," *Proceedings of the Conference on Applied Natural Language Processing*, ACL and NRL, Santa Monica, CA, February, 1983.

Hendrix82.
Hendrix, G.G., "Natural-Language Interface," *American Journal of Computational Linguistics*, vol. 8, no. 2, April-June 1982.

Konolidge79.
Konolidge, K., A Framework for a Portable Natural- Language Interface to Large Data Bases, SRI International, Report 197, Menlo Park, CA, October, 1979.

Moore82.
Moore, R.C., "Natural-Language Access to Databases - Theoretical/Technical Issues," *Proceedings of the 20th Annual Meeting of the Association of Computational Linguistics*, 1982.

Salveter84.
Salveter, Sharon, Natural Language Database Update, TR# 84/001, Computer Science Department, Boston University, 1984.

Schwartz82.
Schwartz, S.P., "Problems with Domain-Independent Natural Language Database Access Systems," *Proceedings of the 20th Annual Meeting of the ACL*, Association for Computational Linguistics, Toronto, Ontario, Canada, June, 1982.

Sondheimer81.
Sondheimer, N., "Panel: Evaluation of Natural Language Interfaces to Database Systems," *Proceedings of the 19th Annual Meeting of the ACL*, Association for Computational Linguistics, Stanford University, June, 1981.

Sondheimer80.
Sondheimer, N.K. and R.M. Weischedel, "A Rule-Based Approach to Ill-Formed Input," *Proc. 8th Int'l Conf. on Computational Linguistics*, pp. 46-54, Tokyo, Japan, October, 1980.

Templeton83.
Templeton, M. and J. Burger, "Problems in Natural Language Interface to DBMS with Examples from EUFID," *Proceedings of the Conference on Applied Natural Language Processing*, ACL and NRL, Santa Monica, CA, February, 1983.

Thompson83.
Thompson, B.H. and F.B. Thompson, "Introducing ASK, A Simple Knowledgeable System," *Proceedings of the Conference on Applied Natural Language Processing*, Santa Monica, CA, February, 1983.

Walker81.
Walker, D.E. and J.R. Hobbs, Natural Language Access to Medical Text, Technical Note 240, SRI International, March, 1981.

Waltz77.
Waltz, D.L., "Natural Language Interfaces," *SIGART Newsletter 61*, February 1977.

Waltz78.
Waltz, D.L., "An English Language Question Answering System for a Large Relational Database," *CACM*, vol. 21, no. 7, pp. 526-534, 1978.

Weischedel79.
Weischedel, R.M. and J.E. Black, Responding to Potentially Unparseable Sentences, University of Delaware, February, 1979.

Weischedel80.
Weischedel, R.M. and J.E. Black, "If The Parser Fails," *Proceedings of the 18th Annual Meeting of the ACL*, June 1980.

Weischedel81.
Weischedel, R.M. and N.K. Sondheimer, A Framework for Processing Ill-Formed Input, University of Delaware, October, 1981.

Woods81.
Woods, W.A., "Procedural Semantics as a Theory of Meaning," in *Elements of Discourse Understanding*, ed. A. Joshi, B.L. Webber and I. Sag, Cambridge University Press, 1981.

Anticipating False Implicatures: Cooperative Responses in Question-Answer Systems

Julia Hirschberg

Department of Computer and Information Science
Moore School/D2
University of Pennsylvania
Philadelphia, PA 19104

1. Introduction

Research on cooperative question-answering [Pollack82, Joshi84a] has shown that a natural language (NL) capability provides more than just "syntactic sugar." Emulation of natural discourse in computer-human interaction can permit the generation of more cooperative responses to user input, which may correct user misconceptions, avoid the licensing of misconceptions, convey information concisely, provide appropriate explanations of system reasoning, and so on; [Joshi82, Mays80, Kaplan81, Mercer84 Schuster83, McCoy83, Allen80, Pollack84, Hirschberg84, Joshi84b, Joshi84c] such emulation can also permit systems to infer information that may be implicitly conveyed by a user and so make explicit questioning unnecessary [Webber84]. In some cases, these benefits may be generalized to non-NL interfaces to make them more cooperative. This paper outlines a strategy for improving the cooperativeness of NL interfaces with database and expert systems that can also be applied to non-NL interaction with them.

In existing database query systems, users' yes-no questions generally elicit a simple *yes* or *no* from the system. The query in (1), for example, might

(1) Q: Has the Acme shipment come in?

a. R: No.

Q: Have they sent it?

R: No.

Q: Was it ordered?

R: No.

Q: Was the requisition filed?

R: Yes.

b. R: The requisition was filed.

initiate an exchange such as (1a), for example. Note that Q is forced to play Twenty Questions to elicit the information that could, in natural discourse, be provided in an indirect response such as (1b). If Q is not persistent, or does not fully recognize the system's limitations, she may never obtain this information, and may never learn that, while the shipment in question has been requisitioned, as far as the system knows it was never ordered.

The difficulty of supporting such responses in question-answer systems is due in part to the fact that accounts of them to date have been heavily domain and exchange-dependent [Hobbs79, Hoeppner84]. However, the concept of **scalar implicature** (SI) provides a more general interpretation that is, consequently, more amenable to computational use. A formalization of this concept promises a powerful and versatile tool for cooperative question-answering. Among other uses, it provides a principled basis for the generation of cooperative responses to yes-no questions, both in NL interfaces which may be extended to use in formal language interfaces.

In Section 2, I explain the concept of SI. In Section 3, I discuss a primary reason for employing it in a system's response strategy, i.e., lest the questioner otherwise draw false conclusions from the system's response. I give a detailed example of the use of such a strategy in database question-answering in Section 4. Finally, in Section 5, I mention the related problems I am currently working on.

2. Scalar Implicature

In 1967, Grice [Grice75] proposed certain conventions governing cooperative conversation. His **Cooperative Principle** postulates that, without evidence to the contrary, participants in conversation assume that their partners share certain conversational goals, specified by some maxims of cooperative conversation. Based upon Grice's **Maxims of Quantity**:

a) Make your contribution as informative as is required (for the current purposes of the exchange).

b) Do not make your contribution more informative than is required.

and **Quality**:

Try to make your contribution one that is true.

a) Do not say what you believe to be false.

b) Do not say that for which you lack adequate evidence,

Horn [Horn72] proposed that, when an utterance refers to a value on some scale defined by **semantic entailment,**[1] that value represents the highest value on its scale that the speaker can truthfully affirm. That is, the speaker is saying as much (**Quantity**) as he truthfully (**Quality**) can. Higher values on the scale, i.e., those that entail the asserted value, are implicitly marked as either not **known** to be true or known **not** to be true, depending upon how far away such values are from the affirmed value.[2] Values lower on the scale than the value affirmed, i.e., values entailed by that value, will be implicitly marked as true. Horn called this notion **scalar predication**.

Simple scalar predication might thus account for (1b) in the following terms: R affirms the furthest stage in a *stages-of-a-process* scale that he truthfully can, here, *filing the requisition*. So, later stages, or higher values, such as *ordering the shipment* and *sending the shipment*, are implicitly marked as unknown or false. However, it is not clear that such process scales are in fact defined by entailment. And other exchanges, such as (2), which seem to

(2) Q: Did Senator Smith testify at the hearing?

R: His aide did.

permit implicatures similar to (1b), clearly cannot be explained in terms of any entailment ordering.

2.1. Redefining Scale

Relations that support SI can be distinguished from those that do not in that they are asymmetric, transitive, and can be defined to be irreflexive. These characteristics in fact define the class of **partial orderings**, i.e., irreflexive, asymmetric, and transitive relations.[3] Using this

---

[1] **M** semantically entails **T** iff **T** is true under every assignment of truth values (i.e., in every model) in which **M** is true.

[2] While Horn believes that some higher values are marked as false and others as unknown, I have argued elsewhere [Hirschberg84] that they should be treated uniformly as licensing epistemic disjunctions, using Hintikka's [Hintikka68] **K** ("speaker knows that") and **P** ("for all a speaker knows") operators. So, on a $\mathbf{b_i} \langle \mathbf{b_j} \langle \mathbf{b_n}$ scale, by asserting b_j, R licenses the implicature $\mathbf{K_R}\neg(b_j)\backslash/\mathbf{P_R}\neg(b_j)$. For economy of reference, this disjunction will be abbreviated by a **U** operator, subscripted for speaker. So, by asserting b_j , R licenses the implicature $\mathbf{U_R}\neg(\mathbf{b_j})$. While I will assume below a database that does permit *false* to be distinguished from *unknown*, i.e., that does not make the **closed world assumption**, [Reiter78] SI may also be adapted for databases that permit only a two-valued logic.

correspondence, we can redefine scales as **partially ordered sets (posets)**. That is, a scale supporting SI may be defined in terms of a **partial ordering** relation and the set of referents that relation orders. Not only must every scale be representable as a poset, but every poset may, **in appropriate contexts**, serve as a scale.

With this poset definition it is possible to provide a more precise statement of the notions of **higher**, **lower**, and **alternate** values used above. For a scale Σ defined by a partial ordering **O** and set of referents $\mathbf{B} = \{\mathbf{b}_1, \mathbf{b}_2, \cdots, \mathbf{b}_n\}$:

1. For any $\mathbf{b}_1, \mathbf{b}_2 \in \mathbf{B}$, $\mathbf{b}_2$ is **higher** on Σ than $\mathbf{b}_1$ iff $\mathbf{b}_1 \mathbf{O} \mathbf{b}_2$;
2. Similarly, $\mathbf{b}_1$ is **lower** on Σ than $\mathbf{b}_2$ iff $\mathbf{b}_1 \mathbf{O} \mathbf{b}_2$;
3. Any pair $\mathbf{b}_1, \mathbf{b}_2$ of **incomparable elements**[4] of Σ will be said to be **alternate values** on Σ.

2.2. Scalar Implicature Conventions

Other exchanges that seem also to rely for their interpretation upon an ordering of values in query and response do not involve the affirmation of a lower value on some scale. For example, in (3a), **alternates** to the queried color *avocado*

(3) Q: Is Model 8704 available in avocado?

a. R: It's available in white and beige.

b. R: It's available in white, beige, and avocado.

are affirmed to convey $\mathbf{U_R}$ ¬(avocado), while, in (3b), a higher value is affirmed.

The dual to the assertion of a highest affirmable value is the denial of a lowest deniable value, as in (4).

(4) Q: Has Smith asked for a transfer?

R: He hasn't received an answer yet.

Q is entitled to infer that Smith **has** requested a transfer. Denial of a scalar value $\mathbf{b}_j$ licenses the implicature that R knows lower values to be true or that he does not know their truth value.[5] Implicatures licensed by a speaker's denial of higher or alternate values and by a speaker's assertion of ignorance about higher, lower, or alternate values may also be defined.

With the definition of scale and the observations made above, we can define a set of conventions $\mathbf{IMP}_{1-3}$ which, for a given scale, a value on that scale, and an utterance affirming, denying, or asserting ignorance of that value, permit the calculation of a set of potential implicatures for that utterance.

> For a speaker R's utterance **Utt** affirming, denying, or asserting ignorance of a proposition represented by the **sentence**[6] $\mathbf{S}_{\mathbf{b}_1}$ which, via some subexpression, refers to a value $\mathbf{b}_1$ on some scale Σ, one can calculate sentences representing the set of potential implicatures $\mathbf{PSI}_{\mathbf{Utt}}$ of **Utt**, as follows:
>
> $\mathbf{Imp}_1$: If **Utt** affirms $\mathbf{S}_{\mathbf{b}_1}$, then for all $\mathbf{b}_2$ on Σ such that $\mathbf{b}_2$ is higher on Σ than $\mathbf{b}_1$, $\mathbf{U_R}\neg(\mathbf{S}_{\mathbf{b}_2}) \in \mathbf{PSI}_{\mathbf{Utt}}$; and, for all $\mathbf{b}_3$ such that $\mathbf{b}_3$ and $\mathbf{b}_1$ are alternate values on Σ, $\mathbf{U_R}\neg(\mathbf{S}_{\mathbf{b}_3}) \in \mathbf{PSI}_{\mathbf{Utt}}$

---

[3] Partial orderings may equivalently be defined as reflexive, antisymmetric, transitive orderings. Although orderings that support SI may also be specified as reflexive orderings, e.g., by defining $<$ relations as $\leq$ relations, this definition seems intuitively preferable.

[4] Elements are incomparable if they are not ordered with respect to one another by **O**.

[5] That is, the denial of $\mathbf{b}_j$ licenses the disjunction $\mathbf{K_R}(\mathbf{b}_i) \vee \mathbf{P_R}(\mathbf{b}_i)$ for lower values $\mathbf{b}_i$. This disjunction can be represented as the dual of $\mathbf{U_R}\neg(\mathbf{b}_i)$, i.e., $\mathbf{U_R}(\mathbf{b}_i)$.

[6] **Sentence** is used here to denote the semantic representation of an utterance. An **expression** or subpart of that sentence may refer to a value $\mathbf{b}_i$ on a scale.

Imp$_2$: If **Utt** is a denial of S_{b_1}, then for all $\mathbf{b_2}$ such that $\mathbf{b_2}$ is lower on Σ than $\mathbf{b_1}$, $U_R(b_2) \in \mathbf{PSI_{Utt}}$; and, for all $\mathbf{b_3}$ such that $\mathbf{b_3}$ and $\mathbf{b_1}$ are alternate values on Σ, $U_R(S_{b_3}) \in \mathbf{PSI_{Utt}}$

Imp$_3$: If **Utt** is an assertion of ignorance of S_{b_2}, then for all $\mathbf{b_1}$ on Σ, such that $\mathbf{b_1} \langle \mathbf{b_2}$, $U_R(S_{b_1}) \in \mathbf{PSI_{Utt}}$; and, for all $\mathbf{b_3}$ on Σ such that $\mathbf{b_3} \rangle \mathbf{b_2}$, $U_R \neg (S_{b_3}) \in \mathbf{PSI_{Utt}}$; and, for all $\mathbf{b_4}$ such that $\mathbf{b_4}$ and $\mathbf{b_1}$ are alternate values on Σ, $K_R(b_4) \in \mathbf{PSI_{Utt}}$

3. Avoiding False Implicatures

Given the ability to determine the implicatures a given utterance licenses, how can this information be useful in computer-human interaction? In his modification of the Gricean Maxim of Quality, Joshi [Joshi82] highlights the importance of avoiding the conveyance of false information:

> Do not say anything which may imply for the hearer something which you the speaker believe to be false.

While SI conventions may be used to achieve a variety of goals, [Hirschberg84] one stands out as particularly important in light of this revised maxim: the avoidance of the licensing of false implicatures. That is, a system that "understands" SI might anticipate the conclusions a given statement entitles a hearer to draw, and, if they are inconsistent with the system's knowledge base, avoid such statements.

The **potential false implicatures** a given utterance might convey can be determined by comparing the implicatures that utterance licenses with the state of the speaker's knowledge base. Recall that if speakers are expected to affirm the highest value on a scale they can truthfully affirm, a simple and truthful *yes* to a query of some scalar value $\mathbf{b_2}$ on a scale Σ may implicate to Q that all higher values $\mathbf{b_3}$ on Σ than $\mathbf{b_3}$ are false or unknown to R. Hence, if R **does** believe some $\mathbf{b_3}$ to be true, then a simple *yes* to the queried $\mathbf{b_2}$ will license a (potential) **false implicature**, so long of course as Q views $\mathbf{b_2}$ as a scalar value and R as cooperative. More generally, for any speaker R, a proposition Π_{b_3}[7] is a potential false implicature of an utterance conveying a proposition Π_{b_2} iff in some context **D** R's conveyance of Π_{b_2} implicates a truth value for Π_{b_3} that is inconsistent with R's knowledge of Π_{b_3}. If so, then R should try to formulate an alternative response that will not mislead Q.

The justification for this analysis rests upon the following assumptions: First, Grice's maxims permit hearers to assume that speakers will provide as much information as they truthfully can that will be relevant to the exchange. Speakers recognize this expectation. Second, if speakers view some query as invoking a scale, they may reasonably assume that other values on this scale will thereby be relevant to the exchange. If indeed a speaker can supply information about an unqueried value that will not be conveyed by a simple direct response to the queried value, and if that information will convey truthful information about the queried value as well, that speaker may cooperatively provide that information. Moreover, failure to provide it may indeed convey to the hearer some false implicature about the unqueried value. This false implicature may of course not be conveyed to the hearer. However, if a cooperative speaker recognizes the possibility, it seems reasonable that she avoid a response that would license it and provide instead a response that, as far as she knows, licenses no false implicatures.

Consider again the exchanges in (1a) and (1b). The indirect response in the latter can be explained as an attempt to avoid those false implicatures which the simple direct responses in (1b) license and to provide an alternative response that does not license such implicatures. In (1a), R's first simple direct *no* according to **Imp$_2$** entitles Q to conclude that R has denied the lowest value on the process scale that he can truthfully deny. Thus, the response implicates that prior stages,

[7] A proposition P that is conveyed by an utterance referring to a scalar value $\mathbf{b_3}$.

such as *sending the shipment* and *ordering the shipment*, which R believes false, as well as *filing the requisition*, which R believes true, are all marked as true or unknown. The indirect response in (1b), on the other hand, marks higher values as false or unknown by $\mathbf{Imp}_1$; such implicatures **are** consistent with R's knowledge. Thus, R should prefer (1b) to (1a) to avoid false licensing false implicatures. Note also that, in exchanges such as (3b), this goal accounts for R's decision to affirm a higher value, the set of colors, rather than simply and truthfully affirming *avocado*.

Clearly it is not always possible for a speaker to anticipate **all** the implicatures a response may convey; so it is not always possible to anticipate all those **false** implicatures that a given utterance may license. For instance, R may not recognize as salient some scale on which a value he refers to may appear — a scale which may, in fact, appear salient to Q. Or, R may define some scale differently from Q. In either case, he may not anticipate the implicatures his response will license for Q. However, failure to anticipate particular scalar implicatures need not always lead to misleading responses. For example, in (3a), R might not realize that Model 8704 was also available in gold; however, his response would license only $\mathbf{U_R} \neg$ (it's available in gold) for Q, which is consistent with R's lack of knowledge that Model 8704 comes in this color. Even though R is unaware that he has conveyed this information, the implicature licensed is consistent with his ignorance. In sum, it seems reasonable to require that all a cooperative speaker or system do to anticipate and avoid false conclusions arising from some response is to ensure that the implicatures that response licenses be consistent with his own knowledge base and with his knowledge of Q.

4. Calculating Cooperative Responses

Given such a goal, together with the conventions and definition of scale discussed above, it is possible to outline a strategy by which scalar implicatures can guide the selection of cooperative responses to YNQs in the following terms:

1. Some proposition having as its semantic representation the sentence **S** enters a discourse context **D**, either through assertion or as the **desideratum**[8] of a query or imperative or through non-linguistic means;
2. Some $\mathbf{b}_1$ in **S** becomes salient to a speaker R, ($\mathbf{S}_{\mathbf{b}_1}$);
3. R perceives this $\mathbf{b}_1$ lying on some scale Σ , whose salience must be determined from **D**;
4. R creates an open sentence $\mathbf{S}_x$ by substituting a variable **x** for $\mathbf{b}_1$ in $\mathbf{S}_{\mathbf{b}_1}$;
5. for each $\mathbf{Imp}_i$, R finds those values $\mathbf{b}_i$ on Σ (which may include $\mathbf{b}_1$ itself), which, when substituted for **x** in $\mathbf{S}_x$, will **not** license false implicatures, i.e., for which the affirmation or denial or assertion of ignorance about $\mathbf{S}_{\mathbf{b}_i}$ licenses no implicatures inconsistent with R's knowledge base;
6. R may choose from among these $\mathbf{S}_{\mathbf{b}_i}$ a cooperative response.

Say R is a question-answering system for a simple naval database that has the following information encoded:[9]

[8] Hintikka's [Hintikka78] term, simply defined as "That which the questioner desires to be made known to him."

[9] Note that, in this example, the system represented **does** make the closed world assumption, i.e., only true information is represented and *unknown* is assumed *false*. In the discussion of this example, truth-values in parentheses represent the disjuncts that would also be predicted in a system that represented false information explicitly, thus permitting a distinction between *false* and *unknown*.

in_port(First_Battle_Division)
part_of(Pacific_Fleet, First_Battle_Division)
part_of(Pacific_Fleet, Second_Battle_Division)
part_of(Pacific_Fleet, Third_Battle_Division)

Then the exchange in (5) can be explained in terms of the model outlined above.

(5) Q: Is the Pacific Fleet in port?

R: The First Battle Division is.

The proposition "The Pacific Fleet is in port" enters the discourse context **D** as the desideratum of Q's query and is given a semantic representation **S**. The expression *Pacific Fleet* is perceived by R as both salient and as referring to a value on a whole/part scale **parts of the USN** defined by inclusion. This scale can be represented in terms of entities and relationships in the database itself: a set of referents defined by membership in a database hierarchy and an inclusion relation that orders them. The open sentence $\mathbf{S_x}$ formed from $\mathbf{S_{b_1}}$ is some semantic representation of the open proposition "**x** is in port."

Then for $\mathbf{Imp_1}$, R can determine that the affirmation of the value *the First Battle Division* licenses the implicatures that, all higher values such as *the Pacific Fleet* and alternate values such as *the Second Battle Division* and *the Third Battle Division*, are false (or unknown); since these implicatures are consistent with R's knowledge, "The First Battle Division is" represents a possible cooperative response to Q's query. However, using $\mathbf{Imp_2}$, R can also find a cooperative response. By denying any single value on *parts-of-the-USN*, R would license false implicatures. For example, if R merely denied *Pacific Fleet*, he would license the implicature that lower values, in particular the *Second Battle Division* and the *Third Battle Division* are known by him to be true (or are unknown); but in fact these division are **not** known to be in port. By denying either *the Second Battle Division* or *the Third Battle Division* — alone — R would also license the false implicature that the other was true (or unknown), via $\mathbf{Imp_2}$. However, by denying both, "The First and Second Battle Divisions aren't," R licenses no false implicatures. The third alternate value in this case, the *First Battle Division*, **is** known to be in port. So, at least in terms of the goals discussed here, R may choose either response to Q's question.

It should be noted that the semantic representation from which scalar implicatures are calculated above might easily represent the formal specification of a query in systems where NL interface is not available. The same conventions which predict that "No" and "The Third Battle Division isn't" will convey false implicatures and that "The First Battle Division is" will not, can predict similar results for the formal counterparts of these responses. So, insights gained from the study of NL interaction can be applied to exchanges conducted on a less "natural" basis.

5. Concluding Remarks

SI provides a principled account of indirect responses to yes-no questions, by indicating

1. how R might determine that a simple direct response is misleading, and thus inappropriate,
2. how R might choose the information to include in a more appropriate response, and
3. how Q might derive the simple response and additional inferences from the information R provides.

However, while SI promises some general answers to the question of why indirect responses to YNQs are generated and how they are interpreted, many specific questions arise about how such insights can be put to use. The role of domain, speakers, and discourse history in the generation and interpretation of particular scalar implicatures is nonetheless made easier to investigate by the particular perspective SI defines. For instance, the concept of SI and in particular the notion of scale lead us to ask specific questions of any exchange: How do participants determine that mention of a possible scalar value does indeed invoke a scale? When several scales might be invoked by a mentioned value, how do participants determine **which** invocation is salient in a given exchange? How does a hearer determine whether a speaker's implicature commits the speaker to denial or affirmation of other values, and when to ignorance of those values? How much and what kind of knowledge must speaker and hearer share for felicitous SI, e.g., of how some scale is defined? When may a speaker choose a **modified direct response**[10] over a simple direct or indirect response? What may serve to cancel potential scalar implicatures? These questions are discussed in [Hirschberg84] and are the focus of my current research.

Much current research in natural language processing focuses upon making computer systems more cooperative. However, as Joshi [Joshi82] has pointed out, the more cooperative and "natural" computer interaction becomes, the more users may expect these systems to be even **more** cooperative than other humans. Since most such systems must also assume the cooperativeness of their users, it seems reasonable to accept Grice's Cooperative Principle as a model for human-machine communication. If so, question-answering systems should benefit from a notion of SI in four ways:

1. it should enable systems to interpret indirect responses to queries and thus to permit users to respond in a natural manner;
2. it should help systems to recognize unrequested information derivable from user assertions and hence to avoid unnecessary questioning of the user;
3. it should help systems avoid licensing false inferences in their responses by allowing them to predict the inferences a potential response may permit; and
4. it should guide the selection of additional unrequested information that systems might appropriately provide either in indirect responses or in modified direct responses to YNQs.

Thus the broad concepts discussed above should have more general applicability to computer-human interaction.

References

Allen80.
Allen, James F. and C. Raymond Perrault, "Analyzing Intention in Utterances," *Artificial Intelligence*, vol. 15, pp. 143-178, 1980.

Grice75.
Grice, H.P., "Logic and Conversation," in *Syntax and Semantics*, ed. P. Cole and M. L. Morgan, vol. 3, Academic Press, New York, 1975. From 1967 lectures.

Hintikka68.
Hintikka, J., *Knowledge and Belief*, Cornell University Press, Ithaca, 1968.

Hintikka78.
Hintikka, J., "Answers to Questions," in *Questions*, ed. H. Hiz, pp. 279-300, Reidel, Dordrecht (Neth.), 1978.

Hirschberg84.
Hirschberg, J., Scalar Implicature: Generating Cooperative Responses to Yes-No Questions, University of Pennsylvania, April 1984.

Hobbs79.
Hobbs, J. and J. Robinson, "Why Ask?," *Discourse Processes*, vol. 2, 1979.

Hoeppner84.
Hoeppner, W., K. Morik, and H. Marburger, Talking it Over: The Natural Language Dialog System HAM-ANS, University of Hamburg, May 1984.

Horn72.
Horn, L.R., On the Semantic Properties of Logical Operators in English, Univ. of California

[10] A direct response plus some additional information

— Los Angeles, 1972. PhD thesis

Joshi82.
Joshi, A.K., "The Role of Mutual Beliefs in Question-Answer Systems," in *Mutual Belief*, ed. N. Smith, Academic Press, New York, 1982.

Joshi84a.
Joshi, A.K. and B.L. Webber, "Next Steps in Natural Language Interaction: Beyond Syntactic Sugar," in *Proceedings of the Conference*, Fourth Jerusalem Conference on Information Technology, May 1984.

Joshi84b.
Joshi, A.K., B.L. Webber, and R. Weischedel, "Preventing False Inferences," in *Proceedings of COLING-84*, COLING-84, Stanford CA, July 1984.

Joshi84c.
Joshi, A.K., B.L. Webber, and R. Weischedel, "Living Up To Expectations: Computing Expert Responses," in *Proceedings of AAAI-84*, AAAI-84, Austin, TX, August 1984.

Kaplan81.
Kaplan, S.J., "Appropriate Responses to Inappropriate Questions," in *Elements of Discourse Understanding*, ed. Joshi, A.K., Webber, B.L., and Sag, I.A., pp. 127-144, Cambridge University Press, Cambridge, 1981.

Mays80.
Mays, Eric, "Correcting Misconceptions about Data Base Structure," in *Proceedings of the Conference*, Canadian Society for Computational Studies of Intelligence, 1980.

McCoy83.
McCoy, K., Cooperative Responses to Object-Related Misconceptions, University of Pennsylvania, November 1983.

Mercer84.
Mercer, R. and R. Rosenberg, "Generating Corrective Answers by Computing Presuppositions of Answers, not of Questions," in *Proceedings of the 1984 Conference*, pp. 16-19, Canadian Society for Computational Studies of Intelligence, University of Western Ontario, London, Ontario, May 1984.

Pollack82.
Pollack, M.E., J. Hirschberg, and B.L. Webber, User Participation in the Reasoning Processes of Expert Systems, Univ. of Pennsylvania, July 1982. A shorter version appears in the AAAI Proceedings, 1982

Pollack84.
Pollack, Martha E., Goal Inference in Expert Systesm, University of Pennsylvania, 1984. Doctoral dissertation proposal.

Reiter78.
Reiter, R., "Closed World Databases," in *Logic and Databases*, ed. H. Gallaire and J. Minker, pp. 149-177, Plenum Press, 1978.

Schuster83.
Schuster, E., Custom-made Responses: Maintaining and Updating the User Model, Computer & Information Science, Univ. of Pennsylvania, September 1983.

Webber84.
Webber, B.L. and T. Finin, "In Response: Next Steps in Natural Language Interaction," in *Artificial Intelligence Applications for Business*, ed. W. Reitman, Ablex, Norwood, N.J., 1984.

Supporting Natural Language Database Update by Modeling Real World Actions†

Sharon Salveter

Computer Science Department
Boston University
111 Cummington Street
Boston, MA 02215

ABSTRACT

One way to increase the usefulness of database systems is to support natural language database access. Although a great deal of research effort has been expended to support natural language database *query,* little effort has gone to support natural language database *update.* In this paper we describe a model of action that supports natural language database update. and the implementation of a system that supports the model. Another goal of this research is to design a system that is transportable both to different domains and different DBMSs

1. INTRODUCTION

One way to increase the usefulness of database systems is to support natural language database access. Although natural language (NL) querying of databases (DBs) has been an active research area for many years [Ha77. Da78, Wo76, Ka79, Wa78, Wz75], and at least one commercial system is available that supports NL DB query [Ha79], little effort has been expended in support of NL DB *update,* as noted by Wiederhold et al. [Wi81]. Thus, end-users of DBs must alternate between easy-to-use NL DB query systems and harder-to-use formal DB update systems.

Salveter and Maier [SM82] have shown that, because NL DB update is a fundamentally different problem than query, it is not possible, in a natural manner, to extend NL DB query systems to also support update. To interpret values of the objects in the DB as statements about a real world, we must be able to connect values in the DB with entities and relationships in the real world. A semantic data description indicates a set of real world states (RWS), a DB definition gives a set of allowable DB states (DBS). The correspondence between the semantic description and the DB definition induces connections between DB states and real world states. The situation is depicted in Figure 1. This *stative correspondence* between DBS and RWS, while adequate for querying, is not adequate for NL DB modification. In Figure 2 we see that when some action in the real world causes a state change from RWS1 to RWS2, we must perform some modification to the DB to change its state from DBS1 to DBS2.

We have a means to describe the action that changed the state of the real world: active verbs. We also have a means to describe a change in the DB state: a data manipulation language (DML) command sequence. But given a description of a real world action, how do we find a DML sequence that will accomplish the corresponding change in the DB? We need a method of specifying *what* is to be modified and *how* to make the modification. We need to connect active verbs, such as "schedule" or "enroll" with some structures that dictate appropriate DML sequences that perform the corresponding updates to the DB. We need to represent an *active correspondence* between descriptions of real world actions and DML sequences.

† This research is partially supported by NSF grants IST-8214622 and IST-8408551.

```
            ----------------                        ----------------
           | RWS1    |<----------------------->| DBS1    |
set of     |         |                         |         | set of
real world | RWS2    |<----------------------->| DBS2    | database
states     |         |                         |         | states
           |   :     |            :            |   :     |
           | RWSn    |<----------------------->| DBSn    |
            ----------------                        ----------------

                          stative
        semantic <================> database
        description    correspondence       definition
```

Figure 1
Real World State - Database State Connection

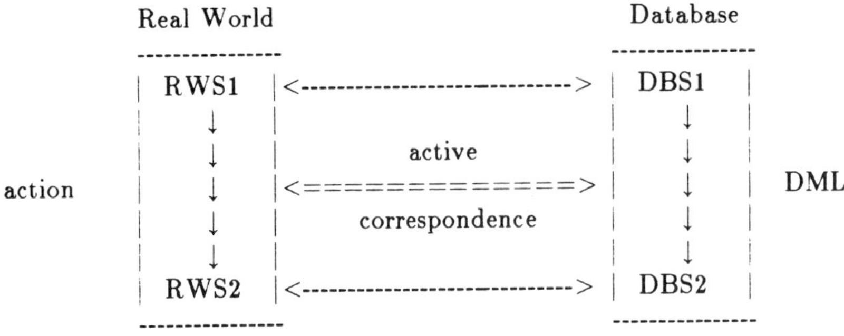

Figure 2
Real World Action - DML Sequence Connection

The goal of this research is the design of a computer system that will support both NL query and update access to DBs. An additional goal is to design a system that is transportable. NL DB access systems must incorporate at least two types of information: domain-independent general linguistic knowledge, and domain-dependent knowledge about a particular DB. When these two types of information are integrated, it is extremely cumbersome and time-consuming, even prohibitively expensive, to transport the system to another DB. The architecture of such an integrated NL DB access system is shown in Figure 3. Here the front-end must perform several tasks: syntactically parse the NL input sentence, semantically analyze the sentence, link sentence elements to DB objects, and generate a program in the DML required by the database management system (DBMS). The DBMS executes the DML to produce the result: response to a query or modification to the DB. Such an approach does not facilitate transportability; the entire front-end must be rewritten whenever a new database is used.

Our approach is to separate domain-independent general linguistic knowledge and domain-dependent knowledge about the DB. This architecture is shown in Figure 4. In this approach, the parser embodies the domain-independent knowledge: from the NL input, it produces a caseframe representation [CW76] that represents the linguistic meaning of the NL input. (Briefly, a caseframe representation is a collection of named slots, such as AGENT or OBJECT, which can be instantiated.) Program X embodies the

```
              ---------------              --------------
NL ------> | front end | -------> DML ------->| DBMS   | -----> result
              ---------------              --------------
```

Figure 3
Architecture of an NL DB Access System

```
         ---------------                            -----------------------                          -------------
NL -----> | Parser    |----> caseframe ----> | Program X       | -----> DML ------> | DBMS | ----> result
         ---------------                            -----------------------                          -------------
```

Figure 4
Architecture of a Domain-Independent NL DB Access System

domain-dependent knowledge: it takes as input a formal structure that represents the linguistic meaning of the NL input, links linguistic elements to DB objects, and produces a DML sequence that represents what the NL command means ***with respect to*** this DB. These components comprise a system that is more expert than a DBMS because the correspondence between a real world and a database is formally represented. The formal representation of domain-dependent information, which heretofore resided only in a programmer's head, can now be used to support some applications that require "intelligence."

Here is an example of the distinction we are trying to achieve between domain-independent and domain-dependent knowledge. Suppose both Harvard University and Boston University have computerized their student registration process. Each school has a DB, but they are quite different in format, information stored, names of files, constraints on registration, and other requirements. If a command such as "Enroll Jane Doe in CS574 for 4 credits with Prof. Jones" is issued, one can "understand" the command at a general linguistic level: course enrolling actions require someone to be enrolled, a course to enroll in, credit hours, professors who teach courses, and sections of courses. A clerk for Boston University would update one set of files and check a set of constraints, say that undergraduates cannot register for more than 16 credits. A Harvard clerk might update a completely different set of files, and perhaps check that a 20 credit limit is not exceeded.

The architecture shown in Figure 4 is an attempt to capture the first type of information in the parser ("enrolling"), and the second type in Program X (how does one "enroll" in this DB, and what are the constraints). Such an architecture supports transportability by limiting the changes required in the parser when the system is transported to a different DB. Rewriting is only required for Program X.

The first problem we have to address is the design of a representation for domain-specific knowledge. This paper describes a structure that is designed for this task, called a ***verbgraph***, and a system that executes the verbgraphs.

2. RELATED WORK

Few attempts have been made to support NL DB update, or transportable NL DB query. Sparck-Jones [SJ82] is designing an NL DB query system with an architecture similar to ours. A long-term goal is to combine our systems to achieve full NL DB access. Bates et al. [Ba85] have also designed a transportable NL DB query system. Several other domain-independent NL query interfaces are described in [CANLP83].

Kaplan and Davidson [KD81] have looked at the translation of NL updates into transactions, but the active verbs they deal with are synonyms for DB terms. This limitation is intentional. Their goal is to be domain-independent, while we are attempting to exploit domain-dependent information and support arbitrary update transactions. Their work is complementary to ours.

Carbonell and Hayes [CH81] have looked at parsing a limited set of NL update commands, but they do not say how to generate transactions for the commands. Skuce [Sk80] addresses the problem of representing DB change by providing an English-like syntax for DB procedure specification.

3. SYSTEM OVERVIEW

From Figure 4, we see that the proposed system is composed of three major components:

```
                    ----------------
1)  NL ------>    |  parser    | ------> caseframe
                    ----------------


                          ----------------------
2)  caseframe -------> |  Program X      | -------> DML
                          ----------------------


                    ---------------
3)  DML -----> |  DBMS    | -----> result
                    ---------------
```

Our research concentrates on the second component, the caseframe to DML translation. The other components are being acquired externally. We hope to use the RUS parser developed at Bolt, Beranek and Newman [Bo78, Ba85]. The output of RUS is a caseframe representation first suggested by Wilks [Wl75], and extended by Sparck-Jones [SJ82]. For the third component, we are using the INGRES DBMS, with its DML QUEL [He75].

Our research goal is to design and implement the second component: the caseframe to DML translator. Actually, we do not want to be restricted to a particular DBMS, as Figure 4 implies. We want our system to produce a formal representation in some intermediate language (IL) that can be translated into the DML of a given DBMS. Thus the overall architecture looks like Figure 5.

```
              ------------                           -------------------
NL -----> | parser | -----> caseframe -----> | Program X | ------> IL
              ------------                           -------------------         ↓
                                                                                  ↓
                                                                                  ↓
                     ------------               -----------------                ↓
result <-------- | DBMS | <---- DML <----| translator | <----------
                     ------------               -----------------
```

Figure 5
Architecture of a Transportable NL DB Access System

Now the second component of our system consists of two major subcomponents:

```
                    ----------------------
caseframe -----> | Program X       |-----> IL
                    ----------------------

                    ----------------------
       IL ------> | translator      |------> DML
                    ----------------------
```

An IL-to-QUEL translator has already been implemented [As84]. Thus our attention is limited to the nature of the caseframe-to-IL conversion. The architecture of this component is shown in Figure 6.

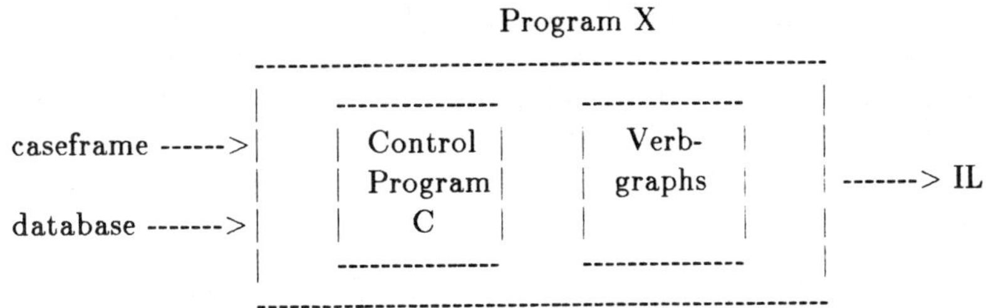

Figure 6
Architecture of a Caseframe-to-Intermediate Language Translator

Because the IL-to-DML translation is a well-understood problem, and not of further interest here, we will often speak of the IL as the language that actually updates the DB.

As Figure 6 shows, the purpose of Program X is to produce IL that will update the DB as indicated by the NL command. However, the program does not have direct access to the NL statement. Its sources of information are the caseframe, which represents the general linguistic meaning of the NL command, and the DB, which may have to be accessed in order to determine how to update it.

The verbgraphs are a set of structures that represents what various update commands mean with respect to this particular DB. Control program C directs execution of the verbgraphs. It is important to note that control program C need *never* be rewritten. If the DBMS changes, then a new IL-to-DML translator must be written. Because all of the domain-dependent information resides in the verbgraphs, a new set of verbgraphs must be constructed when transporting the system to a new domain (assuming the DBMS remains constant). Our design is analogous to expert systems, where domain-dependent information is represented in production rules. There, the control program is domain-independent: it controls selection and execution of production rules.

4. AN EXAMPLE

Let us consider an example that will illustrate the function of each component of the overall system and the nature of the input and output of each component. Suppose we have an office database of employees, their scheduled appointments and seminars, reservations for meeting rooms, and messages from one employee to another. We capture this information in the following relations:

EMP(name, office, phone, supervisor)
APPOINTMENT(name, date, time, duration, who, topic, location)
MAILBOX(name, date, time, from, message)
ROOMRESERVE(room, date, time, duration, reserver)

with domains (permissible sets of values):

DOMAIN	ATTRIBUTES WITH THAT DOMAIN
personname	name, who, from, reserver, supervisor
roomnum	room, location, office
phonenum	phone
calendardate	date
clocktime	time
elapsedtime	duration
text	message, topic

One type of update we may want to make is to schedule a meeting (appointment or seminar). There are four basic variants we are attempting to capture; they are distinguished by whether or not the meeting is scheduled with someone in the company, and whether or not a room is to be reserved. There is also the possibility that the supervisor must be notified of the meeting. The different operations for each variant are described below. In every case, the person scheduling the meeting gets an entry in the APPOINTMENT relation.

Variant 1. Meeting with a person in the company, no reserved room. (Appointment with another employee.)
Also make an APPOINTMENT entry for the schedulee and leave a message. The location of the meeting must be one of the two offices of the persons involved; the default is the office of the scheduler.

Variant 2. Meeting with a person not in the company, no reserved room. (Appointment with a person not an employee.)
The meeting will be in the scheduler's office.

Variant 3. Meeting with another employee, reserve a room. (Seminar with an employee.)
Make an APPOINTMENT entry for the other person and send a message. Reserve a meeting room for the same time.

Variant 4. Meeting with a person not in the company, reserve a room. (Seminar with a person not an employee.)
Reserve a meeting room for the same time. Supervisor must be notified.

We can see that our four variants share some aspects of this sense of the word "schedule." All require an insertion into APPOINTMENT for the scheduler. If the schedulee is also an employee, there are additional insertions into APPOINTMENT and MAILBOX for the schedulee. If a seminar is being scheduled, an insertion is made into ROOMRESERVE. A seminar with a person who is not an employee requires supervisor notification.

We have a number of defaults in this example. These are values that are assumed unless otherwise specified. For an appointment, the location of the meeting is the scheduler's office. All seminars are held on Wednesday at 3 pm. All appointments and seminars are one hour in duration.

5. THE VERBGRAPH

The verbgraph represents what a class of NL update commands means with respect to a particular DB. An NL may have a number of different senses. A sense of a verb roughly corresponds to the different definitions that might be given in a dictionary. In our scheme, a verbgraph represents a single sense of a verb. We avoid the sense selection problem because it is equivalent to the frame selection problem in Artificial Intelligence [CW76], and a solution to this problem is not yet at hand. Thus, one verbgraph might represent the "enrolling" action, and another the "hiring" action, regardless of how these actions are specified in NL. A given verb sense, or action, may have a number of different variants. For example, enrolling an undergraduate may require different DB actions than enrolling a graduate student; hiring faculty may be different than hiring secretaries. A verbgraph represents all legal variants of a verb sense, and is also used to determine which variant is specified in the NL command.

A verbgraph is a repository for several kinds of information, which are outlined below.

- Linkage of linguistic entities to DB objects and updates. (Use the AGENT caseframe slot as the value of attribute NAME in EMP, "hiring" results in insertion into relation EMP.)

- Constraints on the DB. (Only 40 students may enroll in a course.)

- Default values. (All courses are 4 credits unless otherwise specified.)

- Parameterized IL commands.

- Questions to ask the user if insufficient information is specified in the NL command.

- Retrievals that may have to be performed on the DB in order to process an update.

- Templates for tuples to be inserted into, deleted from, or modified in the DB.

A verbgraph is composed of a tree and a blackboard, as shown in Figure 7a. The blackboard contains objects that will ultimately determine the IL sequence. The tree controls instantiation of the blackboard. The tree has at most two levels†. There is a distinguished root node and an arbitrary number of leaf nodes. Each node contains a *guard,* which is a boolean expression. The root node has guard true. A variant of a verb sense is defined by the accumulation of all the nodes in the tree whose guards evaluate to true for a given input. The order of execution of leaf nodes is unimportant. When control program C executes a verbgraph, it evaluates the guards of all the nodes, chooses all nodes whose guards evaluate to true, and executes each node in turn. Node execution may cause access to the caseframe, the DB, the user, or the blackboard. When all the selected nodes have been executed, the blackboard will contain a correct IL sequence that will properly update the DB. It is important to note that no update action is taken on the DB until all the selected nodes have been executed, at which time the IL is translated to DML and executed by the DBMS.

Next, we describe the nature and form of nodes and the blackboard, and how they interact. First we describe the blackboard, followed by a description of the nodes, and an explanation of how the execution of the nodes comprising a variant manipulates blackboard objects.

5.1. The Blackboard

The blackboard, shown in Figure 7b, is a common repository of information that any node can access. It is composed of four types of information:

- variables,
- parameterized IL update commands,
- IL database retrieval commands, and
- questions that may be asked of the user.

Variable are of two kinds, *tuple* and *local,* which are instantiated during node execution. A tuple variable is a composite type. It is bound to a relation name and is composed of fields that correspond to the attributes of the named relation. The type of each field is the domain of the attribute.

† We could allow N-level trees, as discussed in Section 5.2.

```
--------------------------------------
| Verbgraph <vgname>                 |
|   node                             |
|    :                               |
|   node                             |       tree
|    :                               |   specification
|   node                             |
|    :                               |
|   blackboard                       |
|         :                          |
--------------------------------------
```

Figure 7a
Verbgraph Schematic

```
-----------------------
| Blackboard          |
| variables           |
|        :            |
|  IL                 |
|   :                 |
|  retrievals         |
|        :            |
|  questions          |
|        :            |
-----------------------
```

Figure 7b
Blackboard Schematic

```
--------------------------------------
|  Node <nodename>                   |
|    guard <guardspec>               |
|    prerequisites <prereqs>|
|    actions <actionspecs>           |
--------------------------------------
```

Figure 7c
Node Schematic

Figure 7
The Verbgraph

Recall relation EMP from our example in the previous section. Variable t1 in Figure 8 is an example of a tuple variable associated with relation EMP; it has fields name, office, phone, and supervisor.

```
t1 : EMP ;                          t2 : EMP :
  t1.name ;                           t2.name ;
  t1.office ;                         t2.office := t1.office + 1 ;
  t1.phone ;                          t2.phone ;
  t1.supervisor ;                     t2.supervisor := t1.supervisor ;

temp : integer ;
newguy : domain(t1.name) ;
```

Figure 8
Blackboard Variables

Fields of a tuple may be linked. That is, we can force a field of one tuple variable to take on a value that is a function of the field of another variable. In Figure 8, variable t2 is also associated with with relation EMP. It is restricted to taking the value of t1.supervisor as the value of its supervisor field, and one greater than t1.office as the value of its office field. Notice that the linkage is one way: t2.supervisor must take on the value of t1.supervisor, but not vice versa.

The other kind of variable is a local variable. Its type is explicitly or implicitly defined by referring to any base type or the type of any local variable or tuple variable field. In Figure 8, we see two local variables, "temp" and "newguy." Temp is explicitly typed as integer, newguy is implicitly typed to be the type of t1.name, which is domain(name) in EMP.

The blackboard IL component is a set of labeled IL sequences. The form of each set is <label> : (<ILcommand>)*. In our notation, * represents any number of repetitions, {} indicate optional fields, and [] indicate a choice. Each sequence consists of parameterized IL update operations: insert, delete, modify. An IL update command may cause insertion, deletion, or modification of zero or more tuples in the database. During node execution, the label of an IL sequence may be "checked off." The accumulation of the "checked off" sequences will comprise the transaction to be translated into DML.

The three types of IL update commands are insertion, deletion, and modification. The general form of each statement is shown below:

insert <tvar> into <rel> take <attrset> from [<retrieve-label> | <set> | <interval>]

delete <tvar> from <rel> { where <boolexp> }

modify <tvar> from <rel> where <boolexp> assign <attrspecs>

Here we are not concerned with the particular semantics of these statements. It is only important to note their flavor: a pseudo-DML with a high-level insert command that can cause the insertion of many tuples.

The retrievals component of the blackboard is a set of labeled IL retrieval commands. The commands are retrievals that need to be performed against the DB to determine the correct variant of a verb sense, instantiate blackboard variables, or process IL update commands as described above. The form of the command is:

<label> : retrieve <attrset> from <relset> { where <boolexp> }.

The relations mentioned in <relset> are joined, those tuples satisfying <boolexp> are selected, and the result is projected onto <attrset>.

It may be the case that the NL update command did not contain sufficient information to complete processing. It may be impossible to select a variant ("Are you scheduling an appointment or a seminar?"), or the variant may be known, but the required data is incomplete ("I know you're scheduling a seminar, but what room will it be in?"). The questions component of the blackboard is a place for specifying NL questions to be asked of the user. The format is: <label> : <string>.

We have designed our own IL because we do not want to tie our system to a particular DBMS. It is a straightforward task to write a translator that takes IL as input and produces a particular DML, such as QUEL or SQL.

5.2. The Tree

In the previous section, we saw how the blackboard component of the verbgraph stores information needed by the verbgraph tree. However, Program C does not directly access blackboard variables: it selects a set of tree nodes and executes them. Thus it is the tree nodes that have the responsibility for ensuring that the correct IL transaction is generated. It is in the tree, then, that linguistic objects are linked to DB objects, DB integrity and consistency constraints are specified, and blackboard objects are manipulated.

The tree has at most two levels: the root level and the leaf level. Conceptually, the root node represents that which is the case for all variants of this verb sense, and each leaf represents that which is the case for some aspect of a variant for this verb sense. We can conceptually analyze our "scheduling" example from the previous section as a tree, as shown below.

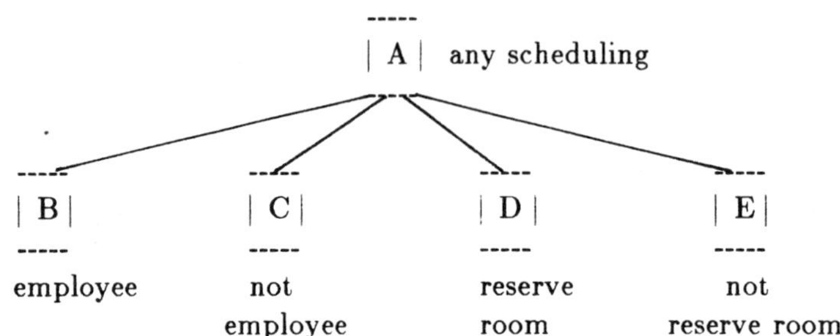

Each node of the tree represents one aspect of a variant. For example, if we are scheduling an appointment with an employee, the variant is represented by the accumulation of nodes A, B, and E. If we are scheduling a seminar with an outside speaker, the variant is the accumulation of nodes A, C, and D. The root node will always be chosen. In this example, we will always choose the root, exactly one node from B and C, and exactly one node from D and E.

We have limited ourselves to a two-level tree. Our analysis of DB updates has convinced us that actions are usually composed of subactions (aspects), and the subactions that make up the action can usually be independently specified. The two-level tree structure allows the designer to specify these subactions independently, without explicitly specifying all their possible interactions. In addition, for any multi-level tree where a variant is represented by a path from the root to a leaf, it is always possible to construct an equivalent two-level tree. Our control structure is simplified by assuming a two-level tree, and a two-level tree is generally appropriate for specifying the aspects of composite actions.

A schematic of the tree specification is shown in Figure 7a. The tree is specified by a series of node definitions. One of the nodes is the distinguished root node, the remaining nodes are leaves. The format of a node is shown in Figure 7c. A node consists of three parts: guard, prerequisite, and action. We discuss each component in turn.

5.2.1. Guards

The form of the guard is: guard : <boolexp>. The guard determines whether or not a node will be selected for execution. All nodes whose guards evaluate to true for this input will be selected. The guard is a boolean combination of terms. Because all node selection is performed before any node other than the root is executed, terms are not allowed to reference blackboard variables. Because variant determination is done by analyzing information in the caseframe, the terms of <boolexp> can only compare caseframe values against constants, other caseframe values, and the result of retrievals against the DB.

5.2.2. Prerequisites

The form of prerequisite specification is:

prereq : (<cfref> : <question-ref>)*

The prerequisites indicate those caseframe slots that must have values before node execution can proceed. That is, information the user must have supplied for this aspect of a variant. Each caseframe slot referred to by <cfref> is inspected. If it does not have a value, the blackboard question labeled by <question-ref> is asked of the user. Processing is suspended until the caseframe slot <cfref> is instantiated.

5.2.3. Actions

Action specifications take the form action :(<actionspec>)*. Actions perform a wide variety of functions:

- instantiate blackboard variables,
- ask the user for further information,
- "check off" blackboard IL,
- retrieve values from the database,
- specify default values, and
- database integrity and consistency constraints.

An <actionspec> is one of three types:

- <checkoff>
- <assignment>
- <conditional>.

Because an <actionspec> can take a number of different forms, it is best illustrated by example. A <checkoff> is the simplest type of action. The statement check (A3) causes the IL sequence labeled A3 to be checked off on the blackboard. This IL sequence will now be part of the final IL transaction.

The <assignment> action type has a number of forms. Its basic function is to instantiate a blackboard variable. The value may be:

- A constant: t.X := 5

- A system variable: t.X := clocktime

- A blackboard variable: t.X := t.Y

- A caseframe value: t.X := cf//location

- A default value: t.X := cf//duration | default(1hour);
If the caseframe slot duration has no value, use one hour.

- The result of a database retrieval: t.X := R3
R3 is the label of a blackboard retrieval that returns a single value.

- Required to be in a range of values: t.X := cf//location in R1 #Q8;
R1 is the label of a blackboard retrieval, Q8 is the label of a blackboard question. If the cf//location value is in the result of R1, then use it. Otherwise ask question labeled Q8 and wait for a response.

- Required to be in a range of values if it exists, otherwise a default is used:

t.X := cf//location in R1 #Q8 | default(R2);

If cf//location has a value and it is in R1, then use it. If it has a value, but is not in R1, ask Q8 and wait for the response.
If cf//location does not have a value, use the default, which is the result of executing blackboard retrieval labeled R2, which must return a single value.

A conditional statement is provided as a programming convenience to facilitate action specification; it adds no computational power to the language. The conditional takes the form:

```
if <boolexp>
    then <then-action-set>
    else <else-action-set> .
```

6. THE EXAMPLE REVISITED

Recall our scheduling example from Section 4. We present here the verbgraph for the variants of "schedule." Annotations are enclosed in {}.

```
verbgraph : SCHEDULE;

node : ROOT;
    guard : true;        {the root aspect is true of all variants}
    prereq:        {caseframe slots that must be instantiated}
        cf//actor;  {always set to system user}
        cf//date : Q1;
        cf//indobj : Q5;
        cf//topic : Q3;
    action:        {instantiate values of tuple to be inserted for scheduler}
        t1.name := cf//actor;
        t1.date := cf//date;
        t1.who := cf//indobj;
        t1.topic := cf//topic;
        check (A1);        {insert entry for scheduler}


node : EMP;        {schedulee is an employee}
    guard : (cf//indobj in R1);        {R1 returns names of employees}
    prereq : null;
    action :
        t4.name := cf//indobj;        {for MAILBOX entry}
        whom-to-meet := cf//actor;
        check (A2,A4);        {insert into MAILBOX and APPOINTMENT for schedulee}


node : RESERVE;        {an aspect of seminar}
    guard : ((((cf//obj = 'meeting') or (cf//obj = null ) and (cf//location. not in R2))) or (cf//obj =
    'seminar'));        {R2 returns employee offices}
    prereq: cf//location : Q4;        {no default for seminar location}
    action:
        t1.time := cf//time | default(14:15);
        t1.duration := cf//duration | default(1);
        t1.location := cf//location not in R2 #Q8;        {cannot have a seminar in office}
        t3.room := t1.location;
        t3.duration := t1.duration;
        {room reserved for same day and time as seminar}
        t3.date := cf//date;
        t3.time := t1.time;
        t3.reserver := cf//actor;
        check (A3); {insert into ROOMRESERVE}
```

```
node : NOT-RESERVE;        {an aspect of appointment}
    guard : (((cf//obj = 'meeting') or (cf//obj = null )) and ((cf//location = null ) or (cf//location in
    R2)));     {R2 returns employee offices}
    prereq : cf//time : Q2;      {no default time for appointments}
    action:
        t1.time := cf//time;
        t1.duration := cf//duration;
        if (cf//indobj in R1)      {if schedulee an employee}
            then      {location must be one of the two offices}
                begin
                t1.location := cf//location in R3 #Q7 | default(R4); {default is scheduler's office}
                end
            else      {location is scheduler's office}
                begin
                t1.location := R4;       {R4 returns scheduler's office}
                end


node : NOTIFY {notify supervisor}
    guard : ( not ( guard (EMP)) and ( guard (RESERVE)));       {not an employee, a seminar}
    prereq : null;
    action:
        t4.name := R5;       {R5 returns scheduler's supervisor}
        whom-to-meet := cf//indobj;      {schedulee}
        check (A4);      {insert into supervisor mailbox}


BLACKBOARD

VARIABLES

    t1 : APPOINTMENT              t2 : APPOINTMENT
    {for scheduler}               {for schedulee}
        name                              name := t1.who
        date                              date := t1.date
        time                              time := t1.time
        duration                          duration := t1.duration
        who                               who := t1.name
        topic                             topic := t1.topic
        location                          location := t1.location

    t3 : ROOMRESERVE              t4 : MAILBOX
    {for a seminar}               {for supervisor or schedulee}
        date                              name
        room                              date := t1.date
        time                              time := t1.time
        duration                          from := t1.name
        reserver                          message := 'Meeting with %whom-to-meet
                                          on %t1.date at %t1.time'

    whom-to-meet : dom(t1.name)
```

IL:

A1 : insert t1 into APPOINTMENT;
A2 : insert t2 into APPOINTMENT;
A3 : insert t3 into ROOMRESERVE;
A4 : insert t4 into MAILBOX;

RETRIEVALS:

R1 : retrieve name from EMP;
R2 : retrieve office from EMP;
R3 : retrieve office from EMP where ((name = cf//actor) or (name = cf//indobj));
R4 : retrieve office from EMP where (name = cf//actor);
R5 : retrieve supervisor from EMP where (name = cf//actor);

QUESTIONS:

Q1 : 'What is the date of the appointment?'
Q2 : 'What is the time of the appointment?'
Q3 : 'What is the topic to be discussed?'
Q4 : 'What is the location of the seminar?'
Q5 : 'With whom are you making the appointment?'
Q6 : 'What is the expected duration of the appointment?'
Q7 : 'Location must be either %R3, enter one of these locations.'
Q8 : 'Seminars cannot be held in employee offices, enter another room number.'

An example of how execution of this verbgraph results in the correct IL for an input sentence is given in Appendix A.

7. CONCLUDING REMARKS

We have discussed the problems of defining a model of actions in a database environment, and designing a transportable system architecture that supports the model. Verbgraphs are structures that can represent the correspondence between linguistic entities and DB objects, between real world actions and DB updates, as well as represent DB integrity and consistency constraints, and default values. A prototype of this system is implemented in C on a VAX 11/780 running Berkeley UNIX.

In the future we plan to implement a toolbox for verbgraph specification, which will include a structured editor. We will also provide an interactive verbgraph debugger, which will allow the verbgraph designer to test the correctness of the verbgraphs. We also need to address the complex question of run-time interaction with the user. For example, the user may supply additional information that changes which nodes guards evaluate to true. We propose to design our user interaction package so that a minimum of reprocessing is necessary, while allowing maximum flexibility. An important design criterion is to avoid forcing the user to restate information that has been given previously.

ACKNOWLEDGEMENTS

I am indebted to David Maier for our early work on the nature of the database update problem. Four students have contributed to the project. Sandra Assiff implemented the IL-to-QUEL translator. Tom Schutz has worked on the implementation. Michael Siegel participated in the vergraph design, and checked the BNF specification. Douglas Stumberger has been involved in the design of the verbgraphs and the system architecture, and is responsible for the majority of the implementation.

REFERENCES

[As84] Assiff, S., Intermediate Language to QUEL Translation. Boston University Computer Science Department Masters Thesis, 1984.

[Ba85] Bates, M., M. Moser, and D. Stallard, The IRUS Transportable Natural Language Database Interface. In this volume.

[Bo78] Bobrow, R. The RUS System. BBN Report #3878, 1978.

[CANLP83] *Proceedings of the Conference on Applied Natural Language Processing,* Santa Monica, CA, 1983.

[CH81] Carbonell, J. and P. Hayes, Multi-strategy Construction-specific Parsing for Flexible Database Query and Update. CMU Internal Report, July, 1981.

[CW76] Charniak, E. and Y. Wilks, *Computational Semantics,* North Holland, 1976.

[Da78] Damereau, F., The Derivation of Answers from Logical Forms in a Question Answering System. *American Journal of Computational Linguistics,* microfiche 75, 1978, pp. 3-42.

[Ha77] Harris, L., Using the Database itself as a Semantic Component to Aid the Parsing of Natural Language Database Queries. Dartmouth College Mathematics Department TR 77-2, 1977.

[Ha79] Harris, L., Experience with ROBOT in 12 Commercial Natural Language Database Query Applications. *Proceedings of the International Joint Conference on Artificial Intelligence,* Tokyo, 1979, pp.365-368.

[He75] Held, G., M. Stonebraker and E. Wong, INGRES - A Relational Database Management System. *Proceedings of the 1975 National Computer Conference,* 1975.

[Ka79] Kaplan, S.J., Cooperative Responses from a Natural Language Database Query System. Stanford University TR HPP-79-19, 1979.

[KD81] Kaplan, S.J. and J. Davidson, Interpreting Natural Language Updates. *Proceedings of the 20th Annual Meeting of the Association for Computational Linguistics,* Stanford, 1981.

[SJ82] Sparck-Jones, K. and B. Boguraev, A Natural Language Analyzer for Database Access. *Information and Technology: Research and Development,* 1, 1982, pp.23-39.

[Sk80] Skuce, D., Bridging the Gap between Natural and Computer Language. *Proceedings of the International Congress on Applied Systems and Cybernetics,* Acapulco, 1980.

[SM82] Salveter, S. and D. Maier, Natural Language Database Updates. *Proceedings of the 20th Annual Meeting of the Association for Computational Linguistics,* Toronto, 1982, pp.67-73.

[Wa78] Walker, D., *Understanding Spoken Language.* American Elsevier, 1978.

[Wi81] Wiederhold, G., S.J. Kaplan and D. Sagalowicz, Research in Knowledge Base Management Systems. *SIGMOD Record,* 7, *3,* April 1981, pp.26-54.

[Wl75] Wilks, Y., An Intelligent Analyzer and Understander of English. *Communications of the Association for Computing Machinery,* 18, 1975, pp 264-274.

[Wo76] Woods, W. et al, Speech Understanding Systems: Final Technical Report. BBN Report #3438, 1976.

[Wz75] Waltz, D., Natural Language Access to a Large Database: An Engineering Approach. *Proceedings of the International Joint Conference on Artificial Intelligence, 1975.*

APPENDIX A - Example Verbgraph Execution

Recall our example of Variant 2 from Section 4:

"Schedule Joe at 2:15 today regarding Fall courses."

Its caseframe representation is:

cf//action	schedule
cf//actor	Sharon
cf//indobj	Joe
cf//date	systemdate
cf//time	14:15
cf//topic	Fall courses

Assume that the SCHEDULE verbgraph has been selected for execution. We now step through the execution process. In each snapshot of the blackboard, we indicate what has changed with a ☞ and checked off IL with a √.

The root node is always selected and executed before evaluation of the guards of the leaf nodes. (Because the prerequisites of the root ensure that all the leaf guards can be evaluated.) In this case, all of the root prerequisites are satisfied. Executing the root actions sets the blackboard as shown below.

BLACKBOARD {after ROOT execution}

VARIABLES

t1 : APPOINTMENT	t2 : APPOINTMENT
☞ name <- Sharon	name := t1.who
☞ date <- 15 Dec	date := t1.date
time	time := t1.time
duration	duration := t1.duration
☞ who <- Joe	who := t1.name
☞ topic <- Fall courses	topic := t1.topic
location	location := t1.location

t3 : ROOMRESERVE	t4 : MAILBOX
date	name
room	date := t1.date
time	time := t1.time
duration	from := t1.name
reserver	message := 'Meeting with %whom-to-meet on %t1.date at %t1.time';

whom-to meet : dom(t1.name)

IL :

☞ √ A1 : insert t1 into APPOINTMENT
A2 : insert t2 into APPOINTMENT
A3 : insert t3 into ROOMRESERVE
A4 : insert t4 into MAILBOX

The following nodes are selected for execution.

EMP {retrieval R1 determines Joe is an employee}

NOT-RESERVE {cf//obj = null and cf//location = null }

Suppose node EMP is processed first. Executing its actions results in the blackboard shown below.

BLACKBOARD {after EMP execution}

VARIABLES

```
t1 : APPOINTMENT
     name <- Sharon
     date <- 15 Dec
     time
     duration
     who <- Joe
     topic <- Fall courses
     location

t2 : APPOINTMENT
     name := t1.who
     date := t1.date
     time := t1.time
     duration := t1.duration
     who := t1.name
     topic := t1.topic
     location := t1.location

t3 : ROOMRESERVE
     date
     room
     time
     duration
     reserver

t4 : MAILBOX
  ☞  name <- Joe
     date := t1.date
     time := t1.time
     from := t1.name
     message := 'Meeting with %whom-to-meet
     on %t1.date at %t1.time';

☞  whom-to meet : dom(t1.name) <- Sharon
```

IL:

```
     √  A1 : insert t1 into APPOINTMENT;
☞   √  A2 : insert t2 into APPOINTMENT;
        A3 : insert t3 into ROOMRESERVE;
☞   √  A4 : insert t4 into MAILBOX;
```

Next, node NOT-RESERVE is processed. Its prerequisites are satisfied. After executing its actions, the blackboard is in the state shown below.

BLACKBOARD {after NOT-RESERVE execution}

VARIABLES

t1 : APPOINTMENT
name <- Sharon
date <- 15 Dec
☞ time <- 14:15
☞ duration <- 1
who <- Joe
topic <- Fall courses
☞ location <- 416

t2 : APPOINTMENT
name := t1.who
date := t1.date
time := t1.time
duration := t1.duration
who := t1.name
topic := t1.topic
location := t1.location

t3 : ROOMRESERVE
date
room
time
duration
reserver

t4 : MAILBOX
name <- Joe
date := t1.date
time := t1.time
from := t1.name
message := 'Meeting with %whom-to meet on %t1.date at %t1.time';

whom-to meet : dom(t1.name) <- Sharon

IL:

√ A1 : insert t1 into APPOINTMENT;
√ A2 : insert t2 into APPOINTMENT;
A3 : insert t3 into ROOMRESERVE;
√ A4 : insert t4 into MAILBOX;

At this point all selected nodes have been executed. The checked off IL is:

A1 : insert t1 into APPOINTMENT
A2 : insert t2 into APPOINTMENT
A4 : insert t4 into MAILBOX

where tuple variables t1, t2 and t4 have values

t1: <Sharon, 15 Dec, 14:15, 1, Joe, Fall courses, 416>

t2: <Joe, 15 Dec, 14:15, 1, Sharon, Fall courses, 416>

t4: <Joe, 15 Dec, 14:15, Sharon, Meeting with Sharon on 15 Dec at 14:15>

After translation to QUEL, the database will be correctly modified.

Semantic Query Optimization
in
Expert Systems and Database Systems

U. S. Chakravarthy — University of Maryland

D. H. Fishman — Bell Communications Research

J. Minker — University of Maryland

Abstract

Knowledge representation is an integral part of any knowledge base or expert system. The usefulness of first order predicate logic to represent knowledge is well understood. Using logic, problem specific knowledge can be represented as a set of general laws (intensional axioms or production rules), assertions (facts) and integrity constraints. In this paper we are concerned with the use of problem specific semantics expressed in logic to answer queries over the knowledge base in an efficient manner, in the presence of general axioms. The semantics is expressed as clauses in predicate logic generally termed as integrity constraints. The proposed approach termed *semantic compilation* compiles the semantics (integrity constraints) together with the general laws of the system and permits queries to be answered efficiently. Usage of semantics in relational databases (without deductive axioms) is a special case of the formalism presented in this paper.

1. Introduction

One of the characterizations of expert systems [Nau83] is the way in which the knowledge pertaining to the domain of the expert system is organized. Most expert computer systems organize knowledge on three levels: data, knowledge-base and control. Knowledge based systems is another term used for systems that conform to the above description. On the data level is declarative knowledge about the particular problem being solved and the current state of affairs in the attempt to solve the problem. On the knowledge-base level is the knowledge specific to the particular problem area which the system utilizes to solve problems or answer queries. Knowledge is used by the system in reasoning about the problem and is often given in the form of rules termed production rules. In the control structure is a computer program that makes decisions about how to use the specific problem solving knowledge. Decisions are made, for example, about which rules to apply and how to use them.

The usefulness of first order logic in a knowledge representation context became evident during the 1960's, primarily as the result of research in mechanical theorem proving [Robi65]. Logic provides a uniform representation to express and organize knowledge on all three levels. Assertions (facts or extensions) are used to represent declarative data. Intensional axioms along with integrity constraints can be used to represent domain dependent knowledge. Reasoning can be performed as deductions using logic. Even control can be expressed as meta-level constructs as shown in Kowalski [Kowa79].

In this paper we delimit ourselves to the representation of knowledge based systems using logic. The discussion is applicable to any deductive database system which uses logic to represent facts, axioms and to query.

The paper is organized as follows. Section 2 deals with knowledge bases, querying on them and the limitations as the knowledge base grows. Section 3 introduces the compiled approach to answering queries with an illustrative example. Section 4 introduces query processing and the relevance of integrity constraints to semantic query processing. Section 5 provides intuitive explanation for compiling integrity constraints into axioms with examples. Section 6 sketches the proposed approach formally. In section 7 we discuss query processing informally, in the wake of semantic compilation and provide an example. Section 8 summarizes the scope of the work.

2. Knowledge Bases and Query Answering

In a small database system where the amount of facts (extensional database (EDB)) and the number of rules (intensional database (IDB)) are relatively few, a simple control mechanism is enough to generate the entire search space of answers for a given query. The search space is small and hence answering queries can be done efficiently even with exhaustive search strategies. PROLOG has been used for small database systems. PROLOG provides facilities to represent facts as assertions and rules in the form of definite Horn axioms (A definite Horn axiom is a disjunction of atomic literals having exactly one positive literal). It has a simple depth-first left-to-right control strategy. Warren [Warr81] has used PROLOG for Chat-80 and proposed a control strategy in terms of rearrangement of predicates to increase the efficiency of the query answering system.

When both the EDB and IDB are large, PROLOG is inefficient. The search space needs to be generated so as to reduce the amount of data accessed from the EDB. The sequence in which general laws are applied also affects the efficiency of a search strategy. Heuristics in the form of clause and literal selection have been proposed [Mink78] to guide the state space search. Alternative representations for the clause form ([Fish75], [Mink73], [Wils76]) have been proposed for the generation of the search space in parallel.

When the EDB is large in comparison to the IDB, it is meaningful to separate the deductive or reasoning process from the data access process. Interleaving the inference and lookup processes as in PROLOG leads to inefficient query processing. The compiled approach of Reiter [Reit78b] decouples the deductive and data access processes. It has been shown in Chakravarthy et al. [Chak82] that compilation as specified by Reiter can be achieved in a PROLOG environment, with little modification to PROLOG.

3. Compiled Approach

In the compiled approach, there are two processors, the extensional query evaluator (EDB processor) and the intensional processor (IDB processor). The IDB processor uses theorem proving. It uses only the intensional axioms without interleaving access to the extensions of the database. The output of the IDB processor is a set of axioms, all of which reference only relations stored explicitly in the EDB. After the compiled axioms are produced, deduction is no longer necessary to answer any query on the database and the theorem prover used to compile the axioms is no longer needed. In effect, this decoupling of EDB and IDB processors relegates the search task over the IDB to the theorem prover, and the "search-free computation" task over the EDB to the extensional query evaluator. Queries are then answered using conventional relational database techniques. (See Reiter [Reit78b] for details.)

We illustrate the notion of compiling non-recursive general axioms by the following simplified example. The example is used later to illustrate semantic compilation of integrity constraints. Fully extensional predicates will be denoted throughout this paper by an asterisk (*). Thus Dept* is fully extensional, while Teach is fully intensional.

Example 3.1:

The database consists of the following relations (EDB relations are starred):

E3.1: Teach*(Tname, Dname, courseno)

E3.2: Enrolled*(Sname, Dname, courseno)

E3.3: Dept*(Dname, courseno, credits)

The IDB contains the following axioms:

A3.1: "GILBERT teaches all courses offered in the chemistry department."

Teach(GILBERT, x, y) ← Dept*(x, y, z), (x=CHEM)

A3.2: "MINKER teaches all courses offered in the computer science department."

Teach(MINKER, x, y) ← Dept*(x, y, z), (x=CS)

A3.3: The rest of the IDB relation Teach is the same as the EDB relation Teach*

Teach(u1, u2, u3) ← Teach*(u1, u2, u3)

A3.4: "If teacher x teaches a course r belonging to the department y and student z is enrolled in course r of department y then x is the teacher of z."

Teacher_of(x,z) ← Teach(x,y, r), Enrolled*(z, y, r)

Teach and Teacher_of are intensional relations.

In the compiled approach, each intensional predicate is considered as a query(in its most general form, that is, containing variables), and all possible proofs with the query as the top clause are derived. A proof is obtained if the null ( ) clause or a clause consisting entirely of EDB literals can be derived. In this example we have

← Teacher_of(u1, u2)

as the most general form of the query for the intensional predicate Teacher_of. This clause resolves with A3.4 to give

← Teach(u1, y, r), Enrolled*(u2, y, r)

The above clause contains an EDB reference as well as an IDB reference. The Teach predicate can be further resolved with respect to A3.1, A3.2 and A3.3 separately to obtain the following:

← Dept*(y, r, z), Enrolled*(u2, y, r), (u1=GILBERT), (y=CHEM)

← Dept*(y, r, z), Enrolled*(u2, y, r), (u1=MINKER), (y=CS)

← Teach*(u1, y, r), Enrolled*(u2, y, r)

The above clauses are compiled forms of the corresponding intensional predicates in the IDB. It should be clear that there is no need to save the entire proof tree. Instead only the top clause and the leaf nodes of the proof tree are retained. Each leaf node in the proof tree gives rise to a Horn clause. The Horn clause corresponding to a leaf node has the top literal of the proof tree as its consequent and the literals in the leaf node as its antecedent. For the above example there are three Horn clauses which are

CA3.1: Teacher_of(u1, u2) ← Teach*(u1, y, r), Enrolled*(u2, y, r)

CA3.2: Teacher_of(u1, u2) ← Dept*(CHEM, r, z), Enrolled*(u2, CHEM, r), (u1=GILBERT)

CA3.3: Teacher_of(u1, u2) ← Dept*(CS, r, z), Enrolled*(u2, CS, r), (u1=MINKER)

In the above compiled axioms the equalities (y=CS) and (y=CHEM) have been substituted into the axioms. We assume throughout the paper that the compiled version of the IDB axioms is available in the form of Horn clauses.

The compilation of an intensional predicate may give rise to several Horn clauses as shown in the above example. This implies that the intensional predicate can be computed in several ways corresponding to each Horn clause generated by the proof tree. The virtual relation corresponding to the intensional predicate is the union of relations produced for each axiom in which the intensional predicate is the consequent.

For the above example, if the intensional predicate Teach(u1, u2, u3) is used as the top clause then we obtain the following compiled axioms:

CA3.4: Teach(u1, u2, u3) ← Dept*(u2, u3, z), (u1=GILBERT), (u2=CHEM)

CA3.5: Teach(u1, u2, u3) ← Dept*(u2, u3, z), (u1=MINKER), (u2=CS)

CA3.6: Teach(u1, u2, u3) ← Teach*(u1, u2, u3)

4. Query Optimization and Semantics Usage

Query optimization can be regarded, in simplistic terms, as the process of transforming a query into an equivalent form (in the sense that it produces the same answer as the original query for any database state), which can be evaluated efficiently.

The techniques developed for query optimization can be broadly classified into two basic categories, namely, conventional query optimization and query optimization using semantics.

4.1. Conventional Query Optimization

Conventional query optimization research has identified a set of problems, has produced useful models for data storage and file operations, and has yielded insights into factors that influence the cost of query processing. This research confined itself to query modification and transformation strategies involving the operators of the query language such as equivalence of expressions, algebraic transformations such as commutativity, associativity, changing the computational order of operators etc., and properties such as factoring in conjunction with the cost estimation associated with file manipulation (or physical data extraction level). Conventional optimization techniques, however, did not take into account the knowledge about the domains or the relations that were associated with the query, except for statistical information about data in the database. In fact, one can view the manipulation of a conventional query optimizer as a process which reorganizes the query using syntactic information to take advantage of the physical representation in the context of the query. Several methodologies using heuristics, statistical and probabilistic measures have been proposed to interface the query modification stage and its evaluation in terms of the physical support. The logical/physical correspondence is exploited to reduce as much as possible the size of the data that must be handled without suitable physical support. See Ullman [Ullm82] for details.

4.2. Role of Integrity Constraints

The role of integrity constraints in processing queries needs some elaboration. It has been shown by Reiter [Reit78a] that integrity constraints play no part in the derivation of answers to an existential query in Horn databases. That is, integrity constraints are not necessary to obtain answers to a given existential query in a Horn database. Nevertheless, the role of integrity constraints as semantics (knowledge) expressed over the database has been well recognized and made use of in several ways. See Hammer and McLeod [Hamm75], McSkimin and Minker [McSk77], Hammer and Zdonik [Hamm80], King [King81], Kohli and Minker [Kohl83], Xu [Xu83], Futo [Futo84] and Jarke et al. [Jark84] for details. Integrity constraints can aid/guide and act as heuristics in searching the space of answers. In some cases they can help terminate queries that have no answers as they violate some database integrity constraints and hence require no search over the database. Integrity constraints can also be used to generate semantically equivalent queries (queries that produce the same answer as the original query for any database state), which can be executed more efficiently over the database than the original query. Thus, integrity constraints have been used either to aid the search process or to transform the original query into a set of semantically equivalent queries.

In this paper we sketch a formalism to use integrity constraints together with compiled axioms. Compiled axioms are extended using integrity constraints and these extended axioms are used for answering queries. The compilation of integrity constraints is done once and in advance of all processing on the database. When a specific query arises, a modest amount of work is essential to revise the query to account for compiled axioms as already modified by the integrity constraints. Doing so can, in some instances, obtain answers without the need for database search. The role of integrity constraints in the deduction process (to obtain answers for the query) is formalized through the notions of subsumption and partial subsumption. We illustrate the approach through examples. We are not here concerned about the use of integrity constraints for the update/insert/delete operations on a database.

4.3. Format of Integrity Constraints

We consider a class of integrity constraints represented in the form of clauses (which need not be Horn). A variety of semantic knowledge can be expressed elegantly using the clause forms given below. Another reason for resorting to clause form is to use the procedural semantics associated with clause form for the purpose of

a) transforming a set of integrity constraints and

b) integrating integrity constraints with the general axioms used for deduction.

The clause form of integrity constraints described in this paper can be one of the following:

1) ← P1, P2, ... , Pm

2) Q1, Q2, ... , Qn ← P1, P2, ... , Pm

3) Q1 & , ..., & Qn ← P1, ..., Pm
which is equivalent to
Q1 ← P1, ..., Pm and , ..., and Qn ← P1, ..., Pm

4) All of the above (except 1) where the implication (←) is replaced by equivalence (≡).

In the above clause forms we assume that the Ps and Qs are either extensional relations of the database or primitive relations which can be evaluated (also known as evaluable predicates such as EQUAL, LESS, etc.). If the integrity constraints are not in this form originally, they may be transformed to this form (see Chakravarthy et al. [Chak84]). All variables in the above clause forms are assumed to be universally quantified and that there are no function symbols and Skolem constants/functions. Although we have listed four clauses of integrity constraints all of the above clause forms can be reduced to the format of 2) with varying values for m and n.

The following examples of integrity constraints illustrate the above formats. Each integrity constraint given is presented first in English and followed immediately by its translation to clause form. Some of the examples are drawn from Chang [Chan78].

IC4.1: "Any company that supplies GUNS does not supply DRESSES."
← Supply(x, GUNS) & Supply(x, DRESSES)

IC4.2: "An individual cannot be both male and female."
← Male(x) & Female(x)

IC4.3: "Any company that supplies GUNS also supplies BULLETS."
Supply(x, BULLETS)← Supply(x, GUNS)

IC4.4: "Only SMITH teaches HISTORY courses."
(x=SMITH) ← Teach(x, HISTORY, z)

IC4.5: "The item supplied is either in the department or in stock."
Dept(y), Stock(y) ← Supply(x, y)

IC4.6: "Every department has only one floor."

(y=z) ← Loc(x, y) & Loc(x, z)

4.4. Assumptions

We make the following assumptions:

1) Axioms are universally quantified, non-recursive and definite Horn clauses.

2) Integrity constraints are universally quantified, non-recursive, and comply with the above formats.

3) Both axioms and integrity constraints are function-free.

4) The closed world assumption is assumed to pertain([Reit78a]).

5. Intuitive Explanation of Integrity Constraint Usage

This section informally explains the usage of integrity constraints in the context of general axioms. Consider the database of Example 1 with the following integrity constraints.

IC5.1: "BAKER teaches only History courses."

(x=HIST) ← Teach*(BAKER, x, v)

IC5.2: "All Chemistry courses are 4 credits each."

(z=4) ← Dept*(CHEM, v, z)

IC5.3: "JOHN is enrolled in computer science or history courses"

(d=CS), (d=HIST) ← Enrolled*(JOHN, d, cno)

As part of semantic compilation we associate the "relevant" integrity constraints with axioms. For example the axiom CA3.1 and the integrity constraint IC5.2 have no predicates in common and hence IC5.2 is not relevant to CA3.1. Formally, we say that IC5.2 is not merge compatible with CA3.1. See King [King81] for a related definition of merge compatibility. If we consider the axiom CA3.1 and the integrity constraint IC5.3, we should be able to attach the condition (y=CS), (y=HIST) ← (u2=JOHN) to the axiom. The reason why we can attach this condition is that if a query for Teacher_of had its argument u2 bound to JOHN, then from the axiom we know that JOHN had to be enrolled in a course taught by the teacher. The integrity constraint states that if JOHN is enrolled in a course then the course must be either CS or HIST. The above condition when added to the axiom states this precisely. If the variable u2 is instantiated to JOHN when using the axiom CA3.1, the attached condition is evaluated and y=CS V y=HIST can be attached to the query. Thus, the value of the variable y is obtained without accessing the database, using only the semantics of the integrity constraint.

We can derive this condition if we try to subsume the body of the compiled axiom CA3.1 by the integrity constraint IC5.3. The subsumption algorithm as given in Chang and Lee [Chan73] does not derive the above condition. A modification to the subsumption algorithm is described that extracts simpler conditions which can be attached to the axioms. The subsumption algorithm described in the next section, produces clauses (termed residues) when an integrity constraint is partially subsumed by an axiom. We integrate this clause produced as a result of partial subsumption with the axiom as follows:

SCA5.1': Teacher_of(u1, u2)← Teach*(u1, y, r),Enrolled*(u2, y, r),
{(y=CS),(y=HIST) ← (u2=JOHN)}

The above axiom is referred to as the semantically constrained axiom. The list {...} is termed constraint list which contains the residues generated by the modified partial subsumption algorithm. The implication in the constraint list helps to bind the variable y to CS and HIST if in any query u2 is instantiated to JOHN. If the relation Enrolled* is indexed on the attribute Dname it helps in accessing the relation Enrolled* using the index.

When we try to integrate IC5.2 with axiom CA3.3 using the modified subsumption algorithm, we are left with the residue

(r=4) ← (CS=CHEM)

Since (CS=CHEM) is never true, this residue cannot be used during query processing. The residue is considered trivial (or the corresponding clause is a tautology) and is not integrated with the axiom. The integrity constraint is not considered to be merge compatible because of the trivial residue generated as a result of partial subsumption.

Using the modified subsumption algorithm to generate non-trivial residues, we obtain the following semantically constrained axioms when the axioms CA3.1 to CA3.3 are merged with IC5.1 through IC5.3.

SCA5.1: Teacher_of(u1, u2) ← Teach*(u1, y, w), Enrolled*(u2, y, w),
{(y=HIST) ← (u1=BAKER),
(y=CS), (y=HIST) ← (u2=JOHN)}

SCA5.2: Teacher_of(u1, u2) ← Dept*(y, w, z), Enrolled*(u2, y, w),
(y=CHEM), (u1=GILBERT),
{(z=4) ←
← (u2=JOHN)}

SCA5.3: Teacher_of(u1, u2) ←Dept*(y, w, z), (u1=MINKER), Enrolled*(u2, y, w),(y=CS),
{}

Once semantic compilation is achieved, these constrained axioms contain semantic information which can be utilized to answer queries. A similar set of semantically constrained axioms can be derived for the intensional axiom Teach. The integrity constraints can also be associated with EDB relations to answer queries involving EDB relations only. When IC5.1 through IC5.3 are merged with Enrolled* and Dept*, the following results:

SCE5.1: Enrolled*(x, y, z) {(y=CS), (y=HIST) ← (x=JOHN)}

SCE5.2: Dept*(x, y, z) {(z=4) ← (x=CHEM)}

Below we take a query and show how the residues are used to answer queries.

Q5.1: "Who is the teacher_of JOHN?"

To obtain the answer for the corresponding query

← Teacher_of(ans, JOHN)

it is sufficient to use only the semantically constrained axioms SCA5.1 to SCA5.3.
It is easy to observe that SCA5.2 produces the answer nil as one of the clauses is violated in the constraint list, namely ← (JOHN=JOHN). Using the clause (y=CS), (y=HIST) ← (u2=JOHN) in the constraint list of SCA5.1, the query can be simplified to

← Teach*(ans, y, w), Enrolled*(JOHN, y, w), (y=CS V y=HIST), (ans=BAKER)

The above axiom is more instantiated than the original axiom and this has been achieved using the semantics. A search is needed only on two departments, namely, CS and HIST. The axiom SCA5.3 cannot be simplified, and the answer MINKER cannot be given because we do not have an integrity constraint to assert that JOHN is actually enrolled in a CS course. Hence access to the Enrolled* and Dept* relational tables cannot be avoided in the absence of other integrity constraints.

The above example provides an overview of the formalism described in detail below. See Chakravarthy et al. [Chak84] for additional details.

6. Semantic Compilation

The motivation behind semantic compilation is to associate integrity constraints in a simplified form with the compiled axioms, as illustrated by the examples in the previous section. The simplified fragments of integrity constraints are usually in the form of simple conditions over variables belonging to the predicates of the general axioms. The purpose of doing so is to make it relatively inexpensive to evaluate these simplified conditions at query execution time, and thereby hopefully reduce the processing time to obtain answers.

The process of semantic compilation is achieved through several stages termed *integration, merging* and *compilation.* An integrity constraint is integrated into an axiom to obtain *semantically constrained axioms.* When several integrity constraints are integrated into an axiom it is termed merging. When merging is performed for all the axioms of the database semantic compilation is achieved.

Definition: A *Semantically Constrained Axiom (SCA)* is defined to be of the form

$$H \leftarrow P_1, ..., P_m \{C_1, ..., C_n\}$$

where

H is the procedure head of the axiom, each literal P_i, i = 1 to m is either a predicate or an evaluable predicate (for example inequality, less_than etc.).

$H \leftarrow P_1, ..., P_m$ denotes the procedural semantics of a Horn clause, C_1 to C_n are fragments of integrity constraints that are associated with the axiom. This format is an extension of clause form that separates the semantics from the intensional definition.

The fragments of integrity constraints, namely, C_i, i = 1 to n are termed residues and are obtained through the process of partial subsumption.

Definition: A *substitution* is a finite set of the form $\{t_1/v_1, ..., t_n/v_n\}$, where every v_i is a variable, every t_i is a term different from v_i, and no two elements in the set have the same variable after the stroke symbol.

The substitution denotes that the term t_i is to be substituted for the variable v_i. When $t_1, ..., t_n$ are ground terms, the substitution is called *ground substitution.* The substitution that consists of no elements is called the *empty substitution* or *identity substitution* and is denoted by ϵ. We shall use Greek letters to represent each substitution. We shall use lower case letters from the end of the alphabet to represent variables and lower case letters from the beginning of the alphabet to denote constants.

Definition: A clause C *subsumes* a clause D if and only iff there is a substitution σ such that $C\sigma \subseteq D$. D is called the subsumed clause.

Our interest in subsumption is to test whether the body of an integrity constraint subsumes the body of a general axiom. This is unlikely for integrity constraints with no consequents, since the computation of the relation implied by the conjunction of the atoms which implies the relation would not lead to any data in the database and hence the axiom should not be part of the IDB. At the same time, a subset of an integrity constraint may partially subsume the body of an axiom, thereby obtaining a partially satisfied integrity constraint (residue or a fragment) along with a set of bindings. These fragments of an integrity constraint (along with the bindings) can be used during query processing in a variety of ways. We use the notion of partial subsumption to obtain the fragments of integrity constraints, which are referred to as residues.

Definition: An integrity constraint IC *partially subsumes* an axiom A if and only if there is a set of substitutions $\sigma_1, ..., \sigma_n$ and a set of clauses $IC_1, ..., IC_n$, where each IC_i, i = 1 to n is a subset of IC, and each $IC_i\sigma_i$ is a subset of A (that is, each IC_i subsumes A), but there is no substitution γ, such that $IC\gamma$ is a subset of A (IC does not subsume A).

For example (y=CS), (y=HIST) ← (u2=JOHN) is the clause obtained when the integrity constraint IC5.3 partially subsumes the axiom CA3.1.

Definition: Let E be a wff and $\theta = \{t_1/v_1, ..., t_n/v_n\}$ be a substitution. Then $E\theta^{-1}$ is an expression obtained by replacing simultaneously each occurrence of the term t_i, $1 \leq i \leq n$, in E by the variable v_i. The expression $E\theta^{-1}$ is called *back substitution* of θ in the wff E.

The form of an integrity constraint as given in earlier examples is not suited for partial subsumption especially to obtain simpler conditions for variables. Hence they are modified to an equivalent form by replacing each distinct constant by a distinct variable and adding the fact that the constant equals the variable. For example the integrity constraint IC5.2 is represented

as
(z=4) ← Dept*(x1, y, z), (x1=CHEM).
The above format is termed ***variable substituted*** form. For a discussion of variable substitution, its utility and correctness see [Chak84].
Definition: Let IC be in variable substituted clause form. A ***residue*** of the integrity constraint IC with respect to an axiom A, is defined as the set of literals $((\text{IC} - \text{IC}_l)\ \sigma_l)\theta^{-1}$ for each IC_l which is a subset of IC and subsumes A. σ_l is the substitution which makes $\text{IC}_l\sigma_l$ an instance of $A\theta$, where θ is a substitution used to reduce A to a ground instance as discussed earlier.

When IC subsumes A, the subset of IC that subsumes A is IC itself (when IC has no consequent). Hence the residue generated is ϕ, which is denoted by R_ϵ and referred to as ***null residue***. Similarly it is easy to observe that IC could partially subsume A by virtue of IC_l being empty (that is IC_l is FALSE), which is a subset of any clause. In this case the residue IC - IC_l is the same as IC. We refer to this as the ***maximal residue***. A residue is termed ***trivial*** if it evaluates to true.

For example the residue (r=4) ← (CS=CHEM) is trivial. Trivial clauses evaluate to true in the interpretation and hence do not contribute to query evaluation.
Definition: An integrity constraint is ***merge compatible*** with an axiom if at least one of the residues generated (as a result of partial subsumption between the axiom and the integrity constraint) is non-trivial.

The modified subsumption algorithm given below generates all the non-trivial residues when an integrity constraint is partially subsumed by an axiom. Consistent residues are appended to the constraint list of the axiom.

6.1. Modified Partial Subsumption Algorithm

INPUT: An integrity constraint IC and a compiled axiom CA.
OUTPUT: Residues if IC is merge compatible with CA, MAXIMAL_RESIDUE is set to true if IC is not merge compatible with CA, FULLY_SUBSUMES is set to true if IC subsumes CA.
Let IC_v be the variable substituted form of IC.
Let $\theta = \{k_1/v_1, \ldots, k_n/v_n\}$ where each v_i for i = 1 to n are variables occurring in CA, and k_i for i = 1 to n are special distinct constants not occurring in either IC or CA. Suppose CA is Q ← $L_1, \ldots, L_n$. Then $\text{CA}\theta = Q\theta \leftarrow L_1\theta, \ldots, L_n\theta$. Note that $\text{CA}\theta$ contains only ground literals. $\neg\text{CA}\theta$ is a set of unit literals.

Algorithm:

```
UNIT_CLAUSES := {← Qθ, L_1θ ←, ..., L_nθ ←};
FULLY_SUBSUMES := FALSE;
MAXIMAL_RESIDUE := FALSE;
if (there are NO literals between UNIT_CLAUSES and IC_v that can resolve)
then
   MAXIMAL_RESIDUE := TRUE    /* case of maximal residue */
else
   k := 0; /* used as a counter */
   RESOLVENTs_k := {IC_v};
   RESIDUEs := {IC_v};
   While ( ¬(null ∈ RESOLVENTs_k) and ¬(RESOLVENTs_k = ∅) )
      k := k+1;
      RESOLVENTs_k := ∅;
      For each clause C ∈ RESOLVENTs_{k-1} do
         Choose a predicate P (other than the evaluable predicates introduced during
         variable substitution) in C
         For each occurrence of the predicate P (say P_i) do
            Let R = {R_1, ..., R_m} be the resolvents obtained when P_i is resolved with
            as many literals in UNIT_CLAUSEs as possible.
```

```
                If (R ≠ ∅) then RESIDUEs := RESIDUEs – {C};
                Simplify evaluable predicates in resolvents ∈ R and factor them out wher-
                ever possible.
                For each (Rl ∈ R) do
                    if ( Rl is non-trivial)
                    then
                        RESIDUEs := RESIDUEs ∪ {Rl};
                        RESOLVENTSk ← RESOLVENTSk ∪ {Rl};
                    end If
                end For
            end For
        end For
    end While
    Replace all the variables in RESIDUEs that were introduced during variable substi-
    tution with the corresponding variables or constants from the evaluable predicates.
    The above is performed for all types of variable substitutions. This can always be
    done. This reduces each element in RESIDUEs into a clause having only the vari-
    ables and constants that were in IC or CA, or special constants ki that were intro-
    duced.
    if ¬(null ∈ RESOLVENTSk) /* non-null residues */
    then
        if ¬(RESIDUEs = ∅) /* some resolvents are non-trivial */
        then
            RESIDUEs := (RESIDUEs)θ^-1
        else
            MAXIMAL_RESIDUE := TRUE; /* case of trivial residues */
        end If
    else
        FULLY_SUBSUMES := TRUE; /* null residue */
    end If
end If
```

For the correctness of the algorithm and the generation of non-trivial residues see [Chak84].

6.2. Integration Process

The process of integration is to make sure that only merge compatible integrity constraints are associated with a compiled axiom. The residues generated using the modified subsumption algorithm are added to the constraint list of the compiled axiom. Only non-maximal and non-trivial residues are added to the constraint list. The algorithm given below describes how to construct the constraint list for a given integrity constraint and an axiom.

6.2.1. Integration Algorithm

Input: An integrity constraint IC and a compiled axiom CA.
Output: Semantically constrained axioms (denoted by SCA) obtained when the given IC is integrated with the axiom CA.

Algorithm:

Apply the modified partial subsumption algorithm of section 6.1 on IC and CA.

```
If MAXIMAL_RESIDUE is true then
    SCA := CA /* not merge compatible */
else
    if FULLY_SUBSUMES is true
    then
```

the consequent of CA is ϕ; IC subsumes CA. Hence IC is violated in the computation of the intensional predicate of the axiom (that is, the consequent of CA). A warning needs to be issued to the Database Administrator.

else

for each clause $R_i \in$ RESIDUEs do

If all the literals in R_i are positive, add it as an element to the constraint list of SCA as an assertion.

If all the literals in R_i are negative, add it to the constraint list as a query.

If some literals are positive and some are negative in R_i, add it to the constraint list as $P_1, \ldots, P_n \leftarrow Q_1, \ldots, Q_m$, where P_i, i=1 to n were positive literals in the R_i and Q_i, i=1 to m are negative literals in the R_i.

end For

end If

end If

As an example SCA5.1' is obtained when IC3 is integrated into C1.

6.3. Merging of an Axiom with a Set of Integrity Constraints

A database is likely to contain several integrity constraints. When an axiom is semantically compiled, the effect of all the integrity constraints needs to be reflected in the final version of a semantically constrained axiom. Merging is the process that integrates all the merge compatible integrity constraints separately into the compiled axiom.

It is possible that the given set of integrity constraints derive additional integrity constraints. The algorithm for merging can be simplified if we take into account all the derivable integrity constraints. We are not concerned with derived integrity constraints in this paper and assume that all derivable integrity constraints have been incorporated in the set of integrity constraints. See [Chak84] for alternative strategies for merging.

6.3.1. Algorithm for Merging

Input: A compiled axiom CA and a set of integrity constraints $IC_s = \{IC_1, \ldots, IC_n\}$.
Output: A semantically constrained axiom SCA, which is the result of merging CA with IC_s.

Algorithm:

Integrate CA and IC_i (any $IC_i \in IC_s$ for that matter) using the integration algorithm. Let SCA be the semantically constrained axiom produced. Let C be the constraint list and let P be the antecedent list. SCA is of the form H $\leftarrow$ P, $\{C\}$, where H is the consequent of the compiled axiom CA.

For each ic $\in IC_s$ (except the IC_i used above) do

Integrate ic with SCA as follows.

Use H $\leftarrow$ P as the axiom.

Add generated residues to C. Note that C is a set.

end For

SCA5.1, SCA5.2 and SCA5.3 are obtained as a result of merging C3.1, C3.2 and C3.3 respectively with the integrity constraints IC5.1 through IC5.3.

6.4. Semantic Compilation of Axioms of a Database

The process of integration and merging generate semantically constrained axioms which contain residues obtained through modified partial subsumption. Semantic compilation is the process of merging each compiled axiom of the database with all the integrity constraints of the database

The algorithm described below compiles the databases axioms by repeatedly applying the merge algorithm.

6.4.1. Algorithm for Semantic Compilation

Input: A set of compiled axioms CAs = $\{CA_1, ..., CA_l\}$ and a set of integrity constraints $IC_s = \{IC_1, ..., IC_m\}$.

Output: A set of semantically constrained axioms SCAs = $\{SCA_1, ..., SCA_n\}$.

Algorithm:

SCAs := $\emptyset$;

For each ca in CAs do

  Merge ca with IC_s to generate a set of semantically constrained axioms sca_s.

  SCAs := SCAs $\cup$ sca_s.

end For

7. Query Processing Using Semantic Compilation

In this section we provide an informal discussion of the usage of semantically constrained axioms during query processing. We will not discuss control strategies and heuristics that are possible (see [Chak84]). Once the semantic compilation has been performed, integrity constraints are no longer needed for query processing. All the information is retained in the constraint list of the compiled axiom in a form which can be readily used during query processing. To keep the discussion simple, we distinguish two types of query processing, namely, atomic query processing and general query processing. In both cases we assume that only positive literals are present in the query.

7.1. Processing Atomic Queries

An atomic query is either an extensional predicate or an intensional predicate. Since there is a constraint list associated with every axiom and base relation, we use the constraint list to simplify the query. If the atomic query is a base relation, simplifications using the constraint list may

a) answer the query without need to access the database;

b) generate a nil answer if an integrity constraint is violated;

c) variables in the query instantiate thereby reducing the number of tuples retrieved;

d) have no impact on the query.

If the atomic query is on an intensional predicate, the simplifications mentioned above can be performed and in addition, the order of join (if any) computation can be determined depending on the simplifications performed. In any case, the semantically constrained axiom provides all the information needed to simplify and evaluate the query. If there are several axioms for the given predicate, a decision can be made (after simplification) as to whether the query can be evaluated using multiple-query evaluation techniques.

7.2. Processing General Queries

When a query consists of more than one atom (either intensional or extensional), query simplification needs to be done using the constraint lists of the individual atoms in the query. We will not go into the details of merging and factoring constraint lists to generate the resultant constraint list in this paper. Instead, we will illustrate general query processing and the use of constraint lists on an example database taken from [Jark84].

Example 7.1:

EDB:

E7.1: Employee*(Eno, Name, Salary, Deptno)

E7.2: Dept*(Deptno, Function, Managerno).

IDB:

A7.1: Works_dir_for(Name1, Name2) ← Employee*(e1, Name1, s1, D), Dept*(D, f1, M),
Employee*(M, Name2, s2, d2).

Integrity Constraints:

IC7.1: "Salaries of all employees are less than 90000 and greater than 10000"

(s1 > 10000) & (s1 < 90000) ← Employee*(e1, n1, s1, d1)

IC7.2: "Employee name functionally determines employee number"

(e1=e2) ← Employee*(e1, n1, s1, d1), Employee*(e2, n1, s2, d2)

IC7.3: "Employee number functionally determines name, salary and department number"

(n1=n2) & (s1=s2) & (d1=d2) ← Employee*(e1, n1, s1, d1), Employee*(e1, n2, s2, d2)

When the above integrity constraints are compiled into the axiom A7.1, using the algorithm of section 6.1, the following semantically constrained axiom is generated.

SCA7.1: Works_dir_for(N1, N2) ← Employee*(eno1, N1, sal1, D), Dept*(D,f1,M),
Employee*(M, N2, sal2, dno2),
{(sal1>10000) & (sal1<90000) ←,
(sal2>10000) & (sal2<90000) ←,
(eno1=M) ← (N1=N2),
(N1=N2) & (sal1=sal2) & (D=dno2) ← (eno1=M)}

The residues that can be associated with the base relations are:

SCE7.1: Employee*(Eno, Name, Salary, Deptno),
{(Salary>10000) & (Salary<90000) ←,
(Eno=e2) ← Employee*(e2, x1, s2, d2), (x1=Name),
(e1=Eno) ← Employee*(e1, x1, s1, d1), (x1=Name),
(Name=n2) & (Salary=s2) & (Deptno=d2) ← Employee*(x1, n2, s2, d2), (x1=Eno),
(Name=n1) & (Salary=s1) & (Deptno=d1) ← Employee*(x1, n1, s1, d1), (x1=Eno)}

SCE7.2: Dept*(Deptno, Function, Managerno) {}

Of the five residues associated with Employee*, two of them (the third and the fifth) can be factored out as they differ only up to renaming of variables.

Suppose we want to answer the query

Q7.1: "Who works directly for Smith and earns less than 40000?"

This query is translated into

← Works_dir_for(ans, SMITH), Employee*(e, ans, s, d), (s<40000)

Using the semantically compiled axiom SCA7.1 for the intensional predicate Works_dir_for and the semantically constrained base relation SCE7.1 for Employee* predicate, query Q7.1 can be expanded to

Q7.1a: ← Employee*(eno1, ans, sal1, D), Dept*(D, f1, M),
Employee*(M, SMITH, sal2, dno2),
{(sal1>10000) & (sal1<90000) ←,
(sal2>10000) & (sal2<90000) ←,
(eno1=M) ← (ans=SMITH),
(ans=SMITH) & (sal1=sal2) & (D=dno2) ← (eno1=M)},
Employee*(e, ans, s, d), (s<40000),
{(s>10000) & (s<90000) ←,
(e=e2) ← Employee*(e2, x1, s2, d2), (x1=ans),
(ans=n2) & (s=s2) & (d=d2) ← Employee*(x2, n2, s2, d2), (x2=e)}

Note that the terms from the query are substituted into corresponding variables in the constraint lists. Retaining only the residues that contribute to the simplification of this query, and discarding the rest, the above expression can be rewritten as

Q7.1b: ← Employee*(eno1, ans, sal1, D), Dept*(D, f1, M),
Employee*(M, SMITH, sal2, dno2),
Employee*(e, ans, s, d), (s<40000),
{(e=e2) ← Employee*(e2, x1, s2, d2), (x1=ans),
(ans=n2) & (s=s2) & (d=d2) ← Employee*(x2, n2, s2, d2), (x2=e)}

How simplifications of constraint lists are accomplished is outside the scope of this paper. Using the first Employee* predicate in the query and the residue
(e=e2) ← Employee*(e2, x1, s2, d2), (x1=ans), we can derive (e=eno1). Using the residue
(ans=n2) & (s=s2) & (d=d2) ← Employee*(x2, n2, s2, d2), (x2=e) and the same Employee* we can derive (ans=ans) & (sal1=s) & (D=d2). Applying these substitutions to the last Employee* predicate makes it identical to the first Employee* predicate and hence can be factored out. Therefore the query simplifies to

Q7.1': ← Employee*(eno1, ans, sal1, D), Dept*(D, f1, M),
Employee*(M, SMITH, sal2, dno2), (sal1<40000)

The above query has one less join than the previous one and this has been accomplished using the functional dependency as an integrity constraint, demonstrating the utility of semantic compilation in query optimization.

8. Summary and Scope

In this paper we have sketched the concept of semantic compilation formally and have illustrated the query answering process with examples. Our formalism provides a unified approach to compile a class of integrity constraints into the general axioms. The approach is based on logic and is uniform for all types of integrity constraints considered. Our approach helps in answering any query using the constraint list in one of the following three ways:

a) Queries can be answered using only the semantics expressed through integrity constraints. That is, using only the constraint list;

b) queries can be answered without using the semantics accumulated in the constraint list whenever it is not efficient;

c) queries can be answered using both the semantics as well as the intensional definitions by deriving semantically equivalent queries which can be answered efficiently;

As the integrity constraints are compiled into the axioms only once, the process is efficient even in the presence of a large number of integrity constraints and axioms.

Our formalism extends the work of King [King81] and Xu [Xu83] in a number of ways. We consider a wider class of integrity constraints such as non-Horn integrity constraints, and also deductive axioms. Databases which do not have general axioms are only a special case of our approach. Our formalism also extends the work of Jarke et al. [Jark84]. Again we consider a wider class of integrity constraints. Our approach is different and uses partial subsumption and resolution. We consider deductive axioms and compile semantics into axioms.

We are investigating extensions to other classes of integrity constraints. Further work is also required in simplifying constraint lists. In addition, when the number of integrity constraints are very large we are investigating control strategies which evaluate cost estimates of answering a query with and without semantics.

9. Acknowledgements

We gratefully appreciate support received under NSF grant MCS-83-05992 for U. S. Chakravarthy and J. Minker which made this work possible; and to Bell Communications Research for D. H. Fishman and J. Minker.

REFERENCES

[Chak82]
U. S. Chakravarthy, J. Minker, and D. Tran, Interfacing Predicate Languages and Relational databases, *Proc First International Logic Programming Conference*, Marseille, Sept 1982.

[Chak84]
U. S. Chakravarthy, D. H. Fishman, and J. Minker, Semantics Usage and Query Optimization in Deductive Databases, Tech Report 1413, University of Maryland, College Park, June 1984.

[Chan73]
C. L. Chang and R. C. T. Lee, *Symbolic Logic and Mechanical Theorem Proving*, Academic Press, New York, 1973.

[Chan78]
C. L. Chang, DEDUCE 2: Further Investigations of Deductions in Relational databases, pp. 201-236 in *Logic and Databases*, ed. H. Gallaire and J. Minker, Plenum Press, 1978.

[Fish75]
D. H. Fishman and J. Minker, PI-Representation: A Clause Representation for Parallel search, *Artificial Intelligence* **6**, 2, pp. 103-127, 1975.

[Futo84]
I. Futo, A Constraint Machine to Control Parallel Search of PRISM, Tech. Report, Department. of Computer Science, University of Maryland, College Park, Feb 1984.

[Hamm75]
M. M. Hammer and D. J. McLeod, Semantic Integrity in Relational Database Systems, *Proc First International Conference on Very Large Databases*, pp. 25-47, Sept 1975.

[Hamm80]
M. M. Hammer and S. B. Zdonik, Knowledge Based Query Processing, *Proc Sixth International Conference on Very Large Databases*, pp. 137-147, Sept 1980.

[Jark84]
M. Jarke, J. Clifford, and Y. Vassiliou, An Optimizing Prolog Front-End to a Relational Query System, *Proc of ACM SIGMOD* **14**, 2, Boston, pp. 296-306, June 1984.

[King81]
Jonathan J. King, Query Optimization by Semantic Reasoning, Ph.D Thesis, Department of Computer Science, Stanford University, May 1981.

[Kohl83]
M. Kohli and J. Minker, Intelligent Control Using Integrity Constraints, *Proc. of AAAI*, pp. 202-205, 1983.

[Kowa79]
Robert Kowalski, *Logic for Problem Solving*, Elsevier North Holland, Inc., 1979.

[McSk77]
J. R. McSkimin and Jack Minker, The Use of Semantic Network in a Deductive Query Answering System, *Proc of Fifth International Joint Conference on AI,* pp. 50-58, 1977.

[Mink73]
J. Minker, D. H. Fishman, and J. R. McSkimin, The Q* Algorithm - A Search Strategy for Deductive Question-Answering Systems, *Artificial Intelligence* **4**, 3, pp. 225-243, 1973.

[Mink78]
J. Minker, Search Strategy and Selection function for an Inferential Relational System, *ACM Transactions on Database Systems* **3**, 1, pp. 1-31, Mar 1978.

[Nau83]
D. S. Nau, Expert Computer Systems, *Computer* **16**, 2, pp. 63-85, 1983.

[Reit78a]
R. Reiter, On Closed World Databases, pp. 55-76 in *Logic and Databases,* ed. H. Gallaire and J. Minker, Plenum Press, 1978.

[Reit78b]
R. Reiter, Deductive Questioning-Answering on Relational databases, pp. 149-177 in *Logic and Databases,* ed. H. Gallaire and J. Minker, Plenum Press, 1978.

[Robi65]
J. A. Robinson, A machine-Oriented Logic Based on the Resolution Principle, *JACM* **12**, 1, pp. 23-41, Jan 1965.

[Ullm82]
J. D. Ullman, *Principles of Database Systems, 2nd Edition,* Computer Science Press, 1982.

[Warr81]
D. H. D. Warren, Efficient Processing of Interactive Relational Database Queries Expressed in Logic, Tech Report, Department of AI, University of Edinburgh, 1981.

[Wils76]
G. Wilson, A Description and Analysis of PAR Technique - An Approach to Parallel Inference and Parallel Search in Problem Solving Systems, Ph.D. Thesis, University of Maryland, 1976.

[Xu83]
G. D. Xu, Search Control in Semantic Query Optimization, 83-9, Univ. Of Massachusetts, Department. of Computer Science, Amherst, 1983.

EXTERNAL SEMANTIC QUERY SIMPLIFICATION:

A GRAPH-THEORETIC APPROACH AND ITS IMPLEMENTATION IN PROLOG

Matthias Jarke

Computer Applications and Information Systems Area
Graduate School of Business Administration
New York University
90 Trinity Place, New York, N.Y. 10006

Abstract

Semantic query simplification utilizes integrity constraints enforced in a database system for reducing the number of tuple variables and terms in a relational query. To a large degree, this can be done by a system that is external to the DBMS. The paper advocates the application of database theory in such a system and describes a working prototype of an external semantic query simplifier implemented in Prolog. The system employs a graph-theoretic approach to integrate tableau techniques and algorithms for the syntactic simplification of queries containing inequality conditions. The use of integrity constraints is shown not only to improve efficiency but also to permit more meaningful error messages to be generated, particularly in the case of an empty query result. The paper concludes with outlining an extension to the multi-user case.

1.0 INTRODUCTION

A research project at New York University investigates the integration of logic-based expert systems into existing management information systems. Prototype expert systems in life insurance [CLIF85; SIVA85] and management science are being built which rely heavily on access to large databases containing, e.g., customer data or health scoring information.

The interaction between expert systems and existing databases requires coupling two independent software systems: the expert system, e.g., written in Prolog, and a database system accessible through a relational query language, e.g., SQL. Rather than writing application-specific access routines as customary in the expert systems area, it was decided to build a generalized software tool that provides information to the expert system as and when required for the expert's deduction, much in the same way a human expert might consult a database for certain facts [JARK84; VASS84].

While the original motivation for building such a tool was its use as a data management backend to an expert system, it is not hard to see that the other direction of interaction is at least equally desirable. Very high-level user interfaces to databases employ deductive components but often lack an efficient interface between these components and an existing database. So-called deductive database systems partially solve this problem but stress a very deep integration with the underlying database or attempt to build one integrated system (see, e.g., [KELL82; SCIO84]). In contrast, our approach assumes independent existing systems and attaches the translation procedure to the expert systems language rather than to the DBMS (which may be used for many additional purposes other than as an expert system backend).

A second aspect of enhancing DBMS with semantic knowledge has been worked upon to a lesser degree so far: the knowledge-based execution of conventional database operations. Current DBMS are typically good in evaluating alternative strategies for processing a query on the physical level. They are often less strong in transforming a query submitted by the user into a (possibly different) representation which lends itself to the creation of more efficient processing alternatives, in particular when queries to views are concerned [OTTH82]. Moreover, processing a sequence or set of related queries is rarely supported.

A coupling mechanism allows the creation of an 'expert system' <u>external to</u> the DBMS that might employ syntactic and semantic knowledge about the database schema, as well as about strengths and weaknesses of the query optimizer of the underlying DBMS, to rephrase and organize a query or set of queries in the most efficient way. While in theory inferior to a fully integrated intelligent DBMS query optimizer (which would have full access to all internal data structures and full information about the database state at any given time), such an external 'database programming expert' may well benefit many existing databases in which the code of the DBMS is not accessible or should not be touched for reliability reasons.

The purpose of the present paper is twofold. First, it tries to clarify the concept of semantic query simplification, as compared to other approaches to utilizing general laws (or AI rules) in DBMS. In particular, it is argued that results obtained by database theory research should be employed as a crucial part of the knowledge bases and inference mechanisms in knowledge-based query evaluation methods although there is additional knowledge that has to be captured and utilized in a less structured manner, both in the application domain and in the query optimization domain itself. In this reliance on the efficient algorithms resulting from database theory, our approach differs from the one presented in [CHAK85] which combines general resolution and subsumption-based inference with control heuristics.

Second, the paper reports preliminary experience with a working prototype of a semantic query simplifier implemented in Prolog whose knowledge base may contain key dependencies, general functional dependencies, certain types of domain and inclusion dependencies, and some 'expert' rules added to the system to reduce optimization time (although these may in rare cases prevent optimality of the result). An overall algorithm has been described in [JARK84]. This paper presents a more efficient, integrated method that is based on a graph-theoretic representation of tableau techniques and handles arbitrary conjunctive queries with inequalities. The paper concludes with an outline of extensions currently under study, in particular with the concept of a multi-user querying front end.

2.0 SEMANTIC QUERY OPTIMIZATION, DATABASE THEORY, AND PROLOG

2.1 Rules In Database Systems

While the main purpose of most current DBMS is the management of large amounts of formatted specific facts, some DBMS support general rules that govern which data can be stored in the database (integrity constraints) or how to derive new facts from the stored ones; the latter are called deduction rules if applied at query time and generation rules if used to store derived facts explicitly. In other words, deduction and generation rules increase the number of facts retrievable from the database beyond the originally inserted facts, whereas integrity constraints reduce the number of facts that can be stored and retrieved [1].

Semantic query optimization employs integrity constraints for

---

[1] Note, that we use integrity rules as a meta-theory of the DBMS of which the database state is a model; in this respect, the approach taken here differs from [BOWE82] and others who see the database state (including rules) as a theory and define correctness in terms of consistency of the theory rather than integrity of the data. In the latter approach, it may be difficult to distinguish between deduction and integrity rules. [REIT84] describes a proof-theoretic way of enforcing integrity rules but does not address the efficiency issues of query evaluation which are the focus of this paper.

transforming queries, in the extreme to the degree that they can be answered without looking at the stored facts at all. The underlying principle of semantic query optimization is simple. One can add to each query predicate, P, an arbitrary number of integrity constraints, C1, ..., Cn, to form a new predicate:

P AND C1 AND ... AND Cn

without changing the result of the query (since all integrity constraints are always true by definition). The new predicate can then be converted -- by syntactic transformations -- into a form that lends itself to more efficient evaluation. We speak of semantic query simplification if the query resulting from this process never has more terms or tuple variables in its predicate than the original one. This will be the case if a subpredicate of P is implied by the added integrity constraints (i.e., the subpredicate is redundant and can be omitted) or contradicts them (i.e., the query result will be empty by definition). Interestingly, the basic ideas underlying this kind of optimization appeared almost simultaneously in a database theory [AHOS79] and in an AI context [HAMM80; KING81]. However, it seems that the connection between the two approaches has not generally been recognized. Demonstrating the practicality of this relationship is one of the goals of the present paper.

2.2 Knowledge Bases For Semantic Query Optimization

A major issue in semantic query optimization has been the reduction of the search space for applicable integrity constraints and efficiency-enhancing query transformations [XU83]. It is our perception that the type of integrity constraints existing in the system has a substantial influence on how this reduction can best be achieved.

In particular, there may be a discrepancy between the scope of typical integrity constraints in a relational database system and in AI-based knowledge representation (e.g., a semantic net or a set of Prolog view definitions). With few exceptions (e.g., [KLUG80]), database theory has concentrated on those types of general laws that are applicable to all elements of one relation (e.g., domain or functional dependencies), or to a combination of relations (e.g., inclusion dependencies). For this type of rules, it is (relatively) easy to recognize the applicability of an integrity constraint to a particular query, and to develop powerful -- sometimes provably optimal -- inference mechanisms. The task may be further simplified by the fact that the same laws are also used in the database design process to structure the database.

In contrast, published work in semantic query optimization has focused on more specific constraints that capture chunks of knowledge about smaller sets of data; simple examples of such constraints include: "only tankers have more than 400,000 tdw" [KING81] or "assistant professors do not have tenure." Here, it is not sufficient to look at a relation name in the constraint definition, since the applicability of a constraint to a certain tuple depends on membership in a subrelation. Moreover, the number of constraints is potentially very large and tends to be a function of the number of tuples (database size) rather than of the number of attributes (schema size). Finally, it is often not clear whether, how, and to what degree the addition of an integrity constraint will improve the efficiency of query evaluation: the optimal query may contain fewer or more terms than the old one. Artificial Intelligence-type heuristics and information about the database state at query execution time are frequently required for making these decisions.

Ultimately, the feasible extent of semantic query optimization depends on two factors: (a) what types of integrity constraints are enforced by the DBMS? and (b) what amount of search for optimization strategies is justified by the expected savings in query execution time? For an external semantic query optimizer, the heavy reliance on database theory and generally applicable laws has the advantage that the number of integrity constraint definitions (to be kept consistent between the optimizer and the DBMS) is relatively small and that little knowledge is required about the current database state; the latter type of knowledge is assumed to be handled by the DBMS query optimizer (this distinguishes our approach from Warren's who duplicates DBMS functions in his optimizer [WARR81]). Additionally, although there is a trend towards more sophisticated integrity assertions, most current database systems do not go beyond relatively simple concepts, such as bounds for numerical attribute values, key or at most general functional dependencies, and certain types of inclusion dependencies, e.g., unary ones [COSM84] or referential constraints.

As demonstrated in the sequel, these constraints can be employed quite efficiently in integrated query simplification algorithms that rely heavily on partial results provided by database theory. Such an algorithm has been implemented in DEC20-Prolog. Runtimes for a set of 14 test queries with four to six tuple variables and 5 to 20 join and restrictive terms were in the range between .5 and 1.2 seconds for interpreted Prolog (the compiled version is supposed to be about twenty times faster), including the times for translating from Prolog to the internal representation used by the optimizer, and from the optimized internal form to the DBMS query language. The usage of additional 'expert rules', obtained by observing systems behavior and intended to cut off less promising searches, even at the expense of guaranteed optimality, further reduces these times and, in particular, their growth rate with respect to the size of queries and the number of integrity constraints.

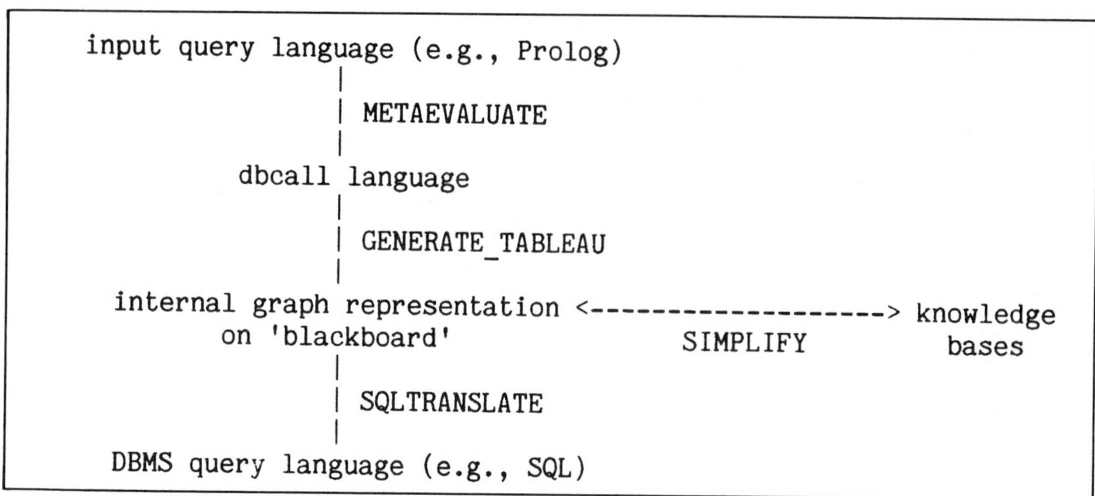

Figure 1: Structure of the External Semantic Query Simplifier

3.0 STRUCTURE OF THE SEMANTIC QUERY SIMPLIFIER

The semantic query simplifier consists of two translation mechanisms, a knowledge base, and the simplifier inference engine working on it, using a 'blackboard' [ERMA75] for intermediate results accessed and altered by multiple, largely independent algorithms (Figure 1). Thus, multiple 'experts' can be created for different kinds of integrity constraints.

The knowledge base is specific to a particular database; it contains a schema definition and predicates describing the integrity constraints. The current implementation will utilize [2] key dependencies (one per relation), general functional dependencies (standardized so that they have only one attribute on the right-hand side), value bounds for numerical attributes, and referential integrity constraints, i.e., inclusion dependencies, in which the superset side must be a key and in which each attribute appears in at most one referential constraint on the subset side [JARK84]. An example of such a constraint may be that "a manager must be an employee." Referential constraints were selected since they are central to the relational data model, yet have easier inference algorithms than general inclusion dependencies.

Key dependencies have been implemented separately from other functional dependencies for three reasons. First, many systems support keys but much less handle general functional dependencies. Thus, being able to state key dependencies directly may be convenient for a user. Second, in tableau optimization, equal keys mean that two complete rows become equal and one of them can be removed, leading to

[2] Additional constraints can be specified but will be ignored by the simplifier, since -- in this respect -- Prolog is purely declarative.

the removal of one join operation in query evaluation. Finally, the use of key dependencies speeds up the simplification algorithm in comparison to the usual representation in which a functional dependency would have to be defined for each non-key attribute.

In summary, the knowledge base would be roughly appropriate for a database in Fagin's [FAGI81] domain/key normal form, except that we allow the use of general functional dependencies. Figure 2 contains the Prolog description of the knowledge base for a two-relation database describing employees and their departments. There is a value bound on the salary attribute of the employee relation; note that the bounds could be defined either by the domain type, or they could represent the actual maximum and minimum value for the current database state if those are maintained [BLAU80]. The two referential integrity constraints say that employees work only in departments that exist, and that managers are employees.

```
schema(employee,[eno, ename, salary, dno]).
keydep(employee, [eno]).
funcdep(employee, [ename], [eno]).
valuebound(employee, salary, 1000, 9000).

schema(department,[dno, dname, mgr]).
keydep(department, [dno]).
funcdep(department, [mgr], [dno]).

refint(employee, [dno], department, [dno]).
refint(department, [mgr], employee, [eno]).
```

Figure 2: Example of a knowledge base for the simplifier

The two translation mechanisms make the core simplifier more or less independent of its input (from the user) and output (to the DBMS) query languages. There are currently experimental interfaces for Prolog input [VASS84], and for relational algebra and SQL output. The simplifier itself expects its input in a tableau-like subset of Prolog [JARK84]. Essentially, each query is a list of "dbcall" predicates corresponding to the rows of a tableau:

```
dbcall(Relationname, List_of_tableau_entries)
```

or to the inequality comparisons:

```
dbcall(Operator, Left_operand, Right_operand)
```

where the operator may be one of: equal, notequal, lessequal, greaterequal, less, greater. The operands are either domain variables appearing as tableau entries or constants. The simplifier does a limited amount of input checking by comparing the form of the input to the schema information, and constant values to the value bounds stored in the knowledge base. Domain variables are expected to be indicated syntactically by beginning with "t_" (for target variables) or with "v_" (for nondistinguished variables).

```
[dbcall(employee, [v_Eno1, t_X, v_Sal1, v_D]),
 dbcall(department, [v_D, v_Fct2, v_M]),
 dbcall(employee, [v_M, smiley, v_Sal3, v_Dno3]),
 dbcall(employee, [v_Eno, t_X, v_S, v_Dno]),
 dbcall(greaterequal, v_S, 4000),
 dbcall(lessequal, v_Sal1, v_Sal3),
 dbcall(lessequal, v_Sal3, 4000)]
```

Figure 3: An example dbcall query

```
/* example view definitions in Prolog: it is known that no manager
   makes more than 4000, but nobody makes more than his manager */

works_directly_for(X, Y) :-
        employee(Eno1, X, Sal1, D),
        department(D, Fct2, M),
        employee(M, Y, Sal3, Dno3),
        Sal1 =< Sal3,
        Sal3 =< 4000.

/* Prolog query: who works directly for smiley and makes at least 4000? */

:- works_directly_for(X, smiley), employee(Eno, X, S, Dno), S >= 4000.
```

Figure 4: Original Prolog query from which Figure 3 is generated by METAEVALUATE mechanism

Figure 3 presents an example input query. If Prolog is used as the user query language, such queries are derived by processing deduction rules (view definitions) defined by Horn clauses. (The method for this [VASS84] is based on the amalgamation of language and metalanguage concept first presented in [BOWE82].) For instance, the query in Figure 3 could have been derived from a view definition and Prolog query as given in Figure 4. The principle of the inference engine has been described in [JARK84]:

1. For each tableau variable that has a value bound constraint, add two inequalities to the query.

2. Set the Boolean variables REPEAT and FIRSTTIME to true.

3. Apply an inequality simplification algorithm; if a contradiction is detected, stop with an empty query result; if variables have to be renamed due to newly detected equality conditions or if FIRSTTIME, set REPEAT to true and FIRSTTIME to false, else set REPEAT to false.

4. If REPEAT then do the following: apply a functional dependency chase algorithm with deletion of duplicate rows; if a contradiction is detected, stop with an empty query result; if variables have been renamed return to 3.

5. Remove tableau rows that serve no other purpose than establishing the existence of certain tuples in a relation which can already be inferred from referential integrity constraints.

A shortcoming of this procedure is the complete separation of processing inequalities and functional dependencies which leads to substantial superfluous work. In the subsequent section, a new algorithm is described that integrates these two steps and results in less overall complexity (and real time savings, as shown by the comparison of the two implementations). In this method, a blackboard is used for managing predicates that are inserted for temporary, shared use by both subalgorithms and erased later. The overall algorithm always starts and ends with a 'clean' blackboard.

4.0 A GRAPH-BASED ALGORITHM AND ITS IMPLEMENTATION IN PROLOG

4.1 Two Graph Representations

The query simplifier uses two interacting graph representations: a query graph for representing a query containing inequalities, and an FD/KD graph for representing the application of functional and key dependencies. The former extends ideas by [ROSE80] whereas the latter is based on concepts introduced in [DOWN80] who also proposed a fast congruence closure algorithm for determining the lossless join property of a tableau, a variation of which is used as part of the algorithm presented here. Both graphs share a common set of nodes but differ in edge semantics.

The query graph is a labelled directed graph. The node set contains all entries appearing in the tableau (i.e., the dbcall predicates that reference relations), plus a node O(d) for each ordered domain d. Arcs represent inequality conditions. There are two types: those representing lessequal conditions, and those representing notequal conditions. Equality terms are handled by renaming; the remaining three operators are converted to lessequal arcs, as indicated in Figure 5. In Prolog, tableau element nodes are represented as 4-ary predicates asserted in the blackboard:

```
in_tableau(Tableau_entry, Level, Tableau_row_no, Attribute_name).
```

The latter two parameters characterize the position of a tableau entry in the input query. The Level parameter provides information when the entry was created with respect to the simplification process; it is necessary because the application of either of the two algorithms working on the blackboard can change tableau entries. Edges are represented by 5-ary predicates:

```
inequality(Identifier, Operator, Left_node, Right_node, Length).
```

where the Identifier is used for fast retrieval on the blackboard (e.g., for erasure or change of operand names) and Length is determined as indicated in Figure 5.

```
                                                 0
var-1 <= var-2                      var-1  ---------> var-2

                                                -1
var-1 < var-2                       var-1  ---------> var-2

                                               const
var-1 <= const                      var-1  ---------> 0(integer)

                                              const-1
var-1 < const                       var-1  ---------> 0(integer)

                                                 0
var-1 >= var-2                      var-1  <--------- var-2

                                                -1
var-1 >  var-2                      var-1  <--------- var-2

                                               -const
var-1 >= const                      var-1  <--------- 0(integer)

                                              -const-1
var-1 >  const                      var-1  <--------- 0(integer)
```

Figure 5: Construction of query graph from inequalities [ROSE80]

In the FD/KD graph, a bundle of directed edges connects each node whose attribute name appears on the right-hand side of a functional or key dependency in the knowledge base, to all the nodes corresponding to the left-hand side of that dependency. An example of a combined query and FD/KD graph is given in Figure 6 for the example in Figure 3. The FD/KD edges are not stored explicitly but derived when needed, utilizing Prolog's efficient pattern matching capabilities.

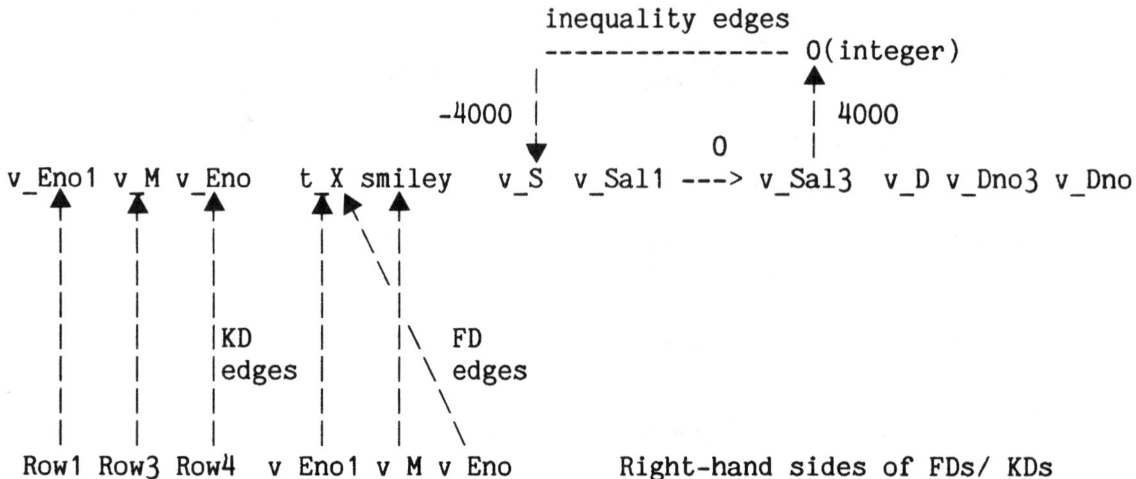

Figure 6: A functional and key dependency graph overlayed with the inequality graph for the query example

4.2 Two Graph Algorithms And Their Integration

The two representations could now be used as in section 3 to simply implement a repeated execution of two separate algorithms until nothing changes any more. Instead, we shall first describe each of the algorithms and then present a better integration. The two algorithms below are extensions and adaptations of work by [ROSE80] for the query graph, and by [DOWN80] for the FD/KD graph.

1. Inequality optimization: The algorithm can be summarized by the following Prolog rule:

```
process_inequalities :-
      remove_multiedges,
      compute_shortest_paths,
      postprocess_graph(0).
```

Remove_multiedges succeeds after removing multiple redundant comparisons between any pair of nodes. A (deliberately extreme) example is given in Figure 7. Note, that the first inequality (greater, v_S, 200) is removed since it is implied by the valuebound on the salary attribute. (The output of the simplifier does not really have the same format as its input; the example has been translated back to the dbcall language for readability.)

```
/* a query with redundant inequality comparisons */

      [dbcall(employee, [v_Eno1, t_X, v_Sal1, v_D]),
       dbcall(department, [v_D, v_Fct2, v_M]),
       dbcall(employee, [v_M, v_Man, v_Sal3, v_Dno3]),
       dbcall(employee, [v_Eno, t_X, v_S, v_Dno]),
       dbcall(greater, v_S, 200),
       dbcall(equal, v_Man, smiley),
       dbcall(lessequal, v_S, 4000),
       dbcall(notequal, v_S, 6000),
       dbcall(notequal, v_S, 6000),
       dbcall(lessequal, v_S, 6000),
       dbcall(notequal, v_S, 4000)]

/* equivalent query after removal of redundant inequalities */

      [dbcall(employee, [v_Eno1, t_X, v_Sal1, v_D]),
       dbcall(department, [v_D, v_Fct2, v_M]),
       dbcall(employee, [v_M, smiley, v_Sal3, v_Dno3]),
       dbcall(employee, [v_Eno, t_X, v_S, v_Dno]),
       dbcall(lessequal, v_S, 3999)]
```

Figure 7: Example for removal of multi-edges

Compute_shortest_paths creates, on the blackboard, a Prolog representation of the shortest paths between all pairs of nodes, using a simple algorithm of cubic (in the number of nodes) complexity, as described, e.g., in [REIN77]. The algorithm has been enhanced in the sense that it stops with an error message and an empty query result as soon as a negative length cycle (meaning 'A < A' for any node A on the cycle -- see the example in Figure 8) is detected, and that it considers only nodes that actually appear in inequalities.

```
| ?- query8(Q), generate_tableau(0,Q), process_inequalities.

warning: contradiction among inequalities

Q = [dbcall(employee,[v_Eno1,t_X,v_Sal1,v_D]),
     dbcall(department,[v_D,v_Fct2,v_M]),
     dbcall(employee,[v_M,v_Man,v_Sal3,v_Dno3]),
     dbcall(employee,[v_Eno,t_X,v_S,v_Dno]),
     dbcall(lessequal,v_S,4000),
     dbcall(greaterequal,v_Sal3,5000),
     dbcall(greater,v_S,v_Sal3)]
```

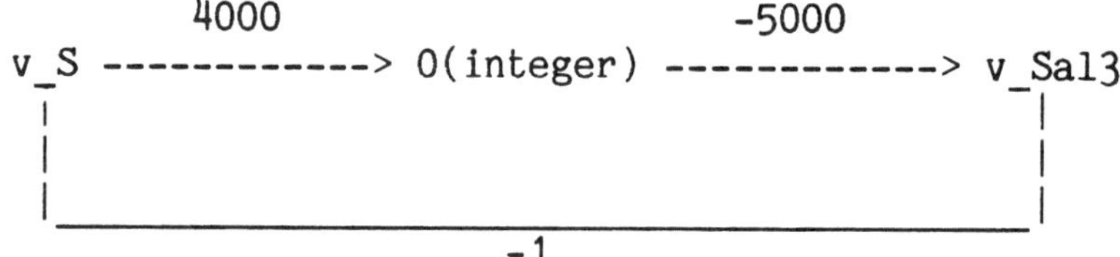

Figure 8: Prolog log and query graph showing a contradiction between inequalities by a negative length cycle.

Postprocess_graph (the parameter corresponds to the previously mentioned Level parameter in the in_tableau predicates) follows the cycles with a total length of 0 and renames all variables appearing on such cycles, either to a single variable name or -- if any node 0(d) is on the cycle -- to a constant corresponding to the total length of the path from each node on the cycle to node 0(d). In the query graph, renaming leads to the removal of nodes and all their related arcs and shortest paths.

2. FD/KD optimization: A fast chase algorithm computes the congruence closure of the FD/KD graph in a breadth-first fashion, using the Level parameter to prescreen the tableau entries to which an FD or KD might be applicable at a given point in time. The algorithm terminates when, at a given level, there are no further in_tableau predicates with that level. In other words, the algorithm tries first to apply all directly applicable FDs/KDs; afterwards, only such FDs/KDs can be applicable that

have as their left-hand side tableau elements changed in the previous step. KDs are tried before FDs since their application leads to the deletion of a row and therefore renders the application of further FDs superfluous. As an example, consider the preprocessed query in Figure 7. At level 0, only one functional dependency is applicable, leading to the new query:

```
[dbcall(employee, [v_Eno1, t_X, v_Sal1, v_D]),
 dbcall(department, [v_D, v_Fct2, v_M]),
 dbcall(employee, [v_M, smiley, v_Sal3, v_Dno3]),
 dbcall(employee, [v_Eno1, t_X, v_S, v_Dno]),
 dbcall(lessequal, v_S, 3999)]
```

At level 1, the key dependency for the employee relation becomes applicable, leading to the deletion of the fourth row and to renaming of v_Sal1 to v_S in the first row. Another example is given in Figure 9; here, the notequal predicate prevents successful application of the key dependency and the query result will be empty.

```
| ?- query10(Q), generate_tableau(0,Q), simplify.

warning: contradiction by \= condition:
v_Dno cannot be equal to v_D
as required by a functional or key dependency

Q = [dbcall(employee,[v_Eno1,t_X,v_Sal1,v_D]),
    dbcall(department,[v_D,v_Fct2,v_M]),
    dbcall(employee,[v_M,smiley,v_Sal3,v_Dno3]),
    dbcall(employee,[v_Eno,t_X,4000,v_Dno]),
    dbcall(notequal,v_D,v_Dno)]

yes
```

Figure 9: Example of a contradiction detected by application of functional and key dependencies

A closer look at the interplay of these two algorithms shows that the results of each algorithm can be expressed in the notion of the other by integrating the two graph representations as shown in Figure 6; this in turn leads to a better integration that avoids full repetition of both algorithms at each stage of the algorithm given in section 3.

The most important observation concerns the application of a functional dependency by the second algorithm. Its result is that two tableau entries are made equal. If both entries, say X and Y, are variables, this corresponds to introducing zero-length edges from X to Y and from Y to X [4]. If previously there was a negative-length shortest path in either direction, this immediately leads to a negative length cycle and thus to a contradiction in the query. Otherwise, all of the shortest paths must be recomputed to look for new zero length cycles which could lead to variable renaming, using the postprocess_graph predicate at the current Level. However, the complexity of this recomputation is at most quadratic (rather than cubic as originally), since only each of the previous shortest paths has to be compared with a path through the new edges between X and Y.

```
simplify :-
      process_inequalities,
      one_relation_simplify(0),
      remove_deletable_danglers.

one_relation_simplify(Level) :-
      rowrel(Row1, Rel), rowrel(Row2, Rel), Row2 > Row1,
      prescreen_and_simplify(Level, Row1, Row2, Rel),
      fail.
one_relation_simplify(Level) :-
      Level1 is Level + 1, in_tableau(_, Level1, _, _),
      !,
      one_relation_simplify(Level1).
one_relation_simplify(_).

prescreen_and_simplify(0, Row1, Row2, Rel) :-
      one_level_simplify(0, Row1, Row2, Rel), !.
prescreen_and_simplify(Level, Row1, Row2, Rel) :-
      (in_tableau(_, Level, Row1, _); in_tableau(_, Level, Row2, _)),
      !,
      one_level_simplify(Level, Row1, Row2, Rel).

one_level_simplify(Level, Row1, Row2, Rel) :-
      equal_key(Level, Row1, Row2, Rel), schema(Rel, Schema),
      !,
      coerce(Level, Schema, Row1, Row2),
      delete_row(Schema, Row2).
one_level_simplify(Level, Row1, Row2, Rel) :-
      equal_LHS(Level, Row1, Row2, Rel, RHS),
      coerce(Level, RHS, Row1, Row2),
      fail.
one_level_simplify(_, _, _, _).
```

Figure 10: High-level Prolog predicates for simplifier implementation

For an example for the integrated procedure, consider again Figures 3 and 6. Adding zero length edges between v_S and v_Sal1 in Figure 6 through the application of a functional (level 0) and a key (level 1) dependency simplifies the query of Figure 3 to:

[4] If one entry (say Y) is a constant of domain d, the same procedure will follow but the edges to be added to the graph will be one from node X to node 0(d) with length Y, and one from 0(d) to X with length -Y. When X and Y are (different) constants, there is again a contradiction leading to a message and an empty query result.

```
[dbcall(employee, [v_Eno1, t_X, 4000, v_D]),
 dbcall(department, [v_D, v_Fct2, v_M]),
 dbcall(employee, [v_M, smiley, 4000, v_Dno3])]).
```

Vice versa, changes in the tableau caused by the inequality algorithm will be indicated by the Level parameter of the in_tableau predicates on the blackboard, such that they can be exploited by the FD/KD algorithm in the same way as changes caused by previous FD/KD applications.

The implementation of this interplay makes use of the recursion features of Prolog. Figure 10 contains a sketch of some of the high-level predicates (the whole system currently has about 200 clauses). The predicate, coerce, tries to make the values of the attributes in the list RHS equal between rows Row1 and Row2, gives appropriate error messages should this prove impossible due to contradictions, and indirectly activates the recomputation of shortest paths.

5.0 CONCLUSIONS AND EXTENSIONS

The practical relevance of tableau-oriented simplification techniques inspired by database theory has repeatedly been questioned by practioners, as evidenced by the fact that they are hardly implemented in any of the well-known relational systems. Our preliminary experience with an actual integration of these concepts into a working system seems to refute this negative opinion. On one hand, the need for semantic simplification invariably arises when higher-level interfaces such as natural language are to be implemented that rely heavily on view mechanisms.

An important if trivial observation in this context is that -- in contrast to integrity checking in update operations -- the query simplifier has complete freedom to use just as many constraints as justified by the expected benefit. The modular implementation enabled by logic programming in connection with the blackboard concept is particularly flexible in allowing the easy addition of 'expert rules' that tell the system which constraints to use in a given environment. For example, the current implementation tries to avoid the exponential search incurred by full handling of notequal conditions [ROSE80] by ignoring certain notequal-related simplification strategies. Similarly, the initial shortest-path procedure currently appears to be the major performance bottleneck. We are therefore experimenting with 'expert rules' that reduce the number of inequalities based on valuebound conditions, and thus the number of nodes in the algorithm based on 'reasonable' -- but not failproof -- assumptions.

The implementation of the simplifier has demonstrated another, quite surprising advantage (although it may seem obvious in hindsight): the capability of the system to provide meaningful warnings where previous query evaluation subsystems would just return an empty result. The need for such enhanced feedback was especially felt during our earlier work on empirically evaluating a natural language query system where users were helpless when the system returned an unexpectedly empty result [JARK85b]. The empty answer problem is also addressed in [MOTR85] and treated therein through query generalization methods.

Apart from our work on an improved interface from Prolog to the simplifier (handling recursion and buffer management), two extensions to the simplifier itself look particularly promising. The first is the analysis and optimization of predicates handling aggregate functions over database data which should lead to improved database interfaces to decision support systems, statistical databases, recursive databases, etc.

Additionally, work is underway to extend the simplifier to the multi-user case. This idea is presumed to have several advantages. First, since all users would be read-only, the simplifier requires only rudimentary concurrency control and can thus be a relatively small and simple system. Second, since the simplifier is external, it can interact with the DBMS as a single user, thus reducing DBMS concurrency control problems. Third, as a consequence of the previous two, the simplifier has full freedom to perform common subexpression analysis to share query evaluation costs and to create common temporary access paths [JARK85a]. Finally, as a consequence of its global architecture (section 3), the simplifier can easily accept multiple input languages, although, from the viewpoint of error messages and efficient common access path analysis, a single input language, e.g., Prolog, may be more desirable since it would allow the addition of view definitions to the knowledge base.

We view the multi-user query front-end as a first step towards a more general concept of database controlling in which the external system implements a multi-level model-theoretic approach that observes strengths and weaknesses of the underlying database system (or systems in the case of distributed systems), in order to provide expert helpers (see also [FURT85]) or to reorganize the workflow of transactions. The merits of such a system that may include update operations remain to be studied.

In summary, it appears that narrowing the scope of semantic query optimization to database theory-based simplification -- while keeping the general idea in mind -- has some benefits of simplicity and efficiency. This should by no means be constructed as a criticism of general semantic query optimization. On the contrary, we see our approach as a kernel around which more sophisticated knowledge bases can be constructed, whose corresponding inference techniques work on the same blackboard data structure, hopefully with little interference with existing algorithms. Further classification of integrity constraints may be desirable for such extensions; in particular, those types of constraints should be investigated for which the range of applicability is easily detectable and does not, in itself, require answering a complex query.

References

[AHOS79] Aho, A.V., Sagiv, Y., Ullman, J.D., 1979. "Equivalences among relational expressions", SIAM Journal of Computing 8, 2, pp. 218-246.

[BLAU81] Blaustein, B.T., 1981. "Enforcing database assertions: techniques and applications", Ph.D. thesis, Harvard University, Cambridge, Mass.

[BOWE82] Bowen, K.A., Kowalski, R.A., 1982. "Amalgamating language and metalanguage in logic programming", in Clark, K.L., Taernlund, S.-A. (eds.): Logic Programming, Academic Press, New York, pp. 153-172.

[CHAK85] Chakravarthy, U.S., Fishman, D., Minker, J., 1985. "Semantic query optimization in expert systems and database systems", this volume.

[CLIF85] Clifford, J., Jarke, M., Lucas, H.C., 1985. "Designing expert systems in a business environment", Proceedings IFAC Workshop on Artificial Intelligence in Economics and Management, Zurich, Switzerland.

[COSM84] Cosmadakis, S.S., Kanellakis, P.C., 1984. "Functional and inclusion dependencies: a graph-theoretic approach", Proceedings ACM Symposium on Principles of Database Systems, Waterloo, Ont., pp. 29-37.

[DOWN80] Downey, P.J., Sethi, R., Tarjan, R.E., 1980. "Variations on the common subexpression problem", Journal of the ACM 27, 4, pp. 758-771.

[ERMA75] Erman, L.D., Lesser,V.R., 1975. "A multi-level organization for problem solving using many diverse, cooperating sources of knowledge", Proceedings 4th IJCAI Conference, 1975, pp. 483-490.

[FAGI81] Fagin, R., 1981. "A normal form for relational databases that is based on domains and keys", ACM Transactions on Database Systems 6, 3, pp. 387-415.

[FURT85]. Furtado,A.L., Moura, C.M.O., 1985. "Expert helpers to data-based information systems", this volume.

[HAMM80] Hammer, M., Zdonik, S.B., 1980. "Knowledge-based query processing", Proceedings 6th VLDB Conference, Montreal, pp. 137-147.

[JARK85a] Jarke, M., 1985. "Common subexpression isolation in multiple query optimization", in W.Kim, D.Reiner, D.Batory (eds.): Query Processing in Database Systems, Springer-Verlag, pp. 191-205.

[JARK84] Jarke, M., Clifford, J., Vassiliou, Y., 1984. "An optimizing Prolog front-end to a relational query system", Proceedings ACM-SIGMOD Conference, Boston, pp. 296-306.

[JARK85b] Jarke, M., Turner, J.A., Stohr, E.A., Vassiliou, Y., White, N., Michielsen, K., 1985. "A field evaluation of natural language for data retrieval", IEEE Transactions on Software Engineering SE-11, 1.

[KELL82] Kellogg, C., 1982. "A practical amalgam of knowledge and data base technology", Proceedings AAAI Conference, Pittsburgh, Pa.

[KING81] King, J.J., 1981. "QUIST: A system for semantic query optimization in relational data bases", Proceedings 7th VLDB Conference, Cannes, France, pp. 510-517.

[KLUG80] Klug, A., 1980. "Calculating constraints on relational expressions", ACM Transactions on Database Systems 5, 3, pp. 260-290.

[MOTR85] Motro, A., 1985. "Query generalization: a technique for handling query failure", this volume.

[OTTH82] Ott, N., Horlaender, K., 1982. "Removing redundant join operations in queries involving views", IBM Scientific Center Heidelberg Technical Report TR-82.02.003.

[REIN77] Reingold, E.M., Nievergelt, J., Deo, N., 1977. Combinatorial Algorithms. Theory and Praxis, Prentice Hall.

[REIT84] Reiter, R., 1984. "Towards a logical reconstruction of relational database theory", in Brodie, M., Mylopoulos, J., Schmidt, J.W. (eds.): On Conceptual Modelling, Springer-Verlag, New York, pp. 191-233.

[ROSE80] Rosenkrantz, D.J., Hunt, M.B., 1980. "Processing conjunctive predicates and queries", Proceedings 6th VLDB Conference, Montreal, pp. 64-74.

[SCIO84] Sciore, E., Warren, D.S., 1984. "Towards an integrated database-Prolog system", position paper, Proceedings First Intl. Workshop on Expert Database Systems, Kiawah Island, SC, pp. 801-815.

[SIVA85] Sivasankaran, T.R., Jarke, M., 1985. "Logic-based formula management strategies in an Actuarial Consulting System", Decision Support Systems 1:3.

[VASS84] Vassiliou, Y., Clifford, J., Jarke, M., 1984. "Access to specific declarative knowledge by expert systems: the impact of logic programming", Decision Support Systems 1, 2.

[WARR81] Warren, D.H.D., 1981. "Efficient processing of interactive relational data base queries expressed in logic", Proceedings 7th VLDB Conference, Cannes, France, pp. 272-282.

[XU83] Xu, G.D., 1983. "Search control in semantic query optimization", TR# 83-09, University of Massachusetts, Amherst.

Author Index

List of Participants

Mark Abdelnour
NCR Corporation
3325 Platt Springs Road
West Columbia, SC 29169
USA

Hassan Ait-Kaci
Microelectronics and Computer
Technology Corporation (MCC)
9430 Research Blvd.
Echelon One, Suite 200
Austin, TX 78759
USA

Peter M.G. Apers
Dept. of Math & Comp. Sci.
Vrije Universiteit
1081 HV Amsterdam
The Netherlands

Vic Askman
Advanced Information &
Decision Sciences
201 San Antonio Circle, Suite 286
Mountain View, CA 94040
USA

Bruce N. Ballard
AT&T Bell Laboratories
600 Mountain Avenue
Murray Hill, NJ 07974
USA

Robert Balzer
USC/Information Sciences Institute
4676 Admiralty Way
Marina del Rey, CA 90292
USA

Madeleine Bates
BBN Laboratories
10 Moulton Street
Cambridge, MA 02238
USA

Rudolf Bayer
Institut fur Informatik
Der Technischen Universitat Munchen
D-8000 Munchen 2, Postfach 20 24 20
Federal Rep. of Germany

David Beech
Hewlett-Packard Laboratories
1501 Page Mill Road
Palo Alto, CA 94304
USA

James Bezdek
Computer Science Department
University of South Carolina
Columbia, SC 29208
USA

Sena H. Black
University of South Carolina
College of Business Administration
Columbia, SC 29208
USA

Robert W. Blanning
Owen Graduate School of Management
Vanderbilt University
Nashville, TN 37203
USA

Alex Borgida
Rutgers University
Dept. of Computer Science
New Brunswick, NJ 08903
USA

Ronald J. Brachman
Fairchild Laboratory for
Artificial Intelligence Research
4001 Miranda Avenue
Palo Alto, CA 94304
USA

B. Alton Brantley, Jr., MD, Ph.D.
Duke University Medical Center
Box 3942
Durham, NC 27710
USA

Michael L. Brodie
Computer Corporation of America
Four Cambridge Center
Cambridge, MA 02142
USA

Peter Buneman
University of Pennsylvania
Moore School of Elec. Eng.
Philadelphia, PA 19104
USA

Stephanie Cammarata
The Rand Corporation and UCLA
1700 Main Street
Santa Monica, CA 90406
USA

Robert L. Cannon
Computer Science Department
University of South Carolina
Columbia, SC 29208
USA

Michael J. Carey
Computer Sciences Dept.
University of Wisconsin
1210 West Dayton St.
Madison, WI 53706
USA

Upen S. Chakravarthy
Dept. of Computer Science
University of Maryland
College Park, MD 20742
USA

Ralph Cherubini
Digital Equipment Corporation
77 Reed Road, HLO2-3/N10
Hudson, MA 01749
USA

Craig M. Cook
Smart Systems Technology
6870 Elm Street
McLean, VA 22101
USA

Francisco Corella
Fairchild Laboratory for
Artificial Intelligence Research
4001 Miranda Avenue
Palo Alto, CA 94304
USA

Andrew S. Cromarty
Advanced Information &
Decision Sciences
201 San Antonio Circle, Suite 286
Mountain View, CA 94040
USA

James F. Cunningham
Advanced Information &
Decision Sciences
201 San Antonio Circle, Suite 286
Mountain View, CA 94040
USA

Xavier Debanne
Data Base Informatica
Via del Mare, 67
00040 Promezia (Rome)
ITALY

Michael Deering
Fairchild Laboratory for
Artificial Intelligence Research
4001 Miranda Avenue
Palo Alto, CA 94304
USA

Nigel Derrett
Hewlett-Packard Laboratories
1501 Page Mill Road
Palo Alto, CA 94304
USA

David J. DeWitt
Computer Sciences Dept.
University of Wisconsin
1210 West Dayton St.
Madison, WI 53706
USA

Joseph Faletti
University of California, Davis
Computer Science Division
Davis, CA 95616
USA

Tim Finin
University of Pennsylvania
Computer and Information Science
Philadelphia, PA 19104
USA

Daniel H. Fishman
Hewlett-Packard Laboratories
1501 Page Mill Road, Bldg. 3L
Palo Alto, CA 94304
USA

Mark S. Fox
Carnegie-Mellon University
Robotics Institute- DH 3317
Shenley Park
Pittsburgh, PA 15213
USA

Andrew U. Frank
University of Maine at Orono
Dept. of Civil Engineering
Boardman Hall 103
Orono, ME 04469
USA

J. Stanley Fryer
Associate Dean for Development
University of South Carolina
College of Business Administration
Columbia, SC 29208
USA

Forouzan Golshani
Arizona State University
Dept. of Computer Science-ECG 252
Tempe, AZ 85287
USA

Jiawei Han
Dept. of Computer Sciences
University of Wisconsin
Madison, WI 53706
USA

Forest Woody Horton, Jr.
Management Consultant
500 23rd St. N.W., Suite B901
Washington, DC 20037
USA

Cathie Hughes
University of South Carolina
College of Business Administration
Columbia, SC 29208
USA

Matthias Jarke
Grad. School of Business
New York University
90 Trinity Place
New York, NY 10006
USA

Paris Kanellakis
MIT
Laboratory for Computer Science
NE43-520
545 Technology Square
Cambridge, MA 02139
USA

Charles Kellogg
Microelectronics and Computer
Technology Corporation (MCC)
9430 Research Blvd.
Echelon One, Suite 200
Austin, TX 78759
USA

Larry Kerschberg
University of South Carolina
College of Business Administration
Columbia, SC 29208
USA

Jonathan J. King
Teknowledge
525 University Avenue
Palo Alto, CA 94303
USA

Roger King
University of Colorado
Dept. of Computer Science
Campus Box 430
Boulder, CO 80309
USA

Gilles M.E. Lafue
Schlumberger-Doll Research
Old Quarry Road
Ridgefield, Conn. 06877-4108
USA

Phillip Latham
SC Budget & Control Board
Division of IRM
1203 Gervais Street
Columbia, SC 29208
USA

William E. Linn, Jr.
Cullinet Software, Inc.
1800 Century Blvd.
Atlanta, GA 30345
USA

Eugene Lowenthal
Microelectronics and Computer
Technology Corporation (MCC)
9430 Research Blvd.
Echelon One, Suite 200
Austin, TX 78759
USA

Eliezer L. Lozinskii
The Hebrew University of Jerusalem
Institute of Mathematics
Jerusalem 91904
ISRAEL

David Maier
Oregon Graduate Center
19600 N.W. Walker Road
Beaverton, OR 97006
USA

Donald A. Marchand
University of South Carolina
College of Business Administration
Columbia, SC 29208
USA

William Mark
USC/Information Sciences Institute
4676 Admiralty Way
Marina del Rey, CA 90292-6695
USA

Robert E. Markland
Management Science Department
College of Business Administration
University of South Carolina
Columbia, SC 29208
USA

Manton M. Matthews
Dept. of Computer Science
University of South Carolina
Columbia, SC 29208
USA

Eric Mays
IBM T.J. Watson Research Center
P.O. Box 218
Yorktown Heights, NY 10598
USA

Lawrence J. Mazlack
University of Cincinnati
QA/IS Dept., ML#130
1118 Crosley Tower
Cincinnati, OH 45221
USA

John L. McCarthy
Lawrence Berkeley Lab
50B-3238
Berkeley, CA 94720
USA

Herbert N. McCauley
Harris Corporation
1025 W. Nasa Blvd.
Melbourne, FL 32919
USA

Norman C. McEntire
NCR Corporation
3325 Platt Springs Road
West Columbia, SC 29169
USA

Tim H. Merrett
McGill University
School of Computer Science
805 Sherbrooke St. West
Montreal, Quebec H3A 2K6
CANADA

Michele Missikoff
Instituto di Analise dei
Sistemi ed Informatica
Viale Marzoni, 30
00185 - Rome
ITALY

Jun Miyazaki
Department of Elect. Eng.
Keio University
2-25-11, TODOROKI, SETAGAKA-KU
TOKYO, JAPAN
JAPAN

Matthew Morgenstern
SRI International - CSL
333 Ravenswood Avenue
Menlo Park, CA 94025
USA

Amihai Motro
University of Southern California
Computer Science Department (SAL 200)
Los Angeles, CA 90089
USA

Claudio M.O. Moura
IBM Latin American
Systems Research Inst.
IBM do Brasil
P.O. Box 1830
22.071 Rio de Janeiro - RJ
BRAZIL

John Mylopoulos
University of Toronto
Dept. of Computer Science
10 King's College Road
Toronto, ONT M5S 1A4
CANADA

Masahiro Nakazawa
Department of Elect. Eng.
Keio University
2-25-11, TODOROKI, SETAGAKA-KU
TOKYO, JAPAN
JAPAN

Dana S. Nau
University of Maryland
Department of Computer Science
College Park, MD 20742
USA

Sham Navathe
University of Florida
Comp. and Information Sciences
512 Weil Hall
Gainesville, FL 32611
USA

Erich J. Neuhold
Technical University of Vienna
Inst. for Applied Informatics
Paniglgasse 16
A-1040 Vienna
AUSTRIA

G.T. Nguyen
IMAG-University of Grenoble
Laboratoire de Genie Informatique
B.P. 68 - 38402 St.-Martin D'Heres
FRANCE

D. Stott Parker
UCLA-Computer Science Department
3732 Boelter Hall
Los Angeles, CA 90024
USA

and

SILOGIC, Inc.
6420 Wilshire, Suite 2000
Los Angeles, CA 90048
USA

Charles Petrie
Microelectronics and Computer
Technology Corporation (MCC)
9430 Research Blvd.
Echelon One, Suite 200
Austin, TX 78759
USA

Alain Pirotte
Philips Research Lab
2 Ave. Van Becelaere
1170 Brussels
BELGIUM

Harry Pople
University of Pittsburgh
Decision Systems Lab
1360 Scaife Hall
Pittsburgh, PA 15261
USA

Don Potter
University of South Carolina
Dept. of Computer Science
Columbia, SC 29208
USA

Darryn Price
Cericor, Inc.
716 East 4500 South
Salt Lake City, UT 84107
USA

Steve Rehfuss
Tektronix, Inc.
Delivery Station 50-662
P.O. Box 500
Beaverton, OR 97077
USA

Ulrich Reimer
Universitat Konstanz
Informationswissenschaft
Postfach 5560
D-7750 Konstanz 1
West Germany

Neil C. Rowe
Naval Postgraduate School
Department of Computer Science
Code 52
Monterey, CA 93943
USA

Enrique H. Ruspini
Hewlett-Packard Laboratories
1501 Page Mill Road
Palo Alto, CA 94306
USA

Sharon Salveter
Boston University
Computer Science Department
111 Cummington Street
Boston, MA 02215
USA

Richard E. Sansom
TRW Inc.
One Space Park
Redondo Beach, CA 90278
USA

Joachim W. Schmidt
Johann Wolfgang Goethe Universitat
Fachbereich Informatik Dantestr. 9
6000 Frankfurt/Main
Federal Republic of Germany

Edward Sciore
Boston University
Dept. of Computer Science
111 Cummington Ave.
Boston, MA 02215
USA

J. Allen Sears
DARPA/IPTO
1400 Wilson Blvd.
Arlington, VA 22209
USA

Allen Shepherd
Hewlett-Packard Laboratories
1501 Page Mill Road, Bldg. 3L
Palo Alto, CA 94304
USA

Oded Shmueli
Technion
Dept. of Computer Science
Haifa,
ISRAEL

Edgar H. Sibley
George Mason University
4400 University Drive
Fairfax, VA 22030
USA

David L. Silverman
Intellicorp, Inc.
707 Laurel St.
Menlo Park, CA 94025-3445
USA

John Miles Smith
Computer Corporation of America
Four Cambridge Center
Cambridge, MA 02142
USA

Rolf Stachowitz
Microelectronics and Computer
Technology Corporation (MCC)
9430 Research Blvd.
Echelon One, Suite 200
Austin, TX 78759
USA

Donald Steiner
Microelectronics and Computer
Technology Corporation (MCC)
9430 Research Blvd.
Echelon One, Suite 200
Austin, TX 78759
USA

Michael Stonebraker
Univ. of California - Berkeley
Dept. of Comp. Sci. and E. E.
549 Evans Hall
Berkeley, CA 94720
USA

Stanley Su
University of Florida
500A Weil Hall
Gainesville, FL 32611

Naomichi Sueda
Engineering Division
Toshiba Corporation
1-1, SHIBAURA 1-CHOME,
MINATO-KU
TOKYO 105, JAPAN

Richard M. Tong
Advanced Information &
Decision Sciences
201 San Antonio Circle, Suite 286
Mountain View, CA 94040
USA

Robert Trueblood
University of South Carolina
Computer Science Dept.
Columbia, SC 29208
USA

Shalom Tsur
Microelectronics and Computer
Technology Corporation (MCC)
9430 Research Blvd.
Echelon One, Suite 200
Austin, TX 78759
USA

Marco Valtorta
Duke University
Department of Computer Science
Durham, NC 27706
USA

Adrian Walker
IBM T.J. Watson Research Lab
P.O. Box 218
Yorktown Heights, NY 10598
USA

Prof. David S. Warren
SUNY at Stony Brook
Dept. of Computer Science
Long Island, NY 11794
USA

Gio Wiederhold
Stanford University
Computer Science Dept.
Stanford University
Stanford, CA 94305
USA

Prof. Eugene Wong
University of California - Berkeley
Dept. EECS
Berkeley, CA 94720
USA

Mark Wright
Inference Corporation
Fifth Floor
5300 West Century Blvd.
Los Angeles, CA 90045
USA

Dr. Ramin Yasdi
University of Stuttgart
Azenberg Str. 12
D-7000 Stuttgart 1
Fed. Rep. of Germany

Carlo Zaniolo
Microelectronics and Computer
Technology Corporation (MCC)
9430 Research Blvd.
Echelon One, Suite 200
Austin, TX 78759
USA

Gian Piero Zarri
CNRS-LISH
54, Boulevard Raspail
75270 PARIS Cedex 06
FRANCE

As Benjamin/Cummings accelerates its exciting publishing venture in the Computer Science and Information Systems, we'd like to offer you the opportunity to learn about our new titles in advance. **If you'd like to be placed on our mailing list** to receive pre-publication notices about our expanding Computer Science and Information Systems list, just fill out this card **completely** and return it to us, postage paid. Thank you.

NAME____

STREET ADDRESS________________________________

CITY____________________STATE________ZIP________

BUSINESS______________________________________

ASSOCIATION AFFILIATION:_________________________

TELEPHONE (_______) _____________________________

AREAS OF INTEREST:

41 ☐ Operating Systems (Please specify)__________________

42 ☐ Programming Languages (Please specify)______________

43 ☐ Systems Languages (Please specify)_________________

44 ☐ Artificial Intelligence
45 ☐ Computer Graphics
46 ☐ Software Documentation
47 ☐ Systems Analysis and Design
48 ☐ Systems Architecture
49 ☐ Data Communications
50 ☐ Software Engineering
51 ☐ Microcomputer Literacy

52 ☐ Other (Please specify)________________________

☐ I am writing.
Area:_______________________________________

cut along dotted line

MAILING LIST • MAILING LIST • MAILING LIST • MAILING LIST • MAILING LIST • MAILING LIST

No Postage
Necessary
if Mailed in the
United States

BUSINESS REPLY CARD
FIRST CLASS PERMIT NO. 450 MENLO PARK, CA 94025

Postage will be paid by Addressee:

Product Manager
The Benjamin/Cummings
Publishing Company, Inc.®
2727 Sand Hill Road
Menlo Park, California 94025